BEYOND DESIGN

BEYOND DESIGN

FIFTH EDITION

The Synergy of Apparel Product Development

SANDRA KEISER

DEBORAH VANDERMAR

MYRNA B. GARNER

FAIRCHILD BOOKS

NEW YORK · LONDON · OXFORD · NEW DELHI · SYDNEY

FAIRCHILD BOOKS
Bloomsbury Publishing Inc
1385 Broadway, New York, NY 10018, USA
50 Bedford Square, London, WC1B 3DP, UK
29 Earlsfort Terrace, Dublin 2, Ireland

BLOOMSBURY, FAIRCHILD BOOKS and the Fairchild Books
logo are trademarks of Bloomsbury Publishing Plc

Third edition published 2012
Fourth edition published 2017
This edition published 2022

Cover design by Louise Dugdale
Cover image: Plume Creative / Getty images

Library of Congress Cataloging-in-Publication Data
Names: Keiser, Sandra J., author. | Vandermar, Deborah A., author. |
Garner, Myrna B., author.
Title: Beyond design : beyond design / Sandra Keiser, Deborah Vandermar, Myrna B Garner.
Description: Fifth edition. | New York, NY, USA : Fairchild Books,
Bloomsbury Publishing Inc., 2022. | Includes index. |
Identifiers: LCCN 2021028290 (print) | LCCN 2021028291 (ebook) |
ISBN 9781501366611 (paperback) | ISBN 9781501366604 (pdf)
Subjects: LCSH: Clothing trade. | Fashion design. | Clothing and dress—Marketing.
Classification: LCC TT497 .K42 2021 (print) | LCC TT497 (ebook) | DDC 746.9/2—dc23
LC record available at https://lccn.loc.gov/2021028290
LC ebook record available at https://lccn.loc.gov/2021028291

ISBN: 978-1-5013-6664-2

Typeset by Lachina Creative, Inc.
Printed and bound in India

To find out more about our authors and books visit
www.fairchildbooks.com and sign up for our newsletter.

BRIEF CONTENTS

EXTENDED CONTENTS

PREFACE

Beyond Design: The Synergy of Apparel Product Development takes students step by step through the decision making involved in the preproduction processes of apparel product development—planning, forecasting, fabricating, color management, line development, creative design, technical design, quality assurance, sourcing, and pricing. It demonstrates how these processes must be coordinated to get the right product to market, when consumers want it, through their preferred distribution channel, and at a price they are willing to pay.

With new virtual and hybrid models of education, a textbook takes on renewed importance. It serves as a reference, available to students 24/7, anytime they don't have access to faculty. Professional business transactions are also increasingly virtual. This means that being conversant in the vocabulary of product development is an essential element of career preparation. The authors immersed themselves in researching professional periodicals and listening to industry experts as they navigated the pandemic and adapted their business strategies. As a result, the new edition incorporates current language and vocabulary as it is used in the industry.

The COVID-19 pandemic accelerated economic, cultural, social, and technological changes that impacted our lifestyles, the business environment, and the way the fashion system works. These changes make synergy and collaboration more important than ever. This edition represents a major revision. It retains what is constant in the product development process while providing a context for change. New business imperatives include:

- responding to the increasing consumer demand for transparency, traceability, and sustainability and implementing standards for accountability;
- recognizing and participating in emerging business models such as supply chain collaborations and recommerce;
- adopting 3D design software and automated manufacturing technology; and
- implementing sophisticated data gathering and machine learning tools that allow for the accurate analysis of individual customer behavior and a customized marketing response.

These directional shifts impact small and large businesses differently. An attempt has been made to address strategies for businesses of all sizes.

ORGANIZATION OF THE TEXT

Beyond Design provides an overview of the processes involved in the creation of an apparel line and develops a framework for the creative and technical tasks required within the reality of the current business environment. It is divided into four parts: business, creative, technical, and production planning. Each part is discussed in relation to the role it plays in product development.

Part 1 focuses on the supply chain and business infrastructure that supports and directs apparel product development processes. Chapter 1 introduces product development vocabulary and describes the apparel supply chain that facilitates product development processes. It introduces the UN Sustainable Development Goals which are now the global blueprint for attaining a more sustainable future. The focus of Chapter 2 is on business planning that provides the foundation for decisions affecting the development of apparel products in a dynamic marketplace. The chapter explains the language of branding and introduces new recommerce business models. Chapter 3 explores the new dynamics of an articulate and demanding consumer-centric marketplace. The technology of data analytics and its use in marketing are explained. The touchpoints and pain points of the customer purchase journey are discussed in relationship to an omni-channel distribution network.

Part 2 explores concepts within the creative design process. Chapter 4 looks at an evolving fashion system that is finding new ways to respond to and communicate with diverse consumers. As sensitivity to slow fashion exposes the waste of the fast fashion system, trend analysis is becoming more nuanced. Trend analysis is evolving to support and promote investment dressing over disposable fashion. The trend analysis process is discussed, explaining how macro- and micro-trends in the zeitgeist inspire design ideas in terms of color, fabric, silhouette, and details. Various approaches to trend analysis are explored. Chapter 5 builds on the concept of color science and how it must be managed during the product development process. Chapter 6 presents textile choices, organized by properties such as luster and drape, to facilitate decision making. Chapter 7 explains the criteria and methods for planning a brand's seasonal line and ensuring that all tasks are completed to support timely delivery. Chapter 8 is concerned with silhouette development and the process of designing individual garment styles. This chapter concludes with a visual appendix of apparel silhouettes and details.

Part 3 focuses on the technical product development process. In recognition of the international audience for *Beyond Design*, many topics have been rewritten. A tech pack based on a single product is introduced in Chapter 9 and then brought in again, page by page, in the chapters that follow as each stage of technical specification is explained. Although the measurements in the tech pack pages are given in the imperial system, instructors can find metric system equivalents in the Instructor's Guide. Chapter 9 reviews traditional methods for creating first patterns and samples as well as 3D design and digital tools for tracking the product development process end to end. Chapter 10 discusses garment sizing and fit with a focus on the role of technology in the evolution toward customization. An appendix has been added with size charts for selected countries. Chapter 11 explores production methods and standards in relation to various product categories, providing choices that impact cost and quality. The section on labeling reflects international changes in labeling requirements and new uses for labels.

Part 4 discusses supply chain partner selection, pricing, and costing. Chapter 12 examines brands' selection of partners within the supply chain, balancing production demands with ethics, with a focus on traceability. Resources will be provided for students to do their own research so that they can stay abreast of changing conditions in partner countries. Chapter 13 defines the elements of cost at retail and wholesale, considering strategies for managing cost variables such as the Environmental Profit and Loss Statement.

Reviewers requested a greater focus on sustainability. Each chapter of the fifth edition includes a sustainability header where the topic is discussed in relation to the chapter focus. These discussions encompass sustainability initiatives throughout the supply chain with an emphasis on linking goals to metrics and accountability.

PEDAGOGICAL FEATURES

The text is targeted to sophomore- and junior-year college and university students. It may be used in its entirety to provide a one-semester overview of the apparel product development cycle or, alternately, in a more project-oriented mode over two semesters, where the first semester emphasizes the creative design processes and the second semester focuses on the technical design aspects of product development. It provides enough flexibility to accommodate students with varying learning styles. The process of product development is presented as a series of choices to prepare students for an industry that is constantly evolving.

Suggested prerequisites include an introductory textile course, a basic illustration course, a technical drawing course, and, for design majors, garment construction and patternmaking courses. A basic understanding of business—accounting, marketing, and management—will provide a foundation for merchandise management majors utilizing the text.

A number of pedagogical features have been designed to enhance both the overview and the project-oriented approach to courses adopting this text. Each chapter begins with a set of objectives and concludes with a summary, a list of key terms, discussion questions, activities, a list of references, and additional resources, if applicable. New case studies have been added within chapters to amplify the chapter topic. Additional resources have been included in the **STUDIO** content developed to supplement the text.

To ensure an accurate and current presentation, the authors have relied on industry contacts, many of whom provided images as well as information about their practices and procedures. The text aims to prepare career-minded students of apparel product development to enter the job market with a realistic, up-to-date understanding of this evolving, dynamic industry.

INSTRUCTOR AND STUDENT RESOURCES

Student Resources

Beyond Design STUDIO

We are pleased to offer an online multimedia resource to support this text—Beyond Design STUDIO. The online STUDIO is specially developed to complement this book with rich media ancillaries that students can adapt to their visual learning styles to better master concepts and improve grades. Within the STUDIO, students will be able to:

- Study smarter with self-quizzes featuring scored results and personalized study tips
- Review concepts with flashcards of essential vocabulary

STUDIO access cards are offered free with new book purchases and are also sold separately through Bloomsbury Fashion Central (www.BloomsburyFashion Central.com).

Instructor Resources

- Instructor's Guide provides suggestions for planning the course and using the text in the classroom, including supplemental assignments and lecture notes
- Test Bank includes sample test questions for each chapter
- PowerPoint presentations include images from the book and provide a framework for lecture and discussion

Instructor's Resources may be accessed through Bloomsbury Fashion Central (www.BloomsburyFashionCentral.com).

ACKNOWLEDGMENTS

The isolation of the COVID-19 pandemic turned out to be a mixed blessing in researching the fifth edition of *Beyond Design*. With in-person professional meetings and trade shows cancelled, there were a plethora of symposiums, webinars, and interviews accessible online which informed this new edition. We were able to learn firsthand how leaders in the industry were responding to the crisis, adapting to market changes, and adopting new technology.

We are grateful to our families, friends, and colleagues who have supported us through this experience, especially Bob Poor, Deborah's patient and encouraging husband. We are particularly indebted to the many industry professionals, colleagues, and alumnae who generously shared their time and expertise for not only the original book but also the follow-up editions. Their efforts have contributed significantly to ensuring that the processes identified are up-to-date and based on accurate industry practices. These individuals represent some of the best in their field at all levels of the product development process.

Support came from Trend Union, First Insights, Evie Lou, Lectra, Optitex, Gerber, Alvanon, Stars Design Group, BeProduct, Scarborough Co., and so many others who provided insights into their processes and visuals for the new edition. Special thanks to the Industrial Sewing and Innovation Center (ISAIC) for sharing their experience in efforts to revitalize the sewn products industry.

We are grateful to all those faculty members who use this text and so generously provided feedback for the newest revision of *Beyond Design*. Their insights into how product development is taught in their curricula informed the direction taken for this fifth edition. We appreciate and have relied upon the research of our colleagues who are advancing our understanding of complex issues and developments in technology, global trade, and ethics.

Bloomsbury Publishing wishes to gratefully acknowledge and thank the editorial team involved in the publication of this book:

Senior Acquisitions Editor: Emily Samulski

Development Manager: Joseph Miranda

Editorial Assistant: Jenna Lefkowitz

Art Development Editor: Edie Weinberg

In-House Designer: Louise Dugdale

Production Manager: Ken Bruce

Project Manager: Courtney Coffman

We also wish to thank the reviewers for their insightful feedback:

Kat Roberts—New York City College of Technology, CUNY

Fabiana Vannuccini—Kent State University, FIT, and Polimoda

Tricia Carlos—Columbus College of Art and Design

Barbara Skuczik—Paris College of Art

PART 1

BUSINESS ORGANIZATION
AND STRATEGY

CHAPTER 1

PRODUCT DEVELOPMENT AND THE APPAREL SUPPLY CHAIN

To succeed, fashion players will have to come to terms with a new paradigm. Regardless of size and segment, players now need to be nimble, think digital-first, and achieve ever-faster speed to market. They need to take an active stance on social issues, satisfy consumer demands for ultra-transparency and sustainability, and most importantly, have the courage to 'self-disrupt' their own identity and the sources of their old success. (MCKINSEY & COMPANY, THE STATE OF FASHION 2019)

OBJECTIVES

- To define the product development process
- To recognize how the fashion system impacts product development
- To examine the changing dynamics of apparel product development
- To comprehend how a global apparel supply chain has evolved to meet the needs of the product development process and a consumer-centric marketplace
- To be aware of the structural organization of apparel companies and their supply chains
- To understand the opportunities of a circular supply chain as a means of making the apparel industry more sustainable
- To recognize the harms caused by the fashion system and the textile and apparel industry as it is presently structured

PRODUCT DEVELOPMENT AND THE FASHION SYSTEM

Fashion has always been defined by change, but consumer desire for newness and self-expression has been accelerating at breakneck speed since the advent of fast fashion. This has been compounded by ongoing changes in the business climate as well as global economic, political, and environmental challenges. A commitment to sustainability is now an imperative. Product developers have struggled to adapt their processes accordingly.

Fashion today is consumer-centric. As such it is increasingly difficult to predict future popularity and adoption by studying the past or the present. To succeed, businesses must learn to pivot quickly as conditions warrant; they need to integrate available and emerging technology and transform their business model to meet the demands of an interconnected global marketplace. This requires a working synergy up and down the supply chain.

Product development is an end-to-end process that includes marketing, merchandising, creative and technical design, sourcing, production, and distribution planning of goods that have a perceived value for a well-defined consumer group. These goods should be made to reach the marketplace in the right quantity when consumers are ready to buy. This requires coordinating an increasingly complex product development process across a global supply chain.

Apparel product developers respond to the demands of the fashion system. In western culture the **fashion system** refers to the organizational structures and activities employed to promote change and novelty in apparel, generally for economic gain. The fashion system encourages the ongoing identification of new trends, promotes seasonal runway shows and fashion presentations, and drives new product development and distribution that propels customers to continually want new product whether or not what's in their closets is still functional. Product developers constantly reevaluate what products they will offer, how those products will be produced, and how and when they will be marketed and distributed to customers, hopefully translating change into opportunity and profitability. The concept of a fashion system is universal; however, it may encompass subsystems specific to culture and place. Fashion systems evolve with time, technology, and consumer lifestyles.

For large brands and entrepreneurial designers both, there is always a tension between being creative and running a profitable business. The pause of the 2020 pandemic and the business challenges that resulted has forced the industry to rethink the fashion system and adapt product development processes. There is great opportunity to be part of a new industry that thinks about, produces, and consumes fashion differently.

This chapter provides a context for understanding the role product development plays in meeting the needs of the fashion system. It describes the organizational dynamics and global partnerships that connect human, material, and intellectual resources to produce consumer-centric goods and services in a timely way. It explains how the product development calendar and digital technology support this business ecosystem. It underscores the need for businesses to become more sustainable and socially just and looks at how entrepreneurs can adapt the product development process to their specific markets. These themes will be further developed throughout the text.

The Dynamics of Product Development

Product development processes vary, depending on:

- *Who* is doing the developing—brand wholesalers or retailers
- *What* kind of products they are developing—basic, seasonal, or fashion forward; whether they are products that require high skill and/or high technology as opposed to those that are low skill, low tech
- *Where* the products will be distributed—regionally, nationally, or globally
- *How* the products will be distributed—online, in stores, or through catalogs
- *When* the products need to be delivered

Figure 1.1
Influencer Sonia Lyson wears a Chanel hat, H&M sweater, Zara pants and coat, and Jacquemas mini bag. H&M and Zara are store brands. Chanel and Jacquemus are wholesale brands.

Wholesale Brands vs. Private Brands (Private Labels and Store Brands)

Wholesale brand businesses design, produce, and market products under a proprietary label and distribute those products to retailers or third parties, who sell them to the final consumer. Mass merchants, department stores, specialty stores, chain stores, and boutiques frequently carry wholesale brands. Wholesale brand product developers may also distribute their products digitally or through their own signature or outlet stores, but typically, these sales do not constitute the bulk of their business. Retailers that carry wholesale brands are sometimes referred to as **multi-brand**.

Private brand product developers develop and merchandise products for exclusive distribution by a particular retailer. Chain stores such as Zara and Lululemon sell only private brands. Private brands sold by mass merchants and department stores typically compete with wholesale brand products also carried by the retailer. They may also be referred to as *exclusive brands* or *own brands*. To distinguish between these two approaches, in this textbook brands developed for stores that sell only private brands will be identified as **store brands**; private brands developed to compete with wholesale brands will be referred to as **private label brands** (Figure 1.1).

Private brand products (both private label and store brand) may be developed in any one of the following ways:

- Product may be developed by the retailer's in-house product development team.
- Buyers may purchase a portion of their private brand merchandise from a wholesale product developer. These products are adaptations from the wholesaler's brand line that are customized in color or fabric to make them exclusive. The wholesale brand supplier adapts the styles purchased to the private brand's sizing specifications and ships the goods with the private brand's label.
- A product developer may contract with an offshore supplier to design and manufacture product.
- A large retailer may buy or license the rights to a wholesale brand, transforming it from a wholesale brand to an exclusive private brand.

Private brands offer the following advantages:

- Prices are usually lower than competing wholesale brands.
- They provide retailers with control over quality and marketing.
- They generally yield higher profit margins.
- They provide retailers with the opportunity to enhance their brand image and differentiate themselves from the competition.
- They are can be a means of cultivating consumer loyalty.

Mass merchant and department stores serve a diverse range of consumers. Most have found that a mix of wholesale brands and private label brands meet the needs of this diverse customer base. A typical merchandise mix is 15 to 50 percent private label and 50 to 85 percent wholesale brands. In spite of the sophistication of today's private label brands, many retailers have found that once the percentage of private label goes beyond 50 percent, the brands lose their cachet.

A store brand strategy attempts to cater to a particular market niche and lifestyle which influences their merchandise curation. This focus can also make these retailers vulnerable to shifts in consumer loyalty. As one generation grows out of a particular retailer's brands, there is no guarantee that the next generation will consider that same brand desirable.

Like everything in the industry, these definitions continue to evolve. Some store brand retailers are adding wholesale brands to their mix. H&M announced in the fall of 2019 that it would add select wholesale brands to its product mix in order to attract new shoppers.

Likewise, store brands are beginning to show up in big box and department stores either as part of a concession strategy, a licensing agreement, or as a temporary pop-up store. A **concession strategy** is a leasing agreement between a retailer and a brand whereby the retailer leases out designated space to the brand which can then operate somewhat autonomously curating its product and services and staffing with its own personnel. Topshop operated a concession store in Nordstrom between 2012 and 2021 in order to expand its American distribution. When Topshop's owner, Arcadia Group, went bankrupt in 2021, online retailer ASOS bought the Topshop brand as well as

Table 1.1 Brand Types

	Definition	Customer	Examples
Wholesale Brands	Brands that are designed, produced, and marketed under a proprietary label and distributed to retailers or third parties who sell them to the final consumer	• Mass merchants • Department stores • Some chain stores • Boutiques • Small quantities may be sold in the brand's own signature stores	• Levi • BCBG • Free People
Private Brands	Brands developed and merchandised for exclusive distribution by a particular retailer		
• Private Label	Brands that are sold by retailers and websites that sell a mix of private and wholesale brands	• Mass merchants • Department stores	• LC Lauren Conrad and FLX for Kohl's • Charter Club and And Now This for Macy's • Wild Fable and Original Use for Target
• Store Brand	Brands that are sold by retailers and websites that sell only private brands	• Chain stores	• Gap • Lululemon • Zara

Topman, Miss Selfridge, and HIIT. Nordstrom acquired a stake in the four ASOS brands in July of 2021 giving Nordstrom exclusive multi-channel distribution rights in North America based on their successful experience with Topshop as a concession brand. Nordstrom entered into licensing agreements with the Madewell and J. Crew brands in 2015. In these agreements, the Nordstrom buyers curate the merchandise in Nordstrom stores. To test out these collaborations, some department stores and big box stores are utilizing the pop-up store concept, entering into agreements for a limited time in order to discern whether or not the partnership is a good match.

These examples illustrate the blurring of lines between wholesale and private brands. New developments are a result of fierce competition, a decrease in brand loyalty, and a rapidly changing distribution landscape with many retailers and wholesale brands closing their businesses. In an effort to offer innovative fashion forward product, brand partnerships are an appealing opportunity. Table 1.1 summarizes the differences between wholesale brands, private label brands, and store brands.

Fashion Level

Consumers have a range of demands for the apparel products they purchase. Their needs vary from basics to fashion. The apparel supply chain that a product developer puts together for any given product is dependent on the product's fashion level.

- **Basic product** is produced in high volume, with predictable demand, and is very price sensitive; the consumer can purchase it from a variety of competitors. Since these products change minimally from season to season, design decisions can be made early, providing a longer production lead time. This longer lead time in combination with high volume means product can be produced at relatively low unit cost offshore.

· **Seasonal product** differentiates a brand and establishes its fashion aesthetic. These items are produced in moderate quantities. Product developers prefer to put off decision making until the last minute to better predict demand. Prices must be competitive, but consumers will pay more for this product's on-trend aesthetic. These products must be in- store when the consumer is ready to buy, so reliable delivery is critical.

· **Fashion forward product** may only be distributed online and in prime store locations. Geared to the store's leading-edge customers, it helps a product developer test the market for upcoming seasons. Made in relatively small quantities and often more complex in design, these items are the most expensive to produce and carry the highest risk. Yet having some fashion forward product in each seasonal delivery is one way of gauging customer sentiments going forward. Fashion forward product may gain its edge through fabrication (organic cotton, leather, or high-tech performance fabrics), through styling (a short-term designer collaboration), or through customizable features.

Most product developers include a combination of all three categories of merchandise in their seasonal lines.

The type of product produced will impact the decision of where it will be produced. Fashion forward product is designed and ordered closer to season; these products may require a higher skill level on the part of the worker or a factory with more sophisticated technology, making them more expensive. Producing this product closer to where it will be marketed helps to shorten the lead time. Basic product may require less skill and technology and can be planned farther in advance; therefore, factory/labor costs tend to be lower. Although more expensive, net margins on fashion forward products may be lower than those for basic products. Hopefully, total sales volumes will average out to the desired net margin. Figure 1.2 summarizes the implications of fashion level on product production.

Product Distribution

The scope of a brand's distribution may be local, regional, national, or global. This will impact their product design as well as their delivery calendar. Entrepreneurs who produce locally for a local market don't need to factor in time for shipping, although they

Figure 1.2
A brand's merchandise mix is generally made up of basics, seasonal goods that define the brand, and fashion forward, co-branded, or specialty items. Each type of product varies in terms of volume, costs, associated risks, development cycle, and distribution.

· Low volume
· Higher cost
· Higher risk
· Short development cycle
· Limited distribution

Fashion Forward or High-Tech Product

Seasonal Product Key Items

Basic Product

· High volume
· Low cost
· Low risk
· Longer development cycle
· Broad distribution

may have to order fabrics and trims from a distance. In terms of design, product developers must deal with cultural differences, as well as variations in weather patterns, holidays, and sizing needs. For example, seasons may be reversed in some parts of the world; some locales don't require cold weather coats and boots but need warm weather apparel year round. Global and cultural differences may require modifications to both the product design and the time and action calendar. Product produced for the United States may be manufactured in one plant and product for Asia or Europe in another in order to best respond to distribution specifications and to minimize transportation costs.

Digital sales had been growing significantly before the COVID-19 pandemic. The global quarantine accelerated that trend. Brands with strong digital platforms were ahead of the game in delivering a satisfactory experience. Digital sales require sophisticated distribution systems in order to respond to orders quickly and efficiently; customers expect delivery to be prompt and, if possible, free. Distribution systems that are set up to ship from either a warehouse or directly from a store maximize product inventory and minimize markdowns. The growth of digital sales is creating a new role for brick-and-mortar stores. Store footprints can be smaller and their environments more engaging as they become a showroom where customers can touch and try on. That symbiotic relationship works both ways. The customer can discover a style they like online, try it on in-store, and purchase it immediately or order it to their specifications. When stores don't have to carry as much stock, the percentage of stock that is discounted due to damage will be lessened.

The Product Development Calendar

A key element of product development is getting the product to consumers when they are ready to buy. The goal is to get customers to pay first price rather than wait until a product is marked down. Product development calendars are developed to ensure that the line is ready to be shown and that stock delivery arrives when retailers have specified. Traditionally, delivery dates are set based on advertising and marketing plans; all deadlines in the product development process are counted back from these dates. Problems may arise when supply chain partners are not sufficiently brought into discussions regarding calendar development. Their ability to meet deadlines is dependent on fabric deliveries, available capacity, and getting completed tech packs on time. As lead times contract and order quantities get smaller, coordination is key. Multiple delivery dates for different parts of the country or different parts of the world further complicate this process.

Fashion timing is an ongoing industry challenge; seasonal deliveries traditionally drop weeks before local weather patterns put the consumer in the mood to buy. This means that just as consumer interest is picking up, product has been on the floor for four to six weeks and is already being marked down. The inventory glut after the shelter-at-home requirements of the global pandemic gave many brands the impetus to re-evaluate their product development calendars. Placing smaller orders informed by shorter product development calendars as well as delivery dates that provide *buy now, wear now* product is the goal (Table 1.2).

Table 1.2 Comparison of Three Product Development Calendars with Same Retail Delivery Date

	Total weeks											
	54	50	45	40	35	30	25	20	15	10	5	0
Traditional calendar	Trend and color		Design and sampling				Buy		Production		Logistics	Set floor
Today's basics/core merchandise						Trend and color	Design and sampling	Buy	Production		Logistics	Set
Today's fashion goods									Trend and color	Design and sampling / Buy	Production / Logistics	Set

Source: Olivier 2008.

Scaling Production

The ability to produce apparel in the right quantities has been a long-standing problem in the industry. Large corporations commit to larger quantities than they have orders for in order to negotiate the best price. Suppliers that require long lead times make it challenging to project an accurate order size. Excess inventory dilutes margins in the best of times because it must be offered at a discount. Excess inventory in a time of economic crisis, such as the COVID-19 pandemic, can put a brand and their supply chain partners out of business. As the fashion system reinvents itself, there is an imperative to correct these inventory issues. The implementation of digital approvals, placing smaller orders with supply chain partners that don't require long lead times, and implementing data analytics to get order sizes right will all help to right-size orders and inventories. Data analytics programs are used to define, collect, cleanse, interpret, and model data points in ways that extract meaning. They can be used to inform decision making and project trends and behaviors throughout every step of the product development process through the use of artificial intelligence and machine learning.

Stakeholders

Every individual, group, or organization that affects or is affected by the fashion system and product development process can be considered a **stakeholder**. Stakeholders include (but are not limited to) raw materials providers, manufacturers, service providers, brands, distribution partners, governments, industry associations, nonprofits, and academia as well as consumers, employees, and investors. Each stakeholder may have other stakeholders to whom they are responsible. Affecting change is challenging because each stakeholder has different expectations and behavioral motivations. Key stakeholders may have the authority to impose requirements and/or constraints that shape the business outcome. Ultimately progress is best made when a majority of stakeholders are in general agreement as to future outcomes and goals (Figure 1.3).

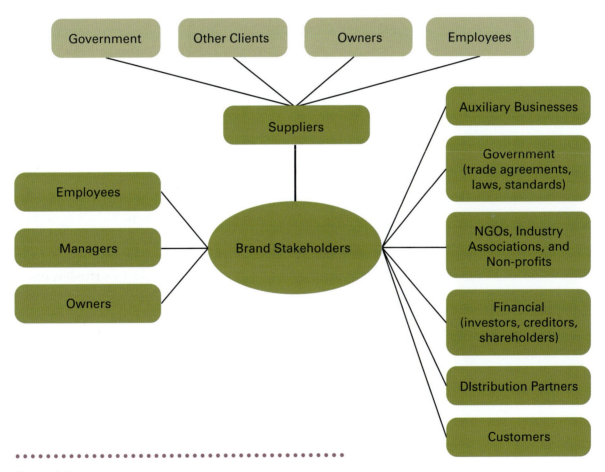

Figure 1.3
Brands have both internal (left) and external (right) stakeholders. Each stakeholder has stakeholders of their own as illustrated by the supplier callout. Collaboration is critical but not easy when goals and expectations differ.

SUPPLY CHAINS THAT MEET PRODUCT DEVELOPMENT NEEDS

Product development is a defining step in assembling the complex network of suppliers and service providers involved directly or indirectly in fulfilling customer demand for apparel.

Supply Chain Definitions

The **apparel supply chain** comprises the flow of all information, products, materials, and funds between different stages of creating and selling a product to the end user. Supply chain management addresses how a designed product can be manufactured from an operational perspective (Tarver, March 24, 2020). Every step in the process—including creating the product or service, manufacturing it, transporting it to a place of sale, and selling it—is part of a company's supply chain.

The supply chain is sometimes referred to as a value chain. From a business management perspective, **value chain** managers look for opportunities to add significant benefit to the product rather than negotiating solely on price. They may look for ways to cut back on shortages, improve quality or functionality, and work with others in the chain to add value for the customer (Tarver, March 24, 2020).

Specialty businesses that support apparel product development are referred to as **auxiliary businesses**; they include design bureaus, software providers, sourcing agents, factors (credit agents), patternmaking services, testing labs, consultants, and advertising agencies with which businesses might contract if they don't have the capacity to perform those tasks in-house. Auxiliary businesses are also a good resource when demand for a task is greater than the in-house team can handle and still meet deadlines.

Product developers must assemble a unique supply chain from a network of suppliers for each product in their line. These supply chains operate for as long as that product is in demand. The individual links of the chain may become part of numerous supply chain variations within a given season, depending on how many diverse styles they have the core competencies and capacity to produce. The best supply chain for an order with a delivery date four months in the future may be very different from a supply chain for the same order that is due in four weeks.

Moving forward, the trend in apparel manufacturing is to deliver carefully edited product ranges, produced in smaller lot sizes in order to avoid inventory overages. According to the American Apparel and Footwear Association, 97.5 percent of apparel purchased in the United States is made offshore. With the trend toward smaller orders and shorter lead times, all levels of the supply chain will need to adapt. This means implementing more technology, automating manufacturing processes, and re-evaluating where product is made. **Near-shoring**, also referred to as *proximity manufacturing*, describes the strategy of producing product closer to the market where it will be sold. It is one more way of shortening the product development calendar though it may negatively impact the millions of workers who are currently employed for low wages in developing countries not located near large consumer markets.

Sourcing is the continuous review of the need for goods and services against the purchasing opportunities that meet quantity, quality, price, sustainability, and delivery parameters in order to leverage purchasing power for the best value. Any goods that a brand can't produce or functions that a brand can't perform cost effectively are outsourced to other vendors. With proper oversight and communication, the expertise of each supply chain participant or sourcing partner contributes to the efficiency of the entire chain and increases the value of the resulting products.

Whether a company is developing high fashion or basic apparel, whether its product development cycle is four weeks or nine months, the goals are the same. Shorten cycle times, drive down costs, eliminate non–value-adding steps (such as warehousing) and right-size inventory levels. This must be accomplished in an environment of decreasing natural resources, volatile costs, increasing expectations for quality and sustainability, and an ever-increasing mix of products. Even entrepreneurial and new businesses must consider how they will be able to meet demand as they grow their business.

Supply Chain Dynamics

The way a supply chain is structured and managed impacts its efficiency and agility. With an unpredictable global economy, supply chains need to be nimble in responding to unexpected fluctuations in demand.

Push vs. Pull Systems

Historically, designers and product developers anticipated consumer demand based on last season's data as to what consumers had already purchased; they produced the products they thought consumers would want and *pushed* them into the marketplace. However, when the forecast is wrong in a push system, retailers are forced to get rid of excess inventory, take unplanned markdowns, and settle for lower profit margins. Nevertheless, push systems have their advantages. Orders can be placed earlier, in bigger quantities, often for a lower price. On the other hand, placing orders early may mean missing a late-developing trend. Push systems continue to work for basic product, but they have limitations when it comes to seasonal and fashion products. Push systems work on a four- to twelve-month product development calendar.

In a *pull* system, designers and product developers wait to commit to product until the last possible minute so that they can collect timely and accurate data about consumer wants and needs. They place smaller, more frequent orders, adapting to consumer buying behavior within the season. This may mean paying higher prices for small orders and may necessitate shipping by air rather than boat in order to reach stores on time. Orders are in response to what consumers say they will buy, resulting in less excess inventory and higher profit margins. In order to be successful, pull systems must have agile supply chain partners capable of responding quickly to new orders. Pull systems typically work on a four- to twelve-week product development calendar.

Today's most efficient apparel supply chains are *pull* driven rather than *push* driven; however, a product developer need not commit to one or the other system. Many

Table 1.3 Push and Pull Systems: Pros and Cons

	Advantages	Disadvantages/Challenges
Push System	• Early orders in large quantities may mean lower prices	• Large orders early in the season may result in excess inventory, necessitating unplanned markdowns • May miss late developing trends • Lower profit margins due to markdowns taken to clear excess inventory
Pull System	• Based on accurate data regarding consumer behavior throughout the season • Smaller, more frequent, and more accurate orders result in less excess inventory and fewer markdowns • Higher profit margins	• Requires agile supply chain partners with business savvy and manufacturing sophistication • Higher shipping costs for smaller orders; may require shipping by air rather than boat

product developers use a combination of push and pull supply chains—a push system for basic goods and a demand-driven pull system for seasonal and fashion goods. See Table 1.3 for an outline of the advantages and disadvantages of the push and pull systems.

Supply Chain Visibility

Most brands partner with the companies that manufacturer their product. They often expect these manufacturers to source the fabrics and findings that go into their products. Product manufacturers may routinely subcontract some of their production commitments to others. To understand supply chain visibility, it may help to look at supply chains in tiers. *First tier* suppliers consist of cut-and-sew factories that make or assemble the final product. *Second tier* suppliers include processing factories such as washing, dyeing, tanning, printing, finishing, and parts manufacturing. *Third tier* suppliers provide fabrics, yarn, notions, and trims to factories (Figure 1.4). Most brands are challenged to track the production of their products all the way back to the fiber source.

Companies are under growing pressure to share their sourcing decisions. Supply chains have long been a closely guarded secret; sourcing managers did not want to share the names of supply chain partners that offered the lowest costs or superior quality. Today, stakeholders from investors to the final consumer are demanding that brands make their supply chains public; they want brands to prove the marketing claims they make. The process starts with **traceability**—being able to track each component of an item throughout the supply chain from the raw material to the thread to the final garment. Supply chain **transparency** requires companies to know what is happening up and down the supply chain and to communicate this knowledge both internally and externally (Bateman and Bonnani, August 20, 2019). The terms upstream and downstream are often used when describing supply chain communication. **Upstream** refers to the supply side of the supply chain—those producers that provide raw materials. **Downstream** refers to points in the supply chain that manage

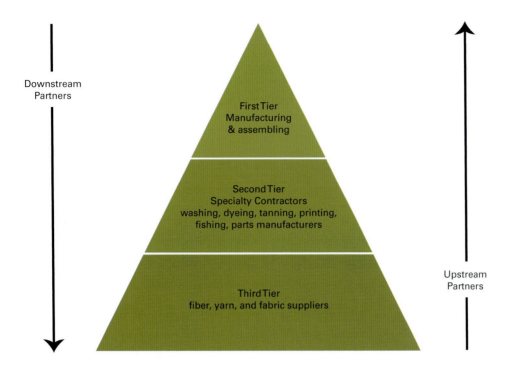

Downstream
Partners

First Tier
Manufacturing
& assembling

Second Tier
Specialty Contractors
washing, dyeing, tanning, printing,
fishing, parts manufacturers

Third Tier
fiber, yarn, and fabric suppliers

Upstream
Partners

Figure 1.4
The supply chain
can be visualized as
tiers, representing
manufacturers, specialty
finishers, and fiber
and fabric suppliers.
Oftentimes brands do
not know their upstream
tier 2 or 3 suppliers,
making it difficult to be
transparent.

distribution to the final consumer. Communication in both directions is critical to transparency.

Transparency helps to end the use of hidden supply chains that abuse workers, hire underage children, and pay substandard wages in order to meet a brand's price and deadline requirements. It is critical in regulating processes and holding the industry accountable for the environmental harms of textile and apparel manufacturing. It also drives new technology that will lead the industry into a more sustainable future. Supply chains are more than a cost to be minimized; they are a source of resilience and an engine for profit that should not be disrespected.

Collaborative Supply Chains

A **collaborative supply chain** is an interactive network of manufacturing specialists who join forces operationally to integrate complementary resources in response to a market opportunity. The goal is to strike strong and mutually beneficial long-term relationships with suppliers while retaining the ability to pivot to meet market needs. To be competitive in today's marketplace requires assembling the most reliable, efficient, and skilled array of supply chain partners. The knowledge, experience, and skills of all team members contribute to the supply chain's success. To be truly collaborative, product developers must:

- gather input up and down the supply chain as to how a product or process can be improved; what the real costs are; and whether or not the delivery schedule is reasonable;

- pay a fair price rather than haggle for a price that necessitates that vendors cut corners;
- require vendors to use processes that do not jeopardize the health and safety of workers;
- help suppliers to do no harm to the planet in the course of supplying their service; and
- honor contracts and share risk in times of national and international crisis.

Authentic collaborative supply chains are better prepared to respond to planned, anticipated, or unexpected external circumstances that present unforeseen challenges and opportunities. Globalization of the apparel business means dealing with communication issues, time zones, language barriers, technology, logistics, and infrastructure complications, as well as less predictable disruptors such as natural disasters, terrorism, wars, politics, and outbreaks of disease. These events require nimble responses and an agile supply chain.

The Covid 19 pandemic of 2020 brought to light the fragility of this system. The pandemic peaked in different parts of the world at intervals. As the US reached its peak, it cancelled orders; many brands did not pay for work in process. Workers in China and Asia were the first to be allowed to return to work within social distancing guidelines. Even where there were sufficient orders to return to production, supply chains often encountered one critical link still under shelter-in-place orders. Some US and European brands opted to skip an entire sales season, denying their supply chain factories their livelihood. The pandemic underscored the power imbalance within the global supply chain where brands assume their right to cancel orders and manufacturing partners in low-wage countries have no work to offer their already impoverished workers. Collaboration is only as good as the communication and sharing that goes into it. Collaboration in name only means nothing.

Circular Supply Chains

A **circular supply chain**, also known as a *closed loop supply chain*, is a zero-waste supply chain that reuses, recycles, or composts all materials. It requires product developers to design out waste and pollution, keeping products and materials in use and regenerating natural systems. Traditional linear supply chains have been concerned with manufacturing and distributing product, assuming no responsibility for what happens to the product when consumers no longer find it useful. The linear supply chain characterized by "take-make-dispose" focuses on producing and selling as much product as possible; it's a system that is no longer sustainable. A circular supply chain is based on reduce-reuse-recycle. Reduce resources used in production and consumer consumption; reuse products until no longer useful; and recycle discarded materials so that they can be collected and repurposed into new items. In this system value is maintained by value preservation. Instead of producing and selling as much product as possible, profits can be generated by upcycling discarded products into new products or converting products into services such as facilitating sharing and renting (Kuebix, June 21, 2019) (Figure 1.5).

Figure 1.5
Circular Supply Chain

Regenerate natural systems

WE ARE SHIFTING TO A SYSTEM WHERE WE

Design out waste and pollution

Keep products and materials in use

NIKE, Inc.'s *Reuse-A-Shoe* program is an example: NIKE, Inc. collects all brands of athletic sneakers and repurposes them into NIKE GRIND. NIKE GRIND is used for new shoe components, apparel, and athletic surfaces for playgrounds, tracks, and tennis courts.

Adidas has pledged to make 11 million sneakers out of recycled plastics pulled from the ocean. Patagonia has its own robust recycling program and offers care and repair instructions on its website. The company also collects garments at the end of their lives for credit to be used on future purchases; it collaborated with Alabama Chanin as part of its *Worn Wear* program to create scarves and wraps from old, discarded jackets. Eileen Fisher takes back their old, discarded clothes. Pieces in good condition are cleaned and resold; pieces that are no longer wearable are turned into new one-of-a-kind designs (Figures 1.6a–b).

Figure 1.6a
The Adidas x Parley sneaker is made from recycled plastic waste from the ocean.

Figure 1.6b
Eileen Fisher's Renew + Remake program collects used garments and remakes them into new designs for resale.

a

b

Vertical vs. Horizontal Supply Chains

Product developers must assess whether ownership or partnership up and down the supply chain is more advantageous in terms of costs, agility, and efficiency. **Vertical integration** is a strategy whereby a company seeks to own its suppliers, distributors, or retail locations in order to control the supply chain's value and efficiency. Companies may follow a vertical integration strategy if they feel it will enhance their access to production capacity, improve quality, or offer economies of scale. On the flip side, it is expensive to own all tiers of a supply chain and ownership can limit a brand's flexibility in adapting to fashion trends. The legalities of owning a business in another country can be complicated.

Spanish retailer Zara has embraced vertical integration. Their supply chain ownership allows them to deliver fashion-right merchandise in a matter of weeks. Luxury brands like Chanel and Kering have been buying up their most unique suppliers, from farms to artisanal specialty providers, to ensure the sustainability of the finest materials and artisanal skills on which they rely. Chanel has a subsidiary named *Paraffection* through which it owns thirteen artisanal suppliers and twenty-one manufacturers that do embroidery, mill cashmere, and make hats and shoes. These *fournisseurs* or luxury suppliers can be hired by any other fashion designer, although Chanel is definitely their biggest patron (Figures 1.7a–b).

Wholesale brands may invest in upward integration by opening their own stores. These stores may be run as off-price outlets or as full-price signature stores. **Outlet stores** provide a means of controlling the distribution of excess goods; **signature stores** provide a direct line to their ultimate consumer (Figure 1.8a–b).

Most product developers, both wholesale and retail, prefer to work with fewer, larger, and more capable suppliers strategically located around the world. Vertically integrated sourcing partners or those who have relationships that enable them to act vertically are sought after since each company in the supply chain represents another

Figures 1.7a and b
Chanel's Paraffection division owns thirteen artisinal suppliers and twenty-one manufacturers that specialize in artisinal skills such as embroidery, pleating, hat making, and shoe making.

a

b

a

b

Figure 1.8a
The Ralph Lauren Rhinelander mansion store on Madison Avenue in New York City is a signature store for men.

Figure 1.8b
Polo Ralph Lauren outlet stores are located in outlet malls across the country.

line of communication and scheduling and a separate profit center. With fewer links in the supply chain, communication is simplified, cycle times are reduced, and profit centers can be eliminated. As offshore manufacturers get more sophisticated, they are able to use their supply chain knowledge to meet the needs of developing regional markets; this can be useful when global markets are disrupted. The next step is for the most sophisticated vertically integrated suppliers to launch their own direct-to-consumer global brands.

Horizontal integration is an alternative growth strategy. **Horizontal integration** prioritizes the acquisition or licensing of companies or brands that make or sell similar products to expand market penetration, reduce competition, access technology, and take advantage of business synergies. It may be used to acquire brands at the same price level, which reduces competition, or to penetrate multiple price points in the same product category, which expands reach.

Like vertical integration, horizontal integration can also apply to supply chains. Some forward-thinking off-shore manufacturers are investing in factories in the US, Mexico, the Caribbean basin, and Europe in order to offer both low-cost manufacturing and near-shore speed-to-market manufacturing. In this way they can be nimbler in meeting all of a brand's manufacturing needs.

Diversification is a strategy in which a firm expands its product mix to capitalize on brand recognition or experience in a particular segment of the business. An apparel company might purchase a jewelry company or a shoe company to increase the company's product mix and facilitate brand extensions. Like horizontal integration, diversification may be achieved through licensing or by the acquisition of related or unrelated companies.

The Michael Kors brand is an example of a brand that has diversified through licensing. Parfums Givenchy Inc., the North American unit of LVMH Fragrance and Cosmetics Group, holds the license for Michael Kors fragrance. Schwartz and Benjamin holds the Michael Kors license for shoes; Le Tannem & Cie holds the license for small leather goods; and The Charmat Group holds the license for eyewear. Michael Kors profits from royalties earned but doesn't have to develop a new unfamiliar supply chain. Brands are vulnerable to diluting the brand image of their premier brand when they launch too many lower-priced sub-brands. Michael Kors has been faulted for this.

In a volatile economy, having the experience in a particular segment such as luxury can be a valuable tool. LVMH owns a number of brands in the luxury market; their reputation gives them access to resources and supply chains that can be advantageous to any brand they own.

Historically, in times of economic prosperity, corporations have had the inclination to become larger. The tumultuous economic ups and downs of the past twenty years is bringing into question the wisdom of the *bigger is better* (and more profitable) philosophy. Many companies are finding that it is easier to forge a strong connection with consumers if they right-size, whatever that means to them as a business. Only time will tell how this plays out.

DISRUPTIVE TECHNOLOGY TRANSFORMING PRODUCT DEVELOPMENT AND SUPPLY CHAIN MANAGEMENT

When innovation and new technology significantly alter the way consumers, businesses, and industries operate, it is described as **disruptive**. Disruptive technologies are so superior that they make previous systems obsolete. The disruptive technologies currently transforming the apparel industry have led some experts to suggest that we are going through a fourth industrial revolution (4IR), characterized by the blurring of boundaries between the physical, digital, and biological worlds (McGinnis, October 20, 2020). Advances in artificial intelligence (AI), robotics, the Internet of Things (IoT), virtual and augmented reality (VR, AR), 3D printing, data analytics, digital twinning, blockchain, and more make new technology adoption and integration imperative. See Appendix 1.1 for technology definitions.

The goal of this transformation is to build a resilient business foundation able to weather social, environmental, economic, and health crises—those unpredictable black swan events with severe consequences that seem to surprise us with increasing frequency. Disruptive technologies will help businesses to anticipate, prepare for, pivot, and survive these events with more collaboration and agility. Value is now measured in terms of benefits to the company, consumers, and society as a whole.

Evaluating Technology Options

Entry-level employees will not need to make technology decisions, but they may be asked to help evaluate options. It is beneficial to recognize the criteria that provide the most value to the evolving fashion system and apparel industry.

Technology investments should focus on cloud-based, open platform, end-to-end digitization that facilitates collaboration and visibility up and down the supply chain. Applications should not be siloed to service a single business function or a single supply chain partner. When data is shared on open platform systems, the supply chain, auxiliary partners, and even competitors can engage in more robust dialog that results in timely cross-functional solutions.

Central to coordinating the product development and production of garments up and down the supply chain are product lifecycle management systems. **Product lifecycle management (PLM)** applications integrate the product development process with supply chain management, enabling internal and external teams to communicate and collaborate on product-related information in order to define roles, streamline processes, meet deadlines, ensure quality, and authenticate product integrity from initial concept to a product's retirement.

Technology that supports ongoing improvement in its ability to produce customized, innovative products and services while minimizing waste should take precedence over an emphasis on high volume, low-cost, homogenized products built for obsolescence. This includes faster recognition of customer preferences with the use of data science and predictive analytics as well as process innovation that reduces time to market and helps to pivot to smaller order sizes in order to right-size inventory and reduce markdowns.

Data analytics will drive zero waste initiatives. Design technology will condense the design development process as digital approvals replace physical samples. Customers will play an increasingly active role in co-curating, co-designing, and customizing their products. Digital fashion presentations, accessible to all, are already replacing expensive runway shows. Traceability initiatives will help to identify waste throughout the supply chain.

As direct-to-consumer and digital distribution channels take over a larger share of the marketplace, systems that enhance shopping across distribution platforms, including virtual store experiences and virtual try-on technology, will be important. Likewise, systems that track transparent pricing, traceable sourcing, and environmental impact will be essential.

Work environments are changing at both the corporate and factory level. Systems that facilitate secure remote working environments and enable collaboration have already resulted in businesses downsizing their corporate footprint. There are advantages and disadvantages associated with remote working environments; however, some form of it appears to be here to stay. At all levels, workforce development will be critical. The pace of technology adoption and automation will transform the workplace, replacing low-skill, low-pay jobs with high-skill, higher-paying jobs. To maintain an adequate workforce and keep workers employed, who might otherwise be replaced by machines, investment will need to be made in workforce development. New training techniques including gamification and on-demand virtual- and augmented-reality work instruction will help workers upskill and reskill for the future.

Digital twin technology is being used to create virtual replicas of processes, tasks, products, or services to run simulations that inform decisions, facilitate remote implementations, and prepare multiple scenarios for an uncertain future. It bridges the physical and virtual world using a composite of available technology including data analytics, AI, ML, and VR. In the apparel industry a digital twin of a product can test a designer's vision against the practical constraints of production; be used to replace physical sampling and facilitate virtual try-ons; or to simulate the flow of supply chain assets in order to better manage production need (Apparel Resources, September 6, 2018).

Technology will be a critical tool in meeting the needs of the new fashion ecosystem. As our vision for sustainable fashion evolves, technology that has never been fully commercialized will now have a role to play.

SUSTAINABILITY

The fashion industry is one of the largest industries in the world. According to Common Objective, the global fashion retail industry including footwear was worth approximately $1.78 trillion in 2019 and generated over 1.8 billion dollars in revenue. It employs more than 60 million people. In its current configuration, it is also one of the most polluting in the world. Apparel and footwear industries were responsible for

8.1 percent of global climate impacts in 2016. Every second, a garbage truck's worth of textiles is dumped in a landfill or burned. Fashion accounts for 20 to 35 percent of microplastic flows into the ocean (Commonobjective.co, 2019 Update).

The **sustainability movement** promotes changes in the fashion system that support environmental integrity, social justice, and economic fairness. These changes would impact planning, design, production, distribution, and consumption of fashion products and services.

The fashion industry has not yet taken its environmental responsibility seriously. The industry culture must transform from one that is resistant to change, secretive, siloed in its communications, turns a blind eye to injustice, and believes that bigger is better, to one that is transparent, cutting edge, relevant, considered, collaborative, synergistic, and socially just.

The sustainability movement calls us to work toward a balanced state where resources used can be forever renewed and nothing goes to waste, without sacrificing a fashion aesthetic. The UN adopted the *2030 Agenda for Sustainable Development* in 2015. The agenda identifies seventeen Sustainable Development Goals (SDGs), which have become the standard for benchmarking sustainable practices. These goals recognize "that ending poverty and other deprivations must go hand-in-hand with strategies that improve health and education, reduce inequality, and spur economic growth—all while tackling climate change and working to preserve our oceans and forests" (UN website). Appendix 1.2 identifies the seventeen UN Sustainable Development Goals and the logo for each.

Transformative change must be holistic. Sustainability starts by re-evaluating the fashion system in terms of how trends start and are disseminated. From there, sustainability impacts everything from the design process to the materials used, manufacturing processes, distribution, consumption, and ultimately collection and repurposing. It is a shared vision embedded throughout the product development process, owned by all supply chain partners, and supported by all stakeholders. It is easy to see that sustainability is difficult to achieve if a supply chain is not truly collaborative.

Fashion search site Lyst saw searches related to sustainability increase 66 percent in 2019. Other studies have shown that two-thirds of consumers believe that brands that publicly promise to be more sustainable are also more trustworthy. Respondents all over the world want fashion to be more environmentally friendly but they can't tell if it is. Sixty-seven percent of the consumers surveyed can't tell if brands are meeting their promises. Too many brands practice greenwashing, where they pretend to be more environmentally friendly than they are and ignore important aspects of sustainability.

The UN's sustainability goals are comprehensive. They offer a universally understood language for the need to change. The pause forced upon us by COVID-19 gave us a moment of stillness—valuable perspective on what's important. For a few short months the skies cleared, the air we breathe was less polluted, and waterways were bluer. As we adapt to a new post-COVID reality, there is an opportunity to work in tandem with our planet.

Case Study 1.1
Levi Strauss & Co. Managing through Crisis

"From our California gold Rush beginnings, we have grown into one of the world's largest brand-name apparel companies. A history of responsible business practices, rooted in our core values, has helped us build our brands and engender consumer trust."
(LEVI.STRAUSS.COM, 2019 ANNUAL REPORT)

The 2019 Annual Report for Levi Strauss & Co.® (LS&Co.) struck a confident tone. After a decade-long turnaround effort, the company went public, with shares selling above the expected market price. The brand was connecting with a new generation of customers. They were confident that the mission-driven strategies they had in place would propel them into the future.

Prior to the pandemic, the company's strategic plan focused on driving growth through diversification in terms of geography, category, and channel. By the end of 2019, 60 percent of their business was international and the women's business, always a secondary category, had grown 14 percent, making it the second-largest US women's denim brand. Their ambition to focus on growing their direct-to-consumer (DTC) and e-commerce businesses proved to be omniscient. This is the story of how one company pivoted to meet the most significant crisis of its more than 150-year history.

LS&Co. was not over-leveraged like some of their competitors; they went into the pandemic with access to about $1.8 billion in accessible cash. Once the pandemic started, the company quickly closed all of its US stores and furloughed 4,500 retail workers, with global stores following suit. They cut 2020 capital expenditures by 40 percent, re-evaluating all budgetary initiatives. Marketing was slashed to almost zero with the exception of a newly launched loyalty program and investments in technology that facilitated its direct-to-consumer business. Investments in sustainability were cut and deadlines delayed, but not eliminated.

High-ranking corporate employees, not immune to the cuts, were asked to take a 50-percent pay cut. In making decisions, Chip Bergh, LS&Co. president, recognized that after a growth trajectory for the four years prior to the pandemic, management was top-heavy. When the company last faced hard times in 2014, it eliminated too many positions without rebalancing the workload. After a thorough assessment and restructuring, the company slashed 15 percent of its global corporate workforce in July of 2020, impacting about 700 jobs (Trefis Team and Great Speculations, December 16, 2020).

LS&Co. was forced to cancel or reduce product orders for the second half of 2020 and into 2021. Cognizant that they utilize a majority of their supplier's production capacity, they recognized the impact that cancelled orders would have. LS&Co. paid for any products already made and shipped, as well as for any raw materials already sourced. (Most US sourcing agreements expect their supply chain partners to pay for fabrics up front.) They worked with smaller niche suppliers, individually offering them various forms of assistance. Recognizing that the pandemic would impact garment workers the most, the Levi Strauss Foundation donated $1 million to communities near their suppliers where unemployed garment workers would need food and health care.

When the pandemic started, the company pivoted hard to support and promote DTC and e-commerce sales. In 2019, wholesale channels accounted for 64 percent of net revenues, and DTC and e-commerce accounted for 32 percent. No single customer represented 10 percent or more of the total, which ensured that the loss of a single customer would not significantly damage the brand. US sales accounted for 53 percent of revenues and Europe and Asia accounted for 47 percent of revenues (LS&Co. 2019). By the end of 2020, direct-to-consumer levels alone were almost 40 percent of global revenues and US wholesale was under 30 percent overall. This rebalancing was by design to protect the business from the volatility of the wholesale market and give it more control in brand presence (Lockwood, December 16, 2020).

As high-end wholesale retail brands such as Neiman Marcus struggled, LS&Co. embraced its mass market partners. Target introduced Levi's Denizen® brand in 2011 and Levi's Red Tab line in 2019; both brands offer value-conscious consumers quality, craftsmanship, great fit, and style at affordable prices. In January of 2021, LS&Co. announced Levi's for Target, a limited-edition collection of over 100 items for the home, for pets, apparel and accessories all based on the two companies shared values of thoughtfully designed durable, sustainable pieces.

Before the pandemic, LS&Co. had ambitious goals around climate change, worker's rights, and resource conservation.

- To reduce carbon emissions in owned factories by 90 percent and across its entire supply chain by 40 percent.

- To launch a program that gives factories financial incentives for decreasing water and chemical use.
- To source all of its cotton from either Better Cotton Initiative farmers, organic cotton farms, or recycled cotton suppliers by the end of 2020.
- To continue their investment in "cottonised" hemp research.

With the supply chain so disrupted, those deadlines had to be extended, but not forgotten.

Project FLX (future-led execution) is part of the company's end-to-end digital transformation. They are now finishing about a third of their total bottoms business with lasers. This allows them to postpone finishing decisions closer to market and better manage inventory. Design functions are digital throughout the entire supply chain. They have invested in artificial intelligence to predict traffic patterns and plan their labor to inform marketing strategies which. ultimately allows them to promote less and maintain gross margins (Lockwood, December 16, 2020).

In October of 2020, LS&Co. launched Levi's SecondHand. It's a logical extension of their business, since authentic vintage Levi's have long been sought after. Consumers receive a store credit or gift card when they bring in any pair of old Levi's. Collected jeans are then refurbished and sold in signature stores.

From the start, the company based decisions on an assumption that it would emerge as a smaller company, but one better able to right-sized inventory levels with products that could hold their value. Ultimately, LS&Co. was able to build market share through the pandemic which is an indication of the strength and overall health of its business. They are comfortable being a somewhat smaller company because they feel closer to the consumer. As consumers are more considered regarding their purchases, they are trading up to brands they know, respect, and trust.

References

Fernandez, Chantal. (2020), "How Levi's Is Navigating the Purpose and Profit Trade-Off," *The Business of Fashion* Case Study. https://wwd.com/business-news/markets/how-levis-navigated-through-the-pandemic-and-emerged-stronger-1234667811/ (accessed on January 30, 2021).

Levistrauss.com. (accessed on January 1, 2021)

Lockwood, Lisa. (2020), "How Levi's Navigated through the Pandemic and Emerged Stronger," *Woman's Wear Daily*, December 16. https://wwd.com/business-news/markets/how-levis-navigated-through-the-pandemic-and-emerged-stronger-1234667811/ (accessed on January 30, 2021).

Thomas, Lauren. (2021), "Levi's Holiday-quarter sales fall 12% despite online gains," *cnbc.com*, January 27. https://www.cnbc.com/2021/01/27/levis-levi-reports-q4-2020-earnings-sales-beat.html (accessed on January 30, 2021).

Trefis Team and Great Speculations. (2020), "Levi's Stock to See Declines in Long Term?" *Forbes*, December 16. https://www.forbes.com/sites/greatspeculations/2020/12/16/levis-stock-to-see-declines-in-long-term/?sh=71c89c27184a (accessed on January 30, 2021).

SUMMARY

The apocalyptic events that have taken place already this century have forced the fashion system and the supply chain that supports it to re-evaluate how they function. To meet increasingly sophisticated consumer expectations, global supply chains must adjust by continuing to shorten lead-times and be more agile. Supply chain decisions are shaped by whether the product developer is a wholesale brand or a retailer, the kind of product they are making (basic, seasonal, or fashion), the channels through which it will be distributed, and the delivery calendar.

Brands are typically classified as either wholesale brands or private brands, although the growth of direct-to-consumer distribution channels is blurring that distinction. Digital channels of distribution are becoming increasingly important, giving consumers greater selection than ever before no matter where they live and creating a more competitive business climate. The industry is coming to terms with issues of product timing and overproduction. Long lead-times result in inaccurate supply and demand predictions and overproduction which ties up capital; this in turn leads to unsustainable discounting and over-consumption which results in clothing being discarded before it's worn out. An emphasis on volume, rather than quality and innovation, has created a homogenous marketplace that erodes clothing's appeal as an outlet for discretionary spending.

Going forward, successful supply chains must be collaborative. Brands need to commit to their partners downstream—at the fiber, fabric, and production level—by offering technical expertise and coaching; they need to engage with them as equal stakeholders in decision making in order to base orders on realistic and fair expectations. Supply chains must also be circular. Starting at the fabrication and design level, planning must anticipate how garments will be recovered, repurposed, and recycled so the garment or its components remain useful in the system rather than ending up in landfills. Brands and supply chains must change their focus from volume to creating value.

Supply chain ownership may be vertical or horizontal depending on a company's core competencies. Vertical integration gives brands more control over available capacity, quality, and transparency along the supply chain; however, it may limit agility. Horizontal integration helps a company leverage their core strengths across multiple brands.

Changes occurring in the fashion ecosystem are supported and driven by new technology that is so disruptive that businesses must adopt it or fail. Savvy customers expect no less. These technologies focus on agility, accuracy, and resiliency never before achievable.

KEY TERMS

apparel supply chain
auxiliary businesses
basic product
circular supply chain
collaborative supply chain
concession strategy
digital twin
disruptive technology
diversification
downstream
fashion forward product

fashion system
horizontal integration
multi-brand retailers
near-shoring
outlet stores
private brand
private label brands
product development
product lifecycle management
seasonal product
signature stores

sourcing
stakeholder
store brands
sustainability movement
traceability
transparency
upstream
value chain
vertical integration
wholesale brand

DISCUSSION QUESTIONS

1. Identify some of your favorite stores/brands. Are they wholesale brands, store brands, or private label brands? Why do you prefer them?

2. Are most of your apparel purchases basic apparel, seasonal apparel, or fashion apparel? Do stores in your area carry their most expensive fashion offerings or do you need to search online to find their most fashion forward products?

3. Fashion is re-evaluating the fashion calendar. Do you typically wait to buy apparel until it goes on sale? If it was shipped closer to season, would you pay full price? Would you buy as much apparel?

4. A circular supply chain focusses on collecting worn apparel and refurbishing and reselling or recycling pieces. Have you taken any pieces of clothing back to a collection point? Have you bought refurbished or secondhand apparel pieces? Have you bought articles of clothing that use recycled fibers?

ACTIVITIES

1. Look at the country of origin on labels from a variety of items of a single brand. How many different countries of origin can you identify? Discuss how the country of origin might have an impact on the product development process for this brand relative to cost, lead time, and quality.

2. Select a brand to follow throughout this class. It may be a regional brand or a company for which you aspire to work. Do some research and identify the following:

   • Is it a wholesale brand, store brand, or private label?
   • Research its distribution network, i.e. stores where it's sold, distribution channels, geographic reach, where the brand manufacturers product, and the primary fashion level of the product.

- Is the brand vertically or horizontally integrated? (A smaller brand may be neither.) Has the brand diversified its product offerings?
- Assess the brand's commitment to sustainability. On which of the UN goals does the brand appear to focus?

STUD!O RESOURCES

- Take the chapter quiz with scored results and personalized study tips.
- Review glossary flashcards to build your vocabulary.

REFERENCES

Apparel Resources. (2020), "Digital Twin—Overlapping Real World with Virtual," *Oracle*, September 6. https://www.oracle.com/sa/a/ocom/docs/dc/em/lpd100807811-impact-of-emerging-technology-on-cx-excellence.pdf (accessed on January 29, 2021).

Bateman, Alexis and Bonnani, Leonardo. (2019), "What Supply Chain Transparency Really Means," August 20. https://hbr.org/2019/08/what-supply-chain-transparency-really-means (accessed on January 23, 2020).

Common Objective. (2018), Mapping the Fashion Industry (February 2019 update), May 14. https://www.commonobjective.co/article/the-size-of-the-global-fashion-retail-market (accessed on January 30, 2021).

Kuebix. (2019), "How the Circular Supply Chain Model Will Replace the Linear Supply Chain," June 21. https://www.supplychain247.com/article/how_the_circular_supply_chain_model_will_replace_the_linear_supply_chain (accessed on January 30, 2021)

McGinnis, Devon. (2020), "What Is the Fourth Industrial Revolution?," October 20. https://www.salesforce.com/blog/what-is-the-fourth-industrial-revolution-4ir/ (accessed on January 29, 2021).

McKinsey & Company. (2019), The State of Fashion 2019. https://cdn.businessoffashion.com/reports/The_State_of_Fashion_2019_v3.pdf (accessed on January 23, 2020).

Nikegrind.com. (accessed on January 30, 2019).

Tarver, Evan. (2020), Value Chain vs. Supply Chain: What's the Difference? March 24. https://www.investopedia.com/ask/answers/043015/what-difference-between-value-chain-and-supply-chain.asp (accessed on January 23, 2020).

United Nations Department of Economic and Social Affairs: Sustainable Development. (2015), The Seventeen Goals. https://sdgs.un.org/goals (accessed on November 30, 2020).

Appendix 1.1 Disruptive Technologies Glossary

Fourth Industrial Revolution (4IR). The advent of technology that uses artificial intelligence and machine learning systems that results in new capabilities for people and machines.

application program interface (API). An application programming interface that enables interactions between multiple software applications or mixed hardware-software intermediaries.

artificial intelligence (AI). The ability of a digitally controlled device, such as a computer or robot, to perform tasks or solve problems that normally would require human intelligence, such as visual perception, speech recognition, and decision making.

augmented reality (AR). A technology that superimposes a computer-generated image on a user's view of the real world, thus providing a composite view. It is used in gaming and virtual try-on technology including virtual mirrors.

big data. Extremely large data sets that may be analyzed digitally to identify patterns, trends, and associations.

block chain. A distributed ledger technology in which a digital record of transactions is linked together in a single list that can be stored globally on thousands of servers while letting anyone on the network see all entries in near real time. Maintained across several computers that are linked in a peer-to-peer network, it is considered one of the most secure technologies because any of the involved blocks of data cannot be altered retroactively without the alteration of all subsequent blocks. It is an important tool in tracing apparel supply chains.

data analytics. Programs that are used to define, collect, cleanse, interpret, and model data points in ways that extract meaning. They can be used to inform decision making and project trends and behaviors throughout every step of the product development process through the use of artificial intelligence and machine learning. Subsets of data analytics include descriptive analytics, diagnostic analytics, and predictive analytics.

digital twin. Technology that is used to create virtual replicas of processes tasks, products, or services to run simulations that inform decisions, facilitate remote implementations, and prepare multiple scenarios for an uncertain future. A digital twin bridges the physical and virtual worlds.

internet of things (IoT). The network of physical objects that are embedded with sensors, software, and other technologies for the purpose of connecting and exchanging data with other devices and systems over the internet. Simply stated it refers to devices that can communicate with one another.

machine learning (ML). Computer systems that are able to recognize patterns in order to learn and improve through experiences without the input of explicit instructions and with minimal human intervention. Machine learning uses algorithms, statistical models, and artificial intelligence to analyze and draw inferences from patterns of data.

supply chain resilience. The ability of a given supply chain to prepare for and adapt to unexpected events; to quickly adjust to sudden disruptive changes.

virtual reality (VR). Computer-generated simulations of a three-dimensional image or environment that can be interacted with in a seemingly real or physical way by a person using special electronic equipment such as special goggles or a helmet with a screen, or gloves fitted with sensors.

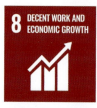

CHAPTER 2

BRAND STRATEGY AND BUSINESS OPERATIONS

"We . . . came to the fashion industry along different paths but for the same reason: a belief in the beauty, imagination and craft that remain at the core of this business. It's time to slow down and rediscover the storytelling and magic of fashion."
#REWIRING FASHION

OBJECTIVES

- To understand the role of branding in defining a product line
- To explore means of differentiating a brand to achieve competitive advantage
- To recognize how brands are positioned in the marketplace
- To understand how a brand's mission, vision, and values shape its strategic plan
- To comprehend how business functions and organizational structure enable the operational tasks required to reach the goals set out in the strategic plan
- To appreciate the collaboration required between business functions to bring a product from concept to delivery
- To appreciate new, more sustainable business models that begin to address overproduction and overconsumption while satisfying our desire for apparel that serves as a means of self expression

Professionals working in the fashion industry need to be bilingual in the languages of business and fashion. They need to think strategy and speak fashion—to become fluent in the subtle nuances of fashion and design as well as the realities of business and brand management (Wang, September 4, 2014). Fashion casts a spell as a means of self-expression, but it is also a business, and as such it must deliver a return on investment. This chapter looks at the importance of branding to create an emotional connection between the product line and the consumer. A branding strategy helps to differentiate products and position them in a competitive marketplace. Once brands are established, they must be managed to address evolving consumer values and preferences, a changing competitive landscape, and macro events that impact the business climate. Brands are guided by their mission, vision, and values. These are the foundation for strategic planning and the benchmark for corporate culture and brand image. Business functions and operational structure are organized to support brand goals and the strategic plan. The goals of the strategic plan guide the financial plan in allocating resources and setting incremental benchmarks. Functional area operations execute the tasks required to reach the benchmarks of the financial plan. The fashion industry has long relied on selling increased volume to grow profits; this chapter will introduce new models for creating value and distributing fashion that are more sustainable while still generating profits.

BRAND STRATEGY

Definitions

A **brand** is the name, logo, tagline, and/or other unique feature that identifies a businesses' goods or services with a promise to its customers that is distinct from its competitors. Competition for consumer dollars is fierce; the growth of digital commerce means that often the customer is making a purchase decision without the opportunity to touch a fabric and try on garments. Brands help to convey a set of standards and build trust that drives repeat business. Brand names, logos, symbols, and slogans are generally proprietary and legally protected through intellectual property laws (Figure 2.1).

Branding is a competitive strategy used to create, communicate, and strengthen a brand's promise to its target market. Branding integrates a brand's visual identity, product differentiation, level of service, marketing, and market positioning in the minds of the consumer.

A **brand image** is the consumer's set of assumptions and feelings about products and/or services provided under the brand name. Building a brand's image is more challenging than ever before. Consumers are increasingly independent and less brand loyal. Traditional forms of advertising in magazines, emails, and newspapers where the brand controlled the message have given way to influencer marketing and the use of social media where consumers craft much of the message. A misstep in living up to brand promises or claims can cause long-term damage, particularly in this era of viral marketing. A brand's image is, in essence, its promise of authenticity, customer satisfaction, and quality.

a

b

Figures 2.1a and b
a. The Nike swoosh logo is recognized globally.
b. The Chuck Taylor All Star basketball shoe has been made since 1932.

Brands need to stay relevant in a dynamic market. **Brand equity** refers to the value that accrues to a brand for customers, who may be willing to spend more for the promise of a brand-name product, and as a corporate asset that can be leveraged in launching new product categories, influencing mergers and acquisitions, maximizing revenue streams, and justifying capital investment.

Product Differentiation, Competitive Advantage and Brand Positioning

Product differentiation means to distinguish a product or service from others in order to make it more desirable in the marketplace. Brands may be known for one or more attributes including, but not limited to, superior quality (Everlane), unique product features or aesthetic (Burberry, Moncler), superior service (Nordstrom, Zappos), minimal carbon footprint (Patagonia), unique fit (Wacoal), speed-to-market (Zara), extensive category selection (Zappos), product technology (ECOALF), artisanal details (Alabama Chanin), circular supply chain (Eileen Fisher), or unparalleled delivery (Amazon).

Product differentiation isn't forever. Once an inventive product is launched in the marketplace there are bound to be competitors that try to improve upon it. Some product developers have been successful in transforming a stagnating brand that has lost its competitive advantage into a dynamic brand with new appeal. The term **sneakerization** describes the process of transforming or redefining a product line that is losing its relevance into a cutting-edge specialty product. Sneakers used to mean an inexpensive canvas shoe with a rubber sole. Companies like Nike and Adidas have developed expensive, high-tech, function-specific products, dependent on extensive research and development for specific sports. Sneakerization is not limited to shoes. Burberry, founded in 1856, designed their classic gabardine trench coat for use during WWI and launched their signature plaid in the 1920s. The brand was emblematic of British history but had grown stodgy when they hired Christopher Baily to revive the brand in 2001. He injected a sexiness into their image by hiring Kate Moss to be the face of the brand. Through sneakerization brands can be transformed to appeal to new customers and thereby gain competitive advantage (Figure 2.2a–b).

Attributes that add value in the customer's eyes are important to maintaining and growing market share and building customer loyalty. **Competitive advantage** refers to attributes that allow an organization to outperform its competitors. If a brand has not sufficiently differentiated their products, the default means of competition is to offer the *lowest-price* products (Walmart, Primark). A low-price strategy is most often used on commodity products where there is little market differentiation or segmentation. Low prices are achieved through high volume and compromised quality. When products aren't made for long-term wear they may end up in landfills. Corporate social responsibility tends to be a casualty of firms that pursue this strategy. As the fashion community comes to terms with the fact that high volume, low-cost production is not sustainable, value creation through competitive advantage is even more important. It is

a

b

especially important for entrepreneurial businesses whose products or services must be unique in order to offset their limited distribution and lower volume.

Competitive advantage along with volume, market share, profit margins, capital investment, and inventory levels all contribute to the ability of a business in a mature industry to remain solvent. Businesses must be vigilant in order to maintain their advantage in an ever-changing business climate.

Once a brand has differentiated its product, it must catch the attention of the intended target customer. **Brand/product positioning** is a marketing strategy that crafts a brand image to highlight the brand's products and services in a way that customers perceive it to be more desirable than the competition. Brand positioning matches product characteristics (size range, fit, colors, logos, fabrication, styling) to decisions regarding channels of distribution, distribution partners, location, presentation (website design, social media, and/or store design), and pricing. It is dependent on identifying and analyzing other players in the competitive landscape and thoroughly understanding the target customer.

To successfully position a brand in the marketplace it is important to know who is already competing in the market, what they do well, and where their weaknesses are; their weaknesses are opportunities for competitive advantage. Internet research and

Figure 2.2a and b
Burberry has used sneakerization to keep its classic British styling and signature plaid relevant. The trench coat in 1973 and Billie Eilish wearing one from 2020.

competitive shopping both in-store and on digital platforms can provide the necessary information for a competitive analysis:

- What are their product offerings?
- Identify the brand's customer; does the brand have a loyal following?
- What do they believe to be their competitive advantage?
- Is their website easy to navigate?
- Does their photography clearly reflect the product?
- How detailed are their product descriptions?
- Do they include customer reviews and are customers satisfied with the product they get?
- How does the website handle abandoned carts?
- Do they use incentives to build an email list?
- What are shipping costs and how are returns handled?
- What is the vibe of the website and in-store experience?
- Do they have brick and mortar stores? If so, where are they located?
- What is their price range and how frequent are promotions?
- What type of social media presence do they have and how engaged are customers?

A positioning grid can be used to assess competitors based on two attributes. Figure 2.3 compares leggings on the basis of price and size inclusivity.

Brands also need to thoroughly study their target customer to understand their shopping motivations and product preferences. Target customer research addresses these questions:

- Who needs the product you're offering?
- What problem does it solve for the customer?
- How do they prefer to shop?
- What are they willing to pay?

Target customer analysis must avoid making assumptions. Markets are dynamic; ongoing market research helps to anticipate shifts in consumer preferences, providing an opportunity to change course or pivot if necessary. Target markets are fully discussed in Chapter 3.

Once a competitive analysis and target customer analysis is complete, brand positioning decisions can be made. One of the most important aspects of product positioning is price. Price impacts where the product can be made, its speed-to-market, distribution partners, selling environment, and levels of service.

Price as it Impacts Brand Positioning

Price point refers to an understanding of the price range that the intended target customer is willing to pay for the value offered; it may also be referred to as *price zone*. The traditional lexicon of price points comes out of department store shopping; department stores were intended to appeal to a wide variety of customers at diverse prices so

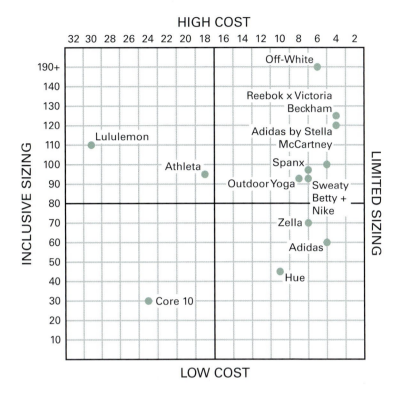

Figure 2.3
Brand comparison placement grid based on quality and price.

a family could do all of their shopping in one place. Department stores might choose to offer merchandise in some combination of moderate, better, bridge, contemporary, and/or designer prices. Stores such as Nordstrom, Harrod's, and Bon Marché start at the better price point and go up from there. Mid-tier department stores, such as Macy's and Marks & Spencer, feature merchandise from moderate to contemporary. Mass merchant stores such as Kohl's, Target, and Primark focus on moderate to better price points. As department stores play a less important role in apparel merchandising and distribution, the use of price point labels is disappearing. Even so, when it comes to decision making, price continues to be at or near the top of the list of factors that motivate consumer behavior; however, any given customer may be willing to pay more for items in a particular garment or accessory category. For example, a customer may spend more on a designer bag or a name brand pair of jeans that they know they will use many times than they would for a dress.

Customers today are aspirational; they don't like to be categorized. They mix and match price points as easily as they do their outfits. The names in given traditional price point categories may be descriptive but not inspiring; the *moderate department* has little cachet with fashion savvy customers on a budget. Instead, chain stores and brands carefully curate their product offerings toward a particular customer in a way that price is implicitly understood. Price positioning becomes more about identifying competitors in the marketplace and the price points that they sell. Table 2.1 defines

Table 2.1 Traditional Women's Price Point Categories
from Most to Least Expensive

Price Point	Description	Examples
Couture	Made to order; client goes to the designer's salon for custom fittings.	Chanel Couture, Dior Couture, Alexis Mabille, Frank Sorbier, Jean Paul Gaultier
Designer	Designer brands available off the rack in a range of sizes.	Prada, Dolce & Gabbana, Ralph Lauren, Armani, Marc Jacobs, MICHAEL Michael Kors, The Row, Alexander Wang, Burberry Prosum, Herve Leger, Marchesa
Contemporary designer	A price point similar to that of bridge or a bit higher; this category includes many new designers who target a younger, fashion-savvy customer.	Tracy Reese, Nanette Lepore, Catherine Malandrino, Tory Burch, Kate Spade, Derek Lam 10 Crosby, Isabel Marant, McQ Alexander McQueen, Thakoon, CO
Bridge	A price point between better and designer, with a focus on career wear and weekend wear.	Lafayette 148, Eileen Fisher, Theory
Better	Products with wide market appeal; often the highest price point available in department stores.	CK Calvin Klein; Lauren Ralph Lauren; Kenneth Cole; MICHAEL Michael Kors
Moderate	Large, price-conscious market; styling appeals to more mature customers.	Lands' End, Uniqlo, Carhartt, Universal Standard, Chaus
Low-end contemporary/ fast fashion	A relatively new category that offers fast fashion at a moderate to better price point.	Zara, H&M, Forever 21, BCBGMAXAZRIA, Cos
Junior/tweens	Apparel with styling and fit geared to teenagers.	PacSun, Urban Outfitters, American Eagle, Brandy Melville
Mass market	A variety of brands that appeal to many different market segments, all at low, affordable prices.	LC Lauren Conrad, FLX, All In Motion, AVA & VIV, Original Use

the traditional price point categories. The terms used in market positioning continue to have a price connotation. Anyone in fashion must understand the meanings of mass market, high street, contemporary, designer RTW, and couture/haute couture.

Mass market may be used to describe a brand, a price point, or a category of retailers/distribution channels. A mass-market strategy attempts to cater to the highest number of customers making up for lower margins with high volume. Most global clothing purchases are made at this price point. Examples of mass-market stores include big box stores such as Kohl's, Target, C&A, and Primark and chain stores such as Old Navy and Uniqlo. Generally, mass-market price points range from budget to low-end better price points. Big box merchants further cut costs by offering minimal in-store services with front-of-store checkouts and few dressing rooms. Their store environment is somewhat generic, preferring stand-alone locations with large parking lots to expensive mall locations. A strong online presence helps to maximize business volume. The design of mass-market merchandise is accessible though not necessarily memorable. Disadvantages of this strategy are that it lacks focus, is of lower quality, is difficult to differentiate in a competitive marketplace, and thereby fails to develop brand loyalty. In order to move large quantities of inventory they tend to be very promotional in their pricing which means they start out with high initial margins, anticipating that most stock will sell at a discounted price. Alternatively, they may offer rock bottom, every-day low pricing and only use sales to clear merchandise.

Fast fashion is the quick and inexpensive design, creation, and marketing of trend-driven apparel. Most fast fashion brands are offered at a mass-market price point though they have more contemporary styling. Fast fashion brands offer clothing that is so affordable that it has led to overconsumption of unsustainable clothing. Unfortunately, because of its low price, consumers feel little guilt when they dispose of fast fashion garments after wearing them only a few times. If that same amount of money would be spent on fewer, more sustainable pieces of clothing that could be worn over the course of several years rather than a single season, it would have a significant positive impact on the industry's sustainability record.

Similarly, in the UK, the term **high street** is often used to describe mass-market chain stores that offer trend-right and affordable fashion that can be readily found on any main street. High street brands are the equivalent to chain stores typically found in US malls. The term *contemporary* is sometimes used to describe mass market or chain store apparel with a fashion forward vibe promoted to a younger customer.

The most expensive garments that can be bought off the rack are known as **designer ready-to-wear (RTW)**. These brands are more profit-oriented than haute couture and may be produced in quantities that vary from one hundred garments to several thousand; they are beautifully designed, impeccably made, and use high-quality fabrics. Designer RTW labels include Gucci, Louis Vuitton, Marc Jacobs, Prada, and many others. Designer RTW is available in specialty department stores, high-end boutiques, signature stores, and more recently direct-to-consumer, online. The accessibility of these garments (as opposed to haute couture) appeals to the busy lifestyles of today's designer customer. Trend forecasters and purveyors of fast fashion look to designer RTW runways to identify the right shade of the next hot color, new fabric developments, and the newest silhouette, detail, or accessory.

A newer subset of designer goods is referred to as **contemporary designer**. These designers/brands offer clothes with a younger vibe and somewhat lower price point than found at designer RTW. Brands include Tori Burch, Alexander Wang, Theory, and M Missoni. They distinguish themselves with a less traditional color palette, more streetwear influence, and a more relaxed fit (Figure 2.4a-c).

The term *couture* is used to denote garments that are one of a kind, custom made with luxury fabrics, often with hand detailing or finishing—the use of the term is not

a

b

c

Figure 2.4a–c
Fast fashion, contemporary designer, and designer RTW versions of the 2020 plaid trend.
(Zara, Rag & Bone, and Miu Miu)

controlled. **Haute couture** is a legally protected designation in Paris that can only be used by houses registered with the French Ministry of Industry. Haute couture designers must adhere to a strict set of standards administered by the Chambre Syndicale de la Haute Couture. Current rules require each house to employ at least fifteen people in a Paris atelier and present a minimum of thirty-five new designs twice a year. Haute couture garments are made of the highest quality fabrics, often require handwork, and are custom made, requiring one or more fittings. At present there are fifteen designers who hold an official haute couture designation. Designers whose ateliers are outside of Paris may request guest member status which allows them to show during couture week; after two years of showing as a guest member, design houses may apply for foreign correspondent status. Giorgio Armani, Valentino, Versace, and Elie Saab all have foreign correspondent status, but do not qualify as haute couture members because their ateliers are not in Paris.

Haute couture garments prioritize creativity over commercialism. Garments can take anywhere from 100–800 hours to make; some very special garments have taken as much as 1500 hours. Prices start at $10,000 for a simple day dress and climb to $350,000 or more for an elaborate evening gown or wedding dress (Figure 2.5). Couture houses claim they make no money on the creations—the House of Chanel and Elie Saab may be the rare exception. They do it for the prestige that sells lesser priced ready-to-wear collections, perfumes, and handbags. Estimates are that there are only 2,000 occasional customers of couture worldwide; 300 to 400 of them purchase couture garments regularly. The majority come from China, Russia, and the Middle East. American couture customers have increasingly disappeared as younger customers find that they can meet their more casual social needs off the rack without the four- to five-month lead time, personal fittings, and intricate construction required for couture garments.

The *luxury market* is a term that is widely used but difficult to define. It is used to refer to haute couture, designer RTW, contemporary designer, and entry-level luxury brands. Simply stated, the **luxury market** consists of goods and services that are highly desirable due to their cost. They are perceived to have superior value, quality, and craftsmanship that project status and taste. Classic symbols of luxury include the Hermès Birkin bag, a Chanel jacket, and Christian Louboutin red-soled shoes. The luxury industry was founded on the premise that price corresponds with value, but that is not necessarily the case. It is true that many brands can justify their high prices by the quality of the materials used as well as their superior fit, workmanship, and artisanal details; but high-profile designers, expensive marketing campaigns, celebrity promotions, and slick fashion shows also add greatly to the cost of garments without necessarily adding to the value. Since luxury apparel is sold in much smaller quantities, these products must be sold at a higher margin to be profitable. Stores catering to a luxury customer tend to offer a higher end shopping experience. Free delivery, personal shoppers, and special events build an emotional connection with these customers.

Luxury fashion has been focused on growth. Young designers are attempting to expand the customer base for luxury; they are replacing ladies-who-lunch suits with *luxury* streetwear and sneakers. Digital sales represent a growing distribution channel; their share of the market was enhanced by digital fashion presentations during the COVID-19 pandemic. Regular designer collaborations with fast fashion merchants, designer outlets, and diffusion lines have introduced younger customers to designer and contemporary brands, making them more attainable and cultivating a new customer base. Further growth potential is coming from the commercialized rental (Rent the Runway) and resale (The RealReal) markets. Much of the geographic growth in the luxury market is coming from China.

The focus on a younger customer has nurtured entry-level luxury brands such as Kate Spade, Coach, GANNI, and Rachel Zoe. As many mid-tier better and bridge brands are struggling to survive, entry-level luxury brands have attempted to fill that void. Ultimately, luxury is a term defined by brand marketing and consumer perception (Figure 2.6 Levels of Luxury graphic).

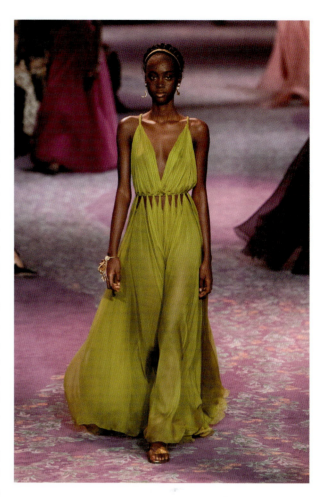

Figure 2.5
This Dior Haute Couture Gown from the Spring 2020 collection took a team of petits mains over 250 hours to complete over the course of a month. It used 67 meters of silk chiffon.

Speed-to-Market

Purveyors of fast fashion, such as H&M and Zara, have promoted product ranges that are broader, produced in smaller lot sizes, and made available for shorter periods than ever before; they deliver product directly to their stores rather than warehousing it.

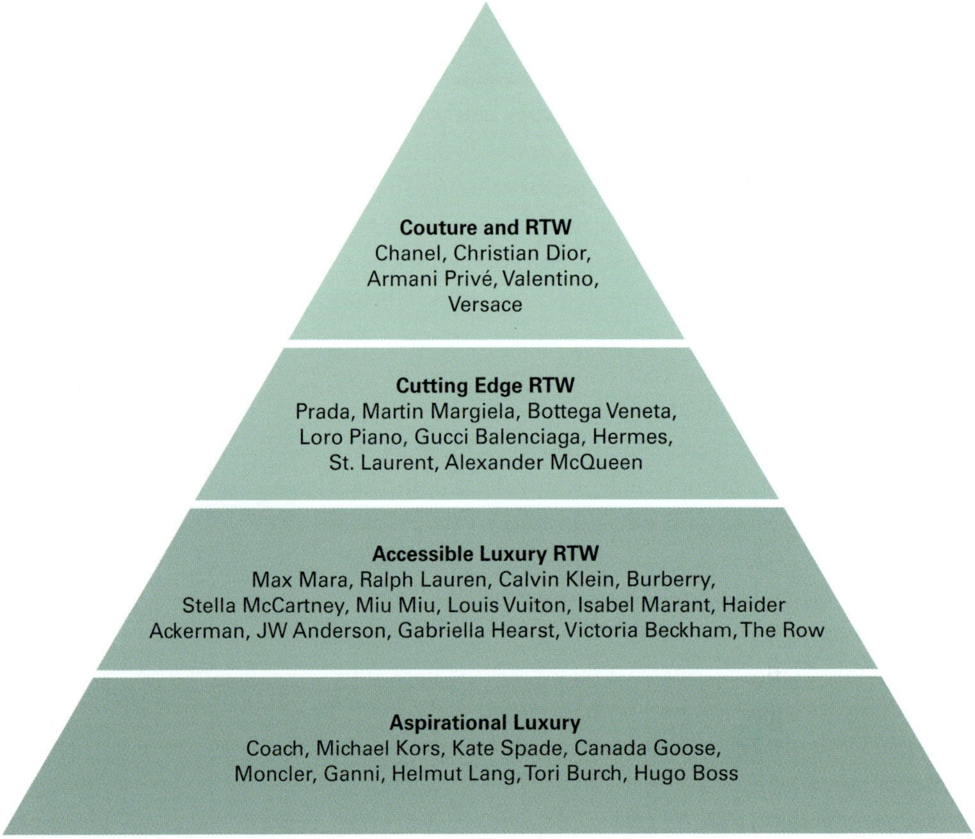

Figure 2.6
Levels of Luxury graphic

Couture and RTW
Chanel, Christian Dior,
Armani Privé, Valentino,
Versace

Cutting Edge RTW
Prada, Martin Margiela, Bottega Veneta,
Loro Piano, Gucci Balenciaga, Hermes,
St. Laurent, Alexander McQueen

Accessible Luxury RTW
Max Mara, Ralph Lauren, Calvin Klein, Burberry,
Stella McCartney, Miu Miu, Louis Vuiton, Isabel Marant, Haider
Ackerman, JW Anderson, Gabriella Hearst, Victoria Beckham, The Row

Aspirational Luxury
Coach, Michael Kors, Kate Spade, Canada Goose,
Moncler, Ganni, Helmut Lang, Tori Burch, Hugo Boss

Though fast fashion comes with many negative connotations, as a system it has challenged our supply chain expectations. Companies like Zara have created a value chain that cuts lead time from years and months to weeks, offers smaller but more frequent shipments tailored to the needs of the market, and eliminates markdowns except at the end of the season because it avoids overproduction. The goal of circular supply chains includes some of the principles of the speed-to-market of fast fashion. In fast fashion as we know it, what must change is the level of quality. Products must be designed and manufactured to last and sustain multiple lives. Fast fashion challenges all brands to strive for agility so that styling decisions can be made closer to the selling season.

The opposite of fast fashion is **slow fashion**—more of a concept than a market, slow fashion prioritizes the sustainable use of resources, ethical treatment of supply chain partners, quality that encourages long-term wear, recycling, reuse, and involving the consumer in design. More authentic collaboration with supply chain partners and implementation of advanced technology will hopefully meld the speed-to-market benefits of fast fashion supply chains with the sustainability goals of slow fashion to change the fashion system for the better. This will require a combined effort of all stakeholders, consumers, distribution networks, product developers, manufacturers, and fiber and fabric suppliers.

Marketing

Marketing is critical to brand positioning. Marketing plans have evolved from a focus on traditional media to social media and influencer culture. Product placement and celebrity spokespersons have also been effective tools go get the attention of younger customers. The momentous shifts that took place post COVID-19 and the ongoing impact of the *Black Lives Matter* and the *Me Too* movements have shifted marketing messages further. Brands began to take value-based stances on politics, injustice, and prejudice, putting all the more focus on the link between values and branding.

Digital Platforms and Delivery

The fast fashion phenomena opened the industry's eyes to how product could be designed and produced more quickly and efficiently. Digital platforms enabled the industry to expand their distribution to anywhere in the world and Amazon enabled the rapid-fire delivery of said product. The COVID-19 pandemic closed brick and mortar stores globally for two to three months—a reality no one could have predicted. Wholesalers and retailers of apparel products must have digital distribution platforms to fall back on in times of crisis. Small businesses can develop their own website and/or rely on a multi-brand digital platform. Multi-brand digital platforms such as Farfetch offer solutions. They curate a selection of sought-after brands for which they don't own the inventory. Instead, they have an efficient logistical system that sources the desired product from around the world and makes arrangements with the respective retailer/brand to complete the order. For this service they collect a 20 to 25 percent commission; the customer pays the shipping fee (Noto, 2018). Etsy and Artful Home can do the same for small entrepreneurial design businesses that want to expand their reach but aren't equipped to manage the backend logistics of online distribution. These platforms are immensely valuable and can facilitate the discovery process for new customers. They also provide a service promise that small brands are hard pressed to offer on their own. Amazon for its part has facilitated digital shopping channels with their promise of expedient delivery. Amazon is looking for ways to collaborate with the fashion industry. Their sponsorship of *Making the Cut* on the Amazon Prime channel and their collaboration with CFDA designers during the COVID-19 pandemic have helped them to make inroads into the fashion business.

Brand Management

Once a brand has clearly defined its brand strategy, it must manage the brand for growth and profit. There are a number of ways that brands can expand or structure their offerings.

The term **brand extension** refers to the practice of using an existing brand's reputation to promote a new service or product. This can be achieved by expanding a brand's assortment—launching a women's brand into menswear—or launching a new product category or service under an existing brand label. Zara has launched home stores in select markets; Rick Owens offers a line of furniture. One strategy for brand extensions is to associate the brand with a specific lifestyle. **Lifestyle brands** go beyond their origins in a single product category to include additional apparel and accessory categories, perfumes, cosmetics, travel packages or experiences, or home goods, all related to a particular lifestyle. Giorgio Armani has a group of hotels and resorts. Ralph Lauren has developed one of the most successful lifestyle brands.

A **diffusion line** is a luxury brand strategy utilized to reach a broader market by launching a secondary line at a more affordable price point. Michael Kors offers his collection line and, in addition, MICHAEL, Michael Kors at a considerably lower price point. Brand variations and the revenue streams they provide are made possible by the equity of the namesake brand heritage.

Exclusivity is another means of energizing a store's brand assortments. **Exclusive brands** may be private brands or brands with which a retailer has a licensing agreement that gives the retailer all rights to distribute product under that brand name in a particular product category or categories. Exclusive brands may be a means of:

- Relaunching a brand at a lower price point when it has lost its equity with consumers at a higher price point
- Capitalizing on the popularity of a cartoon character, celebrity, or sports figure
- Collaborating with a well-known designer on a secondary line that is lower in price than that designer's signature line

Co-branding refers to the practice of marketing a product or service under two brand names, linking the competitive advantage of both brands. The terms of the agreement may be for a single collection or for a term of three to five years, renewable at the discretion of both parties. Co-branded collections have the feel of the designer or brand but are modified to meet the needs and price point of the retailer's target customer. Exclusive brands may be designed by the retailer if the license revolves solely around the use of a logo or character image. In other instances, the brand owner designs the product for the retailer, incorporating agreed-upon design parameters. Many co-branding agreements in the past and present represent partnerships with relatively established designers and retail brands. Imagine the possibilities if co-branding transformed its focus to local creators and/or new designers.

Licensing is integral to branding. **Licensing agreements** grant a business partner exclusive rights to produce or sell products under a proprietary brand name. Licensing agreements may be used to:

- Extend a brand's product mix by partnering with a product developer who has expertise in a new category, i.e., shoes or jewelry
- Expand distribution into a global market
- Capitalize on the popularity of a proprietary character
- Partner with another brand to maximize the value of the combined brands
- Extend the lifecycle of a brand whose image at a higher price point is fading
- Provide exclusive product to a particular retailer

Licensing partners must be chosen carefully so that the products, service, and value they provide is consistent with that of the brand. Brands often experience a decrease in brand equity in the form of market shrinkage at the end of their life cycle. At this stage, a brand may enter into a licensing agreement with a mass-market store, agreeing to continue to develop the brand to the store's quality, size, and price specifications for exclusive distribution.

In a global market, brands must protect their equity internationally. Since marketing and distributing a brand in a global market is fraught with challenges, especially counterfeiting, brand owners often use licensing arrangements to protect their brand while capitalizing on the brand's value in a foreign market.

Many apparel manufacturers are focused on applying their brand management expertise to multiple brands in order to create product and process synergies, and to diversify their product offerings. The management of multiple brands by a single company is referred to as a company's **brand portfolio**. Expanding a company's brand portfolio can be a successful strategy when a brand manager suspects that the market is saturated for its existing brands. In most cases consumers are unaware that a single corporation owns the diversity of brands in its portfolio. See Table 2.2 for the brand portfolios of Kellwood and PVH Corp (Figure 2.7).

There are other instances in which brand owners want to make obvious to the consumer that their multiple brands offer the same level of quality and value. Brand portfolios that are transparent or obvious to the final consumer are sometimes referred to as **brand umbrellas**. Most consumers recognize that Gap's divisions include Gap, Old Navy, Banana Republic, Athleta, and Intermix, each with their own set of in-store brands. Each store within Gap's umbrella is directed to a specific consumer segment or lifestyle. Mass-market stores such as Kohl's have large brand umbrellas that consist of private label brands that they develop themselves and licensed brands that are

Table 2.2 Brand Portfolios for Kellwood and PVH Corp.

Kellwood Brand Portfolio	PVH Corp. Brand Portfolio
Rebecca Taylor	Calvin Klein
Parker	Tommy Hilfiger
XOXO	Van Heusen
Devlin	Izod
Democracy	Arrow
JAX	Speedo
Sangria	Warner's Olga
Briggs New York	
Mymichelle	Numerous licensed brands
Jolt	
rewind	

Figure 2.7
Tommy Hilfiger is part of the PVH brand portfolio.

exclusive to their stores. These brand umbrellas are dynamic—private brands are dropped when they are no longer relevant and new brands are developed.

Strategic Planning

The completion of a thorough analysis of a brand's target market and competition, as well as the development of a positioning strategy are all part of the branding strategy. They inform **strategic planning**, a top-level management activity that is used to set priorities, focus energy and resources, strengthen operations, and ensure that all stakeholders are working toward common goals. It informs decision making and links concepts related to the target market and product/service line to the financial goals of the business. The strategic plan should be realistic and achievable, taking into consideration the firm's core competencies as well as those of its supply chain partners. The strategic plan begins by identifying the brand's mission, vision, and values and then develops goals.

Mission, Vision, and Values

The product or service a business offers should be developed to meet a defined need; its marketing message should be delivered in a language that resonates with the targeted customer. Large or small, every brand needs to communicate why it exists. This is done through its mission statement. A **mission statement** reflects a company's heritage by articulating why it's in business, the customer it serves, and what makes it special. It is part of the brand's DNA and readily communicates the brand's relevance and story to all stakeholders—employees, investors, supply chain partners, consumers, and the communities in which it does business. A good mission statement reflects the company or brand's values and sets the tone for business culture and business partnerships. Some businesses use their mission statement as a tagline in promotions. It should be concise, honest, memorable, and identifiable. Table 2.3 provides examples of mission statements.

A **vision statement** outlines the organization's goals for the future; it is aspirational. A vision statement is critical to planning because in outlining goals, it guides decision making and resource allocation in the planning that follows. Some companies combine their mission and vision statements, but while a mission statement generally remains constant, reflecting the company's heritage and the core values of the founder(s), a vision statement may need to be revised when goals have been reached or market conditions change.

Table 2.3 Selected Mission Statements

Patagonia: "Our reason for being: To build the best product, to cause no unnecessary harm, use business to inspire and implement solutions to the environmental crisis."

Kohl's: "To be the leading value-oriented specialty department store offering quality exclusive and national brand merchandise to the customer in an environment that is convenient, friendly and exciting."

The Gap: "We create emotional connections with customers around the world through inspiring product design, unique store experiences, and compelling marketing."

Tory Burch: "Tory Burch is a luxury lifestyle brand defined by classic American sportswear with an eclectic sensibility and attainable price point."

Michael Kors: "Michael Kors is the leading American fashion designer for luxury accessories and sportswear."

Coach: "Coach seeks to be the leading brand of quality lifestyle accessories offering classic modern American styling."

Zara: "Give customers what they want and get it to them faster than anyone else."

H&M: "Fashion and quality at the best price."

Target: "To make Target the preferred shopping destination for our guests by delivering outstanding value, continuous innovation and an exceptional guest experience by consistently fulfilling our *Expect More Pay Less*® brand promise."

A company's mission and vision statements should reflect its **core values**—what it holds to be important as a business. Whether these values are spelled out or merely implied in the mission and vision statements, they must be authentic in order to make an emotional connection with stakeholders. **Authenticity**, in today's business lexicon, refers to a business that is true to its values in relation to its products and services, its supply chain partners, and its final customers. These values should be evident in how it manages its resources (environmental and financial) and the business culture it creates.

Strategic planning defines a company's direction. It is just as necessary for small entrepreneurial businesses as it is for big corporations. It is a dynamic process. Ongoing review is an opportunity to consider new information and re-evaluate whether objectives are still valid, achievable, and appropriate in the current business environment. As goals are reached, new goals can be set.

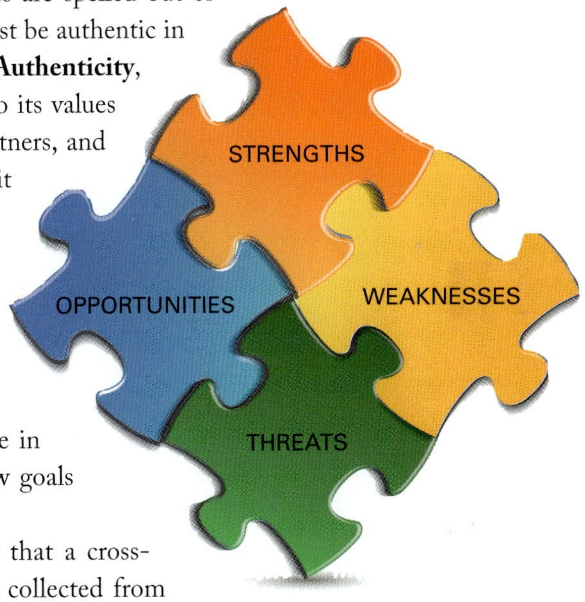

One of the benefits of the strategic planning process is that a cross-functional team shares their expertise in assessing the data collected from internal and external stakeholders up and down the supply chain. The process often starts with a **SWOT analysis** that identifies the internal strengths and weaknesses as well as the external opportunities and threats for a brand (Figure 2.8). This provides context for analyzing the data collected and for evaluating course options going forward. Some of the inputs and outputs of strategic planning are identified in Figure 2.9.

Figure 2.8
A SWOT analysis informs strategic planning.

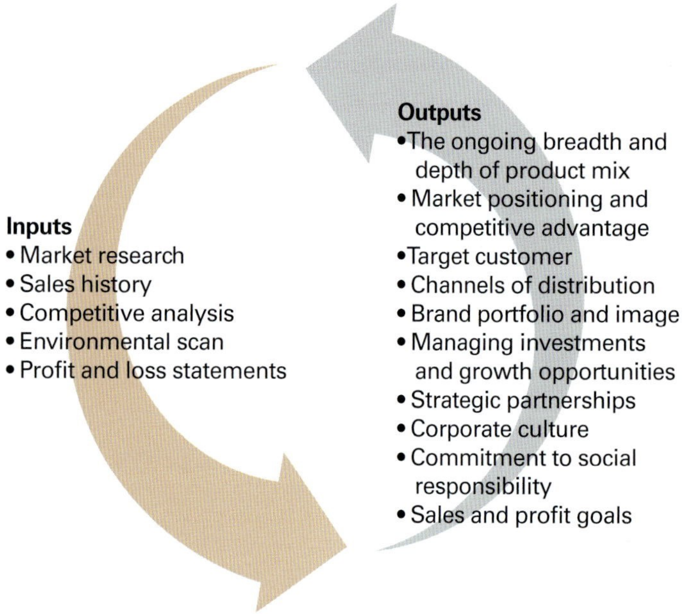

Inputs
- Market research
- Sales history
- Competitive analysis
- Environmental scan
- Profit and loss statements

Outputs
- The ongoing breadth and depth of product mix
- Market positioning and competitive advantage
- Target customer
- Channels of distribution
- Brand portfolio and image
- Managing investments and growth opportunities
- Strategic partnerships
- Corporate culture
- Commitment to social responsibility
- Sales and profit goals

Figure 2.9
The inputs and outputs of strategic planning.

The strategic planning team translates its analysis into priorities and benchmarks necessary to achieve its vision and ensure survival/success in a competitive business climate. Benchmarks are defined in terms of market share, maintaining or increasing sales, lowering returns, maintaining or increasing profit margins, implementing new technology, and meeting sustainability goals. New or entrepreneurial businesses may be happy to achieve profitability, increase brand recognition, and grow their distribution outlets, etc. No matter how lofty the goals, they will take planning to achieve.

Business Plans

Every business should do ongoing strategic planning to guide its operational decision making. New businesses and new divisions of existing businesses require a business plan in order to attract investors and/or secure loans. A **business plan** makes a case for market and operational feasibility by:

- identifying the products and/or services that will be offered;
- analyzing the intended target market and competition;
- identifying required resources and defining goals for the new business;
- outlining the business functions and organizational structure that will be required for the business to function; and
- setting out a budget and sales goals that identify the operating capital required for the first few years of business.

This information provides a rationale for whether or not to move forward with a new business venture or a business expansion. It is the basis on which investors and/or bankers make their investment decisions. It also suggests the business functions and structure that will be required to meet goals.

BUSINESS ORGANIZATION AND OPERATIONS

Business plans and strategic planning focus on the big picture. Each business needs to identify the tasks required to make and deliver their product or service.

Business Ownership and Organizational Structure

Legally, businesses are classified by their ownership. They may be organized as either a sole proprietorship, a partnership, a corporation, or a social enterprise business. Ownership of a company carries legal responsibilities in terms of liability and taxes. Decisions as to business ownership are made based on business size and scope, start-up costs, borrowing/investment capacity, risk tolerance, number of employees and reporting structure, product distribution, and liability considerations. The ownership of a company also impacts investor expectations in terms of a return on their investment, profit expectations, and how those profits are divided. A **social enterprise** is defined as a business that has specific social objectives that serve its primary purpose. Social enterprises seek to maximize profits while maximizing benefits to society and the environment. Their profits are principally used to fund social programs.

A **B Corporation™** is a business that has been certified by B Lab to have met standards of verified, overall social and environmental performance, public transparency, and legal accountability. Patagonia, Eileen Fisher, and Athleta are all examples of certified B Corporations™.

Beyond business ownership, the business structure establishes how decision making, task allocation, coordination, and supervision move the organization toward meeting its goals. Small entrepreneurial businesses may only have a few employees responsible for all tasks and decision making. Large corporations may be so big that they are divided into multiple divisions differentiated by brand, product category (men's, women's, or children's), market (private brand/wholesale brand), or region (domestic or global). Many product developers prefer a team structure to avoid siloed decision making and encourage collaboration. The scope of these divisions will influence business operations.

Business Functions/Operations

For a business organization to work efficiently and profitably, it must identify the jobs or tasks that need to be done. The organization's **business functions/operations** are high-level groupings of processes that describe the workings of a business. Once the basic business functions are identified, an operational flow can be developed to assign responsibilities, chain of command, communication and documentation protocols, and deadlines.

The functional requirements of every business vary depending on business scope. Functional areas include, but are not limited to, Finance, Marketing, Advertising, Design/Product Development, Merchandising, Sales, Research and Development, Information Technology, Customer Service, Human Relations, Production/Sourcing, Legal, Quality Assurance, Distribution/Omnichannel, Global Operations, and Corporate Social Responsibility. Start-up or entrepreneurial business structures may not need and will not be able to afford separate departments or personnel for each function; still, responsibility for these business tasks must be assigned. In entrepreneurial businesses, participants necessarily wear multiple functional hats. No matter how simple or complex the business, all functional areas must work together for the business to run efficiently. Some functional areas are more directly involved with the apparel product development process than others. Figure 2.10 lists some of the responsibilities of those functional areas.

A company's operational structure that provides a clear picture of how a functional area or team will contribute to the organization's goals. Operational planning maps out the day-to-day tasks required to run the business and allocates resources in a way that enables them to reach their assigned goals.

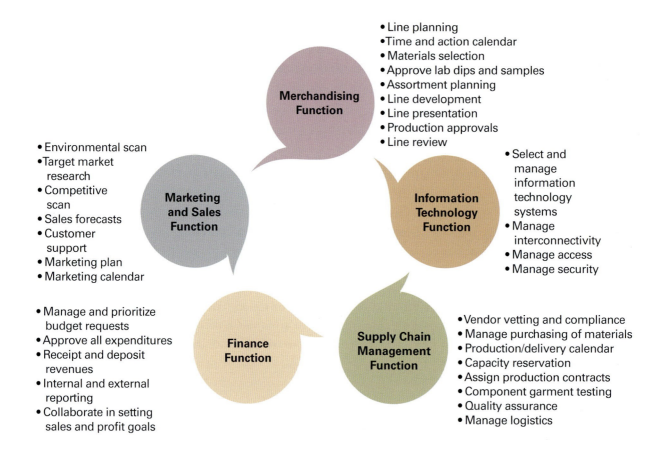

- Line planning
- Time and action calendar
- Materials selection
- Approve lab dips and samples
- Assortment planning
- Line development
- Line presentation
- Production approvals
- Line review

Merchandising Function

- Environmental scan
- Target market research
- Competitive scan
- Sales forecasts
- Customer support
- Marketing plan
- Marketing calendar

Marketing and Sales Function

Information Technology Function

- Select and manage information technology systems
- Manage interconnectivity
- Manage access
- Manage security

- Manage and prioritize budget requests
- Approve all expenditures
- Receipt and deposit revenues
- Internal and external reporting
- Collaborate in setting sales and profit goals

Finance Function

Supply Chain Management Function

- Vendor vetting and compliance
- Manage purchasing of materials
- Production/delivery calendar
- Capacity reservation
- Assign production contracts
- Component garment testing
- Quality assurance
- Manage logistics

Figure 2.10
This graphic outlines the operational areas of responsibility for the basic business functions in apparel product development firms.

Finance

Operational planning is directed by the finance department. Finance is responsible for all of the accounting activities of the business including the profit and loss statement from the past year and the ongoing revenues and expenditures of the current year. From an analysis of past and present, filtered through the prism of the current business climate, the finance department sets benchmarks and allocates responsibility and resources to the functional areas to implement. Benchmarks are set monthly, quarterly, or seasonally according to the business cycle of the product. The budget must also cover all administrative costs and overhead.

Each functional area extrapolates their benchmarks and budget into a more detailed working plan that guides their day-to-day operations. Regular communication and reporting are key to this process to ensure that all functions are able to meet their goals.

Marketing and Sales

The marketing and sales function are responsible for market research, sales forecasting, customer support, and creating and scheduling the marketing plan. The marketing plan is used by the merchandising function to develop a merchandising calendar, in tandem with product development, so that the line is ready for delivery as promised. The sales team may be part of the marketing function.

Merchandising

The merchandising function encompasses the planning, development, and presentation of product lines with regard to price, assortment, styling, and timing. Merchandising provides the framework into which product development/design creates. The merchandising area works with product development to determine the content and diversity of the line, fabrications, styling, pricing, and timing.

Product Development/Design

Product Development is the creation of a product that takes place within the parameters laid out by marketing and merchandising. Product development teams work on three or more deliveries at the same time. Responsibilities include trend forecasting, textile design, color management, garment design, and technical design. Design meets regularly with sales and marketing, merchandising, sourcing, and quality to ensure that everyone's expectations align.

Supply Chain Management/Sourcing

Most apparel manufacturing is done abroad rather than domestically. Supply chain management or sourcing typically vets potential supply chain partners to make sure they have the capacity and proficiency to produce the desired product. They also vet the manufacturer's adherence to a code of conduct, negotiate scheduling and costs, and work closely with quality assurance to ensure that the completed products are made to meet standards.

Quality

The quality function works closely with technical design and sourcing to ensure that the products ordered are produced to specification. When brands over-negotiate on price, it's no surprise that supply chain partners seek ways to make a contract work whether by compromising on quality specifications or subcontracting with supply chain partners that have not been vetted.

Information Technology

The information technology (IT) function is critical to any business as it researches and plans technology investments and oversees implementation and training. The product development function is critically dependent on technology. A collaborative relationship with IT can help the product development team time their technology investments, make good vendor decisions, and implement training programs that maximize those investments.

SUSTAINABILITY

This chapter has laid out the basics of brand strategy, business ownership, organizational structure, and business operations. The traditional business model for fashion has been based on selling new products made from virgin resources. With this model, business growth is dependent on either selling a high volume of low-priced/

low-margin goods (mass market) or selling lower volumes of product at higher margins (luxury). Sustainability is most often treated as an add-on—something nice to have but not essential to the brand's core business. When this is the case, sustainability efforts are limited to a small segment of the brand's offerings, promoting the use of more sustainable materials (organic cotton) and greener packaging materials. These efforts are not consequential enough to promote systemic change.

Brands that build sustainability into their core values are more apt to implement process improvements that design with sustainability in mind, utilize less water, and minimize the industry's carbon footprint. Even these efforts, though positive, do not go far enough to drive impact reduction. Furthermore, most of these efforts add cost to the final product, costs that consumers either can't afford or aren't willing to pay.

According to McKinsey & Company, "the lifespan of fashion products is being stretched as pre-owned, refurbished, repaired, and rental businesses models continue to evolve. Across many categories consumers have demonstrated an appetite to shift away from traditional ownership to newer ways in which to access product (McKinsey & Company, p. 39).

Circular business models look for ways to recapture both textiles and textile products when a consumer is ready to discard them; from there a decision must be made as to how best to extend the life of the garment or the material resources used to make the garment. Extending the life of garments is one of the most effective ways of reducing the environmental impact of the industry. It decreases the production and consumption of virgin resources. Once a garment has truly reached the end of its wearable life, if it was designed with circularity in mind, the textiles used in that garment can be reclaimed and reused. Likewise scraps from garment production can be captured and reused. While zero waste may not yet be feasible, circularity offers the best opportunity for systemic change in the fashion industry.

Business models that focus on the systemic change that circularity can bring have the potential to be profitable for product developers without passing on costs to the consumer. In addition, these strategies reduce our dependence on virgin resources and have the potential to create new skilled jobs. Many of these strategies integrate service into the traditional product distribution model. These new models maximize the lifecycle of fashion garments while eliminating overproduction and overconsumption, truly commercializing the concept of slow fashion. Another way to think about slowing down fashion consumption is to flip the traditional product-focused model into a service-system model that facilitates extended-use or use by multiple customers. New prototype businesses are developing the logistics to test out these models and finding success. New models create environmental and social value while adding new revenue streams realized through services that extend the lifecycle of garments before they are disposed.

New distribution models have been inspired by the popularity of resale and vintage stores combined with do-it-yourself design. As sustainability focused customers have gravitated from fast fashion to vintage fashion, product developers have looked to new ideas that reinforce more sustainable values in fashion consumption.

There is not just one way to set up a circular business model. There need to be options that satisfy the diversity of customer preferences. Figure 2.11 illustrates the circular business strategies that can be combined to yield new business/profit models.

- Materials—For garments to extend their lifecycle, they must be made of high-quality fabrics. Too many garments in the market today have sacrificed fabric quality for price. Using non-virgin fabrics whenever possible is another new strategy. More and more new fabrics are being made from textile waste—off cuts and the fabric from recycled garments can be reprocessed into new

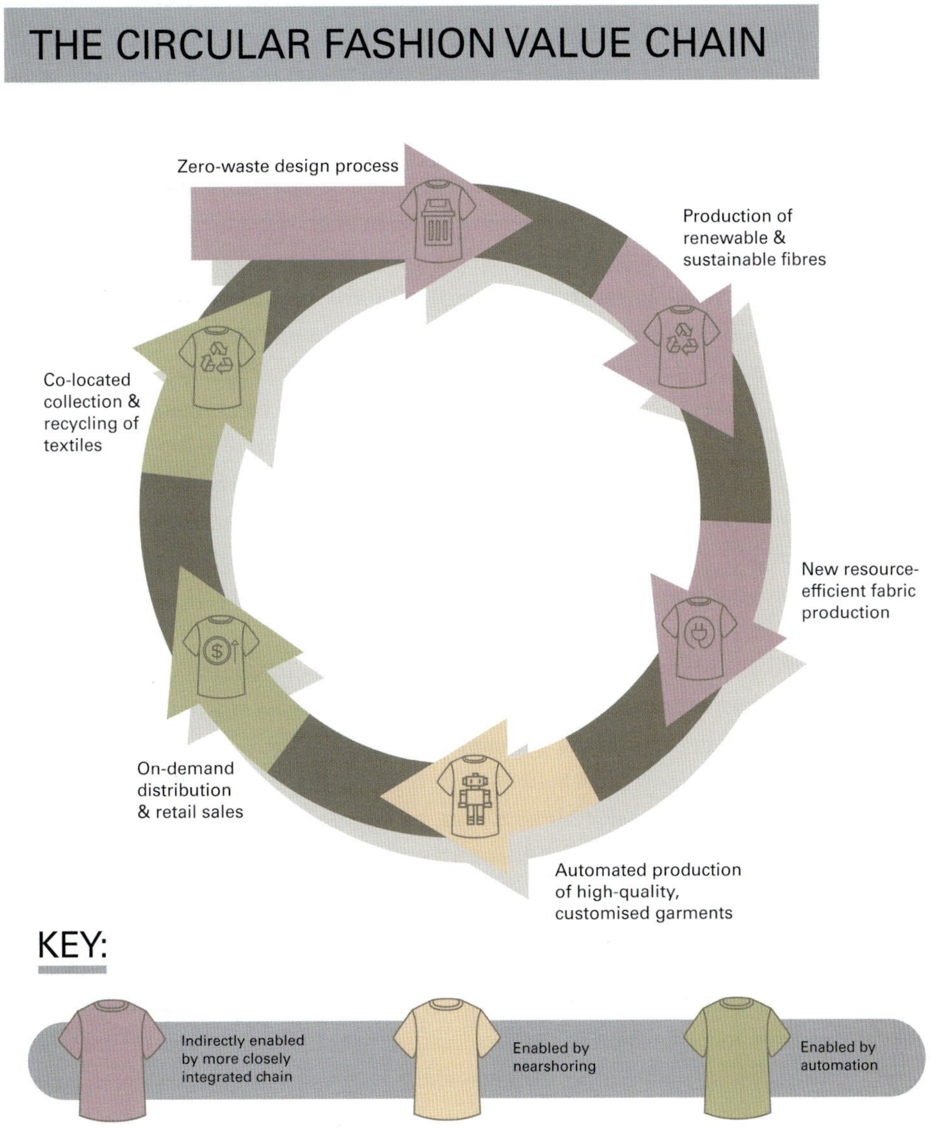

THE CIRCULAR FASHION VALUE CHAIN

Zero-waste design process

Production of renewable & sustainable fibres

Co-located collection & recycling of textiles

New resource-efficient fabric production

On-demand distribution & retail sales

Automated production of high-quality, customised garments

KEY:

Indirectly enabled by more closely integrated chain

Enabled by nearshoring

Enabled by automation

Figure 2.11
Circular supply chain sustainability model.

textiles. New processes are in development to make synthetic leather that is indistinguishable from the real thing. Small designers may be able to procure deadstock fabric of a high quality. Deadstock is excess inventory that was never used—though ideally, deadstock fabric will disappear as orders are right-sized and short lead times replace large orders that are guesstimated and placed months before the selling season.

- Design for circularity—Garments must be designed for extended wear using high-quality fabrics that can withstand ongoing use and care, in classic, time-less styles and colors, and that offer a comfortable fit. Value can be added through artisanal details and great fit, making garments indispensable in the consumer's wardrobe. Designers need to avoid blended fabrics that cannot be separated for recycling and design for easy repair, alterations, and disassembly.

- Collection of discarded materials replaces throwing them away or giving them away. When garments are collected by the brand that created that garment, they may give a credit on the purchase of a new or refurbished garment as an incentive. Of the garments given away to charities such as Goodwill, about 10 percent is resold. The rest is recycled to create industrial quality textiles or shipped overseas where there is an extensive resale market; some is incinerated or goes directly to a landfill. A brand-sponsored collection program offers a better chance that your garments will be recycled in the most sustainable way possible.

- Sorting—An important aspect of circular business models is the sorting process. New companies have positioned themselves to accept used clothing from brands that collect it; they sort it into pieces that can be cleaned, repaired, and resold; donated; or recycled. At present most sorting is a manual process, but research and development is ongoing to automate this process.

- Clean and Repair—Garments built for extended wear can be cleaned and repaired for the same consumer or a new consumer. New cleaning technology removes odors and stains that may have led to the garment disposal in the first place.

- Rental gives customers who value newness and individuality the opportunity to borrow clothes for a fee. When they are returned, someone else can enjoy that garment, keeping the garment in circulation for a longer time and providing customers with a better-made, high quality fashion experience. Some programs offer rental with an option to buy. There are even businesses that advertise their rentals for selfies on Instagram.

- Resale—Thrift stores and vintage apparel stores have seen an increase in popularity for some time. Digital platforms recognized that trend and have expanded upon it. Digital resale platforms may be aligned with a specific brand or may be multi-brand. Multi-brand platforms offer a carefully curated selection of used clothing and accessories; because they are digital, these brands are available in in markets where they might never be found locally.

Digital resale ensures that the garments or accessories a consumer purchases have been cleaned and repaired and are ready for a new life.

- Customized apparel may play a role in extending the life of garments. If a product can be customized and co-designed with the consumer so that it meets that consumer's aesthetic, functional, and fit needs, the customer may be willing to keep it longer. Customization gives the consumer a personalized experience.

It is interesting to study companies that have already structured their businesses for sustainability. Rent the Runway was one of the first online rental business models. Plans are based on four items per shipment; frequency and costs are customizable. Patagonia offers a repair service for their garments and collects discarded garments for repurposing. The company has also collaborated with Alabama Chanin; Patagonia provides discarded down jackets they have collected and Alabama Chanin makes scarves and wraps from the jackets for resale. Eileen Fisher collects discarded garments and repairs them for resale or recycles them for a line of one-of-a-kind textile art. Some companies do their own refurbishment and resale, while others engage refurbishment or resale service providers. Farfetch Second Life has a digital collection and resale program for pre-loved designer bags. Urban Outfitters Nuuly program allows consumers to rent six items a month for $88. Subscribers can wear the garments for one month and then purchase their favorites, return the remaining pieces and select new items for the next month. There is no need to launder or repair returned garments; that's included in the service. These are only a few examples of companies on the cutting edge of the circular business model.

These new service-centered, collaborative business models aren't without their challenges; they require radical changes in both producer and consumer norms as they assume joint responsibility for product reuse and disposal. The collection, sorting, repairing, laundering, redesign, and redistribution are all time-consuming activities that need to be done close to market rather than offshore in low-wage countries. At present the businesses mentioned are small; further development needs to occur in order to scale these business models to the size where they really make an impact.

Those businesses that find a way to launch circular business models have a head start in reaping benefits.

- In the long-term there is less burnout of designers who are currently expected to work on multiple collections simultaneously.
- Resources are reused for as long as possible. This actually gives manmade fiber an edge because they can be reused while maintaining quality more successfully than natural fibers.
- More customization in repairs, fitting, and reuse or redesign will command higher prices and fewer markdowns.
- New domestic businesses and jobs will be created.

This new vision needs to be embraced by all stakeholders—fiber and fabric manufacturers, garment manufacturers, brand product developers, retailers, and consumers—as well as educators, foundations, nonprofits, lobbyists, nongovernment agencies, and governments. If consumers demand more sustainable products there are ways to deliver those products.

SUMMARY

Apparel products are intrinsically linked to the brands they represent. Branding uses words, images, and logos to communicate a brand's promise. Integral to branding is a thorough analysis of competitors and the target market. That research helps brands to position their products in a way that builds competitive advantage. Brands can be positioned through their price, distribution outlets, marketing, speed-to-market, services, and digital presence to enhance the brand's image and ultimately its equity. The recession of 2020 greatly consolidated the industry. Competition based on price alone is a business model that is not sustainable. Successful branding must identify other attributes on which to compete.

Branding research informs the mission, vision, and values of the firm and enables it to develop a strategic plan. The strategic plan provides focus for all activities of the firm. The goals of the strategic plan help to identify the functionality a business needs to operationalize its goals.

Organizational planning is required to execute the strategic plan. The finance department crunches the numbers assessing past performance, tracking current performance, and setting incremental benchmarks and goals for the year ahead. Benchmarks are typically set quarterly, timed to correlate with the product cycle. The strategic plan and budgetary goals inform the business structure. Business functions and responsibilities must be assigned so that day-to-day operations work in tandem to meet objectives and goals.

Apparel product development is a business. As such, it needs to offer a return to its investors, usually in the form of profits. The traditional profit model of the apparel industry comes at an unsustainable cost to the environment. New circular business models focus on replacing virgin materials with more sustainable fibers and fabrics; designing for longevity; collecting apparel discards with the intent of repurposing; sorting; cleaning and repairing; renting and reselling to extend the life of garments; and customizing garments to the specific needs of the customer. This represents systemic change to the product development process. The vision is clear. It will require the effort of all stakeholders to scale this vision into a new reality.

Located in Cascade Locks, Oregon and Amsterdam, Netherlands, Renewal Workshop partners with brands and retailers to recover the value of their unsalable returns, excess inventory, and the discarded used merchandise that the brand collects. When consumers order multiple sizes to get the right fit and then send back the other items, a shocking 30–50 percent of those returned items are never restocked. They are often sent to warehouses where they are shredded and thrown in landfill or incinerated (Martinko, October 11, 2019). There are multiple other recommerce platforms that accept and sell garments in the condition in which they were donated. Renewal offers a unique model; it refurbishes garments to maximize their value. Renewal was launched to solve the challenging problem of apparel sustainability and to create a new system that extends the life of quality apparel. Their proprietary Renewal System takes products typically bound for waste streams and processes them into renewed products, upcycled materials, or recyclable feedstock. They are a certified B Corporation.

Product that is of a quality that can be renewed is either sold back to the brand to be sold through their own sales channels, or sold through the Renewal website. Either way Renewal is a certified partner in optimizing the resources already invested in the product. Their labeling in a refurbished garment acts as a seal of trust and quality.

Data is collected at every stage of the Renewal process and shared with brand partners so that they can continually improve the design and production of future products. Lifetime Cycle Assessment (LCA) is a method of evaluating impacts to the environment and humanity. It identifies all significant inputs and outputs associated with processes related to a portion of a product's life cycle within the scope of study and then applies appropriate factors to calculate impacts on the environment and human health. It provides in-depth reports and scorecards to each of its brands on its impact contributions regarding the amount of water, carbon, and chemicals that were saved through their partnership.

Each partner brand sets up its criteria for collecting used merchandise, typically regardless of the garment's condition. Most brands offer a loyalty reward to be used for new merchandise. Partners include North Face, Mara Hoffman, Coyuchi, Vuori, Tommy Hilfiger, PrAna, Eagle Creek, Pottery Barn, Carhartt, and NAU.

North Face, a major Renewal brand partner, shares its renewal process:

- Pre-sort: Not all products can be renewed. Products are sorted and those items that can't be renewed are upcycled through the REMADE Collection, donated, or recycled.
- Sort: Technicians inspect garments to identify the issues that need to be addressed for renewal and prepare them to be refurbished.
- Identify: Technicians match products to their original data. If a style has been recalled or has known quality issues, it will be removed from the process.
- Clean: Garments are cleaned to factory grade standards using either the Tersus CO_2 cleaning system or high-capacity commercial washing machines.
- Inspect: Repair technicians identify the processes that need to take place to restore garments to either *Like-New* or *Reconditioned* standards. Repairs are assigned based on time, complexity, and capacity.
- Repair: Garments are repaired based on standards provided by the brand's quality control team. Trained technicians ensure that all aspects of the repair meet or exceed requirements.
- Finishing: Finishers complete the process by removing any signs of lint, loose threads, or wrinkles.
- Quality Assurance: Inspectors certify that every garment meets or exceeds the brand standards and there are no signs of exterior visible repairs, defects, or imperfections. Free returns and a one-year warranty are offered if something is missed.

Renewal Workshop's unique model has the potential to divert 30,000,000 unsalable clothing items a year in the US and reintroduce them into the apparel market. "By 2025, they intend to divert over one million pounds of apparel, save over four billion liters of water, mitigate 1.75 million kilograms of carbon emissions, and avoid use of over one million kilograms of toxic chemicals" (drkfoundation.org).

References:
drkfoundation.org. (accessed on June 2, 2021).
Martinko, Katherine. October 11, 2018. https://www.treehugger.com/renewal-workshop-tbd-4857071 (accessed on June 4, 2021).
Renewalworkshop.com. (accessed on June 2, 2021).

Case Study 2.1
Renewal Workshop

With Renewal Workshop, we strive to extend the life of our clothing by adding renew, repurpose, return to the traditional extractive model of the apparel industry. The Renewal Workshop mission allows us to design with circularity in mind, so we are able to move beyond the typical cycle of take, make, use, dispose.

KEY TERMS

authenticity	co-branding	lifestyle brands
B Corporation	competitive advantage	luxury market
brand	contemporary designer	mass market
brand equity	core values	mission statement
brand extension	designer ready-to-wear	price point
brand image	(RTW)	product differentiation
branding	diffusion line	slow fashion
brand portfolio	exclusive brand	sneakerization
brand/product positioning	fast fashion	social enterprise
brand umbrella	haute couture	strategic planning
business functions/operations	high street	SWOT Analysis
business plan	licensing agreements	vision statement

DISCUSSION QUESTIONS

1. What are some of your favorite clothing brands? What differentiates your favorite brands from the competition? Discuss your favorite brands in terms of their market positioning.
2. As a class, discuss what you value in your clothing purchases? Are you able to find apparel that matches your values in the marketplace? What are the market voids as you see them?
3. How long do you wear your clothes once you buy them? What is the average number of times you wear a garment before you discard it? What are the most common reasons that you discard garments?
4. Look up the brand portfolio of several multi-brand conglomerates. How does brand portfolio strategy affect their market penetration? Do the same for a business that has a more obvious brand umbrella. How does their mix of brands enhance their ability to meet the needs of a larger customer base?

ACTIVITIES

1. Select one of your favorite brands (retail or product). What is the brand's competitive advantage? Identify the brand's competitors in the marketplace. Create a grid similar to Figure 2.3. One axis should be price and the second axis should be the attribute you chose as the brand's competitive advantage. Position the brand you chose and its competitors based on the grid.
2. Choose one of your favorite brands. Go to their website and look up their mission/vision/values. Then do a media scan and assess whether their strategic initiatives are compatible with their mission/vision/values. Report back to the class.

3. Research the mission statements of some of your favorite brands. Select one that is weak and try your hand at rewriting it to be more in line with company values and consumer expectations.
4. Select a brand that claims to be sustainable. Research that brand's efforts and imagine two or three initiatives that advance its sustainability claims.
5. Create a co-branding scenario that would appeal to your consumer values. What would be the challenges and the benefits of such a partnership?

STUDIO RESOURCES

- Take the chapter quiz with scored results and personalized study tips.
- Review glossary flashcards to build your vocabulary.

REFERENCES

McKinsey & Company. (2019), The State of Fashion 2019. https://www.mckinsey.com/~/media/mckinsey/industries/retail/our%20insights/the%20state%20of%20fashion%202019%20a%20year%20of%20awakening/the-state-of-fashion-2019-final.ashx p. 39. (accessed on 5/1/2020).

Noto, Anthony. (2018), "Fashion Platform Farfetch Is Going Public," *bizjournals.com*, August 20. https://www.bizjournals.com/newyork/news/2018/08/20/fashion-platform-farfetch-is-going-public.html (accessed on 6/8/2020).

#Rewiring Fashion. (2020), https://www.rewiringfashion.org (accessed on 6/7/2020).

Wang, Lisa. (2014), "Role Call: Jennifer O'Brien, Director of Strategic Planning," Business of Fashion, September 4. https://www.businessoffashion.com/articles/role-call/role-call-jennifer-obrien-director-strategic-planning (accessed on June 7, 2020).

CHAPTER 3

CONSUMER ENGAGEMENT

"CXM (Customer Experience Marketing) equals the art and science of coaxing lifetime loyalty from daily transactions."
STEVE CURTAIN

OBJECTIVES

- To recognize the power shift in consumer engagement
- To learn the language of customer analysis
- To grasp the potential and risks of data analytics
- To understand the new role of marketing in consumer engagement
- To imagine the future of omnichannel apparel distribution
- To examine the purchase journey and the touchpoints that contribute to consumer satisfaction
- To recognize current consumer trends
- To understand the role and responsibility of consumers in creating a more sustainable fashion system

The relationship between consumer and brand is central to product development. There has been a definite power shift in this relationship. Gone is the top-down control brands once had, where they designed aspirational worlds that the consumer bought into without too much thought. Today's consumers are more considered and less loyal. Their relationship with brands is based on shared values and mutually beneficial interactions (McCracken, 2020). This has turned the role of marketing upside down. It has also blurred the roles of brands and retailers in regard to what the customer expects of them. The discussion in this chapter applies to both brands and retailers because ultimately, they are partners in ensuring a value-driven relationship.

Customer engagement is the ongoing, value-driven relationship between the customer and the brand, achieved through providing positive, memorable experiences at every consumer intersection. To be successful, data must be tracked and analyzed every time a consumer engages with the brand to create personalized experiences. The collection of data is an art that is greatly enhanced by technology; the ability to read and interpret data accurately is a science. Ultimately the goal is to lead the customer to acquire brand products and enrich product ownership that leads to repeat customers (Figure 3.1).

Over the years, our ability to analyze the social, psychological, and generational characteristics of consumers has increased dramatically. Market research methods have evolved from simply gathering data through the analysis of transactions and observing behavior to engaging the consumer in a dialogue and, in some cases, making them collaborators. Brands that don't restructure their customer engagement in recognition of this change are destined to fail; they can no longer assume they know their market based on generalized assumptions about market segments. Customers expect personalized relationships for **markets of one**—a strategy that targets each customer as a single market, making them feel special by delivering personalized customer service.

Figure 3.1
Customer engagement occurs at every intersection between a brand and the customer.

THE LANGUAGE OF CONSUMER ANALYSIS

The capture and use of consumer data are the ultimate competitive tools, enabling businesses to personalize their relationships with each customer. Brands and retailers expend a great deal of effort identifying consumers who have the potential to be regular customers. A **target market** is a well-defined customer group to which a business wants to sell. **Market segmentation** is the ability to break down markets into increasingly smaller, well-defined groups based on data collected regarding customer behavior and preferences. Much data is available about individual customers that retailers and brands are attempting to serve (Figure 3.2).

Consumers have traditionally been segmented through the use of demographic data, psychographic analysis, and the study of generational cohorts. This language continues to be helpful in aggregating a brand's customer, but it is no longer sufficient in marketing to customers. Consumers are eager to tell the brands they shop who they are, what they like, and how much they will pay. Marketing based on what a brand thinks a customer wants doesn't work; today it is possible to pinpoint what they actually want. Brands and retailers must work together to collect and share data at every possible juncture. Customers seek one-on-one relationships with the brands and retailers they shop; they will not hesitate to change loyalties to a brand or retailer if they lack transparency and are inauthentic. Not only must brands deliver distinctive

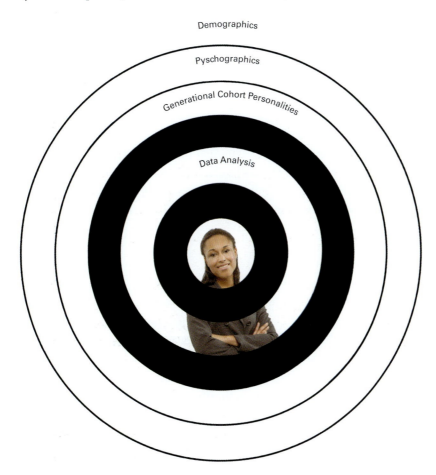

Demographics

Pyschographics

Generational Cohort Personalities

Data Analysis

Figure 3.2
Customers can be defined using demographics, psychographics, generational cohort personalities, and data analytics.

products and services but they must also credibly and authentically relate to customers based on values, diversity and inclusion, the environment, and how workers are treated up and down the supply chain. Ultimately, if consumers do not feel their values aligned with the brand, they will go elsewhere.

Demographics

One of the most simplistic tools for categorizing customers is **demographics**—statistics about a given population with respect to age, gender, marital status, family size, income, spending habits, occupation, education, religion, ethnicity, and region. Market research may be quantitative or qualitative; demographic data is quantitative. **Quantitative research** involves objective methodology in which data are collected about a sample population and analyzed to generalize behavioral patterns statistically. The *Census of Population* is a US federal publication that presents a broad range of demographic data; check the US Census Quick Facts for an overview of the US population. These data can be broken down by zip code to enable companies to target their products according to the demographics of particular geographic markets. Governments of most countries collect and publish similar data.

Demographics provide general categorization data on consumers that can be useful in identifying market voids, launching new products or services, or assessing new markets for distribution. If demographic data supports a new business idea, a deeper dive must be taken to better understand the specific characteristics of the target customer.

Younger consumers tend to resent segmentation based on demographics. They do not classify themselves by age, race, or religious affiliation. Rather they explore a variety of personalities shaped by a combination of creative and social interests; their self-expression is more fluid and can't be captured by static demographic statistics (Hays, January 21, 2020).

Using demographic data alone, for any market, fails to recognize the nuances of consumer niches and individual taste. Assuming that only customers of a certain age or income will be interested in a brand's products could blind a brand to large clusters of potential customers and fail to build a customer base for the future. Categorizing consumers by ethnicity or religion blatantly fails to recognize the diversity that exists within any ethnic culture.

Psychographics

Psychographics is the study of the social and psychological factors that influence consumer lifestyles; this information reveals more behavioral motivations and buying practices. The social aspects of lifestyle include reference groups, life stage, hobbies, interests, and activities. Psychological aspects include personality, attitudes, and level of class consciousness. These lifestyle traits and activities often dictate a consumer's level of interest in apparel, how much of their budget they allocate to apparel spending, and the types of garments they seek. It is **qualitative research**—subjective research that relies on methodologies such as observation, self-reporting, and case studies in which experiences are recorded as a narrative to describe observed behaviors within the context of environmental factors.

We live in a world where consumers don't necessarily age out of their favorite activities; rock climbing may attract young adults as well as people well into their 70s. Popular hobbies and activities may vary due to the geography and weather where consumers live. As a result, demographics and psychographics work synergistically, not in isolation.

Generational Cohort Groups

A **generational cohort** is a group whose members share significant historical and social experiences at a similar stage in life that shape their values and behavior. The study of generational cohorts combines understanding gleaned from both demographic and psychographic data. **Generational marketing** is the study of how the values, motivations, and life experiences of a generational cohort shape its purchasing behavior, reach, and market influence.

Shared life experiences revolve around pop culture, economic conditions, world events, natural disasters, celebrities, politics, and technology. These experiences create a bond that causes a generational cohort to develop similar values and life skills as its members pass through the phases of life—youth, adulthood, midlife, and elderhood.

The generational cohorts most tracked in today's marketplace are *Generation Z, Millennials, Generation X,* and *Baby Boomers* (Table 3.1). The generation born since 2015 is currently being referred to as *Generation Alpha*, though they don't yet have a generational personality. The term *Matures* is now used to describe those who were born before 1946.

Businesses have learned that a product and marketing approach that reaches one generation may be ineffective with another. Because generational characteristics evolve as each generation passes through different stages of life, retailers and brands must constantly reinvent themselves to appeal to a changing customer. They may either follow a generation from one life stage to the next or attempt to capture the attention of the next generation in the life stage they know best. Marketing professionals who understand one generation are often not effective in marketing to another. Many brands and retailers have gone out of business or struggled to stay relevant once the generation to which they originally appealed passed on to another life stage. Forever 21 was very popular with millennials but went into Chapter 11 bankruptcy in 2019. Experts cite a large store footprint that incurred high rents and rapid expansion into forty-seven countries as other chains were downsizing. They were late in building out their e-commerce platform and tone deaf to Generation Z's growing expectations for more sustainable fashion.

Generational cohorts are defined in fifteen- to twenty-year intervals, with their profiles taking shape as they enter adulthood. The years used to define a specific generation may vary slightly depending on the source. Even within a generational cohort, those born in the first eight to ten years of a cohort act and respond somewhat differently from those born during the last years.

Like demographics and psychographics, generational cohort marketing should be just a piece of a product developer's assessment of the target customer. Assuming that all members of a generation share the same attitudes is overly simplistic.

Table 3.1 Generational Cohort Groups Active in Today's Marketplace

Generation	Born	Shared Experience
Baby Boomers	1946–1964	Born during postwar expansion and prosperity, unprecedented employment and educational opportunities; social activists. They are big consumers of traditional media, though 90% have Facebook accounts. They are more apt to use cash for small purchases.
Generation X	1965–1978	Born in the wake of tumultuous political and economic conditions; came of age during a period of business downsizing and reengineering; many were products of broken homes; grew up with MTV and the AIDS epidemic. They consume some traditional media, but are also digitally savvy. They sometimes feel invisible, lost between two huge generations.
Millennials or Generation Y	1979–1995	Raised during the longest bull market in history, they faced a war on terrorism and a recession. They are more diverse than previous generations and more tolerant of diversity. They were schooled with technology. They started their careers in the midst of a recession, many working as contract employees before finding full-time jobs. They were the highest spending generation in 2020 but are saddled with a great deal of debt in the form of student loans.
Generation Z	1996–present	Born and grew up during an era of terrorist threats, extended economic and political gridlock, and increasing awareness of the fragility of our environment and natural resources. More pragmatic about the future and more practical in their purchasing habits. Have been raised with technology and on-demand entertainment. Some have referred to this generation as the loneliest generation because of all the time they've spent working, learning, and communicating digitally.

The characterizations in Table 3.1 reflects the US market; the profiles of generational cohorts in other countries will not necessarily be the same because their peer group experiences are different.

Customer Data Analytics

Every Facebook *like*, Amazon *browse*, Instagram *follow*, or Google *search* is a data point. Anyone that uses the internet can be defined by a data set that companies can catalog and leverage in order to tailor their interactions with any given customer (Stephens, 2019). This data alone offers little value; however when translated into actionable insights, it is indispensable (Figure 3.3).

Customer data analytics is the science of analyzing data points from multiple sources regarding customer behavior; these data points help brands to understand each customer's needs and preferences in order to make strategic marketing decisions. Data analytics uses predictive modeling, data visualization, artificial intelligence, and machine learning to segment buyers based on actual behavior which informs marketing in the development of targeted messaging and promotions delivered at the right time, on the right platform, and on the right device. With the use of data analytics fashion companies can monitor "heat maps" of better-performing geographies, categories, and value segments that serve as a road map for decision making (Figure 3.4).

Skilled use of customer data analytics improves the customer experience, builds brand loyalty, and breaks through the constant noise of traditional advertising. For the most part, digital natives find the benefits of data analytics beneficial; however, there is ongoing concern regarding security risks, privacy, bias, and regulation. The Federal Trade Commission is monitoring how tech companies collect user data and what they do with it. As a result, Google and other search engine providers phased out the use of cookies in 2020. With the presence most brands have on social media and their direct communication with the customer on their websites they will still collect a great deal of valuable data. Appendix 3.1 defines some of the vocabulary of data analytics.

The changes brought on by the COVID-19 pandemic of 2020 illustrate the importance of consumer data analytics. Consumer behavior changed overnight. Work from home became the norm; social lives stopped; and almost everyone's sense of economic security was undermined. Historic sales data from past seasons and past years were immediately obsolete as consumers were unable to shop in-store for several months and the purchases consumers considered necessary were redefined. The pandemic sparked lifestyle changes and value shifts that have transformed the marketplace and accelerated investment in and implementation of new technology. This technology not only collects data but

Figure 3.3
Every Facebook like, Amazon browse, Instagram follow, or Google search is a data point.

Figure 3.4
Heat maps can be generated from data analytics to visually illustrate product performance.

manipulates it to paint a much clearer picture of what each customer is considering in regard to purchases. Brands that had already implemented data analytics were better able to pivot during those unpredictable times and remain viable.

Consumer analytics has moved our basis for marketing from demographic statistics, to lifestyles, to peer group behavior, to individual behavior. With each increasing level of knowledge, the margin for error becomes tighter. Brands that don't find ways to track their customers in real time will find it impossible to remain relevant. With a 360-degree view of each individual customer, brands are able to personalize customer experiences. That data can be aggregated to customer segments and inform product design, services, and brand image.

MARKETING IN THE DIGITAL AGE

The shift to an increasingly digital marketplace has changed the role of marketing. It is no longer advertising focused with budgets planned around coupon promotions and print and broadcast media buys. These forms of marketing have little relevance for younger generations of consumers, though they may still work for older generations. Younger consumers are immune to hard sell techniques; they want to be seen, heard, and acknowledged. They want to curate their own looks and trust their friends and social network groups over the brand. For them, sharing results in better decisions; they want to choose their own experts. Marketing is now data analytics, customer relationship management, customer acquisition and retention, website content and functionality, and social media.

Marketing must be consumer-centric not product-centric. In an era of personal style, it is not sufficient to talk about how great a brand's product is; the customer wants to know why the product is right for them. An ongoing conversation with consumers facilitated by digital interactions has replaced many of the old tools such as focus groups, style testing, and surveys.

Digital platforms provide consumers with more purchasing options than ever before. No longer limited to what's available locally, they can shop a variety of channels for whatever they want, 24/7, and have it delivered to their doorstep. These changes present both opportunities and challenges for brand marketing. Accessible markets are greatly expanded, but new customers may be so diverse that their needs and preferences are too nuanced for a single brand to accommodate. Brands need to carefully evaluate their locations and distribution channels, selecting those that are most relevant to their target market, a match for their core competencies, and true to their values. Customers expect businesses to serve them on their preferred channel. They are exposed to new brands on an ongoing basis so there is less of an inclination to become brand loyal.

The immediacy with which consumers expect to be dealt requires the implementation of state-of-the-art technology and the ability to pivot quickly. Marketing, digital communications, and information technology need to work together seamlessly and without friction to acquire and retain customers. Small entrepreneurial businesses will need to find ways to curate their assortments and personalize their customer experience and service in ways that build trust and an emotional connection.

Predictive Analytics

Predictive analytics is a subset of data analytics that leverages artificial intelligence (AI), machine learning, data models, and algorithms on data assets to predict future behaviors. It assists marketers in understanding consumer behaviors and trends, predicting future shifts, and planning marketing campaigns.

There are three types of models associated with predictive analytics. **Cluster models** use algorithms to segment audiences based on past brand engagement, past purchases, and demographics. **Propensity models** evaluate a consumer's likelihood to engage with a website, act on an offer, or make a purchase. **Recommendations filtering** evaluates past browsing sessions and purchases to understand where there may be additional sales opportunities (Marketing Evolution, June 30, 2020). Amazon has been a leader in this type of modeling. A third of Amazon's sales come from its recommendation algorithm; YouTube's algorithm drives 70 percent of the content watched on its platform (knowledge@wharton, November 23, 2020). Using these three types of models allows marketers to come up with more effective, dynamic media plans that enhance the consumer experience and improve return on investment.

Customer Relationship Management

Customer relationship management (CRM) refers to all strategies, techniques, tools and technologies used by a business to develop, retain, and acquire customers. CRM manages interactions with existing as well as past and potential customers. One critical aspect of CRM is consolidating customer data across channels, which requires that brick-and-mortar stores gather more information about the customers that shop their stores, the products they ask for, and what they try on. These metrics will be most valuable when aggregated with online data. Metrics that silo data from in-store purchases and online purchases in ways that are not shared do little in terms of building the brand.

The Customer Dialogue

Marketing messages must have a purpose. Customers generally appreciate being notified that a product they were interested in is back in stock or on sale. They get annoyed when they receive duplicates of the same message or promotions for merchandise they never purchase. If they don't have a history of buying for men, buying eveningwear, or buying at designer price points, messages promoting those products are just more digital noise. Digital natives are not slaves to email, in part, because email has been overused. They prefer other digital communication channels, especially instant messaging.

Communication in a consumer-centric environment involves two-way dialog. Brands need to understand customer preferences and why they abandoned their cart, but when marketing efforts distract from the brand's message, they run the risk of being blocked. Brands need to invite dialogue when and where the customer wants it and talk to their customers, not at them. There are a variety of ways to do this.

Many retailers and brands are starting to use messaging. **Conversational commerce** represents the intersection of messaging and shopping. It uses text messaging and chat apps like *Facebook messenger*, *WhatsApp*, and *WeChat* with the goal of turning the purchase journey into a two-way conversation rather than a one-way deluge of repetitive promotional messaging. This software utilizes **chatbots**—computer programs that simulate human conversation through voice commands or text chats, which assist consumers with shopping and/or customer service. Chatbots enable brands to have a presence on multiple platforms to learn where the brand has the most impact without hiring additional personnel (Figure 3.5a).

Conversational marketing breaks down the walls between marketing, sales, and support, helping brands gain new insights through a customer's own words: They tell you how they want to interact with your business. Because the conversations are digital, they have context, building from one encounter to the next so that customers don't have to repeat information. They allow conversations to occur whenever the customer prefers (outside of business hours), and they are mobile friendly, especially when they respond to voice commands. Conversational marketing is a variation of clienteling, a long-honed strategy used by small local businesses (Figure 3.5b).

Small retailers may not have the budget for conversational marketing apps; however, they can compete on a more personal level by training sales associates to develop personalized relationships with their customers. Clienteling can make shopping a small specialty store, and its uniquely curated assortment, special for customers. **Clienteling** is a technique where sales associates establish long-term, personal relationships with customers based on data about their preferences, behaviors, and purchases. Brick-and-mortar retailers may use tablets to document each intersection with a customer while websites develop chatbots to facilitate clienteling online.

Figure 3.5a
Chatbots use AI to dialog with customers online.

Figure 3.5b
Sales associates
will increasingly
be expected to
develop personalized
relationships with their
customers through
clienteling.

Websites, Social Media Content, and Connectivity

Websites and social media platforms are invaluable tools, but only if they are continually updated with content of interest to target customers, easy to use, and easily linked. The information on these platforms must engender trust by being informative and authentic.

The website landing page should be designed to give the consumer clear instructions as to the breadth of information available and how to navigate the website at a glance. Websites are often where a customer learns more *about* the brand. This is where a brand can share its mission, vision, and values. If sustainability and the environment are key concerns, then progress on those goals should be shared. It's also a great place to share a bit about corporate culture by focusing on employees and their contributions.

A strong website is the hub of customer engagement. It is generally where a brand's catalog of products is available. The average time a consumer spends on a website is five minutes and only 2.86 percent of e-commerce visits result in a purchase (Appikon, October 8, 2020). The conversion rate for mobile commerce is even lower, perhaps because consumers check their phone constantly but don't generally have the time to follow through on an exploratory search. The faster a site can lead them to what they're looking for and facilitate a transaction, the more successful they will be.

Central to a successful online shopping experience is a well-designed system of **product search filters**. These systems help customers to refine their search by gender, category, brand, price, size, color, and reviews. Availability should be built into search filters so that the site is not showing customers products that are out of stock. In addition to streamlining the customer's product search, each shopping visit to a brand's website gives the brand valuable data points as to how to personalize future conversations. Product search filters are constantly being improved; it is a tool that is definitely worth keeping updated as a brand's online sales grow. The ability to save size, price, and brand searches from visit to visit will enhance a customer's experience with the brand (Figure 3.6).

When a customer is familiar with a brand they can go directly to their website to shop for a specific product and use that website's product search filters. What if the consumer likes a look, but has no idea what brand they are looking at? **Visual search**

Figure 3.6
Search filters make digital shopping more efficient, saving the customer a great deal of time and minimizing the pain point of stockouts.

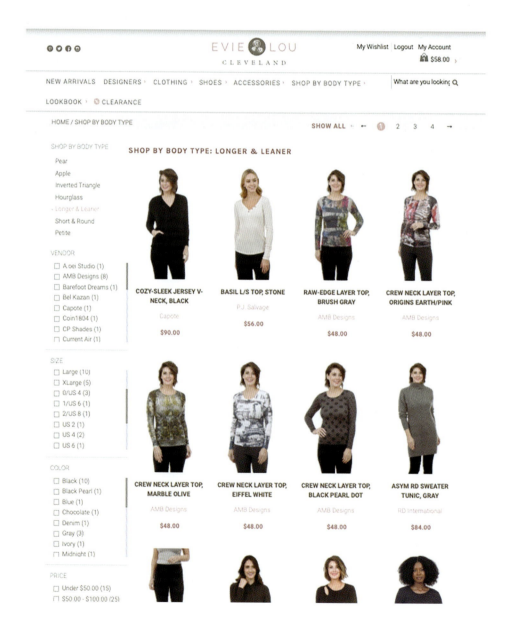

tools enable users to take a screenshot of a look they've seen on the web, on influencers, or social media and find the actual item or similar items, with relevant shopping links. Google has offered image search for some time, although its tool uses verbal searches for image results. Newer visual search tools use AI–powered image recognition technology to identify styles, patterns, colors, and other product characteristics to find exact matches or similar products. Matches are ranked as to whether they are exact or similar products and linked to shopping options. Farfetch uses *Syte*; Amazon offers *StyleSnap*; Pinterest offers *Lens*; ASOS uses *Style Match*. *SnapTech* offers a Snap the Celebrity function; other apps specialize in vintage styles. The search engine is paid based on clicks or purchases that result from the search.

Visual searches improve product discovery. The human brain processes visual searches faster than text searches. Additionally, many consumers do not have a sufficient grasp of fashion terminology to find what they're seeking. Visual searches overcome this deficit. The visual search tool a brand selects will depend on their customer—whether they're desktop-first or mobile first; the social media platform(s) their customer prefers; where their target customer gets their shopping inspiration; and where their brand is positioned in the marketplace.

While visual search tools help consumers identify products for which they don't know the brand or retailer, voice commerce helps consumers complete a transaction without keying in a lot of information. **Voice commerce** is the use of voice commands as a digital assistant to search for and purchase products digitally. This is particularly helpful when the customer has already completed the discovery and research stages of the purchase journey and is ready to buy.

In addition to search filters and visual search tools, shopping sites should encourage and publish reviews. Most digital customers read and rely on reviews in order to make a purchase decision. According to BigCommerce.com, 91 percent of customers read reviews and 84 percent of shoppers trust them more than a personal recommendation. Their research shows that the average customer is willing to spend 31 percent more with a retailer that has excellent reviews. Even when a product receives a high reviewer rating, most customers will also read the most negative reviews. A negative review may give them insight into whether something runs large or small, whether the color of the image is accurate, or how long delivery took. The number of reviews matters; it indicates a consensus opinion on the product's attributes. Reviews can also help designers, buyers, and merchandisers improve product assortments in upcoming seasons. It is the role of marketing to make sure that knowledge gleaned from reviews is shared throughout the organization (Figure 3.7).

Figure 3.7
Featuring customer reviews on a brand or store website helps consumers research a brand and product.

A regular blog can add visibility and create a personal connection with customers. A blog can engage customers by inviting them to submit images of themselves wearing brand product. Guest bloggers and influencers can generate buzz. A photo contest or a crowdsourcing opportunity gives customers a voice in shaping the brand image. **Crowdsourcing** is the process of obtaining input into a decision, usually on a digital platform, from a community of platform users. Including a comment section with your blog creates a community of users that can ask questions or dialogue amongst themselves.

Websites are great points of entry for other social media platforms. Sign-in buttons may request a visitor's email and the creation of a password, or they may sign in using their favorite social media platform. Social share buttons allow visitors to share brand website or social media information with their friends.

Influencer Culture and Product Placement

If a brand is marketing to Millennials and/or Generation Z, they may consider developing an influencer campaign for their brand. **Influencer marketing** uses endorsements and product mentions from individuals who have a dedicated social following and are viewed as experts within their niche. Depending on a brand's budget, they may seek out a celebrity endorsement with a huge following; a micro-influencer with 2,000 or fewer followers; or someone in-between with 5–10,000 followers. Influencer campaigns generally have goals of building brand awareness and increasing sales. These goals may be more specific, i.e., launching a new product or expanding their customer base. The more specific the goal, the easier it is to identify an appropriate influencer. Influencer endorsements once happened organically; today, most are business arrangements. A micro-influencer may be willing to mention a brand in exchange for product, but most influencers expect payment. The average cost per post is $271, but prices range from $83 to $763 (Chen, J., 2020). While millennials were very influenced by celebrities and the glamour and exotic locations that go with them, Generation Z has shown a preference for more casual poses, on real people in relatable settings (Figure 3.8).

Similar to influencer campaigns are product placement campaigns. **Product placement** is when a brand's product is featured in a print image, movie, video, or TV show and gets noticed. Product placement may be paid or by chance. In today's crazy world, an inadvertent mention in or by the next pop culture sensation can do wonders for a brand's visibility.

Figure 3.8
Caro Daur is a popular influencer in the EU.

Entertainment and Educational Events

With the popularity of video, another avenue for brand discovery may be virtual events. Trunk shows were considered a thing of the past as few designers at this time travel to stores and promote their collections. A live-stream video made available to all distribution channels offers a similar experience with far less expenditure of time and money. Local stores can offer their take on new fashion stock and how to wear it. These events don't need to solely focus on fashion. Educational events that pick up on the target customer's interests and causes can help to build an emotional connection.

Customer Acquisition and Retention

Customer lifetime value (CLV) is a key marketing metric. It measures the total revenue a customer can bring to the brand over the course of their lifetime. One-time customers offer little CLV; repeat customers generate increasing value and offer more return on marketing investment. The goal is to maximize sales over a lifetime, not just to force an immediate sale.

When budgets are tight, there's always a tension as to whether to focus on acquisition of new customers or retention of existing customers. The acquisition of new customers is expensive and unless they can be developed into loyal repeat customers, they are not as relevant to the bottom line. In marketing, the 80/20 principle refers to the fact that 20 percent of customers typically account for 80 percent of sales for a brand or retailer. Many brand specialists suggest that rather than focusing budgets on obtaining new customers, brands would be wise to focus their spending on retaining their best customers with personalized attention and service. Research has shown that a 5 percent increase in customer retention can increase profits anywhere from 25 to 95 percent. It costs five times more to acquire a new customer than it does to retain an existing customer; it costs twenty-six times more to get new customers to the same spending level as existing customers (Campbell, May 21, 2020). The word-of-mouth promotion offered by happy customers will help to recruit new customers. Savvy marketers are able to identify the value a customer represents, allowing marketers to qualify and prioritize leads. This allows marketing to devote more attention to customers likely to convert to purchasing and not waste dollars on customers who likely won't respond to marketing.

Marketing Budgets

While social media is generally less expensive than ads in print and traditional media, there are still costs that need to be factored in. First and foremost is the technology that facilitates a presence on multiple platforms. Predictive analytics, conversational marketing apps, product search filters, visual search apps, and other technology that drives brand exposure are all critical. Add to that the commission paid to digital marketplaces for showing product and facilitating transactions. Any savings incurred from selling direct to consumer rather than selling wholesale to a retailer is typically shifted to technology apps and fees to service providers that facilitate customer engagement and transactions.

Budgets must also account for photography, talented web designers, social media specialists, and influencer agreements. During the pandemic, when social distancing was mandated, models were sent garments and asked to style and photograph their own photoshoots. Whether or not this more casual approach to social media and influencer photography takes hold in the long run is yet to be seen. Watch for influencer culture to continue to evolve.

THE NEW FASHION DISTRIBUTION ENVIRONMENT

The global pandemic served to accelerate the technological innovations shaping the experiential nature of both physical environments and digital portals. Experts suggest that change which might have taken five to six years for adoption became imperative in just a year or two. With it, the fundamentals of how apparel is sold and distributed have also changed.

Distribution Channel Proliferation

Channel proliferation has been occurring since the advent of online commerce; one of the first e-commerce companies was Amazon, which began selling books online in 1995. A **channel** is a chain of businesses or intermediaries through which a product or service is distributed. A **channel strategy** is a brand's plan for moving a product or service through one or more chains of commerce to the final customer. Most apparel brands today are **multichannel**; they distribute product through a combination of stores and digital channels.

Distribution channels may be indirect or direct. **Indirect channels** are when a brand sells its products to a retailer or intermediary that ultimately sells to the consumer. Multi-brand department stores, mass-market stores, and boutiques all buy wholesale and add their markup before selling to the final consumer in-store or online. When the same product is sold through brand-owned signature, outlet stores or through their own digital channels, these are referred to as **direct-to-consumer channels (DTC)**. Digital transactions may take place via a website, on social media (social commerce), or using a mobile device (m-commerce). The development of mobile commerce is particularly important in Asia, where many consumers never acquired a computer, but most have cell phones.

Digital marketplaces represent a hybrid variation of digital sales. A **digital marketplace** is a website or app that facilitates shopping from many different sources. The marketplace does not take ownership of inventory. They are experts at presenting a brand's inventory and facilitating transactions, which are fulfilled by the brand. Digital marketplaces are quickly filling the void left by department stores in multi-brand retailing and helping brands to jumpstart their digital presence. They offer immense product choice, representing an array of global brands, which greatly expands the reach of both small and large brands. Most allow the brand to manage pricing. They typically are willing to share relevant customer data with the brand, something that traditional retailers have been hesitant to do. Marketplaces have found unique niches. Yoox specializes in off-season apparel; the RealReal, Depop, Mercari, thredUP, and Poshmark specialize in resale—some peer to peer and some consignment models; Nineteenth Amendment specializes in up-and-coming new designers and made to order; and FarFetch and Pret á Porter specialize in luxury apparel. They may charge anywhere from a 10–25 percent commission for products sold on their site; resale sites charge even higher (Figure 3.9).

Marketplaces that are well established are now offering their own private label and/or white label products. A **white label** is a product or service designed and produced by one company that other companies rebrand to make it appear as if they produced it. Private label product is exclusive to a retailer or marketplace and often customized or co-designed while white label products are already designed when a third party purchases them and are not customized. It is interesting that the private label offerings of mass merchants have been declining in popularity while the private label and white label offerings of digital marketplaces are just taking off. Marketplaces have rich data resources that help them curate and customize their own brand offerings, be they private brands or white brands. Yoox offers *8 by Yoox*; Mr Porter offers *Mr. P.*

The rapid multiplication of distribution channels is great for consumers in terms of choice and flexibility, but it presents challenges for brands that need to determine where they should focus to best reach their customer. Brands need to think about how to leverage their physical assets and their digital assets in ways that complement each other to facilitate and enhance the customer journey. The answer will be different for every brand. Ultimately, the customer expects integrated commerce. They use their

Figure 3.9
Online marketplaces make almost any brand available to all.

phones while they shop to make sure they receive the best possible price and service combination. **Omnichannel merchandising** is a strategy focused on creating a unified customer experience across all possible points of customer engagement for a seamless experience. It recognizes that most customers do not take a linear path to purchasing. They prefer to engage with brands on multiple channels while pausing and resuming their journey at several points before they actually purchase. A customer may discover and research a brand digitally, try on products in-store, purchase an item digitally, and return it in-store. If they can't move frictionlessly from one channel to another while making a purchase, they will likely move on to discover another brand (Figure 3.10).

Given the importance of an omnichannel strategy, brands that measure their sales as either digital or bricks and mortar do so at their peril. It is imperative to break down the silos between bricks and mortar and digital. Businesses must recognize that most purchases are the result of some combination of activities in-store and online.

An omnichannel strategy requires stores to rethink their purpose. They will need to re-evaluate location, square footage, staffing, and activity centers as they become more experiential and more involved in order fulfillment. Most experts believe that there will continue to be a role for physical stores, but the activities and services they provide will look drastically different as they partner with digital commerce to fully address the customer's needs. The level of in-person interaction they provide will be elevated. Omnichannel tools may include live streaming new fashion collections, celebrity and/ or designer virtual appearances, educational events, and online discovery through virtual boutiques, augmented reality-powered try-on tools.

Bifurcated Fashion Market

Consumer spending on fashion is increasingly bifurcated, with retailers and brands in the high-end luxury arena doing well and mass marketers competing on price also doing well. Growing inequality and financial uncertainty have caused the vast majority of consumers to seek out value, leaving brands in the middle to struggle.

A large share of luxury shopping was traditionally done while traveling, especially for Asian customers. During the pandemic, when travel came to a halt, luxury brands needed to find new ways to reach those travel customers. While many stores have shuttered in North America and Europe, luxury brands have been building stores in China. In addition, luxury brands are seeking ways to provide the same level of service online as customers have become accustomed to in-store.

At the other end of the market, mass merchants have increasingly replaced the department store as the go-to resource for family shopping. While some mass merchants tried mall locations, most have reverted to stand-alone locations with big parking lots and easy in and out for customers. Stand-alone locations help them to keep costs down as does the self-service environment in these stores.

The continued popularity of fast fashion makes up much of the remaining value market. As much as younger consumers would like to shop their values with more sustainable brands, they often can't afford them. The rental and resale models are very appealing to Gen Z and millennials who would like to break the fast fashion cycle but don't have the means to purchase full-price investment pieces. The opportunity to expose them to higher quality products should not be ignored.

The New Role of Bricks and Mortar Stores

With a growing share of apparel purchases made online and the demise of the department store anchor, the role of brick-and-mortar stores and the shopping mall are changing significantly. It is no longer necessary to spend a day at the mall shopping when perusing products is more efficiently done on a digital device. Malls are no longer the socializing mecca that they once were. With the contraction of anchor department stores, it is likely that many malls will close and others will need to reinvent themselves. The pivots that had to be made in order to keep fashion retail alive have changed the course of the customer's purchase journey.

To remain relevant, bricks and mortar retail that is not focused on the lowest price will need to reinvent itself—serviceable, but boring retail is out (BOF Team and McKinsey & Co., December 7, 2020). Retailers will need to focus on offering experiences, entertainment, and education (Figure 3.11). They will also play a larger role in order fulfillment and facilitating a seamless omnichannel experience. Traditionally, sales metrics have focused on whether the actual transaction was made in-store or online; store sales were based on sales volume per square foot. To silo transactional data is short sighted. Research shows that most purchases result from a hybrid of in-store and online experiences. To integrate the two experiences, stores need to be better able to capture information regarding their in-store customers and their shopping interests. This can be done anecdotally by training retail staff to record consumer behavior or through the use of new digital tools. The Amazon Go store that opened in Seattle in 2018 scans your mobile device on entry to track every movement and interaction you have with the store and its products. Expect stores of the future to recognize shoppers

as they come into the store. They will track what a customer stops to look at, what they try on, and what they purchase in-store or later online (Stephens, January 29, 2019). At present, consumers are reticent about sharing where they are at any given moment; however, if we expect retailers to give us exactly what we want, we will have to become comfortable with sharing evermore pieces of ourselves. Retail bricks and mortar technology that is already on the horizon includes the following:

- Thermal imaging technology that determines patterns in customer movement throughout the store
- Device-based tracking that keys into a mobile device's unique identifier to track individual consumers throughout retail space
- Computer vision that monitors items that are being removed from shelves by consumers, as well as which items are put back
- Floor sensors that measure footpath and engagement time by location
- Mobile payment apps that identify customers geographically and track and compare their buying patterns
- Radio frequency identification transmitters attached to products to detect their movement and location from a display to the fitting room
- Emotional capture technology used to determine the emotional or cognitive state of shoppers by analyzing facial expression

Once again, this technology walks a fine line in terms of individual privacy. Brands and retailers will need to use it carefully to build a more quality experience; abuse of this information can erode a customer's trust in an instant.

THE PURCHASE JOURNEY

The **customer journey** is a roadmap that tracks every interaction with the brand. The stages of that journey are generally identified as prepurchase awareness and consideration; purchase/acquisition; and postpurchase service and customer retention, evolving into loyalty and advocacy. At each stage there are a number of touchpoints where the brand can interact with the customer to provide a great customer experience. A **touchpoint** is any interaction that might alter the way that the customer feels about the product, brand, business, or service either positively or negatively. The journey will not be the same for everyone, nor will it be the same for every purchase (Figure 3.12).

Technology has the ability to enhance much of the purchase journey, offering personalization, more self-service functionality, expediency, and the ability to compare product offerings based on price and service. Digital natives are comfortable with any technology that makes their purchase journey more seamless. They expect instant gratification—their time is as valuable as the brand's. Long queues on the telephone or delays in receiving an email verification are unacceptable and not tolerated. Self-service is the best option for meeting customer expectations of expediency. Junctures in the purchase journey that cause friction are identified as pain points. Brands and retailers need to be vigilant in identifying pain points and eliminating them. Customers will readily abort a transaction if it takes too long or involves too many steps.

Prepurchase Awareness and Consideration

The first step in the customer purchase journey is awareness of a want or need. Needs are somewhat obvious—a garment no longer fits, something that is worn frequently is no longer serviceable, or another piece is required to complete a look. Most consumers make many more purchases based on wants. They see something worn by a friend, on a mannequin in a store, or on social media and they seek out something similar.

Figure 3.12
There are many touchpoints on the customer's journey to purchase. Failing to meet expectations at any point can result in an aborted transaction.

Needs and wants commence the awareness stage of the purchase journey. A friend's word-of-mouth recommendation, blogs, influencers, and social media visibility are key touchpoints at this stage. Images and posts should reflect diversity. Customers want to see themselves in marketing campaigns and know that the brand sees them for who they are.

Once the desire for a product has been established, customers will likely do further research before making a purchase. During the consideration stage a number of touchpoints may be utilized. If the product is available at a nearby store, they may try it on and check the quality. If the product is being researched digitally, a website and product page are important. All of the information necessary for the customer to make a purchase decision should be available, including fiber content, size, and color.

The ability to try clothes on is one of the advantages of shopping in physical stores. On digital channels, some brands offer videos of a model wearing the garment to show how it moves on the body. Virtual try-on technology has been in the pipeline for some time; the pandemic accelerated its adoption. A variety of augmented reality approaches have been commercialized; they range from a customer inputting their measurements to a customer taking one or more images of themselves, which are uploaded to a website where an avatar is created. Each garment in every size must also be input into the computer for the app to be able to make a size recommendation and create an image of the customer in the garment. Other websites use predictive analytics to recommend sizes based on what the customer has purchased in the past and what size they take in their favorite brands. Small boutiques that can't afford this technology can offer parallel services. They may compose fit notes when they are photographing garments on a model for their webpage. Including anecdotal fit information and recommendations for most appropriate body type on the product web page can be very helpful to digital customers (Figure 3.13).

Figure 3.13
Small businesses can enhance their website interactions by adding anecdotal product and fit notes that set them apart from large marketplaces.

Try-on technology makes buying decisions easier, hopefully increasing conversion rates on digital channels; it also reduces the costs incurred due to returns; and it provides retailers and brands with valuable data points as they design, merchandise, and allocate future seasonal lines.

Customer reviews are another important touchpoint in the research stage. Customers look for insights as to fit, color, and quality. Negative reviews don't always deter a customer from purchasing; rather they can help a customer order the right size or better visualize a color.

No matter which channel customers eventually use to complete their purchase, they will undoubtedly check to see if the price is the same across all channels and whether it's in stock in their desired size and color. If they perceive the price to be too high for their budget, they may place the product on a *wishlist* or put it their cart but not complete the purchase in hopes that it will be marked down. It is at this point that discounts for new customers might help to close the sale. It is important that all channels within the brand's control are offering the same price.

Acquisition

The popularity of new business models means that the acquisition stage of the purchase journey may be completed by purchasing a new or refurbished garment or renting a garment for a specified period of time. Recognizing that transactions aren't complete until the consumer receives the garment and connects with it, subscription services and new variations of personal shopping or clienteling relationships are growing. No matter which platform consumers ultimately use for their acquisition transaction, the process must be seamless.

Payment Options

All distribution channels are challenged to make transactions as fast and easy as possible. Payment options are an important opportunity to streamline transactions and eliminate pain points. Many younger customers are reticent about opening multiple credit cards. They have weathered difficult times and want to avoid the burden of credit card debt that they've seen family members experience. **Payment gateways** are digital services that offer a simple and secure way for businesses to collect digital payments. Customers can link a credit or debit card and not have to enter card information every time they make a purchase. PayPal, Square, Affirm, Klarma, and Alipay (China) are all examples of payment gateways.

Digital wallets, also known as e-wallets, work in a similar way for in-person transactions. They allow payment using a mobile phone, which stores credit or debit card information rather than using cash or the actual credit card. ApplePay and GooglePay work as both payment gateways and digital wallets. These cashless tools not only expedite the purchase transaction, they are also more secure, since store associates never see a credit card number (Figure 3.14a–b).

Increasingly payment gateways are offering flexible payment plans to customers without credit cards, promoted as *buy now, pay later* plans. They offer to divide

a

b

Figure 3.14a–b
Payment portals and
e-wallets speed up the
checkout process and
offer added security.

payments into four or more installments interest free. Many use algorithms on buying history etc., to approve customers for short-term credit lines with approvals coming within minutes. These services are more expensive than traditional credit cards because the brand is paying the fees rather than the customer.

During the pandemic, some retailers devised new variations of clienteling as a means of boosting sales. Local boutiques might offer to bring a selection of garments to a customer's home so that they wouldn't have to venture into a mall setting. Online channels offered to send out three to five styles on approval; the customer could try on the garments before deciding what to keep and what to send back. This is not unlike subscription services, which have grown in popularity since the pandemic. Though these services have been more focused on makeup and accessories, the concept is evolving to include apparel brands. These programs can boost impulse sales and build customer intimacy if they are based on accurate data analytics.

The psychological response to these new purchase/payment options is to make consumers feel less committed to the financial transaction and more emotionally connected to the brand and the product. For many customers it removes a barrier or pain point to finalizing the purchase.

When selecting payment gateways a business must consider their reach. Do they transact business only domestically or do they have customers overseas? Is a chosen gateway functional on the brand's website, on mobile devices, and at least three social media platforms? Other considerations include ease of transaction, transaction fees, ability to process both credit and debit cards, ability to handle gift cards, and security.

The ability to complete purchase transactions on social media platforms without being redirected to a website further streamlines digital purchases. Now brands can go beyond banner ads, reminding the consumer of something they've looked at. E-commerce is firmly embedded within social media, allowing consumers to find products they normally wouldn't search for and purchase those products without being redirected to the brand's website.

Once a transaction is complete, customers should receive a series of notifications, the first of which is a thank you for their purchase. This generally occurs on the transaction page. A copy of the transaction record should be sent via email or text for their records. Additionally, they should be able to retrieve a record of their transaction under their account information on the website.

Order fulfillment can be enhanced when inventory is managed across channels. **Order orchestration** is the ability to fulfill a purchase from either an e-commerce distribution center or a store. Being able to track inventory across all channels helps to avoid overstocks in-store that require significant end of season markdowns while incurring stockouts for the same merchandise online. Using stores for order fulfillment becomes a new responsibility for in-store sales associates. Order orchestration requires an omnichannel understanding of where inventory is at, at any given moment (Chen, C., 2020).

As more and more purchases are made via digital channels, consumers are coming to expect free shipping and free returns. In many cases they would rather get free shipping than get their items faster. Amazon Prime's business model charges a monthly fee for free shipping, but fashion consumers typically don't frequent any one retailer or brand often enough to make that model work. One strategy is to offer tiered service levels or loyalty programs where a brand's best customers get free shipping as a recognition of their *lifetime value*. Or they might offer free shipping once an order reaches a certain dollar amount. An alternative option is to encourage customers to buy online and pick up in-store (**BOPIS or BOPUS**); this allows the customer to avoid shipping fees and receive their merchandise more quickly (Figure 3.15).

Figure 3.15
Buy online pick up in-store was a popular value-added service during the pandemic.

Shopping Events

The concept of making shopping more experiential and entertaining is evolving. One idea that took shape during the pandemic was live shopping events. Reminiscent of television shopping networks, **livestream shopping** events can create community, promote new merchandise, and create a sense of exclusivity and scarcity. They take advantage of consumers' increasing fascination with video on social media. Whether the event is local or international, participants have the first opportunity to purchase what are often limited-edition products. It can be an inexpensive tool for small businesses to generate sales using associates and customers as models. Live streaming events can be facilitated on Zoom, Google Meets, Instagram, TikTok, and FaceTime as social media apps have enabled direct online checkouts. The trend started in China in 2016 and took off throughout the rest of the world during the challenges of the pandemic (Chen, C., 2020).

Limited edition **product drops** are a strategy that was introduced by savvy streetwear brands. Brands specify a day each week or month when limited edition stock will be released at flagship stores and/or online. In-the-know customers wait in line to snag pieces that will be in limited supply (Figure 3.16).

Postpurchase Customer Engagement

There are multiple ways that channels can enhance their customer engagement once a purchase is made. Some opportunities present themselves immediately after the product is delivered. Others are more long term, leading the consumer from satisfied, to loyal, to advocate.

Figure 3.16
Every Thursday skateboarding brand Supreme releases new product at its stores.

Customer Reviews and Returns

Customer reviews have been discussed previously. More and more all types of distribution channels are proactively inviting customers to submit a review. Brands should make it easy by including a form that can be completed quickly and easily. They might also incentivize reviews by offering free shipping or a token discount on the customer's next purchase.

Customer analytics is not just useful for selling to customers, but also for customer service post-sale. It allows functions such as returns to become self-service; authorizing a return can take place on a customer's schedule without the need to reach a service department via phone or email. At the same time data analytics can collect data as to why a product is being returned. This information helps to identify pain points throughout the purchase journey. Was the problem with fit, untimely delivery, or poor quality? This information can be shared throughout the organization as a means of continuous improvement.

Consumers expect to be able to return products via shipping or dropping the product off at a physical store—*buy online, return in store* (BORIS). Return transactions will be less painful when return shipping is free. Brands and retailers may not be able to offer free return shipping to all customers, but it is a much-appreciated perk for first-tier loyal customers. Customers give points for good (frictionless) service even when they don't keep the garment. Satisfied customers are some of the best brand ambassadors and they don't charge a fee.

Loyalty Programs, User Groups, and Next Steps

Customers used to be awarded special perks through their credit card. With the popularity of store credit cards waning, many retailers and brands have created loyalty programs to engage and retain customers. A **loyalty program** is a marketing strategy designed to retain customers and motivate them to buy.

Loyalty programs can be designed in a number of ways. Tiered programs and point programs offer rewards based on annual spending. Point programs award customers a credit, discount, or giveaway as their points grow. Tiered programs offer increasingly valuable perks based on a customer's annual spending level; free shipping and returns plus early access to limited edition merchandise may only go to top-tier customers. Amazon is well known for its paid program; members pay a monthly fee for a full range of perks. While that may not work as readily for fashion brands, subscription models are similar. Customers pay a set fee each month or quarter and receive an assortment of garments tailored to their specifications (Figure 3.17).

Figure 3.17
Subscription services, like Stitch Fix, deliver a customized assortment of products to your doorstep each month.

Mission-based and community-based loyalty programs may not need to give much away; they function as more of a user group based on their customers' shared commitment to a cause or a goal. Brands with an authentic commitment to the environment or a movement like *Black Lives Matter* can engender customer loyalty while taking an activist social or political position. Activewear brands may help customers with encouragement and suggested workouts to meet their fitness goals. These programs can bring many benefits as they support an emotional connection with customers.

Overall, loyalty programs and user groups are a valuable touchpoint for any retention strategy. They boost repeat sales, which increases revenue, and ultimately increases a customer's lifetime value. Furthermore, they can differentiate a brand and drive customer satisfaction. They give a retailer or brand a reason to continue to communicate with offers that are mutually beneficial.

Advocacy and Beyond

In today's consumer-centric market environment the ultimate goal is to build customer engagement that results in advocacy for the brand. The customer is a brand's best marketing tool. Positively engaging them to the point that they enthusiastically promote the brand is authentic and powerful. They serve as a team of influencers, hopefully mentioning the brand on social media and to their friends, family, and colleagues. Consumer advocates are the reward for a job well done, however, the process is ongoing and there is always room for continued improvement.

Brands will increasingly be held accountable to the goals of a circular fashion system. Consumer engagement will be critical to this transformation. Promoting circular business models such as apparel collection, resale, rental, and the use of recycled fiber in a committed and authentic way is a beginning to creating a compelling narrative that prioritizes value, trust, and education. Long-term behavioral change starts with reliable information that results in more conscious decision making.

As more and more brands recognize the importance of making fashion a more circular system, the development of a program to collect and recycle or upcycle gently used garments has the potential to become an integral part of customer engagement. Circularity is an opportunity to reimagine and expand customer engagement. The brands that are able to do it early on will be best situated to meet future consumer expectations.

GENERAL CONSUMER TRENDS

Athleisure

The casualization of fashion is often linked to recessions. The most recent movement probably began in 2008 with Millennials exerting their preference for casual attire in the office and their habit of fitting in a workout before or after work or during a lunch hour. Generation Z followed suit with their fascination for tech-infused apparel. The 2020 pandemic fundamentally transformed the work environment by proving that working from home, telecommuting, flexible hours, and an emphasis on work/

life balance could be both productive and profitable. Athleisure has been embraced across all demographics and lifestyles and at all price points. Nurtured by images of celebrities and influencers on social media, the athleisure movement has driven the market for high end sneakers and workout clothes. Perhaps most surprising is how athleisure has permeated the luxury market. Brands that focused on dated concepts of office wear have struggled to stay in business, indicating that athleisure is here to stay (Figure 3.18).

Seasonless Apparel

With wardrobes becoming more casual, there is an increasing demand for seasonless apparel. Jeans, leggings, tops, and workout apparel can all be layered to adapt to the weather. For the most part, these styles can be worn year round. Seasonless apparel is considered a good investment, especially as consumers become more attuned to cost per wear. It negates the necessity of having two different wardrobes, one for cold weather and another for warm weather, and helps to decrease the fashion industry's footprint.

Gender Neutral

Members of Generation Z are not letting their gender dictate their style. They gravitate to gender-neutral outfits. Forward-thinking labels such as Alexander Wang and Rachel Comey have abandoned separate fashion week presentations; they show their collections on a mix of models, not all professional, with binary looks. Functionality and individuality are central to gender-neutral apparel. Perhaps it reflects a reaction to the divisive culture in which Gen Z has grown up in.

Normcore

Normcore is a trend that celebrates the non-trend. Fashion has moved away from mimicking an outfit seen on social media to personal self-expression—just one more indication that the traditional fashion system must change. Generation Z in particular has no interest in fashion dictates. They intend to call the shots in fashion and most other aspects of life.

Inclusive Culture and Social Justice

Increasingly consumers are expecting the brands to which they are loyal to take a stand on social justice. They are hoping that businesses might help them affect change in ways that divided government has not been able to do. Fashion designer Aurora James spurred a viral movement with her plea asking retailers to commit to buying 15 percent of their products from Black-owned businesses. A number of businesses, including Sephora, have agreed to publish annual breakdowns of the Black brands they support. Other movements include the *Pull Up or Shut Up* Instagram campaign urging brands to publish their overall employment demographics at all levels. Expect consumers teaming with brands to demand change to become a new political force.

Figure 3.18
The popularity of athleisure has changed wardrobe needs.

Digitalization

Digitalization is the use of digital technology and digitized data to get work done faster and smarter. Not only has it impacted how we acquire apparel, it is having a major impact on the jobs in the fashion industry. The ability to identify problems and imagine digital solutions will continue to transform the fashion system as we know it. It will also help to make digital shopping faster, safer, and more satisfying.

Smaller Format Neighborhood Stores

As consumers increasingly work from home, they will expect to be able to shop in their neighborhood. Consumer demand for convenience and immediacy will prompt retailers to create smaller format stores that create a sense of community through experiences and service. While they may not carry a full line of a brand's offerings, they will focus on localized assortments and be organized to procure whatever a customer wants within a day or two, allowing them to try it on and facilitate the transaction. Neighborhood stores will replace locations in large shopping malls with lower overhead and more services.

Global Marketplace

Established fashion brands at all price levels will face increasing competition from global brands. Companies that have previously worked as suppliers within the global supply chain are now spreading their wings, using what they have learned, and launching their own brands. Digital marketplaces make these new brands accessible to a global market.

Gaming Partnerships

A number of savvy fashion brands are partnering with gaming brands as a means to expand their audience. Louis Vuitton sells skins (virtual outfits) to League of Legends players. Burberry launched *B Bounce*, a computer game which promotes the brand's monogram puffer collection. Gaming partnerships serve several purposes. There is no doubt that apparel purchases are losing ground to entertainment spending. These collaborations take advantage of that trend. Also, the artificial intelligence and virtual reality technology that powers gaming is also what is making new try-on technology and visual search tools possible (Figure 3.19).

Figure 3.19
Savvy brands are forming partnerships with game developers to get the attention of customers and to gain experience in cutting-edge technology.

The New Luxury Consumer

Luxury consumers are getting younger. Millennials and Generation Z account for almost half of the global market share and all of the market growth. The luxury market is adapting to the preferences of the younger customer in terms of product offerings, customer engagement strategies, and new distribution channels. Both younger customers and Asian customers are adept at shopping online. Luxury brands have been forced to quickly bring their digital channels up to speed while finding ways to offer the same levels of service they are used to providing in-store. This market has also been forced to acknowledge the reality of cultural and size preferences. These shifts can be seen in the hiring of younger designers and design directors as well as the growing focus on athleisure and streetwear apparel.

SUSTAINABILITY

There has been a longstanding disconnect between Millennial and Generation Z customers' stated values on sustainability and their shopping behavior. Though they believe in climate change, these groups perceived sustainable brands as too expensive when fast fashion brands and a discount culture make cheap clothes so available. Post-pandemic, the fashion system may have finally reached a tipping point:

- New business models allow consumers to satisfy their desire for new fashion by renting or buying gently used garments.
- The work-from-home trend has diminished the need for office apparel and strengthened the athleisure and seasonless trends with function and comfort as key purchase criteria.
- The sustainable fashion message has shifted; brands are focused on the risks of overconsumption, the unsustainable growth of landfills, and the depletion of nonrenewable resources.
- More activist customers have taken seriously the *Me Too* and *Black Lives Matter* movements. Those same customers will be attentive to the plight of the apparel workers and sales associates who lost their jobs during the pandemic.
- Many are hopeful that the Marie Kondo effect that motivated consumers of all ages to tidy up their closets during the pandemic brought home the fact that most consumers have too many clothes. Customers looked at the totality of their wardrobe and asked themselves which purchases made them happy.
- Brands are re-evaluating their production and inventory models. Overproduction and excess inventory lead to early markdowns and deep discounts in the US, making cheap apparel hard to resist. If inventories are right sized and fulfillment orchestration systems put into place, pricing can be more transparent upfront with fewer markdowns.

A good metric for building a more sustainable wardrobe is to calculate **cost per wear**. Estimate how many times a garment has been worn before its discarded. Divide the price of the garment by the number of times the garment was worn. Oftentimes buying a pair of shoes, a bag, or a garment that costs a bit more but is worn weekly over the course of one or more years is a much better value.

Most discussions of sustainable fashion have focused on utilizing sustainable materials and developing systems that engineered waste out of apparel production—worthy goals but little for the consumer to do except buy the resulting products, which were often somewhat more expensive. With the intersection of sustainable fashion and a circular fashion system, there is a more defined role for consumers. In a circular fashion system, the design and production of the garment are equally as important as its end of life. New business models that include the collection, refurbishment, resale, and rental of apparel garments task the consumer with ensuring that discarded garments are collected for refurbishment and resale or reselling the garments at resale stores or on resale marketplaces. These new business models help to close the loop by giving consumers new avenues to acquire clothes affordably. Rather than purchasing a special occasion garment that they will likely only wear once, they can rent it or buy something from a resale channel, and then repurpose it again for someone else to wear and enjoy. These transactions satisfy the consumer's desire for newness while staying within their budget.

The intersection of sustainability and a circular fashion system advocates the goals of both.

- Working to remove nonrecyclable and polluting materials from the supply chain; and using fewer nonrenewable resources in apparel production
- Recapturing everything from garment off cuts to packaging for reuse
- Ensuring use and reuse for as long as possible, including collection schemes and bringing the recycled materials back to a "good as new" state
- Love what you buy and find ways to wear it repeatedly
- Shop second hand wherever possible
- Consider renting for special events
- Host and attend clothes swaps
- Care for your clothes; have them repaired
- Utilize in-store recycling programs
- Choose more sustainable materials when purchasing new clothing
- Talk to people about the benefits of circular fashion
- Make a commitment to not buy brands that don't treat workers fairly and that don't have a vision for becoming more circular.

SUMMARY

Customer engagement is the ongoing value-driven relationship between the customer and the brand. This relationship is powered by consumer data that is captured at every touchpoint the consumer has with the brand. The goal is to deliver personalized service and product recommendations to markets of one. Marketing to markets of one requires a dramatic pivot from product-centric marketing to consumer-centric marketing. Consumers are now in charge and expect brands to deliver what they want, when they want it, all done seamlessly, no matter at which channel a touchpoint occurs. Marketing is now about data analytics, customer relationship management, customer acquisition and retention, website content and functionality, and social media content and functionality. New digital technology tools enable all of these functions. Most notably, game changers include chatbots that power conversational commerce and clienteling, search filters, and visual search tools.

The distribution channels from which consumers can acquire apparel have also expanded. New channels include the traditional indirect route where products are sold wholesale to retailers who sell them to consumer in brick-and-mortar stores or online and direct channels where brands sell directly to consumers. This proliferation of channels requires an omnichannel strategy that manages the touchpoints across all channels seamlessly so that the customer can intersect with the brand both in-store and online seamlessly, receiving the same personalized service no matter from which platform they ultimately buy.

The customer's purchase journey in an omnichannel environment begins with the prepurchase experience involving discovery and research and all of the touchpoints involved. It is followed by the acquisition or purchase phase, which includes payment and delivery. The post-purchase stage of the journey includes facilitating returns, generating feedback, and continued messaging that hopefully results in loyalty and repeat purchases.

The brand/consumer relationship will continue to evolve and with it the consumer's path to acquisition. A circular fashion system will be the foundation for success. Our planet demands it.

Case Study 3.1
Stitch Fix

Stitch Fix is a digital personal styling service founded by Katrina Lake. The concept came out of her love for clothes and a recognition of the human element in shopping—the feeling of finding something that you weren't expecting and delighting in the fact that it fits you and your budget (Lake, May-June 2018). She took that insight and combined it with data to create a new business model for buying clothes. Lake's early career experience was as a consultant to retailers and restaurants. She was fascinated by how untouched those industries were by twenty-first-century technology. As an authority on both fashion and data, she was certain that data could create a better shopping experience.

Lake describes the Stitch Fix business model in her own words. "We send you clothing and accessories we think you'll like; you keep the items you want and send the others back. We leverage data science to deliver personalization at scale, transcending traditional brick-and-mortar and e-commerce retail experiences. Customers enjoy having an expert stylist do the shopping for them and appreciate the convenience and simplicity of the service" (Lake, May-June 2018).

While other brands and retailers attempt to differentiate themselves through the lowest price or fastest shipping, Stitch Fix differentiates its business through personalization. Fix shipments are based on data provided by each customer—first in an extensive questionnaire that is filled out when a new customer signs up, and then in feedback provided after each shipment. They utilize predictive data analytics and machine learning combined with expert human judgement to interpret data for each client and compare individual profiles to those with similar preferences across their active client base of over 4.1 million (Thomas, June 7, 2021).

Stitch Fix is unique in that they own all of the inventory they sell. That ownership provides them with better data to understand what customers want. They are able to turn their inventory faster than most conventional retailers because they buy the right things and get them to the right people. They don't offer special pricing and they don't carry large inventories. Selling the products they have, fast, enables them to pay vendors with cash rather than using a factor—a financial service provider that buys a business's accounts receivable at a discount and assumes responsibility for bill collection—a very efficient financial model. They source directly from a rotating selection of over 1,000 brands, some of which are white label (private) brands available exclusively to Stitch Fix customers (Victor, May 9, 2021). The design of white label products utilizes data to fill in product gaps in the marketplace. The design process first uses an algorithm to suggest clothing items for which there are voids. The second algorithm proposes three different characteristics that are known for complimenting the item for which there is a void. The third algorithm utilizes a bit of randomness to suggest something that makes the item unique. Human designers then use this information to finalize the designs (Victor, May 9, 2021).

The Stitch Fix customer is one that enjoys clothes but hates the time-consuming, tedious, and expensive process of shopping. Stitch Fix is available online or as a mobile app. When a customer first joins Stitch Fix they are invited to take a style quiz. Introductory questions include how they feel about shopping, how much time and effort they put into their look, and how often they try new styles. Once an account is created, they are asked to create a style profile, which is the foundation for customizing fit and styling preferences. Customers are also asked to set their preferred price ranges for each category of apparel and accessories. Customers choose their shipment frequency—every two to three weeks, every month, every other month, every three months—or they may select on-demand scheduling. Some households select to alternate shipments, getting a women's shipment one month and a men's or children's shipment the next. Stitch Fix also offers niche categories including plus sizes, maternity, and petites.

There is a $20 styling fee for each order to cover the personal stylist's time and expertise. That fee is credited if anything from the shipment is purchased. Each box contains five items; a labeled, no-fee USPS return bag; and personalized instructions and a style card to show how to incorporate the clothing into a customer's wardrobe. If the customer decides to keep all five items, they receive 25 percent off the total purchase. A new feature notifies customers two weeks prior to their shipment and invites them to look at ten items their personal stylist has selected. They have forty-eight hours to select their favorite five items before each shipment. Typically, once a shipment arrives, the customer has three days to try on the clothes and complete the return process for any items they don't want. Customers are asked to rate each selection they were sent, adding critical data to their profile. Another new feature is called *Shop Your Looks*. It enables clients to work with their personal stylist to build outfits or capsule wardrobes based on previously kept items without waiting for their next shipment. By the end of the 2021 fiscal year, Stitch fix is scheduled to launch their direct-buy service, which allows customers to purchase individual items from its app without subscribing to the service.

The Stitch Fix team is two-tiered. The technical side of their workforce consists of data scientists, a majority of whom have PhDs in quantitative fields such as math, neuroscience, statistics, and astrophysics. This team ensures that their proprietary algorithms are cutting edge in predicting customer preferences. They also work on projects ranging from automation, to predicting trends more efficiently, to buying assortments and plans. They are able to give their vendors exact information as to what styles, sizes, and color combinations sell best. One project resulted in the creation of Style Shuffle, a digital app where users can swipe right or left to indicate whether they like or dislike certain styles. This app helps to train the company's recommendation algorithms. The other side of their team consists of stylists located all over the US. They're trendsetters and fashion experts who are motivated to understand each customer's personal style needs and preferences. If a customer is consistently unhappy with their stylist's choices, they can ask for a new stylist.

The company encourages clients to link their Stitch Fix accounts with their social media accounts. In this way Stitch Fix is able to capture more data and further personalize their selections. Customer reviews suggest that prices are competitive but not generally the absolute best deal. It's up to the customer to determine whether the convenience of an online stylist is worth a small premium in the price. Their size range is inclusive of a broad range of sizes and fits. A customer can cancel an automatically renewing subscription or a single delivery at any time simply by logging into their account.

References

Cox, Dallas. (2021), "Stitch Fix Review: 4 Things to know before signing up," *clark.com*, March 18. https://clark.com/shopping-retail/stitch-fix-review/ (accessed on June 9, 2021).

Lake, Katrina. (2018), "Stitch Fix's CEO on selling personal style to the mass market," *Harvard Business Review*, May-June. https://hbr.org/2018/05/stitch-fixs-ceo-on-selling-personal-style-to-the-mass-market (accessed on June 9, 2021).

Thomas, Lauren. (2021). "Stitch Fix shares soar as sales top estimates," *cnbc.com*, June 7. https://www.cnbc.com/2021/06/07/stitch-fix-sfix-reports-q3-2021-results.html (accessed on June 9, 2021).

Viktor. (2021), "The Stitch Fix business model--how does Stitch Fix make money?" *productmint*, May 9. https://productmint.com/the-stitch-fix-business-model-how-does-stitch-fix-make-money/ (accessed on June 9, 2021).

KEY TERMS

BOPIS or BOPUS

channel

channel strategy

chatbots

clienteling

cluster models

conversational commerce

cost per wear

crowdsourcing

customer data analytics

customer engagement

customer journey

customer lifetime value (CLV)

customer relationship
   management (CRM)

demographics

digital marketplace

digital wallets

direct-to-consumer channels
   (DTC)

generational cohort

generational marketing

indirect channels

influencer marketing

livestream shopping

loyalty program

market segmentation

markets of one

multichannel

omnichannel merchandising

order orchestration

payment gateways

predictive analytics

product drops

product placement

product search filters

propensity models

psychographics

qualitative research

quantitative research

recommendations filtering

target market

touchpoint

visual search tools

voice commerce

white label

DISCUSSION QUESTIONS

1. Discuss your priorities in shopping for apparel and differentiate those priorities from those of your parents. How do your perceptions of value differ? Distinguish between the types of shopping environments and advertising messages that appeal to you and those that appeal to your parents.

2. In class, identify several brands that do an excellent job of relating to you as a consumer. Discuss the product characteristics and marketing strategies that make your favorite brands relevant. Likewise, identify several brands, intended for your given market, that are not successful in relating to your consumer expectations.

3. Why are demographic data alone insufficient to analyze a market? Discuss examples within your own peer group in which individuals with similar demographic backgrounds exhibit different shopping behaviors.

4. How have companies solicited your consumer input in the past? Has this chapter made you more aware of information that is being collected without your realizing it? What are your concerns regarding data privacy on social media, via voice-activated apps, and across payment portals?

5. Identify several factors that product developers do not seem to understand about your personal product preferences. Where are they missing the mark? How might they learn this information?

6. Identify a store that is on a downward cycle in popularity. Discuss the reasons for the store's waning popularity. Identify a store that is on an upward cycle of popularity. Discuss the reasons for that store's success. Are the reasons you identify for each scenario controllable?

7. What is the most common reason that you dispose of garments?
8. Do you know of any stores or brands that you support that are offering collection points for used apparel? Do you purchase gently used apparel? What are your favorite resources and why?

ACTIVITIES

1. Discuss Forever 21 or another retailer or brand that has recently struggled to stay in business. From your research and experience, why did these once successful businesses falter?
2. Discuss the marketing techniques to which you respond best. Are there brands that have pushed you away due to their incessant and unwanted marketing pitches?
3. Write a blog aimed at shoppers who share your preferences and/or shopping frustrations.
4. As an individual or a class, design a store observation study to better understand consumer preferences. A few examples follow, but feel free to design a study that is of interest to you. Discuss your observations and insights in class.

   - Compare the shopping experiences of male and female shoppers. Jot down notes as to whether they try on clothing or not, whether they shop with someone or alone, how many displays they look at before making a decision, whether they ask questions regarding the product, and whether they make a purchase.
   - Observe customers of a particular age group in a mall. Identify which stores they shop and their shopping behaviors. Do they shop alone or with other people? Observe their interaction with sales associates. What stores do they enter? How long do they spend in a store? Observe how they assess a garment they are considering.

5. Identify a prototype store in your area. Compare the store design and merchandise carried to other stores. If a prototype store is not accessible, compare a company's website and its local stores. Are the store image and merchandise consistent with one another?
6. Write an anonymous description of a particular apparel need using demographic and psychographic information to describe your preferences. Exchange these papers and attempt to interpret the expressed clothing need of the classmate whose description you receive in a series of three to five sketchbook designs. Share the resulting designs in class and discuss your experience in interpreting this information. Did you have enough information? If not, what further information did you need? How did this experience help you to understand the product developer's responsibility for developing customer intimacy?
7. Complete the Customer Profile Worksheet for your favorite brand based on your knowledge of that brand's customer.

STUDiO RESOURCES

- Take the chapter quiz with scored results and personalized study tips.
- Review glossary flashcards to build your vocabulary.

REFERENCES

Appikon. (2020), "How to Use Product Search Filters on Your Shopify Store to Provide a Personalized Shopping Experience," October 8. https://www.appikon.com/how-to-use-product-search-filters-on-your-shopify-store-to-provide-a-personalized-shopping-experience/ (accessed on December 27, 2020).

BOF Team and McKinsey & Company. (2020), "The Year Ahead: The Digital Sprint Will Have Winners and Losers," *Business of Fashion*, December 7. https://www.businessoffashion.com/reports/retail/the-year-ahead-fashions-digital-adoption-optimise-online-customer-experience (accessed on December 12, 2020).

Campbell, Patrick. (2020), "Customer Acquisition vs. Retention: Where Are Your Dollars Best Spent?" *ProfitWell.com*, May 21. https://www.profitwell.com/recur/all/customer-acquisition-vs-retention (accessed on December 12, 2020).

Chen, Cathaleen. (2020), "5 Tech Tools That Should Be on Every Fashion Executive's Radar," *Business of Fashion*, October 5. https://www.businessoffashion.com/articles/technology/5-tech-tools-that-should-be-on-every-fashion-executives-radar (accessed on December 12, 2020).

Chen, Jenh. (2020), "What Is Influencer Marketing: How to Develop Your Strategy," *SproutSocial.com*, September 17. https://sproutsocial.com/insights/influencer-marketing/ (accessed on December 12, 2020).

Hays, Kali. (2020), "Young Consumers Are Done with Demographics, Study Says," *WWD*, January 21. https://wwd.com/business-news/media/young-consumers-are-done-with-demographics-study-says-1203446268/ (accessed on December 6, 2020).

knowledge@wharton. (2020), "Marketing the Future: How Data Analytics is Changing," November 23. https://knowledge.wharton.upenn.edu/article/marketing-future-data-analytics-changing/ (accessed on January 4, 2020).

Marketing Evolution. (2020), "How to Use Predictive Analytics in Data-Driven Marketing," June 30. https://www.marketingevolution.com/knowledge-center/the-role-of-predictive-analytics-in-data-driven-marketing (accessed on December 16, 2020).

McCracken, Jamie. (2020), "The next brand consumer dynamic: the view from the US," *OP Opinium Insight*. https://www.opinium.com/the-next-brand-consumer-dynamic-the-view-from-the-us/ (accessed December 6, 2020).

Stephens, Doug. (201), "Is Surveillance the Future of Service?" *The Business of Fashion*, January 29. https://www.businessoffashion.com/opinions/retail/is-surveillance-the-future-of-service (accessed on December 12, 2020).

A/B testing. A marketing tool that involves launching two different versions of an ad or magazine cover to equal sized audiences and tracking the response based on the version viewed.

algorithm. A sequence of computer-generated rules that produce a predetermined outcome from a set of inputs. They can be used in marketing to automate ad buys and inform decision making to generate the most value and return on investment and reduce ineffective spending.

artificial intelligence (AI). The ability of a digitally controlled device, such as a computer or robot, to perform tasks or solve problems that normally would require human intelligence, such as visual perception, speech recognition, and decision making.

attribution. The evaluation of customer touchpoints and assigning credit to specific channels that played a role in conversion. The goal of attribution is to pinpoint channels, activities, and messages that have the greatest impact on the decision to purchase.

augmented reality (AR). A technology that superimposes a computer-generated image on a user's view of the real world, thus providing a composite view. It is used in gaming and virtual try-on technology including virtual mirrors.

brand loyalty. A consumer's commitment to a particular brand that results in repeat purchases over time.

business drivers. External or internal activities or conditions that impact marketing and business outcomes. Internal factors include media exposure, creative message, and promotional activity; external factors include gas prices, weather conditions, and the economy, which are not controlled by the brand but have an impact on business.

consumer-centric. Marketing that places the individual consumer at the core of all marketing strategies, taking advantage of each consumer's differences and unique tastes. This form of marketing focuses on brand loyalty through personalized messaging and tailored content.

cookies. Pieces of information stored on a user's computer by a website to recall user preferences for future visits. Most search browsers no longer allow the use of third-party cookies.

cross-channel marketing. A strategy for brands to create a seamless and consistent experience for their customers as they navigate interconnected channels. Brands are able to leverage the data collected throughout the customer journey to determine how to improve on those touchpoints and customers can easily transition from channel to channel and experience consistent personalized communication.

click-through rate (CTR). A ratio that measures how often people who see an online ad will click on it.

customer retention rate. The percentage of customers a company keeps actively connected with over a given period of time.

data mapping. A set of rules that accurately matches and integrates data from one information system to data from another information system.

data modeling. Scenario-building technology that helps companies organize data, analyze its implications, and suggest the most effective strategies moving forward.

disruptive technology. An innovation that significantly alters the way that consumers, industries, or businesses operate because its functionality is so superior to what it replaces.

engagement rate. The average ratio of likes and comments to total followers on social media.

key performance indicators (KPI). A means of measuring the impact of marketing efforts on reaching business goals, helping to make business performance quantifiable, time-linked, and transparent.

location-based marketing (LBM). Online and offline technologies designed to help businesses plan and implement marketing based on a consumer's geographic location.

omnichannel marketing. the strategic coordination of all marketing efforts including online, offline, paid, owned, or earned.

optimization. Transforming data insights into action plans that improve marketing impact and/or outcomes at the creative, placement, and campaign levels. Optimization uses past performance and forecasting to determine future marketing budgets.

owned media. Any communication channels controlled by a business or brand, including its websites, blogs, email lists, and social media channels.

page rank. An algorithm that evaluates the quality and quantity of links to a webpage.

path to purchase. A variety of online and offline touchpoints that determine how a consumer connects with a brand and makes a purchase decision. Successful brands focus on delivering a seamless journey from awareness, to engagement, to purchase and eliminating pain points. Also known as the customer journey.

pay per click (PPC). A digital advertising payment model in which the advertiser pays a fee based on each qualifying click-through.

performance marketing. Performance marketing is a comprehensive term referring to an advertiser system where marketing agencies are only paid by brands when a specific pre-established action, like a generated lead, sale, or click, is triggered. It involves less risk than other forms of marketing and is return-on-investment focused.

product listing ad (PLA). A way for marketers to reach targeted consumers by placing images that display during a digital search for a particular product. They are paid image ads used by brands and retailers to drive traffic to specific product pages.

reach. A measurement of the number of people within a defined target audience that will be exposed to a message at least once through a particular medium during a predetermined time period.

return on investment (ROI). A measure of marketing efficiency calculated by measuring the results produced from the amount spent through marketing mediums, calculated at the campaign level to help marketers determine the strategies that are working and inform future spending levels.

search engine marketing (SEM). The process of generating website traffic by paid search, or purchasing ads on search engines, including paid media text and banner ads, search retargeting, and site remarketing display ads, mobile marketing, and paid social media.

search engine optimization (SEO). Digital marketing focused on growing visibility in non-paid search engine results using both technical and creative elements to improve rankings, drive traffic, and increase awareness.

software as a service (SaaS). A method of licensing and delivering centrally hosted applications over the internet as a subscription service rather than the client installing and maintaining the software.

user experience (UX). All aspects of a person's interaction with a company, including its services and/or its products.

user interface (UI). Every visual element that a user might interact with on a technological device, including the device itself as well as apps and websites. UI also refers to the user's experience while interacting, specifically pertaining to the alignment of buttons, scroll bars, icons, menus, and logos.

PART 2

CREATIVE PLANNING

CHAPTER 4

TREND ANALYSIS

"[We all] came to the fashion industry along different paths but for the same reason: a belief in the beauty, imagination and craft that remain at the core of this business. And yet we find ourselves facing a fashion system that is less and less conducive to genuine creativity and ultimately serves the interests of nobody; not designers, not retailers, not customers—and not even our planet. It's time to slow down and rediscover the storytelling and magic of fashion."
#Rewiring Fashion

OBJECTIVES
- To define fashion in contemporary culture
- To recognize the weaknesses of the traditional fashion system
- To reimagine the fashion system in a consumer-centric market
- To comprehend the new role of trends and trend analysis

FASHION AND THE FASHION SYSTEM

Fashion is a culturally endorsed form of aesthetic expression and communication that changes within the context of time and place and reflects the prevailing ideas within a society or group. Fashion is a response to our functional needs and our collective experience; it is a platform for new scientific applications. The concept of fashion is complicated, multifaceted, and ambiguous. It allows us to conceal and reveal ourselves; it helps us to express personal style and manipulate our public persona; it is used to imitate those we admire and differentiate ourselves from others. The concept of fashion applies not only to apparel, but also to styles in architecture, interiors, automobiles, and food. Today those intersections are more important than ever (Figure 4.1). Ultimately fashion is an important global business.

A **trend** is the observable change of direction in ideas, values, purchasing behavior, or style. **Trend analysis** is a means of anticipating consumer demand; it identifies paradigm shifts that cause us to look at things differently. Not only does it promote

newness, but in a business sense, it helps to mitigate risk. There was a time when the interpretation and validation of trends was the prerogative of an elite group of designers, editors, and luxury retailers who curated "fashion." This group of creatives promoted the ideas they considered directional, many of which originated on designer runways. Increasingly, the concept of fashion is much more complex, less homogenous, and a more accurate snapshot of our diverse culture. This chapter will attempt to reimagine the role of trend analysis in a fashion system that is adapting to changes in the product development process, a sophisticated omnichannel distribution system, and a new consumer mindset (Figure 4.2).

A More Consumer-Centric Fashion System

The fashion system has already been defined as the organization, structures, and activities employed to promote change and novelty in apparel, generally for economic gain. In the pre-pandemic fashion world, brands promoted volume consumption based on wants rather than needs. Rapid delivery of new products drove short-lived trends. The fashion system has used trend forecasts, runway shows, and marketing in the form of advertising and editorial placements, to promote an out-of-control pace of change. This system is less and less conducive to genuine creativity and ultimately doesn't serve the interests of its stakeholders or the environment. There is a movement toward a slower-paced fashion system that embraces diversity and innovation and encourages self-expression.

Figure 4.1
The Louis Vuitton Foundation in Paris, France, illustrates how architecture follows trends similar to those of fashion.

Figure 4.2
Consumers today curate their own fashion trends using social media.

The dramatic changes taking place in the fashion system are not new. Failings of the system have been explored and diagnosed for over fifteen years. One of the strongest advocates for change has been Li Edelkoort, who wrote the *Anti_fashion Manifesto* in 2015. In it she identified issues that were pushing the fashion system to the breaking point. The big takeaway was that new ideas increasingly emerge from social change, lifestyle trends, consumer behavior, and new technology rather than fashion runways. She explained how the relentless pace of fashion and incessant cost cutting negatively impacts innovation and sustainability. She spoke to the need for change at every level of the fashion system. The immediate impact of the *Manifesto* was to stimulate spirited discussion, but not much real change occurred. With adversity comes opportunity; Edelkoort's prescient warnings became more actionable during the pandemic.

A cadre of new voices led by designer Dries Van Noten articulated the need for change in 2020. The group included executives, designers, and retailers from around the world. With the support of *Business of Fashion*, they published *#Rewiring Fashion*, which identified problems within the fashion system regarding the fashion calendar, fashion presentations, diversity issues, inventory surpluses, and discounting. The *Council of Fashion Designers of America (CFDA)*, the *British Fashion Council*, the *International Management Group (IMG)*, and other groups proposed their own similar calls for change. This dialogue and the challenges caused by the pandemic gave companies an opportunity to try new solutions.

The current fashion reality is that we don't have the resources to support the pace of fast fashion and the overconsumption that it encourages. Fashion brands of all sizes, no matter their product focus or structure, face the same problems inherent in the fashion system. Solutions will vary depending on a brand's mission, vision, values, and resources. Retailers will continue to develop private brand products that they sell through their own channels; the wholesale model will diminish but continue to exist for the foreseeable future, and the DTC model will continue to grow and evolve. The fashion system and the trend analysis strategies that support these business models will need to be customizable and collaborative. It solves nothing to pass problems along, down the supply chain, and make no changes. A new fashion system must grapple with the following issues.

The Fashion Calendar

The **fashion calendar** is a seasonal schedule that is created to manage the timing of fashion presentations, buying markets, and product deliveries. A year characterized by cancelled orders, delayed product deliveries, and without live fashion presentations reignited a debate over the optimal timing of fashion presentations. The calendar, as it existed pre-pandemic, had turned into a time for the fashion elite to posture and network during a week of social events that were totally disconnected from the seasons as experienced by consumers. The very notion that seasons are relatively universal is ludicrous. While brands were quick to complain about fast fashion knockoffs, the fashion calendar gave these brands ample time to copy ideas which they could bring to market earlier and cheaper than their luxury competitors. Deliveries two to three months before most consumers were ready to wear seasonal apparel meant that the full price selling seasons began too early, particularly in the US, leading to rampant discounting.

Traditional fashion weeks were originally timed to accommodate the long lead times required for manufacturing and print media (especially magazines). Manufacturing lead times have gotten shorter and magazines have far less influence in the current fashion system than they once did. Presentations aimed at the press have led to elaborate garments on the runway, many of which were never produced or had to be modified before being manufactured and delivered, leading to wasted time, materials, and money. The high cost of fashion shows left small brands without the resources to compete. Shows for four to six seasons a year and separate shows for men and women required buyers and the press to expend a great deal of time, money, and energy travelling.

#Rewiring Fashion proposed a new fashion calendar (Figure 4.3) that combines the men's and women's fashion weeks and essentially reverses the seasons. Traditionally designers show fall collections in February and spring collections in September. With the proposed calendar, fashion weeks in late January/early February would feature spring apparel and fashion weeks in June would feature fall apparel—a *show now, sell now* approach. This new timing solves a number of issues. Combining men's and women's fashion weeks saves money and reduces travel. It is also more in sync with the gender-neutral approach to dress that has permeated fashion. Deliveries that are more aligned with real-world seasons require customers to pay full price. Prices can be more transparent when margins don't have to be inflated in anticipation of early markdowns. The opportunity for fast fashion to copy runway ideas is curtailed.

In February of 2021, the CFDA renamed its schedule the *American Collections Calendar*. The move acknowledged that designers may choose to show outside of New York and that, depending on their presentation format and the seasonality of the clothes being shown, a brand/designer's preferred dates may vary.

Likewise, the IMG expanded its calendar to include designers showing in-season and added other types of programming including panel discussions, podcasts, merchandise drops, and cultural programming. Their show lineup will likely continue to include presentations in a wide variety of formats. The IMG has expanded its partnership with the *Black in Fashion Council* to promote diversity and chose TikTok as its official editorial partner, emphasizing the shift from print to social media and illustrating how magazine websites such as *Vogue* are no longer the preferred platform to share fashion presentation imagery.

Ultimately, the fashion system is moving toward a **seasonless fashion model** that slows down the product development and consumption cycle and does not conform to seasonal trends or calendars. A seasonless fashion model focuses on core pieces that are developed to have a longer shelf life, delivered in smaller quantities at intervals throughout the year, without the expense and pageantry of a fashion presentation. Alessandro Michele, designer at Gucci, summed it up this way on Instagram. "I will abandon the worn-out ritual of seasonality and shows to regain a new cadence, closer to my expressive call. Clothes should have a longer life than that which these words attribute to them. We will meet just twice a year, to share the chapters of a new story. Irregular, joyful and absolutely free chapters, which will be written blending rules and genres, feeding on new spaces, linguistic codes and communication platforms (Gucci Instagram Post May 3, 2020)."

#rewiringfashion | A New Fashion Calendar

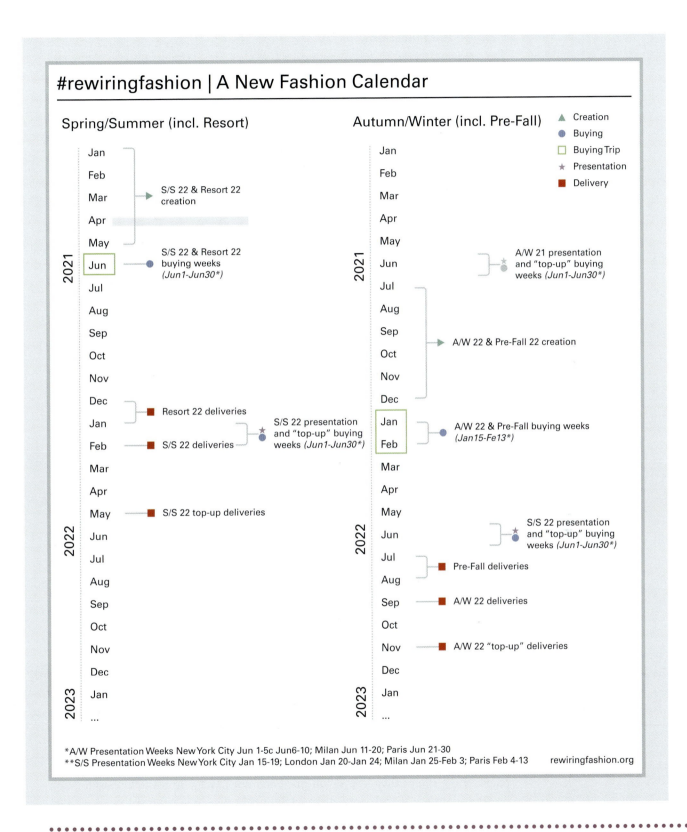

Spring/Summer (incl. Resort)

Autumn/Winter (incl. Pre-Fall)

Legend:
- ▲ Creation
- ● Buying
- ☐ Buying Trip
- ★ Presentation
- ■ Delivery

Spring/Summer column:

2021 — Jan, Feb, Mar, Apr, May, Jun, Jul, Aug, Sep, Oct, Nov, Dec
- S/S 22 & Resort 22 creation
- S/S 22 & Resort 22 buying weeks (Jun1-Jun30*)

2022 — Jan, Feb, Mar, Apr, May, Jun, Jul, Aug, Sep, Oct, Nov, Dec
- Resort 22 deliveries
- S/S 22 deliveries
- S/S 22 presentation and "top-up" buying weeks (Jun1-Jun30*)
- S/S 22 top-up deliveries

2023 — Jan ...

Autumn/Winter column:

2021 — Jan, Feb, Mar, Apr, May, Jun, Jul, Aug, Sep, Oct, Nov, Dec
- A/W 21 presentation and "top-up" buying weeks (Jun1-Jun30*)
- A/W 22 & Pre-Fall 22 creation

2022 — Jan, Feb, Mar, Apr, May, Jun, Jul, Aug, Sep, Oct, Nov, Dec
- A/W 22 & Pre-Fall buying weeks (Jan15-Fe13*)
- S/S 22 presentation and "top-up" buying weeks (Jun1-Jun30*)
- Pre-Fall deliveries
- A/W 22 deliveries
- A/W 22 "top-up" deliveries

2023 — Jan ...

*A/W Presentation Weeks New York City Jun 1-5c Jun6-10; Milan Jun 11-20; Paris Jun 21-30
**S/S Presentation Weeks New York City Jan 15-19; London Jan 20-Jan 24; Milan Jan 25-Feb 3; Paris Feb 4-13

rewiringfashion.org

Figure 4.3
#Rewiring Fashion proposed a new fashion calendar.

Fashion Presentations

The pandemic forced brands to reimagine how they present their collections. The creativity of virtual presentations has gotten better with each season. Live fashion shows were designed for an audience of buyers and the press, but their influence has diminished with direct-to-consumer shopping and social media. The internet makes shows accessible to everyone in real time. New formats acknowledge the role of the ultimate customer as curator and muse. Designs can be shown as they will be shipped rather than exaggerated for the runway and then watered down when displayed on the selling floor. Customer feedback can help to curate and quantify orders, helping to eliminate excess inventory before it's produced.

The new scheduling environment proposed for fashion presentations imposes no rules. Events can be live or virtual or both. They can be made available on the media platforms that their customers follow. The location of shows can move around the world to engage customers where they live. Virgil Abloh chose China as one of the first locations for a live menswear show in 2020. He announced that his shows would span the globe, collaborating with regional offices to find the venue and co-design the event. His on-location events will use all local models and feature local musicians. Other designers have indicated that they might not do live shows every season.

Those designers and brands that prefer to produce live fashion presentations would do so in one of the global fashion capitals during two fashion seasons in order to limit the expense and strain of travel on buyers and journalists. Other designers and brands have already indicated their preference for virtual presentations that could happen anytime (Figure 4.4a–c).

Matching Supply and Demand

Under the guise of creating newness, brands have been offering more and more product. To get the best manufacturing price, they place orders before they have any customer feedback and over anticipate demand. Industry overproduction runs at an incredible 30–40 percent each season (Magnusdottir, May 13, 2020). These practices create a vicious cycle of overproduction and ultimately devalue fashion. Not only is the traditional fashion system financially wasteful, it is also very damaging to the environment. To make matters worse, some luxury brands have been found to be destroying product at the end of a season rather than marking it down.

A new fashion calendar supports short-cycle manufacturing and near-shoring. Placing orders closer to delivery allows brands to be more accurate in order size. Right sizing inventory and delivering when the consumer is ready to buy encourages more full-price sell-through and enables a return to more transparent pricing. A more seasonless fashion system tamps down the idea that a collection must be regularly replaced with next season's offering (Magnusdottir, May 13, 2020).

Controlling inventory creates a sense of scarcity that encourages customers to purchase the things they love at full price and not indulge in wasteful consumption because a product is such a good deal. Ultimately it has the potential to reignite an interest in fashion that has been waning in recent years.

a

b

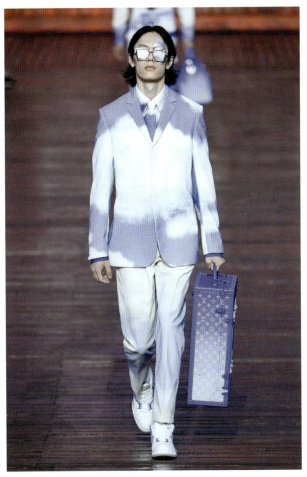

c

Some brands are taking a cue from fast fashion brands like Zara and releasing **capsule collections**—smaller collections of ten to thirty pieces, delivered every two to six weeks—rather than seasonal collections that are released all at one time. Capsule collections have been tried in the past but without a focus on inventory and price controls. This resulted in saturating the market with even more inventory that had to be designed and ultimately reduced. Currently brands are attempting to use a capsule collection strategy to better manage inventory and maintain full-price margins until the majority of stock is sold. New product can be offered on an as-needed basis (most inventory sold out) or on an as-ready basis (when the designer has had the time to finesse product designs). The design team of Proenza Schouler released a twenty-seven–piece capsule collection in the spring of 2021 to use up **deadstock fabric**—fabrics leftover from previous collections. The new styles were variations from past seasons so that the collection could be offered at a more affordable price point with a sustainable message.

These strategies work well for small brands and designers that have limited resources and distribution. The growth of DTC distribution channels gives brands more control over market saturation, pricing, and timing. The amount of merchandise that ends up on seasonal clearance will be reduced and clearing stock for the next season will become less of an issue.

Figure 4.4a
The COVID-19 pandemic forced brands to rethink their fashion presentations. Videos allowed brands to tell a story.

Figure 4.4b
Traditional runway fashion shows are expensive to produce and often feature a prevalence of evening clothes that don't relate to the average consumer's lifestyle.

Figure 4.4c
Louis Vuitton showed their menswear collection in China in 2020. They used local talent to determine venues and hire models.

Inclusion and Diversity

Another focus for a reimagined fashion system is that of inclusion and diversity. For too long, fashion has been managed by an exclusive group of editors, photographers, models, and hair and makeup artists that has profited from promoting an ever-accelerating pace of change. This has been especially evident on the runway and in the editorial content of magazines, where the use of reed-thin, underage models has prevailed. Ethnic diversity has too often appeared as tokenism, with models complaining that hair and makeup teams were inexperienced in dealing with textured hair or insisted that models cover up their hair with wigs to match a designer's reflection of the world. Too many designers have been called out on websites like *Diet Prada* for their tone-deaf creative decisions that were either racist and/or culturally insensitive. They have failed to represent their consumer base in terms of ethnic diversity, gender, size, and age.

For fashion to become more relevant and truly engage with the consumer, it must be more inclusive and better reflect the diversity of the marketplace it claims to serve. Even in developed countries, the industry has failed to nurture and invest in new talent. When it does provide opportunities, entry level talent is often expected to work for free or is underpaid. At the luxury level, designers are hired on a whim and fired when their novelty wears off. Inclusivity and equity at all levels of fashion up and down the supply chain, in corporate culture, on the runway, and from the consuming public needs to be examined and valued. This is often referred to as the **diversity imperative**.

The content requirements of social media and the diversity of fashion customers provides an opportunity to nurture emerging creatives with fresh voices. Mark Guiducci, the Creative Editorial Director for *Vogue* described the contributions of young creatives. "They are pushing and pulling the visual language of fashion and introducing new ideas rooted in their personal experiences (Milner, October 27, 2020)." The fashion industry needs these new ideas to flourish and grow.

Without representation, many consumers have lost interest in the fashion system but not fashion. Blogs and social media now analyze each fashion season as to model representation by race, size, age, and gender diversity. The January 2021 launch of AZ Factory by Alber Elbez made a strong statement toward inclusion. Unfortunately, Elbez passed away of COVID-19 a few months after the brand launched. Other brands that have made inclusion a part of their DNA include, Christian Siriano, Chromat, Pyer Moss, and Rick Owens (Figure 4.5).

Designers are regularly called out for borrowing from cultural traditions and using skilled tradespeople without acknowledgement. **Cultural appropriation** refers to the use of the customs, practices, or ideas of a nondominant culture in a way that does not respect their original meaning, give credit to their source, reinforces stereotypes, or contributes to oppression. Novelty and change in fashion have long been achieved by borrowing from the past, other places, and other cultures. These references allow designers to view the world through another lens by looking beyond their present time and place. Cultural appropriation has been going on for a very long time without

Figure 4.5
Christian Siriano is known for diversity both on the runway and in his client base.

much pushback, but the interconnectedness of a digital world allows for all stakeholders to trace the source of design inspiration. Creatives have massive amounts of information and cultural references at their fingertips. Given the pace of fashion, few give a second thought to using these references as a point of departure for new collections. But those cultures from which traditions and symbolism are borrowed also now have access to what's being shown on designer runways as do those who study fashion. They now have the tools to readily identify borrowing that is not credited or is disrespectful. Creatives should ask the following questions when researching other times, people, and places:

- Has the reference been used as inspiration and changed sufficiently to make it uniquely stand on its own?
- Is the reference acknowledged and credited in runway notes or through curated content?
- If the inspiration originates from a nondominant culture, is there a way to co-curate or co-design, lending authenticity to the collaboration and ensuring that the inspiration is not being manipulated or presented disrespectfully?

a

b

Figure 4.6a
Marc Jacobs was called out in 2016 for styling Gigi Hadid in dreadlocks.

Figure 4.6b
The collection Gucci showed in February 2018 featured men and women wearing full head wraps that closely resembled Sikh turbans. They were sold at retail for $790 before public outcry led to their removal from sales platforms.

- Is there a way to be less extractive—taking inspiration—but giving nothing back? Instead of hiring local artisans to mimic an artisanal technique can cultural artisans be used and paid a similar/fair wage?

Oftentimes the act that causes a reference to be labeled appropriation rather than inspiration is the theatrical way it is shown in a fashion presentation. A fashion environment without historical, cultural, and global references would be boring and colorless. Researching other times, people, and places informs our scope and experience. Doing it in a way that credits those who've come before us and values and acknowledges those who are different from us enriches our global experience and is one small step toward democratizing fashion and making it more inclusive (Figure 4.6a–b).

Innovation

Speed to market, overproduction, and a focus on price is discouraging innovation and burning out designers. "As brands and retailers learn what sells in today's environment they risk leaning too heavily on data [that may stifle] design innovation. A failure to evolve is a big reason that fashion, in the traditional sense, has hit a wall" (Manoff, July 20, 2020). If a new fashion system expects consumers to pay more for fewer garments that are built to last, the fashion industry must deliver designs with more spirit, craftsmanship, and better quality. Designers need time to explore new technologies, reimagine materials, and collaborate with craftspeople. There is a risk that large brands will see the more casual lifestyles that took hold during the pandemic as reason to produce more homogenous leisurewear clothes. Instead of cost cutting through better control of inventory and elimination of waste, they will revert back to delivering high-volume monotonous clothes that fail to register an emotional connection. Innovation in a postmodern world will require a synergy between new ideas, new technology, purpose, and function.

Content Curation and Collaboration

Just as marketing has evolved from a message to a dialogue, the mechanisms of the fashion system have become more interactive. **Content curation**—which refers to the way information is presented to an audience and the interaction that follows—has expanded the tools that a designer can use to communicate their vision to customers beyond fashion presentations. Designers can share their point of view and values through any number of platforms and mediums and get direct feedback. Photography and video can be manipulated through the use of technology to represent a desired vision creating another level of artistry; these images can be published instantly across platforms without waiting for the publication of a magazine or book. Gucci launched a film festival in 2020, called *Guccifest*. The final "Epilogue" of the seven-part release credited the Gucci design team by using them as models. *Guccifest* also used their platform to highlight the work of new emerging designers. Likewise, Virgil Abloh curates Imaginary TV in conjunction with his Off-White brand where he too features new designers and like-minded creatives. The Balenciaga brand launched its own video game as a means of showing new product. Knitwear label PH_5 created their own virtual muse with dark piercing eyes, a cropped bob, and an athletic build who loves Instagram and fights for climate change. Her name is AMA and her title is chief decision scientist (Fernandez, February 15, 2021).

Creatives are now called upon to be storytellers who make a statement by sharing what's important to them, what inspires them, and how they work rather than relying on fashion editors and buyers to interpret their body of work. Authentic content creation can take the customer relationship beyond transactional by adding value to the brand, the product, and the expertise and skill of the designer and their team. Creatives often find that in sharing their process and taking note of feedback, they find more insightful solutions to design problems.

In 2020, Miuccia Prada announced that Raf Simons would become co-creative director, taking designer collaboration to a new level. The two designers are both future oriented, attracted to technology, share a passion for art, and have strong points of view. Simons has been more forward thinking in his approach to business strategies. The partnership, which grows more comfortable with each season, represents a new approach to designer succession. Rather than a disruptive revamp of brand offerings each time a new designer takes the reins, this new strategy appears to be an effort to prepare for more gradual succession that preserves and builds upon the brand's DNA.

Virtual fashion presentations have given creative teams the impetus to embrace artistic collaborations between musicians, artists, videographers, choreographers, and gaming platforms. Not only do these collaborations provide meaningful content and context, multidimensional teams of creatives nurture and invigorate each other, creating a sense of community. These collaborations can expand visibility and grow audience for all collaborators. In an economic environment where fashion has become less important in terms of a customer's discretionary spending, collaborations give fashion a new energy and relevancy by providing entertaining experiences.

TRENDS AND TREND FORECASTING IN A NEW FASHION SYSTEM

Under the old fashion system, trends were tracked on the basis of where they fell within the *diffusion of innovation curve* (Figure 4.7). Stages included innovators, early adopters, early majority, late majority, and laggards. Those categories reflected where a particular trend could be found, ranging from on a runway or worn by a celebrity, to designer signatures stores, mass merchants, and perhaps secondhand shops where it was no longer considered current. In an environment that seeks to promote a more

Figure 4.7
The value of the fashion diffusion curve seems less relevant in a cycle of consumer individualism and a strong recommerce market.

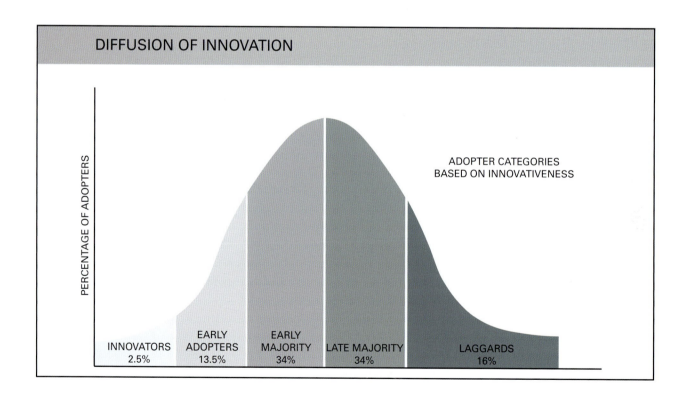

DIFFUSION OF INNOVATION

PERCENTAGE OF ADOPTERS

ADOPTER CATEGORIES
BASED ON INNOVATIVENESS

INNOVATORS
2.5%

EARLY
ADOPTERS
13.5%

EARLY
MAJORITY
34%

LATE MAJORITY
34%

LAGGARDS
16%

circular economy, that visual makes less sense. Rental and resale garments continue to hold their value and play an important role in self-expression. As the fashion system slows down and focuses less on seasonality and volume, trend forecasting must also evolve from seasonal predictions to a non-seasonal, purpose-driven vision that will re-engage consumers with the relevance of fashion.

The adoption of trends has sometimes been described as trickling up, down, or across the socioeconomic spectrum. The **trickle-down theory** is based on the observation that many new fashion ideas start on designer runways, appealing to fashion leaders who have the money and taste level to wear new looks. As new ideas gain visibility, they are reinterpreted at lower and lower price points. The **trickle-across theory** describes a process where there is little lag time between adoption from one group to another—from one price point to another. The **trickle-up theory** explains the phenomenon of street fashions that originate with avant-garde consumer groups rather than a designer or product developer (Figure 4.8). Unfortunately, with the popularity of athleisure, even streetwear has been commercialized by luxury brands who hire streetwear originators and then price the resulting products out of the range of the average consumer. Virgil Abloh for Louis Vuitton and a series of design collaborations at Dior Hommes under Kim Jones are examples.

As fashion ideas have been borrowed, exchanged, and knocked off at a breakneck pace, the direction in which a trend moves is less important than it once was. Identifying and promoting trends from runway shows is no longer a reflection of how people live. Consumers are more apt to get their inspiration from social media, celebrities, influencers, and on the street as opposed to from a retailer, brand, or designer.

Figure 4.8
Cosplay is a street fashion movement that has influenced runways.

Redefining Trends

So, what is the value of trend forecasting in a new fashion system? Fashion continues to be a reaction to the environment and behavioral change. Trend forecasting is perhaps more important than ever in mitigating the risk inherent in product development. Brands are overwhelmed with the amount of data available to them. They don't always have the time or context to know what's important. Trend forecasters can help brands sift through and interpret data in ways that make the brand's mission, vision, and values actionable. Modern day forecasting firms are more holistic, consulting on consumer sentiment, creative direction, market timing, demand planning, and content delivery. Not only have fashion forecasters expanded their role in the ways they assist brands, the content of trend forecasts has also evolved:

- Trend forecasts are becoming more seasonless with no distinct beginning and end to their relevance.
- Trend forecasts are increasingly driven by consumer behaviors, lifestyles, and values rather than runways.
- There is a stronger focus on sustainability, including fabric innovation and upcycling; color evolution; and more functional silhouettes and details all interpreted for a particular brand and its products.
- Forecasts themselves are more customized, helping individual brands to apply trend forecasts with their customer identity in mind. This includes helping brands to regionalize their offerings, rather than offer the same product assortments to customers all over the world.

The Trend Forecasting Process

The first step of trend forecasting is research—the analysis of data and everyday phenomena. The scale and scope of data that a trend forecasting firm is able to access and analyze is generally larger than a brand might be able to do in-house. Trend forecasters are very observant. They either have reps on the ground or they travel to observe nuances in behavior geographically.

The second step of trend forecasting is to correlate observations and data in order to identify the sources, patterns, and causes of paradigm shifts in the status quo. The intuitive ability to connect the dots can be likened to a trained muscle that sees patterns before the average observer.

Once trend forecasters have identified patterns, they are able to conceptualize how these large picture trends might be translated into a given discipline such as fashion. What color does diversity look like? What fabrics (beyond organic cotton) show a commitment to sustainability? How do investment pieces need to function in order to have staying power in an individual's wardrobe? This is where a forecaster's intellectual curiosity comes into play. They stay on top of what's new in the zeitgeist—culture, technology, business models—and they are able to imagine new scenarios.

Finally, the best forecasters have the ability to customize or adapt these scenarios for each of their clients.

- They take into consideration the product a brand makes, the brand's customer relationship, their resources, and their business model to individualize a future strategy.
- They offer new creative concepts that a brand can interpret rather than templates a brand adapts. If brands/designers are going to rightsize supply to match demand, it is more important than ever that they design and produce product that is differentiated in the marketplace.
- They must avoid playing it too safe and offering just one more homogenous option in a saturated market. Rather, they should seek to stand out from the competition by offering their own point of view and unique voice.

In these ways and more, trend forecasting shifts to trend consulting. One forecaster from Stylus in London said that during the pandemic she was doing thirteen presentations a week directly to different brands, retailers, or businesses—up from a typical two meetings per week pre-pandemic (Arnett, April 2020). Forecasting companies are providing more regular updates and in-depth video meetings with Q & A to individualize their services. *See now, buy now* fashion presentations will make it harder for both brands and forecasters to identify trends from runways, which may have the effect of slowing down the pace of change and supporting consumer individualism.

Macro and Micro Trends

The research phase of trend forecasting requires an understanding of macro trends and micro trends. **Macro trends** are long-term paradigm shifts in business strategies, lifestyles, consumer behavior, and global dynamics that affect a major segment of the population. Macro trends evolve over a period of time and tend not to be discipline specific. They tend to reveal the root cause of lifestyle and behavioral change. Macro trends may be triggered by any of the following:

- Major shifts in domestic and international demographics and psychographics (an aging population or a baby boom, a more casual lifestyle)
- Changes in business, industry, and market structures (recommerce model, circular supply chain)
- Changes in consumer interests, values, motivations, and circumstances (sustainability, economic divide)
- Major breakthroughs in technology and science (data analytics, artificial intelligence)
- Shifts in political, cultural, or economic alliances between countries (globalism vs. regionalism vs. isolationism, Paris Climate Accord, EU membership)
- Social, cultural phenomena (Covid, new social media platforms)

The analysis of **micro trends** looks for directional tendencies that are pervasive within a specific sphere of influence and/or for a particular audience. It is more discipline specific; looking for trends that may last a season or several years depending on the audience. Athleisure apparel and luxury streetwear might be identified as micro trends

Figure 4.9
Dimensions of Fashion

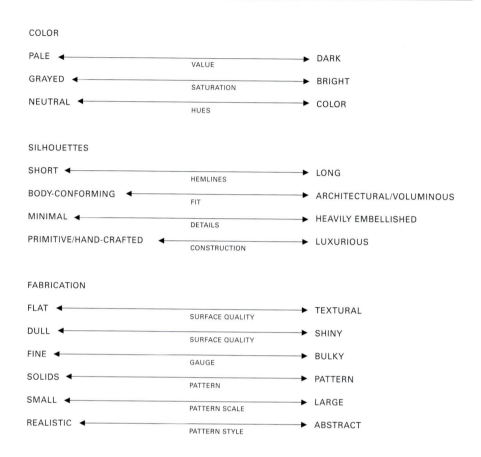

DIMENSIONS OF FASHION

COLOR

PALE ←————— VALUE —————→ DARK

GRAYED ←————— SATURATION —————→ BRIGHT

NEUTRAL ←————— HUES —————→ COLOR

SILHOUETTES

SHORT ←————— HEMLINES —————→ LONG

BODY-CONFORMING ←————— FIT —————→ ARCHITECTURAL/VOLUMINOUS

MINIMAL ←————— DETAILS —————→ HEAVILY EMBELLISHED

PRIMITIVE/HAND-CRAFTED ←————— CONSTRUCTION —————→ LUXURIOUS

FABRICATION

FLAT ←————— SURFACE QUALITY —————→ TEXTURAL

DULL ←————— SURFACE QUALITY —————→ SHINY

FINE ←————— GAUGE —————→ BULKY

SOLIDS ←————— PATTERN —————→ PATTERN

SMALL ←————— PATTERN SCALE —————→ LARGE

REALISTIC ←————— PATTERN STYLE —————→ ABSTRACT

that grew out of the macro trends that identified more casual lifestyles and work-from-home environments. In fashion, the identification of micro trends often suggests the direction of colors, fabrics, garment silhouettes, and details. Figure 4.9 identifies some of the dimensions of fashion that express trends through style change. Micro trends may be inspired by:

- current events (an election, Black Lives Matter, Me Too)
- pop culture and the arts (museum exhibits, dance, movies, videos, music, gaming)
- sports (the Olympics, major sporting events)
- science and technology

Events that speak to a younger market may be very different from those that resonate with a more mature market. Figure 4.10 offers a worksheet for translating macro and micro trends into fashion products and behaviors.

BRAILLE THE ZEITGEIST FOR . . . . .
a story dominating the news with future/ongoing implications. This could be a news topic or a cultural event—preferably scheduled for a future date.

CONNECT THE DOTS . . . .
Identify related stories, happenings, public reactions, historic events or personalities that seem to make the story important or relevant.

IMAGINE HOW THAT LOOKS . . . .
Paint a word picture, write a story or haiku, think of a metaphor. Describe the visual imagery your story brings to mind. Imagine the colors, shapes and patterns that you associate with the story. Name your concept.

TRANSLATE THAT INTO FASHION TERMS . . . .
From those visual images, select a color palette, fabric story, silhouettes, and details that would encapsulate your design concept.

Figure 4.10
A trend map can help to identify micro and macro trends. Use these four steps to practice translating current events into fashion terms.

Approaches to Trend Forecasting

Trend forecasters tend to fall into two camps, each with their own skillsets and expertise. The bigger group is data driven. The ongoing improvements in and applications for data analytics have allowed these firms to invest in applications that monitor consumer touch points and behaviors. Applications take advantage of visual recognition tools to measure the recurrence and popularity of colors, fabrications, silhouettes, and details and are able to provide quantifiable data regarding consumer preferences. Data points and data analysis provide the foundation for their insights. To supplement and verify, they scan current events, attend trade shows, shop fashion markets, follow social media and directional blogs, and track fashion on the streets to identify new ideas. This combination of data analytics, artificial intelligence, visual search and recognition tools, as well as human observation and intuition fuel their concept development and inform the trend reports that forecasters make available to their clients.

Fashion Snoops, WGSN, and Heuritech are examples of data-driven trend forecasters. Though they discuss both micro and macro trends, their focus is more on micro trends. Their reports include color, fabric, silhouette, and detail tendencies as well as runway highlights, trade show recaps, and street images. Colors may be keyed to Pantone's color matching system. Data-driven trend products are designed to make the process of interpreting runway- or street-inspired fashion silhouettes and details fast and efficient. Delivery is primarily digital as the information changes so quickly. Companies that use AI and predictive analytics may be better equipped to modify their forecast for specific global regions. They analyze social media images in each region to customize their reports. Using machine learning Heuritech can analyze 1.5–2 million images a day according to CEO Tony Pinville (Arnett, April 2020). Because they track and analyze so much data, they tend to focus on a more seasonal forecast. Data driven forecasters may be more attuned to the preferences of younger consumers and the rapid pace of change in fast fashion business models.

Other trend forecasters, like Stylus and Trend Union, are more intuitive and conceptual. They base their projections on identifying and explaining macro-trends and their impact. Their general trend books are printed twice a year, in limited editions of between 100 and 250 copies; they project trends two to two-and-a-half years in advance. Trend Union uses expressive imagery and actual samples of textiles. The swatches, many of which are vintage or hand crafted, may be collected from global travels, procured from cutting edge textile manufacturers, or cut from purchased garments that have been deemed prescient (Figure 4.11a–b). All of the firm's seasonal

Figure 4.11a and b
Trend Union subscribers receive trend concept books with fabric color and fabric swatches.

a

b

colors are custom dyed to Trend Union's specifications. Digital presentations that reflect the seasonal trend book are available to clients, presented at trade shows, and presented to nonmembers for a fee. Based on their general trend predictions, they advise clients individually as to how to personalize trend directions to their brand and product. Trend Union's guidance is sought out by companies across many disciplines. One subscriber spoke to the tactile quality of the Trend Union forecasts, "I subscribe to all of them, and there is just nothing like this out there anymore" (Downing Peters, November 29, 2016). Intuitive forecasters, by necessity, are more consultative and individualized. Their forecasts follow more of a seasonless, slow fashion model. What both formats have in common is that their consultants are keen observers, able to connect the dots and interpret societal shifts and behaviors.

Trend Forecasting Resources

Identification of both macro and micro trends relies on a familiarity with and analysis of current events, politics, the business environment, science and technology, culture, and pop culture among other things. Brands may assign the responsibility for trend forecasting to in-house personnel in merchandising or design; very large brands may have separate trend departments. The in-house team selects the trend service(s) that best matches the brand's needs. Generally, no single person or department wants to bear the responsibility of being off base with a collection's direction. Companies expect their creative teams to get trends right. Selecting a trend forecasting partner that aligns with a brand's customers and goals is an important strategic decision. These services can save the trend forecasting or product development team a lot of time by validating their observations and interpreting and alerting them to emerging trends.

Pre-pandemic, attending all of the global events that might have an influence on fashion trends was time- and cost-prohibitive for most brands. A trend service could be a brand's eyes and ears on the ground, sharing photos, summaries, and interviews. Many of those events were forced to go virtual during the pandemic. It remains to be seen whether they find the virtual format able to reach more people in a cost-effective way, revert back to in-person events, or become hybrid events. No matter the answer to that question, a trend forecasting firm can cover more events all over the world than any single brand could hope to attend. Trend forecasting firms have also cultivated special relationships, giving them access to information, new exhibitors, interviews, etc. that provide brands with unique insights and connections. What follows is a discussion of some of the types of events and activities trend forecasters cover as a service to their subscribers.

Thanks to the continued open access of the Internet, there is a wealth of free information available to businesses; however, it requires time and interpretation to be of value. Forecasters subscribe to any number of news aggregators that link to a variety of resources. These subscriptions may not be a huge investment, but it is their job to read them thoroughly and translate daily news into patterns. *Business of Fashion*, *The Sourcing Journal*, *Just-Style*, and *WWD* are excellent sources of fashion-specific news. Trend specialists also scan major global news resources as well as resources that cover culture, pop culture, science, technology, and sports, searching out cross-disciplinary linkages. Previously, imagery of fashion presentations could be accessed on magazine sights like Vogue.com. Brands that have embraced virtual presentations appear to be making their own decisions as to where photographic and video access can be found. TikTok and other social media platforms are now preferred over magazine platforms although traditional print resources still provide collection reviews in their print and digital publications.

Shopping the major fashion markets used to be an important means of identifying how regions around the globe were responding to trends. Trend spotters looked to signature stores in different cities and had representatives on the ground whose job was to document what people were wearing on the street and at events. **Concept stores** are specialty stores, generally located in fashion capitals, that curate their assortments to define the brands, designers, products, and trends currently influencing fashion. DTC platforms, online marketplaces, and digital content curation make shopping the market less important. Several iconic concept stores like Colette in Paris have closed their doors; others are struggling. Wuyong in Bejing; Dover Street Market in NY, Tokyo, Bejing, LA, and London; and L'Eclaireur and Merci in Paris are examples of concept stores still open (Figure 4.12).

Today consumers can access a brand or designer's entire collection from anywhere in the world. Content curation tells the brand or designer's story. Consumer clicks and likes can be registered and collated geographically in order to regionalize preferences. Consumers post images of looks they like and how they've styled their own outfits. With the growing popularity of rental and resale markets, styling takes on new importance. Only time will tell how trend resources will shift in coming years.

Figure 4.12
Dover Street Market has concept stores in most major fashion cities.

a

b

c

One important reference for trend forecasters is museum exhibitions. Both art and fashion exhibitions at major museums are big draws and inform our understanding of time and place, art movements, historic chronology, and artist or designer contributions (Figure 4.13a–c). Color forecasters may respond to the mere announcement of a major art exhibition. In 2021 the Metropolitan Museum of Art's exhibition was entitled *About Time: Fashion and Duration. Africa Fashion* at the Victoria & Albert Museum in London shines a new light on Africa's contributions to fashion. Other museums that offer regular fashion exhibitions include The Museum at FIT in New York, the MoMu Museum in Antwerp, and the Galliera Museum and La Musée de la Mode et du Textile in Paris.

Cultural and pop culture events and celebrities also play a major role in creating fashion trends. Musical and cinematic collaborations with designers in virtual fashion presentations have emphasized the synergistic relationship between fashion and culture. Streamed television platforms now compete with movie theaters in providing video entertainment and have a recognizable influence on popular fashion. Cinematic media can shine a light on a particular period (*Bridgerton*) or a culture (*Emily in Paris*), or a style tribe (*The Duchess*). Technology is on the horizon that will help viewers identify exactly what a character is wearing and where it's available when they spot it on TV or streaming services.

Popular sports frequently influence fashion from skate boarding (Supreme) to soccer, to football. Today, thanks to extensive sports coverage in the media, the stars of such nontraditional sports as snowboarding, surfing, and skateboarding also influence fashion. Skinny jeans, for example, may have derived from the need of skateboarders to do their moves without loose fabric around their ankles interfering. Sports can also be a driver of textile innovation; the technology developed for Olympic competition eventually finds its way into commercial apparel.

Figure 4.13a and b
The Christian Dior restrospective started in Paris and then travelled to London. It was unique in that both finished garments and muslin toiles were on display.

Figure 4.13c
The Metropolitan Museum of Art's 2020 exhibit was titled, *About Time: Fashion and Duration.*

Figure 4.14
Some of the newest textile developments are coming from biotextiles. This jacket is made from a leather-like product grown in the laboratory.

Science and technology affect many aspects of fashion, from the colors we can achieve on different mediums, to the fabrications available to designers, to how garments function, to how we care for and dispose of garments. We can grow cotton in colors; we can 3D print garments to fit the body; and we can wire fabrics to monitor the wearer's vital signs and whereabouts. We can digitally print fabrics, which will eventually allow consumers to customize the pattern they want on a garment. New fibers and modifications of existing fibers are constantly being introduced (Figure 4.14). Perhaps the technological developments that enhance garment fit will be some of the most useful in the future.

There are a number of organizations that specialize in a single aspect of trends such as color or fabrics. They are important resources to know.

Color

Color is one of the first stimuli a customer responds to when shopping. This makes accurate forecasting of colors key. Consumers will not automatically buy a new color that they do not like or that is not becoming. Data analytics are becoming increasingly helpful in identifying the colors customers want to wear and the colors they won't buy, changing the nature of color forecasting.

The decision about a seasonal color palette is one of the first to be made in the product development process. The seasonal color story will be the basis for solids, prints, and yarn-dyed fabrics in a variety of fibers, across all styles in the line. Product developers review a variety of sources before making color decisions.

The process of color forecasting traditionally begins two to two-and-a-half years in advance of a selling season. It would seem that as we move toward short-cycle manufacturing and digital color approvals that this is an area of trend forecasting that can be tightened up. There are several organizations that play a primary role in color forecasting. The Color Marketing Group, the International Colour Authority (ICA), and the Color Association of the United States (CAUS) are the largest color organizations (Figure 4.15). Members of these groups are color specialists representing some of the biggest companies in the world. These organizations provide forums for their members to come together to discuss the various issues of color, network with other industry professionals, exchange information, become familiar with new technology, and forecast color directions. Working in committees and global regions, they forecast colors for industries including fashion, transportation, architecture, communications and graphics, toys, and textiles. Their color palettes project the course or popularity that colors are likely to take—warmer or cooler, lighter or darker, clearer or grayer—and the relative importance of a hue. Pantone Color Institute is a limited liability company rather than an organization, which offers both color forecasting and a color matching system, giving it a unique position in the marketplace.

Figure 4.15
The Color Marketing Group meets in committee several times a year to identify the color trends for upcoming seasons.

Not every color can be obtained on every fiber. Consortiums of textile manufacturers such as the Cotton Council, the Wool Bureau, and the Manmade Fiber Producers, refine early color forecasts for their own markets. Each of these organizations develops a color story that is geared to the end-use categories of the markets it supplies. The predictions come to life as textile manufacturers present their seasonal lines at global fabric fairs that occur about one year before a consumer season. This consensus-building process is, in a sense, a self-fulfilling prophecy whereby each level of color forecasting builds on the one before it so that the color message consumers see is somewhat unified across all markets, brands, and price points. Like fashion, color forecasting is an evolutionary process. Color morphs from season to season, with each seasonal palette taking direction from the season that preceded it and giving a hint of what is to come in seasons that follow. The faster the pace of change in fashion trends, the more drastic the color shift; the slower the pace of change in fashion trends the more evolutionary the color shift. A more seasonless approach would embrace color shifts that move more slowly across the dimensions of color from delivery to delivery so that customers can build on what they already have, rather than discard it.

Fabric

The task of researching fabrics takes place simultaneously with color research and the determination of a color story. Brands need to stay abreast of new technology, fibers, blends, and finishes as well as tendencies in surface texture and prints. Many creatives believe that fabric is a medium that needs to be touched and draped to be appreciated. Toward that end, a number of domestic and international fabric and yarn shows are

held each year to give product developers an overview of what is available. These shows provide an opportunity for yarn and fabric vendors to introduce their seasonal lines (Figure 4.16). During the pandemic, these shows had to run virtually. It remains to be seen whether they will develop some combination of tools and strategies to continue to offer virtual shows or whether shows will return to in-person events. For those brands that do their own sourcing, there may be advantages to virtual fabric fairs. When buying basics and base fabrics that a brand intends to have printed or dyed to their specifications, they can compare more options as to quality, price, delivery, and sustainability. Experiencing the hand and drape of novelty fabrics is more difficult but might be achieved through sampling that allows more people on the merchandising and design teams to weigh in on selections.

Many brands leave the responsibility for fabric sourcing to their manufacturing partners. They purchase samples at fabric shows and share them with offshore sourcing agents who attempt to have the fabric duplicated at a lower cost. This has serious ethical implications and contributes to the disregard of creative intellectual property.

Fabric shows typically feature an area in which trend forecasters can share their seasonal predictions. Seminars and speakers are offered throughout the run of the show to alert product developers to trends and new technology. These offerings took place on streaming platforms during the pandemic and likely reached more people.

Important shows include the Première Vision and Texworld, both in Paris and New York, and Kingpins in New York and Hong Kong. There is growing interest in Asian fabric exhibits because of their proximity to significant production sources. A number of other national and international shows appeal to regional markets or specialize in particular kinds of fibers and fabrics. Product developers must determine which fabric shows best match the needs of their category in terms of product type and price point.

Some large brands and fabric associations assemble representative samples of fabrics for a given season that can be reviewed in their fabric libraries. Using the library can save a designer or product developer the time it would take to visit a number of vendor showrooms in order to identify in advance which sources have the fabric they are seeking. It also lends itself to brands that adopt a capsule collection approach to deliveries as they can make selections at intervals based on what customers are purchasing.

Most of the buying that takes place at large fabric and fiber shows is for sample quantities. Larger commitments are made after the product developer has had time to experiment with the fabric and determine how important it will be to the delivery in which it is featured. Product developers prefer to postpone their final commitment to fabrics until the last possible moment in order to minimize risk.

Fabrics are not always ordered as they are shown. Once a product developer commits to a fabric, the developer may work with the vendor to adapt the fabric by modifying its weight, color, pattern, or scale if the order meets the vendor's minimum yardage requirement.

Product developers in certain categories rely on printed fabrics to make their lines unique. Prints can be acquired in one of several ways. Some product developers select prints from a fabric supplier's seasonal line. Others rely on their creative design teams to develop prints in-house. Prints developed in-house are then sourced out to a textile finisher who prints the pattern on the fabric of its choice. Yet other product developers purchase prints from print studios (Figure 4.17). Most purchased prints are developed on the computer. Prints can also be purchased from print agents, who have showrooms that are open year round. Print agents may design their own prints as well as represent individual domestic and international print designers for a sales commission. The cost of a single print may range from $400 to $500.

Figure 4.17
Fabric prints are exhibited at Direction by Indigo, part of the Première Vision Fabric Show.

Figure 4.18
Trim studios specialize in generating ideas for interesting trims and details. They sell these panels to product developers who can adapt the technique to work with seasonal silhouettes.

In addition to print studios, there are trim studios that specialize in generating ideas for interesting trims and details such as embroideries, pin tucking, lace insertion, and so forth (Figure 4.18). Their swatches are offered as inspiration and generally are not available in yardage. It is up to the product developer to find a sourcing partner that can duplicate the technique. Trim swatches are generally priced about the same as prints. Often these swatches offer multiple ideas. These resources are especially important in seasons when trims and embellishment details predominate.

Silhouettes

In modern fashion, silhouettes appear to be the element that changes least from season to season. **Silhouette** is the term used to describe the outline or shape of a garment. For the most part, western customers are happy with the array of silhouettes available in tops, pants, skirts, jackets, dresses, and outerwear. Although fabric and color may change substantially from season to season, silhouettes usually vary primarily in proportion and details. Periodically, there is a major shift from very fitted silhouettes to less constructed or oversized silhouettes.

Silhouette inspiration comes from a variety of sources. Trend services may generate fashion sketches that incorporate a variety of ideas into single garments. Some sketches may be overdesigned or missing necessary seams and darts for fit, forcing subscribers to reinterpret the ideas for their given market, rather than use them exactly as they were drawn. This helps to minimize the possibility of multiple subscribers coming out with lines that look very much the same.

Other trend services share photographs of looks spotted on the streets in major fashion centers. As more and more fashion ideas trickle up from the streets rather than down from the runways, clothes worn in Saint-Tropez, Paris, London, Tokyo, New York, Los Angeles, and other trend-setting locales can be very inspirational.

More intuitive-focused trend forecasters may only provide research in the form of historical and cultural imagery, allowing the brand's design team to imagine how to reinterpret that inspiration into something that functions in our modern-day society. Chapter 8 discusses silhouette development in detail.

Fashion on Demand

Data analytics has already launched a shift in curation responsibility from merchandisers, designers, and buyers to consumers. In the near future, consumers will be able to co-design the garments they buy.

Crowdsourcing refers to the gathering of input into a particular task by enlisting the services or opinions of a large number of people, who may be paid or unpaid, typically via the internet. Derek Lam was one of the first to use crowdsourcing for a collection he presented on eBay in 2010. After showing a collection of preliminary designs online and listening to customer feedback, the line was edited and presented for sale in the spring of 2011. The concept of crowdsourcing is becoming more and more prevalent. Predictive Analytics providers are offering brands software applications that allow them to digitally present virtual garments to regular customers and ask for feedback. Both Kohl's and Athleta already use this technology. Customers are asked a series of questions about whether or not they would buy a style, what they like or don't like about it, whether they like the color, and how much they would pay. This takes the editing process out of the hands of merchandisers and designers and gives it to consumers.

Stitch Fix delivers monthly clothing assortments to customers, with the help of online stylists. The brand is working with algorithms to identify trends and styles missing from the Stitch Fix inventory based on consumer selections of favorite silhouettes, colors, patterns, and textiles. Then, they used artificial intelligence to design garments that fill in their assortment gaps. These new designs can be reviewed by either a design team or consumer focus group before they are manufactured.

The next step is customizable made-to-order apparel. Nineteenth Amendment is a marketplace for emerging designers. They are required to complete a tech pack, sourcing, a sample, and patterns before showing their designs on the platform. Anything that sells is made on demand, either in-house or with one of Nineteenth Amendment's manufacturing partners. Delivery on sales is promised within nineteen days. Designer brand Prabal Gurung also offers a made-to-order line that requires eight to twelve weeks for delivery. Made-to-order apparel requires lower capital investment, decreased inventories, and a more sustainable production cycle, but lower quantities of garments produced means manufacturing costs are higher. If this mode of ordering takes off, it will support an investment in automated manufacturing which can be done anywhere in the world. The downside is that it would put millions of people out of work in developing countries.

Customizable apparel is a variation of made-to-order. Imagine a shopping experience where the customer can select a silhouette and customize it with the details, color, and fabric they prefer. The application of new fit technology allows it to be made to the customer's measurements and shipped within two weeks' time.

Open-source design is the development of ideas, technology, and systems without the retention of intellectual property rights. Alabama Chanin creates beautiful, rustic, handstitched, applique and reverse applique garments that are sold at high prices. They also sell their applique stencils, preprinted fabrics, books, and kits that teach and enable do-it-yourself customers to make their own versions. Ravelry is a wonderful digital repository for knit and crochet patterns, many of which are freely shared by like-minded creatives. During the pandemic JW Anderson shared the downloadable pattern for a color blocked, knitted, patchwork cardigan worn by singer Harry Styles.

These business models and technologies have the potential to truly personalize apparel procurement and eliminate massive amounts of waste. The technology that supports customization is ready and waiting to be commercialized. In the very near future trends will be determined by the customer.

SUSTAINABILITY

Changes in the fashion system and the way trends are tracked and forecast highlight the differences between fast fashion and slow fashion. Fast fashion is a design, manufacturing, and marketing method focused on producing inexpensive, generally lower-quality clothing, produced rapidly, in response to the latest fashion trends. Fast fashion brands replicate the look of more expensive brands using low-quality materials under the guise of making fashion more democratic. These cheaply made, trendy pieces have resulted in harmful impacts on the environment as well as textile and apparel workers. Ridiculously inexpensive prices entice consumers to purchase garments they don't need. Many have convinced themselves that they can only be seen in the same outfit once on social media. After consumers have worn an item a couple of times, it becomes disposable. Since items didn't cost much, they fail to hold their value. To keep up with demand and deliver the lowest possible price, work is completed in sweatshops where workers are not fairly paid, expected to meet unrealistic timelines, and work under poor conditions. To make matters worse, textile and apparel manufacturing is one of the most polluting industries in the world and fast fashion brands in particular are not doing enough to employ best practices in order to limit environmental harms. As a result of excessive consumption, landfills are filled to the brim with textiles and toxic materials.

It would be remiss to discuss fast fashion without also pointing out its contributions. Fast fashion manufacturers, particularly Zara and H&M, have demonstrated to the industry how product can be designed, manufactured, and delivered in small quantities and in a time frame as short as six weeks. Their process contributions will be critical in a transition to small batch, sustainable manufacturing as long as workers are paid and treated fairly.

The slow fashion movement encourages the design, creation, and purchase of quality garments made from better materials and constructed to last. It encourages small-batch production in factories where workers are paid fair wages, best practices are used to lower the carbon footprint of manufacturing, and business models encourage extending the useful life of garments through repurposing, sharing, renting, upcycling, or recycling. DIY remaking and mending are making a resurgence. Slow design values layering, multipurpose designs, zero waste design, and investment pieces constructed so that they can be upcycled or recycled at the end of their useful life. A seasonless fashion system supports slow fashion by promoting *see now, buy now* fashions that are shown and delivered as needed and/or when ready. When the pace of trends slows down, the consumer can evaluate their purchases based on what they need and love rather than purchasing garments just because they are inexpensive. Designing fewer garments in a more considered environment eliminates a great deal of waste due to samples that never go into production. The exploration of new types of fashion presentations that show garments for both men and women or are gender neutral and are produced for the final consumer rather than the press means that fashion may return to its more functional roots. Slow fashion asks consumers to reconsider their philosophy of consumerism evolving from conspicuous consumption to conscious consumption.

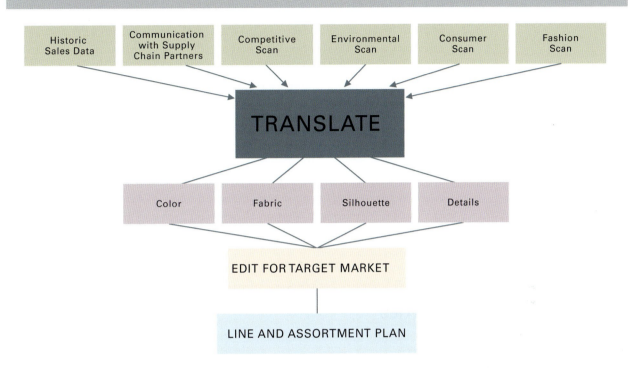

FASHION FORECAST FLOWCHART

Historic Sales Data · Communication with Supply Chain Partners · Competitive Scan · Environmental Scan · Consumer Scan · Fashion Scan

TRANSLATE

Color · Fabric · Silhouette · Details

EDIT FOR TARGET MARKET

LINE AND ASSORTMENT PLAN

The role of trend forecasting is changing. Rather than contributing to an unsustainable delivery of new trends, forecasters are now more consultative. They help brands to interpret and respond to both macro and micro trends in ways that match the brand's DNA and established customer. They may consult regarding marketing, design, market timing, demand planning, and content delivery. They help brands understand the source of new trends and how they've evolved so that they can recognize patterns that will impact their business. This holistic approach helps brands mitigate risk.

Trend forecasting will continue to track color, fabrics, and silhouettes, but hopefully the pendulum between extremes will slow down as consumers come to appreciate better-made, quality garments that are built to last. A consumer shift from fast fashion to slow fashion and recommerce will likely encourage more individuality in fashion with the customer becoming the curator, muse, and stylist.

Figure 4.19
A Fashion Forecast Flowchart

KEY TERMS

capsule collection
concept store
content curation
cultural appropriation
deadstock fabric
diversity imperative

fashion
fashion calendar
macro trends
micro trends
open-source design
seasonless fashion model

silhouette
trend
trend analysis
trickle-across theory
trickle-down theory
trickle-up theory

DISCUSSION QUESTIONS

1. Identify trends in color, fabric, silhouettes, and details that you observe in the assortments at a variety of retailers and brands. Where do you think these trends originated?
2. Identify brands that are widely adapted and copied by other lower-priced brands. What makes those brands more vulnerable to knockoffs? Which brands are doing the copying?
3. Identify several current events in the political, global, and cultural arenas. What impact might they have on fashion?
4. To what extent are you influenced by media and celebrities in your fashion preferences. Where do you get most of your fashion trend information?
5. Do you feel that your generation is demanding change in the fashion system? How important are fashion trends to you when making apparel and accessory purchases?

ACTIVITIES

1. Do a search to identify major art and fashion exhibitions opening within the next year. With these artists and/or designers in mind, what influence do you think these exhibitions will have on fashion trends?
2. Put together a color palette for next season influenced by an upcoming exhibition identified in Activity 1.
3. If your institution subscribes to fashion trend periodicals or web-based services, study the reports for an upcoming season. Then interpret their projections for a particular brand and price point. Your instructor will give you guidelines as to how detailed this report should be.
4. Select a category of apparel to research (active sportswear, denim, dresses, sweaters). Study brands in that category for fabrication. Identify the fabrication trends for that category (i.e., denim finishes, prints and patterns in dresses, sustainability characteristics).

STUDiO RESOURCES

- Take the chapter quiz with scored results and personalized study tips.
- Review glossary flashcards to build your vocabulary.

REFERENCES

Arnett, George. (2020), "Trend Forecasters Predict a More Trendless Future," *Voguebusiness.com*, April 20. https://www.voguebusiness.com/fashion/trend-forecasters-predict-a-more-trendless-future-covid-19 (accessed on February 5, 2020).

Downing Peters, Lauren. (2016), "Seeing the Future? The Methods of Trend Forecasting," *The Fashion Studies Journal*, November 29. http://www.fashionstudiesjournal.org/longform/2016/11/29/seeing -the-future-the-methods-of-trend-forecasting-mepsl (accessed on January 2, 2021).

Fernandez, Chantal. (2021), "The CGI Influencer Gets a Promotion," *Business of Fashion*, February 15. https://www.businessoffashion.com/articles/fashion-week/the-cgi-influencer-gets-a-promotion (accessed on February 16, 2021).

Gucci Instagram Post. (May 3, 2020). https://www.instagram.com/p/CAikqmCCYEw/ (accessed on May 19, 2021).

Magnusdottir, Aslaug. (2020), "How Fashion Manufacturing Will Change After the Coronavirus," *Forbes*, May 13. https://www.forbes.com/sites/aslaugmagnusdottir/2020/05/13/fashions-next-normal /?sh=3b3b0c1978f3 (accessed on February 14, 2021).

Manoff, Jill. (2020). "The End of Fashion: Why Comfortable, Seasonless Styles Will Replace Runway Trends," *Glossy*, July 20. https://www.glossy.co/fashion/there-is-no-fashion-anymore-shoppers -have-changed-out-of-runway-trends-and-into-comfortable-seasonless-styles/ (accessed on February 15, 2021).

Milner, Daphne. (2020), "Is This the End of Fashion's Creative 'Mafia'?" *Business of Fashion*, October 27. https://www.businessoffashion.com/articles/media/fashion-creative-mafia-change-pandemic -inclusivity-social-media (accessed on January 2, 2021).

CHAPTER 5

COLOR MANAGEMENT

"Only those who love color are admitted to its beauty and immanent presence. It affords utility to all but unveils its deeper mysteries only to its devotees." JOHANNES ITTEN

OBJECTIVES

- To review the physics of color science
- To review the impact of color decisions throughout the supply chain
- To define terminology used in color management
- To outline the process for visual and digital color approval
- To identify the variables that affect color management
- To analyze the impact of technology on color measurement

Color is a critical medium of apparel product development. As our scientific understanding of color has grown, a standardized language has developed with a foundation in color theory. Color forecasters, merchandisers, designers, lab technicians, dyers, and quality assurance specialists need both a highly developed color vision and a vocabulary for describing and assessing color that can be understood by supply chain partners working across the globe.

Objects themselves do not have color. **Color** is the visual perception of an object as a result of the way in which it reflects light. **Colorants**, both pigments and dyes, work by reflecting, absorbing, or transmitting light energy that our eye recognizes as color.

Chapter 4 described how color trends evolve as well as the resources on which designers and merchandisers rely, in order to select their brands' seasonal color palettes. As they interpret color trends and current events, designers and merchandisers must consider their target customers—who they are and what they're searching for—to project, to the best of their ability, what customers will want next. The seasonal color palette may be broken out into several deliveries with different color groupings for each delivery. These decisions set in motion the color management function. **Color management** is the process of controlling the outcome of a color, from the initial concept (a chip, swatch, yarn, or sample) to the final production output, in a way that is acceptable to the consumer.

SEASONAL COLOR PALETTE CONSIDERATIONS

Color draws customers in and entices them to explore other aspects of the garment, including fabric and silhouette. Consumers make initial judgments about a product quickly and much of that assessment is based on whether or not the color is appealing. The choice of a seasonal color palette is critical to meeting sales objectives. Color decisions are based on both consumer demand and production efficiencies. Brands strive to offer enough choices to stimulate a broad base of customer interest without offering so many choices that the customer becomes confused. Brands must also consider how their color assortment affects production costs and schedules. In an environment in which responding to new trends as fast as possible is paramount, ongoing advancements in digital color measurement contribute greatly to shortening the product development cycle.

Each size and color in which a style is offered represents a stockkeeping unit (SKU). The more SKUs there are to manage, the more complex color management and its impact on sourcing and buying decisions becomes. Every color that is used in solid, yarn-dyed, or patterned fabric must be included in the seasonal color story. The same color used in several different fabrications must be managed to match throughout the line; the notions used with each style must also be color matched.

Offering too many colors may make each lot size too small to allow it to be produced economically. The color range in a seasonal color palette will be influenced by how the line is merchandised, the number of deliveries, the fashion level, and the price point of the line, and the target market personality.

Merchandising Considerations

Color palettes vary depending on whether the product being developed is going to be sold as separates or as a coordinated group. **Separates** refer to items that are generally purchased as an individual piece rather than a coordinated outfit. A number of factors affect the range of colors available in a separates line. Color ranges for a menswear separates line might be available for an entire season, therefore justifying a broad palette. On the other hand, in a fashion-driven women's wear line, a separates product category might offer one new palette for each delivery. The more deliveries per season, the smaller the color range for each delivery—perhaps three to five colors. If a brand anticipates selling a high volume of a particular style, it may choose to offer it in a wide range of colors; anticipation of a lower sales volume, however, will necessitate a narrower range of colors (Figure 5.1a–b). Separates lines appeal to customers who cannot afford to buy multiple pieces at the same time, who have a more casual lifestyle, and/or who like to create looks that are more distinctive and individual. With more jobs offering work-from-home options and many work environments implementing a casual dress code, separates have become increasingly important for all age groups in the marketplace.

Even though a given customer may only buy one item at a time, product offerings must be planned so that when items are merchandised together on a sales floor or

a   b

webpage, they are pleasing to the eye. When the color range shares a common color attribute, consumers are more confident that whichever color they choose, it is on trend. It also ensures that when merchandised together, the display will be appealing. The colors from one delivery to the next should also relate to some extent since they will occupy floor space simultaneously. Older stock will rotate to the back of the store and newer stock will be merchandised in the front of the store. Customers who buy items from multiple deliveries may hope to wear the pieces together. Therefore, colors should morph from delivery to delivery, rather than change drastically.

Coordinates refer to groups of items that are designed to stimulate the purchase of multiple pieces, e.g., a skirt or pant that pairs with a shirt or sweater and a jacket (Figure 5.2a–e). Product developers of coordinates groups may launch two to four different groups for the first delivery of the season. Subsequent deliveries may update a group already on the floor with more seasonal fabrics and new pieces, or a new delivery might represent a new group concept based on a new color and fabric story. The coordinates method of merchandising a brand appeals to customers who want their looks to be very pulled together, who can spend more money in a single purchase, and who want a wardrobe that can be readily mixed and matched. If a customer invests in both a skirt and pants as well as a jacket, shirt, and sweater, she can wear those pieces in multiple combinations. The range of colors used in a coordinates line will not be as extensive as the range of colors in a separates line. A pair of pants or a jacket may be offered in only one or two colors rather than the three to five colors of a separates line.

As with separates, the colors selected for a group generally share a common attribute or relationship so that they coordinate with each other—all of a similar value or saturation. The color harmonies found in fabric patterns may be the basis for deciding the solid color palette. Just as trends promote particular hues from season to season, trends also impact what is popular in terms of color harmonies.

Figure 5.1a
Uniqlo offered a men's polo shirt in twelve different colors. Male customers are more apt to buy an item they like in multiple colors to streamline the shopping experience.

Figure 5.1b
Galleries Lafayette in Paris offered a sweater set in six colors. Women are less likely than men to buy multiples of the same style.

a b   c   d   e

Figures 5.2a–e
A coordinated group for spring from Elie Tahari combines white, denim, khaki, chambray, and washed indigo for pieces that can be mixed and matched in the wardrobe.

Color harmonies refer to how colors are used in combination in patterns and prints. **Monochromatic** color harmonies utilize a single hue in a variety of tints and shades. An **analogous** color harmony incorporates colors positioned next to each other on the color wheel. **Complementary** color harmonies include colors opposite one another on the color wheel. When interpreting color trends and developing seasonal palettes, it is important to have the right combination of colors that allow for the development of timely color harmonies. The right color used in the wrong combination can have a detrimental impact on sales.

Colors must be consistent within each SKU, between garments that are made from different fabrics that have been dyed the same color, and between solids and patterned fabrics. Whether a product developer focuses on separates, coordinates, or a combination of the two, the color stories of merchandise from several categories or divisions in the same store or adjoining areas should relate. Stores that offer both menswear and women's wear may offer different values of the same palette so that the overall store merchandising suggests a similar aesthetic.

Relating Color Palettes to Target Markets

In today's marketplace, color direction must be interpreted for each apparel category and customer group. Color trends are not necessarily the same for all segments of the market. A well-defined color palette should take into consideration the target market's age and life stage, fashion level, coloring, ethnic diversity, geography and climate, and the garment's function. Merchandisers should attempt to satisfy the preferences of the full range of the brand's customers.

Age and Life Stage

Target customer groups have unique preferences when it comes to color. Young adults are most apt to respond to the extremes of color trends. Their preferences are driven by a need for change, a desire to be on the cutting edge, and pressure to relate to their peers. They are less constricted by dress codes and often see clothing purchases in terms of a single-season life span rather than several years.

As consumers enter the full-time workforce or begin families, their color preferences may become more practical. They develop an awareness of the colors that enhance their personal coloring and the confidence to wear colors that are the most becoming rather than blindly following fashion trends. They begin to conform to unwritten dress codes that reflect their multiple life roles. They shop for clothes with the intention of wearing them for more than one season.

As customers mature, their skin and hair colors begin to change, thus influencing the colors that are the most becoming on them. Older women may reject neutrals such as black, gray, and navy for middle tones that make them look and feel younger.

Fashion Level

Each fashion level interprets color trends somewhat differently. Owing to the real-time availability of fashion information, it rarely takes more than a single season for a new color to become available at all price points; however, product developers at different fashion levels may interpret that color differently. A blue and green trend may appear in very inky dark shades at high-end price points, while at mid-tier and mass market price points the same colors may be interpreted as highly saturated, bright colors used in high-contrast prints.

Within any given market there are customers who are more fashion forward and others who are more conservative. A seasonal color palette should accommodate these preferences by including some fashion forward colors and some mass-consumption colors.

Personal Coloring

Beyond what's on trend, personal coloring may cause customers to prefer warm or cool colors, pastels or brights. Warm-toned skin has yellow undertones and frequently looks best against colors with warm undertones. Cool-toned skin has blue-pink undertones and looks best against colors with cool undertones. Darker skin tones are enhanced by saturated colors; dark neutrals such as blacks, browns, and navy provide little contrast. Hair color has a similar impact. Most colors can be adjusted through manipulation of value and chroma to look becoming with all complexions and hair colors. Yellow and orange hues in their pure state are difficult for most people to wear. When they are in fashion, a product developer should never plan to sell items in those colors in huge numbers. Turquoise, on the other hand, is one of the most universally pleasing colors on most people. For a season in which neutral colors predominate, accent colors should be provided that compliment both warm and cool skin tones.

Geographic Location

Color stories should be appropriate to the geographic markets where the products will be distributed, taking into consideration both weather patterns as well as regional and cultural preferences. The southern part of the United States has warm winters where seasonless clothes can be worn year round, whereas the Midwest has distinct weather patterns for each of the four seasons, ranging from very warm to very cold. In a global marketplace, seasonal considerations can extend the life cycle of a garment because seasons are reversed above and below the equator.

End Use

Each category of apparel (e.g., swimwear, dresses, outerwear) interprets color somewhat differently. Swimwear typically utilizes brighter color palettes, even in seasons where neutrals predominate. The children's wear market also tends to stay with more colorful palettes regardless of season, while neutrals generally dominate the outerwear and menswear markets.

Budget, geographic location, age, lifestyle, and personal coloring all play a role in individual color preferences. As the pace of fashion slows down, it will be increasingly helpful for merchandisers to plan palettes that build on and coordinate with the palettes of previous deliveries in order to promote wardrobe building and brand loyalty. Color palettes that are selected with these considerations in mind will encourage distribution channels to carry the collection in its entirety.

Managing the Color Story

As the seasonal color palette is broken down into deliveries and groups, each is developed around a specific theme. Each color is named to identify it throughout the process of ordering fabric and materials all the way to selling it to the consumer. Some companies use generic color names—red is red from season to season whether it is an orange red or a blue red. Fashion forward companies name their colors to further develop their concept or theme. An orange red might be named flame or poppy, evoking a visual image. A coral red might be called geranium in a floral line for women and watermelon in a fruit-themed line for children. These color names are a marketing tool that can be used in the showroom and in writing copy for catalogs, websites, and print advertising.

Decisions regarding the size (breadth or depth of selections) of the lines to be offered are typically made early in the product development process by the merchandising staff. Multi-brand product developers may manage seasonal color palettes of up to 400 different colors. Each color may start with a paint chip, a piece of fabric, a hank of yarn, or a photo. From that color impression it must be translated into a standard that the entire supply chain can understand.

COLOR SCIENCE

Color management requires an understanding of the variables involved in how we see color. Our perception of color is created through the exchange of information between the eye and the brain. From a scientific perspective, it is the perception of certain wavelengths of light seen by the retina of the eye. Visible light consists of a narrow band of wavelengths within the electromagnetic spectrum, which also includes television and radio waves, X-rays, ultraviolet light, and infrared light. Low frequency wavelengths within the electromagnetic spectrum are quantified in meters, but the visible light waves that allow us to see color are much higher frequency and require a smaller measurement. A **nanometer**, equal to one millionth of a millimeter, is the unit of measurement used to measure light waves. The human eye perceives colors at wavelengths in a range from 400 nanometers (which we see as deep blue) to about 700 nanometers (which we see as deep red) (Figure 5.3a–b). Within this limited range, we are capable of distinguishing about 10 million variations of color, but not all of those colors can be reproduced with available dyes or inks, nor can they be achieved on all available fibers and materials.

Color and Light

Visual color is a function of light. Color cannot be seen in the absence of light: we see no color in the dark. White light is perceived when all wavelengths of the visible spectrum are present in equal amounts; however, true white light is rare. Natural and incandescent lights have yellow undertones; indirect sunlight and fluorescent light have blue undertones. Sunlight is our source of natural light and has become the primary standard by which colors are measured. However, our daily activities take place under a variety of light sources: outdoor activities under sunlight, business activities under fluorescent lights, and activities at home under LED or incandescent lights.

This variety of lighting environments presents a challenge for those responsible for color matching. Different fabrics (and their components—e.g., zippers, thread) dyed the same color must match under a variety of light sources. A shopper will be frustrated if they believe that two garments match in-store under fluorescent lighting only to find that the same two garments are very mismatched under natural sunlight or incandescent home lighting. As digital shopping becomes more prevalent, the consumer's ability to match colors based on how they appear on their screens will be

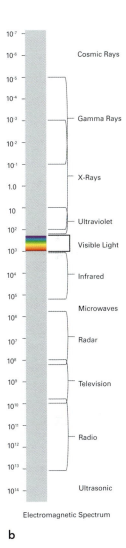

b

Electromagnetic Spectrum

· · · · · · · · · · · · · · · · · · · ·

Figure 5.3a and b
The human eye perceives wavelengths in a range from 400 nanometers to about 700 nanometers as color. Within this limited range, we are capable of distinguishing about 10 million variations of color.

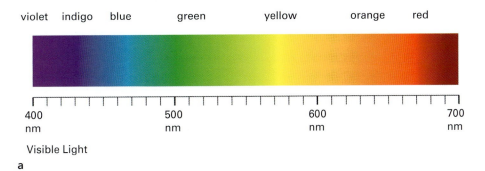

Visible Light

a

Figure 5.4
The same red textile is inconstant under different light sources—tungsten home light (L), cool white fluorescent office light (M), and exterior daylight (R).

a new challenge. Consumers have a greater tolerance for slight color discrepancies between separates. They are less forgiving with coordinates.

Color constancy is a feature of the human color perception system and refers to the perceived color of something appearing relatively constant regardless of the light source. The phenomenon of a single-color sample reading as a slightly different color under different light sources is called **color inconstancy**. Color inconstancy is related to the color hue rather than the color recipe (Figure 5.4). One analysis of 2,300 colors in a textile palette that covered a wide gamut found that 10 to 20 percent of the colors when applied to textile products had a very high color inconstancy going from daylight (D65) to incandescent light. The shades with the highest color inconstancy between daylight and incandescent light are the red-oranges and bright blues, particularly those of medium depth (Agarwal, 2003, 1–4).

Illuminant metamerism is the perceived change in color between a pair of samples that match under one light source but do not a match under another (Figure 5.5). This is because they have different spectral reflectance curves under different illuminants. This poses a problem for product developers who use different fabrics and fibers in garments intended to coordinate or match—a cotton tee shirt designed to be worn

Figure 5.5
Two metameric reds match in daylight but do not match in fluorescent light because they reflect different wavelengths, as shown in their spectrophometric curves (L). In cool white fluorescent light, reds and yellows appear vivid but blues appear gray or greenish (R) when compared to their appearance in daylight.

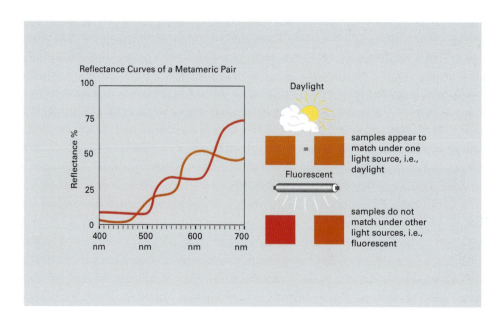

with a rayon skirt, for instance. These may match in the store but not in natural daylight. Illuminant metamerism can usually be controlled by using similar colorants in the color standard and the sample or in the various fabrics being matched to the color standard (Agarwal 2003, 1–4).

Observer metamerism occurs when two observers perceive a match differently—to one's eye the pair matches and to the other's eye the pair does not match. This difference in perception could be due to color blindness in one of the observers, differing sensitivity to light in the medium- and long-wavelength–sensitive cones in the retina, yellowing of the lens, or macular degeneration. **Geometric metamerism** occurs when identical colors appear different when viewed at different angles. **Field-size metamerism** describes a pair that is a good match when viewed from a distance or in a sample that is very small but does not match when viewed up close or in a larger size.

To understand how we perceive color, we must study color as light and as colorant—the dyes and pigments that impart color to another substance. Color is perceived when light strikes a surface that contains a colorant. The colorants of a surface cause some wavelengths to be absorbed and others to be reflected, thus giving the surface its color. The different combinations of reflected wavelengths are the basis for all observed colors.

Color Attributes

Albert Munsell (1858–1918) devoted his life to studying color and developed the Munsell Color Order System to describe and identify color and color relationships. It continues to be the most widely used color system today. Munsell introduced a color vocabulary that describes the various aspects of color and how they interact (Figure 5.6). Color is the quality of an object or substance with respect to the light reflected by the object and can be measured by its hue, value, and chroma.

Hue

A **hue** is the property of light by which the color of an object is classified as one of the hue families of the light spectrum. There is a natural order of hues that follows the sequence of hues seen in a rainbow. That order goes from red to orange to yellow, then green, blue, and purple. Purple does not appear in the rainbow, but it completes the human perception of the hue families. Hue families can be arranged in this order to form a color circle. Within the color circle, one can mix adjacent colors to obtain a continuous variation from one color family to the next. For example, red and yellow may be mixed to obtain all the hues from red through orange to yellow.

In the Munsell system, there are ten basic hue families: five major and five minor. Red, yellow, green, blue, and

Figure 5.6
The Munsell Color Order System defines color by hue, value, and chroma, as illustrated in this three-dimensional model of Munsell color space.

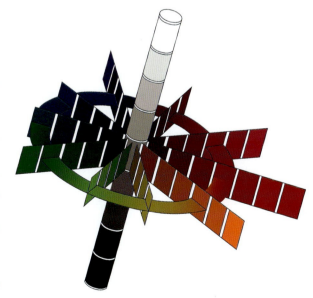

purple are the major families. Halfway between each of these are the five minor hue families of orange, green-yellow, blue-green, purple-blue, and red-purple. These ten hue families are further subdivided into ten more hue steps for a total of 100 hue families. Even finer distinctions can be made between similar hues through the use of decimals. Colors that have a hue are called **chromatic** colors. Black, white, and gray are neutral or **achromatic**, having no hue.

It is important to recognize that the terms "hue" and "color" are not synonymous. Hue has only one attribute—its classification in relation to the dominant wavelength of light—whereas color has three attributes: hue, value, and chroma.

Value

Value is the quality by which we distinguish light colors from dark colors. A light color may be referred to as a **tint**. Painters achieve tints by mixing color with white paint or water, a commercial printer achieves a tint by leaving more space between dots, and a scientist perceives a tint when a colored light is mixed with white light. Tints are sometimes called pastels; examples include pink and peach. A **shade** refers to a color mixed with black to decrease the value and darken the color. Navy blue and forest green are examples of shades.

How we perceive a color's lightness or darkness depends on the percentage of light that is reflected from the colored surface. The lightest color is white; it reflects much of the light that strikes it. The darkest color is absolute black, which reflects no light. Gray is seen when some of the light is absorbed and some of the light is reflected. The value scale applies to chromatic as well as neutral colors. All colors that have the same Munsell value, regardless of their hue, reflect the same amount of light.

The lightness or darkness of any given color can be measured according to a gray scale. The Munsell gray scale is divided into ten value steps, with pure black at zero and pure white at ten. However, the human eye cannot easily distinguish among more than five to seven gray tones. The differentiation is more difficult at the lightest and darkest ends of the value scale.

Chroma

Chroma refers to a color's saturation, or degree of departure from the neutral of the same value. It is determined by the amount of pigment in a color. Hues at 100 percent intensity are fully saturated with pigment; when there is no pigment present, a gray of equal value to the color is left. Figure 5.7 illustrates the difference between value and chroma for one color. In the value direction the color goes from light to dark; in the chroma direction the color goes from gray to fully saturated color.

Color Temperature

Though color temperature is not considered a true attribute of color, there seems to be a universal human perception that hues appear to be either warm or cool. **Color temperature** is used to describe a color's apparent warmth or coolness in relation to another color. Yellow, orange, and red are traditionally known as warm colors, whereas

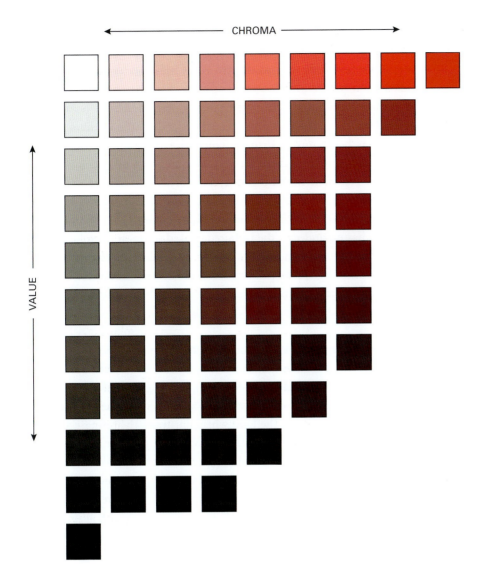

CHROMA

VALUE

Figure 5.7
The many shades of pink can be described by the standardized method developed by the Inter-Society Color Council of the National Institute of Standards and Technology.

green, blue, and violet are considered cool colors. Intermediate colors such as red-violet and yellow-green are considered temperate colors, but they can migrate toward the warm or cool temperatures depending on the proportion of colors mixed and the context of a color within a color grouping. Designers often use the perception of warm and cool colors in their color names to help their customers visualize a particular color. For example, the name "sea green" evokes the image of a cool blue-green color.

Creating and Mixing Colors

Color is a function of light and colorants. Achieving a desired color depends on the material that is being colored. A **substrate**, in color terminology, refers to the material on which one is attempting to apply color. Different materials require different

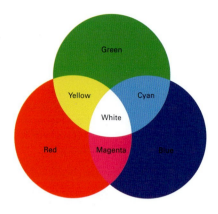

Figure 5.8
The additive color mixing system shows how colored light is mixed using red, green, and blue or blue-violet as the primaries. When all three of the additive primaries are mixed, we see white.

colorants. Colorants are dyes or pigments that give a substrate color. **Dyes** chemically bond with the substrate. **Pigments** lay on the surface of the substrate. Professionals who work with color must understand how color is mixed to create the infinite variety of color that it is possible to achieve with current technology. This understanding is complicated because the hues from which all colors can be created depend on the medium or substance that is being mixed. **Primary colors** are the minimum number of hues that can be mixed to make the greatest number of other colors. When two primary colors are mixed together, they form **secondary colors**. When a primary color is mixed with a secondary color that is next to it on the color wheel, they form tertiary or **intermediate colors**. Our concept of primary colors has expanded as the technology used to create color has grown. Today, three sets of primary colors and two color-mixing systems are recognized. The two color-mixing systems differ in how primary colors are defined, how color is mixed, and the range of colors it is possible to achieve.

Additive System

The **additive color-mixing system** explains how colored light is mixed. It is used in theater lighting, on television screens, and on computer monitors. When using the additive mixing system to mix colored light, red, green, and blue or blue-violet are the primaries; yellow, magenta, and cyan are the secondaries. When all three of the additive primaries are mixed, we see white. The light wheel illustrates the primary and secondary colors in the additive mixing system (Figure 5.8). The greatest range of color can be produced using the additive mixing system.

Subtractive System

The **subtractive color-mixing system** describes how colorants are mixed. Paints, inks, dyes, and other color media all absorb certain wavelengths of light, which enable an object to absorb some light waves and reflect back others. The more colorants that are blended, the more light they absorb and the less light that is reflected, thus the label subtractive color-mixing system.

The **simple subtractive color-mixing system** explains how thin films of color are mixed. Printing inks, drawing inks, watercolor paints, and color photography film are all color media that rely on thin films of color that can be layered one on top of another to create colors. This is important when designers need to print accurate visuals of the fabrics they are using in a line. Scientifically, cyan, magenta, and yellow are considered the subtractive primaries; green, violet, and orange are the subtractive secondaries. These primaries produce the greatest range of colors and, when combined in equal amounts, mix to form black. The process wheel illustrates the relationship of colors using yellow, cyan, and magenta as the subtractive primaries (Figure 5.9).

Theoretically, it should follow that painters would use the same subtractive primaries, since they work with pigments to create color. Because most paints are thick films, mixtures of yellow, cyan, and magenta result in secondaries that are too grey. The **complex subtractive color-mixing system** is used for thick color mediums. Artists using thick paint find two sets of red, blue, and yellow paints—a warm set and a cool set—provide the greatest variety of colors. These colors are sometimes referred to as the complex subtractive primaries (Long & Luke, 2001).

We perceive color on textiles through the subtractive color system. Textiles may be colorized with either dyes or pigments. Dyes are relatively transparent, bonding with the molecular structure of the fabric, giving it some degree of fastness or permanence. For these transparent dyes the subtractive primaries of cyan, magenta, and yellow are best for mixing color. When using more opaque color pigments for silk screen printing, for example, the complex subtractive primaries of red, yellow, blue work best.

Further complicating the subtractive model is the fact that it is a relative rather than an absolute mixing system. Equal amounts of two primaries do not necessarily produce a perceived secondary color. Colorant proportions generally need to be adjusted in order to achieve the desired, balanced mix. Colorists and color systems frequently augment the number of subtractive primary colors they use with additional colors to extend the range of colors that can be mixed. For example, computer printer technology generally uses cyan (C), magenta (M), yellow (Y), and black (K) or CMYK to obtain a truer black than the black that would be achieved from mixing cyan, magenta, and yellow. Colorists that rely on opaque pigments often use two different reds, blues, and yellows to get a full range of color.

Combining Color-Mixing Systems

Unfortunately, it is not possible to create every color in the spectrum with either the additive or subtractive mixing system. While both systems are capable of reproducing a subset of all visible color, there are colors that can only be reproduced with additive color and not with subtractive color, and vice versa. Similarly, the medium and substrate, whether it is paint, dye, ink, or light and whether it is on a computer screen or on a specific type of paper or fabric, affects the possible number of chroma steps or range attainable in any particular medium. The entire range of colors that can be achieved within a medium or on a specific substrate is referred to as its color **gamut**. Understanding color gamut can prevent brands from wasting time developing fabric–color combinations that are impossible to execute or accurately reproduce. Overdevelopment of colorways leads to wasted time and money.

Color systems are rarely used in isolation. The textile artist designs prints using a computer monitor and additive color mixing. When those prints are applied to fabric, subtractive color is used to mix the dyes or pigments. Understanding the basis for the additive and subtractive color systems explains why computer software programs frequently provide two scales for mixing color: RGB (red, green, blue) levers and CMYK (cyan, magenta, yellow, black) levers. Different variations of color can be achieved with

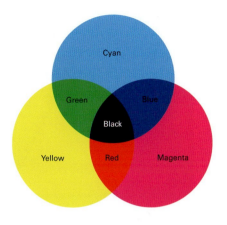

Figure 5.9
There are two types of subtractive color primaries: simple and complex. Transparent inks and paints (shown here), such as printer inks and transparent watercolors, rely on yellow, cyan, and magenta as primary colors to create red, blue, and green secondary colors. Equal amounts of these primaries create black. Opaque pigments and dyes, which dissolve completely to become an integral part of the material, rely on a more complex set of primaries. Artists using opaque paints rely on six primaries—warm and cool reds, blues, and yellows—to obtain the maximum number of colors. Mixing dyes varies by the dye type and substrate used.

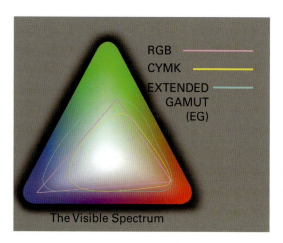

RGB

CYMK

EXTENDED
GAMUT
(EG)

The Visible Spectrum

Figure 5.10
This color gamut comparison chart plots the visible color spectrum and the gamut of color that can be achieved on the computer monitor using CMYK colors, RGB colors, and the extended gamut color system. Achieving all of the colors possible with RGB color is not necessarily possible with the CMYK inks used with most printers.

each. Using RGB levers produces a larger gamut of color that is clearer and brighter, especially in the orange, green, and purple ranges. The RGB gamut is similar to the gamut that can be achieved with fabric dyes. Using CMYK levers typically results in a closer match to printer colors because printers rely on cyan, magenta, and yellow as their primaries, with the addition of black as a key color. Today, professional printers, whose customers require a gamut beyond what can be achieved with CMYK, use a system of extended gamut (EG) colors. Extended gamut printing adds orange, green, and violet inks to the traditional CMYK set, enabling printers to more accurately match and reproduce the gamut of colors that can be achieved with textile dyes and pigments.

The concept of a color medium's gamut is one of the ongoing challenges in color management. A color may be very attainable on fabric but harder to visualize using computer printer inks. Conversely, a designer may develop a concept on the computer in a color they love, only to find that the color cannot be achieved on the fabric they have selected. Figure 5.10 illustrates the gamut of color available when working on the computer using each of three color systems.

Color Notation Systems

Color systems rely on visual representations of color that show how colors relate to one another in respect to their attributes of hue, value, and chroma. These visual sequential arrangements are sometimes referred to as **color solids**. Each color in a color solid can be identified using the color system's numerical notation system, which identifies the specific color in color space. The resulting notation system facilitates the visual identification, matching, and reproduction of colors.

The Munsell system notates color according to the attributes of hue (H), value (V), and chroma (C), which are notated H V/C, each expressed using code numbers that allow users to specify specific colors. The visual of the Munsell Color Order System is organized in the general shape of a sphere. Pure hues are located at the equator of the sphere, number five on the value scale. The vertical trunk represents gradations of value and the horizontal slices represent gradations in chroma or intensity for each hue.

The Munsell color solid does not take the shape of a perfect sphere because not all hue families contain the same number of colors (Figure 5.11). Light colors, such as intense yellow, have a large number of steps on the chroma scale between the fully saturated color and gray. The purest purple is a dark color, which takes fewer steps on the chroma scale between the fully saturated color and gray. The differences in the range of chroma and value for each hue determine the outer shape of the Munsell color solid. Thus, the sphere looks more like an amoeba because the human eye is able to distinguish only so many color variations. The color solid allows for the variations in human perception of color. The National Institute of Standards and Technology (NIST) has adopted the Munsell system as the standard for communicating color.

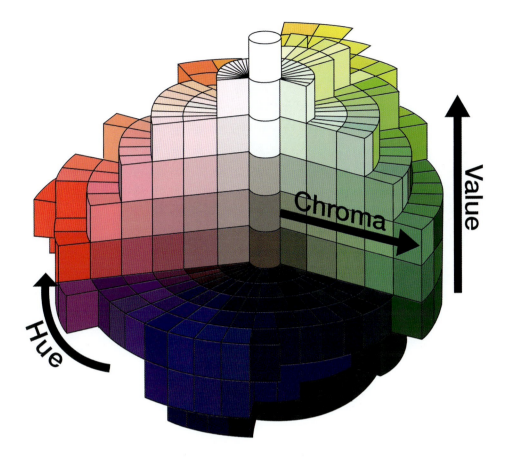

Figure 5.11
The Munsell color solid is shaped like an amoeba. An intense yellow requires more steps on the saturation scale to go from full saturation/value scale to gray than a dark purple does.

COLOR MANAGEMENT

The complexity of seasonal color stories and the unique characteristics of color make it challenging to deliver in a way that it is perceived to consistently match. The remainder of this chapter will introduce the processes, resources, and tools used to measure and approve color throughout the supply chain. While color management may be the responsibility of a color specialist, knowledge of color and the color management process is imperative for every member of the product development team.

Because a seasonal line uses many fabrics and related notions that may be sourced or produced anywhere in the world, color standards allow each partner in the supply chain to match the component it is producing to the same standard. Selecting seasonal color standards directly from a commercial color-matching system that is linked to dye recipes helps to ensure color consistency across the line.

Color Standards and Color-Matching Systems

Once a color concept is determined, a color standard must be specified. The color concept may come from something purchased at a flea market or a high-tech item purchased on a trend-shopping trip. It may be a hank of yarn or a piece of fabric, plastic, or paper. Whatever the source, it must be standardized to a reproducible color. A **color standard** is a visual fabric reference with color code data to which dyed samples can

be measured and compared for accurate color reproduction (Figure 5.12). A **color-matching system** identifies the range of color that can be produced on a given material such as paper, cotton, wool, polyester, or silk and, in some cases, the dye formula to obtain that color.

Physical standards may be available on several different substrates—the underlying material on which a dye or pigment is printed. They are organized in libraries that can be marketed to specific industries in order to represent the gamut of color achievable using available technology. Color standards for textiles and apparel are available on cotton, polyester, and nylon, although not every specification system offers all three substrates. Cotton is the preferred substrate for textile color specification systems because color dyed on cotton can be matched, almost without exception, to other fabric types if the appropriate dye class is used. Colors that can be achieved on polyester, nylon, and silk cannot always be achieved on cotton.

Each color-matching system uses its own method of notation to identify the increments of color by hue, value, and chroma. Today's standards must translate physical colors into data that allow the colors to be replicated digitally and that relate to dye recipes appropriate for a variety of fibers. Dyers and finishers must not only dye a sample that matches the color standard; they must also ensure that production yardage can be produced consistent with the approved sample.

Quality assurance conducts further tests to determine the colorfastness requirements. Colors need to hold up during consumer use and care—that is to say, the color must not bleed, fade, or change under normal conditions. Swimwear needs to maintain its color in chlorine; active sportswear cannot discolor from perspiration; and colors cannot bleed or fade in washing or dry cleaning. Color can affect garment quality in other unanticipated ways. A fabric that is offered in several **colorways** (other colors or different color combinations) may shrink differently during processing or pressing, giving each color-way a slightly different fit. It may also respond under the needle differently.

Color management is a complicated process that can make or break the success of a garment. Even after a careful color approval process, some color deviation may still result. This can be due to uncontrollable variations in the fiber, dyes, and/or environmental conditions during the dying process. Color consistency is imperative because the final customer is mobile and may buy one piece in-store and another online, or he or she may buy several pieces at a store near home and add to that ensemble from a store shopped on vacation or on a business trip.

Commercial Color-Matching Systems

Two commonly used, commercially managed, code-identified color libraries in apparel product development are Pantone and Color Solutions International (CSI). The Pantone Matching System has developed its own color-notation system, which uses a six-digit numerical code to define a color's position in color space. The first pair of numbers represents value, the second pair represents hue, and the third pair represents chroma. The Pantone value scale specifies ten value levels, which are labeled with the numbers 10 to 19, representing the lightest to darkest values. The hue circle is divided into sixty-four sectors from yellow (01) to green-yellow (64). The chroma or saturation scale also has sixty-four steps from neutral gray (00) to maximum color saturation (64). Pantone offers a number of different color libraries suitable for the color gamut of different mediums. The Pantone Textile Color System for textiles is offered on a cotton substrate and includes 2,625 colors (www.pantone.com). Pantone is owned by the X-Rite company, which makes color communication technology, and has a partnership with Clariant, a provider of textile chemicals and colorants.

Color Solutions International (CSI) is another popular commercial color-matching system that offers a library of color standards as well as custom color standards that may be developed from the 4,000 colors in their Color Wall™ (Figure 5.13). Their

Figure 5.13
The CSI Color Wall represents its collection of 4,000 color variations from which certified color standards can be produced.

color standards are available in two-inch by eight-inch physical samples or digital data. They have partnered with Datacolor to support their color quality-control communication abilities and Dystar to support their dye formulas. The use of these color-matching systems allows for the specification of color to be transmitted with accuracy via phone, fax, or the internet.

Color Approval Process

Once seasonal color standards are selected, a master list is developed that identifies the colors for a season by brand, color name, delivery, and the color code that correlates to the color system used. The product developer sends color specifications to the agent, full-package contractor, or the textile or notions vendor specifying that the fabric(s) or notion(s) selected must match the product developer's color standard.

Manufacturing partners may either order physical color standards from the designated color-matching library or rely on digitally communicated spectral reflectance formulas to interpret the colors. Spectral data must be accompanied by color tolerances, illuminant specifications, and measurement protocol.

Visual Color Approval

Visual color approvals match dyed yardage to the physical color standard specified by the brand. Once received, the physical standards need to be carefully stored to protect them from dust and light; they should be touched as little as possible. Even with proper handling, physical color standards cut from the same cloth may not be identical after they arrive at the mills, as they have been exposed to different handling, temperature, and humidity conditions.

Sourcing partners are generally given two weeks to dye a sample of the actual fabric or trim specified to match the color standard as closely as possible. These samples, called **lab dips**, must be submitted to the product developer for evaluation on color evaluation forms, completed by the contracted manufacturer, mill, agent, or dyehouse (Figure 5.14). The evaluation form includes the following information:

- Submission status (first, second, third, fourth, or fifth submission)
- Color standard (number and name)
- Vendor (mill, dyehouse or print facility, and agent)
- Garment description (collection, garment number, group, season, and delivery date)
- Fabrication (fiber content)

Separate lab dips are submitted for each fabric and color specified. If a fabric is being produced at duplicate mills, each mill is required to submit its own lab dips. If the first set of lab dips is not approved, a second, third, or even fourth set is required. With each set of physical lab dips, time and money are lost. Lab dips cost $100–150 a piece, much of which goes to courier services. (Browersox, May 19, 2020).

Visual color reports are written using directional language. For instance, "lighter" means to move the color toward white and "darker" means to move it toward black.

SUBMIT STATUS (CHECK ONE):   ____ 1 ____ 2 ____ 3 ____ 4 ____ 5

DATE LAB DIP SENT: _____   PASS/FAIL RETURN DATE: _____

Submit 4 lab dips per color, one color per page: Minimum 2" by 2" lab dip size

Vendor: Mill: Dyehouse: Agent: Phone #: Email: Season: Color Standard #: Color Standard Name: Fabrication/Fiber Content: Brand Name Collection Name:	Attach swatch here Mill Lab Dip #	Attach swatch here Mill Lab Dip #	Attach swatch here Mill Lab Dip #	Attach swatch here Mill Lab Dip #
VALUE Lighter=move closer to white Darker=move close to black				
CHROMA Brighter=move closer to pure hue Duller=move closer to neutral gray				
HUE Based on CIEL *a*b				
PASS				
FAIL				

COMMENTS: The noted correction is in the direction that the lab dip must change visually in order to match our standard

AUTHORIZED SIGNATURE: DATE:

"Brighter" suggests adding more hue and "duller" suggests moving toward neutral gray. If the hue itself is off, comments suggest adding more or less blue, green, yellow, or red. It can be misleading to make comments in terms of percentages because the amount of colorant it takes to shift a color varies dramatically, depending on the color and fiber content (Figure 5.15).

Figure 5.14
Typically, four lab dips are submitted at a time for approval.

STANDARD　　　LOT SAMPLE

Sample is lighter
and greyer than
standard

Sample is redder
and darker than
standard

Sample is yellower
and lighter than
standard

Figure 5.15
Fabric dyes rely on a
complex subtractive
color-mixing system
with color formulas
varying depending on
the type of dye and
substrate used. As a
result, colorists indicate
the direction they
need a color to move
to meet the standard,
rather than speaking in
percentages.

Visual color approvals can take up a big chunk of the product development calendar, forcing design decisions to be made early to accommodate the approval process. Regionalizing the color approval process by setting up regional color management offices near the factories where fabric is being produced can shorten that time.

A good eye for color is a valuable tool, particularly for those working in color management. Several tests measure color perception, including the Ishihara Color Blindness Test, the HVC Color Aptitude Test, and the Farnsworth-Munsell 100-Hue Test. Globally, about one out of twelve men and one out of two hundred women have defective color vision, commonly called color blindness.

Even among people who are not color-blind, aptitude for judging colors varies. This capability varies even among experts as a result of normal variation in the human eye. Furthermore, color perception can be compromised by fatigue, illness, and age. Most people can only remember specific colors for a period of two to three seconds. Because of all these variables, visual color evaluation will always be subjective. Color differences perceived by the human eye are difficult to quantify and communicate. In spite of these limitations, the human observer will generally be the final judge when there is a question as to whether a color is within an acceptable range of the standard.

Digital Color Approval
Digital color approvals are now the standard for matching solid fabrics. The goal of digital color measurement is to obtain repeatable numeric values that correlate to visual assessment and translate into accurate dye recipes for a variety of fibers and dyes. The implementation of digital color communication can take weeks or even months off the product development calendar and allows designers to make critical decisions closer to the actual selling season. Throughout the supply chain, colors are more apt to be right the first time, saving time and money. The elimination of the need to air ship lab dips between product developer and vendor yields further cost savings. Companies can specify color by numbers and set clear and measurable pass/fail limits or tolerances for color approval, allowing certified suppliers to make decisions and to manage exceptions. The steps to digital color communication include the following:

- A product developer selects a color standard and measures it on a spectrophotometer (a color-measuring instrument).
- Color-matching software identifies the closest color standard from whatever digital color libraries are available or specified.

- The color standard then appears as a digital image on the computer monitor, which has been calibrated for color accuracy.
- The standard, along with clear acceptance tolerances, is electronically sent to the supplier, where the digital color sample is translated to the appropriate dye formula for the fiber/component being produced, and trial color samples are produced and measured on a spectrophotometer.
- The supplier may be certified to approve the sample if it falls within accepted pass criteria or it may electronically send back a digital sample of the best possible color match to the product developer, where it can be compared to the standard on the calibrated monitor. If the match is not accepted, more color matching is requested. The supplier sends additional digital samples until the product developer approves the color match (Mulligan, 2005).
- Colors that need to be dyed on several different fabrics can be presumed to match if the reflectance data are the same.
- Color standards can be digitally archived for quality assurance and future use (Figure 5.16 and Figure 5.17).

Even digital measurements may be subject to irregularity. The surface appearance of a fabric, created by texture—shiny or matte, reflective or diffusive—can add depth to a color's appearance. Pile fabrics absorb light, thus giving the color more depth. Shiny fabrics reflect light, thus making the color appear lighter. In addition, colorants may change a fabric's reflective properties. On a single garment, different fabrics, thread, buttons, and zippers may all be required to match. Mixed fiber materials are more difficult to match than single fiber materials. Although each dyer has the same standard and identification number for matching color, different fabrics and components can end up looking very different.

Figure 5.16
Accurate color management depends on inputting measurable color standards so that they can be translated digitally for accurate output.

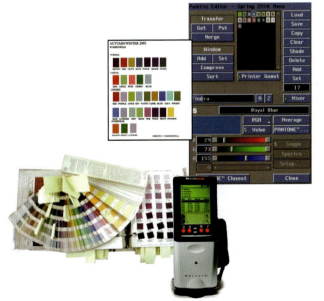

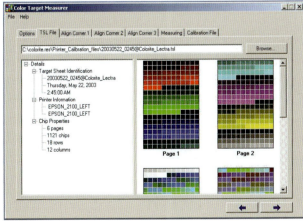

Figure 5.17
Digital color
visualization technology
now allows color
management to
approve lab dips on
the computer screen,
thus maintaining color
integrity throughout the
supply chain.

Once the garment goes into production, the quality assurance department monitors production yardage to ensure that it is consistent with the approved lab dip. Dyeing a sample in a color lab and dyeing production yardage in the dye-house can yield somewhat different results. The source of the fiber, water source, weather conditions, and other variables can cause variation in dyeing the production yardage.

In general, tolerances for matching color standards for separates may be looser than those for coordinates. Some companies are known for repeating neutrals or core colors in their line from season to season so that customers can grow their wardrobes and be assured that what they bought last year will coordinate with new items. These product developers are especially diligent about making sure that colors are within tolerance. Likewise, product developers at higher price points may adhere to stricter tolerances than mass-merchant product developers. Sometimes colors are approved, even though they are out of tolerance, just because time has run out and orders may be cancelled if stores do not receive their full shipment of colors on time.

These variations may result in the need for **shade sorting**, which refers to grouping shades together for distribution to specific customers or regions. Shade sorting of finished goods is a function of quality management. Shade sorting is more challenging in today's multichannel retail environment where a consumer might purchase one piece in-store and a coordinating piece online.

Prints and Yarn-Dyed Fabrics

While digital color approvals have become the standard for solid fabrics, up until recently the same technology could not accurately measure novelty weaves, yarn dyes and printed fabrics which may make up 50 percent of a brand's seasonal fabric story. New technology called **hyperspectral imaging** uses sensors to collect information as a set of images, rather than a single image. It breaks a print down into many different images across the electromagnetic spectrum. The result is an accurate analysis of each color in the pattern.

Print fabrics must still be submitted as one full repeat of pattern in the form of a **strike-off** to approve registration (the actual color placement on the fabric) or a computer-aided design (CAD) file with a color key of all colors that appear within the print. If hyper spectral imagery is not used, then each color in the print must be approved separately. Before this technology a print with twelve to fifteen different colors in it was too costly for most brands. The time it took to approve print colors nullified some of the gains made in digital color approvals. Hyperspectral imaging is a game changer in shortening the product development calendar.

Color Measurement

Whether product developers rely on visual or digital color approval, they must have a basic understanding of the instrumentation used to measure color objectively and how that data can be used for color management. Changes in temperature, humidity, presentation of the cloth, and equipment calibration can cause variations in readings. Most of these conditions can be controlled. Certified color partners must understand these nuances and have the most up-to-date equipment if color approvals are to be made digitally.

The American Association of Textile Chemists and Colorists (AATCC) publishes standards for the visual and instrumental measurement of color. These standards establish procedures and conditions for measuring color for the purpose of achieving a color match. Because application of these standards is typically covered in textile or color curriculums, the discussion that follows provides only an overview.

Instruments

For the most part spectrophotometers have replaced colorimeters for color measurement. **Spectrophotometers** compare the amount of light used to illuminate an object with the amount of light that is reflected back from that object. A ratio is calculated at each wavelength in the visible spectrum in order to measure color accurately. They are the preferred instruments for color identification, detection of metamerism, and color formulation. Handheld versions can help a designer document and read color inspiration without having to buy or collect physical samples. Those initial readings can be used to select color standards from a color library. More sophisticated spectrophotometers are used to match lab dips and production yardage to the color standard, providing measurements that can be compared when the color is viewed under multiple light sources. Hyperspectral spectrophotometers can measure multiple colors in the same fabric. Spectral data can be converted into RGB language for monitor display, into CYMK or extended gamut (EG) language for printers, and to recipes for various dyes.

Illuminants

Generally, lab dips are measured under at least two light sources, commonly known as **illuminants**. One illuminant simulates store light so that the product developer can be sure that the components and resulting garments match in the store. The second illuminant simulates daylight so that an acceptable match is perceived once the garments leave the store. Evaluating lab dips under two light sources reduces problems of metamerism.

SUSTAINABILITY

The implementation of up-to-date color management protocols can have a great impact on sustainability. Efficiencies can be realized from color story management, the color approval process, and new technology in dyeing and printing.

The fashion system has used color to entice consumers to buy new apparel before they've worn out what they already have. Color stories that evolve from delivery to delivery, rather than change dramatically, allow consumers to pair pieces from multiple deliveries and encourage wardrobe building and a slower-paced fashion system. Using the same neutral color standards from season to season encourages brand loyalty. Navy or grey garments purchased over several years' time will still match.

The time and cost savings that can be achieved through the implementation of digital color approvals has been discussed previously. Figure 5.18 summarizes the savings that can be realized throughout the product development process by replacing physical color measurement processes with digital color tools.

The dyeing and printing processes offer some of the most significant opportunities for a more sustainable fashion industry. Not only does the dyeing process require huge volumes of water, but it also uses large amounts of energy to heat that water. The textile industry is the second most polluting industry in the world. Twenty percent of global water pollution can be linked to textile dyeing processes. Excess nonbiodegradable petroleum-based colorants and the toxic agents used to fix those colorants onto the textiles are released into the ecosystem (Figure 5.19). Chemical suppliers are not legally required to list all of the ingredients in dyes, many of which are carcinogenic.

Figure 5.18
Digital color approvals can shave off months from the product development calendar.

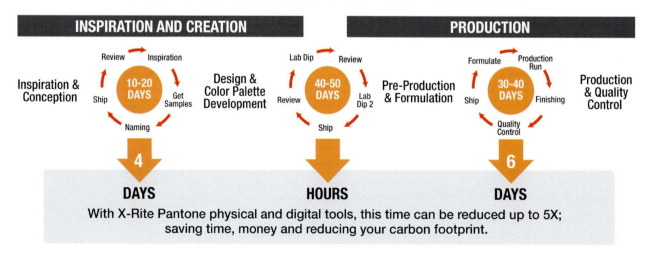

Figure 5.19
The untreated water used in textile dyeing contaminates a river in India; this is the same water that nearby residents rely on as their water source.

Eighty percent of textile supply chains exist outside of the US and EU, making it difficult to track these chemicals in countries where the industry is unregulated by the government. To meet the demand for ever-lower costs, too many dyehouses do not treat the wastewater before it flows into the same water resources on which families rely for drinking and other household needs. Many brands don't even know the companies that are dyeing their textiles as they leave textile sourcing to their manufacturing partners.

New technology and processes for applying color have the potential to reverse many environmental harms particularly in relation to water consumption and contamination. It is imperative for consumers to exert their influence to make sure that brands become more transparent about their textile supply chain and more responsible for unsustainable dyeing and printing practices.

Digital printing technologies are more sustainable than traditional alternatives. The use of pigments rather than dyes on only the areas of fabric that will be used in the garment minimizes water use and eliminates waste that contaminates waterways. Digital printing saved over 40 billion liters of water worldwide in 2018, uses 10 percent the volume of colorant than screen printing uses, and eliminates the need for water and energy in post processing (McGeegan, 2019).

Solution-dyeing is a technique that reduces the use of water and chemicals by mixing the pigment in the liquid polymer solution of synthetic fiber before it is made into filaments. It can be used with raw or recycled fiber and allows the coloration to take place without additional water and chemical waste. For synthetic fibers that require dyeing after fiber extrusion, AirDye uses dispersed dyes that are applied to a paper carrier. With heat alone, AirDye transfers dye from the paper to the textile's surface. The paper can be recycled, 90 percent less water is used, and 85 percent less energy is used. It has the advantage of being able to dye one side of the fabric solid and the other side of the fabric a print.

Huntsman has developed a line of dyes for cotton called Avitera which bonds to the fiber with one-quarter to one-third less water and one-third less energy. They leave little unfixed dye to be removed.

Cotton requires more water than any other textile for dyeing—about 200 liters of water per 1 kg. of fabric. Dow's EcoFast Pure™ and ColorZen™ are both pretreatments for cotton that produce cationic cotton. The pretreated cotton acquires a permanent positive charge that gives it a higher affinity for negatively charged dye molecules. These pretreatments result in cotton that requires less water, less energy, and fewer chemicals during the dye process.

Officina+39 is an Italy-based company that has developed a sustainable dye range called Recycrom. It uses recycled clothing, fiber material, and textile scraps, which are crystalized into an extremely fine powder that can be used as a pigment to dye fabrics and garments made of cotton, wool, nylon, or any other natural fiber. Recycrom can be applied to the fabrics using exhaustion dyeing, dipping, spraying, screen printing, and coating. It is applied as a suspension rather than a chemical solution so it can be easily filtered from water.

Colorfix employs a synthetic biological approach to dyeing that uses bacteria to color textiles and reduce water consumption by ten times. Dye-producing bacteria are affixed to the fabric using a carbon source solution followed by deposition and fixation of dye onto fabrics with a single heating cycle by the lysis of the microorganisms. There is no dye extraction process and no fixing or reducing agents are necessary.

Huntsman Textile Effects has introduced Alvitera, a line of polyreactive dyes for cotton that readily bond to fiber. They use trifunctional chemical reactivity that provides a high reaction and fixation rate leaving very little unfixed dye to be removed or rinsed away.

These technologies and more could revolutionize the impact of the textile dyeing industry but greater transparency and global cooperation will be required. Brands need to know what companies are dyeing their fabrics and they will need to partner with those companies in order for technology adoption to take place.

SUMMARY

Color management begins the moment the seasonal color palette is determined and continues until the product reaches the store. Seasonal color palettes are the colors selected for a given season by the merchandising and/or design teams. This palette should be broad enough to appeal to a diverse range of customers, but not so large that it is unwieldy to manage and costly to produce. Color palettes may vary depending on the age, life stage, ethnicity, geographic location, and fashion level of the target customer, and on the end use of the product. Colors must also be planned so that the garments entice customers to look more closely when the clothes are merchandised on the retail floor.

An understanding of color science is imperative for efficient color management. Color is the visual perception of certain wavelengths of light by the retina of the eye. Color cannot be seen in the absence of light. Colorants impart color to another substance. Color is perceived when light strikes a surface that contains the colorant.

Color attributes include hue, value, chroma, and temperature. These attributes help us to express both what is going on in the zeitgeist and our own personal response to color. The Munsell Color Order System is commonly used to describe and identify color and color relationships. It describes hue, value, and chroma.

One of the challenges in managing color is that we see some color as a function of light and other color as a function of a colorant that absorbs and reflects light. The color we see on a digital device is a function of light and therefore is achieved using the additive color mixing system with red, blue, and yellow as its primary colors. Printed or dyed output on a substrate relies on a colorant which may be transparent or opaque. Printer inks, dyes, photographic films are all examples of transparent colorants that can be mixed using the subtractive primaries of cyan, magenta, and yellow. When using opaque pigments, such as paints and thickened colorants used for some methods of textile printing, a broader gamut of color can be achieved using red, yellow, and blue, the primaries of the complex subtractive color mixing system. As a result, each substrate and colorant combination has a unique range or gamut of color that can be achieved.

The goal of color management is to have every item in the seasonal line match or coordinate with each other. The seasonal color palette is matched to color standards. Pantone and CSI are two commonly used color libraries that offer color standards on a variety of substrates. Each supplier must match all garment components to those standards using visual or digital methods. Digital color measurement can shave weeks off of the product development calendar but until recently could not be used to match colors in prints or yarn dyes. Hyperspectral imaging now allows color matching on multicolored fabrics to be approved digitally. Color matching software is available to link the readings of spectrophotometers to the computer so that onscreen colors match physical samples and can be exchanged digitally among supply chain partners.

Even after rigorous color matching protocols, color variations can occur. The components for each product may be manufactured in different locations which means different temperatures, water sources, etc. Although colors are identified by numbers that represent their hue, value, and chroma, the same color may appear different visually when applied to fabrics with different fiber contents or have different surface texture such as luster and nap. Fabrics of different fiber contents take up color differently and therefore require different dye formulas to achieve the same color.

Up-to-date color management protocols have the potential to shave a great amount of time off of the product development calendar. This helps brands to avoid the overproduction that occurs when they commit to quantities before orders come in. It also allows for more feedback from the ultimate consumer before committing to a color story. Color stories that evolve from season to season and delivery to delivery encourage wardrobe building and slower-paced fashion consumption. New textile dyeing technology can slow or reverse the damage done to waterways in developing countries.

Case Study 5.1
Ralph Lauren
Color on Demand

Color on Demand is what Ralph Lauren describes as the world's first scalable, zero wastewater cotton dyeing system. According to a report from the Ellen MacArthur Foundation, Circular Fibres Initiative, the process of dyeing fabric uses trillions of liters of water; the textile industry is responsible for 20 percent of the world's wastewater (Joe, March 25, 2021). The pollution caused by textile dyeing requires lengthy and costly treatment to make the water reusable.

The new system will reduce water waste and also establish an efficient and sustainable method of dyeing cotton that moves the dyeing process option to any point in product manufacturing compared to the traditional process that gives this option only at the beginning of the production cycle. It also reduces the amount of chemicals, dye, energy, and time used in the cotton dyeing process. This will enable shorter lead times for making product color decisions.

Ralph Lauren's new system has been developed in collaboration with four leading innovators in their respective fields. Agrochemical giant Dow is a leader in materials science and was helpful in tackling the issues of pollution and water scarcity. Jeanologia is a leader in sustainable solutions for garment and fabric finishing, with extensive expertise in garment dyeing and closed loop water treatment systems. Huntsman Textile Effects is a global chemicals company specializing in textile dyes and chemicals. Corob is a global technology leader in dispensing and mixing solutions to reimagine each stage of the coloring process.

During the first phase of *Color on Demand*, the company optimized the use of ECOFAST™ Pure Sustainable Textile Treatment, a pretreatment solution developed by Dow for cotton textiles. When used with existing dyeing equipment, ECOFAST™ Pure uses up to 40 percent less water, 85 percent fewer chemicals, and 90 percent less energy for a 60 percent reduction in carbon footprint compared to traditional cotton dyeing processes. Ralph Lauren is integrating this process into its supply chain (RalphLauren.com, March 22, 2021).

Color on Demand is a part of Ralph Lauren Corporation's *Design the Change* environmental strategy. This strategy is anchored in commitments to creating timeless style; protecting the environment; and championing better lives. Ralph Lauren hopes to eliminate hazardous chemical use and reduce its water usage by 20 percent across its value chain by 2025. The *Color on Demand* system represents a significant step towards these goals. The company hopes that the *Color on Demand* platform will be implemented in 80 percent of their solid cotton products by 2025.

Ralph Lauren is part of the *G7 Fashion Pact*, a group of fashion leaders that are working together to restore biodiversity and protect the earth's oceans. The company is also a signatory to the *We Are Still In* declaration and the *UN Fashion Industry Charter for Climate Action*. In addition, Ralph Lauren supports Natural Fiber Welding, a company researching technology that is commercializing sustainable materials and is looking to set up a new facility to produce plastic-free and plant-based leather.

References

Joe, Tanuvi. (2021). "Ralph Lauren Unveils New System That Recycles & Reuses Water from The Cotton Dyeing Process," March 25. (accessed on June 7, 2021). https://www.greenqueen.com.hk/ralph-lauren-unveils-new-system-that-recycles-reuses-water-from-the-cotton-dyeing-process/

Lockwood, Lisa. (2021). "Ralph Lauren Seeks to Transform How Fashion Industry Dyes Cotton," *Woman's Wear Daily*, March 22. https://wwd.com/fashion-news/designer-luxury/ralph-lauren-transform-how-fashion-industry-dyes-cotton-1234784109/ (accessed on 6/1/2021).

Ralph Lauren Revolutionizes How The Fashion Industry Dyes Cotton. (2021). March 22. https://corporate.ralphlauren.com/pr_210322_ColorOnDemand.html (accessed on June 1, 2021).

KEY TERMS

achromatic

additive color-mixing system

analogous

chroma

chromatic

color

colorants

color constancy

color harmonies

color inconstancy

color management

color-matching system

color solids

color standard

color temperature

colorways

complementary

complex subtractive color-mixing system

coordinates

dye

field-size metamerism

gamut

geometric metamerism

hue

hyperspectral imaging

illuminant metamerism

illuminants

intermediate colors

lab dips

monochromatic

nanometer

observer metamerism

pigment

primary colors

secondary colors

separates

shade

shade sorting

simple subtractive color-mixing system

spectrophotometers

strike-off

substrate

subtractive color-mixing system

tint

value

DISCUSSION QUESTIONS

1. Discuss how the seasonal colors for the current season vary between discount, moderate, and better stores in your area. How do the colors found in the marketplace relate to seasonal color forecasts that you have used?
2. What factors may cause materials that were matched to the same standard to appear as different colors?
3. How can metamerism be avoided?
4. Why is shade sorting sometimes necessary, even after diligent color matching?
5. What are the advantages of digital color matching?

ACTIVITIES

1. Match the color of garments or fabric swatches you have brought to class to Pantone color chips. Do you and your classmates agree on which color chip matches the closest? Do the same for all of the colors in a print.
2. Try to find an example of metamerism—two garments that match under one illuminant but not under another.
3. Test your color sensitivity by taking the Farnsworth-Munsell 100-Hue Test (http://www.xrite.com/custom_page.aspx?PageID=77).
4. Shop a favorite brand both in-store and online. Identify the colors they have chosen for their seasonal color palette. If they stock both women's and men's apparel,

contrast the color palette of each division. Ask store personnel when the various groups on the floor were shipped. Analyze that product developer's seasonal color palette to determine how it relates to their target customer. How does the brand name their colors?

5. Using the research you completed for #4 and any color forecasts that you may have available, develop a color story for the upcoming season. Think about the palette you develop and whether it promotes "fast fashion" or "slow fashion."

6. Select a color story from a color trend forecast resource. Mix those colors on your computer screen and save them as a color palette. Adjust your printer codes to match the screen colors.

STUDIO RESOURCES

- Take the chapter quiz with scored results and personalized study tips.
- Review glossary flashcards to build your vocabulary.
- Read "Color Case Study" and discuss in class.

REFERENCES

Agarwal, N. (2003), "A note on color inconstancy," www.techexchange.com (accessed July 30, 2006).
Long, J., and J. T. Luke. (2001). *The new Munsell student color set*. New York: Fairchild Publications.
Mulligan, S. (2005), "How to ensure effective color in today's manufacturing processes (and why it's more important than ever today)," www.techexchange.com (accessed August 2, 2005).

ADDITIONAL RESOURCES

Color Association. http://www.colorassociation.com. Website for The Color Association of the United States (CAUS).
Color Marketing Group. www.colormarketing.org. Website for the Color Marketing Group.
Color Matters. www.colormatters.com. Website of J. L. Morton, professor of color and color consultant.
Color Vision. www.handprint.com/HP/WCL/wcolor.html. Useful information on color science and color theory.
Commission Internationale de l'Éclairage [International Commission on Datacolor]. www.datacolor.com. Datacolor is a leader in intelligent color management, providing color-matching software, on-screen color simulation software, shade-sorting software, spectrophotometer-calibration software, and more.
Inter-Society Color Council. www.ISCC.org. Access to online quiz on common color myths.
Munsell. http://munsell.com. Information on the Munsell Color System.
Pantone Color Institute. www.pantone.com. Information about Pantone color products and articles about color management.
Techexchange. http://www.techexchange.com/index_libraryTE.php. Good source for articles on color management.
X-Rite. http://www.xrite.com/en/. Information on X-Rite, Pantone, and Munsell color management products and classes.

CHAPTER 6

FABRICATION

"There is no beauty in the finest cloth if it makes hunger and unhappiness."
MAHATMA GANDHI

OBJECTIVES

- To understand the context in which decisions about selecting textiles are made
- To recognize the constraints that mills impose on fabric purchases
- To consider the characteristics of fiber, yarn, construction, and finish in the context of aesthetic properties
- To recognize the effect of fiber, yarn, construction, and finish on utilitarian properties
- To reflect on the consequences of textile production on the environment and on the lives of producers
- To recognize new initiatives and processes that may lead to sustainability of textile production

FABRIC AND TRIM SELECTION

Fabrication is the process of selecting textiles and trims for each style and group in a line. The textiles chosen for the entire line or a group within it are frequently referred to as a **fabric story**. Although a fabric story starts with a concept, it evolves over time as the decisions made become more and more specific (Figures 6.1a and b). Decisions about textiles are made in each phase of the product development process.

Line Planning

During line planning, very general decisions about which textiles to purchase are made by marketing and merchandising teams. Their choices are made based on trend forecasts and an evaluation of how the previous seasonal line performed. If products

Figure 6.1a
This concept or mood board uses references from art, fashion, and documentary photography to create a fashion idea that will appeal to the customer and follow current trends as defined by the merchandisers.

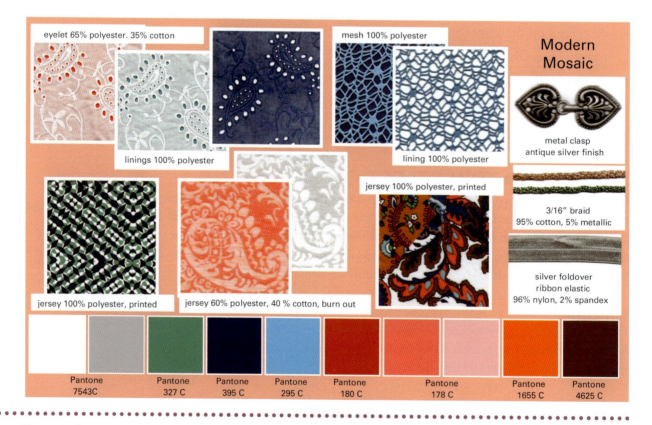

Figure 6.1b
This fabric story board shows textiles and trims that have been selected to reflect the aesthetic represented in the mood board. The materials shown will also suit the target market and the merchandiser's suggested price point.

sold well, the textiles can be repeated. If products did not sell well, there will be an analysis of what went wrong. Was the fabric launched too early? Had the fabric passed its prime? Research will be conducted into consumer needs, trends, and vendor offerings for replacements and a new direction will be established. To reflect current trends and at the same time differentiate the brand from competitors who are following the same trends, a brand might:

- Select a unique color story that follows trends and yet stays true to the brand identity
- Seek fabrics similar to higher-priced competitors
- Avoid fabrics being used by lower-priced competitors
- Integrate innovative performance features
- Spotlight best practices in sustainable textile production
- Include distinctive novelty fabrics and exclusive prints

The search for novelty and innovation brings merchandisers and designers to domestic and/or international fabric and print shows. Texworld USA in New York, International Textile Expo in Las Vegas, and Los Angeles Textile Show are just a few that feature vendors from all over the world with not only fabric but trims as well.

Some vendors may offer products as well as supply chain links. For example, an embroidery vendor may work closely with mills that supply the textiles that are best suited to their machinery. Materials vendors send their representatives (reps) to the shows; they follow up on potential sales afterwards.

Designers can also stay informed about options and trends by maintaining relationships with sales reps from a variety of fabric and trim vendors. In some companies, designers are encouraged to work with specific suppliers because of long-standing relationships based on reliable price, quality, delivery, and sustainability. Reps get to know what a brand is looking for and will send sample cards when new materials arrive on the market.

Large companies maintain their own libraries of samples gathered at shows or sent in by reps so that designers have access to fabric and trim information at a moment's notice.

Online sourcing is becoming an increasingly common method for finding fabric and trim, particularly for basic goods, because of the potential to reduce lead times, increase innovation, decrease the need for travel, and cut costs.

Many companies source their products from agents or factories who supply the whole package. Product developers may specify an exact textile and material that they saw at a show or found in a competitor's garment, or they may specify general characteristics and expect the vendor to do the sourcing. Vendors may offer what they have in stock or what they can obtain in the least amount of time at the lowest cost. They may order the products from vendors recommended by the developer or conduct research until similar products are found.

Line Development

During the development of the line plan, merchandisers and designers collaborate to make decisions about the mix of garment categories and the budget for production. They will balance cost of goods with consumer demands for unique or exclusive looks and sustainability. They will verify the availability of goods from suppliers when they review the merchandising calendar. At this point, the fabric story will include specific types of textiles and a color story. Fabric samples with a paper header or sticker that includes technical information about the textile as well as the price and ordering details (Figure 6.2), or color photos gathered from trade shows and other sources, will be organized and pinned to boards for discussion and selection (Figure 6.3).

As the fashion industry evolves, so will decision-making strategies for designers and merchandisers. In lines developed for traditional women's career wear or casual sportswear, merchandisers decided first what textiles to use for the heavier **bottom-weight** products (typically more than 6.0 ounces per square yard) such as pants, skirts, and jackets. Then lighter weight, or **top-weight** textiles (typically less than 6.0 ounces per square yard), were chosen for blouses, soft dresses, knit tops, and so on. Buying habits are shifting away from coordinated head to toe looks towards item purchases, so some lines such as dresses are organized around a single weight of fabric with variations in surface design. As the influence of active sportswear increases, the concept of layering is becoming more important, so textiles in some lines are referred to as base layer, mid layer, insulating layer, and shell layer, which are distinguished not by weight but by their contribution to managing body temperature.

Another equally important and overlapping criterion for choosing fabric is the mix of basic and novelty goods. Traditional brands with an established presence in the market had an advantage when planning lines. Their loyal customers were familiar with the performance and quality of the brand's **basic goods** (textiles) and did not expect radical changes from year to year; they looked for the gradual introduction of new colors, weave patterns, and weights each season and replaced pieces as they wore out or became outdated. They expected pieces cut in basic textiles, such as pants, skirts, and jackets, which provide a backdrop for items such as tops and sweaters made as **novelty goods**

Figure 6.2
Textile suppliers present samples of their products to designers and merchandisers with paper headers or cards that include technical information about the textile as well as the price and ordering details.

Figure 6.3
Fabric samples and color photos gathered from trade shows and other sources will be organized and pinned to boards for discussion and selection by merchandisers and designers during line development.

(Figure 6.4) featuring fresh print designs, new knit stiches and yarns, or new weaving patterns. Fast fashion brands were less likely to follow this approach. Customers of stores such as H&M found capsule groups with mostly novelty goods that told a story on the floor but were purchased as individual items to be combined for individual looks.

In the wake of COVID-19, consumer demand has led brands to rethink merchandising strategies that drive consumption and waste. Concepts such as durability, wearability (Nishimura, 2020), seasonless dressing (Taylor, 2020) and casual workwear (Young, 2020) are changing the way products are designed, selected, and presented for sale. Terms for textile categories will be likely to change as well.

To keep a line balanced, a large percentage of items need to be cut from basic goods. This is because producing textiles in bulk, with the same specifications, the same color, and the same delivery time, keeps costs down. Fabric mills make little or no money on small quantities, so they establish **minimums**, the smallest orders that they can make at a profit. Novelty textiles may be chosen to add "pop" to a collection, but they must be used in enough items in the line so that the cumulative yardage will meet the minimum. Therefore, designers must be creative and use novelty goods in multiple items as tops, skirts, linings, edge trims, or accessories.

Small businesses face many challenges when they buy textiles. They can rarely meet mill minimums and have to buy fabric from **jobbers**, middlemen who buy in bulk and sell in smaller quantities at higher prices. Because small businesses buy small quantities, they cannot demand exclusive colors or designs. They must buy **off-the-card**, meaning that they have to buy what the mill is offering as shown on sample cards with no changes. All the other small businesses will order from the same cards. When they demand consistent quality or refunds for poor quality, they have little leverage.

The need to balance novelty and yet meet minimums applies to the purchase of trims as well as textiles. Basic closures, such as zippers and buttons, or common trims, such as elastic and ribbon, can be bought in large quantities from the manufacturer's representative or in smaller orders through jobbers. Exclusive decorative items, such as logo zipper pulls, have high minimums.

Assortment Planning

During assortment planning, decisions made by designers, merchandisers, and production planners are far more detailed. Their decisions include descriptions and sketches of silhouettes and design details, as well as the distribution of units per style, fabric, trim, and color. At this point, the fabric story becomes an integral part of assortment planning (see Chapter 8).

Managing **fabric costs** is critical to making a product at the appropriate price point. Fabric costs generally make up 35 to 50 percent of a domestically produced garment and 50 to 70 percent of a garment sourced offshore. When buying a full-package

Figure 6.4
Textiles in this showroom are arranged by color. In each stack there are basic goods paired with novelty goods.

product, the product developer may never know the actual cost of the textile. Vendors will provide a total price for labor, materials, transportation, fees, taxes, overheads, etc., juggling their internal costs to come up with a competitive bid for a contract. The product developers may gain an increasingly clear idea of the relative cost of fabrics when they order the same product (e.g., a classic trouser) in different fabrics across several seasons.

As sustainability becomes an increasingly important criteria for sourcing materials, so does the need for transparency. Many of the choices made by vendors to produce materials without safeguards in place for the environment were hidden behind the veil of "package" pricing. As brands start to demand sustainability certification of vendors, more additional criteria will add complexity to decisions regarding materials.

Because some materials in a line will be more costly than others, product developers may have to take a higher or lower markup to balance the expected revenue. They may ask designers to remove details or simplify sewing methods on items with more costly materials.

Timing Fabric and Trim Decisions

Product developers want to wait as long as possible to make decisions about purchasing materials in order to reduce risk; however, early decisions mean greater selection and guarantee exclusivity. Vendors of textiles and trims want to protect their own business interests. They want to lock in orders as early as possible so that they can keep their factories running without too many or too few orders. They warn developers that an early commitment will guarantee that a fabric will not be sold to a competitor and that space will be held in the production calendar. Early commitment to an exclusive textile or trim will often require a minimum order, so bigger companies have the competitive advantage over smaller ones.

Fabric decisions are best made before designing specific silhouettes. Designing a silhouette before selecting the fabric and trims often results in a design that does not work, because the materials may not perform as the designer imagined either by themselves or when they are sewn together. It is important that new textiles and trims be tested by making samples and laboratory tests (see Chapter 11). New products frequently require special handling and adjustments to machinery to meet quality expectations.

Product development houses that still have their own sample rooms buy **sample yardage**, enough fabric to make one or more samples. Because sample fabric comes from textile shows or sales reps, it may not conform to the brand's quality standards. Small amounts of sample trims are usually sent without charge for sampling. Many product development businesses, however, no longer have sample rooms; rather, they send sketches and the specification packages to their vendors to get samples made.

Sample rooms (Figure 6.5) are usually under pressure to get samples made so that the production planners can commit to purchasing fabric with adequate **turnaround time** (the lead time required for making, dyeing, and finishing the fabric and trims, in order to meet the delivery date determined by the production schedule). Turnaround

Figure 6.5
Whether sample rooms are located in the headquarters of product development houses or in the vendor's factories, they are under pressure to get samples made quickly so that a commitment can be made for purchasing fabrics with adequate lead time.

time is longer for textiles that are made to the developer's specification. Buying off-the-card reduces the turnaround time, but also reduces exclusivity.

Figure 6.6
Sample pieces of novelty textiles have to be tested and approved before they can be adopted. Vendors send in strike-offs of prints, knit-downs, or head ends of wovens. This knit-down represents the gauge and quality of the yarn as well as the stitch pattern.

Fabric Purchasing

Once a fabric is selected for the line, the product developer must commit to an initial production order with the factory, based on early sales projections. With an order in place, the factory can place an order for **production yardage**, the bulk quantity needed to produce the order, made to the brand's technical specifications. When garment sales are finalized, the initial garment order may be increased, triggering an order for additional fabric.

Even after the production yardage is ordered, decisions have to be made about whether the mill has met the standards required. In a coordinated line or group, all of the colors and textures must work with each other and with the trims. Planning can be derailed if approvals for lab dips for custom-dyed fabrics and trims do not match. Mills will send in samples of custom-made prints (strike-offs) or approval samples of knit patterns called (**knit-downs**) or woven patterns (**head ends**). When these samples come in with technical issues, timing of deliveries can be disrupted (Figure 6.6).

Unless an apparel business owns its own production facility and orders its own textiles and trims directly from the supplier, the product developer and production planner may never deal directly with the factory. When suppliers of full package products purchase the materials, they understand that it must meet the quality expectations as specified by the product developer. Product developers generally provide quality assurance manuals in which they specify the fabric tests required for each garment category. They also specify the supply chain partner designated to perform all required fabric testing. The product developer must review all the test results and make sure that the textiles are up to standard and on time.

SELECTING TEXTILES FOR THEIR PROPERTIES

Because textile choices are made for a group of products, not just one piece, it may be necessary to cut costs on some pieces to afford the attractive features in others. Substitute fabrics can be used so that the overall presentation keeps its brand appeal and so that each item meets the needs of the individual customer. During this process of substitution, it is important to keep customer preferences in mind and look for the properties they want.

Aesthetic properties are characteristics of textile products that convey meaning to the consumer. These properties can be employed to create an image of beauty, youth, health, intelligence, commitment, strength, power, flirtation, status, devotion, rebellion, obedience, etc. Meaning is expressed in apparel products through drape and hand, luster, surface interest, and other properties.

Utilitarian properties are characteristics that make the product useful to the consumer. They include safety properties such as resistance to flame or chemicals; value properties such as low cost, easy care, and durability; and comfort properties such as stretch, flexibility, softness, weight, and thermal management.

Sustainability properties are characteristics of the material itself or its production that ensure that it does not cause harm to the environment or people throughout its life cycle.

At each stage of textile manufacturing, a property can be introduced or removed, enhanced, or diminished. Textiles are produced in four stages: raw fiber production, yarn spinning, fabric construction, and finishing. The goal is always to add or change properties and make the least impact to delivery, cost, minimums, and quality.

Fiber

Fiber is the raw material that makes up textiles. Fibers are tiny and hair-like. They must be small and flexible enough to be spun into yarns and stable enough to be woven into fabric. **Natural fibers** are cultivated and harvested from animal and plant sources. Manufactured fibers include **regenerated fibers**, which start as agricultural products that are chemically transformed into liquid and then spun into fiber, and **synthetic fibers**, which are spun from melted thermoplastic compounds distilled from petrochemicals. Many properties found in textiles are caused by the chemical and physical characteristics of the fibers.

Chemical Structure

All fibers, regardless of their source, are made of long chains of molecules called **polymers**. The primary bonds that hold molecules together determine whether a fiber is strong, flexible, dye-able, absorbent, and so on. Plant fibers such as cotton and linen are made of polymers of glucose, and animal fibers such as silk and wool are formed from proteins. Synthetic fibers such as nylon and polyester have very long polymer chains composed of chemicals distilled from petroleum.

Physical Structure

Fiber length is determined by the source. Natural fibers can be short or long; cotton is short (**staple**) while silk is very long (**filament**). **Manufactured fibers** are made from liquid compounds that are forced through tiny holes in a **spinneret** and then hardened.

They can be infinitely long or cut into staple. Long filament fibers stay tucked in, so they make smoother, stronger yarns. Short staple fibers present more ends that absorb light and moisture and add to flexibility. The size of fibers is measured with several systems. In very general terms, fibers are referred to as fine, medium, or coarse. The finer the fiber, the more flexible it is; the coarser the fiber, the stronger.

The **cross-sectional shape** (viewed at 90 degrees to its length) will influence the degree of smoothness of the surface. If the surface is smooth, it is likely to reflect light and heat, repel moisture and dirt, and slip easily past other fibers. The **contour**, the form of the fiber down its length, adds to these properties. The more twisted the fiber, the more it will absorb moisture, heat, and dirt and the more it will tangle with other fibers (Figures 6.7a–c).

Yarn

Yarns are long, thin arrangements of fibers suitable for being fabricated into textiles. During the spinning of yarn, staple fibers are twisted together for strength. The amount of **twist** can add to or diminish the inherent properties of the fiber. Low twist makes yarns soft but weak. Very high twist makes yarns bouncy and dull. Filament fibers are lightly twisted (thrown) together so they can be made into textiles. There are various methods for measuring yarn size, but in general the finer the yarn, the more flexible it is; the coarser the yarn, the stronger. Thin, uniform yarns called **ply** can be spun together to make stronger yarns, and ply of different textures can be spun together to make novelty yarns.

Figures 6.7a–c
Physical characteristics of fibers: smooth fibers reflect light and repel dirt, moisture, and heat; rougher fibers absorb light, dirt, moisture, and heat.

generic fiber name	polyester & nylon	silk	rayon	acrylic	linen	cotton	wool
a. cross-sectional shape: influences the form of the surface							
b. fiber surface: smoother surfaces repel dirt, moisture, heat, and light; rougher surfaces absorb	smoother → rougher						
c. longitude shape: straight fibers make yarns that repel dirt, moisture, heat, and light; twisted or crimped fibers make yarns that absorb	straighter → twisted						

Construction

Wovens

Woven textiles are constructed on looms with two or more sets of yarns. The **warp** yarns are arranged down the length of the loom, parallel to the selvedge, and create the base of the textile. **Weft** yarns are carried across the loom in a shuttle and interlace at right angles to the warp. Garments are generally cut with the warp running vertical to the ground (Figure 6.8a).

Wovens vary by weaving pattern. Yarns in **plain weaves** are arranged very simply so that the surface is uniform. Yarns in twills and satins skip over each other, creating **floats** that reflect light so the surface looks smoother. Because the floats are not interlaced, they are free to move, making the textile more flexible. Extra yarns can be added to the warp and weft of textiles such as **jacquards** to add surface interest, absorption, warmth, weight, and so on.

Knits

Knitted textiles are made on knitting machines by interlooping one or more continuous yarns. Knits vary by the direction in which the loops are formed. **Weft knits** are formed when a yarn passes over a series of hooked needles that pull the yarn into a row of loops called **courses**. The loops of each course are pulled through the loops of the previous row. As each loop connects with the previous loop, they form a vertical chain of loops called **wales (Figure 6.8b).** Weft knits generally stretch in the weft direction. **Warp knits** are more complex. Multiple yarns arranged in the warp direction are pulled in many directions to interconnect with other loops, forming stable, strong fabrics.

Knit patterns in weft knits are formed by dropping stitches or picking up stiches from one row to another. Adding more dropped or picked up stitches adds lots of

Figures 6.8a–c
The characteristics of a textile will be affected not only by the properties of the fiber and yarn, but also by the arrangements of the yarns used in each type of construction. The three basic arrangements are woven, knit, and nonwoven.

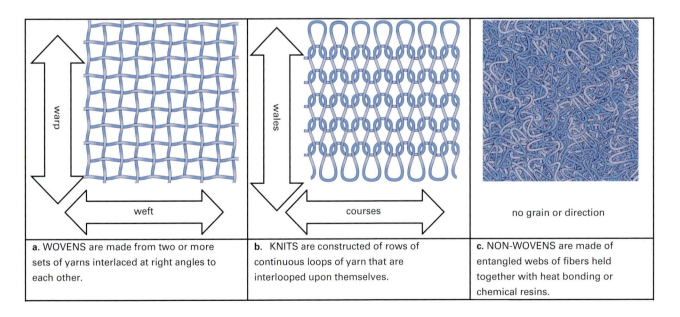

warp / weft	wales / courses	no grain or direction
a. WOVENS are made from two or more sets of yarns interlaced at right angles to each other.	**b.** KNITS are constructed of rows of continuous loops of yarn that are interlooped upon themselves.	**c.** NON-WOVENS are made of entangled webs of fibers held together with heat bonding or chemical resins.

Table 6.1 Finishing Methods That Add or Remove Properties

Chemical Finishes	• Add or remove color • Add or remove stiffness • Add resistance to water, oil, abrasion, insects, mold, etc.
Heated Rollers	• Add luster by smoothing over yarns • Add surface interest by pressing in dips and ridges that imitate woven structures (embossing)
Printing	• Adds visual interest
Brushing	• Adds visual interest • Adds thermal retention
Laminated Surfaces	• Add visual interest by imitating leather or animal skins • Add water repellency

visual texture but weakens the knit. Warp knits can have very elaborate patterns and yet be quite strong.

Nonwovens

Nonwoven textiles are created by entangling fibers and then pressing them into a smooth fabric. Some fibers, such as wool, naturally cling together, but filament polyester and nylon must be bonded together with heat or adhesives. Nonwovens are inexpensive to produce, but they are generally weak (Figure 6.8c).

Finish

Most finishes are applied to textiles after they are woven or knitted to increase or diminish properties. Finishes can also add properties that are not inherent in the fiber, yarn, or construction. In general, adding properties in the earlier stages of production is more costly and time consuming than adding them during finishing. However, finishes tend to wear off over time, diminishing the appeal (Table 6.1).

AESTHETIC PROPERTIES

Successful fashion products rely on matching aesthetic properties to the expectations of the target customer while balancing utilitarian needs and the brand's commitment to sustainability. The more a product development specialist knows about how aesthetic properties are created, augmented, or diminished, the more flexibility they will have in meeting other needs.

Drape

Drape is the tendency of a textile to cling to or stand away from a body when acted upon by gravity. When a textile resists gravity, the drape might be called stiff, hard, firm, or crisp. When the textile gives in to gravity, the drape can be called soft, clingy, swingy, bouncy, or limp. A customer looking for a tailored garment wants a firm drape. A customer searching for a party dress may want a swingy drape. **Hand** (*handle*) is the property that is experienced when a textile is crushed in the hand and then released. Most of the characteristics in fiber, yarn, and construction that produce a soft drape also create a soft hand. Conversely, stiff hand and drape are usually found together.

Fiber and Drape

Chemical structure can contribute rigidity or flexibility to fibers. If the primary bonds that hold the molecules together are strong, the fibers will give when force is applied and then spring back, as in wool. In general, fibers with strong molecular bonds drape well. If the polymer chains that make up the fiber are arranged in a very orderly fashion (crystalline), the fiber will be less flexible and not drape as well. Plant fibers such as cotton and linen are made of glucose molecules that are crystalline, so they have a crisp hand and drape.

Physical characteristics such as fiber shape can also contribute to soft or stiff drape (see Figure 6.7c). Crimped fibers are looped, folded, and twisted. They swing gracefully when the body moves and gravity tugs on them. Wool is naturally crimped and has spring and bounce that can translate into soft drape if it is spun into fine, soft yarns that take advantage of the crimp. Synthetic filament fibers tend to be stiff in their generic form but can be texturized after spinning to imitate the crimp in wool. Some fibers, such as silk, are very fine. When woven into a textile, they bend easily and therefore drape well. Coarser fibers such as hemp, when held together into a woven matrix, do not move as well.

Some fibers are rough on their surface and others are smooth. The smoothness in filament fibers allows them to slip easily past each other as the textile is pulled and moved. Filament silk, rayon, and fine polyester and nylon all drape well if subsequent stages of production do not limit their movement.

All fibers are subject to market forces. The price of cotton soared in 2010 and then went back down. Synthetics go up in price whenever the cost of oil rises. Natural fibers sometimes become scarce when natural disasters disrupt agriculture. Knowing the chemical and physical characteristics of fibers can help a developer look for substitute textiles or blends that have a similar drape and hand and can also meet delivery schedules and maintain mark-ups.

Yarn and Drape

The amount of twist can add or diminish the inherent characteristic of a fiber. The small amount of twist in flannel yarns leaves fibers soft and supple. Average twist will add firmness to fibers. Crepe yarns are twisted so much that kinks and curls make the yarns bounce and swing. Adding crepe twist to filament fibers makes them very drapey, as in polyester georgette. The more ply, the less flexible the yarn and the stiffer the drape. In general, coarse yarns will not drape as well as fine yarns (Figure 6.9a–h).

view at eye level ·· swatches are cut at 2" x 2" ·· bird's eye view

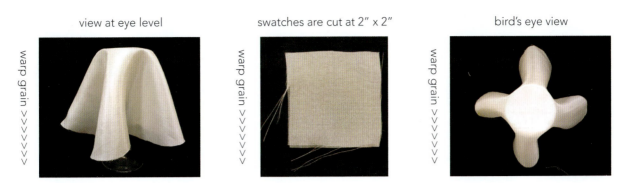

warp grain >>>>>>>>>

a. CHINA SILK: Balanced plain weave. Warp and weft yarns are both spun from the same weight of cultivated silk filament fiber. Four even folds form in the warp and weft directions.

warp grain >>>>>>>>>

b. SILK CHIFFON: Balanced plain weave. Warp and weft yarns are spun from filament cultivated silk with a crepe twist (very high twist per inch (TP)). The crepe yarns are "lively." They bounce and fall gracefully into six even flutes.

warp grain >>>>>>>>>

c. BUTCHER'S CLOTH: Balanced plain weave. Warp and weft medium-weight yarns are spun from a blend of staple-length polyester and cotton. Four folds form evenly at the bias grain and stand out firmly.

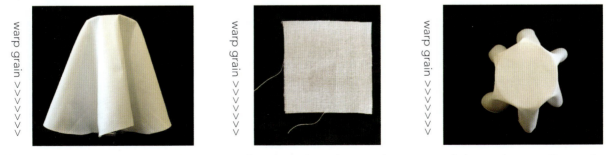

warp grain >>>>>>>>>

d. MUSLIN: Balanced plain weave. Warp and weft are spun from short-staple cotton into light-weight yarns. Six equal folds form evenly spaced in the warp, weft, and bias grains.

Figure 6.9a–d
The drape of a fabric is influenced not only by the characteristics of the fiber, but also by the yarn size, twist, and density. These fabrics (a–d) are all balanced plain weaves so the yarns are the same in the warp and the weft.

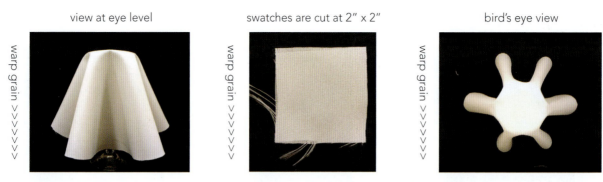

e. SILK BROADCLOTH: Unbalanced plain weave. Warp yarns are fine-filament cultivated silk at twice the count of the weft yarns which are twice as coarse. The result is similar to a balanced weave with flute of equal size evenly spaced.

f. SILK TAFETTA: Unbalanced plain weave. Warp: fine filament yarns. Weft: coarser filament yarns. The wiry weft forces folds to hang toward the weft.

g. RAW SILK: Unbalanced plain weave. Warp yarns are fine filament, cultivated silk. Weft yarns are cultivated raw silk (unwashed so the natural protein sericin acts as a starch and sticks the fibers together in thick bundles). Folds are held out by the warp and thinner flutes formed at the weft.

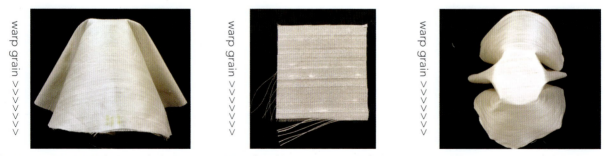

h. SILK DUPIONI: Unbalanced plain weave. Warp: fine filament yarns. Weft: very coarse and naturally uneven filament yarns. Weft forces folds to fan out in the warp direction, leaving narrow folds to form in the weft direction.

Figure 6.9e–h

The drape of a fabric can change dramatically when the warp and weft are made of different weight yarns. These fabrics (e–h) are all unbalanced plain weaves. The heavier yarns can hold out the fabric in wide or stiff folds and the finer yarns allow the fabric to hang in narrower flutes.

Construction and Drape

When a woven textile is cut into a garment with the warp grain perpendicular to the ground, gravity tugs on each yarn, pulling it straight down. The textile will "give" only to the extent of the flexibility in the fiber and yarn. So much of a textile's reaction to gravity depends on the fiber and the yarns, but the weave pattern will also influence the drape.

The **thread count** is the number of yarns per square inch or centimeter in the warp and weft direction. The higher the thread count, the more restricted the movement of the yarns. Textiles with average twist, lightweight cotton yarn, and low thread count, such as batiste, will have a soft drape. The same yarns woven in broadcloth, which has a much higher thread count, will have a crisper hand suitable for men's shirts. Extra yarns (in addition to the warp and weft yarns) tend to restrict movement and make the drape stiffer and heavier in textiles such as brocade.

Weaving patterns with more floats tend to be more flexible and therefore drape more softly. If the yarns from a textile woven with average twist, lightweight cotton yarn in a plain weave were woven with the same thread count but in a twill weave pattern, the twill would have a softer drape (Figures 6.10a–d). Even jeans made from coarse yarns and having a high thread count will drape softly around body contours because of the twill weave.

When a knitted textile is cut into a garment, gravity pulls on the loops, making them narrower and longer. At the same time, the form of the body pushes the loops out. The result is a textile that follows the contours of the body and swings free at the wrists and hem. The loops in knitted fabrics contribute to a soft drape and hand. When the yarn is thick and the stitches are close together, the drape is restricted. The same thick yarn can be knitted with larger stitches to allow more movement (Figures6.11a–c).

Finishes and Drape

Finishes are applied to textiles after they are woven or knitted. Some finishes such as enzyme wash or acid wash on denim alter the chemical structure of the fibers and make them drape more softly. Some finishes add waxes, starches, or other stiffening agents to the textile to add rigidity, such as crinoline. Silicone is sometimes added to allow yarns to slide over each other, enhancing drape, as in rayon challis. Decorative finishes that are added for visual texture, such as embroidery, can add stiffness because of extra yarns. Lamination with plastic layers can add rigidity. Brushing with hooked wire rollers can break surface fibers and soften drape. Embossing such as pleating can add bounce.

Support Materials and Drape

When designers want to create drama or interest to the silhouette, they can use **support materials** that generate contrast by restricting the drape of some parts of the garment while leaving the original drape in other parts.

view at eye level	swatches are cut at 2" x 2"	bird's eye view

 warp grain >>>>>>>>  warp grain >>>>>>>>

a. SILK BRIDAL SATIN: Satin Weave. Warp: fine filament yarns. Weft: coarse filament yarns. The floats in the warp create soft flutes that are held out by the coarse weft.

warp grain >>>>>>>> warp grain >>>>>>>>

b. SILK SATIN WITH COTTON BACK: Satin weave. Warp yarns are fine-filament cultivated silk. Weft yarns are spun from soft, fine, staple cotton.

 warp grain >>>>>>>>  warp grain >>>>>>>>

c. COTTON SATEEN: Satin weave. Warp and weft yarns are made from spun cotton of a similar weight to Figure 6.9c. The floats in the warp allow the fabric to fall in six soft folds.

 warp grain >>>>>>>>   warp grain >>>>>>>>

d. TWILL: Twill weave. The warp and weft are of similar weights but the weft yarns are spun with spandex. The flutes are evenly spaced, but the flutes at 2 o'clock and 8 o'clock are bigger because the floats are aligned with the fold.

Figures 6.10a–d
Floats are formed in a woven textile when a yarn does not interlace with the yarn running in the opposite direction for multiple yarn crossings. The floats move more freely and allow the fabric to drape along the grain in which they are woven.

These images show three fabrics knitted with medium-weight yarns spun with a blend of staple polyester and cotton fibers. Each image shows a different knitting construction. The widest circumference of form is 15 inches. Each of the fabric rectangles is cut smaller than the form. The red lines are 1 inch apart to show how much each fabric stretches.

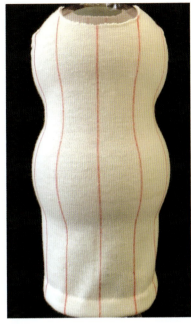

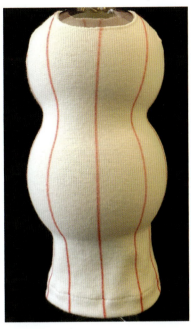

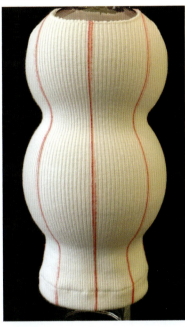

a. JERSEY SINGLE WEFT KNIT
width of knit (rectangle) 11.5″

Even though the fabric is stretched to the maximum around the widest part of the form it does not pull into the narrowest part.

b. 1 x 1 RIB
width of knit (rectangle) 9.5″

The loops in the rib knit open up and stretch over the widest part of the form and pull into the narrowest part.

c. 2 x 2 RIB
width of knit (rectangle) 8.5″

The 2 x 2 rib stretches even more than the 1 x 1. It also molds to the form.

Figures 6.11a–c
When a knitted textile is cut into a garment, gravity pulls on the loops, making them narrower and longer. At the same time, the form of the body pushes the loops out. The result is a textile that follows the contours of the body and swings free at the wrists and hem. The loops in knitted fabrics contribute to a soft drape and hand.

Interlining is a general industry term that includes knit, woven, and nonwoven products. They are rarely seen and remain hidden behind the shell fabric. They can be sewn into the seams (flat lined) or fused to the fabric. As clothing has become more and more industrialized, traditional woven interlining from natural sources such as linen, wool, and horsehair have been replaced with synthetic fibers, knit, and nonwoven construction. **Fusible interlining** was developed to eliminate the need for sewing in the interlining by hand. It has heat-sensitive dots of resin on one side that melt when heat is applied, allowing it to be uniformly bonded to the shell.

For many garments, a single product is enough to add visual contrast between firm and soft parts of the garment. For example, the collar and cuffs of a tailored shirt rely on a firm woven cotton interlining for a stiff, smooth, formal look. The collar on a soft blouse fabric might look better with a knit or woven interlining made of flexible, drapey microfibers. A synthetic jersey track jacket may use a crisp but flexible tricot to keep the stand-up collar from collapsing during exercise. More complex garments, such as formal gowns (Figure 6.12) and suit jackets, utilize a variety of interlinings (see feature on page 191).

coutille or canvas.
Very heavy corset-like foundation fabric that holds boning, cups, and wires to mold the body

grosgrain ribbon.
Used to reinforce a waistband

satin ribbon.
Used to anchor floating parts of the dress together such as the lining and the petticoats

horsehair.
Braided from heavy synthetic filament and sewn into a hem to make it flare out, defying gravity

boning.
Semi-rigid inserts for corsets or bodices made of molded plastic or wire

bra cups.
Molded synthetic foam shapes used in formal gowns, bathing suits, and lingerie

under wires.
Metal "u" shaped device sewn into support material to hold up bust

non-woven sew-in interlining.
Used to flatline the skirt to add body to make the fabric hang smoothly

crinoline.
A stiffened woven cotton layer held up by layers of shirred tulle (netting) make the skirt stand away from the wearer

Figure 6.12
When designers want to create drama or interest to the silhouette, they can use support materials that generate contrast by restricting the drape of some parts of the garment while leaving the original drape for other parts. Many of the support materials for gowns and formal dresses are traditional and require skill to create a sculpted silhouette.

Some support materials are not made entirely from textiles. Semirigid narrow inserts that hold fabric flat and smooth, such as bodice boning and collar stays, are no longer made from whale bone but from molded plastic or metal wire. These materials can be manipulated with heat and sonic waves to create shapes. Victoria's Secret is the leader in molding synthetic foams into bra cups that are manufactured without sewing. As new technology is developed in the performance sportswear industry, materials such as **neoprene**, a laminate of foam rubber and synthetic jersey, have been appearing in runway shows to add shape and volume to silhouettes.

Narrow textiles, made on looms no wider than 12 inches, such as twill tape and grosgrain ribbon and horsehair, play a role in stabilizing and shaping formal and tailored garments (Figure 6.12 and feature on page 191). **Elastic** is a narrow textile that is braided, woven, or knit with insertions of elastomeric filament such as rubber or spandex. When it is sewn in, it can completely alter the silhouette of a garment by

THE COMPASS

A Style Journal from **BLACK LAPEL**

—— SUITING 101 ——

An Introduction to Suit Jacket Construction

CHEST PIECE

CANVAS

SUITING FABRIC SHELL

In this post, we'll discuss the different types of suit jacket construction—namely, fused vs. canvassed—and why they should matter to you.

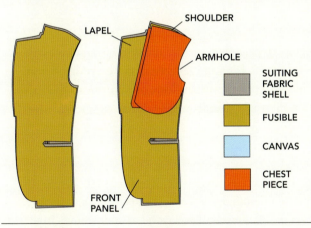

SHOULDER

LAPEL

ARMHOLE

FRONT PANEL

SUITING FABRIC SHELL

FUSIBLE

CANVAS

CHEST PIECE

FULL CANVAS

Canvassed Suit Jacket #1:
Full-Canvassed Suit Jackets are constructed with canvas fabric spanning the entire inside front panels and lapels of the jacket. As a middle structural layer, the canvas is hand stitched to the fabric rather loosely (i.e., a "floating" canvas), so the garment can move with you. Full-canvassed jackets are the most labor and time intensive, requiring a higher level of skill to make, and thus, tend to be pricier. In return for the premium paid, you get a suit that not only molds to you, but will last the longest.

SHOULDER

LAPEL

ARMHOLE

FRONT PANEL

SUITING FABRIC SHELL

FUSIBLE

CANVAS

CHEST PIECE

FUSED

Non-Canvassed Suit Jacket:
Fused Suit Jackets have a fusible interlining that's glued to the wool shell of the suit—both in the front panels and in the lapels. Suit manufacturers started using this construction method to increase production capacity while keeping costs down. It is not only quick, but it also doesn't require any skilled labor. Fusing the jacket gives it shape, but doesn't conform to the wearer, so it may lack the nice, natural drape of canvassed jackets. Poorly fused jackets can bubble (delaminate) in time!

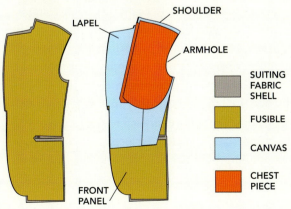

SHOULDER

LAPEL

ARMHOLE

FRONT PANEL

SUITING FABRIC SHELL

FUSIBLE

CANVAS

CHEST PIECE

HALF CANVAS

Canvassed Suit Jacket #2:
Half-Canvassed Jackets have a thin layer of fusible throughout the front panel of the jacket; on top of this layer of fusible interlining, the front panel has a layer of canvassing stitched on that extends from the shoulder down through the chest. Basically, what this means is that you get the benefits of the natural drape and shape that canvas provides where the suit needs it the most—the chest and the lapel. At the same time, you enjoy some cost savings in terms of materials and labor.

Black Lapel is a suit maker in New York. They provide custom-made suits in the store and online. Check out their blog for lots of information about how men's clothing is designed and made.

https://blacklapel.com /thecompass/anatomy -of-a-suit-jacket-fused -vs-canvassed

This case study was edited with permission from February 2013 posting.

Author's note: in addition to interlining, a men's suit is built on shoulder pads, sleeve headers, and chest pieces made of felt that help the tailor sculpt a shape for the fabric to drape on. Felt made of wool is still used in handmade products but has been replaced by polyester needle-punch felt. Woven twill tape or other stable, narrow fabrics are stitched or fused into seams to keep armholes and shoulders from stretching. These have also been replaced by non-woven, fusible products. Percaline, a fine cotton plain weave cut on the bias, smooths the outline of the shoulder pads and keeps the back from stretching out. Wiggins, a firmer bias-cut cotton plain weave, stitched into the hem keeps it smooth, yet clearly defined. Because woven cotton is costly, it is used in more exclusive products, but non-woven products are used in mass production to stiffen cuffs and hems.

restricting its movement at the waistline, wrist, or ankle opening, forcing the shell textile to balloon out. Elastic thread is used to create smocking in children's wear and tube tops.

Some textiles may have a soft drape but, because they have a rough surface, can cling to the body or other garments. **Lining**, a lightweight fabric with a smooth surface, can be added to the inside of a garment to cover the raw edges of seams and help the shell fabric slide easily and yet maintain its drape.

Adding support materials adds cost to garments, and some materials are more costly than others. Nonwovens are cheaper than knits; knits are cheaper than wovens. Natural fibers are more costly than synthetics. Fusible application is less costly than sewing in a product, but over the long term, the appearance can change. Technical designers are expected to have deep knowledge about support materials so that they can work with vendors to deliver the look that is needed without adding cost or jeopardizing quality.

Support materials have to be tested to be sure that they are compatible with the shell—that they do not change dimension, texture, or color during use and care. Large vendors of branded support materials such as Vilene will run tests to help the product developer find the products with the desired drape and hand as well as price, delivery, brand image, and long-term performance. Small companies may not have orders big enough to merit lab services from vendors and may not be able to afford independent lab fees. At a minimum, they can perform wash tests of their own to be sure the product will last.

Luster

Luster is an aesthetic property that is perceived as the amount of light reflected from the textile surface. High luster results from the reflection of a lot of light from a smooth surface. Low luster results from textiles with deep, open areas on the surface that absorb light. At each step of textile manufacturing, luster can be added or removed.

Fiber and Luster

Some fibers are naturally lustrous. Polyester and nylon filament fibers reflect a lot of light. In their generic form they are round, so light rays reflect directly back to the eye. The effect is bright. The cross section of silk is triangular. Rayon has long grooves in the surface (*striations*), and the surface of each lobe is smooth. Light rays bounce around in the grooves before reaching the eye, so the effect is luminous. These fibers can be de-lustered chemically, cut into staple length, or texturized by heating and crimping.

Some fibers are naturally dull. Cotton fiber starts out as a tube shape but folds in half and twists when it is harvested. The pocket that forms catches a lot of light. Because Egyptian and pima cotton fibers are longer staple, they have fewer ends that cast shadows and they appear more lustrous. The surface of wool fiber is covered with overlapping scales, and it is naturally crimped with tangles and loops that capture light (see Figure 6.7b). Linen fiber has smooth sides, but thick bands of cellulose at intervals and a waxy gum on the surface make it dull. The surface of acrylic fibers gets pitted during manufacturing, so even in filament form it is not shiny. Lyocell has striations that peel off over time and give the textile a surface like peach fuzz.

Yarn and Luster

Yarn spinning can add or diminish luster. Yarn spun from carded wool maintains its natural dullness, but wool can be worsted (combed and twisted) so that it appears smoother and more lustrous. Filament fibers are gently twisted (thrown) into yarn so that the reflective surface can shine without being covered up, but when they are highly twisted, as in crepe yarns, their kinks and curls can make filament dull.

Novelty yarns play with luster, breaking it up in interesting ways. Slub yarns can be created by retarding some ply in filament yarns, forming knots and bulbs. Twisted, looped, and knotted ply can be combined with smooth ply of filament for contrast. Metallic yarns made from tiny strips of plastic film can provide sparkling loops.

The definition of luster has expanded from reflected light to include projected light.Companies such as Foster Rohner use the conductivity and flexibility of yarns to embroider low-energy LED yarns into textiles to subtly emphasize surface designs (Figure 6.13) (e-broidery, 2017).

Construction and Luster

Woven patterns with floats reflect the most light. Twills have a soft sheen. When a woven surface has long floats of filament yarns, such as satin, the surface can appear very bright. When a third yarn is added to make a pile, as in velveteen, the surface is deep and very dull. Velvet plays with this depth by using filament in the pile which then twinkles as the textile moves (Figure 6.14c). Most knit constructions do not generally add luster. The loops that create knits capture light and create shadows. Some warp knits build many layers of overlapping loops that act like floats, producing a smooth, reflective surface.

Finishes and Luster

Luster can be added to very dull surfaces. Chinz is a cotton plain weave that is coated with resins and polished to a high luster with metal rollers. Imitation sequins, patent leather, and dazzling holograms can be achieved by laminating thin plastic film on inexpensive tricot (Figure 6.14f). Metallic pigments can be printed onto fabrics with a dull surface to add reflective interest. Embroidery with filament or metallic yarn can add shine (Figure 6.14g).

Luster can be reduced by napping (brushing up) the fibers of low-twist cotton or wool yarns to make flannel. Sanding with rough rollers creates a peach-skin surface on shiny crepe de chine. Finishes are an inexpensive way to add high or low luster to textiles.

Figure 6.13
Designers are using LED lights and flexible circuitry to make a dazzling impact. This suit from Akris has flexible circuits and LED lights from Foster Rohner embroidered into the fabric.

a. Satin is woven with long floats of filament yarns and a high thread count to provide a smooth surface that reflects a lot of light.

b. Chinz is a cotton plain weave that is coated with resins and polished to a high luster with metal rollers.

c. Velvet is woven with a third yarn made of filament fibers. The cut loops absorb light, but the filament reflects it, creating a rich varied luster.

d. Luster can be added to ordinary woven or knit fabric by printing with metallic inks.

e. The loops in a weft knit generally absorb light; however, textiles made with fine filament yarns knitted closely together have a soft luster.

f. Novelty costume fabric use laminates on inexpensive tricot to create very fine shiny films that imitate sequins, patent leather, and even holograms to dazzle.

g. Embroidery with filament or metallic yarns can be used to add luster to any textile.

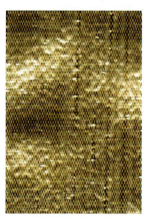

h. Lamé is woven of metallic yarns.

Figure 6.14
Luster can be the result of fiber, yarn, construction, or finish. All images are approximately 150 percent of the original.

Surface Interest

Surface interest in a textile is created by breaking up a surface into contrasting units of light reflection: shiny/dull, rough/smooth, high value/low value, high chroma/low chroma. When surface interest is introduced into a textile in the early stages of production, it is called **structural design**; structural design is added in the fiber, yarn, and construction stages. When surface interest is added to finished textiles it is called **applied design**.

Fibers and Yarns and Surface Interest

The contrasting units of light may be as small as a fiber or a ply of yarn. Yarns that provide surface interest include tweed yarns, which are spun with small "flakes" of

a. slub yarn.
A yarn made of two ply or strands, one of which is retarded during spinning to create knots resembling natural fibers such as linen or dupioni silk.

b. metallic yarn.
A yarn that is actually a very thin strip cut from a film of plastic plated with a very thin layer of metal.

c. tweed yarn.
A two-ply spun yarn into which tiny tufts of colored fiber called "flakes" are sprinkled into the yarn ply during spinning to add visual interest.

flake

flake

d. heather (mélange) yarn.
A yarn made of ply dyed with different colors. There are five ply in the yarn pictured: 2 white, 2 blue, 1 purple.

e. chenille.
A yarn that is actually a thin strip of fabric constructed like velvet. In this jacquard weave the chenille on the face gives a pebbly, soft look.

chenille on face

chenille on reverse

f. bouclé yarn.
A type of three-ply novelty yarn with pronounced loops.

effect ply
base ply
binder ply

contrasting colored fiber. Heather (*mélange*) yarns are spun with ply of various colors. Novelty yarns such as bouclé, snarl, or corkscrew combine two or more ply of vastly different textures and colors (Figures 6.15a–f).

Figures 6.15a–f
Novelty yarns increase surface interest. All images are approximately 175 percent of the original.

Woven and Knit Patterns and Surface Interest
In addition to varying the color, size, and texture of the yarn, the surface of a woven textile can be broken by varying the interlacing yarns (Figures 6.16a–j). The surface of knitted textiles is influenced by the way the loops are formed (Figures 6.17a–g).

a–b. plain weaves. Textiles that are woven on looms with two harnesses (the part of the loom that lifts and lowers the warp yarns so the shuttle can pass between carrying the weft yarn). There are only two possible warp arrangements so the surface of the textile is uniform and unbroken. The easiest way to transform a plain weave into a surface that is visually lively is by using sets of yarns of different colors in the warp or the weft (a) stripes or both (b) plaids.

c–d. rib and basketweaves. Textiles woven with yarns of different weight, texture, or luster in the warp and weft. When fine yarns are packed closely together in the warp and woven over coarser yarns in the weft, the result is a subtle, smooth texture in poplin and broadcloth. Taffeta and faille and (c) ottoman have coarser weft yarns and are more obviously "ribbed." Using multiple yarns in the warp or weft creates basketweaves such as pebbly canvas and (d) oxford cloth.

e–f. twills. Textiles in which the use of 3 to 8 harnesses allows for more warp arrangements. The warp or weft yarns can skip over more than one yarn, creating long, visible sections of yarn called "floats." Floats can be arranged in orderly diagonal rows to create twills, including gabardine, denim, (e) herringbone, or (f) houndstooth. Different colored yarns in warp and weft can bring out these geometric patterns.

g–h. jacquards. Textiles in which harnesses are replaced by wires that raise and lower the warp yarns following patterns on punch cards. The warp arrangements can multiply many times, so it is possible to create complex images combining multiple weave patterns. Damask (g) designs use yarns of different color or texture in the warp and weft, reversing the design from the face to the back. More complex jacquards use multiple colors of yarns and patterns. Brocades (h) employ extra sets of warp and weft and lots of color.

i–j. extra yarn weaves. Textiles in which extra yarns can be added to the warp and weft to make spot weaves of flowers, stripes, or dots as in dotted Swiss (i). Pile weaves use an extra yarn to create loops which can be left uncut, as in terry cloth, or cut to make corduroy (j) or velvet.

Figures 6.16a–j
Complex warp arrangements increase surface interest in wovens. All images are 200 percent of original.

a. yarn-dyed stripe

b. yarn-dyed plaid

c. rib weave: ottoman

d. basketweave: oxford cloth

e. twill weave: herringbone

f. twill weave: houndstooth

g. jacquard weave: damask

h. jacquard weave: brocade

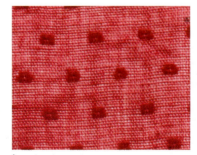
i. extra yarn weave: true dotted Swiss

j. extra yarn weave: corduroy

a. yarn-dyed stripes. Weft knits knitted with changes in yarn color at intervals.

b. tuck stitch. Weft knits with a loop from one course looping onto two or more loops from a course above resulting in lacelike patterns.

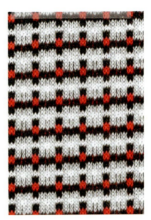

c. missed stitch. Weft knit patterns achieved by allowing a loop to skip one or more stitches causing floats.

d. three-dimensional knit. Weft knit construction with extra courses build onto existing rows. This textile has rows of ruffles knitted into the base.

face　　　　**reverse**

e. double knit jacquards. Weft knits in which two sets of needles and yarns are used. Colored yarns from one ply can be pulled through to the other ply creating intricate images and patterns that are different on each side.

f. warp knits. Knits that take advantage of the possibilities of intricate warp knitting include Missoni inspired zigzag patterns.

g. raschel knits. Include lace-like patterns in textiles for apparel and narrow fabrics for edging.

Pattern Design Development

Structural design has the advantage of being permanent, but it is more costly to produce than applied design. It also must be planned with longer lead times and higher minimums because it involves the planning and production of fiber and yarns and the setup of knitting machines or weaving looms. Although applied finishes are not as durable as structural design, they are applied after the textile is finished so they can provide unlimited variety to a market hungry for novelty and low prices.

Figures 6.17a–g
Complex patterns increase surface interest in knits. Images a,c,e–g are at 90 percent of original. Images b and d are at 180 percent of original.

Whether a surface design is structural or applied, it has to be planned to enhance the appearance of the final product. Historically, patterns for weaving, knitting, and printing were developed by painting images on paper with traditional art media, including gouache, watercolor, acrylic, markers, or pastels. Today, most are developed on the computer; the designer may use off-the-shelf software such as Adobe Illustrator® or Photoshop®, or industry-specific computer-assisted design (CAD) software such as Lectra's Kaledo®, NedGraphics, or Pointcarré. No matter how a pattern is created, it must be translated to a digital format to be scaled, colorized, and manipulated, so it can then be woven, knitted, or printed.

Weaving or knitting textiles with alternating sets of colored yarns can offer a vast variety of stripes, plaids, and zigzags that can be especially dramatic when the yarns contrast each other. These yarn-dyed patterns, however, follow the horizontal and vertical mechanism of the machines and tend to have a structured, geometric look. In woven textiles, curved images must be engineered in jacquard looms. In knitted textiles, curves and circles must be designed as double knits. Images used for prints are not confined by the mechanics of weaving and knitting; they can be much more fluid, representational, and infinitely varied.

Prints and Other Finishes

Printing is the application of a design or pattern to fabric using dyes or pigments applied in limited areas. For many segments of the apparel industry, prints are a critical element in creating novelty from season to season. Categories that rely heavily on prints for brand differentiation include children's, dress, and lingerie markets. Product developers in these categories take an active role in designing their own prints. They take advantage of the wide array of print categories, such as floral, animal, geometric, tribal, and so on, reintroducing them periodically as a way of providing novelty.

The aesthetics of print designs have evolved over time as technology has provided the capacity for expression and variety. Traditional terminology and concepts probably grew out of wood block and stencil printing. There, the visual interest is developed by the relationship first between the printed motif and the background and then between the motifs themselves (Figures 6.18a–k).

The introduction of **engraved roller printing** and **rotary screen printing** in the nineteenth century sped up production, but it confined the repeated image to the size of the roller: approximately 16 inches in diameter and 45 inches in width. Designing for roller printing is focused on disguising the repeat (where the image overlaps on the roller) and planning the colors, which are applied one at a time (Figures 6.19a–e). The design choices are further restrained by merchandising needs such as cost, minimums, width of the base goods, and yardage required, and by quality concerns such as the fiber content of the fabric and the dye or pigment formula required to achieve the range of colors specified (Table 6.2).

A firm may have one or more textile print designers with expertise in graphic design, printing technology, and CAD. The designers may draw inspiration from many sources. Independent print design resources such as Patricia Nugent Textiles store

a. motif. A unit of a larger overall design used to create a larger pattern by repetition.

b. ground. Contrasting background color or texture against which motifs are arranged to create a surface design.

c. loose coverage   **d. tight coverage**

coverage. The amount of ground visible between motifs.
layout. Placement of motifs relative to other motifs taking into consideration direction, repeat, and coverage.
set layouts. Follows an invisible grid, with the motifs arranged in a definite geometric pattern.
one way. One-way layouts—all motifs are placed facing the same direction.

e. half drop. Layout in which the top of the motif is repeated at half the distance from the top of the previously printed row.

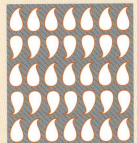

f. two-way. Motifs are alternated in up-and-down or left-and-right directions in the same pattern.

g. four-way layouts. Motifs are alternated in up-and-down and left-and-right directions in the same pattern.

h. radial balance. Motifs are arranged around a central point.

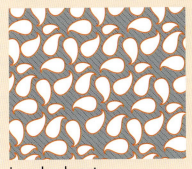

i. random layout.

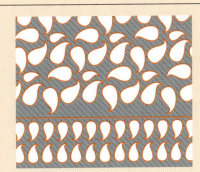

j. border print.

k. engineered print.

Figures 6.18a–k
Traditional terminology and concepts probably evolved from ancient traditions of wood block and stencil printing. Although industrial printing methods do not require that motifs be applied one-by-one by hand, the motif image is usually repeated in patterns to make an overall design.

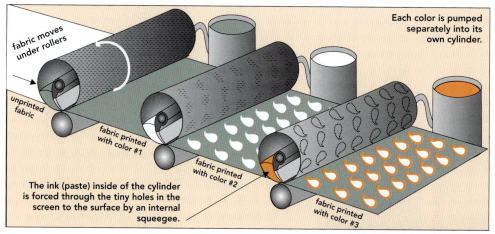

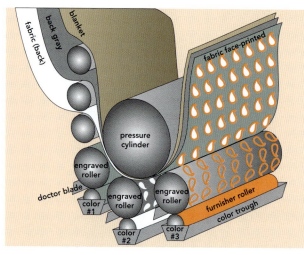

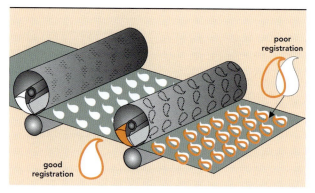

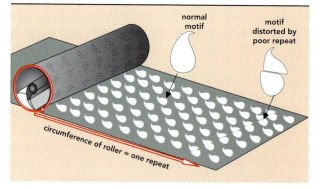

a. Rotary screen printing: Ink (paste) is pumped into the hollow space inside of a cylinder made of a fine metal screen whose surface is blocked in some areas to prevent the paste from printing. Rotary screen printing is used on 70 to 75 percent of all piece goods.

Each color is pumped separately into its own cylinder.

fabric moves under rollers

unprinted fabric

fabric printed with color #1

fabric printed with color #2

fabric printed with color #3

The ink (paste) inside of the cylinder is forced through the tiny holes in the screen to the surface by an internal squeegee.

fabric (back)

back gray

blanket

fabric face-printed

pressure cylinder

engraved roller

doctor blade

engraved roller

engraved roller

color #1

color #2

color #3

furnisher roller

color trough

b. Engraved roller printing utilizes steel cylinders that are coated with an outer layer of copper, into which a design is etched. A furnisher roller passes through a trough of ink (paste) and carries a thin layer to the engraved roller. The doctor blade scrapes away ink, leaving color only in the etched portions of the roller. The pressure cylinder forces the fabric, backed by a cushion of soft material, into the etched areas to pick up the ink.

c. In both methods of roller printing, each color is printed with a separate roller. Some designs use as many as twenty rollers. Lining up all the colors to create a single, coherent image is a challenge.

poor registration

good registration

d. If one of the rollers is misaligned, the colors will not match up. They will not register with each other.

normal motif

motif distorted by poor repeat

circumference of roller = one repeat

e. The circumference of a roller determines the length of the repeat of a pattern. If the design does not repeat in exactly the length of the circumference, the pattern will have an odd, disjoined place.

Figures 6.19a–e
Printing methods using rollers.

Table 6.2 Advantages and Disadvantages of Printing Methods

	Cost	Quality	Minimums	Turn Time	Environmental Concerns
Rotary Screen Printing	• Least costly • Roller width limits cutting area = low yield • One roller per color	• Colors bright • Very fine line detail is limited • Registration can be bad • Size of roller limits the size of the repeat	• Lower than engraved roller	• Preparation of screens is faster than engraved roller	• Toxic inks and lots of water needed to clean up
Engraved Roller Printing	• More costly than rotary screen printing • Roller width limits cutting area = low yield • One roller per color	• Colors can be dull • Registration can be bad • Size of roller limits the size of the repeat	• High: 10,000 yards or more	• Slow preparation of rollers: one per color	• Toxic inks and lots of water needed to clean up
Digital Printing	• More costly than rotary and engraved roller printing	• Colors: wide range, vivid, permanent, flexible • Size of image is limited by the width of the printer or fabric • Inks can run, causing blurred images	• As low as single garment	• Very fast: one printing cycle for all colors • Print from digital file	• No toxic ink cleanup
Sublimation (Heat Transfer) Printing	• Most costly	• Colors: wide range, vivid, permanent, flexible • Size of image is limited by the width of the printer or fabric	• As low as single garment	• Very fast: one printing cycle for all colors • Print from digital file	• No toxic ink cleanup • Waste paper and plastic

thousands of vintage textiles as well as printed media such as wallpaper and original painted designs (Figures 6.20a–b). They assemble packages of samples for a client's design team that reflect a theme, a color story, or a season. Design libraries such as New York's Fashion Institute of Technology also house historic fabric swatches that may be borrowed or purchased. Samples that are used by clients are taken out of circulation for a specified period. Online fee-based resources are also available, providing digital images for downloading and search engines to speed up research.

Although textile mills and converters still design some seasonal lines to be ordered off-the-card, they have greatly reduced their design services over the years. Many firms buy prints from independent studios that employ artists working in-house to develop textile patterns (Figures 6.20c–d). These are then made available to clients through sales reps or at print shows such as Print Source. The average print design generally sells for $400 to $500, but yarn-dye designs can sell for as little as $100 and

a. Patricia Nugent Textiles is a small, independent print design resource with thousands of vintage textiles, other printed media such as wallpaper, and original painted designs from the eighteenth century through the 1970s. Companies large and small will contact the studio, requesting packages of samples that reflect a theme, a color story, a season, and the brand.

b. The value of antique inspiration is the nuanced use of color. Technology is changing the way we see and work with color. Because the samples are the result of direct involvement with the medium, they have richness and variety that may be hard to create on a computer screen.

c. An artist paints a croquis by hand.

d. A team of designers creates new textile designs with inspiration from many sources.

Figures 6.20a–d
Print studios develop new print designs for clients.

embroideries or trim ideas for as much as $1,500. Related prints may be priced as a group. Generally, product developers who purchase prints budget a seasonal dollar amount per division and category.

Purchased prints may be computer generated or painted designs on paper or silk. The purchaser owns the print and the copyright. Once a print is purchased, it can be modified. Computer print technology has greatly reduced the time needed to explore variations in colorways and test options such as variation in scale. A print may be selected because it has multiple components that can be extracted and reworked into several designs from a single purchase.

a

b

a and b. In digital printing, micro-sized droplets of dye are applied to the fabric through inkjet print heads. Patterns created and stored in the computer can be selected, scaled, and printed directly onto a single finished garment (a) or fabric yardage (b) in a single pass through the equipment.

c. Sublimation printing (heat-transfer printing) is a technique in which disperse dyes are first digitally printed on special transfer paper, which is then placed on the fabric and passed through a machine at about 400 degrees Fahrenheit. The temperature and pressure cause the dye to vaporize and transfer onto the fabric. This technique produces bright, sharp, fine-line designs and allows rapid pattern changeover. It can be applied to completed garments or be used to print production yardage on textiles with a minimum of 50 percent thermoplastic content. It can also be used to create a variety of three-dimensional, foil, and special effects.

This sari by Jaish Parathalingam Jayesingha employs a single image that covers the entire piece of fabric.

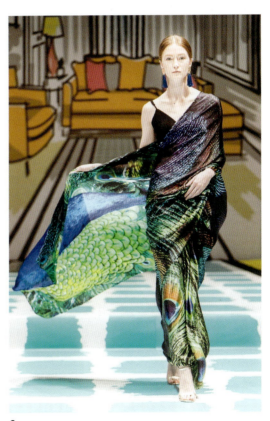

The advent of digital printing has changed the aesthetic rules of surface design. Whereas the challenge used to be to create within the confines of image-to-roller, now the challenge has expanded to create in the field of image-to-body. Two methods print pixel-based images from computer software using dyes forced through ink jets. **Digital printing** applies the image directly onto the fabric. **Sublimation printing** applies the image to paper that is then pressed to the fabric with heat and pressure. Both print all colors at one time. The only limitations are the size of the printer, some of which are as wide as most textiles. A print design can now be conceived from head to toe (Figures 6.21a–c).

While printing creates a two-dimensional change to the surface of a textile, other finishes turn flat textiles into a three-dimensional surface. Hot rollers with engraved surfaces are used to **emboss** dimples, ridges, pleats, and other shapes. Rollers can also apply glue in patterns so that fibers will stick in a design that imitates spot weaves or

c

Figures 6.21a and b
Digital printing.

Figure 6.21c
Sublimation printing.

patterned pile weaves. Chain stitch machines apply sequins, beads, and rows of ribbon and lace in swirls and stripes at high speeds, imitating the richness of fabrics that were once only available in couture studios. Digitally driven embroidery machines create dazzling detailed images. Laser cutters make lace-like patterns in synthetic fabrics (Figures 6.22a–i).

Trims That Add to Surface Interest

Narrow textiles have all the characteristics of wide textiles. Satin, velvet, grosgrain, and jacquard ribbons; twill tape; and edging laces are all narrow versions of wide textiles. They can be inserted in edges and seams or arranged into flowers and bows and applied (Figures 6.23a–m). Elastic trims are functional and used as decoration, too (Figures 6.23n–p). **Braid** trims are made of heavy yarns, sometimes with cord wrapped by filament or metal yarns. Braid is often used for military or formal looks on the borders of collars and cuffs or worked into epaulettes, frogs, and tassels (Figures 6.23q–x).

Trims called **hardware**, such as buttons, buckles, rings, chains, and grommets, can be made of almost any material. They may be variously carved, molded, punched, or etched, and then engraved, covered, laminated, painted, or dyed. Although these trims have functional purposes, they provide a great opportunity to add surface interest and brand identity. Some resemble jewelry and are made in factories that produce costume jewelry. Tack buttons, snaps, studs, and rivets can all be made to match in western looks. Hooks and eyes when painted or covered can be used to fasten as well as decorate lingerie, coats, and dresses (Figures 6.24a–h).

Zippers can be purely functional, but some are quite decorative. Each of the parts— the teeth, tape, or pull—can be made in a contrasting color or texture to add interest (Figures 6.25a–e).

UTILITARIAN PROPERTIES

Research and development for textiles are expensive. New technology in textiles is often funded by organizations that have practical problems that need solving and the money to find solutions. The US military and law enforcement need protective clothing. Medical institutions need products that protect injuries, promote recovery, or deliver medication. Sports teams need a competitive edge to win. Once new technical developments are discovered in specialties such as these, they may be commercialized and made more widely available to the general consumer.

Stretch

Since the introduction of "sportswear" as a clothing category in the 1920s, knits have become a part of every category of apparel. Because they stretch, they suit our active, casual lifestyle. **Stretch** imparts the abilities to a yarn, fiber, or textile both to elongate with stress and to recover its original shape and size when the stress is removed. Even woven fabrics that are inherently stable have evolved to include "comfort stretch" using stretch yarns. Compression has become an important attribute of garments that stretch.

a. embossing. Fabric is passed between heated rollers to press shaped relief into the surface to imitate woven structures such as seersucker.

b. pleating. This fabric is laid between paper and passed through heated rollers after being pushed into folds by a blade.

c. flocking. Fine, loose fibers are shaken onto areas of adhesive screened onto fabric in shapes that imitate dotted Swiss and other shapes.

d. sequins and beads. Automated chain stitch machinery is now used to apply beads and sequins, replacing hand work.

e. embroidery. Multiple head machines add motifs in elaborate or simple patterns to running yardage. Machines replace hand embroidery.

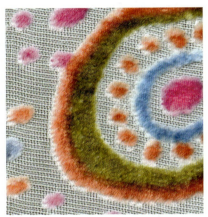

f. burnout (devoré). Fabric is woven or knitted with yarns of different fiber contents. After weaving, some of the yarns are dissolved in chemicals, creating a pattern.

g. laser cut. Fabric made with synthetic fibers can be cut with holes to imitate lace. Wear marks can be added to distress jeans.

h. laminates. A thin layer of vinyl can be laminated to jersey or print cloth and embossed to create the illusion of leather, exotic animal skins, or other effects.

i. moiré. The original method for creating a "watermark" pattern calls for passing two layers of taffeta through hot rollers. Adding a moiré effect by embossing or printing an image is less costly.

Figures 6.22a–i
Applied finishes add surface interest. All images are approximately 175 percent of the original.

NARROW TEXTILES can be manufactured with the same fibers, yarns, and constructions as wide textiles.

a. satin ribbon

b. grosgrain ribbon

c. hem tape

d. jacquard ribbon

e. velvet ribbon

f. twill tape

g. webbing

h. hook & loop tape—loop side

i. hook & loop tape—hook side

LACE. Any textile designed with large open spaces between yarns organized in a pattern.

j. embroidered lace

k. raschel lace

l. raschel lace

m. eyelet lace

ELASTIC. Primarily a support material, but it can also be decorative.

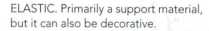

n. lingerie elastic

o. ribbon elastic—fold over type

p. bungee cord

BRAID. A narrow textile made of heavy yarn woven on the bias. Some fancy types are made with yarns that are spun by wrapping a cotton or linen cord with filament or metallic yarns.

q. fold-over braid

r. athletic wear draw cord

s. rick rack

t. gimp spiral cord

u. soutache

PASSAMANTERIES. Very elaborate trims made with cord and braid.

v. gimp three ply cord

w. gimp braid trim

x. frog

Figures 6.23a–x
Textile trims add surface interest when sewn into the edge of on the surface of a garment.

a. NATURAL MATERIALS. These materials can be used for buckles, cord ends, zipper tabs, etc.

shell	horn	leather	wood	tropical nut	bone	glass	cloth covered

b. METAL FINISHES. These finishes can be used for any metal hardware including buttons, buckles, rivets, snaps, zipper pulls, d-rings, etc. Each vendor has its own names for these finishes. Finishes are electroplated unless listed as "enamel." Other finishes names include brushed, etched, polished, brilliant, shiny, etc.

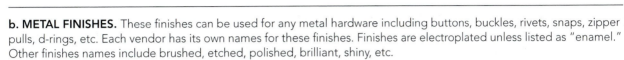

silver	matt silver	antique silver	enamel painted	nickel	black nickel	gold	antique brass	gun metal	copper	antique copper	titanium

c. METAL FABRICATION. **d. PLASTIC.** Plastic surface can be smooth, matte, etched, or molded. Colors are unlimited.

stamped metal	molded metal	imitation shell	imitation horn	imitation leather	imitation tortoise	etched	dyed

e. BUTTON SHAPES. The silhouette of the button adds surface interest. Novelty buttons can be any shape possible. The method of attachment also contributes to the look. Two-hole and four-hole buttons add the texture of the thread for casual looks. Dome and ball buttons are attached by a hole under the button (shank) so the top is smooth for a more formal look.

rimmed	flat	dome	ball	toggle	novelty	novelty	novelty

f. WESTERN LOOK

tack button	snap	rivet	buckle

g. DRESSES

hook and eye

studs   buckle

h. OUTDOOR LOOK

side release buckle	cam lock	ladder lock	grommet	cord lock	D-ring

Figures 6.24a–h
Hardware is trim made of any material that can be carved, molded, punched, etched, engraved, covered, laminated, painted, or dyed. The material, finish, and color add surface interest.

Figures 6.25a–e
Zippers.

a–b. Designers can add surface interest with zippers by simply changing the angle of the seam or the location the zipper is set in or by using a contrast color, texture, or luster. Zippers can be ordered with special features (see c, d, and e).

a.

b.

c. Contrast color of teeth and/or tape

d. Crystals embedded in the teeth

e. Jacquard tape

Fiber and Stretch

As discussed earlier in the section on drape, flexibility of fibers can vary for many reasons. The crimp of wool or texturized synthetic filament elongates when pulled. The polymer chains of some synthetics such as nylon are somewhat disorganized and tend to "give" more than polyester, which is more crystalline. The molecules that make up elastomeric fibers are made of two types of polymer chains: one set gives and the other maintains stability, so the fibers stretch out a lot and then recover. Rubber in filament form is used in elastic trim and thread. Spandex has the most stretch and is much finer than rubber.

Yarn and Stretch

Spandex fibers are too fine to be woven or knit alone, so they are wrapped with one or more ply of cotton, spun polyester, wool, or other fiber with properties that are desirable for comfort or appearance. Spandex can have up to 10 percent elongation and still recover. Yarns with no elastomers can still be engineered with texturized synthetic yarns to have 2 to 5 percent mechanical stretch.

Stretch yarns have improved traditional knit textiles such as jersey and rib knit by adding recovery to the property of stretch. Garments hold their shape on the body and don't lose their fit over time. The athletic wear and lingerie industries continue to create new constructions such as powernet, a warp knit that provides four-way stretch, to lift and support the body.

Construction and Stretch

Some knit constructions, such as ribbing, allow the loops of yarn to open up when stressed (see Figure 6.11). Others, such as double knit, stretch less. Stretch yarns have improved knit textiles such as jersey and rib knit by adding recovery to the property of stretch. Garments hold their shape on the body and do not lose their fit over time.

Runners, swimmers, and other athletes have become reliant on compression knits. When the LZR Racer, a neck-to-ankle swimming suit with a nylon and spandex shell laminated to a film of polyurethane, was introduced at the 2008 Olympics, it was so effective at reducing drag and adding buoyancy that a number of world records were broken (Just-Style, 2010) (Figure 6.26). Afterwards, controversy broke out such that full coverage suits were banned in 2010 to keep the competition fair. Nevertheless, compression is a property still sought out by athletes. Recent research has not been able to definitively connect garments with increased speed or endurance (Shaw, 2017).

Seamless knitting technology, introduced in 1995, results in garments with no bulky or irritating stitches and seams. Seamless panties and bras have become staples in the lingerie category, especially in shapewear (Figures 6.27a and b).

Trims That Stretch

Elastic trims control stretch in knit and woven garments. In addition to woven, knit, and braided elastic, bathing suit elastic is cut in strips from a thick film of solid white or transparent polyurethane. Bungees, bundles of monofilament rubber held together in braided covers, are used for drawstrings in activewear.

Durability

Durability is strength of a textile exhibited through time and use. A durable textile lasts because it resists the mechanical stress of abrasion, cutting, ripping, and tearing. Textiles can lose their durability because fibers may be weakened or destroyed by mold, fungus, insects, ultraviolet light, chemicals, or flame. Some fibers are naturally strong but resistance to various threats can be added during the stages of production.

Figure 6.26
Swimmers at the Beijing Olympics in 2008 shattered records wearing Speedo's LZR Racer, a suit that provided a high level of compression. FINA, the international governing body for swimming and other water sports, introduced restrictions regarding a swimsuit's material, coverage, and thickness in future Olympics to keep the competition fair.

Figures 6.27a and b
The Santoni machine (a) produces seamless knits such as the Puma performance wear shown in (b).

Fiber and Durability

Fiber chemistry determines many aspects of durability. Fibers such as nylon and polyester with strong primary bonds in the polymer chains (molecule to molecule) will withstand a lot of mechanical stress but they melt with heat. Kevlar® is even stronger (used for bullet-proof vests!). Natural and regenerated cellulosics have weak bonds. The chains break apart with bending and the fibers weaken, so cotton and linen crease easily. Cotton can be treated with chemicals to make it stronger (e.g., mercerization). Secondary bonds (the force that holds polymer chains to each other) are easier to weaken with chemical action, heat, and even water. Protein fibers (silk and wool) weaken with steam and alkaline body sweat. Acetate is very weak. It partially dissolves when wet and melts with heat.

Fibers such as hemp and bamboo naturally resist the action of fungus and other microorganisms, perhaps due to a combination of natural oils and the way they absorb water. Synthetic fibers can be engineered for specific purposes. Nomex® is flame retardant without the use of coatings or treatments. Polymer chains can be designed so that they do not interact with the destructive action of specific toxic substances.

Yarn and Durability

Twist is the physical principle that makes fibers into yarn. Tensile strength is the ability of a fiber to resist the destructive force of tensile load (pulling from both ends). Twist transfers the pulling force across the yarns and holds them together. Lower-twist yarns fall apart easily. Average-twist yarns hold together better, but very high-twist

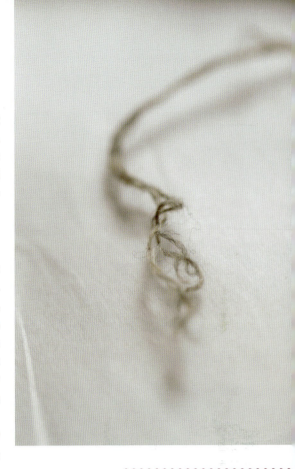

yarns kink and lose strength. More fiber makes thicker yarns, but not necessarily stronger ones. Spinning fibers in strands (ply) and then spinning the ply together makes much stronger yarns. Yarns can be spun to the left or the right (Figure 6.28). Mixing ply with left and right twist makes them even stronger. Staple yarns can be strengthened by adding strong filament ply or cores.

Construction and Durability

Traditional weaving constructions were developed centuries ago to make abrasion-resistant clothing from yarns made of natural fibers. They use heavy, plied yarns and high thread count to make dense, thick textiles such as canvas, drill, gabardine, covert cloth, and denim. The same weaving patterns are used with lighter weight yarns such as nylon and polyester for outdoor sportswear. Work shirts made in weaves such as poplin and broadcloth pack light-weight yarns closely together, making smooth surfaces that shed dirt and resist abrasion (Figures 6.29a–d).

Nonwovens may not seem to be durable, but when made of very strong fibers such as olefin and coated with resistant finishes, they can be used for protective clothing because they do not tear and because they resist holes that might allow toxic gases or liquids to enter.

Finishes and Durability

Traditional protective finishes include waxes, oils, and laminates of rubber or plastic. These finishes prevent liquids and chemicals from penetrating fibers, but also make the clothing stiff and uncomfortable because sweat cannot evaporate.

A nanoparticle is so small that more than 750 would fit across the diameter of one strand of your hair. **Nanoparticles** are applied in solution to fibers, yarns, or finished textiles by spraying, dipping, soaking, or printing. Because nanoparticles attach readily to fibers and fabrics, they do not need a medium. They neither wash out nor do they affect the breathability or hand of the fabric. Common commercial applications impart resistance to abrasion, wrinkles, stains, soil, water, bacteria, and ultraviolet light (Patel& Chattopadhyay, 2007).

Weight

Technically, the **weight** of a textile is measured by cutting a swatch of a specific size, weighing it on a scale, and then calculating the number of ounces per yard or grams per meter. Fabric weight for clothing typically varies between 2 and 16 ounces per square yard.

Weight is also a subjective response to what the user senses is appropriate for a product. A down jacket may appear to be heavy because of its visual bulk but, when worn, may feel surprisingly light. Weight has become a focus of research as competitive athletes such as bicyclists and swimmers seek to shed every ounce of weight that might impede their performance.

Figure 6.28
By spinning yarn ply with alternating twist, the strength of the yarn is increased. The yarn in this image is twisted with S twist and the smaller ply are twisted with Z twist.

a. gabardine. The warp yarns, though finer than the weft, are woven with a higher thread count. The twill floats create a smooth surface that resists abrasion, dirt, and, if treated, repels water.

b. canvas. The yarns are tightly spun in the warp direction. One version of canvas doubles up the warp yarns, making them pack together between interlacings to help canvas resist abrasion and dirt.

c. broadcloth. The warp yarns, though much finer than the weft, are woven with a higher thread count—almost double! The warp yarns pack together and resist abrasion and dirt.

d. tricot. A warp knit that is more durable than weft knits because the interlocking diagonal loops keep the yarns from slipping apart down the wales (running).

• • • • • • • • • • • • • • • •

Figures 6.29a–d
Textile construction can enhance resistance to abrasion, tears, and dirt. All images are approximately 150 percent of the original.

Fiber and Weight

There are many systems in existence that are used to measure the size of fibers. Several of them compare weight to length, but there is no simple way to compare the weight of all fibers to each other. In general, silk is the lightest of natural fibers. The introduction of microfibers in the 1960s brought fibers that were even finer than silk. Microfibers are highly desirable for fabrics used in outdoor and expeditionary wear because they have thermal properties, are durable, and are very lightweight.

Trims and Weight

Synthetic fibers replaced cotton for tapes and webbing for utility purposes (sacks, bags, packs, luggage, etc.) because they are stronger and lighter (see Figures 6.23g, h, i, and p). The outdoor industry has pushed the development of nylon and polypropylene fittings for packs, tents, and clothing because of weight (see Figures 6.24h, i–iv). Nylon coil teeth have made zippers much lighter than metal ones and just as strong.

Thermal Management

Thermal management is a category of textile properties that give apparel products the ability to keep the body at its ideal temperature regardless of exterior conditions, activity level, or health. These properties include heat retention and conduction and are affected by moisture absorption (or repellency) and wicking.

Fiber and Thermal Management

Traditionally, hair fibers such as wool have been used to trap heat close to the body. Three properties that make wool fiber warm have been imitated in engineered synthetic fibers. Wool fiber has a porous center that traps heat from the body. Nylon and polyester can be spun with hollow cores and used for insulation in apparel and bedding. Wool has a rough surface. Acrylic has a pitted surface that is not as efficient as wool but does hold heat. The natural crimp of wool is reproduced by texturizing filament synthetics with pockets and loops that capture heat (Figure 6.7c).

Cotton, linen, and rayon are all cellulosic fibers that do not naturally trap heat and do absorb moisture. They feel cool and comfortable for normal activity, but when they are saturated with sweat, they remain wet and rapidly feel cold. Athletes look for thermal management that is consistent. Wicking fibers transport moisture away from the body out to the surface of the textile where it can evaporate without cooling the body. Synthetic fibers wick rather than absorb.

Construction and Thermal Management
Weaving and knitting patterns can add tiny pockets that trap body heat. Waffle weave used for bathrobes adds a grid of extra warp and weft yarns with a dobby loom to make little cup shapes. Waffle knit (thermal knit) uses a simple drop stitch to create dimples and dips. Extra yarns in knit velour or woven velvet and velveteen weaves add air-trapping pile. Knit and woven terry cloth does the same thing with uncut yarns. Faux furs insulate with long hanks of unspun texturized yarns (Figures 6.30a–d).

Weaving and knitting patterns can also let body heat pass through, cooling the wearer. Thin yarns with low thread count woven into classics such as batiste, basketweaves, and voile let air pass through on summer days. Mesh knits are used to provide ventilation in the side panels of shorts and jerseys and in the underarms of jackets (Figures 6.30e–h).

Nonwoven entangled yarn padding has been used for decades as a heat-retentive layer between water-repellent shell and lining in outerwear. The many little spaces between the fibers hold heat. The outdoor industry continually refines insulation materials, seeking the lightest, warmest, and least bulky. PrimaLoft®, a company that makes some of the best insulation materials, developed a new concept in 2019, weaving the insulation into the shell fabric so that the fibers stay in place and do not migrate. The fibers are designed to imitate animal fur in varying lengths to promote air circulation when moving and insulation when at rest (Innovation in Textiles, 2019a).

Heating elements can be added to clothing to keep the wearer warm using energy that is not generated by the body. Companies such as Gerbing provide outerwear for motorcyclists who can plug their jackets into their batteries as they ride (Gerbing, 2020).

Weaving, knitting, and embroidering can now include microcircuits that sense changes in body temperature—as well as other vital signs—and are able to transmit information to monitoring devices. Although many advances have been made in fibers and yarns that act as circuits, integration with transmitters, power sources, and control mechanisms is still a challenge. Research in this field of Wearable Technology is driven by workwear and medical equipment rather than consumer goods (Innovation in Textiles, 2019b).

Textiles with lots of loops and pockets that trap air tend to insulate the wearer and provide warmth.

a. waffle weave   b. waffle knit   c. terry cloth   d. terry knit

Textiles with open areas in the construction tend to let air pass through providing evaporation and cooling.

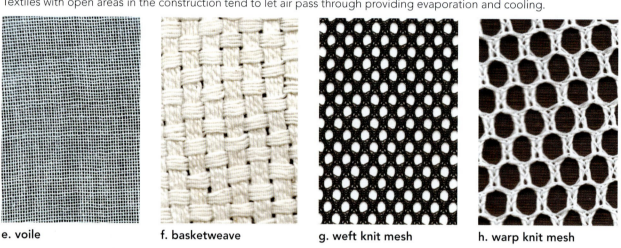

e. voile   f. basketweave   g. weft knit mesh   h. warp knit mesh

Figures 6.30a–h
Textile construction can enhance thermal properties. All images are approximately 150 percent of the original.

Finishes and Thermal Management

Traditional methods for adding warmth include weaving textiles with low thread count and low-twist yarns so that loose, heat-trapping fibers can be napped with hooked wire brushes to bring up the fibers. Napped fabrics made of natural fibers include cotton flannel for pajamas. A less costly alternative is brushed tricot. Wool flannel and cotton sweatshirt fleece can be replaced by brushed synthetic knits such as thermal fleece.

Textiles with wicking properties can be made water resistant by laminating the inside with PTFE, a microporous coating of polytetrafluoroethylene (commonly known by a major brand name, Gore-Tex). PTFE allows droplets of sweat, which are very small, to escape from the body to the shell textile where they are transported to the surface and evaporated. Raindrops are too big to penetrate the film. Even though it is lightweight and flexible, PTFE does stiffen the shell somewhat.

A finish of nanoparticles of carbon from coconut shells helps wick moisture away from the skin so efficiently that the core temperature of an athlete can be maintained in a range close to its ideal performance level of 37.5 degrees Celsius, hence the brand name "Thirtysevenfive". Nanoparticles in fibers do not diminish the properties of the polymers with which they are combined. Polyester continues to be strong and easy to combine with other fibers even when filled with nanoparticles (Thirtysevenfive, 2020) (Figure 6.31).

Trims and Thermal Management
Many trims used in the outdoor industry have been developed to hold warm air close to the body. Seam-sealing tape closes the tiny openings between stitches in PTFE–laminated shells. Linear trims such as bungees, webbing, hook and loop tape (such as Velcro‍), and elastics close up openings where heat can escape at wrist, neck, hem, and hoods. They are secured with durable plastic cord locks, slide locks, ladder locks, and rings. Water-resistant zippers help keep out water and wind.

Figure 6.31
One form of nanotechnology embeds nanofibers into other fibers to add properties. Nanoparticles of carbonized coconut add wicking properties to textiles without changing the other properties of the fibers. This technology is used in performance sportswear brands such as Saloman as well as leisure brands such as Tommy Bahama.

SUSTAINABILITY PROPERTIES

In addition to designing products with aesthetic and utilitarian properties that meet their customers' needs, a third criterionis becoming increasingly important in making decisions about textiles: sustainability. Media attention and social activism is increasing awareness about the harm that pollutants have done to animal and human life, water, soil, and air. Companies such as Patagonia have made sustainability synonymous with their brand image. Marketing departments that once enticed customers with the latest performance or fashion details are now seeking to engage them as partners in protecting the planet from further degradation.

It is no longer enough to use organic cotton or fibers made from soda bottles. Brands are now building their reputations on their efforts to make products that have circular pedigrees. To do this, brands must ask

- Do they or their suppliers use harmful chemicals that pollute the water, air and soil?
- How much water and natural resources do they consume in fiber and textile production processes?
- How much energy and water will be consumed and how much pollution will be caused when consumers are caring for garments?
- Are the garments they make biodegradable? Do they have potential for easy recycling? Or do they end up in landfills continuing to release toxic chemicals?

In order to change the direction of destructive manufacturing, brands have been reaching out to partners in the supply chain who manufacture with new energy- and resource-saving processes. To tell authentic stories about their efforts and products they need independent groups to lend credibility to their claims through inspection and support. There are over 400 organizations that offer environmental certification. The plethora of labels can be confusing for customers but some of the variety may be necessary

Table 6.3 Standards and certification groups are essential for reaching the UN Sustainable Development Goals.

The Sustainable Apparel Coalition (SAC) have made tangible progress in setting standards with input from many stakeholders so that they will be adhered to more readily. The SAC created the Higg Index, a tool for self-assessment of sustainable practices, promulgated in 2012. It reflects equally the input of all members of the apparel supply chain, nonprofits, and academics (The Sustainable Apparel Coalition, 2020).

The Textile Exchange produced the Global Recycle Standard in 2014. The criteria were established by a consortium of major brands and retailers, NGOs, fiber suppliers, and chemical companies. The Textile Exchange also provides annual reports on most fibers so that product developers and their companies can make informed choices. It also offers webinars and conferences to promote the exchange of best practices and solutions in several areas of textile production (Textile Exchange, 2020).

OEKO-TEX®, International Association for Research and Testing in the Field of Textile Ecology, is a team of eighteen laboratories in Europe and Japan. They set standards, define testing criteria, and certify that a product is free from toxins and manufactured with sustainable practices. (OEKO-TEX®, 2020). Companies such as Hanna Andersson promote their children's clothing as safe for the consumer as well as the environment (Figures 6.32a and b).

Bluesign® Technologies Group conducts factory audits with a team of chemists and textile professionals. Their labels assure the customer that the product some or all of the components have been fabricated with the highest standards of chemical safety and pollution control. In addition, bluesign® consultants assist factories in improving their efficiency, water, energy and chemical usage (bluesign®, 2020).

because of the many steps in the production of textiles and the number of countries involved (Schaer,2020). See some examples in Table 6.3 and Figures 6.32a and b.

Reforming a complex industry whose many players are spread around the world takes collaboration throughout the supply chain and among competitors. Collaborators include brands and retailers who work together with their suppliers to implement

a   b

Figure 6.32a
Hannah Andersson produces approximately 60 percent of its line for children from organic cotton.

Figure 6.32b
Companies such as Hannah Andersson can send their products to consortiums such as the International Association for Research and Testing in the Field of Textile (OEKO-TEX®) to obtain certification of their organically sourced textiles, then use the OEKO-TEX® certification to reassure their customers and build brand loyalty.

circular processes and to discover, test, and adopt sustainable components for apparel products. Foundations and nonprofits promote forums, education, and partnerships and fund scientific research, looking for solutions to recycling and clean production challenges. Celebrities have used their media presence to guide consumers to responsible choices and their wealth to fund new businesses and brands that offer sustainable choices (Figure 6.33). Activists and lobbyists circulate petitions and demonstrate to raise consciousness. Individuals shop wisely, join clean-up brigades and vote.

Many of these stakeholders are guided by the Sustainable Development Goals (SDGs) a conceptual framework laid out by The United Nations Sustainable Development Summit in 2015 (Appendix 1.1) (Sustainable Development Goals, 2020). The UN Alliance for Sustainable Fashion in 2019 was established internally to coordinate all agencies of the UN who promote projects and policies that contribute to the achievement of the SDGs. (UN Alliance for Sustainable Fashion, 2020). Five of the SDGs are directly related to the production, use and disposal of textile-based products.

Figure 6.33
Pharrell Williams, Grammy award–winning artist and producer with his own fashion brand has been involved with many projects that draw attention to environmental issues. For example, he is a partner in BIONIC® Yarns, a company that spins fiber from plastic harvested from polluted waterways.

Water

SDG 6
Ensure availability and sustainable management of water and sanitation for all.

Cultivation of one kilo of cotton uses a minimum of 10,000 gallons of water and run-off water carries the 16 percent of pesticides globally used to waterways. Cotton is the obvious target for galvanizing efforts to conserve and clean up water. (Figure 6.34).

Organic cotton looks, feels and performs just like conventional cotton; however, it is cultivated with natural methods that reduce water consumption by 91 percent, uses no synthetic pesticides, herbicides, or fertilizers. Groups around the world who had previously developed their own standards and certifications for organic cotton came together in 2002 to develop harmonized standards. Led by organizations from Japan, Germany, England, and the USA, the Global Organic Textile Standard (GOTS) was written, implemented, and expanded to include standards organizations in five more

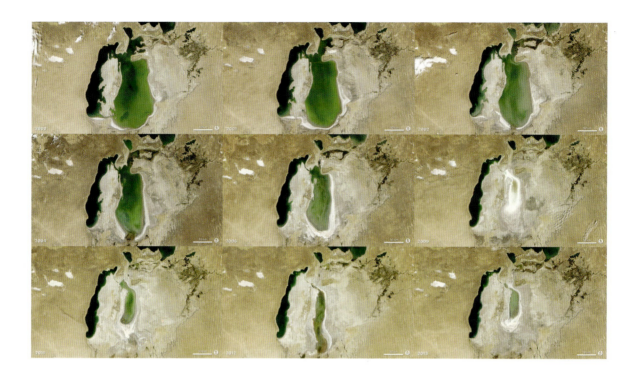

Figure 6.34
These satellite images show the shrinking of the Aral Sea from 2000 to 2013. The Aral Sea, located between Kazakhstan and Uzbekistan, was one of the four largest lakes in the world. It dried up because rivers that fed it were diverted during the Soviet Era irrigation projects, mostly cotton cultivation.

countries. (Global Organic Textile Standard, 2019). At the end of 2019, 7,765 factories in seventy countries were certified by GOTS (Friedman, 2020).

It takes at least three years for most farms to convert to organic. Collaborative groups such as the Better Cotton Initiative recognize that there may never be enough time and unsullied resources to grow sufficient organic cotton to replace current demand for cotton with crops that are organically grown. Cotton can, however, be grown with more sustainable practices that lead to cleaner water and better lives for those who produce it. This international, multichanneled consortium has established best practices and standards as well as stimulated their use in many cotton-producing areas (Better Cotton Initiative, 2020).

The treatment and finishing of textiles are responsible for an estimated 20 percent of industrial water pollution because so much water is needed: about 200 tons per one ton of dyed fabric (Noble, 2017). Denim uses about 20 percent of the cotton fiber produced annually and dyeing denim is responsible for consuming and polluting large amounts of water. Major denim brands have been seeking alternatives. In one of The Gap's water saving initiatives, their brand Banana Republic sources denim dyed with a process called Dry Indigo which uses virtually no water. The dyes are applied with a foam (not water!), using technology that evolved over ten years and involved denim mill Tejidos Royo in Spain along with Indigo Mills and Gaston Foam Systems in the USA (Innovation in Textiles, 2019c).

Ecosystems

SDG 15
Protect, restore, and promote sustainable use of terrestrial ecosystems, sustainably manage forests, combat desertification, halt and reverse land degradation, and halt biodiversity loss.

The popularity of viscose/rayon has increased in recent years. These fibers, Man Made Cellulosic Fibres (MMCFs), are made from plant material, mostly trees, so deforestation has increased to meet demand. Forest ecosystems already supply more than 150 million trees each year for the manufacture of viscose/rayon and that figure may double by 2028 if alternative plant sources are not used (CanopyPlanet, 2019). In the right circumstances MMCFs are biodegradable and therefore a solution to microplastic pollution caused by synthetic fibers. However, the tradeoff in a circular economy is not acceptable until alternative sources of cellulose replace trees. Fibers such as lyocell (Trade name Tencel™), Modal, and Naia™ are sourced from managed tree plantations, not virgin forests.

Since 2013, nonprofit organization Canopy has been supporting Next Generation Solutions (Next-Gen) which include the use of cotton from manufacturing waste and discarded clothing as **feedstock** (raw material) for MMCF production. Enough waste from cotton and viscose/rayon textiles is generated each year to satisfy the demand for MMCF spinning three times over! Efficient reclamation of cellulosic waste could eliminate the need to harvest trees altogether! In addition to saving trees, Next-Gen Solutions could keep textile waste out of landfills, use less energy, less water, and fewer chemicals (CanopyPlanet, 2019).

The CanopyStyle initiative monitors progress being made by fiber manufacturers such as Lenzing™, Aditya Birla in India, and TangShan Sanyou in China. CanopyStyle advises and updates brands when advance have been made so that they can encourage manufacturers to use the fibers in Next-Gen textiles. Some mills have been able to spin MMCF with increasingly large percentages of cellulose from manufacturing waste and recycled clothing, some up to 50 percent!

Hemp is fast growing, producing more fiber than any other plant source—250 percent more yield per acre or hectare than cotton. It does not deplete the soil, requires only a small amount of irrigation, and no pesticides or herbicides. As a fiber, hemp has many advantages. It is stronger and more insulating than cotton and it has antimicrobial properties, but it is scratchy and stiff. Brands who want to use hemp for its green message must blend it with softer fibers or soften it with non-toxic enzymes (Fang et. al., 2017). In a collaborative effort, Levi's® partnered with Outerknown to designWellthread™ X Outerknown, jeans and tee shirts using 70 percent "cottonized" hemp blended with 30 percent cotton(Unzipped Staff, 2019) (Figure 6.35).

The production of hemp to meet demand for sustainable fibers is increasing in some parts of the world such as the US (following legalization in 2018), Canada, Europe, and China (Innovation in Textiles, 2018a). However, because hemp is botanically similar to marijuana, expansion of cultivation is being hampered by legal and procedural issues related to controlling drug use in countries such as India (Jayan, 2018) and Australia (Martinello, 2018). In India, social enterprise, Bombay Hemp Company (BOHECO) partnered with the Council of Scientific and Industrial Research to develop the most productive strains of hemp, in preparation for the hoped-for industrial expansion of the crop. They see themselves as educators and advocates spreading the word about the economic and social possibilities of hemp (Grin. news, 2018).

Figure 6.35
Outerknown partners with other brands and suppliers to create products with textiles that address sustainability issues. For example, Levi's® partnered with Outerknown to design jeans and tee shirts using 70 percent "cottonized" hemp blended with 30 percent cotton for their Wellthread™ X Outerknown line.

Oceans

SDG 14
Conserve and sustainably use the oceans, seas and marine resources for sustainable development.

A 2016 report, *The New Plastics Economy: Rethinking the Future of Plastics* predicted that "there may be more plastic than fish in the ocean, by weight, by 2050" (Ellen MacArthur Foundation, 2016).Some collaborative projects have developed entire supply chains for collection, recycling, and spinning new yarns. Italy-based textile group Aquafil partnered with Outerknown to develop Econyl©, a nylon fiber spun from recycled fishing nets reclaimed from the ocean. It is now featured in Outerknown's Evolution jackets and shorts (Outerknown Journey, 2020). Parlay for the Oceans combs coastlines of remote communities and spins fibers from recycled plastic that are used by brands such as Adidas® to make shoes (Parlay for the Oceans, 2020). Sustainable Spanish brand Ecoalf joined forces with Spanish textile group, Santanderina, and spinning mill, Antex, to commercialize Seaqual™, yarns spun with fibers made with plastics harvested from the sea (Eurovet.com, 2017).These and other plastic reclamation projects are often affiliated with sustainability groups that educate, engage volunteers in clean-ups and challenge consumers to change their behaviors.

The spinning of new polyester and nylon fiber from sea rubbish has come under criticism. About 35 percent of sea waste is made up of microfibers shed from textile products made of synthetic yarns, that includes yarns made from recycled plastic (Wang, 2018). Microplastics are not only deadly for marine life to ingest, but they also spread toxins into the water (Bernstein, 2009). Dr. Mark Brown found that one single synthetic garment can shed more than 1,900 microfibers per wash in a home machine (Browne, et.al., 2011). Recent studies performed by multinational teams of researchers have found that that estimate may have been low (Chua, 2019) and that wearing clothes causes even more shedding. (Chua, 2020a). So far, microfibers have proven difficult to gather from bodies of water for recycling. The UN Environmental Program recommends redesigning products to avoid the use of primary microplastics and stimulating innovation in more sustainable directions (United Nations Environment Program, 2012).

Fiber, yarn, and textile manufacturers are working with researchers to tackle this urgent issue. In Australia, Deakin University's Institute for Frontier Materials and Swiss fiber manufacturer, HeiQ, teamed up to invent NoFuzz, a fiber that resists pilling (Innovation in Textiles, 2018b).In another project, German performance sports brand Vaude founded TextileMission (with government funding) in concert with Italian textile producer Pontetorto and global fiber company, Lenzing™.The goal was to foster teamwork to lower microfiber particle shedding, to search for biodegradable fibers as substitutes, and to improve wastewater treatment so that it can remove microfibers. Their first success was the performance fleece textile Biopile, which uses Tencel for the pile yarns that rub against the skin. When cellulosic Tencel fibers rub or wash of, they biodegrade in ninety days (Innovation in Textiles, 2017).

Production and Consumption

SDG 12
Ensure sustainable consumption and production patterns.

The recycling of textiles into manufacturing feedstock for new products has not yet been established as part of an efficient and productive supply chain. Sorting materials that can be recycled or regenerated has proven to be labor intensive and costly (Chua, 2020b). In 2016 the Fibersort Project was funded by the EU to explore methods for sorting and preparing clothing to be recycled into new fiber. The Fibersort process, now operational and ready to be adopted anywhere, uses optical technology to sort clothing by fiber type using near-infrared spectroscopy (NIRS).NIRS is helpful in sorting bulky clothing because it penetrates deeply and has a broad spectrum for detecting chemical components. Automated equipment speeds up sorting and prepares bundles by fiber and color for recyclers (Smart Fiber Sorting, 2020) (Figure 6.36). The Fibersort team included Worn Again Technologies, along with nonprofit Fashion for Good, business accelerator Future Tech Lab, and brands such as H&M and Kering. Worn Again invented and now provides an "end of life solution" for clothing

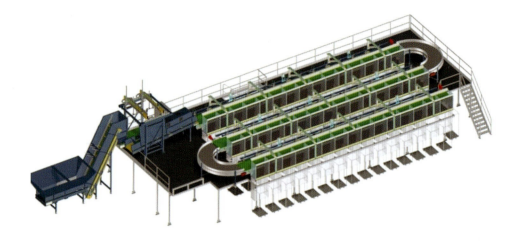

Figure 6.36
The Fibersort process uses optical technology to sort clothing by fiber type using near-infrared spectroscopy (NIRS), which penetrates deeply and has a broad spectrum for detecting chemical components. Automated equipment speeds up sorting and prepares bundles by fiber and color for recyclers.

that cannot be recycled because of blended fiber content. The Worn Again process breaks down a textile into polymer groups such as cellulose, polyester, and nylon. The polymers are separated reverted into their original state. Dyes, metals, and harmful chemicals are also removed. The creators of the Worn Again process believe that it has the potential to eliminate the need for growing, harvesting, or manufacturing any new raw materials, ever again! They hope that it will also clean up landfills, provide jobs and business opportunities, ushering in a truly circular textile system (Worn Again Technologies, 2020).

Recognizing the challenges of preparing end-of-life products for recycling, Italian performance sportswear company Napapijridesigned their iconic Skidoo jacket with all nylon-based components. Mono-material (one polymer) composition is more easily sorted and reduced to fiber for recycling. The shell fabric is Econyl®, made from recycled ocean plastic. It is called "Infinity" because Napapijri will take back the jacket from the consumer after two years and recycle it (Innovation in Textiles, 2019d) (Figure 6.37).

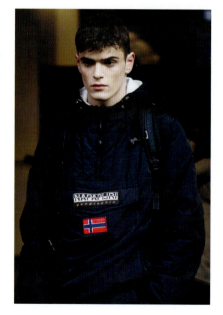

Figure 6.37
Mono-material (one polymer) composition is more easily sorted and reduced to fiber for recycling. Napapijri's "Infinity" jacket is constructed with all nylon-based components including the shell, which is made fromEconyl®, recycled ocean plastic. Napapijri will take back the jacket from the consumer after two years and recycle it.

Spandex/elastane is a synthetic fiber widely used to add elastic recovery to textiles that stretch. It cannot be separated from plant-based textiles or those made of other synthetic polymers. A tee shirt that is 95 percent polyester and 5 percent spandex/elastane cannot be shredded into feedstock for recycling into new yarn. DuPont's Sorona® has stretch properties like spandex/elastane. It is being used by textile firms to replace spandex because garments using Sorona® can be recycled as mono-material polyester. In addition, the stretch does not diminish or wear out like spandex so the consumer can use the product longer. Sorona® has

the added benefit of being derived from corn, a renewable resource. Because the fiber is so versatile, it can be spun into yarns for outerwear, insulation, or even faux fur, so that an entire jacket can be made of recyclable materials (Innovation in Textiles, 2020). Sorona® is a bluesign® systems partner which means everyone in the supply chain who is involved with products using Sorona®, chemical suppliers, spinners, textile mills, dyers, cut-and-sew factories, and brands are all responsible for the sustainability maintaining the of the final product (Innovation in Textiles, 2018c).

●●●●●●●●●●●●●●●●●●

Figure 6.38
Whole garment machines knit two layers of a garment (front and back) at the same time, joining those layers during the knitting process. The process is waste free, eliminates the need for linking (a process that can be harmful to workers' vision), and provides greater fit and styling than tubular knitting. This product is made on Shima Seiki MACH2S 12G.

An important way to reduce textile waste is to eliminate it during the production process. The knit-to-shape method of making sweaters and other clothing generates little waste. The joining of garment panels, or "linking," is very labor intensive. Seamless knitting minimizes or eliminates linking, shaving time as well as cost from the production cycle and resulting in garments with no bulky or irritating stitches and seams. Seamless knitting was first introduced in the hosiery and lingerie category but is now used for sweaters and dresses. Shima Seiki and Stoll are the leaders in this technology, which can also be used to knit made-to-measure garments (Figure 6.38).

Health

SDG 3
Ensure healthy lives and promote well-being for all at all ages.

Outerwear that keeps the wearer dry is highly desirable in outdoor and athleisure markets. The most common Durable Waterproof Finishes (DWRs) use PFASs (polyfluoroalkyl substances) in manufacturing, which end up in the water supply, soil, and food. These chemicals accumulate in the body and are related to numerous health concerns including cancer and damage to the immune system (US Environmental Protection Agency, 2018). Outdoor clothing customers, many of whom are committed to preserving the environment, find themselves in an ethical dilemma. They have come to expect high performance DWRs that are compatible with properties such as stretch, durability, and flexibility but want the DWR to be sustainable. Green Science Policy Institute lists brands such as North Face and Helly Hansen that have introduced some less toxic DWRs in their higher cost products. There is still room for more and better products (PFAS Central, 2020). An international group of scientists published the Madrid Statement in 2015, calling for collaboration among scientists, governments, chemical and product manufacturers, brands, retailers, and consumers to find alternatives to PFASs (Blum, Balan, Scheringer, et al., 2015). In one example of information sharing, Helly Hansen is considering open-sourcing technology developed for their textile, Lifa Infinity Pro. This textile needs no chemical coating to repel water. The fiber and fabric do not absorb water and the structure of the weave does not permit droplets to pass through (Cochrane., 2020).

SUMMARY

The selection of textiles is a process that starts with the first conceptualization of a product line and ends with the final approval of the fabric for production. Knowledge of textile manufacturing can help designers and merchandisers find ways to offer properties that are important to the customer that also fit into the budget, schedule, and assortment plan of the brand. Aesthetic properties (such as drape, hand, luster, and surface interest) and utilitarian properties (such as stretch and compression, durability, weight, and thermal management) can be added, altered, or removed in the fiber, yarn construction, or finish stages of textile manufacturing. Innovation has played a role in offering more and more choices.

The consumer quest for novelty has pushed the fashion industry to ever shorter production cycles and ever lower prices. In this competitive arena, manufacturers of textiles and apparel have often made decisions based solely on their own business survival and have neglected to protect the environment and social welfare.

Things are changing! Brands, fiber producers, yarn spinners, textile manufacturers, and sewing operations are adopting ethical practices at a more rapid pace. Promising methods of recycling are being expanded. Consortiums and collaborative groups are supporting these efforts by sharing information and resources. Governments, universities, trade groups, nonprofits, and certification agencies are working together to support the healthy revitalization of an entire industry.

KEY TERMS

aesthetic properties	cross-sectional shape	fabric costs
applied design	digital printing	fabric story
basic goods	drape	fabrication
bottom-weight	durability	feedstock
braid	elastic	fiber
contour	emboss	filament
courses	engraved roller printing	floats

To get started, C&A was required to engage independent bodies accredited by C2C, McDonough Braungart Design Chemistry (MBDC) and Eco Intelligent Growth (EIG) to perform testing, analysis, and evaluation.

Then C&A, with the help of Fashion for Good, selected supply chain partners. In conventional sourcing practices when a brand is looking for suppliers, there are many factors to consider such as price, lead time, quality, and availability. In addition to these factors, brands seeking certification may only engage suppliers who have already earned or are willing and capable of earning C2C certification for the specific component or process specified.

C&A engaged Arvind, a large textile mill in India known for its commitment to sustainability. Their challenge was to weave and finish the denim with yarns and dyes that were developed specifically for the project. Many trials were run so that the dyes did not change the elasticity of the yarns.

The yarns were spun with a newly released elastomer, ROICA™ from Japanese fiber manufacturer Asahi Kasei that breaks down at end-of-life without releasing toxins. Asahi had not worked with C&A before but wanted to be a part of a C2C certification project.

The finishing chemicals that DyStar first proposed from existing formulas did not meet C2C standards, so DyStar had to research their own formulas, then reach out to other manufacturers for their formulas. They were not able to meet C2C standards until they redeveloped the chemical formulas with the help of the assessors.

Freudenberg, global supplier of nonwoven interlinings, found that C2C would not approve their polyester product because of the presence of toxic chemicals. They sourced woven organic cotton interlining instead. When it was tested, it was approved.

Coats worked with the cut-and-sew factory, Pacific Jeans, Ltd. in Bangladesh, to find a substitute for polyester thread, which is often used for jeans because of its strength. Again, C2C would not approve polyester because of the presence of toxic chemicals. Coats' first offering of organic cotton thread was not strong enough until it was mercerized.

Similar challenges with metal trims, pocket lining and logo patch were encountered and solved to earn C2C Gold certification for all components and therefore for the jean itself. At each step, Fashion for Good identified how the component was brought up to standard. They also proposed ways to reduce and perhaps eliminate the need for troubleshooting in the future.

- design the product with components that are already certified in the Assessed Materials Almanac.
- cultivate a culture of sharing information in the textile and apparel community

Case Study 6.1
Collaboration and "The World's Most Sustainable Jean"

If a brand wanted to demonstrate their commitment to sustainability by creating a product certified by Cradle to Cradle (C2C), how would they go about ensuring that every component was able to pass the approval process? Nonprofit Fashion for Good in the Netherlands and global retailer C&A teamed up to find out by creating "The world's most sustainable jeans." They documented each step and then shared what they learned with everyone on Fashion for Good's website.
(FASHION FOR GOOD, 2018)

Overview of knowledge partners on the C2C Certified™ denim jeans project

Arvind	Fabric	99% cotton, 1% elastane 98% cotton, 2% elastane
Coats	Sewing Thread	Cotton (Gold level) and polyester (Bronze level) sewing thread
DyStar	Fabric dyes	DyStar® Indigo Vat 40% Solution
Freudenberg	Interlining	Cotton interlining for waistband
Lowatag/Charming	Patch	Laser cut jacron patch
Pacific Jeans Ltd.	Cut-make-trim	Product manufacturing Laundry
Roica	Premium Stretch Fiber	Environmentally compatible Stretch Fiber (Roica® V550)
YKK	Metal trims	Metal buttons Metal rivets
Zaber and Zubair	Pocket lining	Organic cotton pocket lining
Various	Axiliaries, printing and laundry chemicals	Washing chemicals Printing chemicals

References

C & A. (2020), Our vision: Making Sustainable Fashion the New Normal. https://www.c-and-a.com/uk/en/corporate/company/sustainability/#c36568

Chua.(2018), "Here's How C&A Made the 'World's Most Sustainable Jeans,'" *Sourcing Journal*, August 17. https://sourcingjournal.com/denim/denim-innovations/c-and-a-cradle-to-cradle-jeans-115581/.

Cradle to Cradle Products Innovation Institute. (2020), What Is Cradle to Cradle Certified™? https://www.c2ccertified.org/get-certified/product-certification (accessed May 27, 2020).

Fashion for Good. (2018), Developing C2C Certified™ Jeans. Fashion for Good. August. https://fashionforgood.com/wp-content/uploads/2018/08/FashionForGood_Denim-Case-Study-FINAL-1.pdf (accessed May 27, 2020).

fusible interlining	novelty goods	sustainability properties
hand	off-the-card	synthetic fibers
hardware	organic cotton	thermal management
head ends	plain weave	thread count
interlining	ply	top-weight
jacquards	polymers	turnaround time
jobbers	printing	utilitarian properties
knit-down	production yardage	wales
knitted textiles (knits)	regenerated fibers	warp
lining	rotary screen printing	warp knits
luster	sample yardage	weft
manufactured fibers	spinneret	weft knits
minimums	staple	weight
nanoparticles	stretch	woven textiles
narrow textiles	structural design	yarns
natural fibers	sublimation printing	zippers
neoprene	support materials	
nonwoven textiles	surface interest	

DISCUSSION QUESTIONS

1. Name the three stages of product development in which decisions about selecting textiles are made. Describe what the main focus is in each stage. Consider decisions such as finding the right balance of novelty and basic goods, cost per yard, sourcing, and turnaround time.
2. What is meant by the term "minimum"? What options does a small business have when faced with large minimums?
3. Look in your own closet and dresser. Choose at least ten items: five items that you regularly wear and five that you wear less. Make a list of the fiber content of each piece. Look at the content label, which you will find in the neck, waistband, or side seam. Now reread the text about the environmental impact of the clothing that you buy. How could you make choices that would contribute to sustainability? If you are already making conscious choices, describe what they are.

ACTIVITIES

1. Go shopping! Find specialty stores or departments in larger department stores that specialize in formal wear. Find an example of an inexpensive way of providing the customer with one of the aesthetic properties discussed in this chapter. Take a photo and describe what the expensive or exclusive product or process is that is being imitated. Examples would include finishes that imitate woven surfaces, machine-set beads or sequins, neoprene bodices, and scuba knit skirts.

2. Go to a store or website of a brand that specializes in high-tech outdoor clothing, such as The North Face, Arc'teryx, or First Ascent. Find an outerwear jacket and read the description. Identify as many features as you can that add to thermal retention, weight, and durability. List whether the feature is a result of fiber, yarn, construction, or finish. Copy the image for your answer. Are any of these features advertised as innovations?

STUDIO RESOURCES

- Take the chapter quiz with scored results and personalized study tips.
- Review glossary flashcards to build your vocabulary.

REFERENCES

Bernstein, M. (2009), "Plastics in oceans decompose, release hazardous chemicals, surprising new study says," *American Chemical Society*, August 19. https://www.acs.org/content/acs/en/pressroom/newsreleases/2009/august/plastics-in-oceans-decompose-release-hazardous-chemicals-surprising-new-study-says.html (accessed May 11, 2020).

Better Cotton Initiative. (2020), http://bettercotton.org (accessed May 11, 2020).

bluesign. (2020), https://www.bluesign.com/en (accessed May 26, 2020).

Blum A., Balan S.A, Scheringer M., et al. (2015), "The Madrid Statement on Poly- and Perfluoroalkyl Substances (PFASs)." *Environmental Health Perspectives*. 123(5). May 1. https://ehp.niehs.nih.gov/doi/10.1289/ehp.1509934 (accessed May 26, 2020).

Browne, M.A. et.al. (2011), Accumulation of Microplastic on Shorelines Woldwide: Sources and Sinks. *Environmental Science Technology*. 45, 21, 9175–9179.

CanopyPlanet. (2019), "Lay of The Land for Next Generation Solutions," *CanopyPlanet.org*, December 1. https://canopyplanet.org/wp-content/uploads/2019/12/Canopy-Green-Paper.pdf (accessed May 22, 2020).

Chua, J.M. (2019), "New Study Puts Zara, Adidas Under Spotlight for Microfiber Shedding," *Sourcing Journal*, February 15. https://sourcingjournal.com/topics/sustainability/plastic-soup-foundation-microfibers-139822/(accessed May 20, 2020).

Chua, J.M. (2020a),"Wearing Polyester Clothes May Shed More Microplastics Than Washing Them," *Sourcing Journal*, March 13. https://sourcingjournal.com/topics/sustainability/microplastics-microfibers-polyester-shedding-pollution-200033/ (accessed May 20, 2020)

Chua, J.M. (2020b), "Report: Obstacles Abound for Post-Consumer Textiles Seeking End Markets," *Sourcing Journal*, February 27.https://sourcingjournal.com/topics/sustainability/fibersort-consortium-post-consumer-textiles-circle-economy-worn-again-clothing-197679/ (accessed May 24, 2020).

Cochrane, A. (2020), "The Race to Design a Rain Jacket That Won't Kill the Planet," *Wired*, April 22. https://www.wired.com/story/pfas-free-waterproof-apparel/ (accessed May 25, 2020).

e-broidery®. (2017), "A new dimension in textile design," http://www.e-broidery.ch/en/fashion/ (accessed May 28, 2020).

Ellen Macarthur Foundation. (2016), "The New Plastics Economy: Rethinking the Future of Plastics,"https://www.ellenmacarthurfoundation.org/publications/the-new-plastics-economy-rethinking-the-future-of-plastics (accessed May 20, 2020.)

Eurovet.com. (2017), "New, eco-designed SEAQUAL™ fibre, created by recycling plastic from marine debris, reveals its ambitions, new fibres, yarns and fabrics," https://eurovet.com/en/news/new-eco-designed-seaqual-fibre-created-recycling-plastic-marine-debris-reveals-ambitions-new-fibres-yarns-fabrics/ (accessed May 20, 2020).

Fang, G., Chen, H. G., Chen, A. Q., Mao, K. W., and Wang, Q. (2017), "An efficient method of bio-chemical combined treatment for obtaining high-quality hemp fiber," *BioRes*. 12(1), 1566–1578. https://bioresources.cnr.ncsu.edu/resources/an-efficient-method-of-bio-chemical-combined-treatment-for-obtaining-high-quality-hemp-fiber/ (accessed May 16, 2020).

Friedman, A. (2020), "GOTS-Certified Facilities Jumped 35% in 2019," *Sourcing Journal*, March 6. https://sourcingjournal.com/topics/raw-materials/global-organic-textile-standard-certified-facilities-cotton-wool-india-198900/ (accessed May 11, 2020).

Gerbing. (2020), http://www.gerbing.eu/en (accessed May 28, 2020).

Global Organic Textile Standard. (2020),https://global-standard.org/ (accessed May 11, 2020).

Grin.news. (2018), "Bombay Hemp: Inside India's coolest cannabis company," *Grin.news*, February 12. https://grin.news/bombay-hemp-inside-indias-coolest-cannabis-company-7e4328204af9 (accessed May 21, 2020).

Innovation in Textiles. (2017), "Vaude and Pontetorto Receive Eco Performance Award," *Innovation in Textiles*, November 27. https://www.innovationintextiles.com/vaude-and-pontetorto-receive-eco-performance-award/ (accessed May 20, 2020).

Innovation in Textiles. (2018a), "Reintroduction of industrial hemp is in full swing," *Innovationintextiles.com*, June 6. https://www.innovationintextiles.com/reintroduction-of-industrial-hemp-is-in-full-swing/ (accessed May 11, 2020).

Innovation in Textiles. (2018b), "New treatment does away with fabric pilling," *Innovation in Textiles*, June 19. https://www.innovationintextiles.com/new-treatment-does-away-with-fabric-pilling/ (accessed May 20, 2020).

Innovation in Textiles. (2018c), "DuPont Sorona becomes bluesign system partner," *Innovationintextiles.com*, July 24. https://www.innovationintextiles.com/dupont-sorona-becomes-bluesign-system-partner/(accessed May 24, 2020).

Innovation in Textiles. (2019a), "Insulation meets fabric with PrimaLoft Next," *Innovation in Textiles*, June 6. https://www.innovationintextiles.com/insulation-meets-fabric-with-primaloft-next/ (accessed May 28, 2020).

Innovation in Textiles. (2019b), "Smart materials and wearable technology at Techtextil," *Innovation in Textiles*, May 31. https://www.innovationintextiles.com/smart-materials-and-wearable-technology-at-techtextil/ (accessed May 28, 2020).

Innovation in Textiles. (2019c), "Gap to release waterless dyed denim in 2020," *Innovationintextiles.com*, August 5. https://www.innovationintextiles.com/gap-to-release-waterless-dyed-denim-in-2020/ (accessed May 24, 2020).

Innovation in Textiles. (2019d), "Napapijri launches 100% recyclable jacket," *Innovationintextiles.com*, July 22. https://www.innovationintextiles.com/napapijri-launches-100-recyclable-jacket/ (accessed May 24, 2020).

Innovation in Textiles. (2020), "DuPont Sorona's recyclable spandex-free stretch jacket," *Innovationintextiles.com*, January 2020.https://www.innovationintextiles.com/dupont-soronas-recyclable-spandexfree-stretch-jacket/ (accessed May 24, 2020).

Jayan, TV. (2018), "Cannabis cultivation is now legal in Uttarakhand," *Business Line*, July 10. https://www.thehindubusinessline.com/economy/agri-business/cannabis-cultivation-is-now-legal-in-uttarakhand/article24381601.ece# (accessed May 11, 2020)

Just-Style. (2010), "Textile fabrics get a boost in performance swimwear," *Just-style.com*, January 5. http://www.just-style.com/analysis/textile-fabrics-get-a-boost-in-performance-swimwear_id106315.aspx (accessed May 11, 2020).

Martinello, A. (2018), "5 questions you may have about the hemp industry,"*AustralianFarmers*, November 30.https://farmers.org.au/blog/5-questions-you-may-have-about-the-hemp-industry/ (accessed May 11, 2020).

Nishimura, K. (2020), "WWDMagic's Fast-Fashion Trends Favor Wearability Over Newness," *Sourcing Journal*, February 11. https://sourcingjournal.com/topics/fashion-trends/wwdmagic-fast-fashion-trends-rust-coats-turtleneck-70s-midi-skirt-194716/ (accessed May 28).

Noble, B. (2017), "Fashion, The Thirsty Industry," *Good On You*, March 21. https://goodonyou.eco/fashion-and-water-the-thirsty-industry/ (accessed May 24, 2020).

OEKO-TEX. (2021), https://www.oeko-tex.com/en/ (accessed May 21, 2020).

Outerknown Journey. (2020), "Turning Waste into Nylon." https://www.outerknown.com/blogs/journey/turning-waste-into-nylon (accessed May 21, 2020).

Parlay for the Oceans. (2020), Ocean Plastic®. http://www.parleyfoundation.org/global-cleanup-network#global-cleanup-network-1 (accessed May 20,2020).

Patel, B. H., and D. P. Chattopadhyay. (2007), "Nano-particles & their uses in textiles," *Indian Textile Journal*, December. http://www.indiantextilejournal.com/articles/FAdetails.asp?id=693 (accessed May 28, 2020).

PFAS Central. (2020), "PFAS Basics: PFAS-Free Products," *PFAS Central*. https://pfascentral.org/pfas-basics/pfas-free-products/ (accessed May 25, 2020).

Shaw, A.(2017), "Study reveals compression tights don't help runner performance," *Ohio State University College of Engineering*, June 11. https://engineering.osu.edu/news/2017/06/study-reveals-compression-tights-dont-help-runner-performance (accessed May 28, 2020).

Smart Fiber Sorting. (2020), "From mixed rags to uniform, high-value raw materials." https://smartfibersorting.com/how-it-works/ (accessed May 24, 2020).

Sustainable Development Goals. (2020), United Nations. https://www.un.org/sustainabledevelopment/development-agenda/ (accessed May 11, 2020)

Taylor, G. (2020), "The 6 Supply Chain Trends the COVID-19 Crisis Will Accelerate," *Sourcing Journal*, May 5. https://sourcingjournal.com/topics/sourcing/the-6-supply-chain-trends-the-covid-19-crisis-will-accelerate-209016/ (accessed May 28, 2020).

Textile Exchange. (2020), About Us. https://textileexchange.org/about-us/(accessed May 11, 2020).

Schaer, C. (2020), "Too Many, Too Confusing: What Does the Future Hold for Eco-Labels?" *Women's Wear Daily*, April 22. https://wwd.com/business-news/business-features/too-many-too-confusing-what-does-the-future-hold-for-eco-labels-1203563276/.

Sustainable Apparel Coalition. (2020), The Higgs Index. http://apparelcoalition.org/the-higg-index (accessed May 20, 2020).

Thirtysevenfive. (2020), https://www.thirtysevenfive.com (accessed May 28, 2020).

UN Alliance for Sustainable Fashion. (2020),https://unfashionalliance.org/(accessed May 11, 2020).

United Nations Environment Program. (2012), Microplastics. https://wedocs.unep.org/bitstream/handle/20.500.11822/12079/brochure-microplastics.pdf?sequence=1&amp%3BisAllowed= (accessed May 21, 2020).

Unzipped Staff. (2019), "New Levi's® Wellthread™ x Outerknown Features Groundbreaking Cottonized Hemp," *Levi Strauss & Co.*, March 11.

https://www.levistrauss.com/2019/03/11/new-levis-wellthread-x-outerknown-features-groundbreaking-cottonized-hemp/ (accessed May 11, 2020).

US Environmental Protection Agency. (2018), Basic Information on PFAS. *Environmental Protection Agency*, December 6. https://www.epa.gov/pfas/basic-information-pfas (accessed May 24, 2020).

Wang, T. (2018), "Distribution of ocean microplastics sources worldwide as of 2018*," *Statista.com*, August 30. https://www.statista.com/statistics/909561/sources-of-ocean-microplastics/ (accessed May 21, 2020).

Worn Again Technologies. (2020), "Reclaim Infinity," *Wornagain.co.uk*, http://wornagain.co.uk/ (accessed May 24, 2020).

Young, V.M. (2020), "Remote-Working Consumers Will Swap Suits for Sweats and Hurt These Three Retailers," *Sourcing Journal*, May 22. https://sourcingjournal.com/topics/retail/moodys-apparel-retail-earnings-coronavirus-ascena-ann-taylor-mens-wearhouse-211826/ (accessed May 28, 2020).

ADDITIONAL RESOURCES

Collier, B. J., M. Bide, and P. G. Totora. (2009), *Understanding textiles* (7th ed.). Upper Saddle River, NJ: Pearson Prentice Hall.

Corbman, B. P. (1982), *Textiles: Fiber to fabric* (6th sub-edition). Glencoe, IL: McGraw-Hill.

Dunne, L. E., S. Ashdown, and B. Smyth. (2005), "Expanding garment functionality through embedded electronic textile," *Journal of Textile and Apparel, Technology and Management*, 4(3 Spring).

Ekobai.com. (2016), http://www.ekobai.com.

Humphries, M. (2009), *Fabric reference* (4th ed.). Upper Saddle River, NJ: Prentice Hall.

Kadolph, S. J. (2010), *Textiles*. Upper Saddle River, NJ: Prentice Hall.

CHAPTER 7

LINE DEVELOPMENT

"You can have the biggest marketing budget, the biggest show, a perfect merchandising plan, but at the end of the day, it doesn't mean anything if the design and quality of the product you are offering [are] not compelling."
NICK WOOSTER, MERCHANDISER, DESIGNER, AND FASHION CONSULTANT

OBJECTIVES

- To understand the merchandising function and the central role it plays in product development
- To comprehend how the demand forecast and market trend analysis are interpreted into a merchandise budget and line plan
- To recognize the functional relationship between merchandising and design in translating the line plan and trend forecast into product assortments with specific delivery dates and sales and profit goals
- To understand the strategies that brands use to develop assortments
- To understand the parameters of legal protection for textile and apparel design
- To comprehend the role of merchandising in moving the fashion system toward a more sustainable slow fashion model

The merchandising function plays a central role in product development. Merchandisers integrate the financial goals of the firm with brand strategies, and consumer and product trends to develop detailed forecasts, product plans, and a functional time and action calendar. These tools help to synchronize the design, marketing, pricing, promotion, sales, production, and logistics functions of the brand. Ultimately, merchandisers are responsible for getting the right product to market at the right price, in the shopping channels their customers shop, timed to coincide with when the customer is ready to buy. Figure 7.1 illustrates the relationships that a marketing team must manage in order to meet that goal.

Figure 7.1
Cross-functional
communication is
required for the
merchandising team to
successfully complete its
activities.

There is no universal approach to merchandising. Depending on the organizational structure of the company, the brand size, and its resources, companies develop their own specialized lexicon for tasks and job titles. They structure responsibilities and oversight in a way that suits their brand needs, personnel assets, and budget. Ultimately, successful merchandising requires an alignment of people, technology, and processes.

Merchandising positions are not entry level. Experienced merchandisers enjoy the diversity of responsibilities, the challenges of meeting goals, and the cross-functional relationships required of the job. Successful merchandisers must be:

- analytical and good with numbers
- accurate and organized
- able to cope with pressure and meet deadlines
- able to communicate cross-functionally
- a respected team player
- experienced in product development processes and/or with channels of distribution
- a creative problem solver
- able to visualize the future
- logical

Ultimately, merchandisers are judged by metrics, including meeting sales goals, sell-through rate, and profit margins.

MERCHANDISING ACTIVITIES

Merchandising activities are focused on maximizing return on investment through planning assortments and production in a way that increases profitability and minimizes losses from markdowns, excess goods, and stockouts. Merchandising responsibilities require input from finance, marketing and sales, creative design, technical design, merchant/buyers (in the case of retail product developers), quality assurance, and manufacturing/sourcing. Communication skills and technology that supports cross-functional sharing is central to success.

The following activities are not necessarily sequential. Many things are happening at the same time. Forecasts and budgets are dynamic; they must constantly be monitored and refined as information becomes more concrete. Merchandisers are like traffic controllers. They make sure that all functional units have the information they need to execute their tasks.

Demand Forecast and Merchandise Budget

The first stage of merchandising is to understand the financial targets for the brand. These targets are based on the strategic goals established for the brand, past season sales data, and an analysis of the current market environment. The profit goals of the brand lead to the development of a demand forecast and merchandise budget.

A **demand forecast** is the projection of achievable sales revenues based on historical sales data, strategic growth goals, quality and capacity of supply chain, and market analysis. It may also be referred to as a *sales forecast*. Advanced analytics tools can be valuable in understanding historical sales data by isolating the factors that drove sales, down to the SKU level. By analyzing patterns, analytic tools can determine whether an item's popularity was due to its color, its fabric, its cut, or its fit.

Market trends analysis helps to anticipate any demographic shifts or market conditions that might impact customer traffic and engagement. This information is often tracked by the marketing and sales arm of the brand, so systematic communication and shared data is critical. Market trends analysis tracks the following:

- macro trends that are impacting large swaths of the population
- consumer behavior in terms of value alignment, spending priorities, and customer satisfaction
- seasonal trends such as climate impact and when holidays fall
- geographical trends that identify emerging markets and mature markets
- social media trends
- omni channel distribution trends

These market trends can be triggered by new technology, economic factors, political changes, and social developments.

The demand forecast breaks down financial profit and sales goals into quarter-by-quarter, then month-to-month, and finally week-to-week targets, taking into consideration anticipated margins as well as the marketing plan for the season. All businesses have cyclic ups and downs. More inventory is planned for the busiest times of the year; less product is delivered for historically slow periods.

The demand forecast is used to develop a **merchandise budget**. Using the demand forecast and sales targets, the budget identifies how much inventory needs to be in stock and ready for distribution week by week. It factors in an estimated cost of goods, anticipated initial margins, and seasonal reductions. This early planning must be synchronized with marketing efforts and helps sourcing to reserve sufficient manufacturing capacity.

The Line Plan

The sales forecast and merchandise budget are used to outline a **line plan**. The line plan anticipates the merchandise inventory levels required to maximize sales potential and return on investment. This plan serves as a guide for the design team, setting parameters that help it to create the right product with the right balance and that it can be delivered to the right channels at the right price. It spells out things such as:

- Number of deliveries
- Range of fabrics required
- Product assortments by category
- The proportion of basic to seasonal to fashion products
- Target cost and margins
- Big picture creative goals based on current season trends

The line plan is primarily data and numbers driven. Effective line planning ensures inventory levels of the right merchandise available through the channels where the customer shops, when the customer is ready to buy, at prices and quantities the market demands while minimizing losses from markdowns and stockouts (Table 7.1). Line plans do not get into creative specifics, but they do keep the design team focused so that each delivery is balanced between basics, seasonal product, and fashion product. In an omnichannel marketplace, customers will become frustrated if fashion apparel or special sized apparel is only available online and not in-store. Inventory must be managed and optimized across all channels. Global brands may need to curate geographically in order to conform to cultural practices and preferences.

Line Concept

It is one thing to design a successful garment; it is quite another to understand how to design a group of garments that can be merchandised together. Well-executed merchandising establishes an environment that nurtures the designer's creativity while providing the controls for effective assortments. Without merchandising controls, lines may be too expensive, poorly timed, or lack cohesive styling. In a culture of fashion individualism, designers and merchandisers must work as a team to translate the **merchandise plan** and interpret the fashion forecast into a framework for new product deliveries. Depending on the brand, they may be imagining product that will be delivered anywhere from four to sixty-two weeks out. Figure 7.2 illustrates how the length of the end-to-end fashion cycle depends on the company's business model.

Table 7.1 Line Plan for Modern Mosaic Capsule
April Delivery

Category	Assortment	SKUs
Dresses		
Dress with sleeves	(1 style, 9 sizes, 2 prints, 1 color each)	18
Sleeveless dress	(1 style, 9 sizes, 1 pattern or print in 2 colors)	18
Jackets		
Nehru jacket	(1 style, 9 sizes, 1 fabric, 1 color)	9
Tops		
Jersey top	(1 style, 9 sizes, 1 print, 2 colors)	18
Fitted top	(1 style, 9 sizes, 1 fabric, 1 color)	9
Novelty top	(1 style, 3 sizes, 1 color)	3
Pants		
Slim pant, jersey	(1 style, 9 sizes, 2 prints, 1 color each)	18
Slim pant, woven	(1 style, 9 sizes, 1 fabric, 1 color)	9
Skirts		
Slim skirt	(1 style, 9 sizes, 1 fabric, 2 colors)	18
Novelty skirt	(1 style, 9 sizes, 1 fabric, 2 colors)	18
Total SKUs		**138**

The duration of an end-to-end fashion cycle widely varies by company.

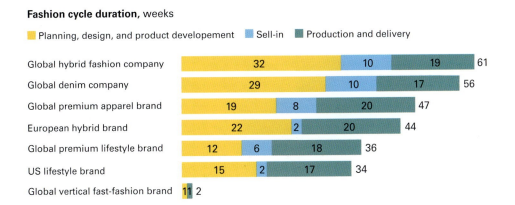

Fashion cycle duration, weeks

- ■ (yellow) Planning, design, and product developement
- ■ (light blue) Sell-in
- ■ (dark teal) Production and delivery

Global hybrid fashion company	32	10	19	61
Global denim company	29	10	17	56
Global premium apparel brand	19	8	20	47
European hybrid brand	22	2	20	44
Global premium lifestyle brand	12	6	18	36
US lifestyle brand	15	2	17	34
Global vertical fast-fashion brand	1	1	2	

Figure 7.2
The duration of the
fashion cycle can take as
little as two weeks and
as much as sixty-one
weeks with planning
and design taking as
much or more time than
production.

Once the parameters of a season have been determined, merchandisers and designers work together to interpret trend research and customer preference data. Companies may have their own trend forecasting team, they may task the merchandising and/or design teams to do this research, or they may subscribe to any number of specialty trend forecasts. The information gathered needs to be edited to fit the image of the brand and the preferences of brand customers.

The data captured by the marketing function can be analyzed for additional insights as to how the customer is responding to current merchandise and what they enter into search functions. Many insights can be gleaned from customer purchasing habits, browsing patterns, personal preferences, typical spend, and purchase timing. Increasingly, medium to large brands are implementing **product experience management programs** that allow businesses to measure customer impressions through feedback on new product categories, styles, fabrics, and colors. All of this information helps merchandisers and designers pursue the trends and themes that appeal to their brand's customer.

Selecting themes for each delivery ensures that functional teams across the brand are working toward the same vision. Concepts may be communicated as digital presentations, as printed booklets, or as collages of tear sheets, color chips and fabric swatches mounted on foam core. No matter the format, they suggest color and fabric direction, silhouette shapes and proportion, key categories, and influential designers or brands (Figure 7.3). The process of deciding which images to include on the board helps the design team to focus their ideas and launch the design process.

Figure 7.3
Concept boards are the starting point of the creative process.

As the design team begins its work, merchandisers are able to share the seasonal vision with functional teams across the brand. Marketing and sales can focus their promotions. Sourcing teams can think about the mix of supply chain partners that are best equipped to produce the product.

The Assortment Plan

An **assortment plan**, also referred to as a range plan, fleshes out the parameters of the line plan using the line concept as a unifying theme. An assortment plan is a detailed chart that shows the number of styles, fabrics, colors, and sizes that will be included in the line. Each style is illustrated and paired with fabric swatches. If the style is to be made in more than one size run (e.g., misses and petites or tall) that is also indicated since every combination will be a separate SKU. One pair of Athleta leggings may be made in three colors; nine sizes for misses, five sizes for petite, and five sizes for tall. That means the company would be manufacturing fifty-seven SKUs for one single style.

Seasonal collections are made up of a combination of basic items, sometimes referred to as core items; seasonal or key items; and cutting-edge items. Basic items are those for which there is little demand for style change. Seasonal or key items help to differentiate the brand from its competitors; they may be unique due to styling, fabrication, or details that are either trend-right or geared to a particular function; these are the products that are typically featured prominently in in-store displays and in advertising. Cutting edge products may be made up of items made from high tech fabrics, complex items that deliver extra performance and function, fashion forward items, or styles the brand wants to test. This group, generally the smallest part of any collection, may use more sophisticated or more expensive fabrications; or more complex cuts and fits; and may only be available through digital channels, in signature stores, or in large stores in major urban areas.

The balance among these categories of merchandise varies from brand to brand. Some brands rely on their fashion styles to produce most of their volume; other brands rely on their basics for volume. A fast fashion store such as Zara brings in new merchandise every two weeks, allowing it to respond to subtle changes in fashion palettes, silhouettes, and details. A brand such as Lands' End might introduce a basic product for fall/winter and offer that same product for a twenty-six–week selling period. Its customer values quality over style change.

One model for assortment planning is the **pyramid plan** (Figure 7.4). The lowest and broadest level of the pyramid is made up of basic styles—core items that carry little risk and can be ordered in large quantities and assortments. In the middle level of the pyramid is where product developers interpret current fashion trends for their

Figure 7.4
A pyramid assortment plan anticipates that the bulk of seasonal sales will come from basic merchandise and that the lowest percentage of seasonal sales will come from fashion items. This type of planning is typically used by mass merchants.

FASHION ITEMS

KEY ITEMS FOR SEASON

BASIC MERCHANDISE

Figure 7.5
A diamond assortment plan anticipates that the bulk of seasonal sales will come from key items for the season with less reliance on basics.

core customer; these key items are critical to maintaining brand loyalty. The top of the pyramid consists of cutting-edge items that help to create an image and expose the customer to new trends in fashion and technology. These items are not produced in great quantities. Uniqlo is a good example of a brand that relies on the pyramid plan to assort its merchandise.

Fashion-oriented brands may prefer a **diamond plan** in which basics represent only a small portion of their product mix, key items make up the bulk of their offerings, and cutting-edge items are again represented at the top. Increasingly, this structure is expected of brands that compete in the fashion arena (Figure 7.5).

As individual garments are designed, a flat with fabric identification is placed into a grid so that the entire team can see how each delivery is developing and what items are still needed. This helps to identify where there are voids in the assortment (Figure 7.6). The assortment plan provides a visual tool to assess things such as whether there are too many sleeveless styles compared to styles with short or long sleeves, the ratio of skirts to pants, or the relationship of core items to fashion items. The assortment plan is used in the early stages of line development to guide planning in merchandising meetings. It helps in fabric development and to quantify fabric orders. It can be used to update the sales forecast and focus marketing efforts. As it becomes finalized, it must be shared with sourcing so that they are reserving appropriate manufacturing capacity.

A well-conceived assortment plan helps designers to focus their efforts on the items that are most likely to make it through the line review process. Each group of styles should express a clear point of view that focuses on a trend-right theme that is relevant to the brand DNA and the target customer. The assortment should reflect the range of customer preferences and constraints, such as aesthetic point of view; price point limitations; and quality, fit, and care expectations. Accurate communication and teamwork throughout the merchandising and design development process will result in a line that is marketable and supports the goals of the brand.

To summarize, the assortment plan is a visual guide that:

- Reflects color, fabric, and silhouette decisions for the brand in relation to current trends
- Establishes the right variety and balance for the brand's target customer
- Serves as a checkpoint to ensure that sufficient inventory will be available to support the marketing plan and meet sales and margin goals
- Anticipates sufficient assortment to meet the needs across geographic locations and channels of distribution

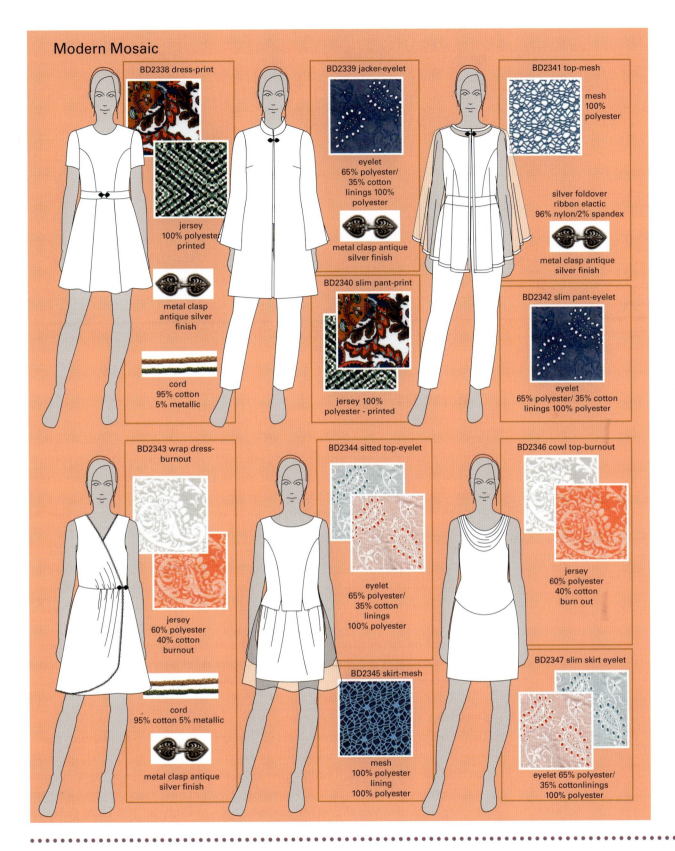

Modern Mosaic

BD2338 dress-print

jersey
100% polyester
printed

metal clasp
antique silver
finish

cord
95% cotton
5% metallic

BD2339 jacker-eyelet

eyelet
65% polyester/
35% cotton
linings 100%
polyester

metal clasp antique
silver finish

BD2340 slim pant-print

jersey 100%
polyester - printed

BD2341 top-mesh

mesh
100%
polyester

silver foldover
ribbon elactic
96% nylon/2% spandex

metal clasp antique
silver finish

BD2342 slim pant-eyelet

eyelet
65% polyester/ 35% cotton
linings 100% polyester

BD2343 wrap dress-
burnout

jersey
60% polyester
40% cotton
burnout

cord
95% cotton 5% metallic

metal clasp antique
silver finish

BD2344 sitted top-eyelet

eyelet
65% polyester/
35% cotton
linings
100% polyester

BD2345 skirt-mesh

mesh
100% polyester
lining
100% polyester

BD2346 cowl top-burnout

jersey
60% polyester
40% cotton
burn out

BD2347 slim skirt eyelet

eyelet 65% polyester/
35% cottonlinings
100% polyester

Figure 7.6
An assortment plan for a capsule collection entitled Modern Mosaic. The assortment plan is updated as fabric availability is confirmed and color matching and pattern strike-offs are approved.

Figure 7.7
Designers present their
silhouettes and fabrics
at concept review
meetings.

Concept Review

Once a design idea has been conceived—whether as a sketch, conceptual drape, fabric development, or purchased prototype—it must be sampled. A few domestic product developers have their own sample rooms, but most expect their supply chain partners to develop sample prototypes for a concept review. The **concept review** is a checkpoint for the design team to present their ideas to the merchandising, sales, and marketing teams to ensure that design assortments are in sync with line plan expectations. At this time, fabric, graphic, color, and silhouette direction are approved. Merchandisers, creative and technical designers, and merchant buyers look to identify any voids in the collection, production challenges, or details that need to be refined. The closer the first prototype matches the brand specifications in terms of final color, fabric, artwork, details, construction, and quality, the faster it can be approved if it's accepted into the line. Once the concept review takes place, discussions ensue to determine target prices based on preliminary costing. The creative design team makes any agreed-upon changes to concepts and the technical design team develops a spec package for those products that will mov e forward to the line review (Figure 7.7).

Sampling

Traditionally, the sampling process added a great deal of time to the product development calendar. Designers might design two to four garments for every garment that made it into the line. Testing those ideas as physical samples is expensive and time consuming. Today, more and more brands have moved toward virtual garment sampling, with the potential of cutting development times in half. Only garments accepted for the line are made into prototypes to check for quality and construction. When prototypes are eventually developed the fit has already been evaluated digitally. Cutting down the time needed for sampling and corrections allows brands to bring products to market faster and respond to shifting trends.

3D **virtual sampling technology** has advanced to the point that it now offers:

- Photorealistic 360-degree images of a true to life garment on 3D avatars that represent a brand's specific fit standards
- Realistic color reproduction through access to the same color libraries used for color matching
- Accurate fabric simulation that allows for print and logo placement
- In-motion fit analysis simulating a real-life fit session with tension maps that measure stretch and pressure points
- Cloud-enabled collaboration that facilitates teamwork between supply chain partners scattered around the globe
- Application program interface (API) that makes them compatible with other prototyping programs for things such as fabric swatches
- A commenting tool that allows designers to make notes directly on the image and collaborate on solutions
- The ability to manage different units of measurement (imperial vs. metric) and adapt designs to ensure size compliance across countries

The use of virtual samples enhances collaboration, allowing more supply chain stakeholders to take part in line review meetings. The more informed supply chain partners are, the better prepared they are to make decisions that support a brand's expectations. Risk can be minimized by finalizing design decisions at the last possible moment, thereby shortening the line development calendar.

Line Review and Distribution Plan

The product shown at the **line review** is fully defined and costed through a technical package; it represents the product that will go into production. It is at the line review that merchants or buyers quantify their orders, taking into consideration product needed for marketing campaigns, visual merchandising displays, and the assortments required for their distribution plan. The sourcing team can finalize their production plan. A distribution plan is developed that determines variations in product assortments geographically, across distribution channels, and between signature stores and lower-performing rural stores.

Time and Action Calendar

This entire process is part of a closely managed **time and action calendar**. The time and action calendar starts from market dates that are set by the industry or, in the case of retail product developers, the delivery dates when new merchandise must hit the stores. These dates are firm and non-negotiable as they coincide with promotional calendars. For fast fashion product, all tasks must be completed in four to eight weeks. To accomplish this turnaround, processes and partners must be in place to make decisions and approvals quickly. Traditional product may work on a thirty- to sixty-week schedule. There is no one-size-fits-all solution; many firms offer both kinds of product. Figure 7.8a and 7.8b shows an example of the tasks managed by a time and action calendar.

Figure 7.8a and b
The Time and Action Calendar manages and assigns responsibility for product development tasks in order to insure delivery by the date promised. Figure 7.8a illustrates how product development tasks for seasonal deliveries overlap throughout the year. Figure 7.8b illustrates the critical importance of meeting task deadlines in order to get a line delivered as promised.

Months (column headers): JANUARY, FEBRUARY, MARCH, APRIL, MAY, JUNE, JULY, AUGUST, SEPTEMBER, OCTOBER, NOVEMBER, DECEMBER

Activity (row labels):
- Market Research
- Fashion Research
- Fabric Research
- Color Research
- Collection Research
- Initial Fabric Selection
- Review Previous Sales
- Line Plan Meeting
- Line Plan Approval
- Order Fabric Sample Cuts
- Concept Boards
- Style Development
- Spec Sheet/Tech Drawings
- Pre-cost
- First Pattern/Prototype
- Fit Model Session
- Pattern Revisions
- Final Cost
- First Adoption
- Order Fabrics for Samples
- Revisions
- Final Adoption
- Review with Top Accounts
- Initial Sales Forecast
- Order Production Fabric
- Receive Fabric for Samples
- Cut and Sew Samples
- Line Preview (Sales Mtg)
- Grade/Production Marker
- Line Release (Start Selling)
- Receive Production Fabric
- Cut. Sew Production
- Sales Forecast Adjustment
- Order Additional Fabric
- Receive Additional Fabric
- Cut/Sew Additional Quantity
- Begin Shipping
- Complete Shipping
- Season Critique

a

"SP" represents the spring line, "SU" represents the summer line, "F" represents the fall line, and "H" represents the holiday line.

Private Brand Development Calendar for Moderate Time Action

		JAN	FEB	MAR	MAR	APR	MAY	MAY	JUNE
DESIGNDEVELOPMENT		SPRING 13				SUMMER 13			
Research and Development/Concept		2/7–2/21*							
Color Overseas		3/4*							
Start Development Packages/Build Blocks and Styles									
Development Packages ex NY to PO									
Samples due to NY		4/25*				6/22*			
MERCHANDISING									
Product Team Travel		4/13*							
Style Count Plans									
Buy Meeting/International Meeting	(3 wks)	6/13–6/17*				8/1–8/5*			
International Buy Meeting		6/20–6/24*				8/20–8/24*			
Finalize Orders/Total Style Count Confirmed	(1 wk)	6/8*							
Team meetings		6/6–6/10*							
FIT APPROVAL									
Early Turnover on Repeat Known Styles				8/1–8/5*		8/5–8/15*			
Style Adopt/Turnover/PE Review	(1 wk)	6/27*	7/18*	8/15*	8/15*	8/29*			10/10*
First Fitting (Style/Initial Fits)	(1 wk)	7/5–7/8*	7/18–7/25*	8/15–8/23*	8/15–8/29*	8/29–9/9*			10/17–10/28*
First PDM Due Date/Factory Allocation	(2 wks)	7/25*	8/12*	9/9*	9/9*	9/23*			11/11*
Approval Deadline	(8 wks)	8/26*	9/30*	10/14*	10/31*	11/9*			1/6
PRODUCTION WINDOW									
Production Start	(1 wk)	9/1*	10/7*	10/21*	11/7*	11/16*			1/13
Production Complete Transit to Consolidate	(8 wks)	10/7*	11/7*	12/5*	12/19*	1/16			3/3
Ship Window	(1 wk)	10/13–10/19*	11/14–11/18*	12/12–12/16*	2/26–12/30*	1/23–1/27	2/13–2/17	2/27–3/3	3/13–3/17
In DC	(8 wks)	12/5*	1/2	1/30	2/13	3/13	4/3	4/17	5/1
On Floor	(3 wks)	Jan	Feb	Mar	Mar	Apr	May	May	June

*Indicates dates are in 2012. Otherwise dates are 2013.

b

ORGANIZING THE LINE

There are two different approaches to organizing a line. One is to view each product as an item to be purchased separately. The other is to structure the line as groups of coordinating products, designed to be purchased as multiples. Increasingly, today's customer purchases items rather than coordinated outfits; however, even item lines need to be merchandized in a way that encourages multiple sales.

Item Line Development

In general, lines created around products that are intended to be sold one piece at a time are considered **item lines**. Sportswear garments, designed as items as opposed to coordinated groups, are sometimes referred to as *separates*. But anyone who has worked at retail understands that when making any sale, associates are challenged to sell more than one piece.

Consumers are increasingly gravitating to brands that specialize in making a certain kind of product. Think Athleta, Lululemon, and Levis (or any other denim brand). By specializing in a particular classification of product, these brands can take advantage of economies of scale—ordering large amounts of fabric at the best price—and of specialized construction expertise. They also become expert in the make of that category—working with the flat felled seams and rivets on jeans or the four-way stretch fabrics in exercise wear. Their designers become knowledgeable about the fit and functionality requirements of the category. These specialist brands are also best poised to integrate and initiate best practices in terms of sustainability for their category.

Item lines frequently start out making a single product or product category to test the market. These products are referred to as **hero products**—a small number of well-designed products that represent a brand's DNA and solve a design problem and serve as a gateway to the marketplace. The brand can then broaden the breadth and depth of their product assortment and categories as they better understand the marketplace. For example, Athleta started out as a specialist in functional exercise apparel and outerwear. They have expanded into swimwear and have explored sleepwear. They also added a robust selection of plus sizes, which they market aggressively.

Item lines frequently include a limited number of styles developed in a wide array of colors. Brands such as Lands' End, Old Navy, Gap, and Uniqlo are known for their item lines. Their color palettes are coordinated across a variety of categories so that goods can be appealingly merchandised in a brand's stores, catalogs, and websites, but their product developers understand that their customers are seeking items that tie into garments they already own; they generally don't purchase an entire outfit at the same time. It is not uncommon for a single tee shirt, sweatshirt, or polo shirt style to be offered in five to ten or more different colors (Figure 7.9a). These assortments have a longer shelf life since they are not designed for their fashion edge. They are more apt to be replenished rather than replaced by new merchandise and often do not need to be marked down until the end of the season, sizes or colors are out of stock, or the store is re-merchandised with a new seasonal color palette. Typically, product developers of separates lines use fit, proportions, styling, color assortment, and/or quality to achieve a competitive edge.

Item lines in categories such as dresses, swimwear, and coats are developed somewhat differently. Multiple small groups of three to six dresses might be designed for each delivery. Each dress group is designed using one to three related fabrics (Figure 7.9b). A solid fabric might be offered in two or three colors; a print group might feature a single fabrication in two or three related prints. Although most customers purchase one dress at a time, the product developer offers the retailer groups of dresses that will hang well together and offer the final consumer some degree of choice.

If the brand's distribution is large enough that it sells to multiple retailers that compete for the same customer, it needs to be able to sell different styles/prints to each vendor. Using a related fabric for several styles also helps these product developers to meet minimum

a

b

yardage requirements. Similarly, a single swimwear fabric may be offered in three or four different styles that appeal to different customers—for example, a tankini, a bikini, and a halter-style suit. Categories such as swimwear and dresses are seasonal, both doing much more business in spring/summer than in the fall.

Item lines are particularly appropriate for markets such as juniors, where disposable income is limited, and fashion interest is high. An increasingly casual lifestyle has also boosted a preference for separates. As the pace of fashion slows, many consumers are seeking out brand specialists that understand a category and build long-lasting, functional garments.

Coordinated Group Line Development

Coordinated group lines consist of items organized around fabric groups and intended to be purchased and worn together. There was a time when a coordinated group line might consist of fifteen to thirty pieces—skirts, pants, jackets, tops, blouses, and sweaters—that consumers could combine in a way that pleased their personal fashion sensibility. This approach has been more challenging with the popularity of separates, the tendency for more casual professional dress, and the consumer's quest for individuality.

New coordinated groups are typically delivered every six to eight weeks; fast fashion suppliers, such as Zara, pride themselves on introducing new items every two weeks. These small collections delivered more frequently are often referred to as **capsule collections**. Early fall collections revolve around seasonless fabrics. As the season progresses and the weather gets cooler, fabric groups will include heavier-weight wools, leather, and specialty fibers. Collections meant for holiday selling may include some dressier fabrications. Items within the group are not replenished; rather, the remaining pieces are marked down and cleared out as new deliveries arrive. This is meant to encourage consumers to make their purchases at full price while their size and styling preferences are still available. In general, coordinates are on the selling floor for six to ten weeks and are sold at full price for four to six weeks.

The fabrics used in a group line are meant to be mixed and matched, allowing customers to personalize their look. A customer can purchase a jacket with either a matched or coordinating skirt or pant and tie it together with a knit tee, a shirt, or a blouse (Figure 7.10). The colors within the fabric story are approved so that no matter what pieces are worn together, they all coordinate. When coordinates groups were larger a store did not necessarily buy every piece in the group. With capsule collections and direct to consumer shopping, the consumer is likely able to make their selection from the entirety of the line.

Coordinated groups are typically designed around a theme that may be expressed through a distinctive color palette, a unique fabric, or repeated use of an interesting detail. The theme helps to attract the consumer to the collection. An advantage of group lines is that if one style within the group does not sell well, the style can be dropped and the yardage that was committed to it can be diverted to production of another style that is selling better than expected.

Figure 7.10
Garments in a
coordinates line
are designed and
merchandised as a
related group to look
appealing on the sales
floor and promote the
sale of multiple pieces.

Those brands still designing coordinated groups have tended to incorporate more casual styles. Brands that embrace a slow fashion philosophy can maintain a related color story across the season, morphing slightly from one delivery to the next while adding new fabrics and layering pieces that evolve with the weather. Capsule collections are great for travel wardrobes. In general, they may hold more appeal for an older customer who has gotten used to that way of shopping and dressing.

LEGAL PROTECTION FOR THE DESIGN OF APPAREL

At the heart of the fashion business is a brand's ability to build and monetize their assets. Distinctive branding elements such as logos and trademarks as well as unique prints and patterns are all considered **intellectual property (IP)**. Intellectual property is an important body of law that protects "creations of the mind" such as novel inventions, ornamental aspects of useful products, literary and artistic works, photographs, and brand names, trademarks, and logos. It is an extremely nuanced aspect of the law. The US law is distinct in the protections it offers from the UK, the EU, and other countries.

In the United States, knocking off fashion silhouettes is more or less legal. The fashion industry has historically operated with no legal prohibition against copying. The fashion cycle is based on the introduction of an idea that is increasingly sought after by consumers and copied or interpreted by other product developers.

Chains such as Forever 21, Zara, and H&M have developed a reputation for their ability to take an idea seen on designer runways and interpret the look for their own stores in as little as six to eight weeks. This practice is often referred to as **design piracy**. Some copy the styling and proportions of the runway garment while adding their interpretation in terms of color and fabrication; others mimic the original design, line for line. The availability of runway photos and video immediately after shows take place gives product developers with a nimble supply chain plenty of time to copy designs and bring them to market at the same time the original designer garment hits the selling floor. These lower-priced copies differ in both quality and fit—but where designers sell several hundred of their ready-to-wear garments for thousands of dollars each, the knockoff may sell hundreds of thousands for under $200. It was interesting to follow fashion presentations during the COVID-19 pandemic where audiences were prohibited. While most designer brands released some sort of video or look book which was available to the public, the normal, editorial, photographic coverage of the presentations was missing. At this writing, it remains to be seen whether the absence of these photos compromised low-cost brands' ability to copy runway designs.

Intellectual property laws include copyright protection, trademark and trade dress protection, and patents. Patents have the least application to fashion; they protect new and useful processes, machines, products, and compositions and so are most likely to apply to the technology used to design or manufacture apparel. The ornamental aspects of fashion are generally not novel enough to be distinguishable from previous types of clothing, and ornamental patent protection is issued only when the design is not dictated by the function of the product. It is difficult to separate apparel design from its function. Therefore, most American courts have ruled that apparel designs do not meet the requirements for a patent (Cox and Jenkins, 2005, p. 10). Securing a patent is relatively expensive and time-consuming; given the brief life cycle of an apparel design, patents are not a viable option for pursuing design protection.

Copyright Protection

In the United States, **copyright law** provides legal protection for authors of non-useful, original compositions, including literary, dramatic, artistic, and musical works. Copyright protection is generally denied to clothing on the grounds that garment designs are intrinsically useful articles. Copyrights can be obtained for two-dimensional fabric designs, unique combinations of knit stitches, patterns on lace, original graphics on a tee shirt, and on occasion, the unique design of ornamental trims such as buttons and buckles. When a work qualifies for copyright protection, protection extends only to the particular manner of expression of the work; it does not extend to the underlying themes or concepts. Artists are free to consult the same source that was used for a copyrighted piece of art for their own original creations. Some accessories may be copyrightable if they have a nonutilitarian purpose.

Copyright protection exists as soon as a work is created; putting a copyright notice on all copies that are distributed to anyone for any purpose can preserve copyright protection. A proper copyright notice consists of the copyright symbol (©) or the word "*copyright*," the year of first distribution, and the name of the copyright owner. Although no action is required to obtain copyright protection, the copyright must be registered with the US Copyright Office before an infringement suit may be filed. In the United States, the copyright for work done while employed by a product developer is owned by the employer, not the employee, unless specific language to the contrary is written into a contract. Freelance designers must address ownership within the terms of their contract.

American courts have been guided by the principle that although copyright protection "might benefit certain designers, it could create monopolies in the fashion industry that would stifle the creativity of future designers, hinder competition, and drive up prices for consumer goods" (Cox and Jenkins, 2005, p. 6). The premise of fashion is that basic elements are constantly mixed and morphed into new combinations that reflect the times. David Bollier and Laurie Racine (2005, p. 6) explain:

> With great speed and flexibility, fashion constantly expresses shifting cultural moods, social demographics, and personal identities with new apparel designs and accessories. This remarkable and turbulent drama is, in turn, seamlessly integrated into a complicated market apparatus of global production, marketing and distribution. It is no accident that fashion permits and even celebrates the appropriation and modification of other people's creative designs; these practices are an indispensable part of the process.

Copyright protection for apparel exists to some degree in both Japan and the European Union. Japanese copyright law covers only apparel items that are unique—no identical or similar design can have existed before—ruling out most apparel products. In the European Union's Community Design System, apparel designs that are registered are protected if the copy is identical; if a minor change is made to a registered design, then it can be registered as a new design.

Proponents for copyright protection for apparel believe that it is necessary to stimulate creativity by providing incentives for creators to control access to their works and collect payment for them. It is challenging for new designers to amass the customers it takes to stay in business. Many a design talent has been forced to close his or her doors due to inadequate funding or been forced to sell out to a conglomerate in order to compete in fashion's high-stakes marketplace.

Those against copyright protection are worried about litigation clogging an already overtaxed court system. Those companies with enough money to hire lawyers will benefit most. Younger start-up designers, who may need protection the most, will likely not be able to afford the lawyers to file suits. Author Johanna Blakley (2010) summarizes her objection to the copyright protection as follows:

> Anyone familiar with the justification for copyright protection—without ownership there is no incentive to innovate—might be surprised by the critical and economic success of the fashion industry. A complex creative ecology has developed in the fashion world that balances a designer's need to both stand out and fit in. Since anyone can copy anyone else, they do. The almost magical result of this process is the establishment of trends. Some designers have ascended to the highest echelons of the fashion world and are well known for setting new trends with their original designs, but all designers admit that they're inspired by "the street," where people mix and match their own personal looks, combining a new Marc Jacobs bag with grandma's vintage sweater with Army surplus boots.

a

b

Figure 7.11a and b
Burberry sued
JCPenney in 2016
for appropriating its
signature plaid.

Given the challenges of proving copyright infringement in the US legal system, few brands bother to wage lawsuits using copyright protection as their defense. Given fashion's rapid cycle, most designers don't even bother to register their designs. This explains why fast fashion companies such as Forever 21, Zara, and H&M run into little legal scrutiny. Laws prohibiting design piracy have been introduced in the US Congress but never received the traction they needed to pass.

Trademark and Trade Dress

For many brands, using trademark and trade dress laws is the best legal strategy to challenge knockoffs of their work. A **trademark** is any word, name, symbol, device, color, or combination thereof that is adopted and used by a manufacturer or merchant to identify goods and distinguish them from those manufactured and sold by others. The Christian Louboutin brand successfully trademarked a particular color of red for the soles of their designer shoes. The brand name *Nike* and its "swoosh" logo are both examples of trademarks, as is the Levi Strauss stitching pattern on the back pocket of jeans. Similarly, the name Chanel and the logo of the interlocking Cs are protected.

Nike filed suit against streetwear brand, Warren Lotas, in October of 2020 shortly after the streetwear brand teamed up with noted Nike collaborator Jeff Staple for what both parties characterized as a reinterpretation of the cult-classic shoe, the *Nike Staple NYC Pigeon*. The Staple/Nike version was released in February of 2005. The Staple/Warren Lotas reinterpretation was released in 2020 and looked almost identical to the original Staple/Nike collaboration. The case was settled confidentially out-of-court. In February of 2016, Burberry sued JCPenney for copyright infringement of its trademark plaid that it has used since the 1920s (Figure 7.11a and b). Similarly, in 2018 Burberry sued Target for use of its trademark plaid on a scarf that was superficially indistinguishable in the use of the plaid, though inferior in fabric and quality. Both cases were settled out of court.

In a more nuanced case, Chanel has been fighting a legal battle against resellers. It filed lawsuits against *The RealReal* and *What Goes Around Comes Around* in what the resale companies have characterized as a bad faith quest to eliminate the market for preowned Chanel products. *The RealReal* argues that Chanel is engaging in an anticompetitive attempt to limit the supply of its products in the market. One of the most interesting arguments in the case centers on whether bags made in an authorized Chanel factory but that were never received by Chanel for quality control and approval are unlawful. Chanel also suggests that if a reseller refurbishes an otherwise genuine bag, it is no longer authentic (The Fashion Law, 2021).

The public recognizes trademarks and expects a certain caliber of product to be associated with the mark. Trademark law protects the designer from unauthorized use of the registered mark but does not protect the actual garment (or accessory) design. **Trade dress** is a broader term that covers the totality of elements in which a product or service is packaged and presented. Trade dress can include the shape and appearance of a product or its packaging, the cover of a book or magazine, or the unique layout and appearance of a business establishment. Marc Jacobs filed a complaint against the Christian Audigier Ed Hardy label asserting trade dress infringement in 2010. Ed Hardy's KOI "*Jana Nylon Tote*" copied the dimensions and overall appearance of the Marc by Marc Jacobs "*Pretty Nylon Little Tate.*" Marc Jacobs asserted that its quilted pattern, the knotted handles, vertical side pockets, metal plaque, and other details were all copied (Misterovich, June 2, 2015).

Counterfeits

In the United States, preventing counterfeit goods from entering the country and investigating intellectual property fraud is the responsibility of Customs and Border Protection (CBP) and Immigration and Customs Enforcement (ICE), both part of the Department of Homeland Security. The CBP's efforts focus on preventing illegal goods from entering the country; the ICE is an investigative branch that looks into human rights violations, financial crimes, cybercrimes, and export enforcement issues. The CBP seized 27,599 shipments of goods that violated intellectual property rights in 2019. The retail value of those goods amounted to $1.5 billion (Richter, February 11, 2020) (Figure 7.12).

Figure 7.12
The sale of counterfeit apparel and accessories is big business. Here a Customs agent displays a pair of counterfeit Christian Louboutin shoes.

Figure 7.13
The Industries Most
Affected by Counterfeit
Products

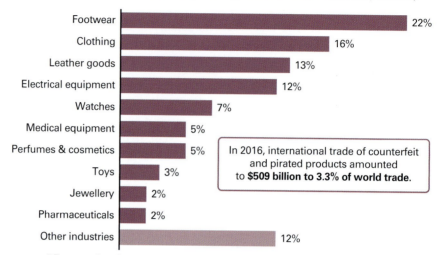

The Industries Most Affected by Counterfeit Products
% of total value of seized counterfeit and pirated goods worldwide in 2016, by industry

Footwear — 22%
Clothing — 16%
Leather goods — 13%
Electrical equipment — 12%
Watches — 7%
Medical equipment — 5%
Perfumes & cosmetics — 5%
Toys — 3%
Jewellery — 2%
Pharmaceuticals — 2%
Other industries — 12%

In 2016, international trade of counterfeit and pirated products amounted to **$509 billion to 3.3% of world trade.**

* Figures are based on customs seizures and therefore do not include domestically produced and consumed counterfeit and pirated products, or pirated digital products distributed over the internet.

Fifty-one percent of the total value of seized goods in the US consists of footwear, clothing, and leather goods (Figure 7.13) (Statista). According to the UN Office on Drugs, 87 percent of the counterfeit goods seized in the United States are from China (Richter, February 11, 2020). China's accession to full World Trade Organization (WTO) status requires that Chinese companies adhere to WTO guidelines when it comes to counterfeit and piracy control. These laws are comprehensive; border customs and inland public enforcement officials have the power to seize offending goods, but implementation of these laws is subject to political cycles (Figure 7.14). On January 15, 2020, the US and China signed a historic agreement on a *Phase One Trade Deal.* Included in the agreement were structural reforms to China's economic and trade regime in the areas of intellectual property, technology transfer, agriculture, financial services and currency, and enforcement against pirated and counterfeit goods. The deal got off to a rough start with China not committed to reducing the trade deficit, however, experts suggest that there are a great number of positive initiatives in the agreements to build upon.

The substantial growth of e-commerce platforms has facilitated growth in the importation of counterfeit and pirated goods. There was a time when these goods were primarily sold on street corners, from the trunks of cars, or in flea markets where consumers might suspect that the goods they were being shown were illegal. On e-commerce platforms, without the ability to physically examine a product, goods may appear to be genuine. Mainstream online markets such as Amazon and eBay don't always own the products they offer on their website. Besides the product they buy directly from brands and wholesalers, they work with third-party sellers that own and

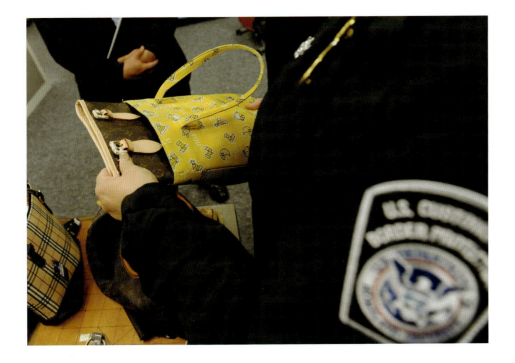

Figure 7.14
World Trade Organization guidelines allow border control customs officials to confiscate goods that violate intellectual property laws.

deliver products that are marketed and sold on the Amazon or eBay platform; this arrangement gives products that are being delivered through third-party providers an aura of authenticity and trust. Third-party sellers that are distributing counterfeit or pirated goods may provide authentic images of the brand product and its packaging but then ship copies.

Social media is often used to distribute counterfeit goods. Businesses set up accounts and post targeted ad campaigns that direct consumers to websites designed to evade detection. They may ask consumers to communicate via a messaging app for purchase details. Purchases are shipped by international air freight in small packages which makes detection more difficult since ICE and CBP efforts are usually focused on large container shipments. Expect to see strategies for controlling counterfeit and pirated products evolve.

SUSTAINABILITY

Merchandisers have a critical role to play if the fashion system is to embrace slow fashion and become more sustainable. Merchandisers are in a position to implement process changes and embrace new technology that:

- directly engages the consumer;
- better supports designers;
- shortens the product development calendar;
- more accurately forecasts customer demand and manages inventory; and
- encourages cross-functional and supply chain communication and collaboration.

The percentage of disposable income being spent on fashion continues to drop yet we have more in our closets than ever before. The availability of fast fashion has promoted overconsumption. Ridiculously low prices encourage impulse buying. For consumers who seek out sustainable apparel, it's not all about price. They are looking for investment value created through a combination of innovation, function, and quality.

Brands are increasingly engaging customers to help curate and edit assortments before garments are put into production. Product **experience management (PXM) software** uses real-time data analytics and customer feedback to find out what customers love and what they'll pay. Corporations as diverse as Saks Fifth Avenue, Athleta, and Kohl's already use this software to obtain feedback from a representative sample of their customers. This sample is asked to evaluate digital product in terms of color, fabrication, silhouette, proportion, and price. Their feedback helps merchandisers to optimize their assortments before costly investment decisions are made and ensures that assortments are priced right. They can also assess how their customer might respond to new product categories. Consumers are not designers and undoubtedly, innovation would be thwarted if the design function was totally democratic. Brands need to encourage innovation and value-driven design over generic, safe product to encourage investment purchases. That said, the small pool of fashion professionals who have curated fashion for so long do not necessarily represent the changing tastes of the consumer.

Shifting product focus to well-designed, *wear now* merchandise that is introduced in smaller, more frequent deliveries further encourages full-price sell- through. Brands are misguided to think that more is always better. It is difficult to compete in today's marketplace with mass-produced undifferentiated product. Furthermore, too much choice makes it difficult for the consumer to make a decision. In the end they defer their purchase until the product is marked down. Ongoing, well-conceived capsule collections delivered every few weeks are a means of minimizing risk. If a silhouette or size range isn't selling, fabric stocks can be diverted to another style and size assortments can be rebalanced. Scarcity of a well-designed product creates an urgency to buy at full price. It is almost always better to maintain margins on smaller inventories than to devalue products by discounting overstocks.

Stockouts can be managed by more agile inventory management or using attribute replenishment. If inventory is managed centrally rather than by channel (stores, DTC, international), when a late spring means that warm-weather garments aren't selling in one region, they can be moved to another where styles are stocking out. Online orders can be fulfilled from stores with excess stock. Using attribute replenishment, a dress silhouette that sells out can be offered in the next delivery in a new fabric with subtle changes to detailing.

Any technology that shortens the product development calendar means assortment decisions can be made closer to product release dates. Implementation of 3D virtual sampling eliminates much of the physical prototyping once required. Time traditionally spent waiting for physical samples can be used to reflect upon consumer feedback and refine design ideas, resulting in smaller but more focused collections.

Mid-market brands have attempted to compete with fast fashion brands on the basis of price. To get the lowest possible price, they've been required to place large production orders before actual sales are quantified. This practice leads to excess inventory and uninspired product. If decisions regarding production quantities can be postponed so that they are based on actual orders rather than forecasts, overproduction and excess inventory can be avoided. This in turn will lower risk, preserve margins, and ultimately improve profitability.

The segment of customers who care about sustainability is growing. As consumers become more sophisticated in their understanding of sustainability, they expect brand strategies that contribute to a circular fashion system. Promoting a line as sustainable just because it uses organic cotton is no longer sufficient. Customers want product that is designed to last, garments that coordinate from one season to the next, and a brand strategy that includes a protocol for extending the life of the garment. Redefining the merchandising function to better engage with consumers, make the design process more efficient, shorten the design development calendar, and better manage demand and inventory is central to sustainability.

SUMMARY

Merchandising a line is a cross-functional responsibility. It begins with the sales and profit goals identified in the strategic plan. These goals are fleshed out in a demand forecast that predicts revenues and projects merchandise needs throughout the year. A line plan is developed by the merchandising team based on the demand forecast and in tandem with a market analysis, generally developed in marketing. The merchandising team works with design to interpret trend forecasting research and customize those forecasts for the needs of the brand.

Once the line plan and line concept have been determined, the design team can begin the design process. Whether the line is organized as an item line or a coordinated group line, each garment will be displayed on the floor, online, or in a catalog as a group that tells a seasonal story. This is accomplished through decisions regarding color, fabric, silhouettes, and details that express the season's trends. Generally, designers come up with more ideas than can be produced. A concept review and line review serve to edit these ideas into those products most likely to meet the expectations of customers and meet sales and profit goals. 3D digital sampling allows designers and merchandisers to edit the line without making physical samples. This can shave weeks off of the design development process.

The line review is where merchants quantify what is needed to support inventory levels geographically and across distribution channels. A production quantity must be determined for each stockkeeping unit within the line.

Case Study 7.1
First Insight
Case Study

Merchandising is at the core of any business, but it is only recently that technology has focused on merchandising efficiencies (Binns, October 17, 2018). First Insight is a *software as a service* (SaaS) vendor leading innovation in the merchandising space. Their goal is to improve decision making with pre-season product testing to support customer-centric merchandising. The cloud-based platform relies on artificial intelligence and machine learning to provide merchandisers with factual data, which replaces a merchandiser's gut instinct.

Data analytics is central to First Insight software products. Data points are continuously collected across product performance, digital touchpoints, and consumer feedback. This data is analyzed using machine learning which helps to train the platform's algorithms to see patterns. These patterns help merchandisers select the right products and quantities (Binns, October 17, 2018).

Digital style-testing is central to the process. 2D or 3-D virtual prototypes of a brand's products are presented to a customer panel before physical samples are developed. Respondents are asked to give qualitative feedback as to what they like about the product, features they don't like, and what they would pay for it. Responses are aggregated and analyzed to determine which products will perform best. The need to develop physical samples is reduced by 40 percent. Users have reported sales increases of 6 percent and inventory reductions of 40 percent (First Insight.com). Furthermore, responses can be aggregated by region or country and into customer groups so that sales teams can make recommendations to merchants about which products will perform best for their business.

First Insight's *InsightPricing* tool brings together historical data and uses AI modeling to accurately predict the price elasticity (the variation in demand in relation to the variation in price) for each product. This gives merchants greater visibility into what a product's sell-through could be and helps them to plan for a reasonable markdown cadence. It also helps them to quantify production overs so they don't end up with a surplus of inventory.

By focusing on merchandise optimization, brands can mitigate the risk of offering too many products. By leaning into digital prototyping early, they can identify the likely winners faster and invest in the products that will be most successful, avoiding costly investment into developing products that are likely to under-perform. Consumers increasingly want to invest in fewer, better products. By identifying what product features the consumer is seeking, designers can leverage that information in future seasons. The savings from developing fewer, but better-targeted products can be invested back into the product. For example, users have found that they can raise prices for truly sustainable products by up to 10 percent. The *Risky Product Alert* feature is designed to enable brands to identify potential controversial or offensive items based on keywords that consumers provide in feedback comments (Taylor, August 27, 2020). The sales team can offer retail buyers *decision confidence* that the products they are recommending have already been identified as what the consumer wants to buy. The software connects via AOI to other "mission-critical" technologies such as CRM, PLM, CAD, and assortment planning systems so that all business functions can benefit from the data analysis that First Insight provides.

Resources

Binns, Jessica. (2018). "First Insight Brings AI, Machine Learning to New Merchandising Platform," *Sourcing Journal*, October 17. https://sourcingjournal.com/topics/technology/first-insight-customer-centric-merchandising-platform-ai-machine-learning-124111/ (accessed on March 3, 2021).

First Insights.com (accessed on June 2, 2021).

Taylor, Glenn. (2020). "Here's What's New in First Insight's Voice of the Customer Analytics Platform," *Sourcing Journal*, August 27. https://sourcingjournal.com/topics/technology/first-insight-voice-of-customer-analytics-risky-products-rue21-wolverine-227980/?__hstc=143860138.882cc674de79573826c6a7aac04f70a5.1627051350285.1627051350285.1627051350285.1&__hssc=143860138.1.1627051350285&__hsfp=304880126&hsCtaTracking=8141ed23-8726-48e1-aba8-865370fdc0b1%7C96ec2927-66d0-4d34-9c11-31f3c7b7453e (accessed on March 15, 2021).

The United States provides minimal legal protection for the design of apparel products due to the fact that apparel is considered functional; somewhat more protection is granted to textile designs. Brands such as Nike, Coach, Burberry, and Louis Vuitton rely on legal protections for trademarks that they use not only in advertisements but also on signature prints and prominent logos on their products.

Merchandisers are critical to building a sustainable brand. They control the scope and timing of the line; they are instrumental in pricing and planning net margins. To become more sustainable, merchandisers must adopt technology that allows them to engage directly with the consumer, shorten the design development calendar, make more accurate demand forecasts, and better manage inventory.

KEY TERMS

assortment plan	experience management	merchandise plan
capsule collections	software	product experience
concept review	hero products	management
coordinated group line	intellectual property	pyramid plan
copyright law	item line	time and action calendar
demand forecast	line review	trade dress
design piracy	market trends analysis	trademark
diamond plan	merchandise budget	virtual sampling technology

DISCUSSION QUESTIONS

1. Identify some of your favorite brands. Are they organized as item lines or coordinated group lines? What is their competitive advantage? How could they be merchandised more effectively?
2. Have you ever been asked to participate on a digital product experience panel? Describe your experience.
3. Brainstorm for reasons that designs might be eliminated from a line, other than their aesthetics?
4. Discuss how your purchasing habits might change if you were presented with well-designed products, available for sale in small quantities, timed to be worn immediately. If less merchandise had to be marked down, how might that impact the first price of garments?

ACTIVITIES

1. Visit an area mall or shop several online marketplaces. Shop a store that focuses on item lines. Identify several styles and how they are assorted by size and color. Then shop a store or department where the focus is on coordinated group lines or capsule collections. Study one group and identify the number of styles, fabrics, colors, and sizes in which this line is available. Which is more appealing to you?

2. Using the line plan developed in Table 7.1 and your own trend research for the upcoming season, complete the following tasks:

   - Develop color and fabric selections for the season.
   - Develop a preliminary line plan for your selected product category, including decisions about the number of styles to include and an estimate of the number of preliminary sketches that will be needed to arrive at a final line plan.
   - Develop an array of croquis sketches for a line of coordinated sportswear or a well-defined item line. (Plan for enough extras to explore your styling ideas and to provide good variety for selection of the final line.)
   - Develop a completed story board presentation for the line, adding flats for each final selection; include technical flats where needed.

STUDIO RESOURCES

- Take the chapter quiz with scored results and personalized study tips.
- Review glossary flashcards to build your vocabulary.

REFERENCES

Blakley, J. (2010), "The costs of ownership: Why copyright protection will hurt the fashion industry," *New Design Observer*, August 19. http://designobserver.com/feature/the-costs-of-ownership-why-copyright-protection-will-hurt-the-fashion-industry/15078/ (accessed July 26, 2011).

Bollier, D., and L. Racine. (2005), Ready to share: Creativity in fashion and digital culture. Conference paper presented January 29. www.learcenter.org/html/publications (accessed September 8, 2006).

Cox, C., and J. Jenkins. (2005), Between the seams, a fertile commons: An overview of the relationship between fashion and intellectual property. Conference paper presented January 29. www.learcenter.org/html/publications (accessed September 9, 2006).

Misterovich, Eric. (2015), Trade Dress in Fashion Design, June 2. https://revisionlegal.com/trademark/trademark-law/trade-dress-in-fashion-design/ (accessed on April 12, 2021).

The Fashion Law. (2020), Fashion Law in 2020: 12 of the Year's Noteworthy Lawsuits, December 28. https://www.thefashionlaw.com/fashion-law-in-2020-12-of-the-years-noteworthy-lawsuits/ (accessed on April 10, 2021).

Richter, Felix. (2020), U.S. Customs Seized Counterfeit Goods Worth $1.5 Billion in 2019, February 11. https://www.statista.com/chart/20787/value-of-shipments-seized-at-the-us-border-for-intellectual-property-right-violations/ (accessed on April 10, 2021).

CHAPTER 8

GARMENT STYLING

"I wish I had invented blue jeans. They have expression, modesty, sex appeal, simplicity—all I hope for in my clothes." Yves Saint Laurent

OBJECTIVES

- To explore the changing role of apparel designers in an evolving fashion system
- To consider the various methods of recording design ideas and experimenting with styling options
- To understand how to use the design elements in combination with design principles to create aesthetically pleasing garments
- To recognize garment classifications and the style variables for each
- To understand how design details add interest to garment styling and how they affect garment cost and production scheduling
- To explore ways that designers can build sustainability into garments

The fashion system is characterized by changes in the zeitgeist. New colors, fabrics, and silhouettes cycle in and out of style. Brand designers can't expect to interpret all of the new fashion ideas at any given moment in time. Instead, they seek to identify the macro and micro trends that impact consumer behavior, and then determine which of those ideas will translate into items that the brand's target customer will buy.

Today's consumers build their wardrobes by adding new items each season that update the basics they already have. As society becomes more casual, fashion has become increasingly **item-driven**. In an item-driven environment, customers tend to buy more single garments than coordinated ensembles. Successful silhouettes must:

- Match the lifestyle and aesthetic preferences of the target customer
- Provide value in terms of quality, function, and fit
- Be produced within a targeted price point
- Be produced to arrive on the retail floor when the customer is ready to buy

Because consumer preferences do not change drastically from season to season, silhouettes tend to evolve, with one style morphing into another. This chapter discusses how to translate design research into silhouette ideas that are appropriate for a specific market. It also explains how to use design elements and principles to create harmonious and salable garments. It points out the style variables of each garment category that can be manipulated in order to differentiate a silhouette.

EXAMINING THE CREATIVE PROCESS

Taste is subjective. In a consumer-centric fashion environment, one might worry that the role of the designer is diminishing, but this is not the case. The role of the designer is changing. It continues to require a designer's eye and ability to identify and interpret new ideas and new attitudes. Their curiosity, exploration, and experimentation add richness to our fashion system. Designers help us to move beyond what's familiar and discover what's new.

In a consumer-centric environment the design process may become more collaborative, but it will continue to require the talent, skill, and training of a designer to interpret the zeitgeist and give apparel meaning. Design in a slow fashion environment is not random; pulling references out of thin air and mimicking the work of others does not create enduring value. Informed design provides relevant solutions that translate insights and influences into meaningful forms of self-expression.

The technical training of design teams is what brings a vision or idea to life. Underlying the creative fashion design process is the relationship between the inside and outside of the garment—between an expressive silhouette and all the technical skill and construction that goes into achieving it. It is important to recognize and value the different levels of design creativity based on experience, technical skill, time, resources, intellectual and creative curiosity, etc.

Some brands offer very few original ideas. These design teams develop **knock offs**—silhouettes that copy the ideas of others, generally in less expensive fabric and poor-quality construction. This is how fast fashion brands such as Forever 21, Zara, H&M, Boohoo, and Primark are able to bring new styles to market in one to four weeks. It is almost impossible to be truly creative in this type of fast-paced environment.

One step up from knocking-off the design ideas of others is **derivative design**. Brands that rely on derivative design adapt the ideas of runway designers or other brands. In essence they are stylists. Derivative designs provide consumers with looks that are similar to what is available at more expensive price points. Examples of derivative design can be found at all price points but are especially prevalent in mass market private brands where basic silhouettes are restyled from season to season.

Interpretive designers and brands are inspired by the zeitgeist. They translate macro and micro trends into wearable, functional designs that are original but break few boundaries. Rather, the added value of these designs comes from higher end, inventive fabrics; more complex construction; and innovative details. Designers are technically experienced and can interpret more complicated silhouettes. They may begin to push boundaries but tend to be more commercial. Adaptive designers typically work for mid- to high-price brands. Athleta, Eileen Fisher, and Giorgio Armani might be considered interpretive brands/designers.

Avant-garde designers break the rules, innovate with new technology, and are masters of fabric manipulation. They value an interdisciplinary approach to design and are more concerned with creativity than commercial viability. The level of original thinking of avant-garde designers can't be learned; only a small number of designers truly achieve it. Examples of avant-garde designers include Iris Van Herpen, John Galliano, and Comme des Garçons (Figure 8.1a–d).

The democratization of design—similar styles available at all price points—comes at a cost. It has resulted in a homogenization of the marketplace. In environments where designers are expected to produce new styles every week or two, there is little time to be creative. To stand out in the future, garments will need to be created not copied. Generally, the price tag of the garment correlates with the level of design creativity.

Methods for Developing Design Ideas

The design process parallels the research process. Just as the researcher tests hypotheses, the designer explores and manipulates fabrics and silhouettes. Ultimately, the best silhouettes are included in the seasonal line and put to the test in the marketplace.

Product developers use a combination of methods to gather ideas and translate their research into a collection. Common approaches include:

- Studying historic or cultural references
- Buying actual garments to study their silhouette, fit, fabric, or detailing
- Exploring designer fashion presentations through trend forecasts and/or the internet
- Sketching design ideas observed while doing market research
- Experimenting with interesting sample fabrics on a dress form
- Creating new styles virtually using 3D technology

Figure 8.1a
The Louis Vuitton signature print is frequently knocked off, with the resulting products sold as copies. The fact that the signature print is actually coated canvas, not leather, makes it easier to knock off.

Figure 8.1b
Armani is an example of an interpretive designer. He has pushed the boundaries of tailoring over the course of his career.

Figure 8.1c
Yohji Yamamato is an example of an avant-garde designer with his mastery of fabric manipulation.

a

b

c

Figure 8.2
The theme or concept
for a collection may
come from travel,
an art exhibition, or
research of a particular
era, culture, topic, or
interest. Images of that
experience or research
serves as a springboard
for seasonal themes that
inspire garment design.

The ability of a designer to communicate creative ideas effectively is pivotal to the success of a brand. The designer must convey not only the appearance of the garment but also its mood and energy. The technique a design team uses depends on their skill level, the garment category, the brand's fashion level, lead time, technology, and budget.

Studying primary resource material frequently results in the most original design ideas. High-end designers may get new ideas from traveling to exotic locales or viewing costume exhibitions featuring the works of great artists or designers (Figure 8.2). Some museums offer memberships that allow designers to study the work of a particular period or designer in their archives.

Many product developers have budgets for purchasing garments. Those who work derivatively have the largest budgets because their lines are developed directly from the samples they buy. Buying samples abroad, rather than from domestic competitors, enables product developers to better differentiate their lines. Brands that are less derivative have smaller budgets; they only buy samples when they want to reinterpret a particular fabric, fit, detail, or construction technique that they cannot capture through sketching or photographs. Very small brands generally have no budget for purchasing garments and are left to interpret trends in other ways.

Forecasting services offer easy access to designer looks as well as images of streetwear taken all over the world. Access to designer presentations can also be found for free on the Internet. The advantage of a forecasting service is that they cull through many images to identify the most important silhouettes and details and group examples to illustrate an emerging trend They help brands interpret the many trend options to the brand's target customer. For time-strapped or less experienced design teams they also offer silhouette templates; however, relying on these templates may result in a lack of differentiation for the brand.

Designers use sketching just as a student or researcher takes notes. Sketches help to quickly document a fleeting idea, so it is not forgotten (Figure 8.3). These quick sketches of the figure with loose drawings of the clothing silhouette and details are called **croquis sketches**. A realistic representation of the female figure is about eight heads high. In contrast, fashion croquis figures are elongated, drawn anywhere from nine to twelve heads high. A skilled artist can quickly sketch a croquis figure freehand, but many excellent designers have not developed that confidence. To ensure that their focus is on the design of the garment, not the proportions of the figure, they may rely on an **underdrawing** or *lay figure*—a well-proportioned pose that can be slid under a page and used as a template to help control proportions and the location of garment details (Figure 8.4). When using an underdrawing, the design idea is drawn first and

then the visible head, arms, and legs are added. There is no need to draw in facial features or hair. Some designers sketch over an underdrawing without adding the body itself. These sketches are called **floats**. The most commonly used croquis poses are full frontal or three-quarter views. As designers select the ideas they are going to develop and present, they will also need to sketch the back of the design. Only very small designers that do custom production would rely on solely on a croquis drawing.

Designers frequently carry a small sketchbook (3 × 5 in. or 5 × 7 in.) with them whenever they shop, making note of unique ideas, details, or proportions. A larger croquis figure may be reduced on a copy machine and used as an underlay for **thumbnail sketches**—very small, quick sketches of design details and/or silhouettes. Where possible, they may try on garments to get a feel for how they relate to the body. The privacy of a dressing room allows the designer to use a tape measure to define key measurements that are integral to achieving a unique proportion, or to study the construction of a garment. Notations in the form of measurements and verbal descriptions can assist a designer in remembering what they saw. Hopefully, the designer will not try to duplicate exactly what they saw, but rather focus on some unique

Figure 8.4
Designers may use an underdrawing of the figure to help them document ideas more quickly.

Figure 8.5
Ultimately silhouettes must be drawn as a flat in order to communicate with the technical design team exactly where to place seams and details. Filled flats include color and/ or digitally rendered fabric.

Figure 8.6
Designers may use draping on the form to explore the characteristics of a particular fabric or to manipulate the fabric into a unique silhouette.

element of the design that they can later interpret and integrate into their own silhouette. Though digital shopping can help a designer cover a lot of ground in terms of quantity of research, there is nothing like shopping in a physical store where one can try on a garment, understand the fit, and feel the fabric. Designers who don't have strong sketching skills may use their phone to capture images.

Many designers develop their ideas as **technical flats** or flats, accurate drawings of the front and back of a proposed garment as it appears in two dimensions spread out on a flat surface. They visually define the proportions, details, and construction techniques required for production purposes. Flats may be drawn by hand to capture a design idea, but most companies utilize the computer for technical flats so that they can be added to the tech package. Hand-drawn flats, used to express a design idea, may be somewhat stylized, showing a little more garment movement. Digital flats can be filled with color or a digital representation of the fabric in which they will be manufactured (Figure 8.5).

With advances in 3D design, there may come a time when even the drawing of flats becomes unnecessary. Garments may be imagined on a 3D avatar, a pattern will be reverse draped from the avatar, and a virtual garment created from which orders can be taken.

Designers who are fabric driven and have well-honed skills in fabric manipulation may use draping to explore silhouette design. Draping allows a designer to explore the personality of a fabric, play with grain, and create more three dimensionally. Luxury designers use draping not only as a patternmaking technique, but also as a design tool. It is also frequently used for dresses, evening wear, and swimwear (Figure 8.6).

Concept Boards

Once the general theme of a delivery has been determined, designers begin to collect ideas for fabrics, silhouettes, and details. The color palette may have already been determined. Designers will usually collect these ideas on a board above their workspace so that they can see how ideas and silhouettes work together. What starts as a collection of tear sheets and random swatches evolves into sketches and fabric samples that are being developed for the season. These working boards help the designer to see voids in the collection as well as identify silhouettes that are redundant. Ultimately the designer is seeking to offer a well-balanced collection that meets the diverse needs of the brand's customer. Designer **concept boards** are an extension of the trend boards developed in the early stages of merchandising. They are collections of images, sketches, color references, and swatches that express the silhouette direction a brand is exploring for a particular delivery. They provide a visual for conversations with the merchandising team and the technical design team (Figure 8.7). Concept boards may be physical or digital depending on how they will be shared.

Figure 8.7
Designers collect tear sheets, sketches, and fabric swatches and use a board to identify voids and redundancies in a given collection.

DESIGN ELEMENTS AND PRINCIPLES

The design of a garment requires the selection and interpretation of color, fabric, silhouette, details, and fit. When these elements work together, the garment enhances the appearance of the wearer, thereby enticing him or her to make a purchase. When these components are haphazardly combined, the resulting design is disappointing, and customers may tire of it quickly. The remainder of this chapter focuses on how to use the elements and principles of design as tools to create appealing garments. Major garment categories are introduced and methods for differentiating and manipulating basic silhouettes are explained. This information, used in combination with the techniques already described, provides the foundation for silhouette development.

Design is the organization of design elements, using design principles, to create products that are aesthetically pleasing to the observer. Professionals who work with the elements and principles of design in a creative, original way are referred to as designers; those who adapt the ideas of others are sometimes called **stylists**. The design process for any product—be it automobiles or apparel, furniture or kitchen appliances—relies on an understanding of design elements and principles. Assuming that these have been taught in other classes, what follows serves as a brief review.

Design Elements

Design elements are the building blocks of design. These elements—line, color, texture, pattern, silhouette, and shape—are intrinsic to every product, including apparel.

Line

Line determines the silhouette of the garment and the shapes formed within the garment. Internal garment lines may be created through the use of garment seams and edges; fabric patterns and textures; and details such as tucks, pleats, darts, gathers, and linear trims. Lines have several aspects that determine their character. These include length, boldness, thickness, and direction (Figure 8.8). The impact of line is further defined by how frequently it is repeated, its placement, and whether it is used symmetrically or asymmetrically.

The use of line can create optical illusions on the body. Rectangular silhouettes and shapes tend to be more slimming than horizontal ones; however, the use of striped patterns may be an exception to that rule. Most of us grew up to believe that the use of vertical stripes elongates the figure, making it appear slimmer; whereas the use of horizontal lines shortens the figure, making it look wider. Figure 8.9 illustrates that the impact of stripes on the figure depend not only on their direction but also on their placement, width, and frequency.

Figure 8.8
The quality and direction of lines used in garments have a physical and psychological impact on how we perceive the wearer.

THE APPEARANCES OR ASPECTS OF LINE

Aspect	Variation	Appearance	Physical Effects	Psychological Effects
Path	Straight		Emphasizes angularity Counters rotundity	Stiff, Direct, Precise Dignified, Tense, Masculine
	Curve	arc	Emphasizes body curves Counters thinness	Dynamic, Feminine, Active, Youthful, Unrestrained
	Jagged		Emphasizes angularity	Abrupt, Nervous, Jerky
	Wavy		Emphasizes roundness	Feminine, Soft, Flowing
Thickness	Thick		Adds Weight	Forceful, Aggressive
	Thin		Minimizes weight	Delicate, Dainty, Calm
Continuity	Continuous		Emphasizes bulges, Smooth	Consistent, Sure, Firm
	Broken		Emphasizes irregularities	Less Certain, Staccato
	Dotted		Spotty, Varied	Interrupted, Playful
Edge/ Sharpness	Sharp		Emphasizes smooth or bumpy area	Definite, Precise, Assertive
	Fuzzy		Gently increases size	Soft, Uncertain
Edge Contour	Smooth		Emphasizes a smooth or textured surface	Suave, Simple, Sure
	Shaped		Varies with shape	Complex, Involved, Busy
Consistency	Solid/Closed		Advances boldly	Sure, Smooth, Strong
	Porous		Advances little, recedes little	Open, Delicate, Less Certain
Length	Long		Emphasizes direction	Depends on the area
	Short		Breaks up space	Abrupt Staccato

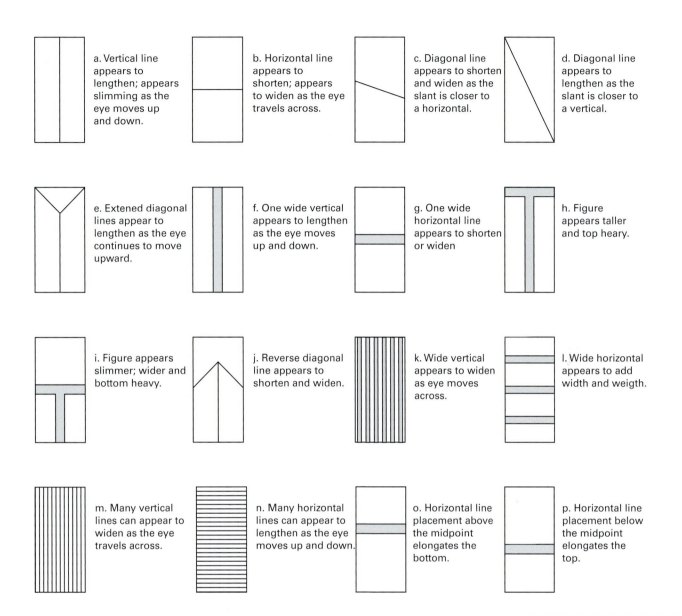

a. Vertical line appears to lengthen; appears slimming as the eye moves up and down.

b. Horizontal line appears to shorten; appears to widen as the eye travels across.

c. Diagonal line appears to shorten and widen as the slant is closer to a horizontal.

d. Diagonal line appears to lengthen as the slant is closer to a vertical.

e. Extended diagonal lines appear to lengthen as the eye continues to move upward.

f. One wide vertical appears to lengthen as the eye moves up and down.

g. One wide horizontal line appears to shorten or widen

h. Figure appears taller and top heary.

i. Figure appears slimmer; wider and bottom heavy.

j. Reverse diagonal line appears to shorten and widen.

k. Wide vertical appears to widen as eye moves across.

l. Wide horizontal appears to add width and weigth.

m. Many vertical lines can appear to widen as the eye travels across.

n. Many horizontal lines can appear to lengthen as the eye moves up and down.

o. Horizontal line placement above the midpoint elongates the bottom.

p. Horizontal line placement below the midpoint elongates the top.

Figure 8.9
The placement and spacing of lines may have the effect of lengthening or widening the figure.

Color

The importance of the element of color was explored in Chapter 5. Because color speaks to individuals on so many levels, it is recognized as one of the first things that attracts a customer to a garment.

How color is utilized in an ensemble can create figure illusions. As previously discussed, color hues are frequently classified as either warm or cool. Warm colors—red, yellow, and orange—tend to draw in the viewer and make an area appear larger. Cool colors—blue, green, and violet—tend to recede and make an area appear smaller. Bright, saturated colors tend to call attention to the figure, creating an illusion of bulk, while darker values (addition of black) or less-saturated colors (addition of gray) absorb light and tend to be more slimming. Wearing a darker shade of a warm color or a less-saturated version of a bright color that is in fashion may be more flattering on some figures. Lighter colors are often more flattering to the face, hence collars are often white or a lighter color than the body of the garment.

Color harmonies also affect how we perceive the figure. Monochromatic ensembles—ensembles made up of a single color or shades of that color—tend to be slimming because they create an illusion of height. When an ensemble consists of a top and bottom of different colors, that long line is broken up into two shorter shapes. Some customer groups are more sensitive to these nuances than others. Understanding how color affects the figure can help to provide options when selecting a color range for a particular silhouette or when determining how to best use color harmonies that are in fashion.

Designers must also be aware of color symbolism. Color palettes are often chosen for their symbolism in an attempt to match the mood of the zeitgeist. Global brands must recognize that the meaning of a color in one part of the world may have a very different meaning in another part of the world. Table 8.1 gives a brief summary of cultural differences in color symbolism.

Texture

Texture is the term used to describe the surface or hand of a fabric and can be attributed to a combination of the fabric's characteristics—fiber, yarn, construction, weight, and finish. A fabric's hand affects how it drapes. The texture of a fabric affects how we perceive color. Shiny surfaces, such as satin or metallics reflect light, emphasizing the color and making the figure look larger. Pile surfaces, such as velvet, chenille, and corduroy absorb light, giving the color more variation. Pile surfaces also have more loft or thickness, thus making the figure look larger. Stiff fabrics, including taffeta and organza, stand away from the body; as a result, the garment silhouette may need some reference to the body to communicate its shape. Drapey fabrics, such as matte jersey, and fabrics cut on the bias tend to cling to the body, identifying its natural curves—which may or may not be desirable. By using a dress form, a designer can explore the natural attributes of a fabric. Fabrics and their textures are used to best advantage when allowed to do what they do naturally.

Pattern

Some fabrics also have pattern. A **pattern** is a repeated decorative design that can be constructed into the fabric through weaving, knitting, or felting or applied to the fabric through printing, embossing, and other specialty techniques such as devoré or laser cutting. The popularity of specific patterns is subject to fashion cycles (Figure 8.10a). In a manner similar to line, color, and texture, patterns can help to create figure illusions. In general, the pattern should be scaled to the wearer. The placement of large

Table 8.1 Cultural Differences in Color Symbolism

Red	China	good luck, celebrations, summoning
	Cherokee	success, triumph
	South Africa	mourning
	India	purity
	Russia	Bolsheviks, Communism
	Eastern	worn by brides
	Western	excitement, danger, love, passion, Christmas (with green), "stop"
Orange	Ireland	religious (Protestants)
	Western	Halloween (with black), creativity, autumn
Yellow	China	nourishment
	Egypt	mourning
	Japan	courage
	India	merchants
	Western	hope, hazards, cowardice
Green	China	worn by cuckolds (green hat), exorcism
	India	Islam
	Ireland	fatherland
	Western	spring, new birth, Saint Patrick's Day, Christmas (with red), "go"
Blue	Cherokee	defeat, trouble
	Iran	heaven, spirituality
	Western	depression, sadness, conservatism, corporations, "something blue" bridal tradition
Purple	Thailand	mourning (widows)
	Western	royalty
	Japan	death (white carnation)
	Eastern	funerals
	Western	brides, angels, good guys, hospitals, doctors, peace (white dove)
Black	China	worn by young boys
	Western	funerals, death, Halloween (with orange), bad guys, rebellion

Source: Kyrnin, J. (2008). Color symbolism chart by culture. *About.com*. Retrieved July 2, 2008, from http://webdesign.about.com /od/color/a/bl_colorculture.htm.

a   b

motifs may need to be engineered on the body to avoid calling attention to certain body parts. This can be more easily accomplished with today's digital printing technology. Large patterns are generally best used in garment silhouettes where there is extra fabric and the pattern can drape in folds over the body or in slim silhouettes where there are few darts and seams (Figure 8.10b).

Silhouette

The garment **silhouette** is the outer shape of a garment. The size and shape of the silhouette is the first thing we see when a garment is on the body. Silhouettes are sometimes described by letters such as A, H, T, V, or Y, in which the silhouette follows the shape of the letter. Silhouettes may also be described as specific shapes (trapezoid, tent, hourglass, pear, or bell) or identified from periods in history (empire or flapper) (Figure 8.11a–d). Aspiring designers should make a point of mastering the language of fashion; terms may evolve any time a silhouette or detail reappears in fashion.

It is not always possible to see a silhouette clearly when a garment is on a hanger. When a garment is hanging, we tend to notice the color and fabric first. The silhouette comes to life when the garment is viewed on the body—which is why mannequins are used to display merchandise in stores.

Garment silhouettes need to be comfortable and functional in order to accommodate the lifestyle needs of consumers. To that end, they tend to evolve more slowly, with silhouettes rotating in and out of fashion. The mass market is likely to reject

a   b   c   d

Figure 8.11a–d
Garment silhouettes may be described in terms of their geometric shape or a historic period including (a) trapeze, (b) empire, (c) bell or hourglass, and (d) shift of flapper.

Figure 8.12
YSL's Mondrian dress illustrates how shapes can add interest within a garment.

silhouettes that are considered extreme. Designers must understand the underlying ideas in a given fashion season. They must also understand patternmaking and construction in order to translate those ideas into garment silhouettes. Understanding the various classifications of garment silhouettes and how they vary is basic to the design process.

Shape

The silhouette is frequently sectioned off into smaller shapes within the garment using seam lines, details, and garment edges (Figure 8.12). These shapes can:

- Add styling interest to the silhouette
- Help to achieve fit
- Allow for the combination of two or more fabrics
- Allow the designer to create optical illusions and/or enhance body proportions
- Add functionality (such as pockets)
- Create symmetrical or asymmetrical balance
- Create equal or unequal proportion
- Create rhythm within the ensemble

The use of shape is an important tool for achieving harmony within the garment. Garments that are sold as coordinates should be evaluated so that their shapes are related.

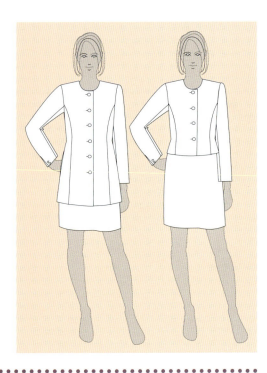

Figure 8.13
A garment with unequal proportions (left) and a garment of equal proportions (right).

Figure 8.14
A garment with symmetric balance (left) and a garment with asymmetric balance (right).

Design Principles

The design process revolves around determining how to combine the design elements we have just reviewed into a pleasing whole. Those decisions are guided by an understanding of **design principles**. Design principles include proportion, balance, emphasis or focal point, rhythm, and harmony or unity.

Proportion

Proportion is the relationship or scale of all of a garment or ensemble's parts to each other and to the body as a whole. Horizontal lines, such as yoke and waistline seams or jacket and top edges, divide a garment or ensemble into sections. The ancient Greeks judged proportions by the rule of the golden mean. They believed that ratios of 2:3, 3:5, and 5:8 were the most pleasing to the eye. Figure 8.13 illustrates unequal and equal proportions.

Balance

Balance refers to the distribution of visual weight of objects, color, texture, and bulk in a garment, giving it a sense of stability or equilibrium. It is determined by dividing a silhouette vertically down the middle. A **symmetric** garment appears to be the same on both sides. A garment with symmetric balance can be easily changed with accessories and can be readily mixed and matched with other symmetrical garments in the wardrobe.

An **asymmetric** garment is different on each side. Asymmetry may be achieved by an off-center closing or a pocket detail on only one side of the garment. Asymmetric garments must be carefully thought through during the patternmaking and cutting processes. Coordinating garments should be similarly balanced or neutral with no visible center point (Figure 8.14).

Focal Point or Emphasis

A garment's **focal point** or *emphasis* is the first place on the garment to which the eye is drawn. It may be created through a convergence of lines, a combination of colors, or a detail. If several elements of the design are competing for the viewer's attention, the garment may be overdesigned. The designer should evaluate whether the second focal point would best be used in another design.

Rhythm

From the focal point, the eye should move naturally through the entire garment. **Rhythm** is the natural movement of the eye through the related elements of a garment. Rhythm can be achieved by strong silhouette lines; through the use of color, line, or shape; or through the use of repetition, sequence, alternation, radiation, or gradation (Figure 8.15).

Harmony or Unity

Successful placement of a focal point that suggests rhythm is key to achieving **harmony** or *unity* in a design. Harmony means that all of the design elements work together in a garment to produce a pleasing aesthetic appearance and to give a feeling of unity to the design.

A designer should assess every garment they create by identifying how they've used the principles of design. With critical observation and experience, fashion designers enhance their ability to identify what makes a garment unique and special and when a garment is overdesigned. Designers use the principles as a form of notation to remember a garment they've seen or a germ of a new idea. Skillful use of the design principles is critical in creating sustainable garments designed for longevity.

Antifashion Movements

Every so often there is a cycle in fashion which is labelled anti-fashion. Anti-fashion movements often occur when a generational cohort is coming of age during challenging times. The movement may trickle up from the street where outliers attempt to express their disenchantment with what is going on socially, economically, or politically. Other anti-fashion movements are initiated by designers who detest the constant barrage of trends and seek to break the rules of design by dismissing traditional construction principles and design aesthetics or by designing for disenfranchised groups of customers. No matter where it originates, anti-fashion movements are bellwethers that call attention to societal issues and are vehicles for highly skilled and expressive designers to expand our thinking and affect change. One of the earliest anti-fashion movements was the Rational Dress Society, which called for the emancipation of women from dress codes that deformed women, impeded movement, and endangered health. Coco Chanel (garçonne), Marc Jacobs (grunge), Vivienne Westwood (punk), and Yohji Yamamoto have all spent major parts of their careers breaking the rules (Figure 8.16). Yamamoto once said, "I think perfection is ugly. Somewhere in the things humans make, I want to see scars, failure, disorder, distortion." Knowing when to follow the rules and when to break or push the rules is another challenge to the designer.

Figure 8.15
The pleats on this jacket lead the eye up and down through the ensemble creating its rhythm, which is continued as the eye follows the wrapped panels on the skirt. The length of the jacket and the skirt are the same, creating equal proportion. However, the jacket features symmetric balance and the skirt is asymmetrical. How do you feel about the overall harmony? Is it over-designed?

Figure 8.16
Punk fashion in the 1980s is an example of an anti-fashion movement often aligned with Vivienne Westwood.

GARMENT VARIATIONS BY CATEGORY

In Western dress, there are basic classifications of garments typically worn by men, women, and children. Within each garment classification, there are certain elements that vary from season to season according to fashion trends and the specific needs of various target markets. Style variables are characteristics of the garment that contribute to its shape, fit, and identity. These may include length, degree of fit, how it hangs on the body, fullness or flare, cut of armscye (*armhole*), and neckline style. When the garment fits close to the body, shaping devices are necessary. **Shaping devices** are darts, seams, pleats, and gathers that help to mold the garment to the contours of the body (Figure 8.17). The use of fabrics made with fibers such as Lycra also helps to shape garments.

For product development purposes, garments for men, women, and children are often broadly classified as tops or bottoms. Included within each broad classification are subcategories of garments worn by each consumer group. Most product developers have at least two sets of specification forms: one set up for the measurements, pattern blocks, and operations involved in making tops, and another for bottoms. Some product developers may have a different set of forms for every category of garment they develop.

Figure 8.17
A simple skirt may be shaped at the waist using darts, seams, release pleats, or gathers to vary the silhouette.

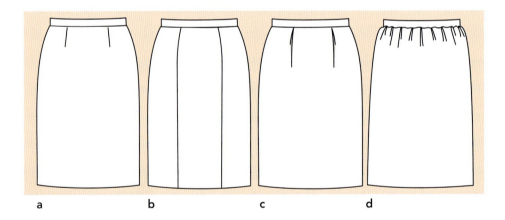

a   b   c   d

Tops

The categories for tops are similar for men, women, and children, but silhouettes vary more dramatically for women than they do for men and children. The term **tops** has two meanings. In the broader meaning, tops must have a front and back bodice; some also have sleeves. Tops include tee shirts, sweaters, shirts and blouses, vests, indoor and outdoor jackets, and coats. Jackets, coats, and dresses are considered tops because they must fit the body torso; they are tops rather than bottoms because they are developed from torso pattern blocks. In the narrower sense, for import and export classification purposes, the tops category generally includes tee shirts, sweatshirts, hoodies, tank tops, crop tops, and the like.

Tops and Tee Shirts

The tops and tee shirts category is generally differentiated from sweaters by their cut-and-sew construction methods. **Cut-and-sew construction** means that the garment pieces are cut from yardage rather than knit to shape. Ribbings, when used, are sewn on with a seam rather than linked. The fit varies from tight-fitting tube tops to oversized tee shirts, sweatshirts, and hoodies.

Tee shirts are perhaps the simplest classification of tops. This is a garment classification with few style variables. A tee shirt consists of a front and a back bodice and sleeves. Tee shirts are dartless and characterized by a ribbed band or other edge finish around the neck. Tee shirts typically are made of cotton jersey or interlock knits. The silhouette can be adapted by using silk, polyester, linen, or rayon knits or woven fabrics for tee shirts that can be worn under suits instead of blouses. The addition of Lycra to any of the preceding fabrics gives the tee shirt a more body-conscious fit without the use of shaping devices. Tops are an important category in active sportswear. The tee shirt silhouette can be elongated to wear as a swimwear cover-up, dress, or nightshirt. Style variables in tops and tee shirts are presented in Table 8.2 and Appendix Figure 8A.1.

Table 8.2 Tops and Tee Shirts

Style Variable	Description
Fit and shape	Varies from body-conforming fit; achieved with stretch fabric, seaming, or darts to dartless and oversized.
Hang from body	Hangs from the shoulders or from above the bust.
Length	Varies from cropped to waist length to hip length to tunic or dress length.
Sleeves	Vary from long or short to cap-sleeved or sleeveless; sleeve cap may be smooth, pleated, or softly gathered.
Armscye	Varies from traditional armhole to extended shoulder to halter style to raglan to kimono.
Neckline	Includes a full range of necklines from jewel to bateau to V-neck and others.

Sweaters

Sweaters are knitted garments worn on the upper part of the body that incorporate some degree of full-fashion construction. In the UK, sweaters are called "jumpers," not to be confused with American jumpers, which are a sleeveless form of dress worn over a blouse or top. **Full-fashion construction** means that some part of the sweater has been knit to shape. At a minimum, sweater lengths are linked together so that the ribbing can be attached through linking as opposed to serging. In other sweaters, shaping for the armscye and neckline are also knit to shape. Sweaters can be categorized as **pullovers** (sweaters that are pulled on over the head) or **cardigans** (sweaters that have a front opening). Sweaters are traditionally thought of as garments that

Table 8.3 Sweaters

Style Variable	Description
Fit and shape	Varies from body-conforming (spandex in yarn, shaped at side seam, knit-in darts) to oversized.
Hang from body	Typically hangs from the shoulders, but off-the-shoulder or strapless styles may hang from above the bust.
Pullover or cardigan	May be designed to be pulled over the head or to open down the front.
Length	Varies from cropped at waist to elongated tunic or dress.
Sleeves	Vary from long or short sleeves to cap-sleeved or sleeveless.
Armscye	Varies from traditional armhole to extended shoulder to raglan to dropped armhole to kimono.
Neckline	Includes a full range of necklines, from turtleneck or mock turtle to cowl, jewel, and bateau or V-neck.

provide warmth, but the advent of **sweater sets** or **twin sets** has popularized sleeveless knit shells that can be worn with or without the cardigan sweater with which they are paired. Sweaters typically have a front and back bodice—the front may be one piece, or two pieces in the case of a cardigan—and sleeves. Sleeves are typical but not mandatory, as are other accessory parts. Style variables in sweaters are presented in Table 8.3 and Appendix Figure 8A.2.

Shirts and Blouses

Shirts and blouses are garments for the upper body. They are generally made from woven fabrics. Shirts feature an extended shoulder, a sleeve with a straighter cap, and a collar band and/or collar. Shirts are typically looser fitting (no darts) although some have side panels for a closer fit. Blouses are similar garments generally worn by women and girls. They may be loose fitting or shaped with darts or extra seams. They are designed with greater styling variation in the neck, collar, and sleeves. Style variables in shirts and blouses are presented in Table 8.4 and Appendix Figure 8A.3.

Jackets and Vests

A **jacket** is a short coat worn for indoor use. Jackets used to be primarily associated with professional dress; however, today casual jackets that can be worn with jeans are equally important. (Jackets intended for outdoor wear are discussed in the next category.) A **vest** is a sleeveless version of a jacket. Jackets are more complicated than other tops. They may be boxy without shaping devices or linings, or they may be very

Table 8.4 Shirts and Blouses

Style Variable	Description
Fit and shape	Varies from straight and oversized to semifitted with darts, a side-front seam, or princess seams.
Hang from body	From the shoulder, a dropped shoulder, or a yoke.
Closure	Traditionally opens down the center front. Blouses may be pulled over the head with a front or back keyhole opening or button down the back, across one shoulder, or asymmetrically down the front.
Length	Varies from the high hip level if meant to be worn out, 6 to 8 inches below the waist when tucked in, or to the thigh for an oversized look.
Sleeves	Shirts generally feature a minimal cap and an extended shoulder seam. Blouses may be sleeveless or with sleeves; sleeves vary from set-in to shirt sleeves to raglan to kimono; sleeve cap may be smooth, gathered, or pleated.
Armscye	Most shirts feature a dropped armhole and extended shoulder that allows the sleeve to be sewn in prior to the side seam joining. Armholes on blouses match the sleeve type.
Neckline	Round necks with band, shirt, or convertible collars. Blouses may be designed with a full range of necklines and collars.

fitted through the use of seams and darts. Very tailored jackets incorporate construction techniques that include taping of seams and roll lines, interfacing throughout the jacket front that is either fused or pad stitched, interfaced hems, and shoulder pads. This construction helps jackets to maintain their silhouette for extended periods of time. It also tends to make them more expensive to produce and often requires them to be dry-cleaned to maintain their shape.

Jacket backs may be one-piece or two-piece; a two-piece back allows for shaping in the center back seam. Jacket fronts may be one-piece if minimal fit is desired, or they may incorporate a princess seam that starts from the shoulder or the armscye if a close fit through the bust is desired. A common jacket body variation is to use a back, a front, and a side panel. In this silhouette, there is no side seam. The side panel starts at the armhole on the front and back and extends down to the hem. This allows for some fit through the bust and waist, but the shaping seams are less distracting. Darts can be used on the jacket front or back to further shape the garment (Figure 8.18). Jacket sleeves may be one-piece or two-piece. Two-piece sleeves are common when the sleeve hem includes a vent, although vents can be included in a one-piece sleeve if the underarm seam is moved slightly to the back of the sleeve. Today, jackets may be made out of anything from cotton denim to double-faced wool to leather, each with a unique target market, price point, and construction and care requirements.

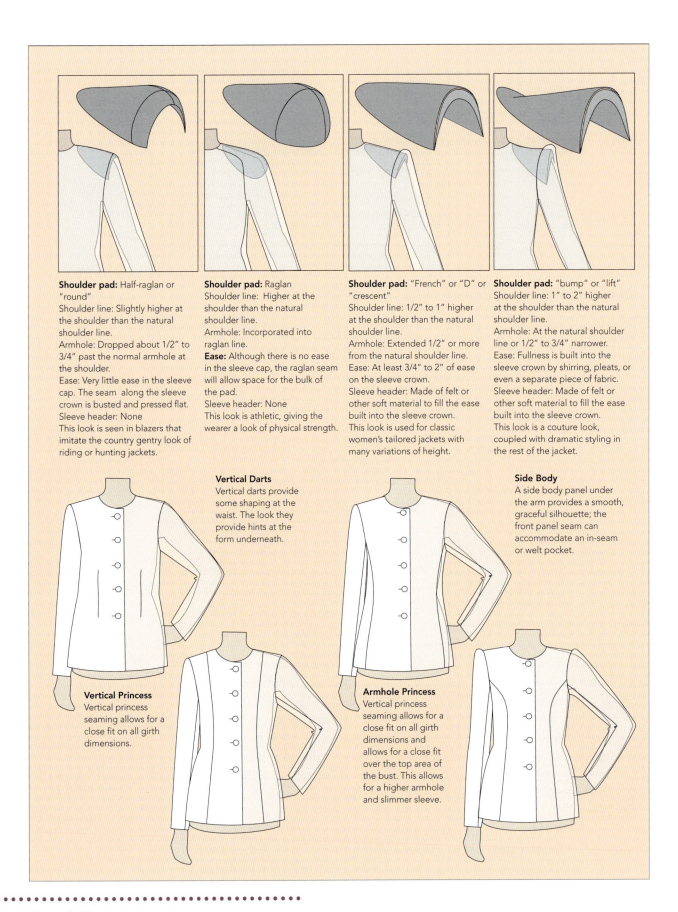

Shoulder pad: Half-raglan or "round"
Shoulder line: Slightly higher at the shoulder than the natural shoulder line.
Armhole: Dropped about 1/2" to 3/4" past the normal armhole at the shoulder.
Ease: Very little ease in the sleeve cap. The seam along the sleeve crown is busted and pressed flat.
Sleeve header: None
This look is seen in blazers that imitate the country gentry look of riding or hunting jackets.

Shoulder pad: Raglan
Shoulder line: Higher at the shoulder than the natural shoulder line.
Armhole: Incorporated into raglan line.
Ease: Although there is no ease in the sleeve cap, the raglan seam will allow space for the bulk of the pad.
Sleeve header: None
This look is athletic, giving the wearer a look of physical strength.

Shoulder pad: "French" or "D" or "crescent"
Shoulder line: 1/2" to 1" higher at the shoulder than the natural shoulder line.
Armhole: Extended 1/2" or more from the natural shoulder line.
Ease: At least 3/4" to 2" of ease on the sleeve crown.
Sleeve header: Made of felt or other soft material to fill the ease built into the sleeve crown.
This look is used for classic women's tailored jackets with many variations of height.

Shoulder pad: "bump" or "lift"
Shoulder line: 1" to 2" higher at the shoulder than the natural shoulder line.
Armhole: At the natural shoulder line or 1/2" to 3/4" narrower.
Ease: Fullness is built into the sleeve crown by shirring, pleats, or even a separate piece of fabric.
Sleeve header: Made of felt or other soft material to fill the ease built into the sleeve crown.
This look is a couture look, coupled with dramatic styling in the rest of the jacket.

Vertical Darts
Vertical darts provide some shaping at the waist. The look they provide hints at the form underneath.

Side Body
A side body panel under the arm provides a smooth, graceful silhouette; the front panel seam can accommodate an in-seam or welt pocket.

Vertical Princess
Vertical princess seaming allows for a close fit on all girth dimensions.

Armhole Princess
Vertical princess seaming allows for a close fit on all girth dimensions and allows for a close fit over the top area of the bust. This allows for a higher armhole and slimmer sleeve.

Figure 8.18
The shaping devices used in a jacket determine its fit.

Vests require less complicated construction than jackets to maintain their shape. In some environments, they can be a viable and less-expensive alternative to the jacket for professional dress. In menswear, the vest is sold as a third piece with a suit during some fashion cycles. Women's wear occasionally offers this same option. Vests are also important in active sportswear; some styles have detachable sleeves so that they function as either a jacket or a vest. Style variables in jackets and vests are presented in Table 8.5 and Appendix Figure 8A.4.

Table 8.5 Indoor Jackets and Vests

Style Variable	Description
Fit and shape	Varies from boxy silhouettes with no shaping devices to a fit achieved through center back and side seams, darts, princess seams, and/or side panels.
Hang from body	Generally hangs from the shoulder, although the location of the shoulder seam may vary.
Length	Varies from cropped to knee-length to floor-length evening jackets.
Front opening	Single-breasted or double-breasted; symmetrical or asymmetrical.
Sleeves	Traditionally long, but three-quarter length or short-sleeve versions are available. Long sleeves may be one-piece, two-piece, or one-piece with the seam toward the back; with or without a vent. Vests are sleeveless.
Armscye	At the shoulder or extended from the shoulder. Raglan, saddle, and kimono sleeves are options.
Neckline	Jacket necklines may be round, V-neck, square, or sweetheart. Jackets may be collarless, but traditional jackets and jackets for men are characterized by collars. Vests are typically collarless.

Outerwear Jackets and Coats

Outerwear jackets and coats are garments that are worn for warmth and protection from the elements. They may be tailored or sporty and made out of wool, cotton, polyester, or nylon insulated with fleece or down. Outerwear jackets and coats have a more generous fit than indoor jackets so that they can be worn over other clothing, including indoor jackets. Style variables in jackets and coats are presented in Table 8.6 and Appendix Figure 8A.5.

Table 8.6 Outerwear Jackets and Coats

Style Variable	Description
Fit and shape	Varies from boxy silhouettes with no shaping devices to a fit achieved through center back and side seams, darts, princess seams, and/or side panels.
Hang from body	Hangs from the shoulder, although the location of the shoulder seam may vary.
Length	Varies from cropped to knee-length to floor-length.
Front opening	Single-breasted or double-breasted; symmetrical or asymmetrical.
Sleeves	Long or three-quarter length sleeves; sleeves on jackets may be removable. Sleeves may be one-piece or two-piece.
Armscye	May be at the shoulder or extended from the shoulder. Raglan, saddle, and kimono sleeves are options.
Neckline	Generally round or V-neck in order to cover the neckline worn underneath and protect the wearer from the elements. Jackets and coats typically have collars.

Dresses

Dresses are one- or two-piece garments that fall from the shoulder or high bust and continue to surround the torso of the body, ending anywhere from the mid-thigh to the floor. For the purposes of this discussion, dresses are categorized as tops because they hang from the body on the shoulder or above the bust and share other characteristics of tops. However, dresses must also accommodate the hip area, and they may be designed as two pieces, consisting of a separate top and bottom. Dresses typically are developed from bodice and skirt pattern blocks that are seamed together or from a torso pattern block that combines the bodice and skirt without a waistline seam (Figure 8.19). Two-piece dresses utilize either a bodice or a torso block for the top and a skirt block for the bottom. Style and silhouette variables in dresses are presented in Table 8.7 and Appendix Figure 8A.6.

Figure 8.19
A princess seam silhouette may be varied by changing how those seams impact the fit and sweep of the garment. Changing the neckline, collar, sleeve, closure, or pockets can further vary the style.

Table 8.7 Dresses

Style Variable	Description
Fit and shape	Like other tops, dresses may be dartless with little shape or they may be fitted with darts, seams, yokes, and/or fullness. The fit above and below the waist may be blended seamlessly or may contrast, utilizing one shaping device above the waist and another below the waist.
Hang from body	Generally hang from the shoulder, although the location of the shoulder seam may vary. Dresses may also hang from the high bust. Two-piece dresses include skirts that hang from the waist.
Length	Varies from mid-thigh length to floor length.
Sleeves	Short or long sleeves, cap sleeves, or no sleeves. Strapless dresses that hang from the high bust typically have no armhole and no sleeve.
Armscye	May be at the shoulder, cut in toward the neck, or extended from the shoulder. Raglan, saddle, and kimono sleeve lines are options.
Neckline	Full range of neckline shapes. Dress necklines frequently have both front and back interest.

Bottoms

Bottoms are garments that encircle the lower body. Bottoms include pants, shorts, and skirts. Bottoms for children vary by age, gender, and activity, but include pants, shorts, and skirts (for girls).

Skirts

A **skirt** hangs from the body at or near the waist and covers the hips and upper legs but is not bifurcated to go around each leg separately as do pants. The basic pattern block for a skirt is a straight skirt with two to four darts in the front and back, and a waistband. From a basic skirt block, many other skirt silhouettes can be designed (Figures 8.20a and b). Culottes and gauchos are sometimes classified as skirts because they are developed from a skirt block, even though they are bifurcated. The common design variables in skirts are presented in Table 8.8 and Appendix 8A.7.

Pants

Pants are bifurcated garments worn by men, women, and children. Pant legs vary from skintight leggings to wide, elephant-leg pants or palazzo pants. Today there is an expanding category of active sportswear pants that includes biker shorts, yoga pants, and ski pants, to name just a few. Style variables in pants are presented in Table 8.9 and Appendix Figure 8A.8.

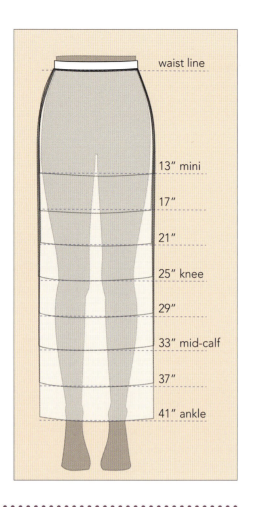

waist line

13" mini

17"

21"

25" knee

29"

33" mid-calf

37"

41" ankle

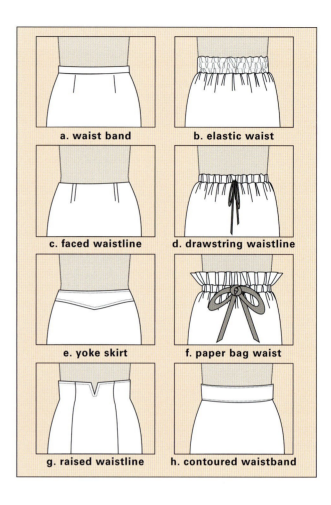

a. waist band

b. elastic waist

c. faced waistline

d. drawstring waistline

e. yoke skirt

f. paper bag waist

g. raised waistline

h. contoured waistband

Figures 8.20a and b
Skirts are often defined by their length and/or
waistline treatment.

Table 8.8 Skirts

Style Variable	Description
Length	Micro-mini length to floor-length.
Fit and shape	The body curve between the waist and hip is generally fitted by darts, pleats, fullness, or flare. Darts can be eliminated in the front for flat figures; this works best in fabrics with Lycra.
Fullness	Gathers or pleats at the waist control some amount of extra fabric, which is released somewhere below the waist.
Flare	A fit that is flat at the waistline and full at the hem.
Waist location	Skirts may hang from the waist, or slightly higher on the rib cage, or fall from the high hip.

Table 8.9 Pants

Style Variable	Description
Waist	May hang from the waist or slightly higher on the rib cage or fall from the hip or high hip.
Length	Ranges from very short shorts (mostly worn by women and children) to Bermuda shorts, Capri pants, and long pants.
Pant leg width	May vary from body-conforming, as in leggings, to wide evening pants for women. Added width may extend all the way up the leg, as in pajama pants, or taper from the thigh or knee, as in flares or bell-bottoms. Men's pant legs tend to vary less in width from a boot-cut jean to a full-cut trouser to a drawstring casual pant.
Fit	May be shaped to fit the waist, hips, and buttocks using darts, pleats, or gathers. Darts can be eliminated in the front for flat figures; this works best in fabrics with Lycra.

Specialty Categories

The previous list covers basic garment categories, but specialty categories may be equally important in a brand's market. The **athleisure** market has become very important with casual lifestyles and jobs where many can work from home. Leggings are almost as ubiquitous as jeans and oftentimes more comfortable. Lingerie, sleepwear, and swimwear are other examples of special garment categories. Designers approach these categories in the same way, identifying the elements that can be changed or varied to differentiate product from delivery to delivery.

GARMENT DETAILS

Garment details provide a means of changing classic silhouettes from season to season. They add to the aesthetics of a garment silhouette and provide a visual link to a fashion theme. **Details** include component parts, decorative embellishments, and trims. **Component parts** are elements of a garment that are not part of its basic structure but add aesthetic interest or provide functionality. Examples include collars, cuffs, pockets, and belts. **Decorative embellishments** add to the fabric of the garment, such as smocking, quilting, tucking, appliqué, and embroidery. These embellishments may be added at the fabric yardage stage or strategically applied to a cut piece. Trims are details added to the garment, such as buttons, braids, and lace.

Details can be added to garments for aesthetics or functionality. Examples of decorative details include a tucked front on a blouse, a ruffle on the hem of a skirt or dress, and a monogram on a blouse. Functional details include pockets, buttons, and hoods. Details should enhance the aesthetics of the garment or add function without making the garment too expensive for its target market.

Designers and product developers should keep files of interesting details because the popularity of details and decorative techniques is cyclic in the world of fashion.

Cycles of minimalism and heavy embellishment frequently alternate in popularity. It is important for product developers to have good working relationships with a variety of trim vendors so that when a new trim or detail becomes important, they readily know where to source it. The remainder of this chapter discusses component parts, including closures, as they relate to the design process.

Component Parts

Component parts are so much a part of the garment that they often are not thought of as details. A good designer is attuned to picking up on the subtle changes in proportion, shape, and placement of component parts.

Necklines and Collars

The neckline of a garment frames the neck and provides an opening for the head. It may be finished simply with a facing, ribbed band, or bias binding; it may be further embellished with a collar. Necklines may be round, square, scooped, sweetheart, or V-shaped. Neckline variations are illustrated in Appendix Figure 8A.9.

Collars are component parts that surround the neck and are attached permanently or temporarily to the neckline of the garment. Detachable collars may make garments easier to clean, but detachable details are a problem for merchants. They are easily stolen or lost, thus compromising the value of the garment. Collars are integral details for many garments—particularly shirts, blouses, jackets, and coats—and are frequently the focal point.

A designer must understand collar terminology in order to design a successful collar. A collar **stand** is the part of the collar that fits close to the neck. The collar **fall** is the part of the collar that turns over the stand or garment. The collar **roll line** is the line where the collar fall turns over the stand. The collar **style line** is the shape of the outer edge of the collar.

Additional terminology applies to tailored collars. The collar **lapels** are part of the garment front and are designed to attach to the collar and turn back over the garment. The **breakline** is the line on which the lapels turn back. The **break point** is the point along the front edge of the garment at which the lapel begins to roll back. The **gorge line** is where the collar and the lapel are joined. The **notch** is the triangular shape between the lapel and the collar, formed where the gorge line ends (Figure 8.21). With that terminology in mind, consider the four factors that determine a collar's shape:

1. The placement of the garment neckline in relation to the base of the neck
2. The shape of the neckline seam in relation to the length and shape of the neck seam on the collar
3. The shape and depth of the fall of the collar
4. Whether the collar has a revere or lapel, and the size and shape of that revere or lapel

Flat collars have neckline curves that are the same shape as the neckline of the garment. This allows them to lie flat on the garment with no roll or stand onto the neck. Examples of flat collars include Peter Pan collars, Bertha collars, and sailor collars. Flat collars are popular on children's clothes because children have short necks. They create a youthful feel on adult garments.

Partial roll collars have neckline curves that are straighter than the neckline of the garment but not perfectly straight. This creates a stand at the back of the collar but allows the collar to lie flat on the garment as it comes around to the front. Convertible collars, Chelsea collars, tailored collars, and shawl collars are examples of partial roll collars.

Stand collars have neckline edges that are straight in relation to the neckline curve of the garment. This straight edge causes the collar to encircle the neck. Turtleneck collars, shirt collars, mandarin collars, and tie collars are examples. Straight collars that are cut on the bias tend to hug the neck and are more easily manipulated in collars that tie. Learn to analyze the grain of collars as well as their shape when researching these details.

Gathered ruffled collars have a longer neck seam on the collar than the neckline and must be gathered or pleated to fit the neckline seam. *Circular ruffle collars* have a neck seam the same length as the neckline seam but a neck curve that is greater than the neckline seam, causing the style line of the collar to fall into soft folds referred to as a flounce. Cowl collars, as opposed to cowl necklines, are a variation of the turtleneck. They are frequently used on a neckline that is placed away from the base of the neck. Extra length is left in the fall of the collar so that it bunches over the stand. Collar variations are illustrated in Appendix Figure 8A.10.

Tailored collars are more complex than other collars and require more careful shaping during construction. They may be used on jackets, coats, and dresses. A well-designed collar can be the focal point of a tailored garment. This is an important detail for designers to explore. Study the relationship between the lapel and the collar at the gorge line and the angle they form at the notch. Tailored collars can be changed dramatically by raising or lowering the break point. This may affect how a jacket is merchandised because a high break point may eliminate the need for wearing a shell or blouse under the jacket. A suit jacket that does not require a blouse for modesty is known as a dressmaker suit. A low break point can be very slimming because it creates a long V-line in the front, but it may be difficult to control gapping at the neck when the garment is worn, particularly on full-figured consumers. Figures 8.22a and b illustrate a few variations of both tailored and shawl collars.

Shawl collars are similar to tailored collars except that they do not have a gorge line. Shawl collars are drafted as an extension of the bodice front. They make a nice foil for decorative techniques or decorative edges. Shawl collars can be varied in width

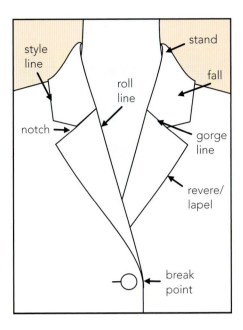

Figure 8.21
A diagram of the parts of a tailored collar.

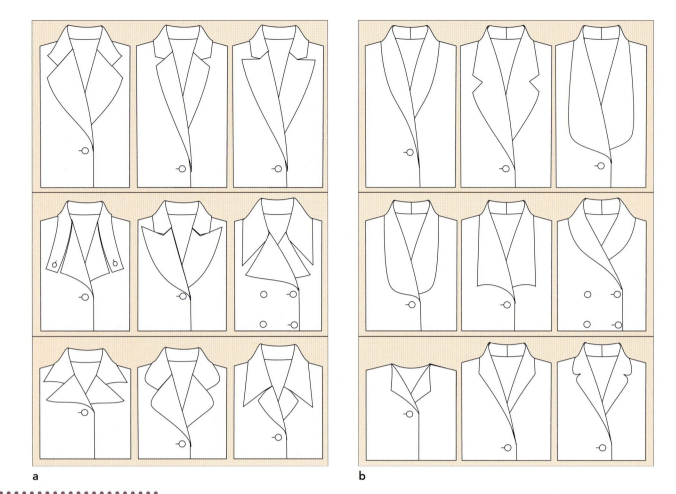

a   b

Figure 8.22a
Tailored collars (a) may be varied by manipulating the collar and lapel length or width, changing the collar shape, changing the location of the break point; or changing the notch or gorge line.

Figure 8.22b
Shawl collars (b) are varied by changing the break point, the width, or the shape of the collar.

by lowering or raising the break point or by shaping the collar style line. Diagonal fabric designs or weaves do not translate well into shawl collar designs and should be avoided in this style.

Sleeves and Cuffs

Although sleeves are a structural part of the garment rather than a component part, style variations for sleeves are discussed here. Sleeves are designed to fit the armscye. The armscye may be cut in at the shoulder as in a halter style, in which case a sleeve is not appropriate. When the armscye is in its natural location on the body, a set-in sleeve is an option. The shoulder line may be extended or the armscye may be lowered, in which case a looser-fitting sleeve is appropriate. A raglan sleeve extends the sleeve line into the neckline as does a saddle sleeve. Kimono and dolman sleeves are cut in one piece with the garment body. Common sleeve variations are illustrated in Appendix Figure 8A.11.

The bottom of the sleeve may be hemmed, finished with a vent, or attached to a cuff. Hems may be blind hemmed, machine rolled, topstitched, or finished with a facing, flounce, or ruffle. Vents are frequently found on tailored jackets at better price points. A sleeve vent is located slightly back from the normal location of an underarm seam. Vents are usually found in two-piece sleeves, or the underarm seam on a one-piece

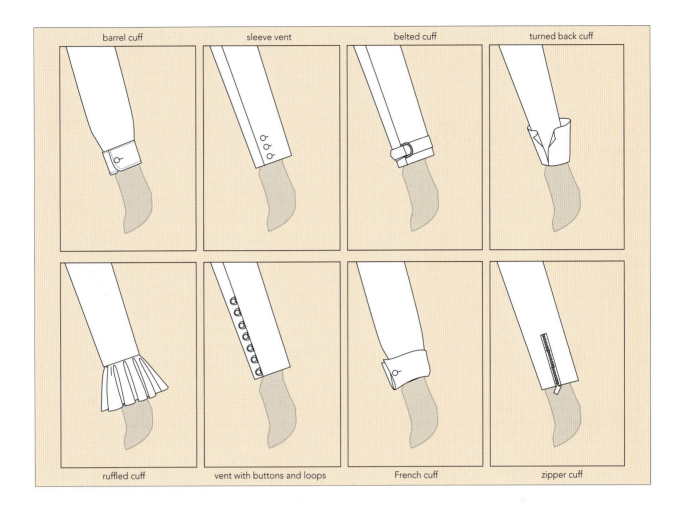

barrel cuff	sleeve vent	belted cuff	turned back cuff
ruffled cuff	vent with buttons and loops	French cuff	zipper cuff

sleeve may be moved to the back in order to accommodate a vent. Designers are aware of the numerous ways to construct vents and will specify the method that suits their quality level, price point, and fabric. Cuffs may be applied to a straight, gathered, or pleated sleeve edge. Figure 8.23 illustrates various ways to finish a sleeve bottom.

Pockets

Pockets consist of extra fabric attached to the inside or outside of a garment to form a pouch with a top or side opening. Pockets play both decorative and functional roles in garment design. Pockets may be classified as inside or outside pockets. On **outside pockets**, the pouch or bag of the pocket is visible from the outside of the garment. On **inside pockets**, the pouch falls inside the garment with only an opening visible from the outside. The pocket opening is traditionally large enough to fit a hand—5.5 to 6.5 inches across the opening for adult women. This measurement may be smaller for a decorative effect. Some pockets are intended to be nonfunctional; they are designed as such to cut costs or prevent distortion of the garment's fit. Pockets may be used symmetrically, in pairs, or asymmetrically. Figure 8.24 illustrates various pocket styles.

Figure 8.23
Sleeves can be varied by changing how the bottom edge is finished.

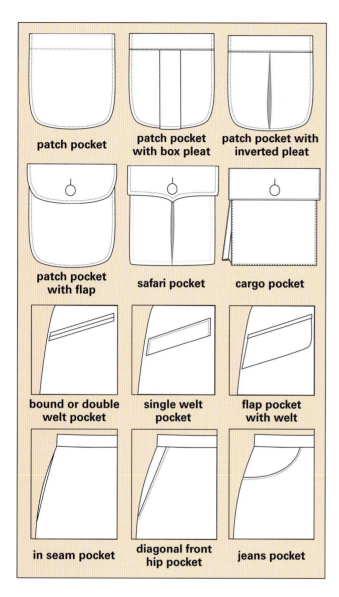

Figure 8.24
Pockets are both a decorative and functional garment component that can differentiate a garment silhouette.

Outside pockets are also known as **patch pockets**. They can be designed in many shapes and sizes to harmonize with the silhouette, details, and feeling of a garment. Patch pockets work best in fabrics that are not too soft and that hold their shape; when made of fabrics that have a great deal of drape or stretch, these pockets may sag. Patch pockets tend to add bulk, which should be considered when determining placement on the body and appropriateness for a particular fabric or figure type. A patch pocket may be embellished with pleats, tucks, topstitching, or buttons, and it may be combined with a flap. Patch pockets may also be made three-dimensional by incorporating a pleat of fabric in the perimeter of the pocket; this accommodates carrying of larger objects. Patch pockets are typically topstitched onto the garment; however, a technique for machine sewing them on invisibly is sometimes used in higher-priced garments. No matter how the pocket is attached, it should be reinforced at the pocket opening.

Inside pockets include slash pockets, pockets hidden in a seam, and front-hip pockets used on jeans. **Slash pockets** are frequently used on tailored garments. They include double-welt or bound pockets, welt pockets, and flap pockets. The pocket opening is slashed into the garment body and finished with a flap or welt, with the pocket pouch hidden inside the garment. The designer may vary the position of the slash by cutting horizontally, vertically, diagonally, or on a curve into the fabric. These pockets are typically basted closed for pressing; the basting must be removed when the garment is purchased to access the pocket. To ensure product quality and consistency, most product developers require contractors that bid on garments with slash pockets to have automated pocket-making equipment.

Double-welt pockets consist of two welts, one sewn to the top edge of the slash and the other sewn to the bottom edge of the slash. They resemble bound buttonholes and are sometimes referred to as bound pockets or besom pockets. Welts are typically ³⁄₁₆- to ¼-inch wide. Bound pockets are accessed in an opening between the two welts.

Welt pockets have a single welt, typically ¼ inch to 1½-inches wide, which is attached to the bottom edge of the slash and flips up over the pocket to cover the opening. This pocket is accessed from the top of the welt. Narrow welt pockets are sometimes used on the back of men's or women's pants. Wider welts are frequently found on tailored jackets, coat dresses, and coats.

Flap pockets consist of a flap that is sewn to the top edge of the slash and that falls over the pocket opening. The pocket flap must be lifted to provide access to the pocket. Flap pockets may be combined with upper or lower pocket welts. Sometimes flaps are attached to a garment to give the look of an inside pocket even though there is no inside pouch. This technique saves costs by making the garment simpler to produce. It may also be desirable when the garment fabric cannot support a functional pocket.

In-seam pockets are designed into an existing seam of the garment. They are most frequently found in vertical garment side seams or princess seams, but they may also be found in horizontal yoke or waist seams. These pockets provide function without disrupting the lines of the garment. The edge may be topstitched for a crisper line or to blend with the detailing on the rest of the garment. There should be a self-fabric extension on the garment back for vertical in-seam pockets, and on the garment yoke or bodice for horizontal in-seam pockets, so that if the pocket opens, the fabric of the pocket pouch is not visible. It is important that garments with in-seam pockets be designed with enough ease so that the pocket does not pull open when not in use.

Front-hip pockets are typically used on jeans and pants. They feature a style line that is cut into the garment front at the hip and faced to form the opening. Many variations can be achieved with this pocket style. They are frequently topstitched.

Belts

If a garment requires a belt, it is best to sell the belt with the garment so that the consumer is purchasing a complete ensemble. Some garments, such as jeans, are designed with belt loops but are typically worn without belts. Therefore, a belt need not be sold with them. Belts can be made of the same fabric as the garment or may be purchased from a belt supplier to coordinate with the garment. Belts that are sold with a garment are generally made of synthetic materials rather than leather in order to keep costs down.

Closures

Closures are an important part of any design. There must be a way to get a garment on and off the body. Sometimes there is sufficient stretch in the garment fabric, making a closure unnecessary. Examples include swimwear and tee shirts. However, most garments require some sort of closure. Closures for tops are typically at the center front or center back, but they may also be located along a shoulder or side seam. Closures on women's bottoms may be located at the center front, center back, or left side seam (as worn); however, on men's pants the openings are always in the center front. Closures include various types of zippers, button closures, tie closures, hooks and eyes, Velcro hook and loop fasteners, and snaps.

Zippers are generally inserted into a seam but may also be applied to the top of a garment, exposing the zipper tape and teeth. To indicate a zipper, place a cross mark at the bottom of the zipper and indicate stitching lines for a centered or lapped zipper. Invisible zippers require no stitching lines. Fly fronts can be stitched in a variety of ways, depending on the garment and fabrication. Study sample garments carefully to make sure you include all stitching lines and reinforcement tacks. The curved line that

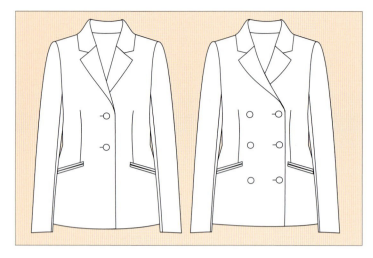

Figure 8.25
Jackets may be single breasted (left) or double breasted (right).

Figure 8.26
Garment closures can be differentiated in a variety of ways including choice of fasteners, topstitching, a framed or bias bound edge, or edge shaping.

forms a fly zipper application is called a J-stitch because of the shape of the line it creates.

To indicate a lapped front or back closure, you must first visualize the center front or center back line with a light guideline. As you look at the garment, women's closures lap left over right and men's garments lap right over left. Determine the size of your button and draw the outer edge of the garment ¾ to 1 button diameter away from the center, making sure that the lap is in the proper direction. Once the lap is established, the neckline can be completed and the center front guideline can be erased.

On double-breasted jackets, the center front line divides the placement of the two rows of buttons. Determine the center front guideline and the direction of lap and place the buttons. Then complete the outer edge, allowing ¼ to ½ inch beyond the edge of the buttons. Join the neckline to the outer edge and erase the center front guideline. Figure 8.25 illustrates a single- and double-breasted jacket. Figure 8.26 illustrates additional closure variations.

Planning and Sourcing for Garment Details

Designers have a variety of options when planning details. Some prefer to use ready-made trims that may or may not have to be color matched. Others work with studios that sell prototypes of trims and decorative effects that may be copied and adapted to the product developer's line. Still others have graphic artists who design exclusive trims for in-house use.

The cost of trims and decorative effects can vary greatly depending on where the garment is sourced. In recent years, any form of handwork for trims and decorative effects has generally become too costly for production in the United States, but such

handwork may be affordable in a lower-wage country such as India or Southeast Asia. Trim houses may specialize in decorative effects that require special machinery. The use of these services and the ordering of trims must be planned early in the development calendar. This planning should include any additional time necessary to obtain approval of color matching and production samples, as well as extra time for shipping. Decisions about all details must be made early enough in the process to ensure availability of these items as needed in the garment production schedule.

SUSTAINABILITY

Designing for sustainability takes on new meaning in the world of slow fashion. It goes beyond fabric selection, although sustainable design decisions start there. Sustainability in the manufacture of fibers and fabrics is thoroughly discussed in Chapter 6. The design team further evaluates the fabric in terms of quality as it relates to the garment's purpose. Quality fabrics should retain their appearance throughout the life of the garment and support longevity. Care of the garment should have minimal environmental impact. That means ensuring that both the fabric and the trims require the same care. Finally, there should be a way to recover the fibers at the end of the garment's life and convert them into new products or fibers. Color palettes should encourage wardrobe building rather than wardrobe obsolescence by standardizing neutrals such as grey and navy and evolving palettes so that new pieces coordinate with things purchased last season.

During the design process, every decision should be put through a filter. A designer should ask, *is this the most sustainable way to design this? Could it be done more sustainably?* To address longevity goals, garments should be designed for easy alterations and repairs. This includes wider seam allowances and more generous hems. Design details that make garments adjustable, transformable, or multipurpose all add value and support longevity. Designers can avoid trims that would make an otherwise washable garment dry clean only. Or they might make the desired trim detachable.

Sustainable design means perfecting a smaller number of garments rather than rushing the delivery of too many new styles. New 3D tools are revolutionizing this process. 3D modeling makes it possible to show a virtual representation of a garment to customers before it's ever made. The Scandinavian brand Carling showed its first digital collection in 2018. The capsule collection consisted of nineteen pieces. They were prepared to sell a limited production of twelve pieces of each of the designs. The design team presented the collection on social media before ever making a sample. Customers provided photos of themselves, and the design team superimposed realistic images of the garments on their photos. The collection sold out within weeks (UFO3D.com, ND). This story illustrates how sustainable design might function in the near future. As 3D fit technology continues to improve, garments will only be made when there is a full-price order; orders will be delivered in a matter of days in a version that fits perfectly. All of this will be done through virtual sampling eliminating wasteful iterations of the same design, overproduction of styles that don't sell, and customized fit without wasting time, money, and energy on shipping samples back and forth.

Clear communication during the design process will ensure that the technical design team gets the pattern and sample right the first time. Collaborating with an experienced patternmaker can ensure that the placement of seams, details, and shaping will preserve the visual intent of the designer while making sure that the garment can be cut to minimize material waste and easily run through production (Bye, 2020). Patterns can be developed on the computer, sewn digitally, and then fit on a digital avatar to create a 3D virtual sample (Bye, 2020).

SUMMARY

The methods a designer employs are, to a degree, determined by the brand for which they work. The timeline for design, the budget for sample garments and fabrics, and the support they get from fabric libraries, trend services, and the merchandising department all impact the garment design process. Brands vary in terms of the level of creativity they expect. Inexpensive brands may be satisfied with silhouettes that are knocked off or copied from the ideas of others. Mass market brands may accept derivative silhouettes but expect their designers to avoid direct copies that could lead to serious financial liability. As clothes get more expensive, design is typically more considered and interpretive. The most creative designers are described as avant-garde.

Designers take inspiration from primary research in the form of artifacts and travel experiences, shopping both their competitors as well as aspirational brands, and following runway presentations, social media, and blogs. They take "notes" using sketching, photos, and tear sheets to document ideas. They may further explore silhouettes by draping sample fabric directly on the form.

Garment design is a process that utilizes the design elements of line, color, texture, pattern, silhouette, and shape to create a garment. Understanding these elements and the principles of design may help the product developer evaluate the potential success of an individual garment. By identifying the proportion, balance, focal point, rhythm, and harmony of each proposed design, the designer can determine whether the elements combine to make an aesthetically pleasing whole.

Garment silhouettes worn today are relatively standard. The silhouettes themselves evolve slowly from season to season, yet the pace of new offerings has created a false sense of need. Understanding the style variables present in different garment classifications can help a designer be more creative. Once a silhouette is determined, garments can be further embellished with details, including collars, sleeves, cuffs, pockets, trims, and closures.

The Ellen MacArthur Foundation is an organization committed to making fashion circular. In 2019, the Foundation challenged denim manufacturers to redesign their products in accordance with circular design principles. The *Jeans Redesign* guidelines provided minimum requirements for denim products in terms of durability, material health, recyclability, and traceability (The Ellen MacArthur Foundation, ND). Philips Van Heusen (PVH) is a core partner of the Ellen MacArthur Foundation. Tommy Hilfiger, a PVH brand, was eager to participate in the project along with seventy other leading brands, manufacturers, and fabric mills.

The Tommy Hilfiger *Jeans Redesign* collection debuted in March of 2021 and consisted of seven pieces—five pairs of jeans and two denim jackets. The brand totally rethought the design of jeans incorporating circular design principles. Garments were made from 100 percent organic fabric and featured detachable buttons; bar tacks replaced metal rivets and metal zippers and leather pocket patches were eliminated. Each piece included wash and care instructions on the pockets, along with advice on how to repair, donate, or recycle the product after use (Lockwood, March 3, 2021). The company already uses low impact processes in finishing its denim, minimizing water and energy use. The brand is committed to eliminating waste and becoming completely circular by 2030. Innovating for circularity requires rethinking the value chain as well as the design process.

The *Denim Redesign* project was a good fit for the brand's *Circle Round* design initiatives. The label partners with STITCH Design Lab to train its designers on circular design principles. The first step has been to create a digital library of fabrics and trims in the 3D design hub, each with a specific sustainability rating. Access to this resource makes designers carefully consider the impact of their design decisions. Along with the digital library, designers have access to a toolbox for creating products that are circular. This means not only selecting recycled or recyclable fabrics and trims, but putting them together in a way that enables easy disassembly to aid with reuse and recycling. The next step will give designers access to a sustainability score of their product during the creative process allowing for design modifications to make garments more sustainable and circular (https://responsibility.pvh.com/tommy).

Tommy for Life is the name of the brand's buy-back initiative, centered on extending the lifecycle of pre-owned Tommy Hilfiger and Tommy Jeans as well as damaged items from retail operations. Pre-owned or damaged jeans become part of one of three collections. The *Reloved* collection offers previously owned products traded in by consumers. The *Refreshed* collection offers damaged and/or returned garments that have been cleaned and repaired. The *Remixed* collection uses materials from items that can't be renewed and makes them into unique new designs. Through these initiatives and more, the brand has vowed to become fully circular by 2030. In line with their mission statement, the brand is committed to twenty-four targets centered around circularity and inclusivity.

References

Ellen MacArthur Foundation. ND. The Jeans Redesign. https://www.ellenmacarthurfoundation.org/our-work/activities/make-fashion-circular/the-jeans-redesign (accessed on 3/5/2021).

Lockwood, Lisa. (2020), Tommy Hilfiger Introduces First Circular Design Denim Collection, March 3. https://wwd.com/business-news/markets/tommy-hilfiger-circular-design-denim-1234762759/ (accessed on 3/4/2021).

Making Revolution Possible: In Conversation with Dominic. No date. https://responsibility.pvh.com/tommy/making-revolution-possible/ (accessed on 3/6/21).

Vision Statement. https://global.tommy.com/en_hk/about-us-corporate-responsibility (accessed on March 6, 2021).

Warren, Liz. (2020), "Tommy for Life Pilot Program Tests Circularity in the Netherlands." *The Sourcing Journal*, November 18. https://sourcingjournal.com/denim/denim-brands/tommy-hilfiger-tommy-for-life-circularity-buy-back-resale-netherlands-245381/ (accessed on March 6, 2021).

Case Study 8.1
Tommy Hilfiger Jeans Redesign

Tommy Hilfiger is on a mission to create fashion that "Wastes Nothing and Welcomes All." Today, the world faces some of the biggest challenges yet—from climate change and resource scarcity to inequality and prejudice. One fashion brand can't change all of this, but through the power of partnership and collaboration we will do everything in our power to create a more circular and inclusive future of fashion. This is our time. It's time to Make it Possible. https://global.tommy.com/en_hk/about-us-corporate-responsibility

KEY TERMS

asymmetric balance

athleisure

avant-garde design

balance

break point

breakline

cardigan

collar

component parts

concept board

croquis sketch

cut-and-sew construction

decorative embellishments

derivative design

design

design elements

design principles

details

double-welt pocket

dress

fall

flap pocket

float

focal point

front-hip pocket

full-fashion construction

gorge line

harmony

in-seam pocket

inside pocket

interpretive design

item-driven

jacket

knock-off

lapel

line

notch

outside pocket

pants

patch pocket

pattern

pocket

proportion

pullover

rhythm

roll line

shaping device

silhouette

skirt

slash pocket

stand

style line

stylist

sweater sets or twin sets

symmetric balance

technical flat

texture

thumbnail sketch

tops

underdrawing

vest

welt pocket

DISCUSSION QUESTIONS

1. Review fashion resources and shop your favorite brands instore or online. Discuss the current silhouette and detail direction for several categories.

2. Practice evaluating runway looks using the language of the design elements and principles. Avoid beginning your assessment with "I like this or I don't like this . . ." and instead begin your assessment with "this works or this doesn't work because . . . ."

3. Bring examples of garments with symmetrical and asymmetrical balance to class. Discuss your experience in wearing these garments. Do you wear some garments more often than others? Are some garments easier to wear than others? How long have you had each garment in your wardrobe?

4. Bring garments from your wardrobe to class that you have worn for several seasons. Share with the class, why the garment continues to be a favorite. Likewise, bring something that you've purchased and only worn once or twice. Share with the class why it hasn't served you well.

ACTIVITIES

1. Study fashion periodicals and shop your local mall for jackets with tailored collars. Try on a few jackets with tailored collars and identify the various parts. In your croquis book, sketch as many interesting variations as you can find, annotating with key measurements to sensitize your eye to proportions. Continue your sketches using catalogs and fashion periodicals. Use this sketchbook as a reference whenever you are designing garments with tailored collars. Continue adding to it as you come across additional interesting variations.

2. Select a trim, such as buttons, zippers, or ruffles. Experiment with using that trim as a design element in garments. Express your ideas in a series of croquis drawings.

3. Design your own logo for the back of a jeans pocket. Select the color of stitching and the type of stitch used.

4. Identify a dress silhouette that you like through shopping or in a fashion periodical. Sketch the dress you identify and then do a series of twenty croquis sketches that maintain the basic silhouette but vary the details, balance, and proportions. Share your work with the class.

5. Select a runway garment that you find in a magazine or on the internet. Do a series of design sketches interpreting the runway design for a particular customer and price point. Then do a second series of sketches interpreting that same design for another market.

6. Select a garment category not covered in this chapter, such as swimwear, sleepwear, athleisure, or a category of your choice. Develop a chart that identifies the identifying features and how they can be changed.

STUDIO RESOURCES

- Take the chapter quiz with scored results and personalized study tips.
- Review glossary flashcards to build your vocabulary.

REFERENCE

Bye, M. (2020), "Sustainability Must Drive Design" in S. Marcketti and E. Karpova (eds), *The Dangers of Fashion*: Bloomsbury.

Figure 8A.1 KNIT TOPS

Tee

Henly

Polo

Tank

Camisole

Racer Back

Sports Bra

Double Layer Tee

Trapeze Tee

Tee Shirt Dress

Sweatshirt

Hoodie

Thermal Fleece Layering

Figure 8A.2 SWEATERS

Pullover Sweater

Mock Turtleneck

Turtleneck

V Neck

Short Sleeve Shell

Cropped Sweater

Cardigan

Twin Set

Sweater Coat

Sweater Jacket

Sweater Vest

Shrug

Figure 8A.3 SHIRTS AND BLOUSES

Shirt

Tuxedo Shirt

Western Cut

Blouse

Shell

Peasant Blouse

Camp Shirt

Tunic

Surplice Wrap Top

Figure 8A.4 JACKETS

Blazer

Double Breasted Blazer

Cardigan Jacket

Smoking Jacket

Chanel Jacket

Bolero Jacket

Spencer Jacket

Nehru Jacket

Cutaway Jacket

Wrap Front Jacket

Princess/Fit & Flare

Swagger Coat

Pea Coat/Reefer Coat

Trench Coat

Balmacaan Coat

Chesterfield Coat

Duster

Clutch Coat

Bomber Jacket

Duffle Coat

Parka/Anorak

Eisenhower Jacket

Vest

Motorcycle Jacket

Warm Up Jacket

Safari Jacket

Poncho

Cape

Shirt Jacket

sheath

A-Line

Princess

Empire Waist

Dropped Waist

Fit and Flare

Tent-Trapeze

Strapless

Figure 8A.6 DRESS SILHOUETTES

Shift

Wedge

Shirt Waist

Shirt Dress

Coat Dress

Maxi

Figure 8A.7 SKIRTS

Straight Skirt   Pegged Skirt   A-Line Skirt   Dirndl Skirt

Flare Skirt   Circle Skirt   Yoke Skirt

Kilt   Sunburst Pleating   Knife Pleating   Box Pleats

Inverted Pleat   Coulotte   Gored Skirt   Wrap Skirt

Figure 8A.7 SKIRTS, *Continued*

Trumpet Skirt

Tiered/Peasant Skirt

Hi-Low Skirt

Handkerchief

Sarong

Gaucho

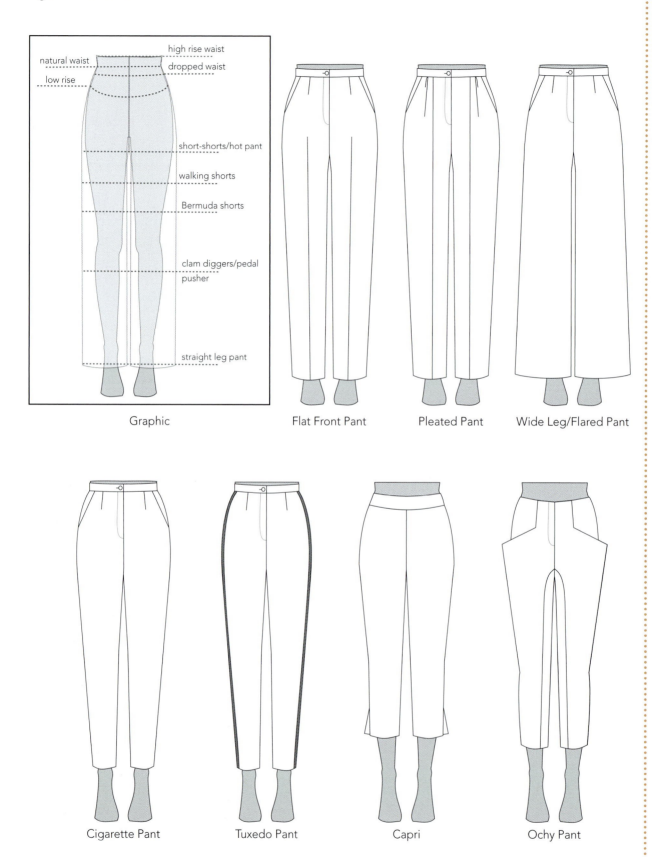

Graphic

Flat Front Pant

Pleated Pant

Wide Leg/Flared Pant

Cigarette Pant

Tuxedo Pant

Capri

Ochy Pant

Figure 8A.8 PANTS

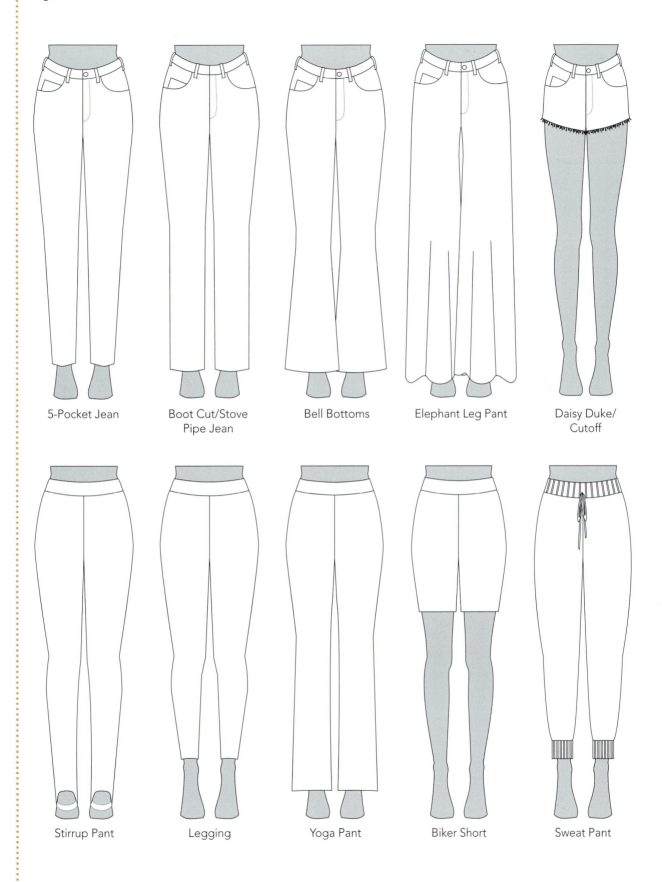

5-Pocket Jean

Boot Cut/Stove
Pipe Jean

Bell Bottoms

Elephant Leg Pant

Daisy Duke/
Cutoff

Stirrup Pant

Legging

Yoga Pant

Biker Short

Sweat Pant

Figure 8A.8 PANTS

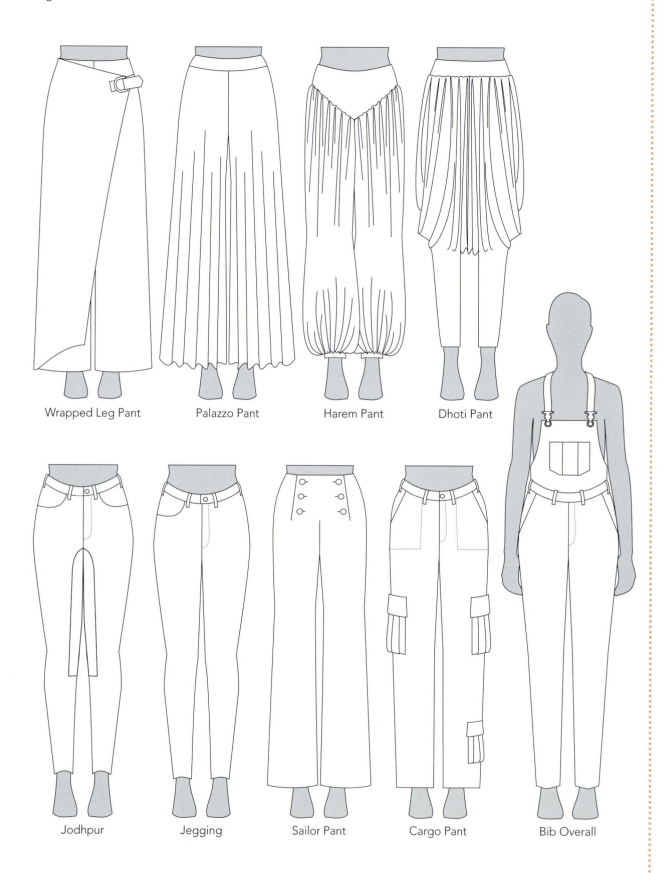

Wrapped Leg Pant   Palazzo Pant   Harem Pant   Dhoti Pant

Jodhpur   Jegging   Sailor Pant   Cargo Pant   Bib Overall

Figure 8A.9 NECKLINES

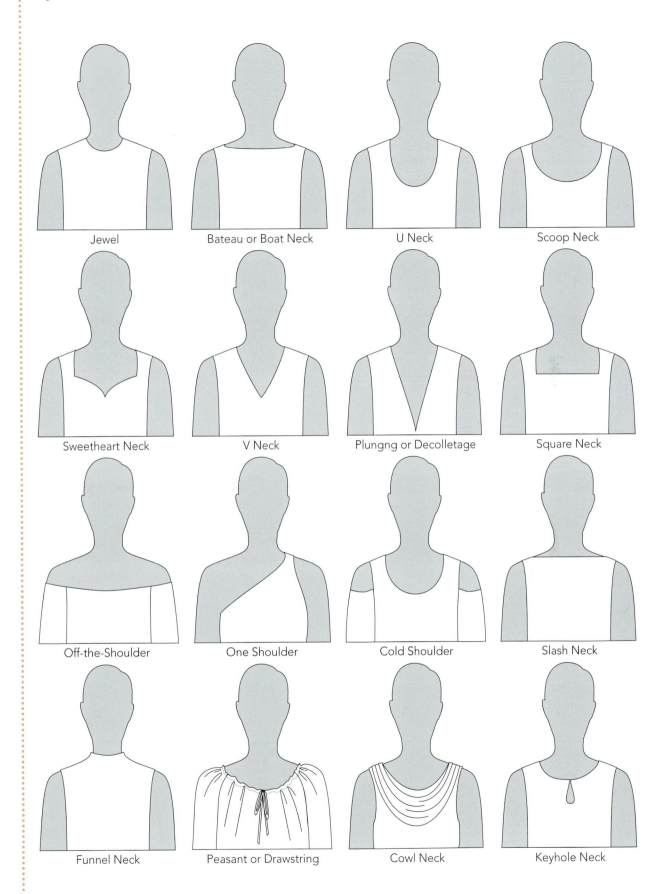

Jewel

Bateau or Boat Neck

U Neck

Scoop Neck

Sweetheart Neck

V Neck

Plungng or Decolletage

Square Neck

Off-the-Shoulder

One Shoulder

Cold Shoulder

Slash Neck

Funnel Neck

Peasant or Drawstring

Cowl Neck

Keyhole Neck

Figure 8A.10 COLLARS

Mandarin or Nehru

Wing

Notched

Shirt

Peter Pan

Chelsea

Convertible-closed

Convertible-Open

Puritan

Bertha

Cowl

Turtleneck

Ascot or Tie

Jabot

Sailor

Shawl

Figure 8A.11 SLEEVES

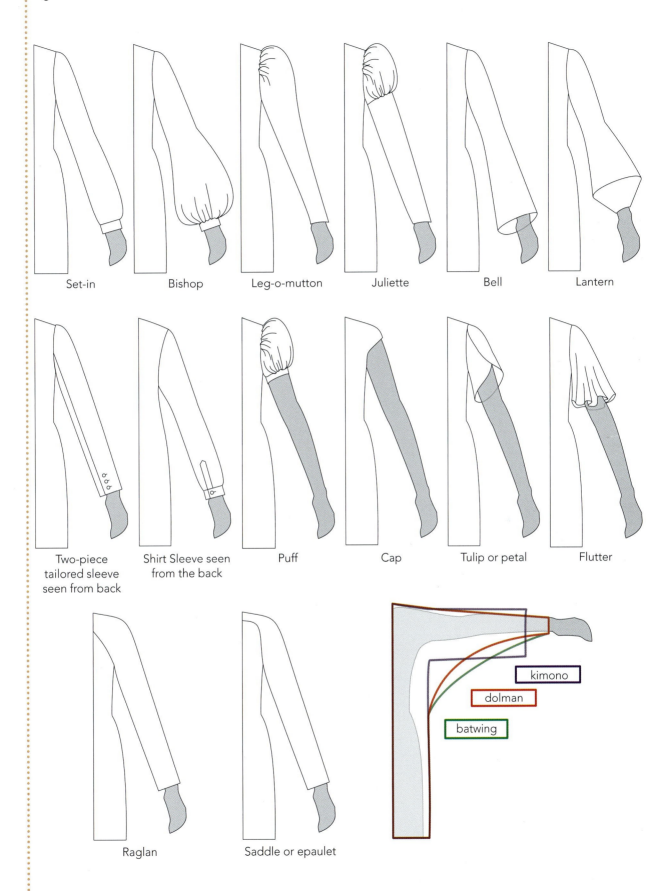

Set-in

Bishop

Leg-o-mutton

Juliette

Bell

Lantern

Two-piece tailored sleeve seen from back

Shirt Sleeve seen from the back

Puff

Cap

Tulip or petal

Flutter

Raglan

Saddle or epaulet

kimono

dolman

batwing

PART 3

TECHNICAL PLANNING

CHAPTER 9

TRANSLATING CONCEPT TO PRODUCT

"Ideas are magical only when they become real and can be appreciated and analyzed. A sketch translated into a sample garment is the realization of an idea. But it becomes complete only when the garment unites with a body moving in space." EVELYN L. BRANNON

OBJECTIVES

- Recognize that the use standards, while creating and maintaining specifications, contributes to efficiency
- Identify the kind of information that is needed in the design spec to begin the sampling process
- Distinguish between various methods used to create a first pattern for a first sample
- Examine the factors that influence decisions about how and where to have patternmaking and sample making sourced
- Compare manual and digital methods for patternmaking, including three-dimensional patternmaking technology
- Understand factors in making decisions about when and how to adopt digital methods of patternmaking
- Recognize the potential contribution that PLMs and three-dimensional tools can make to sustainable business practices.

Previous chapters focused on strategic planning, consumer research, trend forecasting, color planning and management, fabric planning and management, garment design, and merchandise planning. The next stage in the development process is technical planning.

STANDARDS

Standards are characteristics of products and processes that are used as a basis for making decisions. They define expectation for sizing, fit, and quality of materials and performance. They reflect the needs of the target market and allow the brand to stand out in a competitive landscape. Some standards are developed over time as the firm seeks its place in the market and faces competition. Other standards are imposed by governmental agencies where the product is produced or sold.

The application of standards can be built into the process of writing specifications. Standardized specification formats reduce errors and increase efficiency. As seasons pass and new products are added, specification libraries can be built within the firm. Developers can recall and reuse previously developed specifications to be used as the starting point for new styles. Standards that were proven to work in previously successful products can be replicated, saving time and money.

SPECIFICATIONS

Creative and technical designers work as a team to translate each style idea into a set of visual and written directions called **design specifications (design specs),** used to produce the first prototypes. These instructions evolve throughout the development process and are finalized before the product goes into mass production. The document that clearly defines expectations for the final product and the methods used to achieve it is called a **technical specification package (tech pack)**.

Commercial Product Lifecycle Management (PLMs) software packages have been developed specifically for writing, storing, and transmitting standardized specifications. Yunique PLM from Gerber Technology (Gerber Technology, 2020a) and Lectra FashionPLM 4.0 (Lectra, 2020) have been the leaders in apparel (PLMs) but

Figure 9.1
PLMs are one of the many software applications that can be integrated into an **Enterprise Resource Planning systems (ERP)**. ERPs are software programs that include all the applications needed to run a business such as accounting, human resources, corporate governance, customer services, sales, distribution, procurement, and design. ERPs store, share and analyze information using a single data base that updates all linked applications simultaneously. ERPs not only integrate multiple functions within a business but can also allow customers and vendors to articulate their activities with the business.

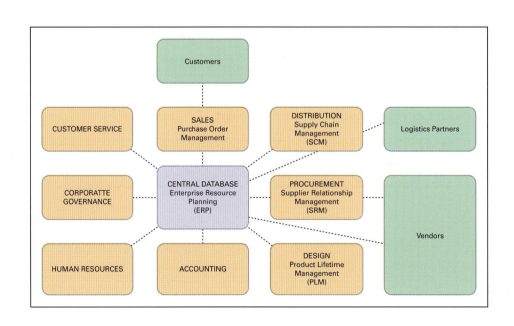

there are many other systems available such as Blue Cherry from CGS (Computer Generated Solutions, 2020) and Infor CloudSuite PLM for Fashion (Infor, 2020). These systems are at the heart of the product development revolution that has driven competition in the apparel business and has contributed to the development of fast fashion.

PLMs focus on merchandising planning and product design, but they may also be combined with a Supplier Relationship Management (SRM) application to handle vendor capacity, compliance, and logistics (Figure 9.1). PLMs may include

- **Computer Aided Design (CAD)** software for creating original design sketches, layout of merchandising boards, color management and illustrations for the tech pack.
- **Specification library** that stores information about materials and drawings of past styles that can be drawn on when developing a new design spec (Figures 9.2a and b).

Figure 9.2a
Gerber Yunique PLM digital raw materials library screen for building specifications.

Figure 9.2b
Note the headers are linked to dropdown boxes that prompt the user to fill in the necessary information from the digital library.

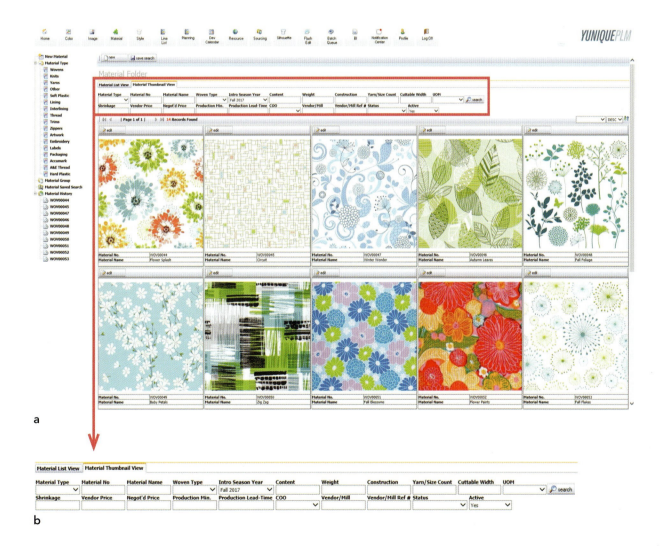

a

b

- **Pattern Design Software (PDS)** for developing the tools needed to prepare a design for industrial production and sales in a commercial environment
- **Three-dimensional patternmaking software** for displaying virtual images of garments to test design concept and fit.

Design Spec

Every company has different name for the design spec and it may contain various levels of information but at a minimum each style should have a style number and include a technical drawing of the product, instructions about cutting, sewing and design details, a list of materials, a preliminary cost estimate, and a set of target measurements from which to create a first sample. In smaller companies using off-the-shelf software, a single page may be used to provide a brief overview of technical information that can be expanded in the tech pack.

In companies with PLM systems, information for the design spec is entered into the system as the first iteration of the tech pack. The technical designer does not necessarily expect to provide full information until after the line review. When samples are made by vendors who are familiar with the client and its product, the design spec may not need the same level of detail as the final tech pack. When dealing with a new vendor, more information may be needed.

Technical Flats

To get a first bid from a vendor, some companies may send a hand-drawn sketch, magazine tear, or inspiration sample purchased from a store. However, the design specs sent for making the first sample is more formal. It usually includes a **technical flat**, an accurate drawing of the front and back of a proposed garment as it appears in two dimensions spread out on a flat surface (Figure 9.3). Technical flats visually define the proportions, details, and construction techniques required for production purposes. They may include measurements and sewing notations. Complex details are sometimes enlarged in **callouts (blowups)**, separate drawings in a larger scale that magnify an area so that a patternmaker or sample maker can understand exactly what is expected. When done by hand, the garment can be drawn on tracing paper over a scale representation of the ideal body form or a standard garment silhouette.

Technical flats that are part of a PLM or pattern design software (PDS) system are developed digitally. Companies that use off-the-shelf software to generate spread sheets for specifications use programs such as Adobe Illustrator to create technical flats so that the images are accurate and easily transmitted online.

When technical flats are drawn digitally, they can be developed in layers, with different information in each layer. The silhouette can be drawn in one layer. It may be copied from a previous season and adjusted as needed or a body template can be used to ensure that the images of garments from the same group and category have the same proportions. When the silhouette is done, the layer with the template is deleted.

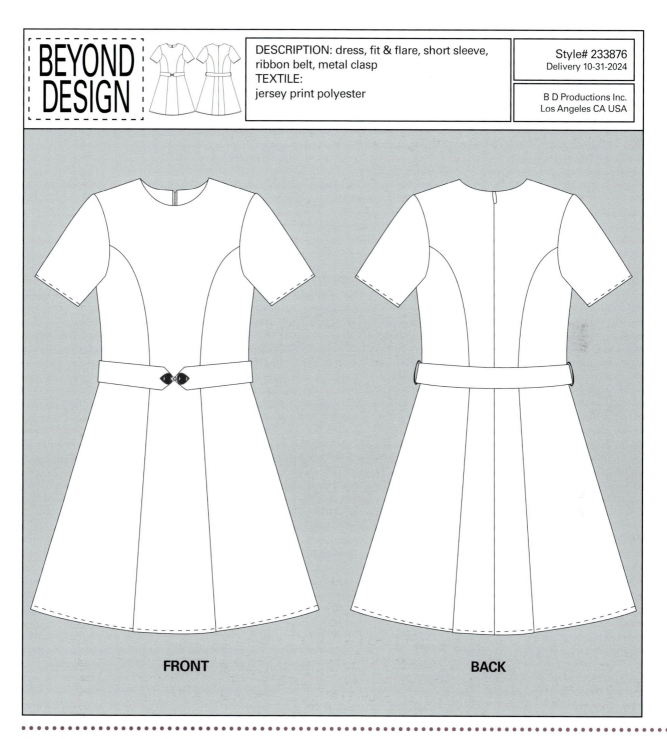

DESCRIPTION: dress, fit & flare, short sleeve, ribbon belt, metal clasp
TEXTILE: jersey print polyester

Style# 233876
Delivery 10-31-2024

B D Productions Inc.
Los Angeles CA USA

BEYOND DESIGN

FRONT

BACK

Figure 9.3

Each company has its own format for documenting the design process. Each page of the design spec should have a header with the name of the company, a description, a style number, and the season and possibly a thumbnail sketch of the garment. The design spec usually includes a technical flat of the front and back of the garment drawn to scale and with standardized line weights.

Design details such as pockets, cuffs, and collars can be stored in libraries, then copied and added in another layer. Topstich detail, which is usually drawn as a broken line and sometimes in a different line weight, can be added in another layer. Components such as buttons can be added in yet another layer.

Many companies draw their technical flats to scale, often at a proportion of 1 to 8. The silhouette is drawn to exact proportions, following the measurements. Every detail is positioned accurately. The sketch must reflect the garment measurements perfectly so that there is no confusion as to what the final product should look like. Discrepancies between the technical flat and the measurement page can result in many emails between the technical designer and the vendor to clarify what is wanted.

Styles of drawing for technical flats vary. Some companies require a bolder line for the silhouette outline. Some expect a consistent line for outline and yoke or panel seams. Because a technical flat is a two-dimensional representation of a product that is worn on a three-dimensional body, there are some areas of the garment that are confusing to draw, such as crotches, underarms, and collars. Solutions for how to draw these areas are usually standardized within a brand or product group. *Technical Sourcebook for Designers* (Lee & Steen, 2019) is an excellent resource for guidance about technical flats and for its discussion of styles and uses.

Measurement Chart

The design spec includes a **measurement chart**, a list of target measurements for the finished garment that guides the patternmaker to create a first pattern (Figure 9.4b). After the sample is approved for production, the measurement chart is graded for each size. Examples of key points to include in measurements of tops are collar circumference or minimum neck stretch (in knits); bust or chest circumference; armhole, sleeve opening, and sleeve length; and center back length. Key points on garment bottoms include waist, hip, front and back rise, functional zipper opening, and pant inseam or center back skirt length.

Bill of Materials

The bill of materials (BOM) is a section of a design spec in which textiles, trims, labels and packing materials are listed with description, sizes, quantities, and other information needed to ensure that the product is made according to the design (Figures 9.4c and d). A BOM for a design spec lists the textiles and trims needed to make the first sample. It may not list everything because the vendor may source and supply materials and then later provide information for the tech pack. At a minimum, the design spec should list as much technical description of the material as possible, or a source and order number of a product already identified from a textile show or sales rep.

Cutting Instructions

Companies that provide paper patterns for their vendors include **cutting instructions** (**pattern chart** or **cutters must**), a list that itemizes all the pattern pieces needed to make one garment, including the patterns for interlining, lining, and contrast as well as how many times each pattern should be cut (Figure 9.4e). If a vendor is making the patterns, the cutting instructions can be used to provide clarity regarding unusual cutting layout such as use of bias or cross grain.

Sewing Instructions

Sewing instructions are given in a section of a design spec in which standards are listed for stitch types and seam types (Figure 9.4f). Measurements are given for seam and hem depths, topstitch gauges, and stitches per inch. At a minimum, for a design spec, instructions or examples should be included for unusual or novel construction procedures or for achieving a unique or uncommon appearance. Some companies include a diagram for complex print layout.

Special Instructions

The designer or technical designer may need to add **special instructions** to their design spec for non-sewing processes that are not done in the cutting room or on the sewing floor such as pleating, embroidery, garment wash, or dyeing

Cost Sheet

As part of the design and merchandising process, it is necessary to establish a **preliminary cost estimate (precost)** for each product based on costs of materials and labor from past styles (Figure 9.4g). It is used for establishing the **wholesale price**, the amount charged by a wholesale product developer or manufacturer when the garment is sold to a retailer or distributor. These estimates are useful for determining whether a garment is suitable for remaining within the line and for comparing bids from competing vendors. Until a sample has been made and materials have been tested, the costs are not definite. The **cost sheet** is created during the early stages of the product development process and used throughout as a dynamic record of decisions made about costs that make up the wholesale price.

In large companies, decisions made by the designer and technical designer impact the cost of goods, which is only one variable in the price that a vendor may ultimately charge. Other variables include packaging, shipping, duty, brokerage fees, etc., which are not usually handled by a technical designer. Negotiating cost is often handled by production planners or sourcing specialists. A cost sheet may not exist in a design spec.

In smaller companies where a design team may be managing the purchasing of materials and running a production workshop, the cost sheet may be added to the design spec.

Figures 9.4a–g

Design Specs. In addition to a technical flat **(a)**, the design spec will include a measurement chart **(b)**, bill of materials **(c** and **d)**, cutting instructions **(e)**, sewing instructions **(f)** and possibly a preliminary cost estimate (precost) **(g)**. The information in the design spec will be updated during the sample approval process and finalized in the technical specification package (tech pack) used for production.

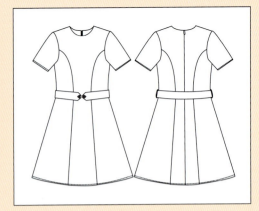

a

MEASUREMENT CHART									
	target spec	first sample	first sample	target spec	second sample	second sample	target spec	third sample	third sample
	size 10	vendor	fit session	size 10	vendor	fit session	size 10	vendor	fit session
date	3/15/22								
bust 1" below armhole	38								
waist 16 1/2" from HPS at back	33								
hip at 26" from HPS	41								
across back	15								
back length from HPS to waist	16 1/2								
neck width shoulder to shoulder	6								
front neck drop from HPS	3								
back neck drop from, HPS	1								
armhole (half)	9 7/8								
sleeve length shoulder-cuff edge	9								
sleeve opening	14								
back length from HPS to hem	42								
belt finished length	34 1/2								

b

BILL OF MATERIALS—TEXTILES								
function	construction	source	color	location	fiber content	width	weight	qty
shell	jersey	Fabtex	#334 tile	shell	rayon	60"	6 oz.	
interlining	tricot fusible #FT 201	Lena Textiles	white	neck & cuff facings	100% polyester	58"	light weight	
trim	gross grain ribbon with cord appliqué	Sohn Ltd.	indigo/terra	belt	polyester / cotton/ metallic	2"		

c

BILL OF MATERIALS—TRIMS							
description	material	source	finish	color	size	location	q'ty
zipper-concealed	nylon coil	tbd		cfc	3mm x 22"	center back	
clasp	molded metal	Bijoux Ltd.	antique	silver	2" x 3/4"	front belt	
spun thread	polyester	tbd		cfc shell	Tex 27	all operations	
thread chain	polyester	tbd		cfc belt	Tex 27	belt loops	

d

CUTTING INSTRUCTIONS

textile	pattern piece	quantity	notes	textile	pattern piece	quantity	notes
shell	center front bodice	1		shell	center back skirt	2 to pair	
shell	side front bodice	2 to pair		shell	side front skirt	2 to pair	
shell	center back bodice	2 to pair		shell	block for neck facings		
shell	side back bodice	2 to pair		fusible	block for neck facings		
shell	center front skirt	1		re-cut pattern	front neck facing	1	cut from fused block
shell	side front skirt	2 to pair		re-cut pattern	back neck facing	2 to pair	cut from fused block

e

SEWING INSTRUCTIONS

	operation & garment part	stitch type (ASTM)	seam type (ASTM)	top stitch	seam allowance	finished width	SPI
SHELL	serge: shoulders, underarms, set sleeve, side panels, center back skirt , waist	4 thread serge (514)	SSa		1/2"		10-12
	serge: center back zipper opening, bottom hem, & cuff, facing edges @ neck	3 thread serge (504)	EFd		1/2"		"
	set: center back zipper	lock stitch (301)	SSaa		1/2"		"
	topstitch bottom and sleeve hems	lock stitch (301)	EFa	1/2"		5/8""	"
BELT	finish ribbon ends (see special instructions)	lock stitch (301)	SSa	1/4"			
	attach clasp (see special instructions)	button tack (304) or hand tack					
FINISHING	stay stitch thread chain for belt loop (see special instructions)	lock stitch (301)			1/2"		2

f

COST SHEET—PRELIMINARY

agent	Nguyen Bros.				TBA							
COO	Viet Nam				Mexico							
min	2000 per color				TBA							
textile	100% polyester jersey				100% polyester jersey							
HTS	6204.43.40				6204.43.40							
TD target	49.00%				49.00%							
	q'nty	per unit	unit	prelim	q'nty	per unit	unit	alternative	q'nty	per unit	unit	FINAL
jersey print	1.50	$3.75	yd	$5.63	1.50	$3.95	yd	$5.93				
fusible	0.07	$0.50	yd	$0.04	0.07	$0.50	yd	$0.04				
ribbon	1.00	$2.00	yd	$2.00	1.00	$2.00	yd	$2.00				
clasp	1.00	$1.00	pc	$1.00	1.00	$1.00	pc	$1.00				
labels	3.00	$0.05	pc	$0.15	3.00	$0.05	pc	$0.15				
hang tag	1.00	$0.05	pc	$0.05	1.00	$0.05	pc	$0.05				
packaging	1.00	$0.05	pcs	$0.05	1.00	$0.05	pcs	$0.05				
labor	29.50	$0.05	SAM	$1.48	29.50	$0.08	SAM	$2.36				
total				$10.39				$11.57				
commission %		0.07		$0.73		0.05		$0.58				
duty %		0.16		$1.78		0.00		$0.00				
shipping	1.00	$0.50	pc	$0.50	1.00	$0.40	pc	$0.40				
total CoG				$13.39				$12.55				
wholesale mark up		0.50		$13.39		0.50		$12.55				
wholesale price				$26.78				$25.10				
trade discount %				48.50%				49.81%				
list price				$52.00				$50.00				

g

Vendor Relationship

The design spec and tech pack are documents that hold the product development process together. The importance of accurate communications cannot be overemphasized. Specifications are not only used for communication within the firm, they also form the basis for contracts with overseas vendors, setting the standards for materials, production capacity, quality standards, and evaluating **vendor compliance**. **Product development** is a process that is conducted across cultural and linguistic boundaries not only offshore, but onshore as well. Product developers must take care to write specifications that can be understood by sourcing partners. They must avoid the use of slang, easily misunderstood terms, or terms that lose meaning when translated into other languages.

PATTERNMAKING

After the design specs are written, the technical development process typically proceeds to a patternmaker who creates a **pattern**, a set of paper or electronic shapes that are used as templates to guide the cutting of fabric panels that are sewn into a product. The dimensions of the **first patterns** are based on target measurements. The **first sample** is cut from the first patterns in the sample size and cut from sample fabric. When it is finished, the first sample is checked for fit and styling in a fit session, which is a collaborative effort that includes the designer, technical designer, and merchandiser. Adjustments to measurements, changes to materials, and sewing details are part of the information that is used to write the first version of the tech pack that is sent to the patternmaker, who revises the first pattern so that it can be used to create a second sample which is sometimes used for the line presentation. The second sample is reviewed, patterns are adjusted, and a new sample is made. This process is repeated as many times as needed until everyone agrees that the style is ready for production. The changes result in a final tech pack and a production pattern and sample.

Developing Patterns for First Samples

Patterns for new, original garments may be created using drafting or draping methods. Patterns can be derived from existing sources using flat pattern, or trace-off methods.

Pattern Drafting

Pattern drafting is a process of translating a three-dimensional form that moves into two dimensions. There are many methods for drafting patterns, but they all start by taking measurements from a body, mannequin, or three-dimensional scan. The measurements are plotted onto a coordinate grid. The x-axis represents a line horizontal to the floor; the y-axis represents the line of gravity, 90 degrees to the floor. The landmark points must be drawn on the grid and connected in a closed figure to be made into a pattern.

Generally, landmark points on the body must be established at positions that relate to the pattern: center front neckline, shoulder point, and so on. Such points may not be visible on the body but need to be identified so that they can be marked on the

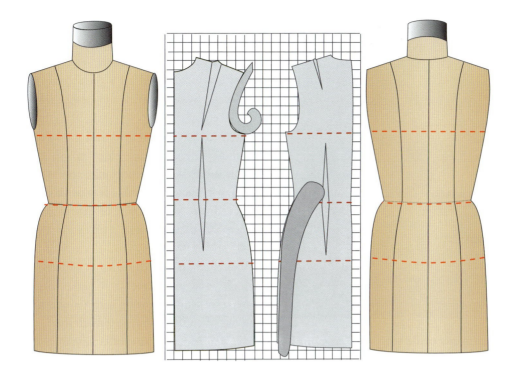

Figure 9.5
Pattern drafting
systems start with body
measurements that are
laid into a coordinate
grid. Ease is added to
the body measurement.
Landmark points
are connected using
formulas to create
depths of curves; a
curved ruler can also be
used.

x- and *y*-axes of a coordinate grid (Figure 9.5). Girth measurements are taken around the circumference of a body part. Length measurements are taken from one landmark point to another, or between circumference measurements, and are taken perpendicular to the floor. Width measurements are taken horizontally from landmark point to landmark point. In some systems, diagonal measurements are taken between landmark points.

First, the landmark points must be placed on the grid in relation to a "zero point." In some systems, the "0" point is the center front neckline; in others, it is the high point shoulder. Then the girth measurements are laid in. They are adjusted according to algorithms dictated by the patternmaking system. These rules include splitting the girth proportionally between the back and front patterns and adding extra measurement for movement and ease. Curves connecting landmark points are also drawn in by formulas or specially designed rulers called French curves. The math used in these systems has evolved over time and reflects the body shapes of the people who created them. For this reason, patterns drafted with rules developed for body types common in one region do not necessarily fit people elsewhere.

Draping

Draping is the method of patternmaking in which fabric is shaped around a body form to create a garment prototype (Figure 9.6). Inexpensive substitute fabric such as muslin can be used for the original prototype. It is critical, however, that the draping fabric has the same properties as the ultimate garment fabric to ensure desired

outcomes. Landmark points are noted on the fabric and correspond to center front and back, neckline, armhole, etc. Once the style is established on a dress form or model, all the seam lines and design lines are marked on the draping fabric. The fabric is flattened out and all lines and marks are transferred to paper and "trued up." If the right and left sides are not quite the same, the draper decides which measurement is correct. If parts do not quite fit together, the pattern has to be adjusted until every seam matches.

This method of achieving a pattern is typically used for garments at higher price points, especially garments with unique silhouettes such as women's formal wear, or garments made with unusual fabrics. Truly creative designs that exhibit subtleties of silhouette and fit usually start with draping. Even though draping may not be used for all parts of a garment, some complex closures, sleeves, or collars cannot be achieved by drafting alone and may have to be draped.

Figure 9.6
Draping is the method of patternmaking in which fabric is draped or shaped around a body form to create a garment prototype. The fabric is removed and a pattern is traced from the markings made by the draper.

Flat Pattern Method

Either draping or drafting can be used to create a pattern for a garment, but both methods are time consuming and costly. Because they both start from the beginning each time, variations in standard measurements and fit can occur from style to style. Either of these methods can be used to create **block patterns (slopers)**. Blocks are the simplest pattern pieces needed to make a garment. In a dress, the pieces would include a front, back, and sleeve with no style lines, design detail, or finishing pieces such as facings. Blocks include ease for comfort and movement, but no extra fabric for silhouettes that extend beyond the body shape.

Block patterns can be developed for each body type (for example, misses, women's, petite). They can be made for each basic silhouette common to the brand, such as pant, skirt, blouse, dress, jacket, and coat, and for fit categories such as "relaxed" or slim. Blocks can be made for frequently recurring styles such as princess seam dresses, four-dart jackets, two-pleat trousers, or polo shirts. Using the **flat pattern method**, blocks can be manipulated in to create a prototype. One technique is called the "slash-and-spread," in which the patternmaker adds fullness to change the silhouette (Figures 9.7a–c).

Developing styles by the flat pattern method is cost effective because the patternmaker does not have to start from measurements each time. Consistency in fit is ensured because the basic pattern is the same from one style to the next. Blocks are proprietary and reflect the fit that is expected by the target customer.

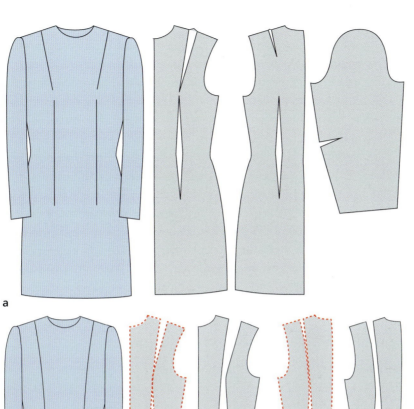

Figure 9.7a
Block patterns can be derived from drafting or draping methods. They include basic pieces such as a front, back, and sleeve for a dress with no style lines, facings, or details.

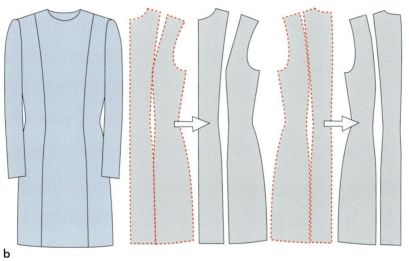

Figure 9.7b
Seam detail can be added by manipulating darts. Here a waist dart bodice block is manipulated into a princess seam.

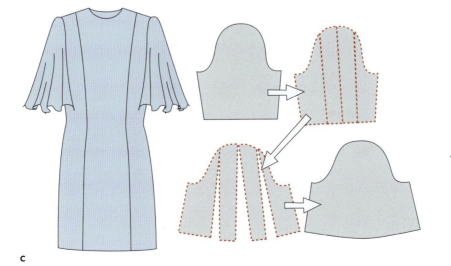

Figure 9.7c
The silhouette for a style can be achieved by slash-and-spread method to add fullness.

Trace-Off

A pattern created from copying an existing garment is called **trace-off**, (**rub-off**, or **reverse engineering**). It involves marking landmark points at various points on an existing garment and measuring the distance between these along lines that run horizontal and vertical to the center front of the garment. Using the same coordinate grid, the marks and measurements are transferred to paper. The curves of necklines, armholes, and placement of details can be followed with a tracing wheel rather than laid in with algorithms. Since the garment may have been stretched or twisted in manufacturing or wear, the measurements may not create a perfect pattern. Therefore, they should be refined by an experienced patternmaker. This method can be cost-effective for the production of basic garments, as it saves the development of the individual patterns or manipulation of blocks, but it is not very effective for copying more complex garments nor do the measurements conform to standard fit parameters. They have to be modified once a fit garment is made and tested. Trace-offs are often used by companies that do not have access to professional patternmakers and are risky as a long-term way of establishing a signature fit and style.

Sourcing Pattern and Sample Services

In-House Pattern and Sample Making

Small entrepreneurial companies with onshore production may do their own patternmaking, sample making, and cost estimation **in-house**, in the same location and same business unit as the marketing and design functions. Because they may also be closely connected with the factory making the production, they may not need extensive specifications.

Pattern and Sample-Making Services

When companies choose to use contract **pattern and sample-making services** instead of their own in-house sample room, the design specs may be generated at the client's firm or by the service. The service goes through all the steps of creating the patterns and samples that form the basis for the final tech pack and production sample. The tech pack and sample can then be sent for bidding to vendors who provide manufacturing services.

Full Package Vendors

Many companies work with **full package vendors** who make their own patterns and samples based on client requirements and then proceed to source the materials, factory labor, and services needed to produce the garment. Design specs may be sent out to more than one vendor for bidding. If the estimated price quoted by the vendor is acceptable to the client, the vendor starts the process of pattern and sample making. More than one vendor may be asked to make a first sample. Once a bid for the contract is accepted, the chosen vendor creates a tech pack and line presentation sample and then, with changes, the final tech pack and a production sample.

Making samples is a very costly process for the vendors and a time-consuming one for the product development team. The goal is always to limit the number of samples to three, but more may be needed at any stage, to verify not only fit and styling, but also the performance of materials and other technical aspects.

Making Patterns for Production

After the final sample is made in production fabric and approved, production patterns are made in order for the factory to manufacture the product.

Manual Method

When a final pattern is made by the **manual method**, it is cut from heavy manila cardboard called **tag board** (**oak tag** or just **tag**) (Figure 9.8). It has accurate seam allowances, grain lines, notches, and all identifying information for each pattern part. One pattern is cut for each piece cut from fabric, including interlining, lining, etc. Left and right sleeves or fronts are cut even if they are mirror images of each other. Top and under collars are cut even if they are the same. The cutting instructions are updated to match the final pattern. Producing patterns manually has many drawbacks. It is very time consuming, uses a lot of paper and is less accurate than digital methods.

Once a final pattern is made in the sample size, a complete set of **production patterns** is produced in a process called **grading**. Patterns for each size must be made using **grade rules**, a list of incremental changes to pattern measurements from one size to the next that are applied to the final pattern to expand the distance proportionally

Figure 9.8
Manual patternmaking uses tag board for patterns. All of the patterns for one style are stored on one pattern hook. A list of patterns, called cutting instructions (pattern chart, cutter's must), is included on the hook.

Figure 9.9a
Once a production sample is made in the sample size, a complete set of production patterns has to be made in each size using algorithms to expand the distance between landmark points proportionally on the coordinate grid.

Figure 9.9b
Fabric is spread on the cutting table in a stack of multiple layers for production. The cutting machine operators need to have a guide for cutting the pieces accurately. For this purpose, the graded patterns are traced onto a large piece of paper that covers the stack of fabric called a marker.

Figure 9.9c
This image shows a layout of all the pieces needed for the dress shown in Figure 9.3. Note that all of the pieces are laid in one direction facing the top of the garment. The fabric is not utilized well, but the quality is higher. Cutting in the right direction prevents the wales from "running."

Figure 9.9d
This image shows a layout of all the pieces needed for the dress shown in Figure 9.3. Note that the pieces are not laid in the same direction. Some are "up", and some are "down" in relation to the top of the garment. This arrangement saves five inches of fabric.

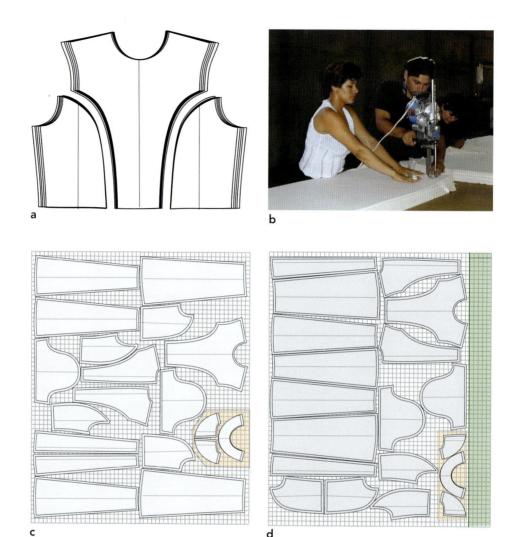

a

b

c

d

between landmark points on the coordinate grid. Each piece of the pattern, including facings, interlinings, tabs, outside and inside cuffs, left and rights sides of all parts, and so on, have to be graded, labeled, and cut out in tag board (Figure 9.9a). Because fabric for production comes rolled in a single layer, not folded, all patterns must be made whole, not on the half. It takes a lot of skill and time to manually cut all sizes accurately in tag board!

In many production factories, fabric is not cut one garment at a time; it is laid **ply** by ply (layer by layer) in a stack and cut with machines (Figure 9.9b). Cutting machine operators need to have a guide for cutting the pieces accurately. For this purpose, the graded patterns are traced onto a large piece of paper called a **marker** that covers the **lay** (stack of fabric) (Figure 9.9c). The pattern pieces must lock together in the most efficient way possible. Since fabric is often the costliest component of a garment, a good marker maker strives to lock all the pieces as close together as possible to reduce waste (Figure 9.9d).

Marker making with manually made patterns is also a slow job, requiring table space in the cutting room. Not only does a marker have to have all the pieces for each size, but a marker must be made for each different type of fabric: one marker for the shell fabric, one for the interlining, and so on. Trying out multiple lay-ups of pattern pieces can require multiple attempts until the best yield is obtained.

Digitization

Most companies use digitized patternmaking, grading, and marker making to create first patterns, production patterns, graded patterns, and markers. Computerized systems save time and money by improving fabric utilization and consistency. Even small startup companies that cannot afford the hardware and software can contract specialty services that digitize handmade patterns so that the grading and marker making can be done electronically. Many computerized patternmaking systems are available, including those from Gerber, Lectra, and EFI Optitex.

Digital patterns are created on an electronic grid just the way they are on paper. Manual patterns obtained from draping or drafting can be digitized onto the grid with a digitizing table or by taking a digital photo (Gerber Technology, 2020b) (Figure 9.10a and b). Firms store both their basic blocks and past-season patterns digitally so that they can be pulled up and modified to create new styles. Once the pattern is made and tested, changes are easy to make in the software. (Figures 9.11a and b).

After grade rules are entered into the software, the graded pattern pieces are created virtually and available on the screen for making markers. Tools in the system prompt the marker maker to lay pattern pieces on grain and without overlapping. The software can calculate the fabric utilization and suggest better layouts of pieces (Figures 9.11c–d).

a

Figure 9.10a
Tag board patterns derived from hand pattern drafting or draping can be digitized into software that automatically grades patterns and make markers. Digitizing can be done on a digitizing table by manually entering points around the tag pattern with a mouse or pen. This method is slow and less accurate than starting a pattern in the digital environment in the first place.

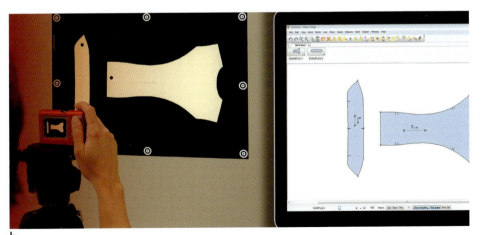

b

Figure 9.10b
Digitizing can also be done by scanning or taking a photo of each tag pattern and importing the photo into the patternmaking software. These methods are less time consuming than using a digitizing table.

Figure 9.11a
Pattern drafting
can be executed in
computer software
such as O/Dev by
EFI Optitex.

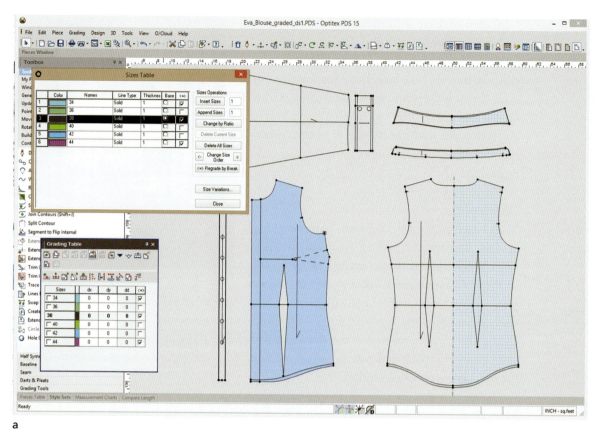

a

Figure 9.11b
Pattern drafting by
Gerber's Accumark
is another pattern
design system
(PDS).

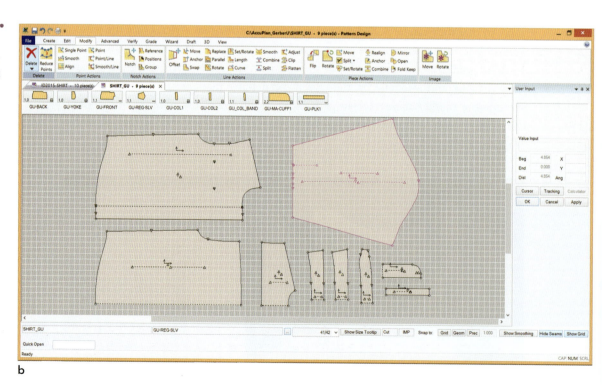

b

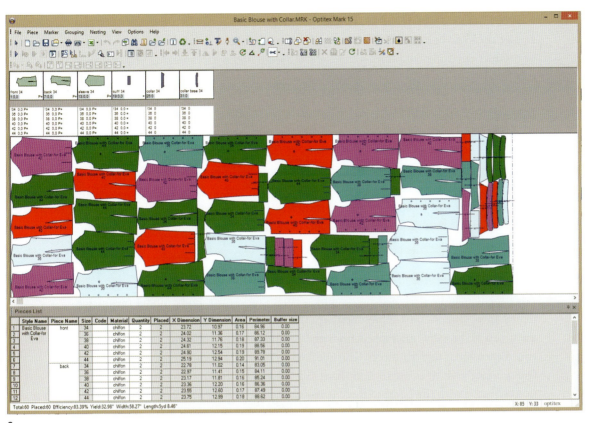

Figure 9.11c
Once patterns are digitized or created in a CAD system, such as O/Dev by EFI Optitex, they can be graded and markers can be made with accuracy and efficiency.

c

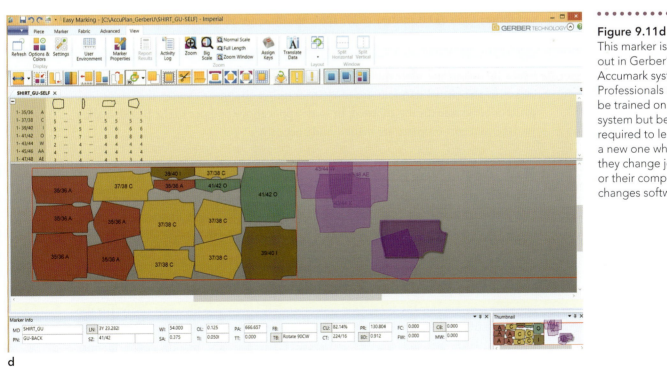

Figure 9.11d
This marker is laid out in Gerber's Accumark system. Professionals may be trained on one system but be required to learn a new one when they change jobs or their company changes software.

d

Patternmaking Technology

In past decades, digitization of patternmaking increased the standardization and speed of product development. Three-dimensional design and patternmaking will continue this trend.

Body Scanning

Body scanning technology enables retrieval of highly accurate three-dimensional body measurements from an individual consumer (Figure 9.12a). These measurements may be directly applied to the development of a customized flat pattern using manual or digital drafting techniques.

The collection of three-dimensional scanning data is being utilized to develop new sizing standards that more accurately reflect the body measurements and proportions of diverse populations.

Three-Dimensional Draping

A garment may be designed by draping virtual fabric on a **body model (avatar)**, a digital three-dimensional representation of a human figure. The resulting virtual garment can be literally unwrapped from the computerized figure and laid flat to form two-dimensional pattern pieces. This method originated for the design of upholstery and accessories such as purses and shoes. Such products are static in shape and to not need to move with the body, so there is less need for complex fit.

Three-Dimensional Patternmaking Technology

Applications such as VStitcher by Browzwear (Browzwear Solutions Pte Ltd., 2020a) or Optitex PDS 3D (Optitex, 2020) allow the designer to "stitch" the panels of virtual fabric in the shape of the electronic patterns of a garment on a body model (Figures 9.12b–d). As the body model moves, stretching, pulling, bunching, and balance issues in the virtual garment are revealed. As adjustments to the length, width, or curves of the virtual garment are made to improve the fit or change the design, the patterns are automatically adjusted. In some applications updates to the BOM, marker yardage, and cost estimate are made simultaneously.

BALANCING BUSINESS NEEDS

As a firm carves out its market share and its business model, it must keep costs affordable for its clients. Three-dimensional technology may offer some new ways to resolve conflicting demands.

Creativity vs. Cost

Patternmaking processes that allow the most creativity, such as draping or drafting one style at a time, are the most time consuming and therefore the most costly. The use of block patterns and flat patterning is faster but tends to give products "cookie cutter" sameness. Trace-offs and rub-offs are fast, but over time the brand's design identity and fit become muddied.

Emerging software programs that allow the designer to drape virtually on three-dimensional body models with highly realistic images of textiles offer more scope for creativity without the investment of time and materials needed for hand draping. Programs such as SmartDesign by Browzewear give instant feedback to the designer about cost of fabric, trims, labor so that they can be inventive within the parameters of the brand's pricing goals (Browzwear Solutions Pte Ltd., 2020b).

Location and Cost

Some firms that make highly technical products or very refined designs keep pattern development in-house or at local studios so that they can control every detail. Other firms prefer patternmaking done with local sensibilities for fit and fit models locally. Some firms are not concerned with pattern skill, only with cost, so they accept flat patterning as part of the overall package cost. The erosion of expertise that has occurred in postindustrial economies has led some firms to seek tailoring and patterning skills in other countries.

One of the major goals of the development of three-dimensional patternmaking is the reduction of the number of samples needed to achieve production-ready patterns and tech packs. Some companies assert that they are able to develop products with only one "real" sample. First, second, and third samples are handled virtually.

SUSTAINABILITY

When PLMs were first introduced, they were costly and used mainly by large brands. When PLMs were developed as cloud-based applications, more companies were able to afford them as they did not require dedicated servers. Now, PLM software is available as open platform applications that can be mixed and matched to suit the needs of smaller, growing companies. This is good news because PLMs, especially those with three-dimensional tools, contribute to brands' efforts to adopt sustainable practices by

- providing tools to reduce fabric waste in cutting
- reducing the number of samples, therefore reducing freight (carbon footprint) and materials waste
- supporting customization of products and small quantities instead of massive production runs that end up in landfills when they do not sell
- supporting transparency in processes through clear communication and reliable information
- supporting collaboration within the supply chain, an emerging trend that is essential to solving the most intractable problems of pollution and unjust labor practices (Harrop, 2020).

For students entering the fashion market, learning how to navigate three-dimensional software is critical not only to support emerging business practices but also to advance sustainability.

Figure 9.12a
Using 3D body scans for measurement speeds up patternmaking, whether in a PDS system such this one from EFI Optitex or in manual patternmaking. Measurements can be stored and analyzed again and again.

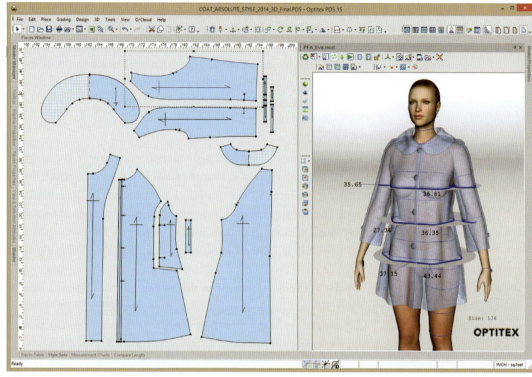

a

Figure 9.12b
Pattern pieces in 3D draping software can be transformed to the images of cut fabric and shaped around the 3D body model.

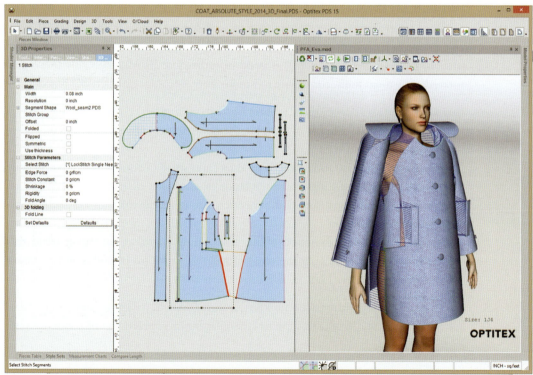

b

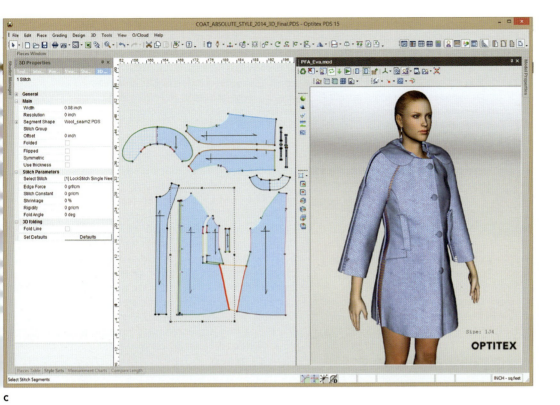

Figure 9.12c
The virtual cut pieces are "stitched" together on the 3D body model.

c

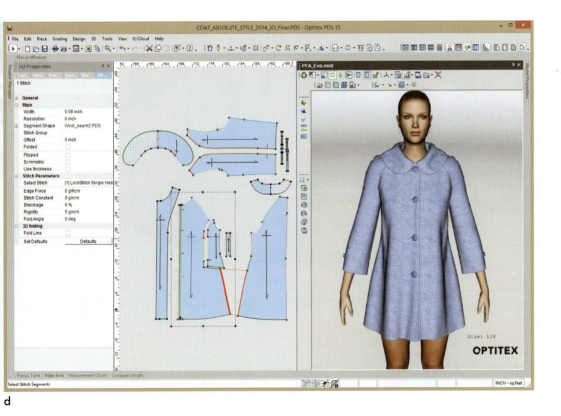

Figure 9.12d
Then the characteristics of drape that are added to the fabric file can be added to see how the garment hang on the figure.

d

Case Study 9.1
Collaboration in the Quest for Product Development Solutions

Stars Design Group (SDG) Incorporated in St. Louis, MO, USA, designs and develops thousands of apparel styles per year for its many clients, which include brands, private label clothing for retailers, and products made under license. They handle primarily menswear, including sportswear, outerwear and uniforms sold in the US, Canada, Europe, and Asia. They are known for their in-depth participation in design process and technical product development. Their global supply chain extends from Ethiopia to India, Vietnam, and China. The diversity of their client base and supply chain partners as well as the complexity of their products challenge their commitment to on-time deliveries, competitive costs, and ethical choices.

Since their founding in 2000, SDG has been through the implementation of several PLM systems. They found legacy systems to be expensive, demanding high investment upfront as well as added customization costs. Once the software is up and running, it becomes outdated quickly, but updates tend to come slowly and need to be installed by the vendor. These older systems were developed during a time when the apparel industry was characterized by large orders from dominant brands whose categories and specifications did not change often.

The landscape in which SDG competes is now populated by clients whose products vary greatly in design detail, fabrication, order size, and turnaround time. The use of 3D design and product development is critical to success. Legacy PLM software that is not built on 3D technology is not easily adaptable. In 2017, SDG started to look for a PLM system with cloud-based software and an open platform that would easily integrate workflow systems with what SDG considered to be the best of 3D solutions for design and merchandising presentations (Browzwear) and the most reliable 3D patternmaking system (Optitex).

Stars International found that BeProduct's real-time, collaborative PLM platform appealed to younger employees.

In 2017, in their quest for the best PLM, SDG embarked on a collaborative beta test of BeProduct's Digital Product Platform. A tailored instance of BeProduct's cloud native solution was specifically configured for SDG to help manage the company's workflows, including uniting design, product development, and production activities based on a single "source of truth".

For Brad Schnitker, CEO and President of SDG, one of the main reasons for the success of the beta test was BeProduct's contemporary platform, which appeals to younger employees and those who have had a less than satisfying experience with traditional PLMs. Matthew Cochran, SVP of Strategy at BeProduct, explained that the platform was designed in a forward-looking manner to work like other popular, real-time collaborative platforms such as Sales-Force and GSuite. Its private environment allows for users to "like," "create notifications and tasks," and "comment" on assets within the platform. Users can extend and invite their preferred partners, facilitating greater collaboration with their external vendor partners. The platform also appeals to brands and retailers who can participate in the design experience drawing on the intelligence of the system and the intuition of the user.

Because BeProduct is extensively configurable out-of-the-box and with open API's included, it can be easily connected to any complementary tools such as 3D design tools. The platform can support a handful of users or thousands. SDG brought on over thirty active users within the first year. It is subscription based and affordable, so it works well for a large company like SDG and is accessible to SMEs as well.

References

BeProduct. (2021), The Best of PLM & Beyond. https://us.beproduct.com/default/public/features (accessed March 25, 2021).

Cochran, M. (2021), Interview, March 29.

Schnitker, B. (2020), Interview. July 7.

Stars Design Group. (2018), BeProduct and Stars Design Group Celebrate PLM Success, August 31. https://starsdesigngroup.com/news/beproduct-and-stars-design-group-celebrate-plm-success (accessed July 3, 2020).

Stars Design Group. (2021), SDG Our Story. https://starsdesigngroup.com/about-clothing-manufacturers/ (accessed March 26, 2021).

SUMMARY

When product development professionals translate a design concept to a commercial product, they begin by applying standards, whether they are making decisions about materials or methods. The creation of the design spec is the foundation for the tech pack that becomes the blueprint for the way the product is manufactured. Product developers can save time by building specs on historical information from specification libraries. Basic information is needed to guide the pattern and sample makers, such as a technical sketch, materials information, preliminary costs, and target measurements.

Some companies still create their patterns in-house, so they have more flexibility with how much information is needed in the design spec. If patterns are made at a contracting facility, the information must be far more detailed. Full-package vendors may require even more information. Patterns for first samples can be created from original drafts or by draping. The flat pattern method, in which block patterns are manipulated to create individual styles, is faster, more efficient, and yields more consistency of fit than drafting and draping. Blocks can be used as the basis for styles that derive their inspiration by knocking-off fit and style details from another brand's products. Trace-offs that reproduce all details, including measurements from an existing product, are another form of knock-off.

Manual methods for making production patterns and graded sets are costly and time consuming. Most companies work with digitized systems or contract with studios that provide services. End-to-end systems are very efficient and give larger companies an edge in the creation of first samples and in managing the production cycle with accuracy and efficiency.

Fashion companies are challenged to meet the demand for novelty while also competing to get their product to market first at the lowest price. Technology may be the key to speed and accuracy and also contribute to better business methods and sustainable practices.

KEY TERMS

bill of materials (BOM)

block patterns (slopers)

body model (avatar)

callouts (blowups)

Computer Aided Design
(CAD)

cost sheet

cutting instructions

design specifications (design
specs)

draping

Enterprise Resource Planning
systems (ERP).

first pattern

first sample

flat pattern method

full package vendors

grade rules

grading

in-house

lay

manual method

marker

measurement chart

pattern

pattern and sample-making
services

pattern design software (PDS)

pattern drafting

ply

preliminary cost estimate
(precost)

production patterns

sewing instructions

special instructions

specification library

standards

tag board (oak tag, tag)

technical flat

technical specification package
(tech pack)

three-dimensional pattern
making software

trace-off (rub-off, reverse
engineering)

vendor compliance

wholesale price

DISCUSSION QUESTIONS

1. Open your browser and enter the keywords "compare clothing pattern design software". You are likely to find several sites that list PDS software applications and compare their attributes. If you were starting your own fashion line or product development business, which software would you choose? Please explain how you made your decision.

2. Compare and contrast the four methods for making patterns. Touch on topics such as brand identity, efficiency, consistency of fit, and creativity and cost.

ACTIVITIES

1. Imagine that you are working for a company that does trace-offs. Your boss has asked you to start off the design spec using a pair of jeans that she purchased from another brand. (Find a pair of jeans in your closet for this activity.)

   - Make a list of all the pattern pieces that would show up in cutting instructions.
   - Make a list of all the materials. Don't worry if you don't know the names of everything. List what you see.
   - Describe the design features, such as the number of pockets, their shapes, embroidery, topstitch, etc.
   - Draw a front and back sketch to $\frac{1}{8}$-inch scale.

2. Assemble a collection of at least twelve knit tops. Work together as a team, bring some from your homes, or, if you have enough people in your household, empty your drawers and closets. Look at the tops and decide whether you can perceive a difference in the quality of fabric, sewing, design, or how well the tops have held up to wear and tear. Lay out the tops on a table and rank them from best to worst. Identify how you made your choices. From this, make a list of your own standards.

STUDIO RESOURCES

- Take the chapter quiz with scored results and personalized study tips.
- Review glossary flashcards to build your vocabulary.

REFERENCES

Brannon, E. L. (2011), *Designer's guide to fashion apparel*. New York: Fairchild Books.

Browzwear Solutions Pte Ltd. (2020a), VStitcher. https://browzwear.com/products/v-stitcher/ (accessed July 31, 2020).

Browzwear Solutions Pte Ltd. (2020b), SmartDesign. https://browzwear.com/products/smartdesign/ (accessed July 29, 2020).

Computer Generated Solutions, (2020), BlueCherry PLM. https://www.cgsinc.com/en/bluecherry/plm (accessed July 21, 2020).

Gerber Technology. (2020a), Yunique PLM. https://www.gerbertechnology.com/fashion-apparel/plan/yuniqueplm/ (accessed July 21, 2020).

Gerber Technology. (2020b), AccuScan. https://gerbersoftware.com/products/accuscan/ (accessed July 31, 2020).

Infor. (2020), InforCloudSuite PLM for Fashion. https://www.infor.com/resources/cloudsuite-plm-for-fashion (accessed July 21, 2020).

Lectra. (2020), Lectra Fashion PLM 4.0 Management Software. https://www.lectra.com/en/products/lectra-fashion-plm-4-0 (accessed July 21, 2020).

Lee, J., and C. Steen. (2019), *Technical Sourcebook for Apparel Designers 3rd Edition*. New York: Fairchild Books.

Harrop, M. (2020), PLM Buyer's Guide 2020. WhichPLM. https://www.whichplm.com/download-our-plm-buyers-guide-2020/ (accessed July 31, 2020).

Optitex. (2020), Pattern Design Software (PDS) 3D. https://optitex.com/products/2d-and-3d-cad-software/ (accessed July 31, 2020).

ADDITIONAL RESOURCES

Armstrong, H. J. (2006), *Patternmaking for fashion design* (4th ed.). New York: HarperCollins.

Myers-McDevitt, P. J. (2015), *Complete guide to size specification and technical design* (2nd ed.). New York: Fairchild Publications.

CHAPTER 10

SIZING AND FIT SPECIFICATIONS

"In analyzing how my competitors communicate fit, I saw a place, an opportunity where we could first use models that have more average size figures and also develop a size chart that is easily understandable. . . . I want to gain trust and loyalty with our customer base." CARRIE PARRY (ALVANON 2014)

OBJECTIVES

- Understand how customer dissatisfaction with fit and sizing has impacted the growth of customer returns at retail
- Understand types of product recommendation software that retailers are using to reduce customer returns for fit issues
- Understand the methods that companies use to define their standard (core) body size
- Recognize the limitation of traditional linear grading systems and explore the potential benefits of new sizing systems
- Recognize common fit issues
- Understand the differences and similarities between fitting of virtual garments on avatars and fitting actual samples on live models
- Understand the role of the measurement chart in monitoring compliance in the factory
- Compare methods of mass customization
- Consider the potential of whole garment knitting and three-dimensional (3D) printing in the arena of finding the perfect fit
- Understand the impact that technological advances can have on reducing waste and lowering the carbon footprint of the fashion industry

CONSUMER PERCEPTION OF FIT

It is estimated that the value of all returns at retail has climbed to over US$1 trillion annually (IHL group, 2020). Apparel is returned at a much higher rate than other goods: clothing and shoes at 56 percent compared to electronics at 42 percent and accessories and jewelry at 30 percent (Charlton, 2020). (Figure 10.1) The Fashion e-Commerce Report found that 78.7 percent of respondents to their survey said that their top reason for returning clothing was fit and quality (Yotpo, 2020).

Size Recommendation Software

In an effort to reduce the impact of returns on their profitability, retailers have turned to **size recommendation software**, digital applications (apps) that match customers to products that are more likely to meet their expectations for size and fit. Information about size and fit is gathered, input, and compared to vast data bases of information about other consumers and a profile is created using algorithms. When the customer selects a product, their fit profile is compared to information from brands' tech packs or measurement charts and choices that similar customers have made, and the app recommends a size. If the customer continues to use the same application over time, the predictions will become more and more accurate. As the developers of these apps partner with more brands and retailers, and as they acquire more users, their data bases grow, and the algorithms become more refined in their predictions.

Developments in size recommendation software have primarily focused on capturing, as accurately as possible, the exact size and shape of the customer (Figure 10.2). Depending on the breadth and accuracy of the product information provided by the brand, the app's ability to make an accurate prediction may be limited.

Figure 10.1
Retail returns have climbed to over US$ one trillion annually. It is estimated that over half of all returns are apparel and accessories. Because retailers cannot absorb all the returns, many are sent to liquidators such as the one in this image. Many are disposed of in landfills or burned.

Figure 10.2
Retailers use size recommendation software to capture the customer's size and shape with various methods.

Questionnaire
Fit Analytics (Taylor, 2020a), Bold Metrics Contactless Fit™ (Taylor, 2020b), and True Fit (Soltes, 2020) base their size recommendations on responses to a handful of questions such as their height, weight, age, or usual size in a favorite brand which are compared to the app's large data base of customer choices. Each app has its own algorithms for analyzing and making size recommendations.

Body scan
Fit:Match asks customers to make an appointment and visit a Pop Up Studio in a popular shopping mall. After answering a few questions, the customer is scanned, the information is entered into the app. The customer is issued a Fitch:ID number which represents their fit profile which they can use when visiting participating brands' websites or stores (Soltes, 2020).

Mobile phone app-measurements
MySize ID gathers body measurement using sensors built into cell phones. The customer glides the phone over their body to capture measurements such as arm length or inseam. The app stores the measurements and retailers can use the information for fit recommendations (Roshitsh, 2018).

Mobile phone app-photos, computer vision and geometry processing
Companies such as Meepl use **geometry (mesh) processing**, algorithms that reconstruct the customer's 3D shape, using computer vision technology and photos taken on the customer's cell phone. (Meepl, 2020). The customer's measurements or avatars can be used to interface with retailers' recommendation software (Jones, 2020).

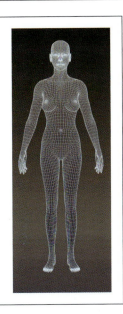

Mobile phone app-photos, computer vision and 3D matching
3DLook Mobile Tailor tool also uses a cell phone. The customer takes two photos of themselves from the front and side.

Using **computer vision technology** to process and analyze digital information from photos and **3D matching technology** to create a shape based on comparing the two photos. This app is especially useful for linking customers with small businesses that customize their products (Hall, 2020).

The degree of impact of recommendation apps on customer satisfaction and the reduction of returns because of fit is not yet proven (Taylor, 2020a). Jason Wang of Alvanon is skeptical that unless brands provide detailed and accurate 3D information about their products, a match with the customer's avatar will be hit-and-miss (see Case Study 10.1).

At present, recommendation software can address some fit issues better than others.

- Availability—Customers can find out quickly if a product is available or not in their size.
- Appropriateness—Many of the software programs provide garment images that can be superimposed over the customer's photo or even be virtually tried on the customer's avatar. A garment might be rejected because it may not appear to align with the customer's personal taste, cultural norms, or expectation of a brand's identity. It might hug the body too closely or hang too loosely. Too much or not enough skin may be revealed.
- Proportion—If the measurements from the customer and from the brand tech packs are accurate, then the image of the garment on the customer's photo or avatar will show whether the garment fits in around all areas of the body and whether the torso, legs, or arms lengths are correct. If either the customer's or the brands's measurements are inaccurate, the product may look good on the app, but may not fit when the garment is delivered.
- Consistency—The recommendation engine will translate the fit of a garment regardless of the brand. But it will not be able to guarantee that fit after the garment is worn and cleaned.
- Ease of movement—Recommendation apps that show a 3D garment on an avatar that moves will be better able to predict ease or restriction of movement.
- Smoothness—Depending on the accuracy of the measurements of both the customer's body and the brand's tech pack, the virtual image of the product might reveal unwanted folds and bunches at crotch, underarms, neckline, waist, elbows, or cuffs.
- Balance—Pattern adjustments that affect balance are subtle and not easily captured by measurements. It may not yet be possible for a recommendation engine to represent a garment that shifts to the front, back, or one side.

Recommendation software apps have the potential to collect valuable data about customers to support brands' efforts to

- Perfect the standard body size as a reflection of the target market: its body dimensions, shape, and proportions.
- Establish grade rules that reflect the target market.
- Discover underserved or unrecognized niche size categories.

Technical Designers' role will be even more essential in providing accurate specifications, assisting in monitoring vendor compliance, and refining patternmaking and construction techniques.

STANDARD BODY SIZE

The mass production of apparel capitalizes on making hundreds, thousands, or tens of thousands of copies of a single product to enhance profitability. The problem is that people are not all the same size and shape. Brands are continually challenged to provide enough size variation to fit the range of customers in their target market and still make a profit.

Once a brand has identified its target market through demographic, psychographic, and lifestyle markers, it defines a **standard (core) body size** by establishing a set of body measurements that most closely represent the shape of their target customer. The measurements of the brand's typical customer usually fall in the middle of a range of sizes that are larger and smaller. Each size will be labeled with a number or letter designation. The actual measurements for the incremental changes between sizes might be borrowed from other brands, taken from lists of standard body measurements, or developed by the brand over time. Manufacturers will seek to minimize the number of sizes they offer to keep inventories down and yet satisfy as many customers as possible. A list of sizes, usually expressed as letters or numbers with corresponding body measurements, is called a **size system** (Petrova, 2007).

Fit Model

Chapter 9 discussed the various methods for creating patterns for mass production. All of these methods start with a body form from which measurements can be taken or on which fabric can be draped. Apparel companies that choose to work with a live **fit model** look for an individual whose measurements match the standard body size with no exaggerated features such as a rounded back or sloped shoulders. Companies may choose a fit model whose shape projects an aspirational ideal that appeals to the target market (Figure 10.3). Small companies may choose a fit model from among

Figure 10.3
Nanette Lapore fits a garment on a live fit model in her studio in New York with staff commenting and taking notes.

acquaintances, family members, or employees based on availability or to avoid hiring expensive professional models.

Body Forms

Some companies use **body forms** (mannequins, dress forms) that represent the whole body or partial sections (such as torso or legs), which are placed on a stand to facilitate patternmaking, draping, and fitting activities. Body forms are available for all genders and ages. Specialized forms are made for bathing suits, pants, maternity wear, and even dogs! Traditional body forms from companies such as Wolf Form Company and Superior Model Form are made by pressing papier-mâché into plaster molds whose shapes are created by master craftsmen (How It's Made, 2015). Although their standard shapes have evolved over the years, reflecting changes in foundation garments and fashion silhouettes, these form companies may have contributed to the perpetuation of idealized body shapes because they make their standard forms based on idealized notions of what the body *should* be rather than on data collected from real people (Figure 10.4a). Although these body form companies will produce customized body forms for a higher price, smaller companies that cannot afford them will buy a standard body form and then base their standard body shape on that body form. An inexpensive way to customize a standard form to meet specifications is to build it out with padding or with molded foam shapes from companies such as Fabulous Fit (Fabulous Fit® Dress Form Fitting System, 2020).

Companies such as Alvanon provide customized forms for clients based on 3D body scans of the customer's fit model or other well-known fit models (Alvanon, 2020a). The process of fabricating the forms starts with milling the 3D shape into poly

Figure 10.4a
Companies that created mannequins for the apparel industry in the past performed a valuable service by making standardized forms, but they may have inadvertently contributed to the perpetuation of clothing being made for unrealistic shapes because the forms they made were based on idealized notions of what the body should be rather than on data collected from real people.

Figure 10.4b
The fabrication of the forms at Alvanon is driven by software with information generated by 3D modeling.

a

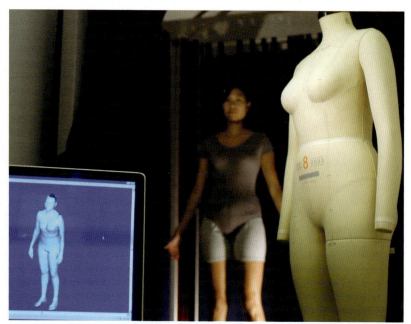

b

foam using digital files. From that precise shape, a mold is made, then a cast is made from the mold in fiberglass. Then, the rigid mold is covered in soft materials (Figure 10.4b) (Alvanon, 2013).

Three-Dimensional (3D) Body Scans

Companies such as Alvanon can also take a 3D scan of a brand's fit model and extract measurements to provide a customized avatar for 3D patternmaking (Alvanon, 2020b). Some companies have their own 3D scanners and use the scans they take to make their own virtual fit models.

Standard Body Size Sources

When a company identifies and routinely uses a standard body shape to make patterns, the result is consistency of fit that strengthens brand identity. There is not and has never been a globally applied or enforced standard for clothing sizes. In the late 1960s the ISO formed the Technical Committee (ISO/TC133) to create a universal sizing system. They concluded that the task was impossible given the vast differences in body structure throughout the world. By 1977 the Committee devised guidelines for creating sizing systems that would be applicable to unique populations in different countries. By 1991, the Committee had established procedures that included the selection of key dimensions, and suggested intervals between sizes and methods for gathering data (Figure 10.5). The committee published updated guidelines in 2018 based on statistical analysis and body dimensions data. They urge flexibility in creating sizing systems in order to adapt to change. (ISO. 2018).

England, Japan, South Korea, and Hungary have so far made efforts to adopt the ISO methodology, each country with different key dimensions and intervals based on their own populations (Petrova, 2007). Although there have been some initiatives to standardize sizing of apparel, such as EN 13402 in the European Union, Shape GB in Great Britain, and Size India (Saini, 2018), a universal sizing system within a single country is still an elusive goal.

Consumers, manufacturers, and retailers agree that voluntary sizing standards have not fully represented women's actual body measurements, so they have not been widely used. It may be a good thing that the use of these lists has been voluntary, because manufacturers have been free to create garments that fit their particular target populations. Consumers whose needs have not been met by one brand have at least been able to shop until they find brands and products that fit better.

Standardization of measurements may seem to be a solution for inconsistency of fit from one brand to the next; however, the populations of some countries such as the United States are composed of people from all over the world with different body structures. Intermarriage, lifestyle changes, and an increase of obesity have added to

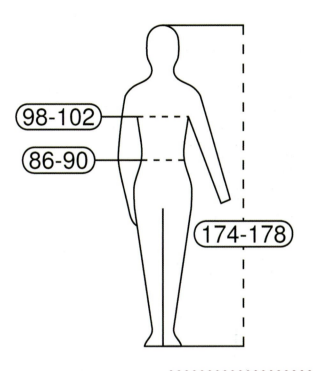

Figure 10.5
The ISO sizing guidelines for sizing information provided to the consumer call for the identification of a key dimension on the body that is relevant to the category of garment so that the consumer can compare sizes across brands.

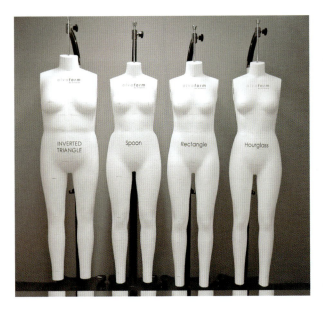

Figure 10.6
Alvanon has a database of scans of thousands of bodies. They analyze the data and create body forms and size charts that reflect real bodies. These shapes were identified in studies that were based on data from SizeUSA.

the diversity of body shapes. Cultures with more genetically homogeneous populations, such as Korea, have fewer sizes in the stores, reflecting fewer body variations (Lee et al., 2007).

Analysis of data from 3D scanning has resulted in the creation of more size categories and sizes rather than a single standard. One of the first comprehensive studies, SizeUSA, created a pool of actual body measurement data from more than 10,000 participants (SizeUSA, 2008). When the results of SizeUSA were released to the press in 2004, it was clear that the industry standard "hourglass" size 8 female was a myth. In all populations, the average bust size was at least 5 inches larger than the "industry standard" median size 8. Not only was the average woman larger, but *more importantly*, her proportions were different. The "hourglass" silhouette with a small waist that had been used for decades by brands only represented 21.6 percent of the population. Other shapes with substantial representation were identified such as "spoon" and "rectangle" (Figure 10.6). SizeUSA study findings were shared with fifty companies, including Victoria's Secret, Jockey, Chico's, and JCPenney (Weathers, 2007), some of whom adjusted the proportions in their clothing immediately.

In 2011 ASTM International D5585-11 Standard Tables of Body Measurements for Adult Female Misses Figure Type, Size Range 00–20, created new standards for misses' apparel sizes by analyzing data from the apparel industry, Department of Commerce, Civilian American and European Surface Anthropometry Resource Project (CAESAR) Study, and SizeUSA. The new measurement tables were documented utilizing 3D avatars developed by Alvanon, Inc. This new sizing standard for misses' sizes introduced numerous changes from previous versions, many of which were directly attributed to the availability of new scanned body measurement data and previously unavailable computerized modeling capabilities. The most visible change in the new ASTM apparel sizing standards is the inclusion of two body types for each of the sizes, straight and curvy, with different measurements applied to these two body silhouettes (Appendix 10.1a and b) (ASTM International, 2015).

Alvanon has continued to partner with brands and standards associations to expand its collection of data outside of the United States, now providing measurements for standard body sizes in China, France, Germany, Japan, EU, UK, and Australia (in progress). Their size ranges include adults, children, extended sizes, and niche markets such as athletic specialties and protective clothing (Alvanon, 2016c) (see Appendix 10.1c–p). Some companies develop libraries of avatars for 3D product development from proprietary sources. Tukatech scans hundreds of fit models from brands (Nishimura, 2019). BodyBlock AI gathers body data using its own scanners at fitness and wellness centers around the world to create their versions of virtual body forms that represent large segments of the population (Roshitsh, 2019).

SIZING

Traditional Grade Rules

After the dimensions of the standard body size have been determined and the block patterns have been made, a style is designed and approved. The patterns are scaled using **grade rules,** lists of incremental changes to pattern measurements from one size to the next. Grade rules may have been created by the company, borrowed from other companies, or taken from published sizing systems. Research into the validity of grade rules in sizing systems, which began in the 1980s, has continued to question customary grade rules and show that their use contributes to ill-fitting garments in the sizes furthest from the base size. Although there are many sizing systems, some misconceptions about variations from the standard body size in a given population are common (Figure 10.7a).

- People who are taller than the standard are also proportionately wider in girth.
- People who are wider than the standard in the chest are proportionally wider in the waist and hip (seat).
- Girth measurements are distributed evenly between front and back on all people
- People who have one measurement longer than the standard such as arm length will have proportionately longer measurements everywhere, including pant inseam, crotch depth and overall height.
- People who have wider girth measurements will have proportionally wider across-body measurements such as shoulder width.

Researcher Nancy Schofield makes the argument that the application of grade rules that are linked to each other and follow a proportional internal system were developed when graded sets of patterns were hand made in tag board. It was easy to check that all the pieces related to each other in a nested set (Schofield, 2007). The poor fit resulting from proportional grade rules in American companies has rarely been challenged because testing of sizes beyond the base size is time consuming and costly (Bougourd, 2007).

New Sizing Systems

The time is right to apply new systems of sizing.

- Patterns are almost universally graded by computer software, so visual truing in oak tag is no longer necessary.
- Anthropometric data are readily available.
- 3D fitting on avatars of all sizes is becoming more available and increasingly accurate.
- Digital retail companies are clamoring for solutions that build customer trust and reduce returns.

Data from scanning projects have been used to test, analyze, and amend existing sizing systems. For example, ASTM found that 65 percent of the women in the USA measured for Standard D5585-11e1 were 5 feet 5 inches tall, so the new standard lists body grade rules for girth only, not height. These efforts perform much needed

Figures 10.7a1–3
The patterns shown in Figure 10.7a are graded using traditional linear grade rules. As sizes increase or decrease in girth, they increase or decrease in length. (Simulation)

Figure 10.7a1. In traditional liner grading systems, a pattern is made for a size that is chosen as a median size. The back is on the left. The front is on the right.

Figure 10.7a2. In this image, the largest size XL (gold) and the smallest XS (red) are nested from the waist and center. The grade rules increase the overall length of the back and front by the same amount.

Figure 10.7a3. In this image, all of the sizes XS–XL are graded in length and width by the same proportion and placed together in a nest. Notice that the armhole "grows" evenly both vertically and horizontally. The shoulder width widens for each size.

Figures 10.7b1–3
The patterns in Figure 10.7b are made for same demographic group as Figure 10.7a. Note that the length does not necessarily increase or decrease from size to size in proportion to the girth and that the shapes such as the shoulder slope do not have the same angle. Measurements that come from data mining body scan information will not necessarily fall into size groups that are proportioned in the same way. (Simulation)

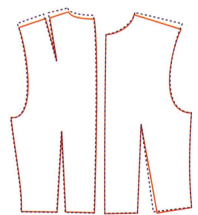

Figure 10.7b1. The largest size from the XS–XL nest above (solid gold) is compared to a pattern made from data (simulated) that has been analyzed with data mining techniques (dotted line in brown). Note that the armhole is not as deep and the shoulder slope on the front is a different angle. The front dart is deeper.

Figure 10.7b2. This image is also a simulation. In it the smallest size (solid red) demonstrates that the traditional grade does not allow enough length in the back. The bust dart is too deep, making the waist too small in relation to the bust area.

Figure 10.7b3. This image places the simulated XL, M and XS in a nest, aligned at the bust and center just as the nest above. For this group of customers, the back does not need to be graded as the front. The armhole depth does not need to change. The shoulder width does not change in the larger sizes.

revision, but they perpetuate a system based on regular, predictable intervals between sizes. The consistency of these size systems may be convenient for production and understandable to the customer on the sales floor, but they do not reflect the reality of fit for individual consumers.

The development of new sizing systems that accommodate the greatest number of people calls for an entirely new way of thinking. Intervals between sizes may need to be irregularly spaced and not easily predicted by an algorithm (Figure 10.7b). If size intervals serve more customers when they are not evenly spaced, then how will sizes be defined and marketed?

As product recommendation software becomes more prevalent, it is possible that the need for sizing systems will disappear. The algorithms used to analyze data gathered about the dimensions of the target market will lead to ever more refined understanding of the shape of the customers. As matching software relies more on the 3D shape of the customer and product and less on lists of measurements, the right product will increasingly be selected for the customer without the need for size labels.

GARMENT FIT

When a firm has done the research to find a sample size body and method of sizing up and down (grading) that accurately reflects the shape of its target market, there is more work to be done. Customer expectations of **fit** are subjective, influenced by fashion trends, textile characteristics, social and cultural context, function, and demographics (Lee & Steen, 2019, p. 280) as well as taste and personal preference. Perceptions that are driven by feelings must be transformed by the technical designer into changes in measurements and by the patternmaker into changes to the pattern.

Ease

Ease is the amount of difference between the body measurements of the intended wearer and the corresponding measurements of the finished garment.

Functional Ease

Functional ease, or wearing ease, is the number of inches added to the garment over and above the body, corresponding measurement to allow body movement and comfort. It is the minimum required for the garment to be worn. Women's garments made of stable, woven fabrics typically provide wearing ease of approximately 2.5 inches in the bust, 1 inch in the waist, and 2 inches in the hip. Functional ease also varies with the garment category and intended end use of the garment itself. For example, bicyclists need clothing that is very snug to avoid folds of fabric that catch air and create drag.

Functional ease requirements in general are significantly less for knit fabrics. The textile must be tested before patterning to establish the amount of elasticity and recovery in both the warp and weft direction. The amount of stretch can be expressed in a percentage of the usual ease found in a stable woven. Woven block pattern dimensions can then be adjusted by that percentage to create patterns for first fit sample

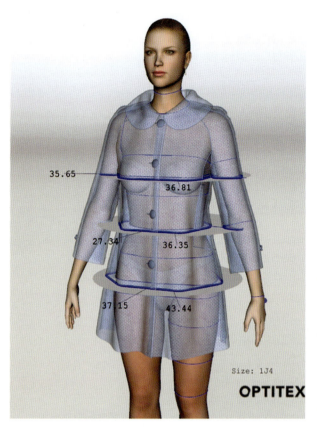

35.65

36.81

27.34

36.35

37.15

43.44

Size: 1J4

OPTITEX

(Richardson, 2008). Because spandex has been incorporated into so many textiles, the same process can be used for wovens with added stretch.

3D technology allows the designer to analyze the amount of functional ease while creating a style. When a garment is draped on an avatar, the system calculates the space between the shell and the body. Notice the two sets of measurements at the bust, waist, and hips on the 3D image in Figure 10.8. These measurements show the circumference of the avatar compared to the pattern.

A useful tool called a tension map (Figure 10.9) considers not only the ease in the pattern but also the characteristics of the textile; then it shows areas where the fabric is stressed more than others with various colors. As the designer changes the dimensions of the pattern, the color indicating the stressed area will change.

Design Ease

Design ease reflects the number of inches added to or removed from garment measurements (over and above the corresponding body measurement and functional ease) to produce the silhouette desired by the designer. Appropriate design ease varies by brand image, season, culture, generational cohort, gender identity, lifestyle, and ability level. The amount of ease will also change within each group over time.

Figure 10.8
When a garment is draped on an avatar in 3D pattern design software, the system calculates the space between the shell and the body. Notice the two sets of measurements at the bust, waist, and hips. These measurements show the circumference of the avatar compared to the pattern.

Drag Lines

In some cases, **drag lines** (unintended folds) that form horizontally across the bust, hip, or shoulder will improve with added functional ease. Noticing that fabric is pulling is just the beginning of solving the problem. Patternmaking is a process of creating shapes that will work together. The issue may be that there is no dart, princess line, or other shaping seams to allow for the fullness of the bust. The solution to a problem may not only be how much to add, but where and how to shape the fabric to fit a body curve. Customer complaints such as "this garment is bunching (too much fabric) under the crotch or armhole" may be caused by a crotch depth (rise) that is too long at the back or front or a sleeve cap that is unevenly distributed in an armhole.

Balance

The panels or textiles that make up a garment are subject to gravity when they are hanging from the shoulders or waist. Most bodies are not cylinders, so the panels on the front and back will not hang freely from top to hem. The contoured parts of the body such as bust or seat will hold the panels out. If all the panels of a garment have

a   b

Figure 10.9
Tension map in a 3D
virtual fitting. The red
and yellow areas over
the bust and shoulders
of the avatar show
stress. In the blue areas
the fabric is draping
with no stress.

the proper ease, they will hang vertical to the ground. If the panels swing out at the hem at the front or the back, then the shoulder slope must be adjusted until the panels hang vertically and the garment shows **balance (pattern)** from front to back.

In general, digital patternmaking systems automatically mirror patterns from left to right. Left-right imbalance in a garment is more likely to be a textile- or production-related problem rather than poor patternmaking. When a garment twists, it may have been improperly designed or laid into the marker with the warp grain on an angle that is not vertical to the ground. Sometimes textiles, wovens, or knits, are not finished correctly and the yarns on the weft direction are stretched or pulled to an angle that is not 90 degrees to the warp direction (skewed). When a skewed textile is cut and worn without correction, the garment will twist around the body. Occasionally pieces from one size are mixed with pieces from another garment during assembly, thus creating an imbalance.

SAMPLE APPROVAL

Even before the pandemic of 2020, many companies were seeking ways to reduce the number of approval samples necessary to be reviewed before starting production. Digital tools that reduce the number of samples needed such as 3D draping on avatars were essential during times when **fit sessions** were impossible because the technical designer, designer, and/or the merchandiser were not able to meet in person to view a sewn garment on a body form or fit model, to assess conformity with specifications and standards, and to make comments.

With the advent of open platform software, it is possible for small and mid-sized companies to work with a company such as Alvanon to identify their target body size and size system. They can purchase body forms and block patterns that conform. The patterns can be used in most of the patternmaking software to develop styles from the blocks that already fit the forms. If their patternmaking software has 3D design and draping capability, they can license the avatars that reflect the body forms and block patterns. The first two to three prototypes can be designed, tested, and specced and if they have PLM software as well, the virtual samples can be costed very rapidly.

Companies who continue to develop prototypes by having offshore vendors make sample after sample from specifications will find themselves spending money and time on development that will be hard to recover in a landscape defined by ever more available and less costly technology. Even vertically integrated companies who have the luxury of having sample services in the same building or city will still choose to start development virtually because all the data will be captured and transmitted through a data base.

Face-to-face fitting sessions for which technical designers must physically measure samples (Figure 10.10), gather the product development team in a physical location, take photos or videos, and write and distribute comments may become obsolete for all

Figure 10.10
Before the fitting, the garment will be measured to see if any parts are out of tolerance.

except the final fitting. Some of the information gathered in a face-to-face fit session can be decided in an iterative process in 3D patternmaking tools in PLM such as

- testing assumptions about garment when displayed on the standard body size
- confirming that the amount of ease is appropriate for function and style
- observing the performance of the textile used in the specific style
- confirming balance
- eliminating drag lines and bunching
- analyzing the appropriateness of the design for the customer

Follow-up tasks such as making pattern corrections and updating the measurement charts can be done automatically in a PLM (Figure 10.11).

Figure 10.11
The measurement chart from a design spec lists target measurements and records actual measurements of the sample garment taken by the vendor and the technical designer before fittings (see the technical flat from Figure 9.3).

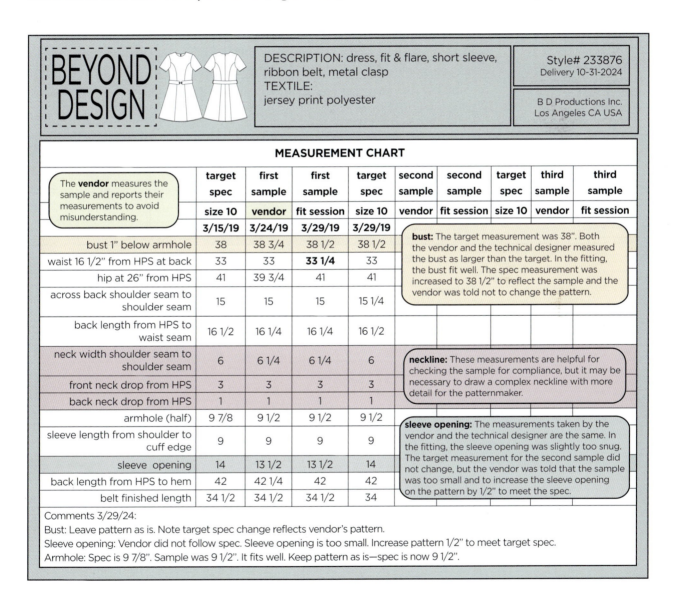

BEYOND DESIGN

DESCRIPTION: dress, fit & flare, short sleeve, ribbon belt, metal clasp
TEXTILE:
jersey print polyester

Style# 233876
Delivery 10-31-2024

B D Productions Inc.
Los Angeles CA USA

MEASUREMENT CHART

The **vendor** measures the sample and reports their measurements to avoid misunderstanding.

	target spec	first sample	first sample	target spec	second sample	second sample	target spec	third sample	third sample
	size 10	vendor	fit session	size 10	vendor	fit session	size 10	vendor	fit session
	3/15/19	3/24/19	3/29/19	3/29/19					
bust 1" below armhole	38	38 3/4	38 1/2	38 1/2					
waist 16 1/2" from HPS at back	33	33	**33 1/4**	33					
hip at 26" from HPS	41	39 3/4	41	41					
across back shoulder seam to shoulder seam	15	15	15	15 1/4					
back length from HPS to waist seam	16 1/2	16 1/4	16 1/4	16 1/2					
neck width shoulder seam to shoulder seam	6	6 1/4	6 1/4	6					
front neck drop from HPS	3	3	3	3					
back neck drop from HPS	1	1	1	1					
armhole (half)	9 7/8	9 1/2	9 1/2	9 1/2					
sleeve length from shoulder to cuff edge	9	9	9	9					
sleeve opening	14	13 1/2	13 1/2	14					
back length from HPS to hem	42	42 1/4	42	42					
belt finished length	34 1/2	34 1/2	34 1/2	34					

bust: The target measurement was 38". Both the vendor and the technical designer measured the bust as larger than the target. In the fitting, the bust fit well. The spec measurement was increased to 38 1/2" to reflect the sample and the vendor was told not to change the pattern.

neckline: These measurements are helpful for checking the sample for compliance, but it may be necessary to draw a complex neckline with more detail for the patternmaker.

sleeve opening: The measurements taken by the vendor and the technical designer are the same. In the fitting, the sleeve opening was slightly too snug. The target measurement for the second sample did not change, but the vendor was told that the sample was too small and to increase the sleeve opening on the pattern by 1/2" to meet the spec.

Comments 3/29/24:
Bust: Leave pattern as is. Note target spec change reflects vendor's pattern.
Sleeve opening: Vendor did not follow spec. Sleeve opening is too small. Increase pattern 1/2" to meet target spec.
Armhole: Spec is 9 7/8". Sample was 9 1/2". It fits well. Keep pattern as is—spec is now 9 1/2".

MONITORING COMPLIANCE

In spite of extensive sizing research and careful design, customers may still receive products that do not fit as intended due to incorrect cutting, sewing, or textile performance. Some of these problems can be dealt with during production if the factory has the correct specifications and conducts quality checks throughout the manufacturing process.

Measurements

After the sample is approved for production, the measurement chart is updated for the tech pack. Only measurements required for production of the garment are listed. They may be expanded or simplified to facilitate production and quality monitoring. Graded measurements for each size are listed (Figure 10.12).

Large companies such as Nordstrom develop manuals with lists of precise locations and methods of taking measurements that enable anyone involved in the product development process to communicate exactly (Nordstrom, 2016). Smaller companies can find lists and images of how to measure in sources such as the *Vendor Compliance Handbook* (Secul, 2010).

Figure 10.12
The measurement chart in the tech pack may have more or fewer measurements than the design spec so that it is useful for monitoring quality and consistency in the factory (see the technical flat from Figure 9.3).

BEYOND DESIGN		DESCRIPTION: dress, fit & flare, short sleeve, ribbon belt, metal clasp TEXTILE: jersey print polyester	Style# 233876 Delivery 10-31-2024
			B D Productions Inc. Los Angeles CA USA

MEASUREMENT CHART-GRADED

	tolerance	4	6	8	10	12	14	16
bust 1" below armhole	3 1/2	35 1/2	36 1/2	37 1/2	38 1/2	38 1/2	41 1/2	43
waist 16 1/2" from HPS at back	3 1/2	30	31	32	33	33	36	37 1/2
hip at 26" from HPS	3 1/2	38	39	40	41	41	44	45 1/2
across back shoulder seam to shoulder seam	3 1/8	14 1/2	14 3/4	15	15 1/4	15 1/2	15 3/4	16
back length from HPS to waist seam	16 1/2	16 1/2	16 1/2	16 1/2	16 1/2	16 1/2	16 1/2	16 1/2
neck width shoulder seam to shoulder seam	3 1/4	5 5/8	5 3/4	5 7/8	6	6 3/16	6 3/8	6 9/16
front neck drop from HPS	3 1/8	2 5/8	2 3/4	2 7/8	3	3 3/16	3 3/8	3 9/16
back neck drop from HPS	3 1/8	7/8	7/8	1	1	1 1/8	1 1/8	1 1/4
armhole (half)	3 1/4	8 3/4	9	9 1/4	9 1/2	9 7/8	10 1/4	10 5/8
sleeve length from shoulder to cuff edge	3 1/4	9	9	9	9	9	9	9
sleeve opening	3 1/4	13 5/8	13 3/4	13 7/8	14	14 1/8	14 1/4	14 3/8
back length from HPS to hem	3 1/2	42	42	42	42	42	42	42
belt length (finished tip to tip)	–	31 1/2	32 1/2	33 1/2	34 1/2	36	37 1/2	39

Metrics and Sizing

The metric system is almost universally used for measurement charts; only the United States, Myanmar, and Liberia continue to use the imperial system. A technical designer who develops products with one of these counties must be fluent with manipulating fractions.

Tolerance

Tolerance is the allowable amount of variance from the stated measurement. It is usually stated next to a measurement as +/– and a fraction of an inch. Each company develops its own standards for tolerances, but some guidelines are common:

- Girth tolerance should not be more than half of the grade.
- Tolerance on wovens is less than on knits.
- Tolerance on tiny parts such as collar points must be small enough not to be detected by the customer.
- Tolerance cannot be more than the ability of the machine or method to produce.
- Tolerance should suit the product: a fleece hoody and a bra will not be the same.

MASS CUSTOMIZATION

Mass customization is the application of mass-production techniques to the production of a single customer-configured garment to maximize choice and minimize cost. The dream of being able to walk into a 3D scanner in one moment and walk out of a store a few minutes later with a custom-fit and custom-designed product has not yet been realized. However, progress has been made thanks to the availability of 3D design software and data mining software.

One technique for generating a customized pattern is to import a scan of an individual customer into 3D pattern making software and create an avatar. The system identifies the pattern of the customer's selected style with their avatar and finds the size that is closest to their measurements. The system then recommends pattern alterations that need to be made for a good fit and displays the final virtual garment on the customer's avatar (Figure 10.13). This process needs to be supported by a production system assisted by technology such as electronic single ply cutting in order to be profitable.

Another technique uses data mining on large collections of scans to identify a broad range of figure types. Patterns are created for each of these. Customers are scanned and matched with a pattern that is close to their shape and dimensions.

THREE-DIMENSIONAL (3D) MANUFACTURING SOLUTIONS

Discussions of size and fit are focused on finding the best way to translate a customer's 3D shape into measurements that can be arranged into a 2D pattern in order to cut pattern shapes out of 2D textiles that are then sewn back together into a 3D garment.

Figures 10.13a–g

Browzwear has harnessed the flexibility of 3D design to create a customization app called Made to Measure. The manufacturer creates a style on a stock avatar (a) and edits the patterns until a perfect fit is achieved. The customer sends the manufacturer a 3D body scan and chooses a style (c). The app finds the pattern of the digital garment that is closest to the customer's shape (d). The system drapes a digital garment based on the existing pattern onto the customer's avatar and discovers where it does and does not fit (e). The system makes the pattern adjustment to achieve perfect fit on the customer's avatar (f) and verifies the fit on the avatar (g).

a

b

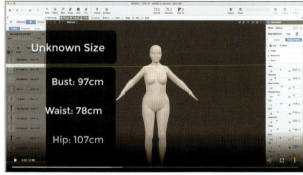

c

d

e

f

g

The technology exists now to create 3D garments without going through the 2D process of making patterns and cutting. Shima Seiki's 3D WHOLEGARMENT® machines can knit the entire garment at one time, eliminating the need for linking. (Flat knit machines knit separate shaped panels that require a process called linking to join the seams.) Shima Seiki's Made2Fit technology exists now to adjust an existing 3D knitting pattern to a customer's shape using a body scan from a smartphone and produce a custom fit garment in 90 minutes. As with many advances in technology, setting up a business that is solely based on custom ordered 3D knitting may require changes in business operations and significant investment (SJ Guest Editorial, 2019), so on-demand custom knit garments are not yet readily available. Companies such as Tailored Industry in Brooklyn, NY are working on a mass customization model that supplies very small batches of 3D knit products with style customizations so that specialty retailers such as Ministry of Supply and startups can get a clear idea of the demand for their size assortment and order only what they can sell (Binns, 2019).

The advent of 3D printing may completely circumvent the need for patternmaking and weaving. The fabric can be produced from interlocking units of varying sizes to conform to the customers' shapes gathered from body scans. In initial experiments with this process, garments are slow and expensive to produce, and the materials are not yet very comfortable (Mok, 2015). If, however, 3D printing of clothing follows the same trajectory as other technology, these issues may become irrelevant (Figure 10.14).

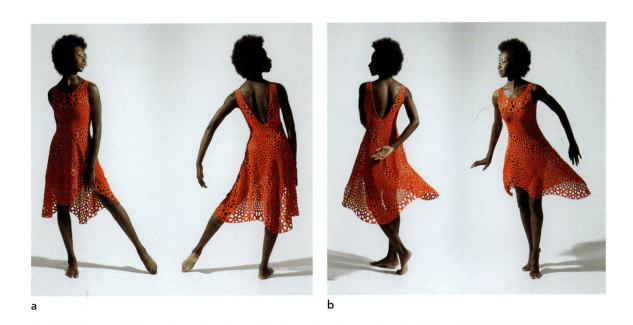

a   b

Figure 10.14
Kinematics Dress #6 was designed and produced by Nervous System Design Studio in Massachusetts using 3D printing that requires no patterning, no sewing, and generates no waste! The program generates thousands of pieces that hinge together and cover the avatar of the body of the scanned customer. The pieces fold up so that the entire garment can fit into the printer. Although the dress is beautiful and a glimpse at future solutions to fit, it took 48 hours to make and cost $3000 (Mok, 2015)!

Case Study 10.1

Authentic Digital Garment

Jason Wang, COO of Alvanon believes that designers of size recommendation software will struggle to provide tools that make accurate matches between customers and garments until the virtual garment that the customer tries on is authentic. Wang uses the term "Authentic Digital Garment" to mean a digital file that contains all the necessary requirements to mass produce a garment in which the fit, the fabric, the pattern, the details, and the grade have all been properly verified to be sure that the digital garment, as viewed on a 3D avatar, is equal to a garment made in the factory.

Currently, recommendation software relies on matching a digital representation of the customer with a measurement provided by the brand, which is not necessarily reliable. When a customer tries an Authentic Digital Garment, their 3D avatar is being compared to an accurate 3D representation of the garment, not a list of measurements.

They conducted a test using the following method for a tee shirt and a pant. They

- chose a size from a size system that is built on research
- chose a block pattern developed in 2D for that size that had been tested and proven fit on the 3D and on the physical form developed for a textile with similar properties to the textile being tested
- used the block to create a pattern for a new style in 2D
- transferred the 2D pattern into the 3D software
- verified the fit of the new style on the avatar in 3D
- made corrections needed
- transferred the pattern back into 2D
- made physical sample using the 2D patterns
- verified the fit on the physical body form that matches the size avatar
- compared the virtual 3D image of the garment on the avatar with a photo of the actual sample on the form.

Though not exactly the same, the image of an actual garment on a real form and the image of the virtual garment on the avatar were very similar.

Alvanon continued the authentication process by grading the core size using grade rules generated from the avatars representing each size. Then they validated the "fit intent" on each size and modified where necessary.

Alvanon continued to test the digital rendering of the same 2D patterns in both Optitex and Browzwear 3D. The results were similar. Although there were some challenges in rendering the drape of the textile accurately, their answer to the question, "Can we trust 3D renderings to accurately represent garments for fitting purposes on customer's avatars?" is YES! if the patterns are made from validated blocks! Creating authentic garments is a process that takes time and skill but will yield high rewards in customer trust and fewer returns.

Figure CS 10.1
Jason Wang, COO of Alvanon

AUTHENTIC DIGITAL GARMENT

=

Figure CS 10.2

Alvanon posed the question: Can we trust 3D renderings to accurately represent garments for fitting purposes on customers' avatars? They created garments using blocks that are designed to fit both 3D avatars and their corresponding real-world body forms. They compared the virtual 3D image of a garment on a 3D avatar with a photo of the actual fabric sample on the body form. The resulting images are very similar.

References

Onuso, C., Rickert, T. (2020), "The New Fundamentals of Digital Transformation," *Motif*, September 16. https://motif.org/3dtf-16-0930-christina-onusko-tracy-rickert/ (accessed September 17, 2020).

Wang, J. (2020), "Authentic Digital Garment," *Motif*, Monday, September 14. https://motif.org/3dtf-14-0915-jason-wang/ (accessed September 17, 2020).

SUSTAINABILITY

The advances in technology that are aimed at solving issues with fit also have the potential of contribution to sustainable practices. It is estimated that 25 percent of returned apparel ends up in landfills (Courtey, 2019) (where toxic chemicals leach into soil and water) or is incinerated (adding to air pollution). Improved fit may not only reduce returns, but perhaps, if customers find their apparel fits well, they may keep it in their closet longer!

The use of virtual fitting for multiple rounds of samples during the approval process not only saves time, it reduces the carbon emissions related to excessive use of materials for sampling and transporting samples by air (Warren, 2020).

Mass Customization reduces the production of excess inventory (which is often destroyed or discarded) because products are made on-demand. Because they are custom made, the likelihood of their being satisfactory is high and the consumer will keep them longer.

The promise of zero waste from 3D knitting and 3D printing will grow as these methods of production are commercialized and improved over time.

SUMMARY

Retailers are reeling from the exponential increase in returns. They understand that fit is a major reason that customers give for their dissatisfaction. Retailers are turning to product recommendation software to help match customers to products that will fit. Until brands can standardize their fit and improve their ability to communicate consistently about it or until mass customization or personal customization becomes more available, customers may continue to be frustrated.

Brands can use many methods to identify a standard body size that reflects their target market. They may seek support in identifying a sizing system that resembles customers' body shapes, rather than relying on outdated linear grading systems.

The process of sample approval is changing rapidly, relying more on an iterative process of approvals of virtual products shown on size-appropriate avatars. Whether in a 3D space or face to face, technical designers must recognize common fit issues and communicate them to other product development team members. Once the garment is approved, the measurement page of the Tech Pack must be updated accurately so that the production product will match the sample.

Even with application of data mining and algorithms and virtual testing of samples, some customers will not find the right fit among mass produced products. They may turn to the many small entrepreneurial companies that are using technology to make a customized product at an affordable price. Some may try custom made garments made on 3D knitting machines. Sometime in the future 3D printing may be the solution to all of our fitting needs.

An added benefit of solving fit issues is the contribution that is made to the environment by reducing returns, sampling, excess stock, and waste during manufacturing.

KEY TERMS

balance (pattern)

body form (mannequin, (dress form)

computer vision technology

design ease

drag lines

ease

fit

fit models

fit session

functional ease

geometry (mesh) processing

mass customization

size recommendation software

size system

standard (core) body size

tolerance

3D matching technology

DISCUSSION QUESTIONS

1. Think about your own experience when you buy clothing. What is the one area of a garment that you know will be a problem for you? Are the sleeves always too short? Does the waist on pants pull down at the back when you sit? Is the bust always too tight? How have you tried to solve this problem? Have you found a brand that fits you better than the rest? Do you alter your clothes? Do you buy one size up and then live with baggy areas in the rest of the garment? Do you cover up the area that does not fit well with another layer of clothes? If you have this problem, so do thousands of other people. Imagine that you are the designer of a line of clothes that will now address your specific fit issues. Describe the clothing you would provide.

2. Now imagine that the line you designed from Question 1 is ready to launch. You have made long sleeves or bigger bust lines. How will you market your line? What will you say to your customers? What about customers with short arms and small busts who liked your line before? What do you think they will do now? How will you deal with customers abandoning your brand when you change fit parameters?

3. The field of 3D printing is changing daily. Do some online research on firms such as Kinematics and report about the latest developments. Would you wear a jacket made by 3D printing?

ACTIVITIES

1. Classroom activity (you will need a tape measure):
   a. Find a garment in your classroom—a jacket, sweater, or coat.
   b. On a piece of paper, make a list of five measurements that are easy to take, such as:
      - Across bust 1 inch below armhole
      - Center back length
      - Across hem
      - Sleeve length
      - Neck circumference

    c. Go around the room and allow each student to take the same measurements and write them down.

    d. Discuss your results and your experience.

- Is it easy to take measurements accurately?
- Does everyone agree on how to take the measurements?
- How do you decide what is the right way?
- How much difference is there between the highest and lowest measurement from the same location?
- Would these challenges create a problem for a brand trying to create trust in customers?
- How would you ensure that the measurements in your company were taken the same by everyone and reported accurately?

2. Classroom activity (in groups of four or five students):

    a. Ask for volunteers to be the fit model, designer, technical designer, merchandiser, and brand manager.

    b. Have the fit model stand in the center of the group (if you have a mirror in the classroom, have that nearby).

    c. Simulate a fit session critiquing the clothing that the fit model is wearing. Pay particular attention to functional and design ease.

    d. Imagine that you are seeing the garments the fit model is wearing from your unique perspective (as designer, technical designer, merchandiser, or brand manager). What will you do to improve the fit?

    e. Have the technical designer write up the fit comments. Ask the other members of the group to review them to see if the technical designer understood the changes.

STUDIO RESOURCES

- Take the chapter quiz with scored results and personalized study tips.
- Review glossary flashcards to build your vocabulary.

REFERENCES

Alvanon. (2013), How We Make Our AlvaForms. https://www.youtube.com/watch?time_continue=2&v=D6z0BOqOdoQ&feature=emb_logo (accessed September 12, 2020).

Alvanon. (2020a), AlvaForm: Production and Development Process. https://alvanon.warkulwiz.com/M03_S04_T01.html (accessed September 12, 2020).

Alvanon. (2020b), Alvanon Takes 3D Design to Next Level with New Digital Body Platform. https://alvanon.com/introducing-the-alvanon-body-platform/ (accessed September 12, 2020).

Alvanon. (2016c) Data Gathering and Analytics. https://alvanon.com/solutions/data-gathering-analytics/ (accessed September 12, 2020).

ASTM International. (2015), *ASTM standards for body measurements*. Conshohocken, PA.

Binns, J. (2019), "Behind Tailored Industry's Ambitious Plan to Revive American Knitwear," *Sourcing Journal*, September 18. https://sourcingjournal.com/topics/sourcing/tailored-industry-american-knitwear-sourcing-alex-tschopp-169743/ (accessed Sept 20, 2020).

Bougourd, J. (2007), Sizing systems, fit models and target markets. In S. P. Ashdown (Ed.), *Sizing and clothing: Developing effective sizing systems for ready-to-wear clothing*. Cambridge, UK: Woodhead Publishing Ltd.

Charlton, G. (2020), "Ecommerce Returns: 2020 Stats and Trends," *SaleCycle*. January 15. https://www.salecycle.com/blog/featured/ecommerce-returns-2018-stats-trends/ (accessed August 31, 2020).

Courtey, R. (2019), "That sweater you don't like is a trillion-dollar problem for retailers. These companies want to fix it," *CBC.com*. January 12. https://www.cnbc.com/2019/01/10/growing-online-sales-means-more-returns-and-trash-for-landfills.html (accessed August 31, 2020).

Fabulous Fit® Dress Form Fitting System. (2020), https://www.fabulousfit.com/professional-dress-form-padding-system/full-fitting-set accessed September 20, 2020).

Hall, Christopher. (2020), "Gerber Partnership Gives Made-to-Measure Brands a Way to Customize Fit Online," *Sourcing Journal*, April 25. https://sourcingjournal.com/topics/technology/gerber-technology-3dlook-partnership-made-to-measure-fit-customization-205949/ (accessed June 8, 2020).

IHL Group. (2020), The Coming Retail Returns Tsunami, June 2. https://www.ihlservices.com/product/researchpaperretailreturnstsunami/ (accessed August 31, 2020).

ISO. (2018), ISO 8559-3:2018 Size designation of clothes—Part 3: Methodology for the creation of body measurement tables and intervals. https://www.iso.org/standard/67334.html (accessed Sept 23, 2020).

Jones, S. (2020), "How Taking Consumer Body Data Upstream Can Close Fashion's Fit Gaps," *Sourcing Journal*, April 6. https://sourcingjournal.com/topics/technology/fit-sizing-shoptalk-fit-analytics-perfitly-savitude-volumental-200076/ (accessed June 8, 2020).

Lee, Y. M., C. L. Istook, Y. J. Nam, and S. M. Park. (2007), Comparison of body shape between USA and Korean women. *International Journal of Clothing Science and Technology*, 19(5).

Lee, J., and C. Steen. (2019), *Technical Sourcebook for Apparel Designers*. New York: Fairchild Books.

Meepl. (2020), Technology. https://www.meepl.com/technology (accessed September 9, 2020).

Mok, K. (2015), Kinematics: Origami inspired 4D printed clothing that might actually be comfortable to wear. *The NewStack*, January 31. http://thenewstack.io/kinematics-origami-inspired-4d-printed-clothing-might-actually-comfortable-wear/ (accessed September 14, 2020).

Nishimura, K. (2019), "Virtual Fit Models Bring Real-life Proportions to 3D Fashion Software," *Sourcing Journal*. September 3. https://sourcingjournal.com/topics/technology/tukatech-fashion-technology-software-3d-design-samples-fit-garments-167381/ (accessed Sept 20, 2020).

Nordstrom.com. (2016), Supplier compliance manual section 3 measuring and folding guidelines. http://www.nordstromsupplier.com/Content/sc_manual/Reference_Documents/MEASURING_AND_FOLDING_GUIDELINES.pdf (accessed September 14, 2020).

Petrova, A. (2007), Creating sizing systems. In Ashdown, S.P. (Ed.), *Sizing and clothing: Developing effective sizing systems for ready-to-wear clothing*. Cambridge, UK: Woodhead Publishing Ltd.

Richardson, K. (2008), *Designing and patternmaking for stretch fabrics*. New York: Fairchild Books.

Roshitsh, K. (2018), A Perfect Fit, No Undressing or Universal Size Needed. *Women's Wear Daily*, December 28. https://wwd.com/business-news/technology/mysizeid-qa-founder-perfect-fit-1202939001/ (accessed June 8, 2020).

Roshitsh, K. (2019), *Women's Wear Daily*, July 15. https://wwd.com/business-news/technology/apparel-industry-actual-size-will-vary-1203219355/ (accessed September 12, 2020).

SJ Guest Editorial. (2019), "Why Just-in-Time Manufacturing is Having a Moment," *Sourcing Journal*, August 26. https://sourcingjournal.com/topics/technology/shima-seiki-on-demand-manufacturing-165112/ (accessed September 20, 2020).

Saini, B. (2018), *Women's Wear Daily*, April 4. https://wwd.com/business-news/government-trade/indian-sizing-project-force-global-brands-adapt-1202642028/ (accessed September 19, 2020).

Schofield, N. A. (2007), Pattern grading. In S. P. Ashdown (Ed.), *Sizing and clothing: Developing effective sizing systems for ready-to-wear clothing*. Cambridge, UK: Woodhead Publishing Ltd.

Secul, D. (2010), *Vendor compliance handbook*. New York: Fashiondex, Inc.

SizeUSA. (2008), SizeUSA user group meeting—[TC]². http://www.techexchange.com/library /SizeUSA%20User%20Group%20Meeting%20-%202008.pdf (accessed February 9, 2016).

Soltes, F. (2020), "Virtual fit's role in retail's recovery," *National Retail Federation*. https://nrf.com/blog/ virtual-fits-role-retails-recovery (accessed August 29, 2020).

Taylor, G. (2020a), "Pandemic Propels Fit Tech to the Fore," *Sourcing Journal*, May 17. https://sourcing-journal.com/topics/technology/fit-tech-ecommerce-returns-coronavirus-yotpo-bigthinx-asos-bon-prix-208999/ (accessed June 10, 2020).

Taylor, G. (2020b), "Scared to Return to the Fitting Room? Contactless Fit Has You Covered," *Sourcing Journal*, May 18. https://sourcingjournal.com/topics/technology/bold-metrics-contactless-fitting-room-stores-coronavirus-mastercard-payments-210996/ (accessed June 8, 2020).

Warren, L. (2020), "Jeanologia Develops Tool Streamlining Digital Design," *Sourcing Journal*, July 20. https://sourcingjournal.com/denim/denim-innovations/jeanologia-edesigner-denim-wash-software-digital-design-222172/ (accessed July 21, 2020).

Weathers, N. R. (2007), "Sizing up garment fit issues," *Just-style*, August 9. http://www.just-style.com /analysis/sizing-up-garment-fit-issues_id98055.aspx (accessed September 15, 2020).

Yotpo, (2020), Fashion eCommerce Report. "The majority of respondents (78.7%) named fit and quality issues a top reason for returning clothing." https://www.yotpo.com/?s=Fashion+eCommerce+Report %3A (accessed August 31, 2020).

ADDITIONAL RESOURCES

Moore, C. L., K. K. Mullet, and M. B. Prevatt Young. (2009), *Concepts of pattern grading: Techniques for manual and computer grading* (2nd ed.). New York: Fairchild Publications.

Simmons, K., C. L. Istook, and P. Devarajan. (2004), "Female figure identification technique (FFIT) for apparel; Part 1: Describing female shapes," *Journal of Textile and Apparel, Technology and Management*, 4(1) (Summer). www.tx.ncsu.edu/jtatm (accessed August 25, 2006).

Appendix A10.1a. Alvanon provides body forms, measurement charts and 3D avatars all based on the virtual shapes that are formulated by research including of extensive proprietary data collection from body scans, demographic studies and digital analysis. For this and all Standard Series in this Appendix, see https://alvanon.com/solutions/dress-forms/.

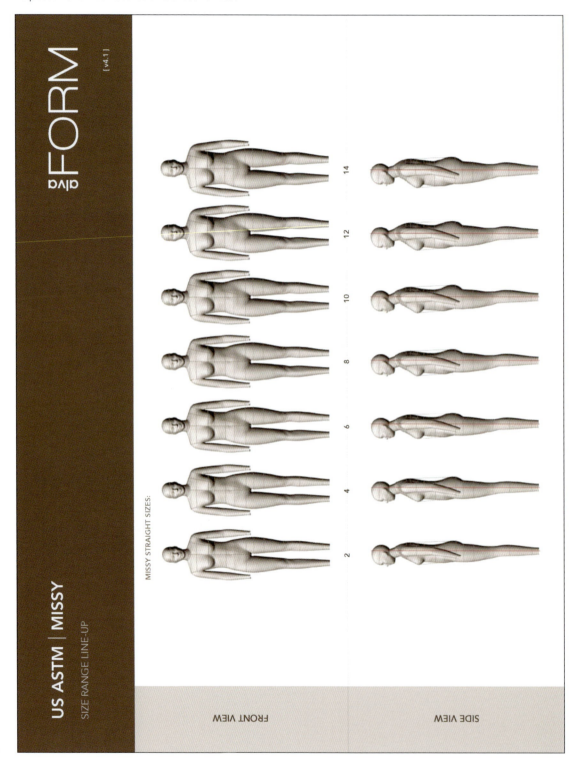

alvaFORM [v4.1]

US ASTM | MISSY
SIZE RANGE LINE-UP

MISSY STRAIGHT SIZES:

2   4   6   8   10   12   14

FRONT VIEW

SIDE VIEW

Appendix A10.1b. This Measurement Chart corresponds to the images of body shapes on the left. This Standard Series represents the US women's market, "straight" silhouette. All of the Standard Series in this Appendix are printed courtesy of Alvanon, Inc.

alva FORM [v4.1]

US ASTM | MISSY
MEASUREMENT CHART

Size Category	Missy Straight		Missy Straight		Missy Straight		Missy Straight		Missy Straight		Missy Straight		Missy Straight	
Size Range	2		4		6		8		10		12		14	
Neck Base	13 3/4	35	14	35.75	14 1/4	36.25	14 5/8	37	14 7/8	37.75	15 1/8	38.5	15 1/2	39.25
Across Shoulder	14 7/8	37.75	15 1/8	38.5	15 1/4	38.75	15 1/2	39.25	15 5/8	39.75	15 3/4	40	16	40.75
Chest	n/a	n/a	n/a	n/a	n/a	n/a	n/a	n/a	n/a	n/a	n/a	n/a	n/a	n/a
Bust	33	83.75	34 1/8	86.75	35 1/4	89.5	36 1/4	92	37 1/4	94.5	38 3/4	98.5	40 3/8	102.5
HPS to Apex	10	25.5	10 1/8	25.75	10 1/4	26.25	10 3/8	26.5	10 1/2	26.75	10 3/4	27.25	11	28
Waist	26 7/8	68.25	27 5/8	70.25	28 1/2	72.5	29 1/2	75	30 1/2	77.5	32 1/4	82	34	86.25
CF Neck to Waist	14 1/8	35.75	14 1/4	36	14 3/8	36.5	14 1/2	36.75	14 1/2	36.75	14 5/8	37	14 3/4	37.25
CB Neck to Waist	16 1/8	40.75	16 1/8	41	16 1/8	41	16 1/8	41	16 1/8	41	16 1/4	41.25	16 3/8	41.5
High Hip	31 3/8	79.75	32 7/8	83.5	34	86.25	35	89	36	91.5	37 1/2	95.25	39 1/8	99.5
Low Hip	35 1/8	89.25	36 3/8	92.5	37 1/2	95.25	38 1/2	97.75	39 1/2	100.25	41	104	42 1/2	108
Inseam	30 1/2	77.5	30 1/2	77.5	30 1/2	77.5	30 1/2	77.5	30 1/2	77.5	30 1/2	77.5	30 1/2	77.5
Total Rise	24 3/4	62.75	25	63.5	25 1/4	64	25 1/2	64.75	25 7/8	65.75	26 1/4	66.75	26 3/4	68
Thigh	20 7/8	53	21 1/4	54	21 3/4	55.25	22 1/4	56.5	22 3/4	57.75	23 5/8	60	24 1/2	62.25
CB Neck to Wrist	30 3/8	77	30 1/2	77.5	30 5/8	77.75	30 3/4	78	30 3/4	78	30 3/4	78.25	30 7/8	78.5
Bicep	10 1/4	26	10 1/2	26.75	10 3/4	27.25	11 1/8	28.25	11 1/2	29.25	11 3/4	29.75	12 1/8	30.75
Total Height	65 1/2	166.25	65 1/2	166.25	65 1/2	166.25	65 1/2	166.25	65 1/2	166.25	65 1/2	166.25	65 1/2	166.25
Head	21 1/2	54.5	21 1/2	54.5	21 3/4	55.25	21 3/4	55.25	22	56	22	56	22 1/4	56.5

■ INCHES ☐ CENTIMETERS

www.alvanon.com

Appendix A10.1c. The US ASTM Standard Series has two versions for women, "straight" and "curvy." This is the Standard Series for Curvy.

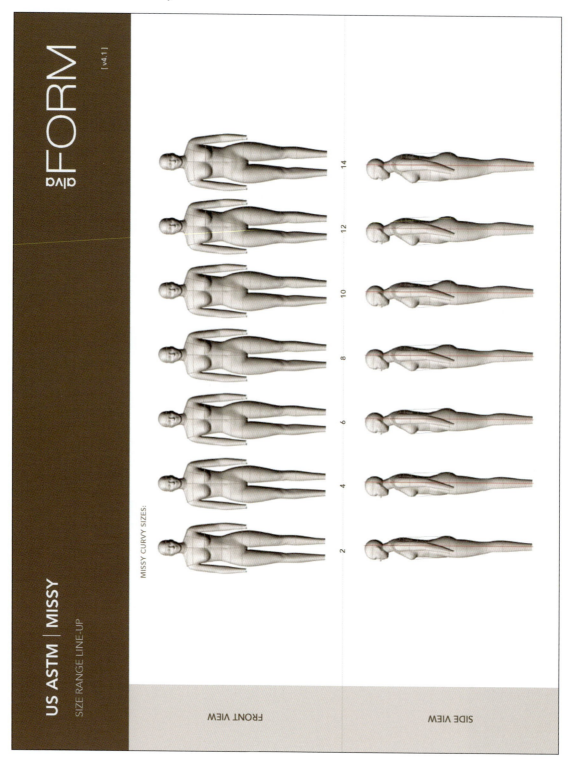

Appendix A10.1d. A10.1c–d represent a group of body shapes that are curvier than A10.1a–b. Compare the bust, waist and hips on both series to see the difference. Note that the overall height of each size is the same.

alva >FORM [v4.1]

US ASTM | MISSY
MEASUREMENT CHART

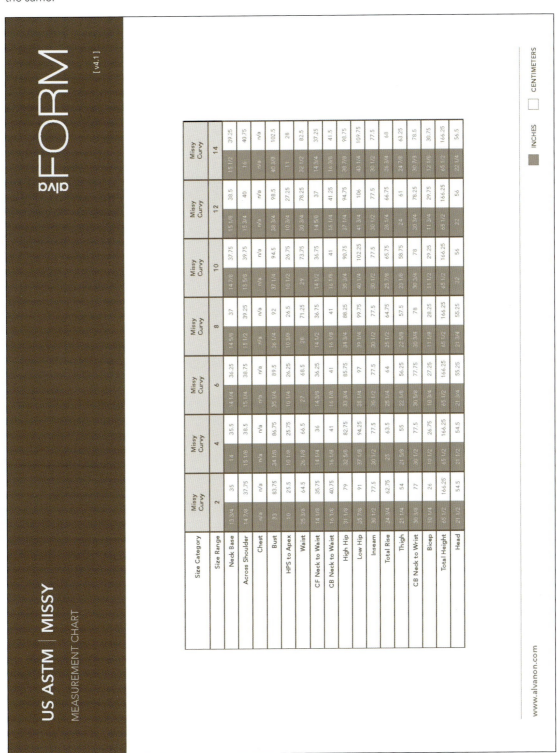

Size Category	Missy Curvy		Missy Curvy		Missy Curvy		Missy Curvy		Missy Curvy		Missy Curvy		Missy Curvy	
Size Range	2		4		6		8		10		12		14	
Neck Base	13 3/4	35	14	35.5	14 1/4	36.25	14 5/8	37	14 7/8	37.75	15 1/8	38.5	15 1/2	39.25
Across Shoulder	14 7/8	37.75	15 1/8	38.5	15 1/4	38.75	15 1/2	39.25	15 5/8	39.75	15 3/4	40	16	40.75
Chest	n/a	n/a	n/a	n/a	n/a	n/a	n/a	n/a	n/a	n/a	n/a	n/a	n/a	n/a
Bust	33	83.75	34 1/8	86.75	35 1/4	89.5	36 1/4	92	37 1/4	94.5	38 3/4	98.5	40 3/8	102.5
HPS to Apex	10	25.5	10 1/8	25.75	10 1/4	26.25	10 3/8	26.5	10 1/2	26.75	10 3/4	27.25	11	28
Waist	25 3/8	64.5	26 1/8	66.5	27	68.5	28	71.25	29	73.75	30 3/4	78.25	32 1/2	82.5
CF Neck to Waist	14 1/8	35.75	14 1/4	36	14 3/8	36.25	14 1/2	36.75	14 1/2	36.75	14 5/8	37	14 3/4	37.25
CB Neck to Waist	16 1/8	40.75	16 1/8	41	16 1/8	41	16 1/8	41	16 1/8	41	16 1/4	41.25	16 3/8	41.5
High Hip	31 1/8	79	32 5/8	82.75	33 3/4	85.75	34 3/4	88.25	35 3/4	90.75	37 1/4	94.75	38 7/8	98.75
Low Hip	35 7/8	91	37 1/8	94.25	38 1/4	97	39 1/4	99.75	40 1/4	102.25	41 3/4	106	43 1/4	109.75
Inseam	30 1/2	77.5	30 1/2	77.5	30 1/2	77.5	30 1/2	77.5	30 1/2	77.5	30 1/2	77.5	30 1/2	77.5
Total Rise	24 3/4	62.75	25	63.5	25 1/4	64	25 1/2	64.75	25 7/8	65.75	26 1/4	66.75	26 3/4	68
Thigh	21 1/4	54	21 5/8	55	22 1/8	56.25	22 5/8	57.5	23 1/8	58.75	24	61	24 7/8	63.25
CB Neck to Wrist	30 3/8	77	30 1/2	77.5	30 5/8	77.75	30 3/4	78	30 3/4	78	30 3/4	78.25	30 7/8	78.5
Bicep	10 1/4	26	10 1/2	26.75	10 3/4	27.25	11 1/8	28.25	11 1/2	29.25	11 3/4	29.75	12 1/8	30.75
Total Height	65 1/2	166.25	65 1/2	166.25	65 1/2	166.25	65 1/2	166.25	65 1/2	166.25	65 1/2	166.25	65 1/2	166.25
Head	21 1/2	54.5	21 1/2	54.5	21 3/4	55.25	21 3/4	55.25	22	56	22	56	22 1/4	56.5

■ INCHES   □ CENTIMETERS

www.alvanon.com

Appendix A10.1e. Alvanon has done extensive research in China using proprietary body scanning, data, demographic and population studies as well as data analysis. They developed fit standards for men, women and children.

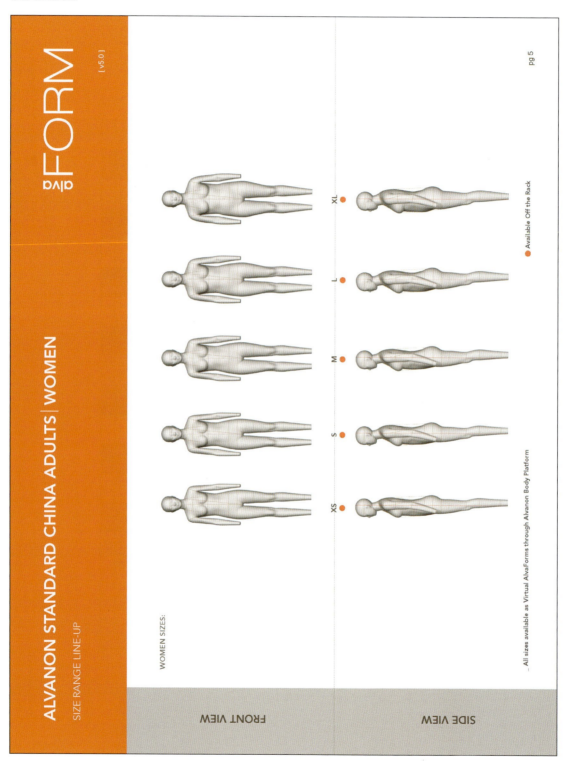

Appendix A10.1f. The overall body structure is different from Standard Series from other regions. Compare bust, waist and hip measurements to UK or EU.

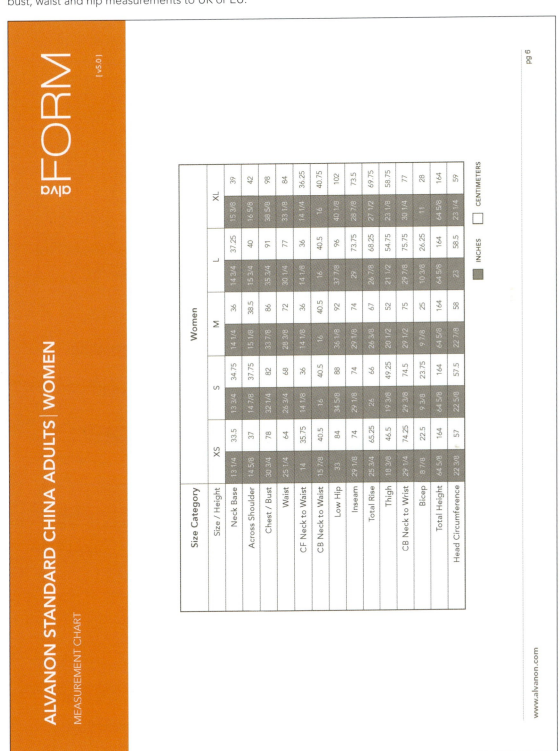

alvaFORM [v5.0]

ALVANON STANDARD CHINA ADULTS | WOMEN

MEASUREMENT CHART

Women

Size Category	XS (in)	XS (cm)	S (in)	S (cm)	M (in)	M (cm)	L (in)	L (cm)	XL (in)	XL (cm)
Neck Base	13 1/4	33.5	13 3/4	34.75	14 1/4	36	14 3/4	37.25	15 3/8	39
Across Shoulder	14 5/8	37	14 7/8	37.75	15 1/8	38.5	15 3/4	40	16 5/8	42
Chest / Bust	30 3/4	78	32 1/4	82	33 7/8	86	35 3/4	91	38 5/8	98
Waist	25 1/4	64	26 3/4	68	28 3/8	72	30 1/4	77	33 1/8	84
CF Neck to Waist	14	35.75	14 1/8	36	14 1/8	36	14 1/8	36	14 1/4	36.25
CB Neck to Waist	15 7/8	40.5	16	40.5	16	40.5	16	40.5	16	40.75
Low Hip	33	84	34 5/8	88	36 1/8	92	37 7/8	96	40 1/8	102
Inseam	29 1/8	74	29 1/8	74	29 1/8	74	29	73.5	28 7/8	73.5
Total Rise	25 3/4	65.25	26	66	26 3/8	67	26 7/8	68.25	27 1/2	69.75
Thigh	18 3/8	46.5	19 3/8	49.25	20 1/2	52	21 1/2	54.75	23 1/8	58.75
CB Neck to Wrist	29 1/4	74.25	29 3/8	74.5	29 1/2	75	29 7/8	75.75	30 1/4	77
Bicep	8 7/8	22.5	9 3/8	23.75	9 7/8	25	10 3/8	26.25	11	28
Total Height	64 5/8	164	64 5/8	164	64 5/8	164	64 5/8	164	64 5/8	164
Head Circumference	22 3/8	57	22 5/8	57.5	22 7/8	58	23	58.5	23 1/4	59

INCHES   CENTIMETERS

pg 6

www.alvanon.com

Appendix A10.1g. Using body scanning, data gathered from many sources and data analysis, Alvanon has developed size and fit Standard Series for adult men and women in Japan.

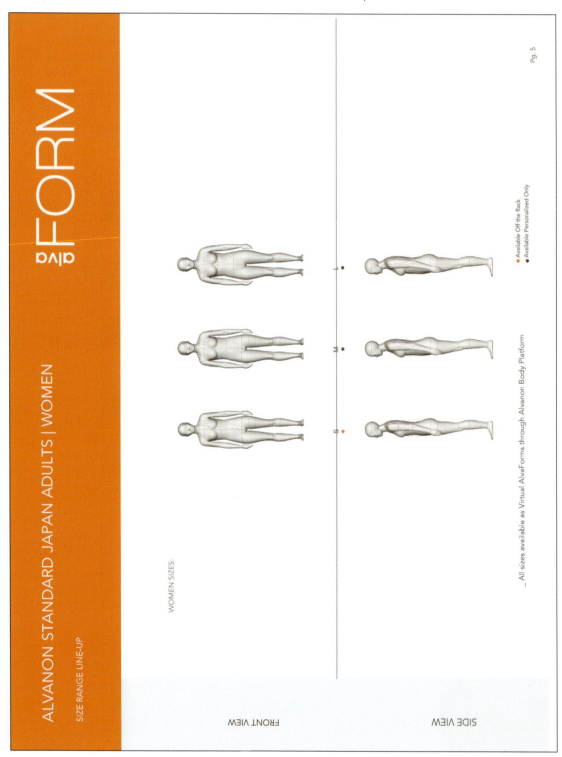

aLva FORM

ALVANON STANDARD JAPAN ADULTS | WOMEN

SIZE RANGE LINE-UP

WOMEN SIZES:

S M L

FRONT VIEW

SIDE VIEW

● Available Off the Rack
● Available Personalized Only

_ All sizes available as Virtual AlvaForms through Alvanon Body Platform

Pg. 5

Appendix A10.1h. As with all Alvanon Standard Series, the Size Range Line-up, the Measurement chart, AlvaForms (the physical body forms) and Virtual AlvaForms (3D Avatars) align so that product developers can all work from the same information whether they are writing measurement specifications, draping on a body form or in 3D.

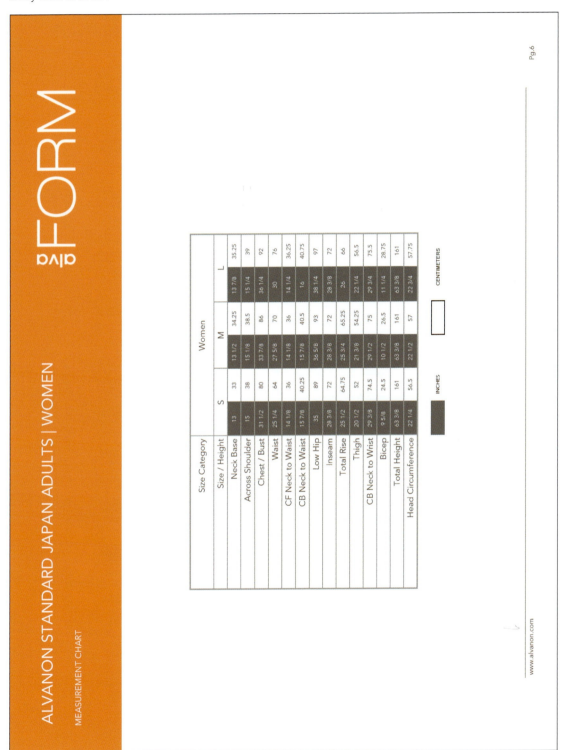

alva**FORM**

ALVANON STANDARD JAPAN ADULTS | WOMEN

MEASUREMENT CHART

Pg.6

Size Category	Women S		Women M		Women L	
	INCHES	CENTIMETERS	INCHES	CENTIMETERS	INCHES	CENTIMETERS
Size / Height						
Neck Base	13	33	13 1/2	34.25	13 7/8	35.25
Across Shoulder	15	38	15 1/8	38.5	15 1/4	39
Chest / Bust	31 1/2	80	33 7/8	86	36 1/4	92
Waist	25 1/4	64	27 5/8	70	30	76
CF Neck to Waist	14 1/8	36	14 1/8	36	14 1/4	36.25
CB Neck to Waist	15 7/8	40.25	15 7/8	40.5	16	40.75
Low Hip	35	89	36 5/8	93	38 1/4	97
Inseam	28 3/8	72	28 3/8	72	28 3/8	72
Total Rise	25 1/2	64.75	25 3/4	65.25	26	66
Thigh	20 1/2	52	21 3/8	54.25	22 1/4	56.5
CB Neck to Wrist	29 3/8	74.5	29 1/2	75	29 3/4	75.5
Bicep	9 5/8	24.5	10 1/2	26.5	11 1/4	28.75
Total Height	63 3/8	161	63 3/8	161	63 3/8	161
Head Circumference	22 1/4	56.5	22 1/2	57	22 3/4	57.75

www.alvanon.com

Appendix A10.1i. Alvanon updated its Standard Series for adult women in Europe 2020.

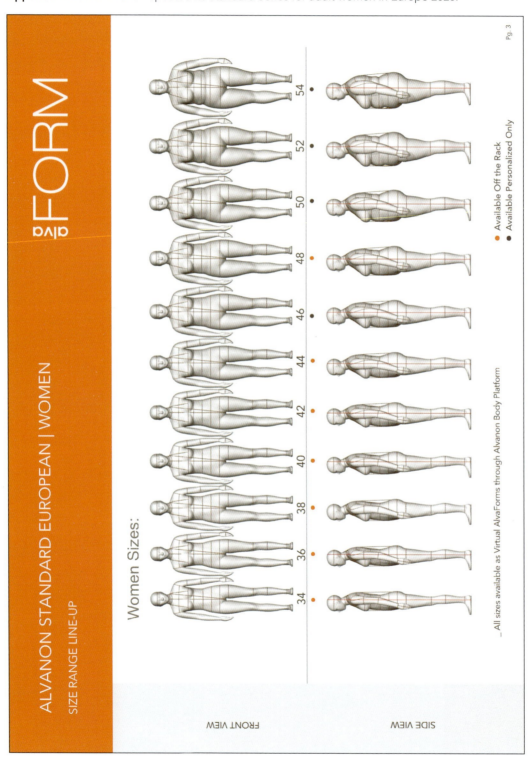

Appendix A10.1j. As with all of the Charts provided by Alvanon, measurements are listed in metric and imperial system. They are given for the body, not the garment. The measurement of each specific part of the body increases or decreases from one size to the next. These differences from size to size can be used to developing grade rules for garments.

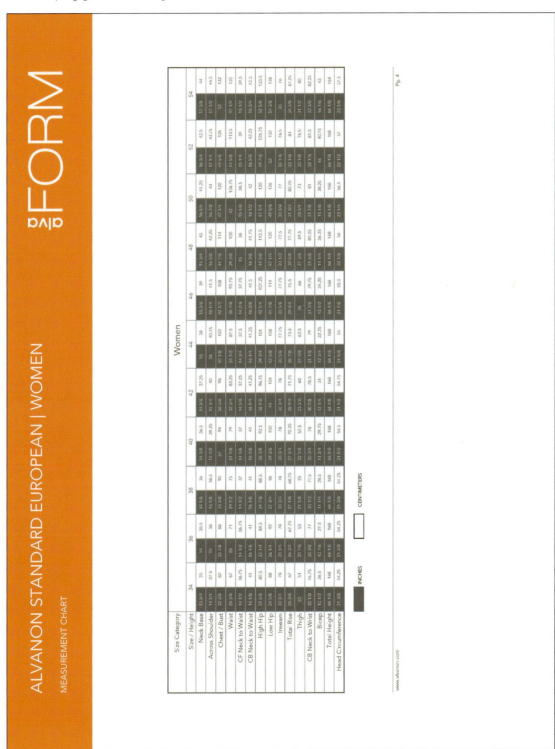

Appendix A10.1k. Alvanon developed two Standards Series for women in Europe in 2020, "Women" and "Atelier Women".

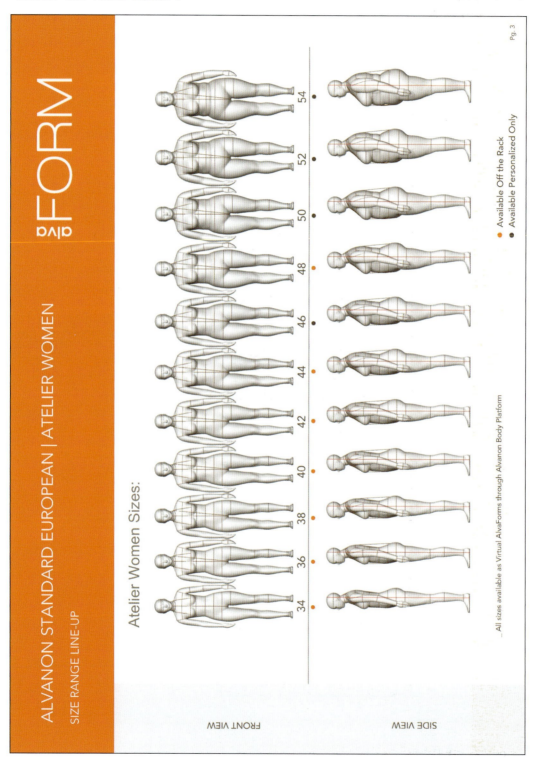

Appendix A10.1l. Compare the bust, waist and hips on the "Women" and "Atelier Women" Standard Series for European women. The Atelier Series is curvier than the Women's. Note that the overall height of each size is the same.

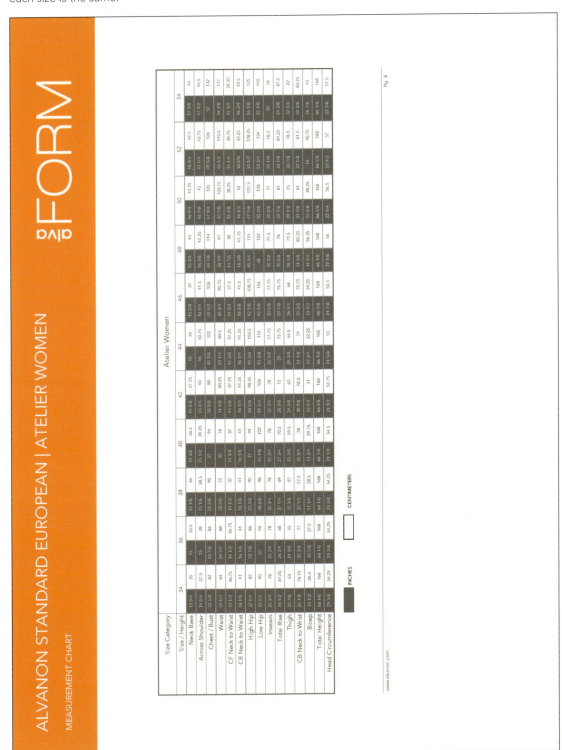

Appendix A10.1m. Alvanon has developed a Standard Series for women in the UK. As with the other Standard Series, they use proprietary body scanning, data from body, demographic and population studies as well as data analysis.

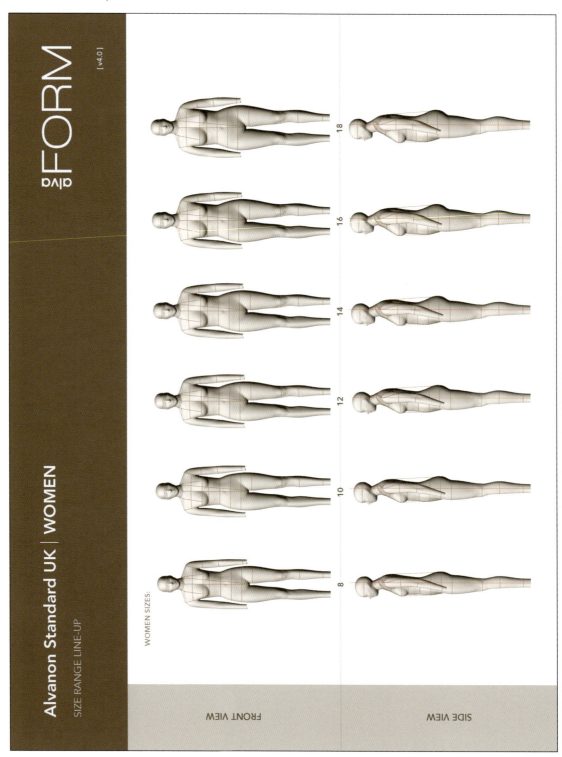

Appendix A10.1n. Using charts from various Standard Series, it is possible to see whether a product developed for one population might be a good fit for a market in another geographical area. How close is the UK woman to her counterpart in Europe?

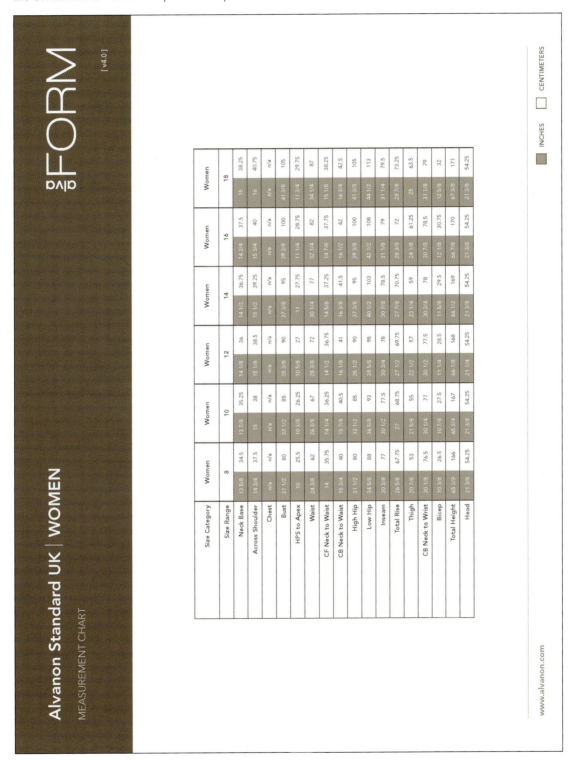

alva FORM [v4.0]

Alvanon Standard UK | WOMEN

MEASUREMENT CHART

Size Category	Women 8		Women 10		Women 12		Women 14		Women 16		Women 18	
Size Range												
Neck Base	13 5/8	34.5	13 7/8	35.25	14 1/8	36	14 1/2	36.75	14 3/4	37.5	15	38.25
Across Shoulder	14 3/4	37.5	15	38	15 1/8	38.5	15 1/2	39.25	15 3/4	40	16	40.75
Chest	n/a	n/a	n/a	n/a	n/a	n/a	n/a	n/a	n/a	n/a	n/a	n/a
Bust	31 1/2	80	33 1/2	85	35 3/8	90	37 3/8	95	39 3/8	100	41 3/8	105
HPS to Apex	10	25.5	10 3/8	26.25	10 5/8	27	11	27.75	11 1/4	28.75	11 3/4	29.75
Waist	24 3/8	62	26 3/8	67	28 3/8	72	30 1/4	77	32 1/4	82	34 1/4	87
CF Neck to Waist	14	35.75	14 1/4	36.25	14 1/2	36.75	14 5/8	37.25	14 7/8	37.75	15 1/8	38.25
CB Neck to Waist	15 3/4	40	15 7/8	40.5	16 1/8	41	16 3/8	41.5	16 1/2	42	16 3/4	42.5
High Hip	31 1/2	80	33 1/2	85	35 1/2	90	37 3/8	95	39 3/8	100	41 3/8	105
Low Hip	34 5/8	88	36 5/8	93	38 5/8	98	40 1/2	103	42 1/2	108	44 1/2	113
Inseam	30 3/8	77	30 1/2	77.5	30 3/4	78	30 7/8	78.5	31 1/8	79	31 1/4	79.5
Total Rise	26 5/8	67.75	27	68.75	27 1/2	69.75	27 7/8	70.75	28 3/8	72	28 7/8	73.25
Thigh	20 7/8	53	21 5/8	55	22 1/2	57	23 1/4	59	24 1/8	61.25	25	63.5
CB Neck to Wrist	30 1/8	76.5	30 1/4	77	30 1/2	77.5	30 3/4	78	30 7/8	78.5	31 1/8	79
Bicep	10 3/8	26.5	10 7/8	27.5	11 1/4	28.5	11 5/8	29.5	12 1/8	30.75	12 5/8	32
Total Height	65 3/8	166	65 3/4	167	66 1/8	168	66 1/2	169	66 7/8	170	67 3/8	171
Head	21 3/8	54.25	21 3/8	54.25	21 1/4	54.25	21 3/8	54.25	21 3/8	54.25	21 3/8	54.25

■ INCHES □ CENTIMETERS

www.alvanon.com

Appendix A10.1o. Although Alvanon has developed Standard Series for Europe, it has also developed Series for specific populations within Europe. This one is for Germany.

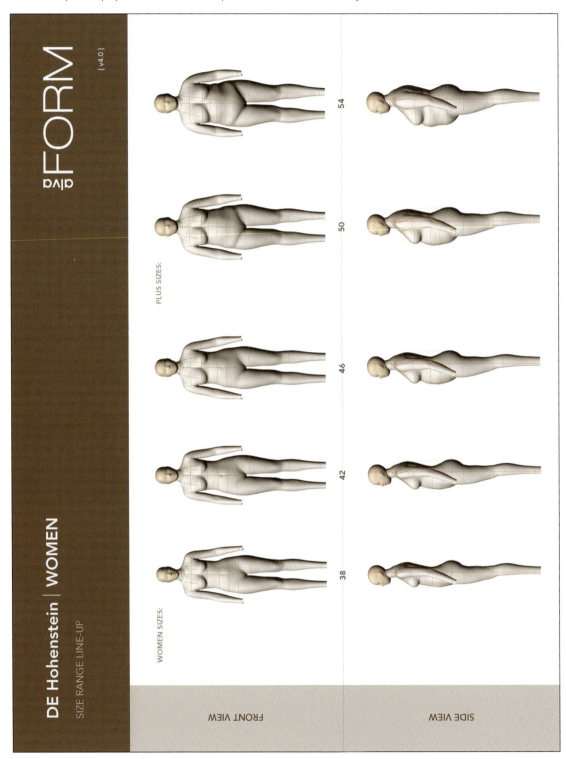

Appendix A10.1p. Compare bust, wait and hip to see how the proportions in the Series for Germany differs from Europe in general.

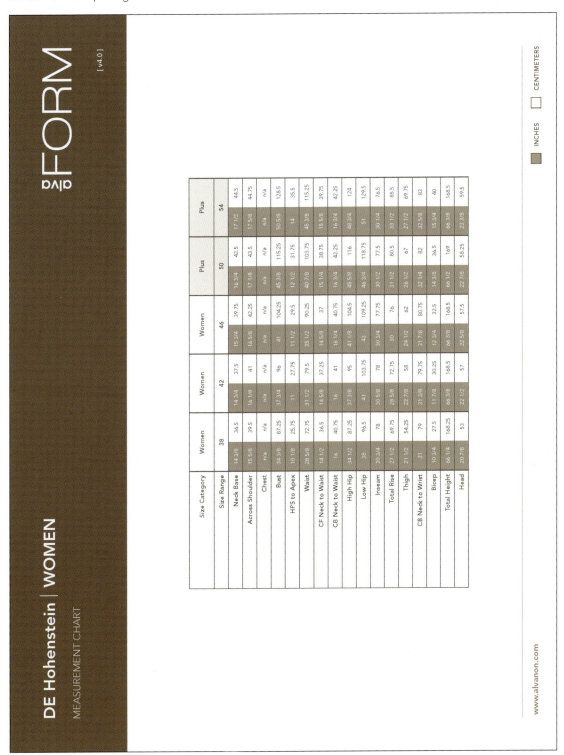

alva**FORM** [v4.0]

DE Hohenstein | WOMEN
MEASUREMENT CHART

Size Category	Women 38		Women 42		Women 46		Plus 50		Plus 54	
Size Range	38		42		46		50		54	
Neck Base	14 3/8	36.5	14 3/4	37.5	15 3/4	39.75	16 3/4	42.5	17 1/2	44.5
Across Shoulder	15 5/8	39.5	16 1/8	41	16 5/8	42.25	17 1/8	43.5	17 5/8	44.75
Chest	n/a	n/a	n/a	n/a	n/a	n/a	n/a	n/a	n/a	n/a
Bust	34 3/8	87.25	37 3/4	96	41	104.25	45 3/8	115.25	50 5/8	128.5
HPS to Apex	10 1/8	25.75	11	27.75	11 1/2	29.5	12 1/2	31.75	14	35.5
Waist	28 5/8	72.75	31 1/2	79.5	35 1/2	90.25	40 7/8	103.75	45 3/8	115.25
CF Neck to Waist	14 1/2	36.5	14 5/8	37.25	14 5/8	37	15 1/4	38.75	15 5/8	39.75
CB Neck to Waist	16	40.75	16	41	16 1/4	40.75	16 3/4	42.25	16 3/4	42.25
High Hip	34 1/2	87.25	37 3/8	95	41 1/8	104.5	45 5/8	116	48 3/4	124
Low Hip	38	96.5	41	103.75	43	109.25	46 3/4	118.75	51	129.5
Inseam	30 3/4	78	30 5/8	78	30 3/4	77.75	30 1/2	77.5	30 1/4	76.5
Total Rise	27 1/2	69.75	28 5/8	72.75	30	76	31 1/2	80.5	33 1/2	85.5
Thigh	21 1/8	54.25	22 7/8	58	24 1/2	62	26 1/2	67	27 1/2	69.75
CB Neck to Wrist	31	79	31 3/8	79.75	31 7/8	80.75	32 1/4	82	32 5/8	83
Bicep	10 3/4	27.5	11 7/8	30.25	12 3/4	32.5	14 3/8	36.5	15 3/4	40
Total Height	66 1/4	168.25	66 3/8	168.5	66 3/8	168.5	66 1/2	169	66 3/8	168.5
Head	20 7/8	53	22 1/2	57	22 5/8	57.5	22 7/8	58.25	23 3/8	59.5

■ INCHES ☐ CENTIMETERS

www.alvanon.com

Appendix A10.1q. Alvanon created a Standard Series for women in Mexico using proprietary body scanning, data from body, demographic and population studies as well as data analysis. For this and all Standard Series in this Appendix, see https://alvanon.com/resources/alvaform-measurements-specs/.

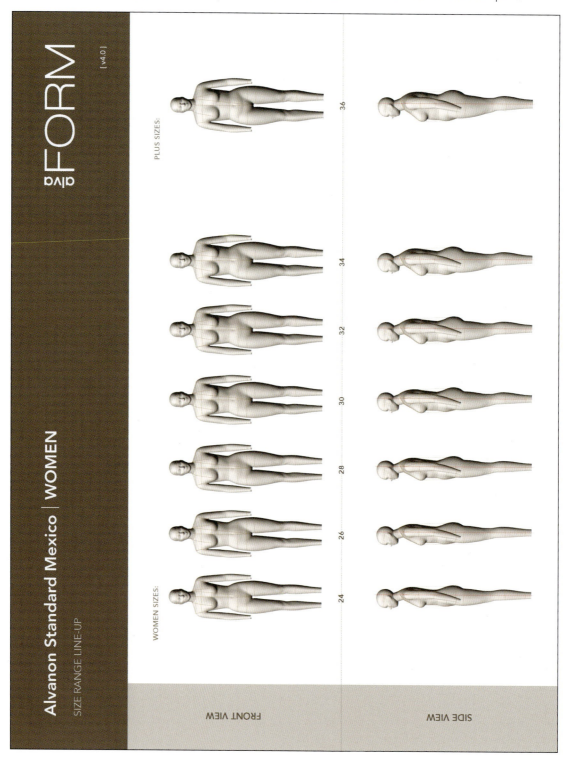

alva**FORM** [v4.0]

Alvanon Standard Mexico | WOMEN

SIZE RANGE LINE-UP

PLUS SIZES:

WOMEN SIZES:

24 26 28 30 32 34 36

FRONT VIEW

SIDE VIEW

Appendix A10.1r. This Measurement Chart corresponds to the images of body shapes on the left. Measurements are in Metric and Imperial System. Some of the Standard Series are posted in more than one language. This one is in English and Spanish. All of the Standard Series in this Appendix are printed courtesy of Alvanon, Inc.

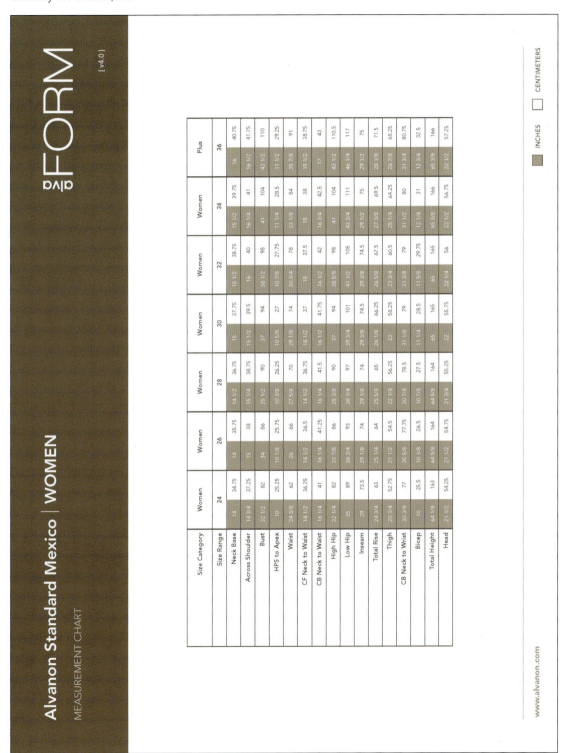

alva FORM [v4.0]

Alvanon Standard Mexico | WOMEN
MEASUREMENT CHART

■ INCHES □ CENTIMETERS

Size Category	Women		Women		Women		Women		Women		Women		Plus	
Size Range	24		26		28		30		32		34		36	
Neck Base	14	34.75	14	35.75	14 1/2	36.75	15	37.75	15 1/2	38.75	15 1/2	39.75	16	40.75
Across Shoulder	14 3/4	37.25	15	38	15 1/4	38.75	15 1/2	39.5	16	40	16 1/4	41	16 1/2	41.75
Bust	32 1/2	82	34	86	35 1/2	90	37	94	38 1/2	98	41	104	43 1/2	110
HPS to Apex	10	25.25	10 1/8	25.75	10 3/8	26.25	10 5/8	27	10 7/8	27.75	11 1/4	28.5	11 1/2	29.25
Waist	24 3/8	62	26	66	27 5/8	70	29 1/8	74	30 3/4	78	33 1/8	84	35 7/8	91
CF Neck to Waist	14 1/2	36.25	14 1/2	36.5	14 1/2	36.75	14 1/2	37	15	37.5	15	38	15 1/2	38.75
CB Neck to Waist	16 1/4	41	16 1/4	41.25	16 1/4	41.5	16 1/2	41.75	16 1/2	42	16 3/4	42.5	17	43
High Hip	32 1/4	82	33 7/8	86	35 3/8	90	37	94	38 5/8	98	41	104	43 1/2	110.5
Low Hip	35	89	36 3/4	93	38 1/4	97	39 3/4	101	41 1/2	105	43 3/4	111	46 1/4	117
Inseam	29	73.5	29 1/8	74	29 1/8	74	29 3/8	74.5	29 3/8	74.5	29 1/2	75	29 1/2	75
Total Rise	24 3/4	63	25 1/4	64	25 5/8	65	26 1/8	66.25	26 5/8	67.5	27 3/8	69.5	28 3/8	71.5
Thigh	20 3/4	52.75	21 1/2	54.5	22 1/8	56.25	23	58.25	23 3/4	60.5	25 1/4	64.25	26 7/8	68.25
CB Neck to Wrist	30 3/8	77	30 5/8	77.75	30 7/8	78.5	31 1/8	79	31 3/8	79	31 1/2	80	31 3/4	80.75
Bicep	10	25.5	10 3/8	26.5	10 7/8	27.5	11 1/4	28.5	11 5/8	29.75	12 1/4	31	12 3/4	32.5
Total Height	64 1/8	163	64 5/8	164	64 5/8	164	65	165	65	165	65 3/8	166	65 3/8	166
Head	21 1/2	54.25	21 1/2	54.75	21 3/4	55.25	22	55.75	22 1/4	56	22 1/2	56.75	22 1/2	57.25

www.alvanon.com

CHAPTER 11

A PRODUCT DEVELOPMENT PERSPECTIVE ON QUALITY

"Employees . . . who work in quality . . . must be the voice of the consumer. They need to know and use information from all facets of the industry because developing a quality product through design, production, and delivery is both a science and an art." DORIS H. KINCADE

OBJECTIVES

- Understand the role of the tech pack in ensuring that a product meets customers' expectations
- Recognize the role of the tech pack as a hub of information that guides contractors and subcontractors with the appropriate level of information
- Recognize the role of the cutting instructions in ensuring that the design concept is fulfilled
- Identify sewing techniques as an expression of brand identity and expected quality
- Distinguish between various requirements for listing characteristics of materials for a bill of materials (BOM)
- Recognize various methods and materials that are used to convey information to consumers, other businesses, government agencies, etc.
- Identify methods for discovering defects at all stages of production before products are shipped
- Understand that production methods that focus on continuous improvement in quality and efficiency share goals with the sustainability movement.

QUALITY STANDARDS

Quality assurance is simply good business. It is the result of everyone doing their job properly, without error. The term **quality assurance** implies defect *prevention* rather than defect *detection*. Each person must perform their part with an awareness of and commitment to meeting customer expectations. Preventing errors translates into saving time, effort, money, and reputation. Phillip Crosby, in his book *Quality is Free* said "Do things right in the first place, and you won't have to pay to fix them or do them over" (Crosby, 1979). Because product developers are involved in the beginning of the process, they can have great impact on keeping the **Cost of Poor Quality (COPQ)** down (Figure 11.1).

Quality assurance requires conforming to standards and specifications that meet or exceed customer expectations, therefore quality is what the customer says it is. Often, consumers associate a certain level of quality with a popular or coveted brand. However, when a customer finds a product of comparable quality (according to their concept) but at a different price, they will generally go for the lower price. For that reason, when faced with choices regarding materials, assembly processes, packaging, etc., product developers must consider cost of goods and labor along with quality standards.

The quality standards of a company may be expressed in general terms. Phrases such as "guaranteed for a lifetime of service," "keeps you warm even in the coldest weather," or "trims inches off your waistline" constitute promises to the customer. These promises are delivered to the customer through characteristics such as durability, thermal retention, or compression. A designer chooses materials and manufacturing processes with properties that contribute to marketing promises made. For example, the warmth of a down coat might come from the ability of down to trap warmth from the body, tight-fitting knitted cuffs, a quick-drying fabric in the shell, and sealed seams. Each step in the manufacturing process can add, remove, increase, or decrease properties. Technical designers must be fluent in standards for the materials and manufacturing methods that deliver these properties. They must review materials and methods against cost, availability of machinery, and skill levels of factories. Their ability to deliver the desired properties within limitations makes them valuable to their companies.

TECHNICAL SPECIFICATION PACKAGES

The design spec, as discussed in Chapters 9 and 10, reflects all the decisions made by designers and merchandisers as they transform concepts such as brand identity, target market preferences, and trends into products with physical features. Consider the sample-making process as a test of their aesthetic and cost decisions, as well as the decisions made by the vendor regarding patterning and construction. When the first design sample is reviewed in a fit session, the appearance of the garment proves that the textile and components are appropriate, that the measurements are accurate, that it is producible, and that the cost of the garment corresponds to its value to the customer. This first dimension of product quality (what the product *is*) is measured by aesthetic standards in relation to economic and production realities.

Figure 11.1

Cost of Poor Quality. Product development specialists can make a great contribution to reducing waste and unnecessary cost during the design and planning of apparel products. Effort spent in the early stages of the lifecycle of a product is far less costly than effort spent in scrambling to find acceptable solutions to problems when thousands of units are already cut and in process on the factory floor.

The later in the design and production process that problems are found, the more costly it is to deal with them.

Each member of the supply chain is involved with the Cost of Good Quality (COGQ)		
Prevention Cost	initial target market research	Sales/Marketing/Merchandising
	continually monitor market needs as products enter market	Marketing/ Merchandising
	design to market needs	Merchandising/Design/Technical Design
	evaluate suppliers	Technical Design/Sourcing
	design within capabilities of materials and factories	Design/Technical Design
	standardize machinery & process	Technical Design/ Sourcing
	test components and processes	Technical Design/ Sourcing
	review samples from vendors	Technical Design/ Sourcing
Detection Cost	establish verification methods and standards	Technical Design/ Sourcing
	target critical characteristics	Technical Design/ Sourcing
	educate & train	Sourcing/Factory
	inspect in-line	Factory
	conduct QA audits	Factory
Each member of the supply chain is involved with the Cost of Poor Quality (COPQ)		
Internal Failure Cost	sort good/poor quality	Factory
	troubleshoot and repair	Factory/Sourcing/Technical Design
	manage personnel for additional hours to make replacements/repairs	Factory
	improve design	Design/Technical Design
	order additional materials for replacements/repairs	Sourcing
	re-inspect and retest replacements/repairs	Factory/Sourcing
	re-train	Factory/Sourcing
	arrange disposal of rejects	Factory/Sourcing
	manage logistics for late deliveries due to replacements/repairs	Factory/Sourcing
External Failure Cost	negotiate penalties for late/unfulfilled delivery	Sales
	handle complaints, returns and allowances	Customer Service/ Sales/Marketing/ Merchandising
	rebuild relationship with customers	Customer Service/ Sales/Marketing/ Merchandising
	rebuild customer confidence in brand	Entire supply chain

After the sampling process is completed and the product is deemed worthy of adoption, the information that was provided in the original design spec is updated to create the technical specification package (aka the tech pack). The tech pack will reflect expectations regarding the second dimension of quality: functional performance (what the product _does_).

Companies usually create formats for tech packs that are consistent across categories of products. They develop procedures and processes about what information will be in a tech pack and how it will be communicated. The style of the tech pack is dictated by the nature of the supply chain and the needs of the vendors. Some companies use a prose style, some use lists. Some use lots of drawings, some do not. Some companies document every change to the tech pack in a running log. For the sake of clarity, companies determine who will be able to change the tech pack and who will give final approval. One of the great improvements offered by Product Lifecycle Management (PLM) systems is the ability to revise and update tech packs simultaneously in real time from anywhere in the world with documentation of all changes (Figure 11.2). Companies with very consistent products such as tee shirts may give common specifications in a manual or general document and only give information on printing or dyeing for individual styles. Some companies, especially in the outdoor industry, may provide very detailed tech packs because of the highly technical nature of their products.

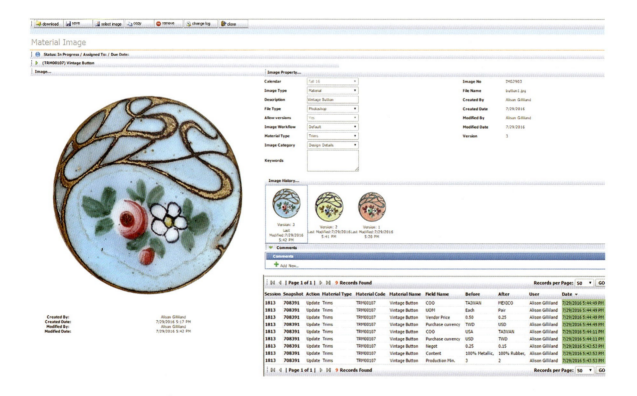

Figure 11.2
One of the most difficult jobs for a technical designer is tracking changes made to tech packs. Product Lifecycle Management (PLM) systems provide a great advantage because they allow everyone involved in the product to make changes in real time. Changes are logged automatically, so everyone can see who made a change and when. This page from Gerber's Yunque system shows the rejected button styles as well as the current choice so that everyone knows what NOT to use.

Page Header

It is advisable for tech packs to have some kind of header on every page that lists the company name and label, the style number, some reference to the timeframe of production such as season or delivery date, and a brief description and/or sketch of the product and the type of textile. This allows translators and engineers to pull out sections for translation, analysis, and planning without losing the context of the whole product.

Technical Flats

The sketch that was included in the design spec will be updated with any changes made during the review of the first sample. Additional callouts may be added for production.

Measurement Chart

The measurement chart in the tech pack will be based on the original measurements from the design spec. More measurements may be added for the exact location of details such as pockets, epaulettes, and cuffs. Some measurements may be restated for ease of taking measurements during quality assurance audits. The graded measurements will be added for each size.

Because finished garment measurements determine the size and shape of pattern pieces for grading, they will impact the layout of the marker and the fabric consumption. Some compromises may be needed. For example, the girth measurement at the hem of a skirt with a wide sweep may be "held" (not graded) so the pieces will fit across the width of the fabric in all sizes and only the waist will grade.

Many companies send materials for testing (Table 11.1) to independent labs such as Intertek (Intertek, 2020). These labs are highly regulated to ensure that they use consistent methods and equipment throughout the world based on testing methods and standards from ASTM, AATCC, and the ISO. The tests that influence decisions about garment measurements might include dimensional stability after dry cleaning or washing (Bubonia, 2015). The report from the lab will state how much a material or garment has shrunk or stretched out during stress and normal care. Once this information is reported, it is up to the technical designer to ask the patternmaker to adjust the patterns to achieve the target measurements or advise the sourcing team to seek another supplier. Some companies will test one or two yards of sample fabric or garments and then test again when production fabric is available.

Cutting Instructions

Because so much of production is conducted offshore, the exact means of cutting a product will vary from factory to factory, so the tech pack does not need to list exhaustive instructions. However, the tech pack should include **cutting instructions** to alert the contractors who make markers or spread and cut fabric about unique requirements of the fabric or style (See Figure 11.3a–d). Other variables include whether to allow the use of drill holes to mark the location of pockets or which pattern pieces are cut from which contrasting color fabric in a **color blocked garment** (Figure 11.3e).

Table 11.1 Quality Assurance Standards:
Basic Testing Requirements for Fabrics, Findings, and Trims*

Test Type	Test Method Recommended	Comments on Requirements
Verification of textile specifications		
Fiber content	AATCC 20 and 20A	Required for permanent label on apparel by U.S. government.
Thread count	ASTM D3775; ASTM D3887	Yarn count; reported separately for warp and filling. Critical in verifying fabric quality.
Fabric weight	ASTM D3776; ASTM D3887	Designated in terms such as "ounces per square yard" or "grams per square meter." Critical in verifying fabric shipped is same as fabric ordered.
Performance during normal wear		
Colorfastness to water	AATCC 107	Sometimes called static wetting; color staining or migration when left wet for periods of time.
Crocking	AATCC 8	Color rubs off onto other surfaces due to poor dye penetration.
Colorfastness to light	AATCC 16	Colors fade or change when exposed to light for periods of time. Time varies, depending on product end use.
Colorfastness to perspiration	AATCC 15	Perspiration causes staining or color change. Useful to test linings.
Pilling	ASTM D3512	Small balls of fiber appear on surface, caused by rubbing or abrasion. Long-staple fiber and higher-twist yarns pill less.
Water repellency, water resistance	AATCC 22; AATCC 35; AATCC 127	These tests verify how much water penetrates a textile in various settings from shower to immersion. None of them will verify a completely waterproof product.
Performance during normal care		
Dimensional stability (shrinkage)	AATCC 135	Excessive shrinkage results in consumer dissatisfaction.
Colorfastness to laundering	AATCC 61	Color fading and staining during laundering is unacceptable.
Durable press or wrinkle-free	AATCC 145	A rather subjective test, but of use to determine whether the finish meets expectations after washing.
Skewing	AATCC 179	Used mostly on knits. Identifies issues of garments twisting when washed, when it is too late to correct.
Colorfastness to laundering	AATCC 61	Color fading and staining during laundering is unacceptable.
Colorfastness to nonchlorine bleach	AATCC 172	Used to determine whether nonchlorine bleach will affect colors during washing. Labeling must be adjusted if color affected.
Colorfastness to chlorine bleach	AATCC 188	If fabric is affected by chlorine bleach only, warning on label to read: "Only nonchlorine bleach if needed." If sensitive to both bleach types, label to read: "Do not bleach."

*Listed tests are for fabrics used in apparel; findings and trims are tested for many of the same criteria to determine compatibility with shell fabrics.

Some companies provide a list of pattern pieces to be sure that all internal components such as interlinings and chest pieces are included. Listing every pattern piece can limit the flexibility of the factory. For example, a fly facing can be cut as one piece with a fold or as two pieces with a seam. The decision is related to the machinery used to set the zipper. Unless the technical designer has a reason to select one or the other, the factory should be left to make this call.

A **cut order plan** will be generated by the production department. It will confirm the exact style, sizes, and quantities that are to be cut to complete the contracted order. The marker may be made in-house by the brand, by a sub-contractor, or by the factory. Whoever is responsible will be expected to arrange the piece in a marker that produces the least **fallout**—scraps of fabric that are left after the patterns are all cut out of the fabric and are generally thrown away. A technical designer can clarify how the marker will be made when issues arise from fabric that can only be cut in one direction or oversized pieces (Figure 11.3f).

Since we know that fabric is often the costliest component of garment production, a marker maker strives for 100 percent utilization (*efficiency, consumption, yield*). Fallout is not only costly, but also accounts for about 15 percent of textile waste. Designers such as Zandra Rhodes, Issey Miyake, and Yeohlee Teng pioneered the concept of designing with **zero waste** to explore ways to reduce or eliminate fallout in the cutting process. Designers such as Tess Whitfort, Julian Roberts, and Holly McQuillan carry on this research. Timo Rissanen, co-author of *Zero Waste Fashion Design* (McQuillan & Rissanem, 2020) says, "It requires a skilled designer to simultaneously imagine the garment as a 3D item and a flat pattern, while trying to fit the pieces together like a jigsaw," (Common Objective, 2019) (Figure 11.4 a-c).

Special Instructions

Some garments call for additional processes that require machinery or skills that are very costly or use up too much space and are not used all the time. Factories will send out this kind of special treatment to subcontractors. Some of the processes, such as pleating and embroidery, are done to cut pieces before assembly (Figure 11.5a). Some finishes are added to the completed garment with wet applications such as garment dye and bleaching (Figure 11.5b). Other finishes are added in dry applications, such as wrinkle free.

A technical designer may work directly with a contractor who does a special process for more than one factory so that the finish is consistent throughout the production run. A pleater will need to know the size and shape of pleats; an embroiderer may need to have CAD images of logos or other designs. A dye house will need color standards.

Figure 11.3a–f

The cutting instructions in the tech pack will alert the marker maker, spreader, and cutter about the unique requirements of each style that will impact layout and fabric consumption. In these examples the patterns are based on the dress in Figure 9.3. All examples are shown to scale on 60-inch wide fabric. The layout of the marker impacts the yield.

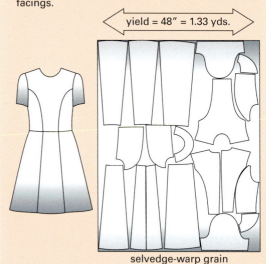

a. Border Print. The skirt and sleeve pieces are laid on the selvedge edge so that the border design will show up on their hems. The entire dress is cut on the cross grain except for the facings.

yield = 48" = 1.33 yds.

selvedge-warp grain

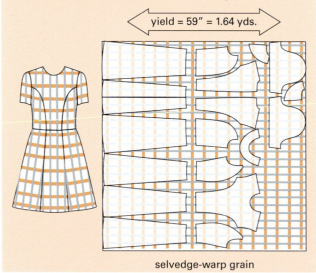

c. 100% Plaid Match. The plaid lines in the panels on this dress line up with each other horizontally. The vertical lines are mirrored from left to right. The fabric yield is higher than the dress below in figure d.

yield = 59" = 1.64 yds.

selvedge-warp grain

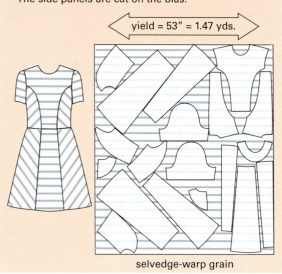

b. Stripes. The center panels and sleeves are cut on the cross grain so that the stripes are horizontal. The side panels are cut on the bias.

yield = 53" = 1.47 yds.

selvedge-warp grain

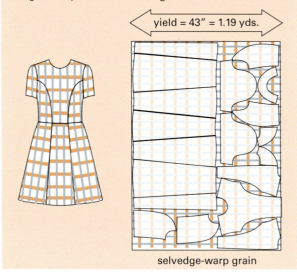

d. Plaid Match. Horizontal and vertical lines do not match everywhere, but they are mirrored from left to right. The yield is less than figure c.

yield = 43" = 1.19 yds.

selvedge-warp grain

Colorway #1

Colorway #2

self

contrast

e. Color Blocking. The color of the center panels and sleeves in each dress match each other. The color of the side panels match each other, but are cut in a contracting color to the center panels. Each color needs to be spread separately and needs its own marker. The pattern chart will list which pieces will be cut in the self fabric and which pieces will be cut in contrast. A list of colorways must be included with the cutting chart using color names listed on the BOM.

PATTERN CHART (CUTTER'S MUST)			
textile	pattern piece	textile	pattern piece
self	center front bodice	contrast	side front bodice
self	center front skirt	contrast	side front skirt
self	center back bodice	contrast	side back bodice
self	center back skirt	contrast	side back bodice
self	front neck facing	fusible	side neck facings
self	back neck facing	fusible	back neck facing
self	sleeves		

COLORWAYS
Colorway #1: Shell-Gray Contrast-Teal
Colorway #2: Shell-Tan Contrast-Brown

f. Splitting Patterns. The patterns for the front and back of this dress are very large and waste a lot of fabric when laid into the marker. By splitting the back pattern down the center back, the pieces fit into the width of the fabric with a better yield.

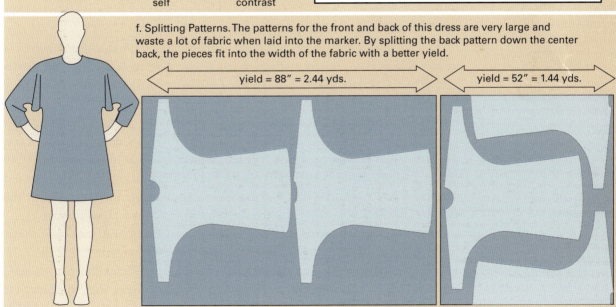

yield = 88" = 2.44 yds.

yield = 52" = 1.44 yds.

a

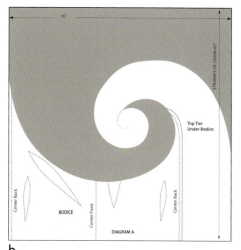

b

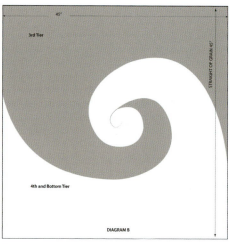

c

Figure 11.4a
Designers Colleen Moretz and Sandra Keiser were inspired to create this award-winning spiral dress, "Macchia Spiral Into Zero-Waste Times Two" by using principles outlined in the book *Zero Waste Fashion Design* by Timo Rissanen and Holly McQuillan (Rissanen & McQuillan, 2020).

Figure 11.4b and c
The pattern shown in figure 11.4b and c for the dress in figure 11.4a demonstrates how none of the fabric was wasted while achieving a dramatic silhouette.

Sewing Instructions

Determining the degree of detail to include in the tech pack for stitch, seam, and edge finishes varies considerably from firm to firm and product to product. Some apparel firms leave decisions regarding these areas up to the engineering staff or the vendor, especially when using full-package contractors. Other firms spell out these specifications to the last detail to ensure that the finished products conform to the original concept for that garment's construction. Detailed construction information aids in establishing criteria for acceptable quality and in determining acceptability of finished products. This approach also makes it possible for garments to be consistent when more than one vendor is used to produce a style.

There are many common names for seams and stitches. These can vary by region, by product classification, and by machine manufacturer. *Serging*, *overlock*, or *merrow* are all used to describe the same stitch. To avoid confusion, product developers can use a standard system provided by ASTM International D6193-20 Standard Practice for Stitches and Seams (ASTM International, 2020). The ISO provides the same naming system for stitch types in ISO 4915:1991 (ISO, 1991a). The ASTM system uses an alpha system for seams and the ISO uses numbers only in ISO 4916:1991 (ISO, 1991b). Easily accessible charts from American & Efird, Inc., are available online and in Appendix 11.1 (American & Eiferd 2009a and , 2009b). The discussion in this book uses the ASTM system for **stitch classification** and **seam classification**.

In both systems, the term **stitch** signifies a row of continuous strands of thread that interlace or interloop to hold fabric together or create a pattern that shows on the surface of the garment. The various types of stitches are discussed in the following sections. A **seam** is a configuration of parts and/or edges of fabric that, when stitched, transforms raw fabric into a garment or product and adds to its visual design. ASTM uses letters to designate groups of seams that are formed in a similar way.

- BS (**bound seam**) includes the application of a folded piece of fabric (a binding) to finish the raw edge(s) of fabric in a seam.

a

b

Figures 11.5a and b
Some garments call for additional processes that require machinery or skills that are very costly or use up too much space and are not used all the time. Factories may send out this kind of special treatment to subcontractors. Some processes such as pleating and embroidery are done to cut pieces before assembly (a). Some finishes are added to the completed garment with wet applications such as garment dye and bleaching (b). Others are added in dry applications, such as wrinkle free.

- EF (**edge finish**) includes a variety of configurations that hide raw edges, such as hems that use the fabric itself, not a separate piece.
- FS (**flat seam**) is used for athletic wear and made on machinery that cuts and butts fabric together before stitching with a web of stitches.
- LS (**lapped seam**) and SS (**superimposed seam**) represent a wide variety of configurations that range from simple to highly complex in which two or more pieces of fabric are laid together and stitched.
- OS (**ornamental stitch**) is decorative and does not necessarily function to hold fabric together into a garment such as embroidery and darts.

These lists are helpful in describing various seams and stitches with images and words, but they do not group seams and stitches together with those that are likely to be used in the same product. How can a product developer know which ones to choose? There are about twenty common stitch types, but there are hundreds of seam types!

When product developers start to work in a company with well-established standards, they will find that each product category and price level has its own **make**. This term is sometimes used to describe the sum total of the perceived quality of the textile, components, seaming, fit, and finish. A blazer without a lining has a sportswear make. Add a lining and it has a tailored make. The concept includes end use as well as manufacturing source. The make of a bathing suit is very different from the make of a dress. Tech packs written for the same garment category and price point will have seams and stitches that are very similar. They will reflect the same make.

Knits vs. Wovens

The ASTM seam SSa (sometimes called a **booked seam**) is the most common configuration of fabric in industrial sewing. Two layers of fabric are lined up along their cut edges and inserted into the machine. The distance between the needle and the raw edges is called the **seam allowance**. Seam allowances vary in depth depending on the make.

- Woven fabrics are sewn with ½-inch seam allowance on seams that will be subject to weight or tension, such as side seams and shoulders. A quarter-inch allowance is used on an **enclosed seam** such as collar and cuff edges or facings where the edges of the seam allowance are concealed inside of the outer layers of fabric. The back crotch seam of men's tailored trousers often starts at 1½-inch seam allowance near the waistline and tapers to ½ inch to provide fabric for alterations.
- Knitwear is sewn with 3/8-inch seam allowance for the majority of seams.
- Other seam allowance widths are found in special categories, such as lingerie, swimwear, and coats.

Machinery is classified in the ASTM system according to the way the mechanism forms a stitch. On a **lockstitch machine** (300 class) one thread is forced by a needle through the layers of fabric and then interlaced with a thread from a **bobbin** (a small spool in the bottom of the machine). The interlaced threads create a row of straight stitches that echoes the structure of weaving. The stitch line does not "give." This stability makes lockstitch suitable for seaming woven fabric (Figure 11.6a–b). Lockstitch can be configured with two needles and two bobbins for a double needle look (301(2)). It can also form as a zigzag that is commonly used for durable buttonholes and bartacks (304) as well as for applying elastic to lingerie and swimwear.

Looper machines do not have bobbins for the lower thread; they have loopers that look like thick curved needles under the machine that force the threads to interloop with each other. These stitches imitate knitting. The loops are also caught by the needle threads so that they do not slip apart. Because the stitches "give," they are most suitable for knitted fabrics (Figures 11.6c–d).

The 500 class includes the three-thread **serging (overlock) machine** (504). When used on an SSa seam, it creates a flexible seam line and an embroidered finish along the seam allowance, which is cut clean with an internal knife. The four-thread serger (512 or 514) is also used for seaming knits and uses two needles. The seam is more secure than the 504 but still very flexible.

The **coverstitch machine** (400 & 600 classes) is used for hemming, neckline binding, flat seaming, and decoration. The topstitching does not break when the knit is stretched during use.

The **chain stitch machine** (401) is used to seam and topstitch knits for flexibility.

Figures 11.6a–e

Single needle lockstitch (301) and chain stitch (401) have different constructions. Lockstitch is more suitable for wovens, whereas looper stitches such as 401 are more suitable for knits.

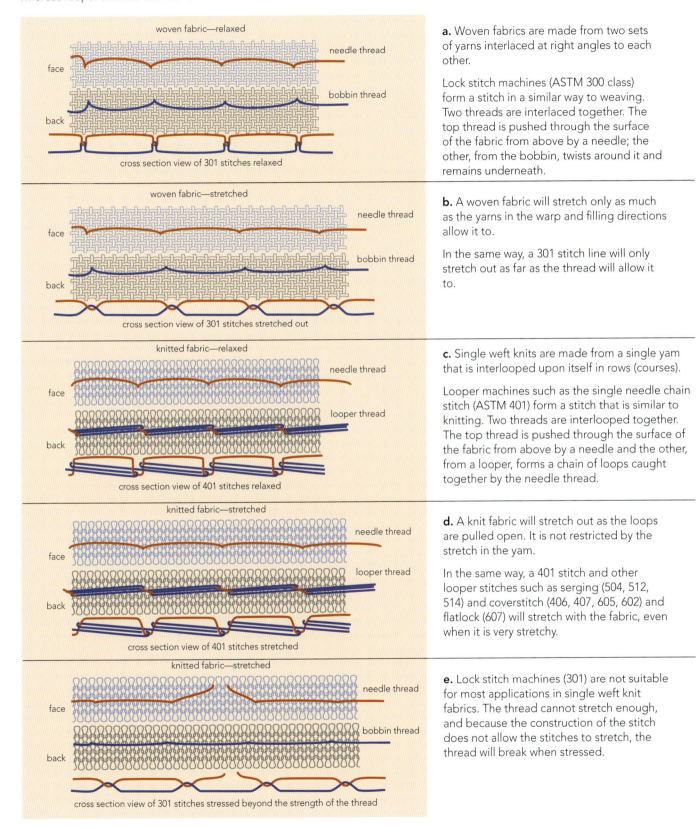

a. Woven fabrics are made from two sets of yarns interlaced at right angles to each other.

Lock stitch machines (ASTM 300 class) form a stitch in a similar way to weaving. Two threads are interlaced together. The top thread is pushed through the surface of the fabric from above by a needle; the other, from the bobbin, twists around it and remains underneath.

b. A woven fabric will stretch only as much as the yarns in the warp and filling directions allow it to.

In the same way, a 301 stitch line will only stretch out as far as the thread will allow it to.

c. Single weft knits are made from a single yarn that is interlooped upon itself in rows (courses).

Looper machines such as the single needle chain stitch (ASTM 401) form a stitch that is similar to knitting. Two threads are interlooped together. The top thread is pushed through the surface of the fabric from above by a needle and the other, from a looper, forms a chain of loops caught together by the needle thread.

d. A knit fabric will stretch out as the loops are pulled open. It is not restricted by the stretch in the yarn.

In the same way, a 401 stitch and other looper stitches such as serging (504, 512, 514) and coverstitch (406, 407, 605, 602) and flatlock (607) will stretch with the fabric, even when it is very stretchy.

e. Lock stitch machines (301) are not suitable for most applications in single weft knit fabrics. The thread cannot stretch enough, and because the construction of the stitch does not allow the stitches to stretch, the thread will break when stressed.

Commodity vs. Fashion Products

Product such as shirts, tee shirts, jeans, and chinos are referred to as **commodity products** because they are mass-produced with few differentiating features so that they can be made available to a large market at a competitive price. Competition in the commodity market drives factories to invent machines and methods that are increasingly faster to run and demand less skill to operate. There are many devices made of sheet metal that guide strips of fabric cut from rolls or fabric edges, folding them into shapes such as plackets and bindings and hems. A **folder** (**assist**) replaces the need for multiple operations to position, join, and turn fabric before topstitching. Because the cut piece of the garment and the folded placket or binding pass under the needles only once, the operation may be given a single ASTM letter designation (Figures 11.7a and b).

Folders have the advantage of increasing production speed and consistency, but they are costly to set up. Hence, production managers rely on recovering costs through high volume. Designers who want to produce fashion product in a commodity factory will be turned away or charged sample rates. Folders are also limited to straight or slightly curved edges. Only a few binders allow the operator to form a corner.

Operations performed on folders cannot be made in a circle because the ends cannot be made to join, so bindings on necklines or armholes have to be joined with the seam, making very bulky and sometimes uncomfortable lumps of fabric at the shoulder or underarm. Garments with a better make apply bindings on circular areas in several steps so that the ends can be joined first, making a smooth circle.

Commodity products are associated more with utility than aesthetics. The finishing of raw seam edges must be durable and fast. There are two methods for joining and cleaning seams at the same time: four-thread (512) and five-thread sergers (504+401) seam and serge the edge at the same time. They are used for seaming SSa seams of jeans and everyday woven shirts to save money because they are fast and secure. Flat-felled seams (LSc and LSas) are joined by feeding the cut garment pieces into a folder that turns the edges under and stitches two rows of chain stitch (401(2)). The seam is very strong, durable, and clean finished.

Seams that trap layers of fabric together are inflexible and do not conform well to the body, so they are not used in makes where the silhouette is important. The exception is the French seam (SSae), which encloses the seam edges, but it is usually very narrow and used only on fine fabrics. Seams shape better over the body when they are sewn first and then **busted** (**pressed open** or **butterflied**). One way to cover the raw edges of open seams on wovens is to sew a lining into the garment, but unlined garments can use three-thread serging (301) or bias binding (BSc) to cover the raveling cut edge. Bias binding can be applied with a folder (BSc).

Commodity hems on woven products are turned twice in one operation using a folder (EFb) and topstitched with lockstitch (301) or chain stitch (410). As with other folders, deep curves do not pass through the folders without twisting, so curved shirt hems are ¼-inch deep. Hems on garments with a higher make may use two operations by cleaning the edge with the use of a three-thread serge (504) or seam tape (LSa) and finishing with a blind hem (101) single-thread chain stitch (no lower looper). Figures 11.8a–d show some of the seams and stitches used in commodity and fashion products.

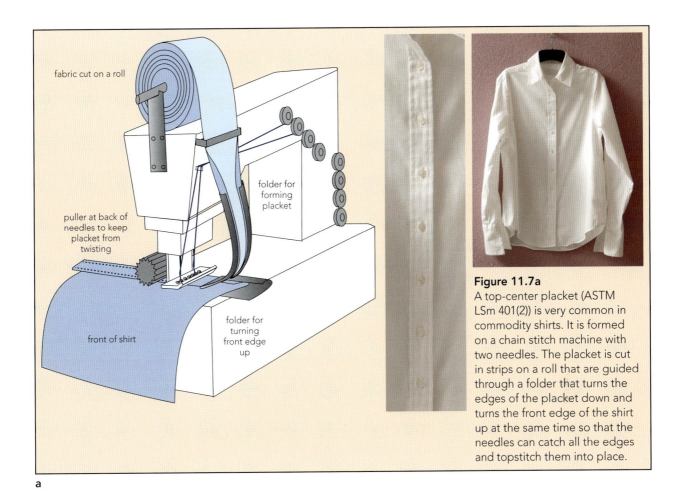

a

Figure 11.7a
A top-center placket (ASTM LSm 401(2)) is very common in commodity shirts. It is formed on a chain stitch machine with two needles. The placket is cut in strips on a roll that are guided through a folder that turns the edges of the placket down and turns the front edge of the shirt up at the same time so that the needles can catch all the edges and topstitch them into place.

b

Figure 11.7b
Waistbands on jeans (ASTM BSc 401(2)) are formed by folding the waistband strips in the shape of a "C" and inserting the top of the jean into the open space between the folds. The ends have to be turned in by hand and finished on a lockstitch machine because the folder cannot form finished corners.

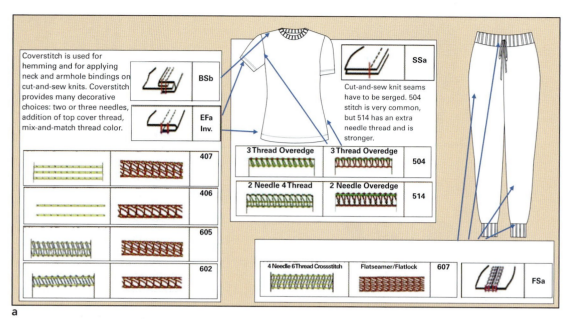

a

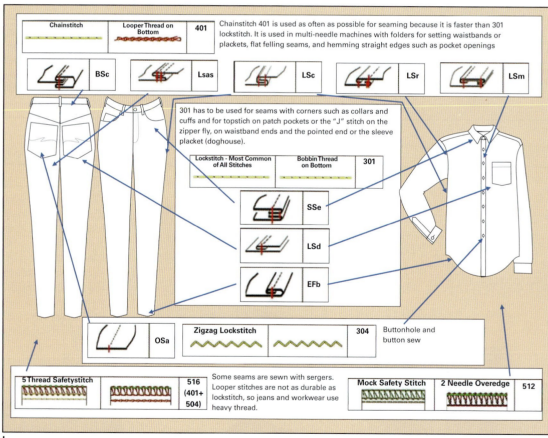

b

Figure 11.8a
Seam and stitch selection for cut-and-sew knits.

Figure 11.8b
Seam and stitch selection for commodity shirts.

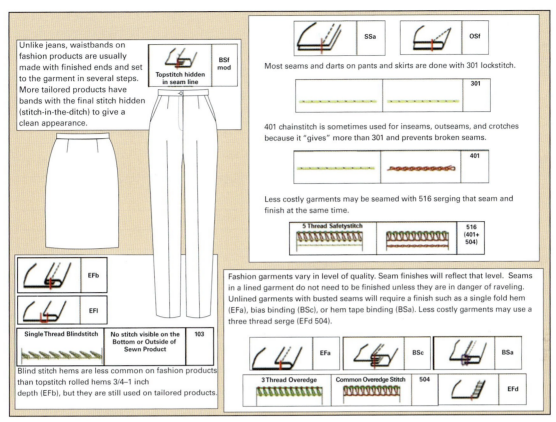

c

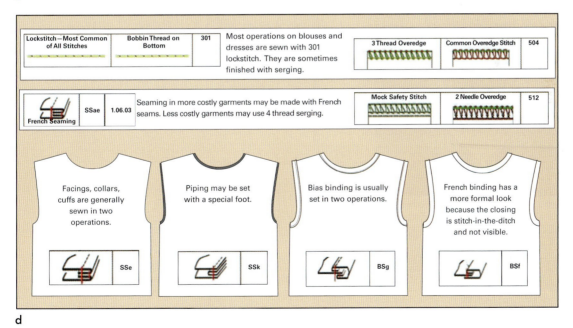

d

Figure 11.8c
Seam and stitch selection for fashion bottoms.

Figure 11.8d
Seam and stitch selection for blouses and dresses.

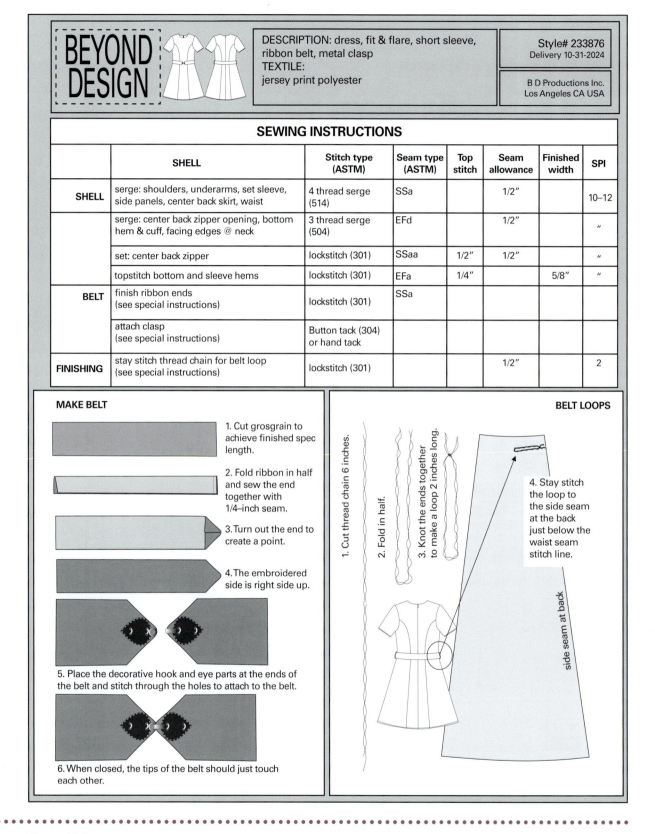

DESCRIPTION: dress, fit & flare, short sleeve, ribbon belt, metal clasp
TEXTILE: jersey print polyester

Style# 233876
Delivery 10-31-2024

B D Productions Inc.
Los Angeles CA USA

SEWING INSTRUCTIONS

	SHELL	Stitch type (ASTM)	Seam type (ASTM)	Top stitch	Seam allowance	Finished width	SPI
SHELL	serge: shoulders, underarms, set sleeve, side panels, center back skirt, waist	4 thread serge (514)	SSa		1/2"		10–12
	serge: center back zipper opening, bottom hem & cuff, facing edges @ neck	3 thread serge (504)	EFd		1/2"		"
	set: center back zipper	lockstitch (301)	SSaa	1/2"	1/2"		"
	topstitch bottom and sleeve hems	lockstitch (301)	EFa	1/4"		5/8"	"
BELT	finish ribbon ends (see special instructions)	lockstitch (301)	SSa				
	attach clasp (see special instructions)	Button tack (304) or hand tack					
FINISHING	stay stitch thread chain for belt loop (see special instructions)	lockstitch (301)			1/2"		2

MAKE BELT

1. Cut grosgrain to achieve finished spec length.

2. Fold ribbon in half and sew the end together with 1/4–inch seam.

3. Turn out the end to create a point.

4. The embroidered side is right side up.

5. Place the decorative hook and eye parts at the ends of the belt and stitch through the holes to attach to the belt.

6. When closed, the tips of the belt should just touch each other.

BELT LOOPS

1. Cut thread chain 6 inches.

2. Fold in half.

3. Knot the ends together to make a loop 2 inches long.

4. Stay stitch the loop to the side seam at the back just below the waist seam stitch line.

side seam at back

Figure 11.9
Sewing instructions for the dress in Figure 9.3.

Woven products look and fit better when seam allowances are trimmed, clipped, and finished by **under-pressing**, a method of pressing seams and darts on the inside of the garment shortly after they are sewn and before the garment is pressed during finishing. Pockets, darts, and other details come out balanced and properly located when shapes and locations are marked by hand on each garment. This kind of attention adds to the fineness of fit and presentation, but it is labor intensive and expensive, so it is not done on commodity products.

In recent years the make of fashion products has been influenced by the deconstructionist aesthetic. Designers have become playful and witty by mixing seams, stitches, and materials that are associated with one make and featuring them on another. The introduction of the heavy brass zipper into eveningwear was shocking when it was introduced. Today, deconstructed design elements such as exposed zippers, raw hem edges, and dropped stitches on sweaters are commonplace.

Technical Detail Sketches

Sewing instructions that are not easily expressed by a standard stitch and seam can be called out with technical drawings of a much larger scale than the flat technical sketch of the whole garment. Such drawings are used to illustrate pocket positioning, button spacing, overlap, location of tabs, method of inserting elastic, style of zipper setting, or the profile of topstitch design (Figure 11.9). Drawings of details avoid confusion that can come from too many words. Occasionally a step-by-step sample of a complex operation may be needed. *Technical Sourcebook for Apparel Designers* (Lee & Steen, 2019) is an excellent resource for the kinds of sewing methods that are available and how to illustrate them.

Non-Sewing

Some processes used in the assembling of textile parts are not addressed in ASTM lists of seams and stitches (summarized in the Appendix 11.1 and 11.2). Victoria's Secret seamless bras use ultrasonic welding, as does high-performance sportswear made by Patagonia and others. Waterproof zippers that are joined into openings with laser welding are now common in technical outerwear (Figure 11.10). Micro-porous polyurethane laminates such as Gore-Tex® require heat-applied water sealing tape on seams (Bubonia, 2015).

Processes such as pressing are not listed as sewing operations. Most garments require finish pressing. This is done in addition to any in-process pressing that might have been required to achieve desired effects during the construction process. Some garments, such as tee shirts, require very little pressing; others, such as tailored pants and jackets, require extensive final pressing. Pressing standards can be established by manuals but are more difficult to express because they are subjective. Pressing is more of an art; it relies on the "hand" of the individual presser.

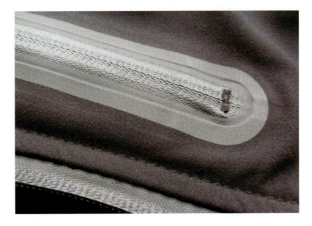

Figure 11.10
The zipper in this jacket has been welded to the shell using lasers that bond the shell material to the waterproof zipper, avoiding the holes made by needles during sewing.

Figure 11.11a
This utility pressing machine is used for in-process and final pressing of trousers and other tailored products. It resembles machines from 150 years ago, but it has vacuum and steam controls that reduce variations in pressing from operator to operator.

Figure 11.11b
This form finishing machine blasts steam from the inside out to smooth out wrinkles, then sets the press with a blast of cool air. This kind of machine not only reduces the number of steps needed to press the garment but also produces uniform results due to computerized controls.

Figure 11.11c
Pressing boards with vacuum assist the presser in several ways. They dry and "set" the press so the presser can move on quickly. They also provide a jet of "up air" against which the presser can glide the iron, eliminating the danger of marking the surface.

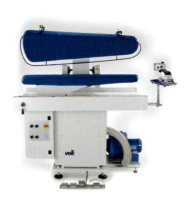

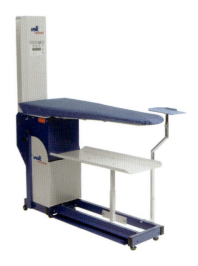

The industry has developed many types of pressing equipment. The traditional **buck** (**utility press**) (Figure 11.11a) has been used for tailored products for over a century. It has two parts that open and close like an oyster. It has seen many improvements, such as steam pressure controls and timers. The whole garment presser in Figure 11.11b employs steam that is blasted from the inside the garment with calibrated temperature and cycle time. The garment is cooled by a blast of air and dried by vacuum. The pressers in Figure 11.11c can reduce marking the surface of the fabric by using blasts of air or vacuum. These techniques have reduced the wide variation in results but have not eliminated them altogether.

Stitches Per Inch

In general, shorter stitches produce more durable seams. However, there is a point of diminishing return at which, if stitches are too packed together, puckering and seam distortion occur. A stitch length of 10 to 12 stitches per inch (SPI) is considered average for light- to medium-weight wovens. Dress shirts often have 14 to 20 SPI to denote higher quality. Some knits need a higher stitch count (up to 16 SPI on swimwear and 18 SPI on knits with spandex) so that when the stitches are stretched out, there is more length to the stitch line (Bubonia, 2015). Jeans require several different stitch lengths: 8 to 10 for internal stitching and 7 to 8 for topstitch.

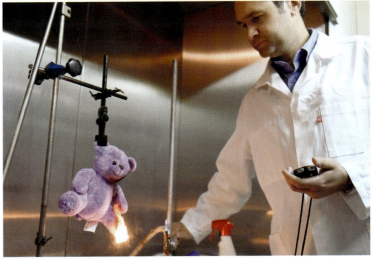

a
b

Bills of Materials (BOM): Textiles and Trims

The **bill of materials (BOM)** is a section within a tech pack in which textiles, trims, labels, and packing materials are listed with descriptions, sizes, and quantities. Many companies test materials for performance over time. Until the test results are back from the lab, technical designers cannot complete their tech packs. If a material does not meet company standards, it will have to be replaced or the supplier will have to improve it unless the company wants to risk loss of brand identity and sales. Common tests include verification of textile specifications such as fiber content, thread count, and fabric weight. Performance of the textile during normal use can be confirmed with tests for color stability when the product is exposed to water, light, and perspiration. Tests will show how the color of the textile stands up to laundering. Tests for outdoor products or protective clothing might include water repellency, durability, elastic recovery, or reflectivity (see Table 11.1). Safety tests, such as flammability and lead content, may be mandatory in children's wear (Figure 11.12b).

Some companies test the whole garment to be sure that all components are compatible. Garments with multiple textile products can be severely distorted if interlinings, mesh pockets, appliqués, or trims shrink or stretch more or less than other parts. Styles with color blocking or contrast trims can be ruined by color migration.

The BOM can be highly detailed or very simple, depending on the relationship with the vendor. Technical designers in charge of developing proprietary textiles may handle the exchange of information outside of the tech pack, instead referring to the textile by an order number. Some brands write separate BOMs for textiles and trims (Figure 11.13).

Figure 11.12a
Labs such as Intertek provide many tests to ensure that the materials that are ordered meet the standards of the brand. Some brands have their own labs. The lab will provide results, but it is up to the technical designer to decide how closely that result meets the standard. Fabrics are tested for strength with an Instron tester. The cloth is pulled until it tears, and the amount of pressure needed to tear the fabric is measured.

Figure 11.12b
Some countries have laws regarding the manufacturing of children's clothing, toys, bedding, and other textile-based products. Some restrict the use of small parts and drawstrings. Some require that the materials pass flammability tests or assessment of poisonous metal content such as lead in buttons and small parts.

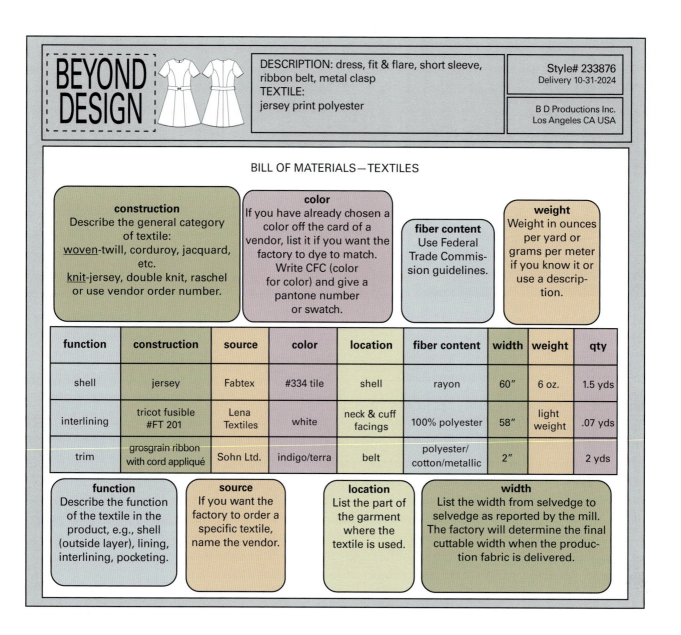

BILL OF MATERIALS—TEXTILES

DESCRIPTION: dress, fit & flare, short sleeve, ribbon belt, metal clasp
TEXTILE: jersey print polyester

Style# 233876
Delivery 10-31-2024

B D Productions Inc.
Los Angeles CA USA

construction
Describe the general category of textile:
<u>woven</u>-twill, corduroy, jacquard, etc.
<u>knit</u>-jersey, double knit, raschel or use vendor order number.

color
If you have already chosen a color off the card of a vendor, list it if you want the factory to dye to match. Write CFC (color for color) and give a pantone number or swatch.

fiber content
Use Federal Trade Commission guidelines.

weight
Weight in ounces per yard or grams per meter if you know it or use a description.

function	construction	source	color	location	fiber content	width	weight	qty
shell	jersey	Fabtex	#334 tile	shell	rayon	60"	6 oz.	1.5 yds
interlining	tricot fusible #FT 201	Lena Textiles	white	neck & cuff facings	100% polyester	58"	light weight	.07 yds
trim	grosgrain ribbon with cord appliqué	Sohn Ltd.	indigo/terra	belt	polyester/ cotton/metallic	2"		2 yds

function
Describe the function of the textile in the product, e.g., shell (outside layer), lining, interlining, pocketing.

source
If you want the factory to order a specific textile, name the vendor.

location
List the part of the garment where the textile is used.

width
List the width from selvedge to selvedge as reported by the mill. The factory will determine the final cuttable width when the production fabric is delivered.

Figure 11.13
This Bill of Materials–Textiles lists the textiles needed for the dress in Figure 9.3. Wide and narrow textiles such as ribbon are listed here.

Components also need to be tested before being included in the final tech pack. Each kind of trim has pertinent ASTM or AATCC tests regarding strength, durability, and compatibility. These tests are crucial in high-performance sportswear, and safety gear but may not be as necessary for everyday clothing. The easiest test to perform is to launder the whole garment according to label instructions. If any of the trims are likely to crock, fall apart, snag, or break, they will do so during this test.

Trim specification will vary depending on method of manufacturing and application (Figure 11.14). Companies often keep cards or packets from vendors with samples of trims. Such cards list the kind of information that is needed in the tech pack. Companies with PLMs store this information in database libraries.

DESCRIPTION: dress, fit & flare, short sleeve, ribbon belt, metal clasp
TEXTILE:
jersey print polyester

Style# 233876
Delivery 10-31-2024

B D Productions Inc.
Los Angeles CA USA

BILL OF MATERIALS-TRIMS

description See Chapter 6 for details.

Buttons are described by shape (rimmed, flat, ball, etc.) and method of attachment (two-hole, shank, tack, etc.).

Zippers are described by the way they function (concealed, waterproof, separating) and the kind of material used in the teeth (plastic coil, metal, molded plastic, etc.).

Hooks & eyes are described by end-use (trouser, fur, coat, dress, clasp, etc.) and kind of material used (wire, stamped metal, plastic, etc.).

finish
metal: antique, brushed, enameled, plastic, and natural materials: etched, laser cut, painted, distressed, etc.

size
Each kind of trim has a different measurement system! Some have to be graded for different sizes. Buttons are measured across the diameter by lignes (1/40th of an inch) or millimeter. Hooks and eyes sizes are related to the gauge of the wire. Buckles and d-rings are measured across the interior clearance allowed for the belt or webbing. Zippers are sized by the number of millimeters across the teeth and by the length in inches.

quantity
Don't forget the extra button!

description	material	source	finish	color	size	location	qty
zipper concealed	nylon coil	factory sourced		cfc	3 mm 22"	center back	1
clasp	molded metal	Bijoux Ltd.	antique	silver	2" x 3/4"	front belt	1
spun thread	polyester	factory sourced		cfc shell	Tex 27	all operations	
thread chain	polyester	factory sourced		cfc belt	Tex 27	belt loops	12"

materials
Metal: nickel, brass, pewter, copper, etc.
Plastic: nylon, acrylic, polyester, composite, etc.
Natural materials: wood, shell, nut, stone, bone, horn, etc.
Methods of fabrication include: molded, carved, stamped, etc.

source
Your company will have a library of samples from known vendors.

color
Hardware and zippers can be dyed to match. You can choose the number of a color provided by the vendor on a sample card or you can send a color standard for matching and list "Color for Color" (CFC) on the Tech Pack.

location
Very important information when a trim like a button or zipper comes in more than one size or type!

Figure 11.14
This Bill of Materials–Trims lists the trims needed for the dress in Figure 9.3.

Hardware

In the tech pack, hardware such as buttons, snaps, rivets, hooks and eyes, buckles, and novelty zipper pulls may require information such as the type of material used, the method of fabrication, and the method of application, as well as color, size, and quantity. Support devices such as collar stays, boning, and underwire will require similar details (Figure 11.15a).

Logos that are molded into, etched onto, or painted onto buttons, zipper pulls, and other hardware are often managed by the marketing department or outside firms that provide technical information and artwork directly to the hardware fabricator (Figure 11.15b). This kind of detailed information is sometimes handled with a manual or technical document other than the tech pack.

Zippers

In the tech pack, zippers will require information about the type and size of the teeth (also called *chain*), the method of opening, the method of application, the kind of zipper tape and zipper pull, the length of the opening, and the color (Figure 11.15c). Choosing a zipper that is compatible with the garment requires understanding of the textile, the end use, and the market. For example, the zipper tape of a garment that is dyed or bleached after production has to absorb color or chemicals like the shell does.

Thread

Thread is a strong, slender form of yarn used for stitching garments. Thread is selected not only for its color, but also for its size, strength, elasticity, and colorfastness. Thread can have a strong impact on the quality of the finished product. It must be compatible with the shell during wear and care. Selection of appropriate threads can help prevent poor formation of stitches during the construction process such as thread breakage, skipped stitches, melting of thermoplastic fiber threads, and puckered seams (Figure 11.16).

Thread is sold using a system called **Tex** (also used for yarn), which has a direct numbering system: the larger the number, the thicker the thread. Tex 24 and 27 are common Tex sizes for everyday wear. Tex 50 is used on seaming of heavier fabrics for work wear and Tex 80 is used for topstitching jeans. Although the amount of thread used to construct a garment is handled by the factory in large offshore orders, for smaller, local companies that may need to estimate their thread needs, American & Efird provides a guide for thread consumption (American & Efird 2016a).

Bill of Materials: Labels and Packaging

Although labels and packaging products are used at different times in the production cycle and are made of a wide variety of materials, they are often designed and produced through the same source. Companies that specialize in branding offer comprehensive services that include labels, hangtags, boxes, bags, tissue paper, hangers, and even textiles used for linings and components. The marketing department of the brand works with this kind of company to develop artwork that reflects the brand image.

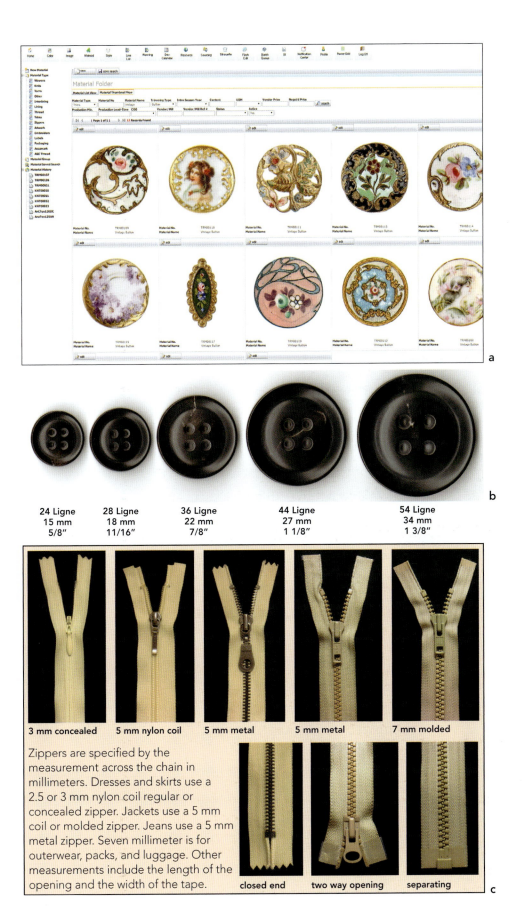

a

b

24 Ligne	28 Ligne	36 Ligne	44 Ligne	54 Ligne
15 mm	18 mm	22 mm	27 mm	34 mm
5/8"	11/16"	7/8"	1 1/8"	1 3/8"

3 mm concealed **5 mm nylon coil** **5 mm metal** **5 mm metal** **7 mm molded**

Zippers are specified by the measurement across the chain in millimeters. Dresses and skirts use a 2.5 or 3 mm nylon coil regular or concealed zipper. Jackets use a 5 mm coil or molded zipper. Jeans use a 5 mm metal zipper. Seven millimeter is for outerwear, packs, and luggage. Other measurements include the length of the opening and the width of the tape.

closed end **two way opening** **separating**

c

Figure 11.15a

Companies often keep cards or packets from vendors with samples of trims. Such cards list the kind of information that is needed in the tech pack. Companies with PLMs store this information in database libraries. Once the designer selects a product, all of the information in the database populates the design spec and, later, the tech pack.

Figure 11.15b

In the tech pack, hardware (such as buttons, snaps, rivets, hooks and eyes, buckles, and novelty zipper pulls) requires information about the type of material used, the method of fabrication, and the method of application, as well as color, size, and quantity. Two systems are used for buttons: Ligne (each ligne = 1/64th of an inch) and millimeters. In this list, both systems are used, along with their equivalent in inches. The buttons are typically used on jackets and coats and are shown in full size.

Figure 11.15c

In the tech pack, zippers will require information about the type and size of the teeth (also called chain), the method of opening, the method of application, the kind of zipper tape and zipper pull, the length of the opening, and the color.

SPUN THREAD

Polyester

- the most commonly used sewing thread in industrial applications
- made of short staple in a variety of weights and twists
- inexpensive
- available in many colors
- strong enough for most clothing in daily use

Cotton

- more costly than polyester
- does not break in high-speed machines
- shrinks more than polyester
- does not melt in high-speed machines, so it does not break
- compatible with cotton garments: changes color as garment during dyeing or washing

CORESPUN THREAD

Polyester wrapped
- made of staple polyester fibers that are twisted around a polyester filament
- stronger than spun thread
- more expensive than spun thread

Cotton wrapped
- more costly than polyester wrapped
- even stronger than polyester wrapped
- cool in high speed machines
- compatible with cotton garments during dyeing and washing

MONOFILAMENT THREAD

- single filament polyester or nylon of very fine denier in various sizes
- sometimes used in blind stitching hems or label setting
- melts at a low temperature, unravels easily, is scratchy
- used only in inexpensive garments

MULTIFILAMENT THREAD (NOT TEXTURIZED)

- made of multiple smooth filaments twisted together
- some multifilament thread is used for very heavy duty applications, such as shoes, upholstery, and industrial applications
- embroidery threads are available in rayon, polyester, and nylon

TEXTURIZED MULTIFILAMENT THREAD

- made of multiple texturized filaments twisted together
- stretchy and soft
- used for serging inexpensive knit garments
- used for pearl edge (fine serging stitch) for edging ruffles

Figure 11.16
Spun and corespun thread are the most common types of general sewing thread, although other types of thread are used.

All of their suppliers are linked electronically. They use compatible software, such as Pantone color systems, so that all logos, typefaces, colors, and verbiage send the same message to the consumer. The branding company works with the technical designer to be sure that labels and packaging will work with the garments. They will then supply information in the tech packs or in technical bulletins or manuals so that the sewing contractor can use all of the products correctly.

Labels are parts of a garment that convey messages by words, images, codes, or electronic signals. Some information about labels will be unique to an individual style and will be listed in the BOM–Labels and Packaging section of the tech pack (Figure 11.17). In a large company, details may already have been determined by the marketing department and may be codified in a manual or technical document. In addition to materials, the information will include the dimensions and shape of the label, the location in the garment, and the method of attachment.

Brands use labeling to convey information to consumers, other businesses, government agencies and nongovernmental standards and compliance organizations. A label may carry a message for one, some, or all of these groups. Some information may be provided by the brand voluntarily for marketing and merchandising purposes. Some may be required in the country where the garment is produced or where it is sold by laws that are designed to protect trade, the consumer, or the environment. Laws governing labels also state what language should be used.

Label Materials

They can be printed, embroidered, or woven onto the garment itself or on pieces of fabric or other material that are attached to the garment. Because labels are made of such a wide range of materials, specification in the tech pack will vary widely. Sewn-in

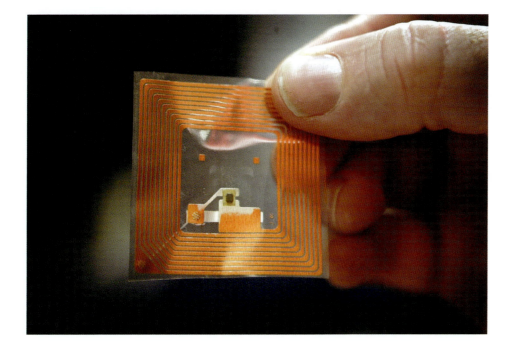

Figure 11.17
Radio Frequency Identification (RFID) tags are being used more and more in clothing to track their progress through the production process.

labels are generally made of some form of narrow textile, such as ribbon or tape woven as satin, grosgrain, jacquard, or twill or cut from nonwovens such as Tyvek®. Details for textile-based labels will follow usual textile description: fiber, yarn, construction, and finish. Novelty labels made of materials such as metal, plastic, rubber, or leather that may be transformed by molding, stamping, printing, dyeing, painting, etching, or other method will have their own terminology in the tech pack similar to specifying hardware. **RFID tags** (radio frequency identification) tags will be specified by durability, range of transmission, size of memory and method of attachment (Figure 11.18).

Fiber Content

Fiber content label requirements vary by country. They may ask the manufacturer to list the generic common name of a synthetic fiber such as polyester or nylon, the plant or animal source of a natural fiber such as silk or cotton, or the animal from which a skin has been obtained such as lamb or goat. Brand names such as Lycra® may be allowed; in some cases spandex, the generic name, may be required instead. In some countries, listing fiber content is mandated to protect the consumer from fraud, allergic reaction, or unknowingly purchasing a garment made with products harvested from endangered species or produced in unethical conditions. In countries where fiber content is optional, brands may include it anyway to show their commitment to consumer protection and/or responsible sourcing.

Fiber content is required by some countries to protect their domestic businesses from foreign competition. By imposing tariffs (taxes) or quotas (restrictions on quantities) on specific fibers, the country may seek to discourage imports.

Manufacturer Identification

Some form of manufacturer's identification may be required on the fiber identification label. This may be for identifying the party who will pay tariffs, taxes, or other fees required by law. It may also be used to trace a manufacturer for purposes of legal action by a government agency or consumer.

Country of Origin

Tariffs and quota restrictions may be assigned at varying rates by a country that seeks to limit trade to address trade imbalance with one country or to encourage trade with a developing country. Some countries prohibit trade with countries that are perceived to be ignoring human rights or sustainability goals. Even when a label stating country of origin is not required by law, brands may choose to showcase country of origin when it is associated with craftsmanship or fashion leadership.

Care

Care labeling can be a controversial topic. Governments sometimes show that they champion consumer rights by mandating that care instructions be sewn into garments. At other times, when governments are faced with demands from the business community to reduce regulation, they may rescind laws requiring care labels or simply not enforce them. Some brands will include care instructions to show their concern

BEYOND DESIGN

DESCRIPTION: dress, fit & flare, short sleeve, ribbon belt, metal clasp
TEXTILE: jersey print polyester

Style# 233876
Delivery 10-31-2024

B D Productions Inc.
Los Angeles CA USA

BILL OF MATERIALS-LABELS AND PACKAGING

product	description	source	material/content	dimensions	location	method of attachment
brand label	jacquard end fold-see manual	Brandtex BDEF01	polyester/rayon	3/4" x 2"	left back neck facing	topstitch see instructions
size tab	jacquard loop-see manual	Brandtex 14BG2	polyester/rayon	3/8"	left back neck facing	under brand label see instructions
COO/care/content label	satin ribbon loop-printed-see instructions	Avery 1-SR-WH	polyester	1" x 2.5 1/4 insert	right back neck facing	under brand label see instructions
brand hang tag	full color	Brandtex BDHT03	card stock glossy	2 1/2" x 3 1/2"	under left arm	swiftach
swiftach	paddle white	vendor source-see manual	nylon	1 1/2"		insert through hang tag hole
swiftach	paddle white	vendor source-see manual	nylon	1 1/2"	belt at center back waist seam at left as worn	insert through hang tag hole
bag	.5 mm clear	vendor source-see manual	acetate	12" x 18"		see packing manual
boxes	see manual					see packing manual

TEXT FOR COO/CARE/CONTENT LABEL
Country of Origin: Vietnam
Content: 100% Polyester
Care: machine wash, air dry flat
RN# 66578

LABEL SETTING

-insert coo label and size tab under center bottom edge of brand label

-topstitch 4 sides of brand label onto left back neck facing 1/2" below finished neck edge and 1" from center back

a

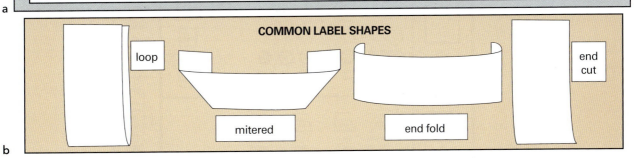

COMMON LABEL SHAPES

loop

mitered

end fold

end cut

b

Figure 11.18a
This Bill of Materials–Labels and Packaging lists the supplies needed for the dress in Figure 9.3.

Figure 11.18b
Although labels come in many shapes and sizes, these are the most common.

a

b

Figure 11.19a
Screen-printed labels are common in knit garments. They are more comfortable than sewn in labels in activewear.

Figure 11.19b
For screen-printed labels, the information is printed directly onto the garment. In this image, socks are being printed.

Figure 11.19c
The use of symbols for care instructions is not mandatory in the United States, but when they are used they must be correct.

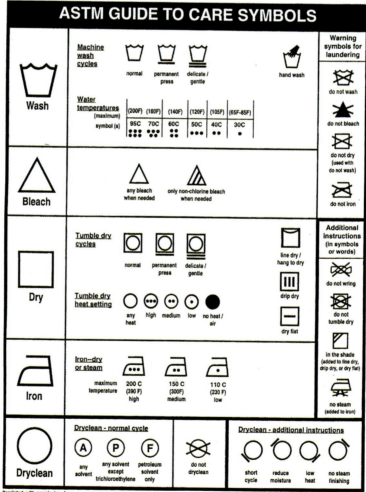

c

for the protection of the consumer or the environment. To facilitate the consumer's understanding of care instructions some brands use symbols provided by standards organizations such as ASTM and ISO (Figure 11.19c).

Size Designations
Not all countries require size labels. Some may only provide guidelines for clarity around sizing systems.

Trademarks
Using a company's trademark is voluntary and considered a good marketing tool, but using someone else's trademark is illegal. Garments carrying look-alike trademarks are considered counterfeit. When such products are discovered entering a country, they may be seized, and the owner may be fined or prosecuted for trademark infringement (Figure 11.20).

Warranties and Certifications
All products have an **implied warranty** that they will do what they are designed to do. For instance, a raincoat should repel water and snow boots should keep feet warm. A **written warranty** that appears on a label or hangtag claiming some characteristic becomes legally binding.

Most voluntary labeling on the product and hangtags, such as union labels or "Made in Italy," are intended to be more of a marketing tool than a legitimate quality claim. For example, the use of the cotton seal from Cotton, Inc., only claims that the product is made of cotton. It does not indicate the quality of that cotton.

Figure 11.20
Customs Officers display fake designer brand jeans in Melbourne, Australia. The goods, valued at around AUS$1 million dollars, were found during an examination of a sea cargo consignment.

Circularity

Brands may want to provide options for consumers who are looking for a robust in-depth story about the circularity of a garment that goes beyond fiber content, care instructions, and country of origin. They may want to describe the origin of a garment's materials, the sustainability of its manufacturing processes, the treatment of the people who produced it, the transparency of the brand's business practices, the predicted longevity, care, and the second and third life of the product. The brand can share this information by instantly connecting the consumer to a website with a scan of a barcode, **QR code** (an arrangement of black and white squares printed on a surface that can be read by a camera or phone which directs a user to a URL), or an RFID tag (Case Study 11.1).

Packaging Materials

Packaging is part of the brand message as well, as a way to ensure that the garment gets to the customer in the best condition possible (Figure 11.21). Packaging can also be mandated by the retailer or distributor. Many warehouses and receiving docks are automated and can only receive goods that are in boxes made of designated materials, sizes, and labeling. Individual products must be folded to the correct size and barcodes have to be positioned for robotic scanners. Large retailers can demand that the product be **floor-ready** (for brick and mortar) or ready for shipment (for direct to consumer) while keeping shipping costs down. They will charge the vendor if the product does not comply in every detail. Smaller companies are often excluded from selling to large retailers because they cannot comply with packaging requirements.

Figure 11.21
Garments are folded and bagged before being packed for shipment in this Villatex factory in Honduras. This factory makes intimate apparel for Vanity Fair and Victoria's Secret.

The packaging on some products can actually cost more than the product itself! Paper products might include hangtags, disclaimer tags, and support cardboard in shirts. Plastic products might include extra button bags, shipping bags, shipping hangers, and free gifts such as key chain fobs. Metal products might include safety pins, straight pins, etc. Most of the materials and methods for packing will be standardized and listed in a manual or technical bulletin. However, the technical designer may choose to include instructions or drawings that are exceptional or new.

QUALITY COMPLIANCE

Quality requirements may be stated as general standards for all products produced by the company, as in a firm's manual of standards, or when dealing with a single garment style, in the tech pack accompanied by an approved garment sample. These written materials become a part of the contractual agreement between the vendor and the firm ordering the garments.

Inspection of Textiles and Components

The first step in vendor compliance is the verification that the materials meet specified standards before production begins. Regardless of whether those materials have already been tested or certified by the vendor, factories generally conduct their own textile inspection, flagging flaws, dirt, varying widths, skew, shading, and other problems that will slow down manufacture, reduce yield, or affect the quality of the product (Figure 11.22).

Figure 11.22
Fabric inspection machines light the fabric from behind so that flaws and holes are visible.

In-Line Inspection

Random checks by QA (quality assurance) inspectors (in-process inspection) help reveal unexpected problems early in the process when change can be implemented quickly. At this point a few basic measurements should be checked to be sure that there are no issues with incorrect size labeling, cutting problems, errors in assembly method, or problems with materials such as shrinkage.

One hundred percent end-of-line inspections find errors in garments before they are moved from the sewing line to the finishing area. At this time flawed parts can be replaced or sewing can be corrected. This inspection should focus on compliance with the tech pack. The materials, components, and general construction of the garment should be verified before leaving the line (Figure 11.23).

- All components should be compatible: no pulling, puckering, or delamination of fusibles.
- Seams should be sewn with even seam allowances and with no twisting.
- Seams should match at intersections.
- All design elements should balance on the left and right side of the garment (e.g., collar points should match in size and shape; pockets should be level with each other).
- Fabric pattern should fall on the garment as required (e.g., plaids and stripes should match).
- Stitches should be neat and straight, with no ruptures or visible thread ends.
- Closures should be firmly attached, functional, and close with both parts matching.
- Random measurement checks help find errors in cutting, seaming, and labeling.

Final Inspection

Final inspection occurs after the garment is pressed, trimmed, and ready for packing (Figure 11.24). It is advisable to have the garments trimmed of all threads before inspection because final inspectors with trimmers in their hands will not be focusing on the whole product. It is not wise to pay inspectors on piece rate because they may pass products without looking carefully so that they make their rate. Productivity and quality can best be accomplished if the inspectors are given a **Standard Inspection Procedure (SIP)** for looking at the garment (Bubonia, 2015). For example, they might start at the top of the front, working their way down to the hem, and then flip to the back and repeat. At each section of the garment, they can look for issues that pertain to that part of the garment.

At this point, basic compliance regarding materials and construction should have been verified in earlier inspections. Now the inspector is looking for errors that show up once the garment is pressed, trimmed, and hanging. Even garments that will be packed flat are best inspected on tilted tables so that problems with cutting such as skew can be detected. In addition to finding anything that has been missed at

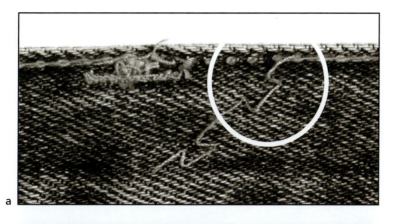

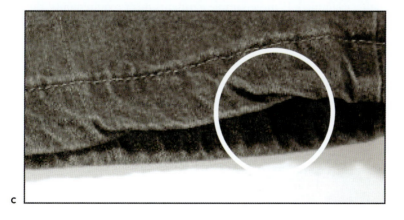

Figure 11.23
Common seam quality defects include **(a)** unraveling caused by a broken or skipped stitch, **(b)** restitched seams reflecting a "splice" in the stitch line where a thread broke or ran out during construction, and **(c)** a ropy hem caused by poor operator handling or too much pressure on the presser foot.

end-of-line review, the final inspector will look for dirt, oil, stains, flaws, and unclipped threads. Spot checks for measurements are also advisable.

For many of the criteria established in the tech pack, there are tolerances listed for accepting or rejecting a product. Perfection is not possible, so some variation will occur in the product yet still be within acceptable parameters. The tolerance is the difference between the allowable minimum and maximum on a process or finished measurements. Tolerances cannot be too rigid, yet some things such as the number of buttons are not flexible. Orders are usually written to compensate for expected problems and

Figure 11.24
Quality inspection: checking measurements as finished garments come off the production line at Gokaldas Exports factory in Bangalore, India.

human error. Some products, such as silk, have higher levels of expected defects, but an average level runs around 6 percent.

If the order is very large, a random sample of garments is pulled from the shipment and thoroughly examined. If these sample garments meet requirements, the entire lot is passed on for distribution; if flaws are found in the sample garments, the decision becomes more complex. A common practice is to increase the sample size to determine the extent of the problem. Some factories have highly standardized procedures for inspection such as *Sampling Procedures and Tables for Inspection by Attributes* provided by the American Society for Quality (ASQ, 2018).

There are many strategies for salvaging a delivery. The most extreme method involves inspecting 100 percent of the garments in the lot that contained defective garments and separating out the flawed pieces, sending them for repair or, if repair is not possible, removing the damaged garments and shipping "short." As soon as the factory knows that it may need to reduce the quantities to be shipped or ship substandard products, it must notify the client firm so they can work out a solution together. The client firm may have strategies for dealing with these challenges that the factory cannot imagine. Even with repair and replacement, one study calculated that waste from discarding products that cannot be made to first quality is roughly one percent of factory waste.

Dealing with Factory Rejected Product

If defective goods are found in a delivery from an offshore vendor, there are few remedies. Re-exporting, reimporting, and reshipping in both directions could take more time than most apparel delivery schedules allow for and more money than the value of the whole shipment. The client can ask for a rebate but given that every country has its own financial laws, this may not be possible. The cost of repair or loss can be deducted from future contracts if the production planners choose to preserve their relationship with the vendor. If not, the last resort is to find another vendor.

Some companies prefer to source their products onshore in order to avoid this issue. Making a claim or sending work back for repair within the same legal and financial systems and within close geographical proximity is obviously easier and faster.

SUSTAINABILITY

During the years when brands and retailers in developed countries increasingly sourced apparel products offshore rather than in local factories, they lost the ability to monitor compliance with their own standards. Losses from returns and mark-downs due to poor quality were offset by the low cost of labor. With ever-rising volume of online sales the cost of returns has made it impossible for brands to ignore consumer demand for reliable quality.

The plague of returns is prompting brands to work more closely with vendors, encouraging or even demanding that they put in place preventative measures to reduce the Cost of Poor Quality (Johnston, 2019). Such measures include:

- matching core competency of factory to product
- allowing new factories time to ramp up to expectations
- practicing partnership not policing
- requiring vendors to report quality issues immediately to brand and work together to solve
- reallocating resources to support vendors improvement
- increasing vigilance of sub-contractors
- improving competence of factory through training
- improving working conditions
- using data capture during production to drive improvement
- implementing continuous improvement strategies

Continuous improvement is a concept originally formulated by W. Edward Demming, one of the founders of modern quality assurance. It involves defining opportunities for improvement, testing solutions, measuring the impact and sharing the learning. The goal is to create a culture that engages and inspires. Continuous improvement is a core idea of production methods such as Six Sigma, Kanban, Kaizen, Toyota Production System (TPS), and Lean. Although these systems differ from each other, they share strategies and goals with the sustainability movement such as transparency, education, fair and equitable treatment of all stakeholders, and zero waste. Whether factories choose to adopt the principles of continuous improvement because they want to improve quality or efficiency, or both, they are also taking steps in the direction of more sustainable practices.

Case Study 11.1
Solving QR Code Labeling Challenges for SMEs through Collaboration

As recommerce grows as a business, brands are seeking ways to track products through their lifecycle from first sale to resale, reuse, and beyond. Major brands such as Adidas (Lijzenga, 2020) and Ralph Lauren (Young, 2021) have already adopted methods for implanting and tracking digital triggers. The most common is the QR code.

Can SMEs (Small and Medium-sized Enterprises) adopt lifecycle tracking easily? We asked a small batch manufacturer in Detroit, MI, USA to describe their experience when they decided to add QR codes to their customized tee shirt line. The team at The Industrial Sewing and Innovation Center (ISAIC) who worked on the challenge included Joseph Lybik, Sustainability Fellow; Anne Fitzpatrick, Marketing & Communications; and Jasmine Onianwa, Supply Chain Manager.

What were the marketing goals that ISAIC was hoping to accomplish by adding lifecycle tracking to their tee shirts?

AF: Our philosophy on sustainability at ISAIC has centered around what we call "Progressive Good." We know we can't be perfect, but we ask ourselves, how can we be better every day? Part of that is helping to raise awareness of the issues facing the apparel industry and solutions to help consumers make more informed choices. The QR code, which links the user to our web site, allows us an opportunity to share up-to-date information about the circular economy in general and specifically about how to care for the tee shirt in a sustainable way.

What were the sustainability goals that ISAIC was hoping to accomplish by adding lifecycle tracking to their tee shirts?

JL: Most brands do not know what happens to their products once they are sold. We wanted to start the process of tracking so that we could build a picture of the lifecycle of our products. We also wanted to provide our customers with support in the resale and reuse of our tee shirts.

How did you decide on QR codes as your digital trigger (rather than RFID or another method)?

JL: We started to work on this project in the middle of the pandemic. QR codes were becoming ubiquitous in retail settings to reduce the spread of the virus through touch and interaction. We knew that customers were becoming more familiar with them.

JO: I thought it was a great idea! I was familiar with getting nutrition information from food with QR codes and found it easy and engaging.

What choices did you discover when you looked for a QR subscription service?

Figure CS 11.1
Startup nonprofit Industrial Sewing and Innovation Center (ISAIC) in Detroit chose organic cotton jersey knit for their customized tee shirt line.

Figure CS 11.2
In order to support their sustainability method, they chose to insert a label with a QR code to guide customers to use the tee shirt responsibly and give them options for the participating in the long-term life cycle of the product in a circular economy.

JL: We discovered that we had two options. A static subscription provides a QR code that leads to a website with information that does not update. We chose a dynamic subscription because we knew that the landscape of recommerce was changing rapidly and we wanted to be sure to provide up-to-date guidance for our customers. We also wanted the flexibility to change the URL that the QR leads to in case we needed to change it for marketing purposes.

We also wanted a subscription service that would be around to support the link of the QR code to the URL. We looked for a service that had been around for a few years, that had clients like us, that was affordable and flexible. We chose uQR.me.

How did you decide how to attach the QR code in the garment?

JO: We have digital direct-to-garment printing capability, but it was not a good option for quality reasons, so we had to go with a sew-in label.

What challenges did you experience when you sought a supply chain partner for the sew-in labels?

JO: First we investigated purchasing our own label printer. The ROI for the machine was not a good decision at the time, so we looked at label suppliers.

Then we tried Avery Dennison, but their minimums were too high for our small, pilot program and their lead time was 6–12 weeks. That lead time included the development of the artwork which included the QR code itself. We wanted to get the program up and running sooner.

Detroit is a great place for collaboration and sharing of resources, so we reached out to SME colleagues who were more experienced in sourcing labels. Detroit Denim owner Brenna Wyatt suggested a supplier in Texas, the Scarborough Company. They were just getting into the QR code business, so they had some experience and were willing to work with us. They were able to offer low minimums (500 pieces) and very short lead times (days, not weeks) if we generated the QR code and sent them the artwork for the label. Although the labels cost $0.15 per piece we knew that the cost would go down once we had higher quantities.

Did you run into any issues with the quality of the labels?

JO: We did not anticipate the quality of the printing in relation to the fabric we chose for the label. There were two ribbon choices at the lowest cost, polyester satin, and a nylon plain weave. We chose the satin for comfort. We wanted the customer to keep the QR code throughout the lifecycle of the product, so we didn't want them to cut it out because it scratched. Unfortunately, the printing on the satin ribbon was not clear enough to be consistently picked up by the QR reader app. We had to scan all the labels and find the bad ones. Scarborough offered other options of both material and printing methods for our next orders.

How did the use of synthetic labels fit into the sustainability "story" of the ISAIC customizable tee? Will you be looking for an alternative?

JL: As with so many decisions about sustainability, it is virtually impossible to create a product with a purely circular story. Although we were sourcing US made organic cotton fabric, we knew that there were few options for cotton at end-of-life that were currently commercialized and widely available. We chose a trade-off strategy, using a QR code on a permanent, durable label (yes, made of polyester) in order to encourage the customer to resell, restore, and donate as long as possible. We will stick with this plan but also keep our eyes on developments for cotton end-of-life.

As major brands, SMEs and suppliers are continuing to experiment with best practices for digital tracking, they are contributing to the development of a "digital passport" that could be a unifying force to make everyone able to participate in the circular economy with ease (Lijzenga, 2020).

References

Lijzenga, C. (2020), "The future of garment technology in circular fashion," *Fashion United*, September 17. https://fashionunited.com/news/business/the-future-of-garment-technology-in-circular-fashion/2020091735503 (accessed April 4, 2021).

Fitzgerald, A. (2021), Interview, April 12.

Lybik, J. (2021), Interview, April 8.

Onianwa, J. (2021), Interview, April 5.

Scarborough, A. (2021), Interview, April 5.

Young, V. (2021), Ralph Lauren's Alagöz on Speed-to Market and Industry Collaboration. *Sourcing Journal: Sourcing Report*. https://sourcingjournal.com/report/sourcing-report-2021/ (accessed March 22, 2020).

uQR.me. (2021), QR solutions. https://uqr.me/qr-solutions/

SUMMARY

Quality is defined by customers' expectations. A technical designer can translate customers' needs into properties that can be specified and measured. Consistency in the organization and presentation of information in the tech pack reinforces the expression of standardized procedures and performance levels. Some information will be carried over from the design specs, such as the page header and the technical flats. The measurement chart will be updated with graded measurements for each size. Results from testing may demand increasing or decreasing measurements to accommodate shrinkage or stretching. Technical designers can anticipate questions from the marker maker and cutting room that will need clarification.

Some processes such as dyeing, printing, and pleating may be handled by specialists, and the tech pack may simply list the subcontractor's information. Because of the complexity of sewing assembly, a tech pack may include instructions about the finished product that guide the factory to use specific machinery or techniques to achieve the quality level demanded by the brand.

Bills of materials may be more or less detailed, depending on how much a brand relies on its vendors to supply the textiles and trims as part of a package. Each component will be described in its unique way, depending on its materials and method of fabrication. Of all the content in a tech pack, labels are the most regulated as to the information they must provide. Information about packaging may also be governed by rules from customers' warehouses.

Compliance with standards is a process that starts with inspection of the raw materials and continues with verification all through the manufacturing process. Final inspection should verify that everyone has done their job well. Practices that have been adopted by factories to improve quality and efficiency also contribute to sustainability of manufacturing processes.

KEY TERMS

bobbin

booked seam

bound seam

buck (utility press)

busted (pressed open, butterflied) seam

chain stitch machine

color blocked garment

continuous improvement

Cost of Poor Quality (COPQ)

coverstitch machines

cut order plan

edge finish

enclosed seam

fallout

flat seam

floor-ready

folder (assist)

implied warranty

labels

lapped seam

lockstitch machine

make

ornamental stitch

QR code

quality assurance

RFID tags

seam

seam allowance

seam classification

serging (overlock) machine

Standard Inspection Procedure (SIP)

stitch classification

stitch

superimposed seam

Tex

thread

under-pressing

written warranty

zero waste

DISCUSSION QUESTIONS

1. Think of a garment you have that you perceive as having a flaw. Describe the flaw and try to imagine when in the production process that flaw could have been detected and corrected. Start with testing of materials and end with final inspection. If you were the technical designer for this product, and the complaint about this product came to you, how would you avoid repeating the flaw in the future? Who would you inform? What procedures would you put in place so this flaw would not occur again?

2. Look in your closet and find a garment with labels. Search for labeling requirements in your own country. How compliant is this garment?

ACTIVITIES

1. Take a garment from your wardrobe. Using the guides from Appendices 11.1 and 11.2, list as many of the seams and stitches that you can find in the garment. Now reread the section "Commodity vs. Fashion Products." Decide whether your garment is more of a commodity or a fashion product. Justify your decision.

2. Look at the pages of the tech pack in Chapters 9 and 11. Imagine that you are a technical designer for the Beyond Design label and your boss has just asked you to make changes to the style found in figure 9.3 immediately. The buyer does not want the buckle closure on the belt and would rather replace it with two buttons. List the pages in the tech pack that would be affected and the changes that you would have to make.

STUD!O RESOURCES

- Take the chapter quiz with scored results and personalized study tips.
- Review glossary flashcards to build your vocabulary.

REFERENCES

American & Efird, Inc. (2009a), ISO Stitch Terminology. http://www.amefird.com/wp-content/uploads/2009/10/Stitch-Type-Matrix.pdf (accessed October 26, 2020).

American & Efird. (2009b), Seam Type. http://www.amefird.com/wp-content/uploads/2009/10/Seam-Type.pdf (accessed October 26, 2020).

American & Efird. (2016), Estimating Thread Consumption. http://www.amefird.com/wp-content/uploads/2012/09/Estimating-Thread-Consumption-.pdf.

American Society for Quality. (2018), ANSI/ASQ Z1.4-2003 (R2018) *Sampling Procedures and Tables for Inspection by Attributes.* Milwaukee: Quality Press.

ASTM International. (2020), ASTM D6193-20 Standard Practice for Stitches and Seams. https://www.astm.org/search/fullsite-search.html?query=ASTM%20D6193& (accessed October 26, 2020).

Bubonia, J.E. (2015), Apparel quality: A guide to evaluating sewn products. New York: Fairchild Books.

Common Objective. (2019), "Design Lessons in Zero Waste," *Common Objective,* June 19. https://www.commonobjective.co/article/design-lessons-in-zero-waste (accessed November 15, 2020).

Crosby, P. (1979), *Quality is Free*. New York: McGraw Hill.

Johnston, L. (2019), "How Untuckit, Toms, VF and More Tackle Quality Control at the Factory Level," *Sourcing Journal*, November 13. https://sourcingjournal.com/topics/sourcing/untuckit-soludos-toms -vf-cosabella-mud-apparel-footwear-quality-factory-170718/ (accessed October 21, 2020).

Lee, J., and Steen, C. (2019), *Technical Sourcebook for Apparel Designers 3rd Edition*. New York: Fairchild Books.

McQuillan, H & Rissanen, T. (2020), *Zero Waste Fashion Design*. New York: Fairchild Books.

ADDITIONAL RESOURCES

Brown, P., and J. Rice. (2014), *Ready-to-wear apparel analysis* (4th ed.). Upper Saddle River, NJ: Prentice-Hall.

Glock, R. E., and G. I. Kunz. (2005), *Apparel manufacturing: Sewn product analysis*. (4th ed.). Upper Saddle River, NJ: Prentice-Hall.

International Organization for Standardization (ISO). (1991a), ISO 4915:1991 Textiles – stitch types – classification and terminology. http://www.iso.org/iso/home/store/catalogue_tc/catalogue_detail .htm?csnumber=10932 (accessed October 26, 2020).

International Organization for Standardization (ISO). (1991b), ISO 4916:1991 Textiles – seam types – classification and terminology. http://www.iso.org/iso/home/store/catalogue_tc/catalogue_detail .htm?csnumber=10934 (accessed October 26, 2020).

Intertek. Textiles and Apparel. (2020), http://www.intertek.com/textiles-apparel (accessed February 26, 2020).

Kadolph, S.J. (2007), *Quality assurance for textiles and apparel* (2nd ed.). New York: Fairchild Publications.

Kincade, D.H. (2008), *Sewn product quality: A management perspective*. Upper Saddle River, NJ: Pearson Education.

Mehta, P. (1992), An introduction to quality control for the apparel industry. Milwaukee, WI: ASQC Quality Press.

Myers-McDevitt, P.J. (2015), *Complete guide to size specification and technical design* (2nd ed.). New York: Fairchild Publications.

Stitch Drawing		ISO 4915 Number	Common Application	Requirements	Stitch Description
Top View As Sewn	Bottom View As Sewn				
Single Thread Chainstitch		101	Basting Stitch for Tailored Clothing; Bag Closing	Specify SPI.	Stitch formed by a needle thread passing through the material and interlooping with itself on the underside of the seam with the assistance of a spreader.
Single Thread Chainstitch or Lockstitch Buttonsew, Buttonhole or Bartack	*304 Lockstitch is preferred when stitch security is a Must.	101 or 304	Buttonsew, Buttonhole, or Bartack	1)Buttonsew - specify stitches per cycle (Ex. 8,16, 32) 2)BH - specify length & width (1/2", etc.) 3) Bartack - specify length & width of tack.	Knit Shirts - Buttonhole length generally is 1/2 inch, is placed horizontally, with approximately 85-90 stitches
Single Thread Blindstitch	No stitch visible on the Bottom or Outside of Sewn Product	103	Blindstitch Hemming, Felling, Making Belt Loops	Specify 1) SPI 3 - 5 SPI 2) Non-skip or 2 to 1 skipped stitch	Stitch is formed with one needle thread that is interlooped with itself on the top surface of the material. The thread passes through the top ply and horizontally through portions of the bottom ply without completely penetrating it the full depth.
Lockstitch - Most Common of All Stitches	Bobbin Thread on Bottom	301	Topstitching, Single Needle Stitching, Straight Stitching	Specify SPI.	Stitch formed by a needle thread passing through the material and interlocking with a bobbin thread with the threads meeting in the center of the seam. Stitch looks the same top & bottom.
Zig Zag Lockstitch		304	Intimate Apparel, Athletic wear, Infantwear, Exercisewear	Specify 1) SPI 2) Throw or width Zig-Zag (1/8", 3/16", 1/4")	Stitch is formed with a needle and a bobbin that are set in the center of the seam and form a symmetrical zig-zag pattern. Also, used to identify bartacking and lockstitch buttonsewing and buttonholing.
Chainstitch	Looper Thread on Bottom	401	Single Needle Chainstitch - Mainseams on Wovens	Specify SPI.	Stitch formed by 1-needle thread passing through the material and interlooped with 1-looper thread and pulled up to the underside of the seam.
Zig Zag Chainstitch	Looper Thread on Bottom	404	Zig-Zag Chainstitch for Infantwear and Childrenswear: Binding, Topstitching, etc.	Specify 1) SPI 2) Throw or width Zig-Zag (1/8")	Stitch is formed with a needle and a looper that are set on the underside of the seam and form a symmetrical zig-zag pattern.

Stitch Drawing		ISO 4915 Number	Common Application	Requirements	Stitch Description
Top View As Sewn	Bottom View As Sewn				
2 Needle Bottom Coverstitch	Looper Thread on Bottom	406	Hemming, Attaching, Elastic, Binding, Coverseaming, Making Belt Loops	Specify 1) Needle spacing (1/8", 3/16", 1/4") 2) SPI	Stitch formed by 2-needle threads passing through the material and interlooping with 1-looper thread with the stitch set on the underside of the seam. Looper thread interlooped between needle threads providing seam coverage on the bottom side only.
3 Needle Bottom Coverstitch	Looper Thread on Bottom	407	Attaching Elastic to Men's & Boys Knit Underwear	Specify 1) Needle spacing (1/4") 2) SPI	Stitch formed by 3-needle threads passing through the material and interlooping with 1-looper thread with the stitch set on the underside of the seam. Looper thread is interlooped between needle threads providing seam coverage on the bottom side only.
2 Needle Chainstitch with Cover Thread	Looper Thread on Bottom	408	Attaching Pocket Facings to Jeans & Chino Casual Pants		Stitch formed by 2-needle threads passing through the material and interlooping with 2-looper threads with the stitches set on the underside of the seam. A top spreader thread is interlaced on the top side of the seam between the two needle threads.
2 Thread Overedge	Single "purl" on Edge	503	Serging & Blindhemming	Specify 1) Width Bite (Ex. 1/8", 3/16", 1/4") 2) SPI.	Stitch formed by 1-needle thread and 1-looper thread with purl on edge of seam for serging or blindhemming ONLY.
3 Thread Overedge	Common Overedge Stitch	504	Single Needle Overedge Seaming	Specify 1) Width Bite (Ex. 1/8", 3/16", 1/4") 2) SPI.	Stitch formed with 1-needle thread and 2-looper threads with the looper threads forming a purl on the edge of the seam. For overedge seaming and serging.
3 Thread Overedge	Double "purl" on Edge	505	Serging with Double purl on Edge	Specify 1) Width Bite (Ex. 1/8", 3/16", 1/4") 2) SPI.	Stitch formed with 1-needle thread and 2-looper threads with the looper threads forming a double purl on the edge of the seam for serging ONLY.
Mock Safety Stitch	2 Needle Overedge	512	Seaming Stretch Knits, Wovens	Specify SPI.	Stitch formed with 2-needle threads and 2 looper threads with the looper threads forming a purl on the edge of the seam. 512 – right needle only enters the upper looper loop. Stitch does NOT chain-off as well as 514 Stitch
2 Needle 4 Thread Overedge	2 Needle Overedge	514	Seaming Stretch Knits, Wovens	Specify SPI.	Stitch formed with 2-needle threads and 2 looper threads with the looper threads forming a purl on the edge of the seam. 514 – both needles enter the upper looper loop. Preferred over 512 Stitch because it chains-off better.

Stitch Drawing		ISO 4915 Number	Common Application	Requirements	Stitch Description
Top View As Sewn	Bottom View As Sewn				
4 Thread Safetystitch		**515** (401+503)	Safetystitch Seaming Wovens & Knits	Specify 1) Needle spacing & bite - Ex.: 1/8"- 1/8", 3/16" - 3/16" 3/16" – 1/4" 2) SPI	Combination stitch consisting of a single-needle chainstitch (401) and a 2-thread Overedge stitch (503) that are formed simultaneously. Uses less thread than a 516 stitch; however, many manufacturers prefer a 516 stitch.
5 Thread Safetystitch		**516** (401+504)	Safety Stitch Seaming Wovens & Knits	Specify 3) Needle spacing & bite - Ex.: 1/8"- 1/8", 3/16" 3/16" 3/16" – 1/4" 4) SPI	Combination stitch consisting of a single-needle chainstitch (401) and a 3-thread Overedge stitch (504) that are formed simultaneously.
2 Needle 4 Thread Coverstitch		**602**	Binding A Shirts, Infants Clothing, etc.	Specify 1) Needle spacing (Ex: 1/8", 3/16", 1/4") 2) SPI	Stitch formed with 2-needle threads, a top cover thread and a bottom looper thread.
3 Needle 5 Thread Coverstitch		**605**	Lap Seaming, Coverseaming, Binding on Knits	Specify 1) Needle spacing (Ex: 1/4") 2) SPI	Stitch formed with 3-needle threads, a top cover thread and a bottom looper thread.
4 Needle 6 Thread Coverstitch	Flatseamer/Flatlock	**607**	Flat or Lap Seaming Knit Underwear, Fleece, etc.	Specify SPI	Stitch formed with 4-needle threads, a top cover thread and a bottom looper thread. Preferred over 606 stitch because machines are easier to maintain.

SEAMS DRAWINGS - INDEX

By Operations	Seam	Pg. #	By Operations	Seam	Pg. #
Attach & Edgestitch (usually 301 stitch)	SSae	5	Joining Bib to Overall	LSar	5
Bag Seaming - 401	SSd	6	Joining Bib to Overall	LSi	5
Bagging Welt Pockets on Trousers (usually 301)	SSc	6	Joining plies	SSv	6
Binding (2 needle - clean finish - 301 or 401)	BSe	2	Lap Seaming	LSa	4
Binding (2 needle - selvedge edge - 301 or 401)	BSd	2	Lap Seaming - top edge turned under	LSb	4
Binding (bottom coverstitch - 406 stitch)	BSb	2	Lining Cuffs for Dress Shirts	SSbc	6
Binding (clean finish - usually 301)	BSc	2	Making Belt Loops (for jeans, chinos)	EFh	2
Binding (coverstitch - 602 or 605)	BSa	2	Making Spaghetti	EFu	3
Binding (Mock clean finish binding - 2 operations)	BSg	2	Making Strap or Belt (1 needle)	EFj	3
Binding (Mock clean finish binding - 2 operations)	BSj	2	Making Strap or Belt (1 needle)	EFp	3
Binding (selvedge edge binding - 301 or 401)	BSa	2	Making Strap or Belt (1 needle)	EFy	3
Bolt-end seaming (501 - single thread overedge)	FSf	5	Making Strap or Belt (1 needle)	EFz	3
Butt seam & tape - generally 301 lockstitch	SSf	6	Making Strap or Belt (2 needle - 2 piece)	EFad	3
Centerplait (Cut-on centerplait - 401/301 stitch)	EFv	2	Making Strap or Belt (2 needle - 2 piece)	EFn	3
Centerplait (Set-on - generally 401 stitch)	LSm	4	Making Straps, Belts (hidden stitch w interlining)	SSaz	6
Cord seam only - generally 301 or 401 stitch	LSq (b)	4	Patch Pocket Setting - 301 stitch	LSd	4
Coverseaming only (straddle stitch - 406 stitch)	SSh (b)	6	Pocket Set (hem & set front pocket - jeans)	SSI	6
Crotch seam (Flatseaming with 607 stitch)	FSa	5	Pocket Set (patch pkt. - 2 operations)	LSs	4
Crotch seam (Flatlock seaming with 606 stitch)	LSa	4	Runstitch & Topstitch - generally 301 stitch	SSe	5
Crotch seam on Jeans - usually 301 stitch	LSas	4	Seam & Cord Seam	LSq	4
Darting (panel not cut - generally 301 stitch)	OSf	5	Seam & Topstitch Seam	LSq	4
Deco Stitching	OSa	5	Seam with Piping	SSk	5
Elastic attaching - 3 or 4 needle 401 stitch	SSt	6	Seam with Piping & Topstitch	SSaw	5
Elastic attaching - 406 or 407 stitch - underwear	LSa	4	Seam with Piping & Topstitch	SSav	5
Facing to front with Zipper	SSj	5	Seaming & Coverseaming	SSh	6
Feiling (Mock Felled Seam)	SSw	6	Seaming (1st part of 2 part operation)	SSa	5
Felling or felled seam (2 or 3 needle 401 stitch)	LSc	4	Seaming (General)	SSa	5
Flatlock seaming (with 606 stitch)	FSa	5	Seaming then Taping Seam	SSag	6
Flatseaming (with 607 stitch)	FSa	5	Seaming with Stay Tape	SSab	5
French Seam	SSae	5	Serging - generally with 503, 504 or 505 stitch	EFd	3
General Seaming	SSa	5	Sleeve Set (2 operations)	LSr	4
Hem Seaming (clean finish)	SSp	6	Stripes attaching - 2 needle - either 301 or 401	SSat	6
Hem Seaming (raw edges)	SSn	5	Taping Edge - generally 301	SSaa	5
Hem Serging	EFe	3	Topstitch only - 2nd part of 2 part operation	SSag (b)	6
Hem with Elastic	EFf	3	Topstitch only - 2nd part of 2 part operation	SSe (b)	5
Hem with Elastic (2 needle)	EFg	3	Waistbanding (1 piece - binding - jeans)	BSc	2
Hem with Elastic (2 needle)	EFq	3	Waistbanding (1 piece)	LSk	4
Hem with Piping	LSn	4	Waistbanding (2 piece band)	LSg	4
Hemming - 2 Ndl. hemming on knits	EFa Inv.	2	Waistbanding (2 piece w interlining)	LSj	4
Hemming - blindhemming w overedge	EFc	2	Waistbanding (with Elastic - 3 or 4 needle)	SSt	6
Hemming - blindstitch hemming (clean finish)	EFm	2	Waistbanding (with Elastic - 406 / 407 stitch)	LSa	4
Hemming - blindstitch hemming (serged or pinked)	EFl	2	Waistbanding (with "stitch-in-a-ditch" topstitching)	BSf mod	2
Hemming - Tunneled Elastic (2 needle)	EFr	3	Yoking (1 operation - w folder)	LSe	4
Hemming (clean finish)	EFb	2	Yoking (1 operation - wo folder)	LSf	4
Hemming (selvedge edge)	EFa	2	Yoking (2 operations)	SSq	4
Join & Tape Front (flatseamer)	LSz	4	Mock Felled Seam	SSw	6

Seam Drawing	751a Number	ISO 4916 Number	Common Application	Requirements	Seam Drawing	751a Number	ISO 4916 Number	Common Application	Requirements
	BSa	3.01.01	Binding Carpets, etc. with selvedge edge binding	1) Specify the Binding finished width.	Topstitch hidden in seam line	BSf mod		"Stitch in a Ditch" - Topstitching Waistband with stitch line on top of previous seam line.	1) May require special PF with Guide so stitch is totally hidden
	BSa	3.01.01	Setting collarettes & Sleeve Binding on Undershirts, etc. Usually sewn with a 602 or 605 bottom coverstitch	1) Specify the needle spacing if 602 or 605 stitch is used; 2) specify the Binding finished width.	Sewn in 2 Operations	BSg	3.14.01	Mock Clean Finish Binding	1) Specify width of Binding
	BSb	3.03.01	Setting collarettes on T Shirts; binding legs and fly on knit briefs, etc. Usually sewn with a 406 bottom coverstitch	1) Specify the needle spacing if 406 stitch is used (Ex: 1/8", 3/16"); 2) specify the Binding finished width.	Sewn in two operations	BSj	3.05.06	Mock Clean Finish Binding	1) Specify the width of the binding. Example: 1/2" Binding.
	BSc	3.05.01	For setting sleeve facings to shirts, piping edges of outerwear, etc. Can be sewn with a 301 lockstitch or 401 Chainstitch	1) Specify the width of the binding. Example: 1/2" Binding. 2) Requires a binding folder.	Waistbanding on Jeans	BSc	3.05.01	For setting waistbands to jeans, etc. Can be sewn with a 401 chainstitch or 301 lockstitch	1) Specify needle spacing; and 2) Specify the width of the binding. (Example: 1-3/8" and 1-5/8" Binding.) 3) Requires a binding folder.
	BSd	3.01.02	Seaming with selvedge edge binding on Outerwear	1) Specify the needle spacing; and 2) Width binding. Example: 3/8" needle spacing and 1/4" Binding. 3) Requires a binding folder.		BSe	3.05.05	Seaming and binding on Outerwear	1) Specify the needle spacing; and 2) Width binding. (Example: 3/8" needle spacing and 1/4" Binding.) 3) Requires a binding folder.
2 Ndl. Hem	EFa	6.02.01	Hemming Selvedge Edge Shirt Front	1) Specify width of hem.	Blindstitch Hem	EFl		Hemming Dresses, Slacks, Coats, Bedspreads. Generally sewn with 103 blindstitch	1) Specify Width Hem
	EFa Inv.	6.02.07	Hemming Tee Shirts, Polo Shirts, etc. Generally sewn with a 406 stitch.	1) Specify width of hem; and 2) Needle Spacing. (Ex. 1" hem with 1/4" needle spacing).	Belt Loops	EFh		Making Belt Loops for Jeans and Casual Pants, Shorts, Etc. Usually sewn with 406 stitch.	1) Specify needle Spacing & 2) Width of Belt Loop. (Ex. 1/4" needle spacing and 3/8" width belt loops) 3) Requires belt loop folder.
Clean Finish Hem	EFb	6.03.01	Hemming Shirts, Jeans, Shorts, etc.	1) Specify width of hem. 2) Generally a hemming folder is required or a hemming PF.	Blindstitch Hem	EFm		Hemming Dresses, Slacks, Coats, Bedspreads. Generally sewn with 103 blindstitch	1) Specify Width Hem
Blindhemming	EFc	6.06.01	Hemming bottoms of Tee Shirts, Undershirts, etc. Usually sewn with a 503 Stitch.	1) Specify width Hem. (Ex. 1" hem); 2) Generally a hemming guide is required.	Centerplaiting	EFv		Cut-on Centerplait. Generally sewn with 2 rows of 401 stitch. (See also LSm - set-on centerplait)	1) Specify needle spacing; and 2) Width centerplait. (Ex. 1" needle spacing & 1 1/2" centerplait. 3) Requires centerplait folder.

Seam Drawing	751a Number	ISO 4916 Number	Common Application	Requirements
Serging				
	EFd	6.01.01	Serging Pants Panels, Flys, Facings, etc.	1) Specify width Bite. (Ex. 3/16")
	EFe		Serging edges of napkins, sheer curtains, etc.	1) Specify width Bite. (Ex. 3/32") 2) A hemming P.F. is required.
Serge & Hem				
	EFf	7.24.02	Hem and Insert Elastic to Infants Panties, etc.	1) Specify the width of hem
Hem & insert				
	EFg	7.24.03	Hem and Insert Elastic to Infants Panties, etc.	1) Specify the needle spacing; and 2) Specify the width of hem. (Ex. 1/4" needle spacing and 1/2" width hem.) 3) Requires hemming folder & elastic guide.
	EFq	7.26.05	Hem and Insert Elastic to Infants Panties, etc.	1) Specify the needle spacing; and 2) Specify the width of hem. (Ex. 1/4" needle spacing and 1/2" width hem.) 3) Requires hemming folder & elastic guide.
	EFr	7.26.05	Hem and Insert Elastic to Infants Panties, etc.	1) Specify the needle spacing; and 2) Specify the width of hem. (Ex. 1/4" needle spacing and 1/2" width hem.) 3) Requires hemming folder & elastic guide.
Tunnelled Elastic				

Seam Drawing	751a Number	ISO 4916 Number	Common Application	Requirements
Making Spaghetti				
	EFu	8.07.01	Making straps. The stitch is hidden and not visible.	1) Specify with of strap.
	EFj	8.05.01	Making straps or belts with clean finish.	1) Specify with of strap.
	EFn	8.19.01	Making straps or belts with clean finish.	1) Specify needle spacing; and 2) Specify with of strap.
	EFp	8.06.01	Making straps or belts with clean finish.	1) Specify with of strap.
	EFad	8.17.01	Making straps or belts with clean finish with interlining.	1) Specify with of strap.
	EFy	8.03.03	Making straps or belts with clean finish.	1) Specify with of strap.
	EFz	8.03.04	Making straps or belts with clean finish.	1) Specify with of strap.

Seam Drawing (category)	751a Number	ISO 4916 Number	Common Application	Requirements
Lap Seaming	LSa	2.01.01	Attaching knitted cuffs - generally sewn with a coverstitch - 605 or 607	1) A seaming guide or trimmer is used to keep the edges even. 2) Specify Needle Spacing. (Ex. 1/4" ndl spacing)
	LSb	2.02.01	Not as common as LSq where the piece is attached and then corded or topstitched.	1) Specify the dimension from stitching to edge of top ply. Example: 1/8" header.
Felled Seam	LSc	2.04.06	Seaming Jeans, Shirts, Jackets, etc. Generally with a two or three needle 401 Chainstitch	1) Specify needle spacing & seam width. (Ex: 1/4 needle spacing w 3/8" seam width). 2) A felling folder with correct capacity is required.
Patch Pocket Setting	LSd	5.31.01	For setting patch pockets, flaps, pocket facings, etc.generally with a 301 Lockstitch	1) Specify margin (example: 1/16" or 3/32"). 2) A pressure foot with a yielding section is used to maintain a uniform margin from the stitch to the edge.
Patch Pocket Setting	LSs	2.05.02	For setting large patch pockets on Suit Coats, Overcoats and Jackets	1) Specify margin (example: 1/16" or 3/32"); 2) A folder consisting of upper and lower scrolls are required.
Yoking	LSe	1.22.01	Seaming yokes to back on Shirts or Blouses in one operation. Not as common as SSq.	1) 1st Operation - highly skilled operation; 2) Specify margin (example: 1/16" or 3/32").
Set-On Center Plait	LSm	7.62.01	Attaching Set-On Centerplaits to Shirts and Blouses	1) Specify margin: 1/16" or 3/32"); 2) Specify width of Centerplait (Ex. 1 1/2") 3) Requires a Folder with Top Strip Folder with
	LSn		Not Common	
Joining & Taping	LSz	2.14.02	Joining & Taping Fronts of Knit Briefs & Thermal Underwear	1) Generally done on a 607 Flatseaming machine with or with the upper spreader thread. 2) Requires an upper Taping Folder.
Lap Seaming / Attaching Elastic	LSa	2.01.01	Setting Elastic to panties or briefs - 406 or 407 stitch; Attaching knitted cuffs - generally sewn with a coverstitch - 605 or 607	1) A seaming guide or trimmer is used to keep the edges even. 2) Specify Needle Spacing. (Ex. - 1/4" ndl spacing)
Seam & Cord Seam	LSq	2.02.03	Sideseam on jeans; Chinos; Jackets; etc.	1) 1st Operation - specify seam width; 2) 2nd Operation - specify number of needles (1, 2, 3) and needle spacing.
	LSk	7.32.03	Waistbanding on Pajamas; Making Rod Pkt.on Curtains & Shower Curtains, etc.	1) Specify needle spacing and 2) Tape width.3) A folder combining a turn down folder and strip folder is required.
Two piece Waistband	LSg	7.57.01	Attaching a Waistband to Chinos or Work Pants	1) Specify the needle spacing; 2) width of W.B.; 3) A folder consisting of an upper strip folder and lower strip folder is required.
Two piece Waistband	LSj	7.76.01	Attaching a Waistband to Chinos or Work Pants	1) Specify the needle spacing; 2) width of W.B.; 3) A folder consisting of an upper strip folder with guide for interlining, and lower strip folder is required.
	LSf		Seaming yokes to back on Shirts or Blouses in one operation.	1) Specify margin from stitch line to edge (example: 1/16" or 3/32")
	Lsas		Crotch Seaming on Jeans & Chinos	1) Specify needle spacing - (Ex. 1/4")
	LSbj	5.30.01	Facing front pockets on jeans	1) Facing should be serged prior to being set.
Sleeve Set	LSr	2.06.02	Setting Sleeves on Dress Shirts or Blouses	1) 1st Operation - specify the seam width - a folder may be required; 2) 2nd Operation - specify topstitch margin.

Seam Drawing	751a Number	ISO 4916 Number	Common Application	Requirements
	LSl	2.28.03	Joining the Bib to Pants of Bib Overall in 1 operation.	1) Needle Spacing and 2) Strip width are required.
	LSar		Joining the Bib to Pants of Bib Overall in 1 operation.	1) Needle Spacing and 2) Strip width are required.
Sewing Darts	OSf	6.05.01	Dart panel on Slacks, Chinos, Blouses, etc.	1) Specify width of Dart and length. (Ex. 3/8" wide and 3" long)
General Seaming	SSa	1.01	Most common seam construction for both wovens & knits.	1) Seam Margin must be specified to maintain fit. 2) A seaming guide or trimmer is used to keep the edges even.
Seaming & Taping	SSab		Joining Shoulders with Stay Tape; Attaching Facing to Jacket Front with Stay Tape	1) Specify width of Stay Tape; 2) Specify Seam Margin
Attaching Tape to Edge	SSaa		Attaching a Zipper tape to Fly Facing; Attaching Stay Tape to Armhole	1) Specify width of tape; and 2) Specify seam margin
	SSe	1.06.02	For making collars & Cuffs on Shirts; attaching front pockets, bagging front pockets, setting fly on Chinos, etc.	1) Seam Margin must be specified on both 1st & 2nd operations. 2) A seaming guide is used to keep the edges even. 3) There is a turning process between 1st & 2nd process.
Runstitch & Topstitch; French Seaming	SSae	1.06.03	For edgestitching front facings on Jackets, Dresses.	1) Seam Margin must be specified on both 1st & 2nd operations. 2) A seaming guide is used to keep the edges even. 3) There is a turning process between 1st & 2nd process.

Seam Drawing	751a Number	ISO 4916 Number	Common Application	Requirements
Flatseaming	FSa	4.01.01	Flatseaming Underwear, Fleese, Exercisewear, etc. Generally sewn with a 607 stitch.	
Bolt End Seaming	FSf		Bolt-End Seaming with a 501 Stitch	
Decorative Stitching	OSa	5.01.01	Decorative Stitch Back Pockets on Jeans; Saddle Stitching	1) Specify Design Pattern with dimensions of stitch location
	SSj	1.11	For attaching a Zipper Tape between the Shell and Facing.	1) Seam Margin must be specified to maintain fit; 2) A seaming guide is used to keep the edges even. 3. A zipper Foot may be required.
Seam with Piping	SSk	1.12	For seam apparel, furniture with piping in seam	1) Seam Margin must be specified to maintain fit. 2) A seaming guide is used to keep the edges even. 2) May require a Foot with grooved bottom if cord is used in piping.
Seam, Fold, & Topstitch	SSax	1.18/1.19	For seaming and piping edges of pillow; Pajama Tops, etc.	1) Specify Seam Margin; 2) Topstitch Heading / Margin; and 3) a Folder may be used to make the piping w/ or wo cord
Seam, Fold, & Topstitch	SSaw	2.19.02	For seaming and piping edges of cushions; pillows; attaching yokes to backs on casual shirts, dresses, etc.	1) Specify Seam Margin; and 2) Topstitch Heading / Margin
Hem Seam	SSn	1.20.01	For seaming fabrics that may be susceptible to Seam Slippage	1) A hemming folder or guide is generally used. 2) Hem width should be specified. Example: 3/8" Hem.

Seam Drawing	751a Number	ISO 4916 Number	Common Application	Requirements
Seam, Fold & Cord	SSq	2.42.04	For attaching Yokes to Back or Shoulder Joining on Shirts, Blouses, etc. Similar to LSe but done in 2 steps.	1) A swing out marging guide is required along with a Yielding Presser Foot. 2) The correct PF with the preferred margin guide should be used (example: 1/16 or 3/32 inch).
Butt Seam & Tape	SSf	4.08.02	For Butt seaming & Taping heel seams on Shoes, etc.	1) Seam margin must be specified on 1st Operation. 2) Needle spacing and Tape width specified on 2nd operation.
Seaming & Coverseaming	SSh	4.04.01	For coverseaming knit tops, undergarments to reenforce the seam and give it a decorative appearance	1) Suggest using a 504 for 1st operation and 406 with 1/4" needle spacing for 2nd operation; 2) Seaming guide on Coverseaming machine.
Seaming, then Taping Seam	SSag	4.10.02	For taping the shoulder and neck of Tee Shirts	1) The finished width of the Tape and 2) needle spacing on the taping operation is generally required. 3) A taping guide folder is required fold and guide the tape on to the seam.
Setting Stripes Shirts, Shorts, etc.	SSat	5.06.01	For attaching stripes to Shirt Fronts, etc.	1) Specify Tape Finished Width and 2) Needle Spacing. (Ex.: 3/4" Tape with 1/2" needle spacing)
Mock Felled Seam	SSw	2.04.06	For Side Seaming Shirts, Blouses, Dresses, etc.	Manual method for making a felled seam. 1) Hem ply 1 around ply 2 - Specify Hem width and 2) Topstitch seam - Heading /Topstitch Margin
Mock Felled Seam	SSw (b)		For Side Seaming Shirts, Blouses, Dresses, etc.	Manual method for making a felled seam. 1) Lay ply 1 on top of ply two with edges uneven; 2) Fold and Topstitch - Heading /Topstitch Margin
	SSd	1.07	Not common.	1) Manual method for making a felled seam. 2) Specify Hem width and 3) Heading /Topstitch Margin
	SSv	5.01	Not Common	

Seam Drawing	751a Number	ISO 4916 Number	Common Application	Requirements
	SSp	1.21.01	For seaming fabrics that may be susceptable to Seam Slippage	1) A hemming folder is generally required. 2) Hem width should be specified. Example: 3/8" hem.
Hem Seam	SSs	7.09.01	Hemming and attaching zipper tape.	1) Specify width of tape; and 2) Specify seam margin.
	SSt	7.09	For seaming knitted or woven elastic to Boxers, Gym Shorts	1) Specify Width of Elastic; 2) Usually 2, 3, or 4 rows of 401 chainstitch are used to make this seam - Specify Needle Spacing. (Ex.: 1 1/4" Elastic with 4 rows 1/4" needle spacing)
Attaching Elastic	SSbc	1.03.01	Attaching Lining to Cuffs for Shirts & Blouses	1) Specify the Width Hem, if necessary.
Lining Cuffs	SSb	1.04	Not common	
	SSaz	8.11.01	Making Straps, Belts, etc.	1) Specify finished width. 2) This seam is made on a special "spaghetti" machine.
	SSl	1.08	For setting front pockets on Jeans	1) A hemming folder is used to hem the bottom ply uniformly. 2) Hem width should be specified. 3) If more than one needle, specify needle spacing (ex. 1/4")
	SSc	1.06.01	Not common. SSe is more common.	

PART 4

PRODUCTION PLANNING

CHAPTER 12

DEVELOPING SUPPLY CHAIN PARTNERSHIPS

"Chasing the cheapest needle has long since fallen by the wayside as a sustainable way forward for sourcing; instead, quality, efficacy and proximity to the end consumer will continue to win out." TARA DONALDSON *(SOURCING JOURNAL, 2020)*

OBJECTIVES

- To understand that the apparel industry has been undergoing a transformation from a "design-make-sell" paradigm to "design-sell-make."
- To recognize the various methods for finding supply chain partners
- To distinguish between types of supply chain partnerships
- To identify criteria for selecting vendors who are able to adapt production methods to support D2C supply chain requirements
- To identify sources for assessing human resource conditions and policies that support reliable and ethical production within a country
- To identify economic indicators that indicate whether the business climate within a country will support supply chain partnerships
- To identify criteria that demonstrate that a country's infrastructure is stable and capable of supporting textile and apparel sourcing partnerships
- To understand the constantly changing context and complexity of global trade relations
- To recognize various methods for tracing the origin of materials, the purpose of compliance certification and to support progress toward Sustainable Development Goals

SUPPLY CHAIN PARTNERSHIPS

The apparel industry's sourcing practices are undergoing increasing scrutiny from consumer activism and investigative journalism. Brands face damage to brand image and cancel culture if they cannot fully trace activities along their supply chain. A *design-make-sell* sourcing environment has created unprecedented waste, pollution, and human exploitation. Stakeholder demand for ethical design and production, coupled with new technology that facilitates traceability and transparency is driving a supply chain transformation to a *design-sell-make* model. This transformation requires a shift in priorities. Rather than seeking out vendors who can supply goods for the cheapest costs, brands are seeking partnerships who can collaborate and conduct business with transparency and ethics.

In a *design-make-sell* model, decision making starts with market research, trend forecasting and design research. Sourcing specialists may be brought into early planning stages to consult about availability of new materials or skills. Their role is not to advise or collaborate, but to produce whatever is required by merchandisers and designers. They use their understanding of the technical demands of the product to find factories with the appropriate skills and machinery. When obstacles arise, they can suggest substitutions of materials or changes in production methods that solve problems without compromising the design of the product. They constantly update their knowledge of trade rules, shipping routes, and internal conditions in multiple countries in order to discover and select vendors who offer the lowest costs and shortest turnaround times.

Many brands have instituted Corporate Social Responsibility (CSR) policies and have engaged in monitoring activities for decades but still have fallen short of being able to track the activities of suppliers up and down the supply chain. For this reason, they have started to narrow their vendor base and are increasingly turning to partners who can help them select components produced in ethical conditions. Stronger relationships with vendors allow for more collaborative decision making during the design process that takes advantage of the vendor's knowledge of ethically sourced materials and efficient production methods. Digital tools help partners share information as well as improve efficiency and shorten turnaround time, allowing brands to control costs without compromising ethical standards.

Finding Supply Chain Partners

The first step that brands must take in developing supply chain partnerships is to find partners who are willing to collaborate and share their ethical values. The application of technology is breaking down barriers, helping brands and supply chain partners find each other.

Trade Shows

Hundreds of international and regional trade shows organized by companies that specialize in mounting large exhibitions bring brands into contact with suppliers. Some shows such as Yarnex (India), Pitti Immagine Filati (Italy), and SpinExpo

(Paris, New York, Shanghai) focus on upstream businesses such as fiber and yarn. Other shows such as Techtextil North America and ISPO (Germany, China) feature finished textiles for specific sectors such as the outdoor industry. Other shows such as The London Textile Fair serve a more generalized fashion market (Apparel Entrepreneurship, 2020).

The role of the in-person trade show is in transition. Digital platforms designed for suppliers to offer their products and services have been available and continue to improve. Until the COVID-19 pandemic, digital platforms had been used primarily as marketing support for trade shows. Because most in-person trade shows were cancelled in 2020, trade show companies such as Kingpins, Messe Frankfurt, and Liberty Fairs partnered with software companies to launch fully digital trade shows. The success of these shows proved to many vendors and clients that they can conduct business virtually.

It is likely that trade show companies will build on their success and invest in developing shows that are primarily digital, with longer selling periods, value-added webinars, and other educational resources. In-person shows will no doubt continue, but with less emphasis on sales and more as networking forums for discussing issues and opportunities for suppliers to showcase innovation (Warren, 2020).

The scope of digital platforms is opening the way for trade fair organizers such as Messe Frankfurt France to work on creating marketplaces where exhibitors from multiple trade shows can interact with buyers. These proposed interactive environments will provide not only descriptions of products and services but all the criteria needed to make good business decisions such as minimums and turnaround times, as well as lists of certifications to guide ethical choices. Interactions conducted on such a platform can provide data and analysis from which to improve relationships between brands and vendors and to assist in matchmaking. It is hoped that by extending the buying period of a digital trade fair, beyond the two or three days of an in-person event, strong relationships can form and flourish (Fiber2Fashion, 2020). Digital platforms provide opportunities for smaller companies and startups who might not have had the ability to attend an in-person trade show to get a foothold in the market (Nishimura, 2020).

Some governments or regional trade associations organize trade shows to showcase suppliers in their own countries or regions. For example, Indian Synthetic & Rayon Textiles Export Promotion Council (SRTEPC) hosts textile shows not only in India, but also in developing markets such as Ethiopia (Fiber2Fashion, 2017). These regionally sponsored shows can offer an opportunity for brands to get to know the scope and capabilities of vendors more deeply. SRTEPC also sends delegations to international trade shows (Figure 12.1).

Other Resources

In response to consumer demand for transparency and collaboration, brands are increasingly willing to share information about sourcing partners. For example, Primark publishes its Global Sourcing Map, showing their vendors listed along with

Figure 12.1

Countries with national trade delegations or trade organizations will send representatives to textile and apparel trade shows to promote the skills and resources of their local businesses. This booth at the International Trade Malaysia (INTRADE 2011) Exhibition in 2011 in Kuala Lumpur, Malaysia, is presented by the India Trade and Promotion Organization, the Synthetic and Rayon Textiles Export Promotion Council of India, and regional Chambers of Commerce and Industry. The goal is to promote trade for many businesses, not just one.

contact information and data about the factories (Primark Stores Ltd., 2020). The Open Apparel Registry aggregates factory lists from brands such as Primark into one interactive open-source map with contact information and affiliation (Friedman, 2018) (Figure 12.2).

Small companies can search online sites such as Apparel Search, which is managed by a network of apparel industry experts. Trade associations, such as the American Apparel and Footwear Association (AAFA), compile and make lists of suppliers that they share with members (American Apparel and Footwear and Association, 2021). Commercial sites such as Global Sources include images of factories and ratings. Alibaba offers product development services as well as factories all over the world with low minimums and affordable prices.

Selecting Partner Relationships

There are a variety of ways to structure sourcing partnerships. Each varies in its level of collaboration, transparency, and control in terms of sustainability of resources and the ethical treatment of people.

Licensing

For an established brand, a low-risk way to add brand extensions to the product mix is to source products through licensing. A **licensee** provides all services to create and distribute a product, including design, development, manufacturing, marketing, and sales. A brand will license its trade name, design characteristics, and logo to the maker under contract and will receive a royalty. Both parties win. The brand gets to sell proven products with its own brand signature in new markets; the licensee increases sales of its own products because of the brand's cachet (Figure 12.3). The brand relies entirely on the licensee to handle compliance with social responsibility issues. Licensing is the least collaborative and transparent of business relationships.

Sourcing Agent / Full Package

Sourcing through agents is a good option for companies that want to focus their attention on their core competencies of marketing and design. A **sourcing agent** manages and delivers full package products, providing all the services necessary for production, including sourcing of fabrics and trims, product testing, color matching, sample making, grading, marker making, cutting, garment assembly, finishing, shipping, and export. Full package contracting places the burden of production financing on the vendor.

Li & Fung, one of the largest sourcing agents in the world, supplies full package products to Kohl's, Carter's, Niki, Target, Benetton, Nautica, Roberto Cavalli, St. John, and many more (Figure 12.4a). Other large agencies include Mast Global Fashions, Lever Style, William O. Connor, and Young One. Such agents charge 7 to 10 percent for their services. Large agents tend to have high minimums, but they also offer a wide range of suppliers from which to choose and have robust compliance departments. Independent agents can provide support for companies with smaller quantities, but they may not be able to provide the same broad range of materials, skills, or oversight as larger agencies (Figure 12.4b). Sourcing agents can be found at trade fairs, through professional associations, and on social media sites.

Agents provide the day-to-day management of the supply chain, which may include goods and services from multiple countries and regions. They overcome communication/language issues and navigate cultural differences. They apply knowledge of internal government regulations and export requirements. For example, an agent in Hong Kong may facilitate

Figure 12.2
Open Apparel Registry is an interactive open-source map that represents aggregated lists of suppliers from industry stakeholders. The entries for each facility show their credentials and with whom they are affiliated. (Open Apparel Registry 2021).

Figure 12.3
Disney's Mickey Mouse licensed character motifs are featured on the runway at Jean-Charles Castelbajac RTW show.

a

b

Figure 12.4a
Li & Fung with its main offices in Hong Kong is one of the largest apparel full-package sourcing agents in the world.

Figure 12.4b
Art Atlas is a full package contracting firm in Peru that offers full package design, patternmaking, cutting, and manufacturing services. They are a small niche agent that specialized in sustainable products.

the sourcing of shell fabric from Japan, lining from Taiwan, interlining from Hong Kong, zippers from Shanghai, and production in Shenzhen. Among the many benefits of working with an agent is that it greatly reduces the time needed to establish supply chain relationships abroad. Compliance monitoring may be difficult. Agents may provide monitoring, but can it be trusted? Brands may monitor compliance themselves or send independent monitoring agencies, but will they be able to identify all links in the supply chain or be able to monitor them all?

OEM (Original Equipment Manufacturing)

Under **OEM (original equipment manufacturing)** contracts, the brand retains more responsibility for technical planning and design than with full package contracting. It will source materials and create samples, patterns, and markers, as well as provide written standards, assembly instructions, and materials specifications. The OEM vendor sources and finances materials from specified sources while providing cutting, sewing, finishing, and packing. This model has become common with vendors in Bangladesh, Indonesia, Sri Lanka, and Mexico (Gereffi & Frederick, 2010). In relationships with OEM partners, a brand can be involved in the sourcing of materials and the treatment of people not only in the production factory but in suppliers' facilities. The brand can not only expect increasing levels of transparency in its dealings with the factory, but also support its attainment of goals.

CMT (Cut, Make, and Trim)

Under **CMT (cut, make, and trim)** contracts, the company provides the designs, patterns, and markers and selects, purchases, and arranges delivery of fabric and decorative trims. The contractor cuts, assembles, and finishes the garments. Contractors charge for production labor, thread, basic trims, and overhead. CMT allows control of the design, patterning, grading, marking, and materials selection, but risks poor sewing quality, late delivery, and intellectual property theft. CMT is more common in countries where technical skills are less well developed or where trade agreements demand that fabric is sent from the United States. Because the brand has total control over the supply chain and has direct involvement with the factory, it can collaborate with the factory to meet standards of sustainability and treatment of workers.

Direct Sourcing

When a company obtains its products by **direct sourcing**, it does not use an agent or intermediary. The sourcing professional seeks out factory capacity through personal networking, the internet, or sourcing fairs. The company can select from a range of vendors—from cut, make, and trim factories to full package facilities. The costs are less because there are no agent fees to pay; on the other hand, there is no oversight or support. US firms that utilize direct sourcing for the majority of their production include Walmart, Gap, Nike, VF Corporation, and PVH Corporation, although many of these firms also utilize sourcing agents for a portion of their **sourcing mix**. When sourcing directly, these very large companies with multiple brands can have close involvement with materials sourcing and labor relations.

Offshore Facility and Joint Ventures

When US firms build their own offshore production facilities, they are taking advantage of less expensive labor sources abroad while increasing the company's control of the production process, quality, and scheduling. However, they carry a great deal of risk and responsibility. Initial investment costs are high in obtaining a building, bringing in equipment, and training staff. Finding American managers willing to relocate and run an offshore facility may be difficult. Relying on local management brings its own issues of loyalty and communication. Owning a plant locks a company into a fixed asset. A sudden change in the host country's political climate can end favorable tax breaks or concessions. If the market for the firm's product changes overnight, it may be difficult to quickly get new machinery brought in to convert to new production methods. Opening offshore plants in free trade zones avoids some of these risks. In **free trade zones**, a piece of property owned by a host government is set aside for foreigners to conduct business with freedom from import duties, relaxation of some local regulations and taxes, relaxed export procedures, and added security.

A slightly less risky alternative to owning offshore production facilities is a **joint venture**. A joint venture entails the shared ownership of a facility with a business based in another country. In some countries, joint ownership is required. Offshore partners understand the local culture and legal context. Control of production and quality can be maintained while some of the risks to the foreign investor can be avoided. The initial investment cost is lower, startup time is reduced, and local access is improved. Brands that have full or joint ownership of the businesses that produce their products have the highest level of control over transparency and social responsibility.

A mix of partnership options is common for many companies (Figure 12.5). They may license sunglasses or fragrance, produce their signature lines in their own factories, send out simpler garments to CMT factories where costs are low and high skill is not needed, and have the bulk of their product made through full package sourcing agents.

Figure 12.5
When choosing a sourcing option, a product development company will balance the degree of control they have with the overall cost of goods.

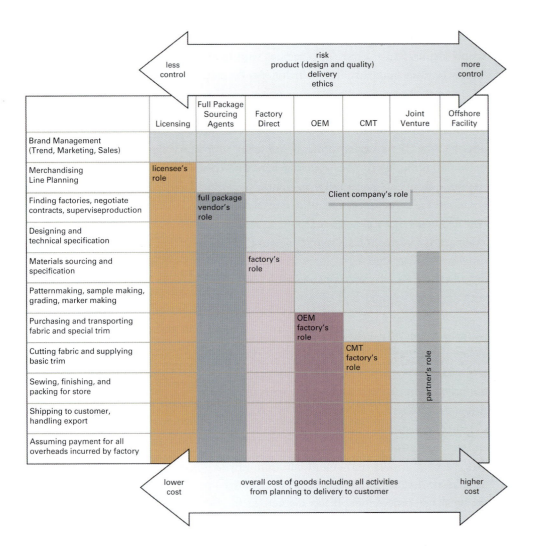

In times of economic crisis, the commitment to partnership can be tested. In a severe crisis a brand may not be able to sell inventory and may not have the liquidity to pay vendors for incoming orders. The brand has a responsibility to pay the partner for the services it has provided. Consumers watch as brands make the choice whether to work out financial remedies with sourcing partners so that they can continue to operate or leave them with the financial burden. Brands that do not treat their partners responsibly face the possibility of damaged brand identity and sales.

Criteria for Selecting Partners

Consumers are driving the rapid expansion of the Direct-to-Consumer (DTC) model of retail distribution and production. DTC brands want to order small quantities to test the market and then be able to reorder quickly. In response to the competition posed by DTC brands, retailers and other brands are also reducing order sizes and days-to-delivery. They expect suppliers to fulfill their orders without increasing costs or risking social responsibility obligations. Brands and retailers seek partners who can evolve to meet their needs.

Minimums and Turnaround Time

Traditional sewing factories are organized to produce mass quantities of apparel products. Their **minimum order quantities (MOQs)**, the smallest order a supplier can make and still make a profit, range from thousands to tens of thousands of units. Their turnaround times (the time it takes from the day that an order is started by the factory until it is shipped) range from weeks to months. They employ assembly line models such as the **progressive bundle system** in which small parts are completed first, and then attached to larger sections that are finally assembled into a whole garment. The operators in a bundle system are paid by the piece based on standardized rates. This system encourages the operators to become specialists in one operation and complete their tasks quickly. Although the bundle system can be very efficient when supported by automated and computerized equipment it can also be inflexible. As retailers and brands reduce order sizes, large factories are challenged to find ways to produce constantly changing small batch orders, ranging in size from one unit to dozens with turnaround times of a few days.

Factories can use **modular manufacturing systems** in which operators work in teams on small quantities of product, often conducting multiple tasks at one machine. Quality assessment takes place during assembly, so errors are identified and corrected quickly, rather than passed on down the line to be found and repaired during final inspection. Payment is made to the team and divided among the members, calculated by the number of garments completed to standard and by the level of training the operator has achieved. This system produces high quality, high value products with great flexibility and fast response time.

Some factories have expanded their sample rooms into small workshops that make small quantities. When orders increase, they can be transferred to mass production lines. Other factories set up partnerships with smaller factories that are already expert in small batch, offering a steady supply of orders and the benefits of being part of a larger business with access to easier credit and better pricing from materials suppliers.

Technology

Advances in technology can help factories produce small batch or customized products rapidly. Brands can offer basic products such as shirts or knit tops with a range of customizable features such as color, size, and design details. Using 3D design and PLM applications, unique products can be transferred digitally, one by one, to be cut with single-ply cutting machines (see Figure 12.6c). The individual garments can be assembled in modules, small workshops, or with a **Unit Production System (UPS)**. Regardless of how many units are in an order, each garment moves through the factory one at a time. All the parts of one garment are clipped onto a single hanger that is suspended from a maze of overhead rails. The hangers are directed digitally to each operator's station in sequence of operations. After an operator performs a task, the hanger is whisked away on the transporter to the next station until the garment is complete. A UPS shortens turnaround time by reducing many steps needed to organize, mark, and move cut work around the factory. Because all pieces are tracked in the system, it is possible to know exactly where an order is and troubleshoot bottle necks to meet deliveries (see Figure 12.7b).

Figure 12.6a-c
Technology has been incorporated into every aspect of apparel production factories.

a

Materials and finished products are increasing being tagged using RFID and QR codes as well as barcodes to facilitate end-to-end tracking with digital applications such as blockchain.

b

Fabric spreading is accomplished by laying multiple plies of fabric on a table. Although this can be done by hand, the speed and quality of the lay (the stack of fabric) increases with a mechanical spreader. The edges line up and the tension is consistent. Computerized counting ensures the number of ply is correct. Adding electronic sensors can also detect flaws and reduce waste when fabric needs to be spliced (overlapped).

plastic film spread on top of lay

cutting head on gantry driven by software

stack of fabric (lay) is under plastic film

perforated table allows the compressor to pull air from the lay

c

Automated systems add high speed and precision to the cutting process. When fabric is spread, it is laid out on perforated tables. A blast of air raises the lay so it can be slid onto a cutting machine. A layer of plastic is spread over the lay and a vacuum sucks the air out of the fabric, compressing the fabric into a board-like stack. The cutting head floats above the lay on a gantry driven by the computer software. No marker is needed. The cutting is done by a very thin blade or a laser beam. This entire cutting table is on a track and can be moved to the next table where fabric is being spread.

a

• •

Figure 12.7a-c
Technology improves speed and accuracy.

Pneumatic assists (forced air and vacuum) drive many functions in an automated factory. The blue coiled tubes above these machines drive automatic lifting and dropping of the presser foot, thread trimmers, and needle positioners. The sewing machine operator signals these functions with the foot pedal, freeing hands for more skilled tasks. Pneumatic fingers on robotic machines pick up pieces of fabric with suction and move them with puffs of air.

In this image the machines have panels which house digital controls that can be programmed to change stitch length, ease, and other parameters.

b

This factory has a Unit Production System. The garments pieces are suspended from carriers that hang from a rail above the heads of the sewers. The carrier stops at each station for the next operation and then is lifted back onto the rail and carried to the next person. Note the operator is standing to increase efficiency and promote better health.

c

This machine is fitted with a device that is folding a strip of bias cut fabric before it is stitched into a binding along the front edge of a garment. The folder does the job of a third hand, allowing the operator to work quickly and accurately.

Fully automated sewing lines using robots, such as Lowry Sewbots®, exist but are not yet in widespread use (SoftWear, 2021). They offer speed and consistency for commodity products produced in bulk, but they are not yet able to sew entire garments on demand, customized for individual customers. However, much of the technology employed in sewing robots is already in use. Forced air and vacuums are essential tools in speeding up the movement of mechanical parts and for moving fabric into and out of machines without human touch. Cameras, lasers, and optical sensors guide fabric evenly through the machine and machine learning helps feeding mechanisms readjust plies under the needle when fabric stretches or pulls. (Figure 12.7a). Mechanical aids such as the folder in Figure 12.7c add a "third hand" and allow an operator to set a binding or band evenly and quickly. Many of these assists are only suitable for mass production because they are designed especially for large quantities of one product. However, as machine learning is increasingly incorporated into automated sewing, machines are becoming more and more adaptable and flexible.

Location

In order to decrease turnaround time and reduce delays some production factories are buying out their suppliers or building their own materials factories. Some brands are placing orders in factories geographically closer to the markets they serve (near-shoring) such as OnPoint Manufacturing in Alabama, USA to reduce turnaround times, reduce hidden costs from tariffs, freight delays and storage of unsold inventory (Sourcing Journal, 2021).

Flexibility

Whether brands want to source through agents or build their own networks of suppliers, they require a mix of partners that can offer a range of product categories. Their suppliers will need to be able to accommodate the use of raw materials and components from multiple sources, domestic or imported as the market changes.

Working Conditions

Sourcing professionals may be challenged, on their own, to find ethically managed factories that are also affordable. They can seek vendors who are certified by agencies such as FLOCERT (Figure 12.8). These agencies will check that the management is delivering basic amenities such as fresh air, adequate sanitation, clean water, reasonable shift length, and civil treatment. Although the work environment is heavily conditioned by social, cultural, and political forces within a given country the management can reverse negative influences by treating its workers justly and equitably. Some certification agencies have resources to help factories improve conditions and achieve compliance.

SELECTING SUPPLY CHAIN PARTNERS IN A GLOBAL ENVIRONMENT

In recent years, dramatic global changes in political, economic, and social conditions have prompted brands to adopt supply chain diversification as a part of their strategic plans (Figure 12.9). As factors that were once favorable within a country start to shift,

Figure 12.8
This factory in India is a fair trade factory certified by FLOCERT, which not only monitors vendor activities for compliance with standards such as healthy working conditions and fair wages but also helps factories identify areas for improvement and offers training so that they can achieve their goals.

brands want to rely on established relationships with factories in other countries. As brands broaden their base of supply chain partners, they must expand their understanding of conditions within a country and its relationships outside its borders.

Very large firms may hire consulting companies to prepare research about which country to work in, but such reports are usually proprietary and seldom shared. Research companies may initiate their own investigations and sell reports for thousands of dollars to bigger firms. Such **country reports** are sometimes available with subscriptions to databases in colleges and public libraries. Industry associations and news outlets such as Fiber2Fashion, Just Style, the *Sourcing Journal*, and the National Retail Federation publish white papers that are available for a fee, but they often offer abstracts and overviews, as well as digests of current news, for free.

Country reports are available at no cost from well-funded large institutions that have the resources to gather vast amounts of data and pay for research. Privately funded foundations, such as the World Economic Forum, and internationally funded sources, such as the United Nations, the World Bank, and the World Trade Organization, publish periodic reports aggregating data and providing analysis from their unique perspectives. Trade delegations, consulates, and embassies from many countries promote their industries by providing reports, data, contacts and setting up sourcing visits. For example, the US government publishes international trade figures from the Department of Commerce International Trade Administration Office of Textiles and Apparel (OTEXA), as well as reports by the US Trade Delegation, the State Department, and other agencies. International nongovernmental organizations (NGOs) such as the International Labor Organization (ILO), the World Health Organization (WHO), and Transparency.org report on ethical issues.

Human Resources

The apparel industry is labor intensive. The ability of people to do their work with ease and productivity is essential to successful business. Every country has a different understanding of the value of its human resources and supports their development its own way.

Figure 12.9

Countries who were dependent on China for most of their offshore apparel production started a process called "diversification" in the mid-2000s, increasing sourcing from other countries such as Bangladesh and Vietnam.

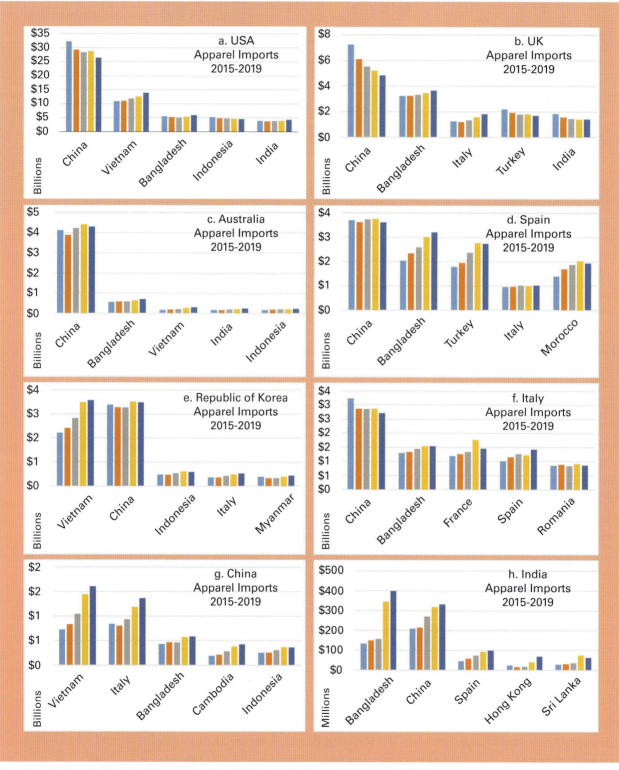

Based on data from UN Comtrade International Trade Statistics Database. All charts are in US$.

Efficiency

For any company, income must be greater than expenses in order to stay in business. Cost containment is crucial. In developed national economies where the cost of labor and materials are relatively stable, cost control centers on efficiency, the reduction of waste through the application of technology, advanced design, good management, and lean systems. Apparel companies in developed countries look for production facilities offshore in less developed countries, where they can benefit from cheaper labor costs. Unfortunately, in the process they often encounter hidden costs due to late deliveries, uneven quality, and lost materials. Sourcing professionals look for countries with lower wages that nevertheless have cultural or social assets that can contribute to efficiency, such as equitable relations between genders, openness to change, fluid social structures, punctuality, and willingness to solve problems. Global organizations such as the World Economic Forum (WEF), publish open-source white papers on topics such as gender equality. Their annual Global Gender Gap Report measures fourteen parameters to create an overall score so that one country's progress can be measured against another (World Economic Forum, 2020).

Labor Relations

In most of the countries where wages are low, there is little institutional support for workers' rights and benefits. The presence of labor unions can be of benefit as a way for workers to get better conditions in an orderly way. If the local government opposes labor organizations, disruption can occur (Figure 12.10). Sourcing specialists look for a balance between affordable labor costs and a climate where workers' conditions, though perhaps less than ideal, are in a process of steady improvement in which the local government has recognized the need for change and dedicated resources to

Figure 12.10
Garment workers march in the streets of Dhaka, Bangladesh, demonstrating to express their demands for higher wages.

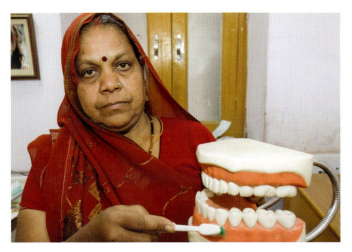

Figure 12.11
General health, reproductive health, and malnutrition are only some of the issues for which the Barefoot College provides training and support. This woman is only one of many Barefoot Dentists and Doctors who provide affordable healthcare services in rural India.

implementing it. The International Labor Organization (ILO) publishes annual World Employment and Social Outlook Trends (ILO, 2020a), Global Wage Report (ILO, 2020b) and periodic World Social Protection Report (ILO, 2017). These reports show trends, not just snapshots, of how countries are progressing in labor relations.

Public Health/Safety

Poor health and safety standards are bad business. Absenteeism and turnover resulting from illness and injury cause communication breakdowns, inconsistent standards, and a need for remedial training—all of which translate into lost time and money. Public health requires the availability of clean water and the maintenance of sanitary conditions as well as access to doctors, medicine, and education about diet, food storage, and disease prevention (Figure 12.11). The Global Health Observatory website run by The World Health Organization (WHO) provides ranked lists of countries searchable by thousands of indicators such as government spending on improving water and sanitation, number of prenatal visits, immunizations, etc. They also provide publications, fact sheets, and graphics on topics such as current trends in urban health and disease control (Global Health Observatory, 2021).

Education

The lack of universal primary education (which includes a fundamental knowledge of reading, writing, math, and civics) can prevent a country from entering the global economy. In many countries, children work rather than attend school (Figure 12.12). Lack of higher education can keep a nation from competing effectively in a marketplace driven by ever-changing demands. Countries that enter the apparel market by offering low prices based on cheap, unschooled labor find that their workers quickly gain communication and technological skills and are drawn away to better paying jobs. In order to demand higher prices to afford to pay competitive wages, vendors must provide training so that their workers can handle increasingly sophisticated production methods, technology, and diversified products. Managers, accountants, purchasing agents, client liaisons, and all employees need continual education to perform their jobs consistently and productively. World Population Review provides country comparisons based on level of schooling attained by percentage of population and test scores (World Population Review, 2020). The World Atlas publishes its List of Countries by Literacy Rate (Burton, 2020).

Business Climate

Sourcing professionals must be aware of business conditions that could threaten manufacturing and the movement of goods. They will also want to be alert to opportunities and changes that will impact their sourcing partners favorably.

Figure 12.12
This young boy is a laborer in a factory making women's clothing in a factory in Dhaka, Bangladesh.

Financial System

Even the most politically stable country can be disrupted economically when outside forces cause currency fluctuations or sudden changes in the balance of trade. In developing economies, apparel manufacture and export have a stabilizing influence, as they increase income and attract investment. Countries that establish substantial bank regulation, standardize taxation, and crackdown on corruption tend to improve predictable revenues and prevent conditions that trigger inflation and the devaluation of currency. TheGlobalEconomy.com allows the user to select hundreds of indicators and 200 countries to compare. Indicators include, "Governance and the Business Environment, "Banking System Access and Depth", and Banking System Efficiency and Stability" (The Global Economy, 2020).

Access to Capital

Public debt strangles countries as they recover from recession, natural disasters, public health crises, military conflict, and other major disruptions. Private individuals also struggle to pay off personal debt, so they do not save or spend as they would in a healthy economy. Banks are reluctant to loan people money until debts are paid back. Without cash, consumers do not shop. Without demand, banks are reluctant to make new investments in business. Lack of available capital and unfavorable interest rates can prevent businesses from investing in technology, education, and other factors that support domestic and export business. A factory that makes goods for export depends on numerous other suppliers and support services. If all businesses in a country are struggling with cash flow, then export manufacturers, even when they have access to capital, are negatively affected. The website *Trading Economics* provides data per country about capital flow and loans to the private sector (Trading Economics, 2021). The Organization for Economic Co-operation and Development (OECD) offers similar data as well as reports summarizing and analyzing financial flow. Some reports are free, some are available for a fee (OECD, 2021).

Access to Markets

When countries or regions have apparel production factories that serve well-established domestic retail markets or growing export markets, they tend to have people available to work who have relevant skills and the ability to discern quality standards demanded in a competitive environment. Such places are also likely to have supply chains in place for sourcing apparel materials and components (Figure 12.13). If information about the apparel and textile industry is not available from country reports published by proprietary or open sources, sourcing specialists may look for reports specifically about the industry in publications from local associations such as Sistema Moda Italia (SMI) or Clothing Manufacturers' Association of India (CMAI), United States Fashion Industry Association (USFIA), or local apparel industry publications such as *Textile Today* from Bangladesh.

Technology Penetration

Today the entire global textile and apparel system is dependent on the Internet. PLM systems are becoming standard communication methodology. Countries that cannot provide consistent access to high-speed internet connections and consistent energy

Figure 12.13
As the economies of developing countries expand, so do the local consumer markets. This shopping center sale in Ho Chi Minh City in Vietnam is a sign that the local population is used to selecting products in a competitive market. These local cultural habits translate into consciousness of quality and cost in the factory, a hidden asset to look for when sourcing.

supplies cannot compete. Without real-time connections to customers on the other side of the globe, the inability to communicate changes to orders rapidly can hurt quality and threaten on-time deliveries.

Innovation

Innovation may be the result of a cultural attitude of problem solving and collaboration which can spark and support fresh, creative solutions to challenges. The proximity of dynamic industries to each other in a region can create synergies that stimulate creativity. One measure of innovation is the number of patents filed and in force in a country in one year. The World Intellectual Property Organization (WIPO), an agency of the United Nations, provides this and more. Innovation can also be nurtured by local and international government, agencies or associations through grants and projects. The United Nations tracks Gross Domestic Expenditure on research and Development (GERD) as a percentage of Gross Domestic Product (GDP) (UNData, 2014).

Public Institutions

Public institutions are unique to each country. They may have been created in accord with religious practices or ideological goals. They may be traditional or newly instituted. They may be easy to navigate or opaque and frustrating. Sourcing professionals will make decisions based on an understanding of how institutions impact their brand's business and ethical goals.

Government

Reliable deliveries cannot be maintained in a setting plagued by political or economic instability. Governments range from dictatorships, where one person makes all of the decisions, to democracies, where people elect leaders and decide on laws. Dictators can provide stability until people rise up and throw them out. Democracies can be stable for many years but then also go through periods of turmoil. While extreme political unrest can lead to destruction of property and violence toward people, less drastic changes of government can also be disastrous when new regimes seize property, change regulations that impact the process of export, raise taxes and fees, and so forth. Weak governance, lack of transparency, and widespread corruption can cause hidden costs, delays, and general lack of respect among managers and workers (Figures 12.14a and b). Choosing countries in which to produce garments is not a matter of choosing one kind of political system over another; rather it requires a deeper understanding of the forces within the country that support or impede foreign investment and trade.

Figure 12.14a
The collapse of the Rana Plaza building on April 24, 2013.

Figure 12.14b
Media coverage put a human face to statistics and reports about unacceptable working conditions in Bangladesh. When the building collapsed, 1,137 people died, and 200 were missing.

a

b

The Fund for Peace has identified twelve indicators of a government's vulnerability at various stages as it is becoming healthy or starting to collapse. FFP tracks these indicators over time and provides tools to use them to compare countries (Fragile States Index, 2021).

Infrastructure

Water is necessary for many steps in the processing of textiles and apparel. However, water is becoming an increasingly scarce resource and its cost and scarcity will likely continue to increase. Brands that are committed to protecting the environment seek partners who operate in countries that can demonstrate progress toward reducing water use, keeping water clean during manufacturing, and managing water reclamation (Figure 12.15). The World Health Organization (WHO) and The United Nations Children's Fund (UNICEF) monitor progress that countries are making toward the achieving Sustainable Development Goal 6, "Ensure availability and sustainable management of water and sanitation for all" through the Joint Monitoring Program (JMP) for Water Supply and Sanitation. The JMP provides searchable data by country about sanitation, drinking water, water treatment and other indicators. (United Nations, 2021a).

Energy to run machines, vehicles, and technology for making products can be derived from burning fossil fuels such as petroleum, gas, or coal by harnessing the flow of water, rays of the sun, the power of the wind or controlled nuclear reaction. Countries that have their own energy resources can run factories without importing fuel, but those without resources must import. Working with partners from countries that are highly dependent on energy imports can be risky. Costs incurred by importing

Figure 12.15
The Noyyal River in Tirapur, India, is awash with effluent from local textile dyeing plants. Efforts to control pollution have been effective in bigger factories that can afford treatment but smaller firms still dump untreated water.

energy rise and fall with the market. Shortages can interrupt production and communication. Apart from avoiding business risk, brands may also consider damage to their image when they work in countries that do not have policies for increasing use of renewable energy. The World Bank in cooperation with the International Energy Agency, and the Energy Sector Management Assistance Program, support the Sustainable Energy for All (SE4ALL) database that tracks energy production, consumption, and trade indicators by country (World Bank, 2021).

A well-developed transportation system is essential for apparel manufacturing to thrive. Few factories are located near all of the materials needed to produce garments. People need to travel to and from work. The condition of railways and roads to and from ports, other factories, warehouses, and homes is critical to the predictable and safe movement of goods and services. Many developing countries do not have the resources to build and maintain efficient networks of roads and railways. They may not be able to buy and maintain fleets of buses, train cars, build fuel stations, repair shops, and parts distributors. Indicators such as the quantity and quality of roads, railways, vehicles, and ports can be compared by country on websites such as *The Global Economy*.

The degree to which **e-government**, the use of web-based communication that governments use to provide or support the delivery of services and information, is fundamental to the success of businesses. The UN tracks nations' e-government improvement from year to year and provides a comparison tool and country reports (United Nations, 2021b).

Import/Export Context

Imports are goods or services that are produced or performed in one country and brought in by businesses or residents of another. **Exports** are goods or services that are produced or performed in one country and sold outside of its borders (Amadeo, 2020).

Shipping

The distance from an exporter's location to the importer's destination will impact lead time. **Lead time** is the length of time spent from the date that an order is placed for a product until it is the hands of the customer. Lead time includes turnaround time for production as well as logistics such as order processing and shipping. Shorter lead times reduce costs in two ways. Most companies borrow money to finance production. Every day that a product is sitting on a dock or in a ship, the company is not delivering and not getting paid and is still paying interest on loans. Shorter lead times also allow a brand to respond to fashion trends rapidly, capturing the market while the demand is high or reducing orders when a trend is no longer popular.

In 2007, all major shipping lines adopted a **slow steam policy** in order to reduce fuel costs and limit greenhouse gas emissions, adding as much as ten to fourteen days to the time a product spends in a container during a trans-Pacific voyage. Shipping time is approximately sixteen days from Shanghai to Long Beach, USA, five days to Vietnam, and twenty-one days to Italy. These times do not include any of the many possible delays that a shipment may encounter along the way (Figure 12.16).

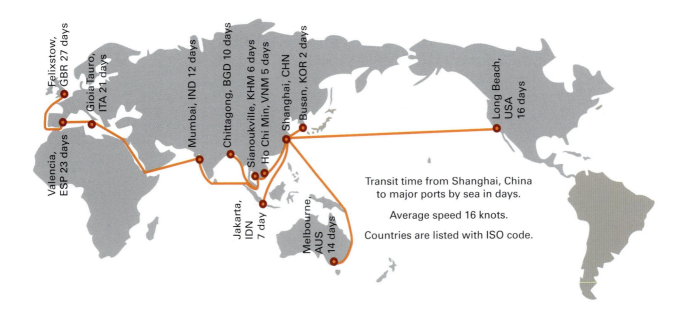

Transit time from Shanghai, China to major ports by sea in days.

Average speed 16 knots.

Countries are listed with ISO code.

Figure 12.16

Transit times from Shanghai, China. Times are quoted as minimum time. All shipping takes longer than the times listed. Goods sit on the dock while awaiting loading and transfer from one conveyance to another. Refueling can take days while vessels wait in line. Shortages of containers can delay shipping for weeks.

(SeaRates, 2021)

Trade Relations

Trade is conducted by businesses, each of which has its own financial goals and strategies. When a business trades with another within the same country, their relationship is governed by internal laws. When a business trades with another outside of its own country, the relationship is governed by rules and restrictions determined by each country.

Some businesses within a country may expect their government to keep tariffs low so that they can offer products at competitive prices. Some citizens may expect their government to protect their jobs from the threat of wage competition from foreign labor. Governments may adopt protectionist trade policies, such as **tariffs** (import and export taxes or duties) or **quotas** (limits that nations impose on the quantity of goods that can be imported during a specific period) that restrict foreign businesses from having a competitive advantage in domestic markets.

Other businesses within the same country may expect that their government will work on their behalf to open up markets in foreign countries. Some citizens may expect to benefit from open access to imported goods and services at low prices. Governments may enter into **trade agreements** with other countries to lower or remove barriers to each other's markets.

When one government enters trade negotiations with another, they must both navigate the conflicting demands of all segments of their populations. Each partner country must give up some level of autonomy or authority over their internal governance to gain a foothold in the other partner's markets. Over time, trade partners build trust that others will not take unfair advantage of privileged access and achieve the gains that they had hoped for. Partners may continue to extend their trading relationship toward ever deeper **economic integration**. This process may start when trade partners lower tariffs or quotas for some products and may expand to unrestricted movement of goods, creation of shared financial institutions or even a common currency (Balassa, 1961).

Trade Agreements

One way of understanding trade agreements is by the number of countries who have signed them. **Unilateral trade agreements or actions** (one country adopting a trade behavior toward another without reciprocity) may be instituted by prosperous nations who wish to offer trade advantages to developing ones. Unilateral actions may also include tariffs, quotas, or bans as a form of sanctions imposed by one country against another for perceived violations of prior agreements or intolerable behavior. For example, in January 2021, the US banned all imports from the Xinjiang Uyghur Autonomous Region in northwestern China to protest China's alleged use of enforced labor to suppress the fair market value of goods produced in the region (Chua, 2021). **Bilateral trade agreements** are struck between two nations or between a nation and a **trade bloc** (inter-governmental trade organization) for mutual benefit in trade. Multilateral trade agreements involve many countries and/or trade blocs. They provide powerful competitive advantage to members (Amadeo, 2020).

The **General Agreement on Trades and Tariffs (GATT)** was a multilateral trade agreement set up in 1948 by twenty-three nations to eliminate tariffs and quotas. The **World Trade Organization (WTO)**, established in 1995, expanded the scope of the GATT rules, formulating the largest set of multilateral agreements in the world, **WTO Rules of Global Trade**. In 2020 the WTO had 164 member countries (22 countries were pending). Although trade agreements do exist outside of its structure, it accounts for 98 percent of world trade. It deals not only with goods, but also services. It is the only global entity dedicated entirely to facilitating trade. It has its own institutions, including mechanisms to rule on disputes between trading partners.

WTO is a voluntary organization that functions through negotiation, it does not govern. Should one member choose not to abide the WTO rules, a complaint can be filed by the injured member with the **WTO Appellate Body** who will hear arguments on both sides and make a ruling. It can authorize remedies for the injured member such as allowing them to raise tariffs. The US in 2019 registered its frustration with the Appellate Body's fair handling of its claims regarding tariffs and refused to send representatives to the Appellate Body, effectively shutting it down and severely weakening the effectiveness of the WTO (Brown, 2020).

Although the WTO claims to support open and fair trade for all countries, many have claimed that WTO rules are skewed toward corporate interests, putting the benefits of international trade over local laws that protect the environment, fair labor practices and health of plants, animals, and people (Guardian, 2011). As the WTO rebuilds itself, it has the opportunity to rewrite its rules and procedures to address issues of sustainability and social justice (Stockman, 2020).

Free Trade Agreements

In 2020 there were over 300 Regional Trade Agreements ratified by various participating member countries of the WTO and the number was growing. Most were **Free Trade Agreements (FTAs)**, which are multinational pacts whose goals include the reduction or elimination of tariffs and other barriers to trade among countries within a **free trade** area. FTAs allow each country to form trade agreements with outside nations.

One of the world's largest FTAs is the **United States-Mexico-Canada Agreement 2018 (USMCA)**, an updated version of the North American Free Trade Agreement (NAFTA), which features the duty-free exchange of goods and a unified, simplified import and export system among its partners, Mexico, Canada, and the USA.

When apparel and textiles are included in its rules an FTA may require that all the steps of production (excluding fiber) must be conducted within the partner countries unless a component product is in **short supply** (not commercially available). This **yarn forward rule** encourages development of a supply chain within each country and with the trading partner, but it also complicates the ease of movement of components through the supply chain. Partners must provide **Rules of Origin Certificates** so that they can prove eligibility for reduced or removed tariffs under yarn forward rules.

The Regional Comprehensive Economic Partnership (RCEP), an FTA between the **Association of Southeast Asian Nations (ASEAN)** (a trade bloc including Indonesia, Malaysia, the Philippines, Singapore, Thailand, Brunei, Vietnam, Laos, Myanmar, and Cambodia) and China, Japan, South Korea, Australia, and New Zealand, requires only one rule of origin, the final manufacturing country. This is expected to encourage trade of apparel and textile products in RECP nations (Elms & Hughes, 2021).

In the early 2020s, because of the liberalization of trade, global tariff rates were relatively low, about 3 percent on average. The attention that used to be spent on negotiating tariff levels in FTAs, had shifted to a focus on standardization of regulations and processes of production. (Jacobson, 2020). Such standards may include strict rules and enforcement to prevent partner countries from unfair trade practices such as **dumping** (selling goods for lower than market rate) and **transshipment** (exporting goods from other countries under the FTA country's label).

The Comprehensive and Progressive Agreement for Trans-Pacific Partnership (CPTPP) signed by Australia, Brunei, Canada, Chile, Japan, Malaysia, Mexico, New Zealand, Peru, Singapore, and Vietnam in 2018 is considered a high-level FTA because of its advanced, detailed standards protecting partners' intellectual property, innovations, and data gathered in digital trade. (Goodman 2018.) These measures, all of which are important in the production of apparel and textiles, improve trust and transparency.

A **customs union** is like an FTA, but members negotiate trade with outside countries with uniform policies. For example, The European Union Customs Union (comprised of most EU member states and a few more countries) trade freely with each other without barriers but agree on common tariffs on imports from nonmembers. In 2019 when the EU chose to raise tariffs on a number of iconic US products, including jeans, in retaliation for increased tariffs imposed by the USA, all EU countries had to abide by the increase (Deutsche Welle, 2018).

In spite of notable challenges to the strength of multilateral agreements such as the exit of the UK from the EU and tensions between Australia and China (partners in ASEAN-Australia-New Zealand), trade agreements have been evolving toward stronger regional alliances as evidenced by the formation of RCEP and the renegotiation of USMCA (Buczynski, 2020).

Preferential Trade Agreements

Most trade agreements are reciprocal. It is expected that increased sales to trading partners in one sector will make up for losses in another sector that must compete with lower prices on imports. Exceptions to WTO rules are made on a unilateral basis to allow **Preferential Trade Arrangements (PTAs)** to be made for the benefit of **Least Developed Countries (LDCs)**, those countries that are deemed by the United Nations to have the lowest indicators of socioeconomic development. For example, Ethiopia's apparel manufacturing has boomed due in part to duty free access to the US under the **African Growth and Opportunity Act (AGOA)** and to the EU under Everything but Arms (EBA). This PTA permits imports (excluding armaments) from LDCs to enter EU countries duty free and quota free (Hailu, 2020).

PTAs tend to be more vulnerable to immediate changes than FTAs. In January of 2021, the US let all PTA agreements, including AGOA, administered under their General System of Preferences (GSP) lapse. This has happened several times in the past and the US has reinstated its PTA agreements, but the disruptions are messy and costly for the recipient country (Friedman, 2021). PTAs (or their cancellation) can also be used to send a message to developing countries about respect for intellectual property rights, human rights abuses, and the deteriorating rule of law (Donaldson, 2007).

Because trade is often a contentious political issue, governments may change, cancel, or ignore their policies and agreements rapidly as power shifts from one faction or party to another within a country. For this reason, product development specialists must stay abreast of the political and economic environment of their own country and that of trading partners.

Larger companies with established import or export trade may have in-house specialists or consultants who advise them about the latest threats to current trade agreements and emerging opportunities offered by new agreements. Smaller companies who wish to find trading partners in countries that already have trade agreements with their country may find that the fee paid for reports or aggregated data published by companies such as Just Style to be of value because they reduce research time (Just Style, 2021).

Some information is available free of charge such as publication from business associations like Asia Business Trade Association (ABTA) (Asia Business Trade Association, 2021), Asia Pacific MSME Trade Coalition (AMTC) (Asia Pacific MSME Trade Coalition, 2021), or Asia Trade Center (ATC) (Asian Trade Center 2021), a research organization that provides reports, white papers and coaching. American Apparel and Footwear Association (AAFA) (American Apparel and Footwear Association, 2020) publishes reports about the changing trade environment for the public and members. The WTO World Trade Organization provides tools for searching its databases.

SUSTAINABILITY

As consumers have become increasingly aware of the damage done to the environment and people during the process of producing apparel products, the marketing departments of some brands have overused the term "sustainability" and sometimes applied it without foundation. As misleading claims have been exposed, consumers have become wary of claims that a product is "sustainable" without infallible verification (Burstein, 2020). They want every aspect of the product to be traceable back to its origin and proven to be authentically sustainable.

Verification

Brands with extensive offshore operations sometimes conduct in-person audits of suppliers. These efforts rely on teams of individuals traveling to suppliers' sites. Their access can be seriously interrupted or stopped during natural disasters, health crises, or changes in political stability.

Many other brands use third-party verification by organizations such as Intertek, Bureau Veritas, or Worldwide Responsible Accredited Production (WRAP). Some brands have partnered with nonprofit groups such as GOTS who certify that a fiber is produced according to the strict requirements of organic farming. Obtaining reports can be slow and cumbersome, sometimes threatening delivery schedules. Suppliers may be tempted to falsify certificates, which are vulnerable due to the use of easily altered PDF files.

Brands with close connections to trusted suppliers have been experimenting with empowering suppliers to take responsibility locally. Some have instituted training programs about ethical practices and encouraged the increased use of video conferencing to build trust and loyalty between supplier and brand.

Authenticity

Forensic science is being used by firms such as Oritain™ to authenticate the geographic point of origin of natural fibers such as cotton and wool. Because these fibers pick up trace elements and isotopes from soil, air and water as they grow, it is possible to create an "origin fingerprint" that can be used for testing all along the supply chain at any time. Although forensic testing is being used primarily for luxury products, such services may become more affordable over time. They are not yet being used for tracing recycled synthetic fibers.

Recycled plastics can be tagged using DNA markers that are added to the polymer melt before spinning it into new fibers by companies such as by Applied DNA Science using CertainT® technology. After tagging, fibers can be tested and tracked at any step of the process from yarn to fabric to garment. The marker can identify fibers that started out as soda bottles or ocean trash. Testing along the supply chain can be disruptive and costly.

Blockchain

Although forensics and DNA markers can verify the source of the fiber, even in a finished product, they cannot authenticate the sustainability of other processes to which the fiber has been subjected such as dyeing or finishing. They cannot testify to the circumstances in which the product was produced such as unfair labor practices or dangerous health threats.

Most certification programs focus on one or a few parts of the supply chain. Brands are beginning to use blockchain technology to protect the whole supply chain, not only the authenticity of raw materials, but also the people who perform the tasks to transform materials into finished products.

Blockchain technology starts with a digital shared ledger which is a synchronized data base. No one person or company owns or manages the ledger. A group of stakeholders "own" the ledger and agree that they will employ it to track transactions during the lifecycle of a product. They cooperate ahead of time to agree on protocols. As the ledger is updated, each transaction must be verified by a majority of participants. Collaboration is one of the most important features of blockchain.

Each transaction is added to the ledger as a "block" which contains information that is required by the participants. Selected bits of information from the block are transformed into a digital "hash" using algorithms generated by designated participants. Each block is linked to the hash of the block before it, making a chain of data that is virtually impossible to alter (immutable). This feature builds trust because it is transparent and readily available to all participants. It exposes fraudulent reports regarding where, when, or how a product is produced. Transparency is another especially important feature of blockchain.

Because transactions are added to the ledger in real time, not only can CSR violations be identified immediately, but participants are alerted to bottlenecks and delivery issues that call for rapid intervention. Speed and efficiency are also important features of blockchain.

The use of blockchain can build on existing efforts to monitor supply chain partners. Companies such as TextileGenesis™ specialize in providing blockchain software for apparel brands, incorporating existing protocols for verifying sustainable and ethical practices. Indeed, blockchain requires collaboration, giving brands a way to fulfill Sustainable Development Goal #17: Strengthen the means of implementation and revitalize the global partnership for sustainable development.

SUMMARY

As consumer demand for transparency and accountability from brands grows, sourcing professionals must seek partners to support corporate CSR goals. Although face-to-face trade shows will probably continue to be an excellent venue at which to find supply chain partners, many other digital means now exist such as video conferencing and matchmaking and open-sourced supplier maps. As brands seek relationships with partners who share their CSR goals, they must weigh the level of control that they are willing to give up and the amount of risk that they will take. Brands are responding to the Direct-to-Consumer model of distribution. Sourcing professionals are looking for factories that can handle low MOQs and short turnaround times as well as being flexible and resilient. Of course, they must monitor compliance with CSR goals.

Sourcing professionals have many ways to study the social, economic, and political environment of the countries in which they do business in order to look for opportunities, and also to avoid threats to their supply chains. Trade relationships also need constant monitoring for changes that impact import and export rules. Compliance with CSR goals has become critical to brands' reputations and new technologies are emerging to make monitoring easier.

Case Study 12.1
Business as a Force for Good: Saitex, The First B Corp Factory in Asia

There are many models for structuring businesses, which vary from country to country. They range from private companies owned by a single person to corporations owned by thousands of shareholders. These legal structures in any country define who is liable for financial losses and who benefits from the profits that result from business activities. Business law generally holds officers and executives accountable to act in the best interest of the corporation which has, until recently, been regarded as monetary gain. A benefits corporation or "B Corp" is a relatively new legal model in which a company operates as a for-profit business but expands its corporate best interests to include social and environmental good. B corps may seek third-party certification to assure shareholders, stakeholders, and customers that they are making progress toward achieving their stated goals (Gee, 2018). Even companies that do not incorporate as B corps can seek certification. B Lab, a nonprofit organization that provides this service, states that in 2021 there were nearly 4000 Certified B Corps in seventy-four countries. Sourcing professionals can find a directory on their website (B Lab, 2021).

B Corps Brands such as Patagonia, Eileen Fisher, and Athleta have been leading the way in making social and environmental good the core of their companies' best interests (Leighton, 2021). Now businesses farther upstream are joining the movement. In 2019, Saitex, a production factory in Vietnam, became the first factory in Asia and the only large-scale manufacturer of denim to earn B Corporation™ Certification (Velasquez, 2019). Because transparency is a hallmark of social and environmental responsibility, they post their B Corp scores for each of four areas: governance, workers, community, and the environment. They pledge attention to areas that need improvement (Saitex, 2021a). Clients such as Edwin USA and Outerknown were not surprised that Saitex earned a score of 105.6 (the bar for certification is 80 points). They already partner with Saitex to support their corporate CSR goals. Saitex has earned the title "the cleanest denim factory in the world" by recycling 98 percent of its water and converting the sludge from water processing into bricks for affordable housing. They reduced their carbon footprint by 80 percent using solar power, natural lighting, recapturing heat, and air-drying their products. Each of these steps has saved the company money, answering the perennial question, "Can sustainability be profitable?"

Saitex' commitment to people is evident in the treatment of their workers. 58 percent of workers are female, some of whom are general managers. Saitex grows its own food with clean farming methods (hydroponic), providing not only healthy food for workers, but also jobs. Training of marginalized people such as orphans and the disabled leads to jobs in the organization with the same pay and respect as other workers.

Sanjeev Bahl, CEO of Saitex discovered that the key to maintaining their commitment to sustainability was having control over upstream suppliers. Lack of transparency and flexibility in textile suppliers in Vietnam led them to build their own denim mill. Saitex intends to replicate their successes with the vertical model in Vietnam in other countries (Nishimura, 2021). Their state-of-the-art production factory opened in March 2021 in Los Angeles, CA (Velasquez, 2021). They are exploring building a textile factory as well (Warren, 2021).

References

B Lab. (2021), About B Corps. https://bcorporation.net/about-b-corps (accessed April 14, 2021).

Leighton, M, Saguin, J. (2021), "B Corps are businesses committed to using their profit for good—these 15 make products we love," *Business Insider.* February 23. https://www.businessinsider.com/b-corp-retail-companies (accessed April 21, 2021).

Nishimura, K. (2021), "After Decades of China Dominance, Sourcing Seeks a New Way Forward," Sourcing State of the Industry Report. *Sourcing Journal.* https://sourcingjournal.com/report/sourcing-report-2021/ 9accessed April 21, 2021).

Gee, D. (2018), "LLC, C Corp, S Corp, B Corp, EIEIO," *Medium.* January 25. https://medium.com/@davidralphgee/llc-c-corp-s-corp-b-corp-eieio-6b927ff02c0d (accessed April 14, 2021).

Saitex. (2021), Purpose Matters. https://www.sai-tex.com/purpose/ (accessed April 14, 2021).

Velasquez, A. (2019), "Saitex is Now the Only Large Scale Denim Manufacturer with B Corp Certification," *Sourcing Journal.* June 27. https://sourcingjournal.com/denim/denim-mills/saitex-b-corp-certification-158230/ (accessed April 1, 2021).

Velasquez, A. (2021), "Saitex Flips on the Switch at Los Angeles Facility," *Sourcing Journal.* March 17. https://sourcingjournal.com/denim-business/saitex-usa-opens-los-angeles-denim-factory-sanjeev-bahl-268748/ (accessed April 1, 2021).

Warren, L. (2021), "Saitex Founder Sanjeev Bahl on Expansion During a Pandemi," *Sourcing Journal.* March 31. https://sourcingjournal.com/denim/rivet-50/2020-sanjeev-bahl-saitex-la-factory/ (accessed April 1, 2021).

KEY TERMS

African Growth and
  Opportunity Act (AGOA)
Association of Southeast
  Asian Nations (ASEAN)
bilateral trade agreements
country report
customs union
CMT (cut, make, trim)
direct sourcing
dumping
economic integration
e-government
exports
free trade
free trade zones
Free Trade Agreements
  (FTAs)
General Agreement on Trades
  and Tariffs (GATT)

imports
joint venture
lead time
Least Developed Countries
  (LDCs)
licensee
Minimum order quantities
  (MOQs)
modular manufacturing
  systems
OEM (original equipment
  manufacturing)
Preferential Trade
  Arrangements (PTAs)
progressive bundle system
quota
Rules of Origin Certificate
short supply
slow steam policy

sourcing agents
sourcing mix
tariff
trade agreements
trade bloc
transshipment
unilateral trade agreements or
  actions
Unit Production System
  (UPS)
United States-Mexico-Canada
  Agreement 2018 (USMCA)
World Trade Organization
  (WTO)
WTO Appellate Body
WTO Rules of Global Trade
yarn forward rule

DISCUSSION QUESTIONS

1. If you were a designer who wanted to start their own DTC line, how would you go about finding supply chain partners?

2. Imagine that you are part of the sourcing team for a company that is buying its products through a full package sourcing agent. Your CEO has asked your team to recommend changes in the sourcing strategy that will allow your company to have more control over issues of fit. What kind of sourcing arrangement would you recommend? Why?

3. If you were working for a brand that was considering local factories as supply chain partners, do you think you would find them ready to produce products that were affordable, sustainable and ethical? What would be their biggest challenge?

ACTIVITIES

1. Work in teams of three or four. Imagine that you are sourcing professionals working for a brand that specializes in cotton athletic clothing that is made exclusively in China. You have been asked by your boss to find factories in two countries, Pakistan and Bangladesh, that your company has not worked in before. She has asked you to conduct research about these two potential supply chain partners. Using the resources in sections "Human Resources," "Business Climate," "Public Institu-

tions," and "Import Export Context," work together to create Country Reports for Pakistan and Bangladesh. Compare the countries using all the criteria in these sections. Which of these countries would your team recommend to your boss? Justify your answer.

2. Go to the Open Apparel Registry website. Locate a pin(s) in your hometown or the closest one you can find. Were you aware that there are (or are not) factories near you? How far away is the nearest factory? What can you find out about it?

STUD!O RESOURCES

- Take the chapter quiz with scored results and personalized study tips.
- Review glossary flashcards to build your vocabulary.

REFERENCES

Amadeo, K. (2020), "Free Trade Agreements: Their Impact, Types, and Examples," *The Balance*. September 24. https://www.thebalance.com/free-trade-agreement-types-and-examples-3305897#:~:text=3%20 Types%20of%20Trade%20Agreements%201%20Unilateral%20Trade,more%20are%20the%20 most%20difficult%20to%20negotiate.%20 (accessed December 31, 2020).

American Apparel and Footwear Association. (2020), https://www.aafaglobal.org/ (accessed December 28, 2020).

Apparel Entrepreneurship. (2020), Material sourcing—fabrics & trims. January 15. https://www. apparelentrepreneurship.com/fashion-trade-shows-and-sourcing-fairs-2019-2020/ (accessed December 29, 2020).

The Asia Business Trade Association (ABTA). (2021), https://asiabusiness.trade/ (accessed January 11, 2021).

Asia Pacific MSME Trade Coalition (AMTC). (2021), https://www.amtctrade.org/ (accessed January 11, 2021).

Asian Trade Centre. (2021), http://asiantradecentre.org/(accessed January 11, 2021).

Balassa, B. (1961), *The Theory of Economic Integration*. London: George Allen & Unwin Ltd.

Brown, C. (2020), "Why did Trump end the WTO's Appellate Body? Tariffs," *Peterson Institute for International Economics*, March 4. https://www.piie.com/blogs/trade-and-investment-policy-watch/ why-did-trump-end-wtos-appellate-body-tariffs (accessed January 11, 2021).

Buczynski, R. (2020), "Globalization: Political, Cultural and Economic Dimensions," *IBISWorld*, October 5. https://www.ibisworld.com/industry-insider/insights-from-our-chief-economist/globalization-part-1/ (accessed January 18, 2021).

Burstein, M. (2020), "Why Scaling Traceability Should Be Fashion's Next Sustainability Goal," *Sourcing Journal*, October 7. https://sourcingjournal.com/topics/sustainability/ngc-fashion-apparel-traceability-blockchain-xinjiang-ban-cotton-forced-labor-236240/ (accessed January 29, 2021).

Burton, J. (2020), "List of Countries by Literacy Rate," *World Atlas*, August 12. https://www.worldatlas. com/articles/the-highest-literacy-rates-in-the-world.html (accessed January 19, 2021).

Chua, J. (2021), "Xinjiang Cotton Faces Sweeping New Western Sanctions," *Sourcing Journal*, January 13. https://sourcingjournal.com/topics/labor/xinjiang-cotton-ban-u-s-cbp-aafa-ncto-forced-labor-255289/ (accessed January 14, 2021).

Deutsche Welle. (2018), "EU's retaliatory tariffs on US products come into effect," *Deutsche Welle*, June 22. https://www.dw.com/en/eus-retaliatory-tariffs-on-us-products-come-into-effect/a-44342588 (accessed January 11, 2021).

Donaldson, T. (2007), "Trump Adjusts Which Countries Will Get GSP Benefits and Which Won't," *Sourcing Journal*, December 28. https://sourcingjournal.com/topics/trade/trump-gsp-agoa-benefits-76499/ (accessed January 14, 2021).

Elms, D., and Hughes, B. (2021), RCEP: What Does it Mean for US Textile and Apparel Sourcing from Asia? Texworld Webinar, January 14 (accessed January 14, 2021).

Fiber2Fashion. (2017), INTEXPO promotes Indian MMF textiles in Ethiopia. https://www.fibre2fashion.com/news/textile-news/intexpo-promotes-indian-mmf-textiles-in-ethiopia-204446-newsdetails.htm.

Fiber2Fashion. (2020), Messe Frankfurt France providing digital platform from Sep, July 20. https://www.fibre2fashion.com/news/textile-news/messe-frankfurt-france-providing-digital-platform-from-sep-268487-newsdetails.htm (accessed December 28, 2020).

Fragile States Index. (2021). Country Dashboard. https://fragilestatesindex.org/country-data/ (accessed January 21, 2021).

Friedman, A. (2018), "Primark Publishes Global Sourcing Map in Transparency Move," *Sourcing Journal*. February 9. https://sourcingjournal.com/topics/compliance/primark-publishes-global-sourcing-map-transparency-78577/ (accessed December 29, 2020).

Friedman, F. (2021,) "$2.5 Billion in Tariffs: What Lapse in Trade Programs Could Cost US Firms," *Sourcing Journal*, January 4. https://sourcingjournal.com/topics/trade/gsp-tariff-bill-congress-duties-sandler-travis-aafa-253343/ (accessed January 14, 2021).

Fund for Peace (FFP). (2021), How We Develop Tools and Metrics. https://fundforpeace.org/ (accessed January 21, 2021).

Gereffi, G., and S. Frederick. (2010), The global apparel value chain, trade and the crisis: Challenges and opportunities for developing countries. The World Bank, Policy Research Working Paper 5281. http://unstats.un.org/unsd/trade/s_geneva2011/refdocs/rds/apparel%20industry%20and%20crisis%20(gereffi%20-%20apr%202010).pdf (accessed May 25, 2011).

Global Health Observatory. (2021), World Health Data Platform: Indicators. https://www.who.int/data/gho/data/indicators (accessed January 19, 2021).

Goodman, M. (2018), "From TPP to CPTPP," *Center for Strategic and International Studies*. March 8. https://www.csis.org/analysis/tpp-cptpp (accessed January 18, 2021).

Hailu, H. (2020), "Ethiopia's Ten-Year Plan to Industrialize," *The Ethiopian Herald*, December 29. https://allafrica.com/stories/202012290316.html (accessed January 12, 2021).

International Labor Organization. (2017), "World Social Protection Report 2017–19," *ILO Global Publications*, November 29. https://www.ilo.org/global/publications/books/WCMS_604882/lang--en/index.htm (accessed January 19, 2021).

International Labor Organization (ILO). (2020a),. World Employment and Social Outlook Trends. https://www.ilo.org/wcmsp5/groups/public/---dgreports/---dcomm/---publ/documents/publication/wcms_734455.pdf (accessed January 19, 2021).

International Labor Organization (ILO). (2020b), "Global Wage Report 2020–21: Wages and minimum wages in the time of COVID-19," *ILO Global Publications*, December 2. https://www.ilo.org/global/publications/books/WCMS_762534/lang--en/index.htm (accessed January 19, 2021).

Jacobson, J. (2020), "International Trade: From Tariffs to Standards," *Insights,* March 11. https://www.ie.edu/insights/articles/international-trade-from-tariffs-to-standards/ (accessed January 7, 2020.)

Just Style. (2021), Create apparel sourcing plans that work. https://www.just-style.com/resource/apparel-tariffs-trade-sourcing-data.aspx (accessed January 10, 2021).

Nishimura, J. (2020), "Why Joor CEO Says Fashion's 'Bar Has Been Raised' This Year," *Sourcing Journal*, December 9. https://sourcingjournal.com/topics/technology/joor-b2b-fashion-wholesale-digitization-trade-shows-online-249664/ (accessed December 28, 2020).

Open Apparel Registry. The open map of global apparel facilities. https://openapparel.org/ (accessed December 29, 2020).

Organization for Economic Co-operation and Development (OECD). (2021), Monetary and fiscal issues. http://www.oecd.org/ /finance/monetary/ (accessed January 21, 2021).

Primark Stores Ltd. (2021), Primark Global Sourcing Map. https://globalsourcingmap.primark.com/en/ (accessed January 29, 2021).

SeaRates.com. (2020), Logistics Explorer. https://www.searates.com/reference/portdistance

SoftWear Automation. (2021), The Next Generation Lowry Sewbots® Are Here. https://softwearautomation.com/products/ (accessed January 25, 2021).

Sourcing Journal. (2020), Sourcing Report 2020. https://sourcingjournal.com/report/sourcing-2020-report/ (accessed January 7, 2020).

Sourcing Journal. (2021), Sourcing Report 2021. https://sourcingjournal.com/report/sourcing-report-2021/

Stockman, F. (2020), "The World Trade Organization is having a midlife crisis," *The Economic Times*, December 18. https://economictimes.indiatimes.com/news/international/business/the-world-trade-organization-is-having-a-midlife-crisis/articleshow/79790481.cms (accessed January 12, 2021).

The Guardian. (2011), "The WTO has failed developing nations," *The Guardian*, November 14. https://www.theguardian.com/global-development/poverty-matters/2011/nov/14/wto-fails-developing-countries (accessed January 12, 2021).

The Global Economy. (2020), Compare countries with annual data from official sources. https://www.theglobaleconomy.com/compare-countries/(accessed January 19, 2021).

Trading Economics. (2021), Loans to Private Sector. https://tradingeconomics.com/country-list/loans-to-private-sector (accessed January 21, 2021).

UNdata. (2014), Gross Domestic Expenditure on research and Development (GERD) as a percentage of Gross Domestic Product (GDP). http://data.un.org/Data.aspx?d=UNESCO&f=series:ST_SCGERDGDP (accessed January 21, 2021).

United Nations. (2021a), UN Water. https://sdg6data.org/ (accessed January 22, 2021).

United Nations. (2021b), UN E-Government Knowledgebase. https://publicadministration.un.org/egovkb/en-us/Data/Compare-Countries (accessed January 22, 2021).

Warren, L. (2020), "Pandemic Offers Rebirth for Trade Shows in Need of Disruption," *Sourcing Journal*, December 14. https://sourcingjournal.com/denim/denim-trade-shows/fashion-snoops-trade-show-coronavirus-digital-opportunities-informa-liberty-fairs-249492/ (accessed December 28, 2020).

World Bank. (2021), Renewable Energy Consumption. https://data.worldbank.org/indicator/EG.FEC.RNEW.ZS (accessed January 21, 2021).

World Economic Forum. (2020), Global Gender Gap Report 2020. http://www3.weforum.org/docs/WEF_GGGR_2020.pdf (accessed January 19, 2021).

World Population Review. (2020), Education Rankings by Country. https://worldpopulationreview.com/country-rankings/education-rankings-by-country (accessed January 19, 2021).

CHAPTER 13

COSTING

"Considering the reality of climate change, our industry can't just wait to 'scale solutions' through collaborations or for technology to catch up to our sustainability needs. We need to be transparent about our total impacts and take full ownership of them right now. This ownership will drive change...we transparently publish all our environmental impacts...every year and all the information about our sustainability activities . . . ." MARCO BIZZARRI, PRESIDENT AND CEO, GUCCI

OBJECTIVES

• To understand that financial management for apparel businesses is complex because brands are engaged in a broad spectrum of activities that generate expenses and income from planning and production to distribution and recommerce

• To identify basic terminology and formulas used in a Profit and Loss Statement

• To trace the development of cost information through the phases of product development

• To recognize the decisions that a product developer can make to manage direct and indirect costs

• To understand the changing impacts of various costs as new distribution channels evolve

• To recognize the cost structures of business models in the emerging recommerce sector

FINANCIAL MANAGEMENT

The purpose of financial planning and management is to support a business in achieving its mission and goals. To do this a business must have enough liquidity to meet unexpected challenges. It also needs to maintain a reputation for prudent management so that it can borrow capital that allows it to grow. Financial activities need to be conducted transparently to encourage trust in its relationships with stakeholders.

Business Activities

At one time the distinction between the wholesale and retail activities in the apparel industry was clear. Wholesalers organized the mass production of finished apparel and sold it in bulk quantities to retailers. Retailers bought ready-made goods in bulk from wholesalers and sold items one by one to individual customers. Since the 1980s, this distinction has become blurred. Some retailers now manage the production of their own in-house brands, essentially becoming wholesalers to themselves.

Wholesalers were at one time vertically integrated. They conducted brand management, marketing, merchandising, design, technical design, and factory production under one organization. Today, brands may contract outside entities to perform some or all aspects of technical preparation, such as patterning, sampling, grading, and marker making as well as factory production. Brands who at one time sold their bulk products exclusively to independent retail stores may now operate their own, distributing items that they produce directly to individual customers.

Both brands and retailers sell directly to consumers on their own e-commerce platforms or through third party marketplace websites. Some brands gather size and fit data from individual customers using in-store or online apps. They may own or contract small factories or studios where garments are produced in very small quantities or one by one.

Recommerce is the process of selling previously owned, new, or used products to private or business customers for the purpose of reusing, repairing, or recycling. It is a growing sector of the apparel industry and its supply chain is still in its infancy. Some business activities may resemble traditional wholesale and retail practices, and some are new.

Profit and Loss Statement

One of the ways that businesses keep track of the cost of their business activities is by recording the money that they spend (**costs and expenses**) and receive (**income or revenue**) over a period of time in a **Profit and Loss Statement (P&L)**.

A typical P&L for a retail store includes line items for

- Income (revenue)
  - **Gross sales**: all of the money earned from sales in a period of time (month, quarter, year)
  - **Other income**: money earned for activities not related to the retail operation
- Expenses (costs)
  - **Cost of goods sold**: the dollar value of unsold inventory from the previous period plus the amount paid to obtain new merchandise
  - **Returns and allowances**: money lost when a product is marked down after a return or to resolve a customer complaint

- **Operating expenses**: all the expenses that the retailer must pay to run the retail business
- **Other expenses**: money spent for activities not related to the retail operation
- Calculations
  - **Net sales**: gross sales – returns/allowances = net sales
  - **Gross margin**: net sales – cost of goods sold = gross margin
  - **Operating profit**: gross margin – operating expenses = operating profit
  - **Profit before taxes**: operating profit + / – other expenses or income = profit before taxes

The P&L can be expanded and itemized. Data from one time period can be compared to another in order to analyze whether the business is reaching its goals for growth in dollars or percentages. The month-to-month comparison of gross margin percentage to sales goals can act as an immediate red flag that can trigger decisions regarding buying more inventory or selling it off through events or markdowns (Figure 13.1).

Figure 13.1
Six-month Profit and Loss Statement.

SIX MONTH PROFIT AND LOSS STATEMENT

	January	February	March	April	May	June	YTD
Gross Sales (GS)	$43,000.00	$45,209.00	$47,199.00	$50,677.00	$47,864.00	$45,864.00	$279,281.00
Returns & Allowance	$1,678.00	$1,578.00	$2,299.00	$1,367.00	$1,607.00	$1,638.00	$10,167.00
Net Sales (NS)	$41,322.00	$43,631.00	$44,900.00	$49,310.00	$46,257.00	$43,694.00	$269,114.00
Cost of Goods Sold (GOG)	$21,500.00	$22,700.00	$23,643.00	$24,954.00	$24,310.13	$22,525.63	$139,632.76
COGS % of NS	**52.03%**	**52.03%**	**52.66%**	**50.61%**	**52.55%**	**51.55%**	**51.89%**
Gross Margin (GM)	$19,822	$20,981	$21,257	$24,356	$21.947	$21,168	$129,481
GM % of NS	**47.97%**	**47.97%**	**47.34%**	**49.39%**	**47.45%**	**48.45%**	**48.11%**
Operating Expenses (OE)							
Salaries & Wages	$7,500.00	$7,875.00	$8,268.75	$8.682.19	$9,116.30	$7.875.00	49,317.24
Rent Expense	$2,700.00	$2,700.00	$2,700.00	$2,700.00	$2,700.00	$2,700.00	$16,200.00
Utilities	$900.00	$900.00	$900.00	$900.00	$900.00	$900.00	$5,400.00
Marketing Expenses	$2,000.00	$2,000.00	$2,300.00	$2,500.00	$2,200.00	$2,000.00	$13,000.00
Other Expenses	$5,500.00	$5,500.00	$5,500.00	$7,500.00	$5,500.00	$5,500.00	$35.000.00
Total Operating Expenses	$18,600.00	$18,975.00	$19,668.75	$22,282.19	$18,416.30	$18,975.00	$118,917.24
Operating Profit	$1,222.00	$1,956.00	$1,588.25	$2,073.81	$1,530.57	$2,193.37	$10,564.00
Other Income or Expense	-$100.00	-$105.00	-$110.25	-$115.76	-$121.55	-$127.63	-$680.19
Net Profit Before Income Taxes	$1,122.00	$1,851.00	$1,478.00	$1,958.05	$1,409.02	$2,063.74	$9,883.81
Profit % of NS	**2.72%**	**4.24%**	**3.29%**	**3.97%**	**3.05%**	**4.73%**	**3.67%**

*Other Expenses including: administration, insurance legal fees, maintenence, depreciation, supplies, communications, ect.

In this simulation representing a small retail business or a department within a bigger store, the target gross margin percent is 48 percent and target profitpercentage of net sales is 4percent. Sales were up in February compared to January (green highlight), but the cost of goods was also high. The gross margin was the same in both months, but because sales were higher, the profits were higher. In April (purple highlight), sales were very good, costof goods was low, so the gross margin was high. Salaries were higher to cover extra hours for a big sale. In addition, an unexpected expense due to legal fees from a law suit was due. Nevertheless, because sales were very good in April, profit, a profit was made, although not reaching the target.

Cost Sheet

The line items for a P&L for bulk production businesses are very similar to those for retail. Some of the data needed to build a P&L for production costing is located in the cost sheets for each product made. The cost sheet may be started by a designer or merchandiser, refined by a technical designer, augmented by a production specialist, and reviewed and approved by a sourcing specialist. Input will come from vendors, brokers, and shippers. The use of PLM software allows sourcing partners in other time zones to add and change information in real time, making the process efficient and reliable. Even smaller companies who do not have PLM systems can use shared web-based spread sheets to be sure no detail is changed without everyone knowing.

A cost sheet will contain two kinds of costs. **Direct costs** are related to the expenses of producing individual products. They include only the materials and labor needed to assemble a specific garment. Collectively they are referred to as Cost of Goods (COG) on a cost sheet. Indirect costs are not directly related to the production of any individual product. They are generalized and apply to all products. All businesses incur indirect costs such as operating expenses, taxes, and profit. Costs generated during the planning stages of product development include brand management, trend analysis, marketing, sales, merchandising, and line planning. These activities pertain to the intellectual property of the brand. On a cost sheet, indirect costs and profit are added and listed as the markup.

Phases of Costing

In the beginning of the development process, the merchandising and design staff will agree on basic design information and generate a design spec so that a sample can be made. At that time, they will create a preliminary cost estimate (precost) based on current cost information about materials and labor. They will consider factors that impact materials consumption such as the size category and range which impact the number of SKUs, the estimated size of the order, or the surface design repeat. They will think about the amount of design detail and level of sewing difficulty. They will include estimates for duty, freight, and insurance if relevant (Figure 13.2).

Brands using full package sourcing agents will send the design spec and arrange for a sample to be made. When the samples are finished, technicians who made the patterns and samples will provide feedback about fabric utilization and labor requirements to help confirm estimated costs. Meanwhile, the supply chain management staff will confirm material pricing, minimums, deliveries, and factory skill and capacity and the cost sheet will be updated (Figure 13.3).

The product development team will then enter a phase of internal and external negotiation. For a brand that offers seasonal lines or groups of items, a merchandiser can manipulate the target markup of each item, balancing gains from one style with losses from another to reach an average markup that is acceptable. If the estimated cost of an individual item is too high, merchandisers may ask designers, technical designers, and production and sourcing specialists to offer cost-saving alternatives. Some styles in the line will be modified, some will be dropped, and some new styles may be added until the cost of goods and markups are in line with financial goals. The challenge for the team is to offer novelty to attract customers and quality to keep them, while offering prices that compete in the marketplace (Figure 13.4). Finally, the cost sheet will be updated with the **production cost** at the same time that the tech pack is created with confirmed technical information.

PRODUCTION COSTS

Product development professionals help gather, verify, and juggle the Cost of Goods throughout the phases of costing. One decision may impact another. For example, a change of fabric may mean a higher duty or a longer lead time due to shipping from a more distant supplier.

Direct Labor Costs

Chapter 11 discusses garment assembly practices in the context of "make," a concept that encompasses the sum total of perceived quality of a garment's components, seaming, fit, and finish. When a design spec and preliminary cost sheet are sent to an in-house or contract sample room or to a vendor, the materials listed and sewing details given will imply the level of make. The pattern and sample maker will do their best to create a garment with the right make, but if the package cost or detailed labor cost comes in above the estimate, the product development team will begin to consider changes.

- If details such as pockets, flaps, tabs, ruffles, or topstitch are reduced, will the product still be attractive to the customer?
- If finishing on the inside of the garment is reduced, will the brand image be damaged? (For example, if five-thread overlock (504+401) machines are used for seaming instead of busted seams.)
- If automated applications are used, will the garment appear cheap? (For example, if a folder is used to apply a binding on a neckline instead of using a facing.)

A product development specialist will have access to labor costs under CMT contracts, but not factory direct and OEM or full package. Factories may believe that the way they formulate labor cost is proprietary and not to be shared with the brand.

Brands with their own factories employ costing engineers so that they can refine their labor estimates on the preliminary cost sheet. Costing engineers start by studying the design spec and then create a detailed list of steps needed to assemble the product (Figure 13.5). They will use historical information to choose machinery, processes, and details that reflect the brand make. They will assign a time value to each operation. Although there are many methods used to measure the time, they commonly employ a stopwatch and observation to measure the motions made by workers as they assemble the product. Some methods group motions together, some divide the motions into minute gestures such as "pick up label," "slide out chair," "lift lever,"

DESCRIPTION: dress, fit & flare, short sleeve, ribbon belt, metal clasp	Style# 233876
TEXTILE: jersey print polyester	Delivery 10-31-2024
	B D Productions Inc. Los Angeles CA USA

COST SHEET-PRELIMINARY

agent	Nguyen Bros.				TBA							
COO	Viet Nam				Mexico							
min	2000 per color				TBA							
textile	100% polyester jersey				100% polyester jersey							
HTS	6204.43.40				6204.43.40							
TD target	49.00%				49.00%							
	qty	per unit	unit	prelim	qty	per unit	unit	alter-native	qty	per unit	unit	alter-native
jersey print	1.50	$3.75	yd	$5.63	1.50	$3.95	yd	$5.93				
fusible	0.07	$0.50	yd	$0.04	0.07	$0.50	yd	$0.04				
ribbon	1.00	$2.00	yd	$2.00	1.00	$2.00	yd	$2.00				
clasp	1.00	$1.00	pc	$1.00	1.00	$1.00	pc	$1.00				
labels	3.00	$0.05	pc	$0.15	3.00	$0.05	pc	$0.15				
hang tag	1.00	$0.05	pc	$0.05	1.00	$0.05	pc	$0.05				
packaging	1.00	$0.05	pcs	$0.05	1.00	$0.05	pcs	$0.05				
labor	29.50	$0.05	SAM	$1.48	29.50	$0.08	SAM	$2.36				
total				$10.39				$11.57				
commission %		0.07		$0.73		0.05		$0.58				
duty %		0.16		$1.78		0.00		$0.00				
shipping	1.00	$0.50	pc	$0.50	1.00	$0.50	pc	$0.40				
total CoG				$13.39				$12.55				
wholesale mark up		0.50		$13.39		0.50		$12.55				
wholesale price				$26.78				$25.10				
trade discount %				48.50%				49.81%				
list price				$52.00				$50.00				

Most of the information on a cost sheet in a PLM will be drawn from the data base and reformatted for calulation. In this simulation, the buyer asked for a list price of $50. The merchandiser asked the sourcing team to look for alternatives.

The sourcing team found that this HTS category was duty free in several countries. (See Figure 13.8). They also found that importing the textile would cost more and the labor was higher, but agent fees were lower. The shipping would be shorter. (These costs are highlighted in yellow.) They warned the merchandisers that they had no established business relationships in the area and advised that the team discuss the impact of a new sourcing strategy before offering a lower price to the buyers.

Figure 13.2
This preliminary cost sheet is a simulation of one that might be generated by a computer software system specializing in apparel. The information reflects the details presented for the dress in Figure 9.3 and in the other tech pack pages in Chapters 10 and 11.

BEYOND DESIGN

DESCRIPTION: dress, fit & flare, short sleeve, ribbon belt, metal clasp
TEXTILE:
jersey print polyester

Style# 233876
Delivery 10-31-2024

B D Productions Inc.
Los Angeles CA USA

COST SHEET-PRODUCTION

	Nguyen Bros.				TBA				Nguyen Bros.			
agent	Nguyen Bros.				TBA				Nguyen Bros.			
COO	Viet Nam				Mexico				Viet Nam			
min	2000 per color				TBA				2000 per color			
textile	100% polyester jersey				100% polyester jersey				100% polyester jersey			
HTS	6204.43.40				6204.43.40				6204.43.40			
TD target	49.00%				49.00%				49.00%			
	qty	per unit	unit	prelim	qty	per unit	unit	alter-native	qty	per unit	unit	final
jersey print	1.50	$3.75	yd	$5.63	1.50	$3.95	yd	$5.93	1.50	$3.75	yd	$5.63
fusible	0.07	$0.50	yd	$0.04	0.07	$0.50	yd	$0.04	0.07	$0.50	yd	$0.04
ribbon	1.00	$2.00	yd	$2.00	1.00	$2.00	yd	$2.00	1.00	$2.00	yd	$2.00
clasp	1.00	$1.00	pc	$1.00	1.00	$1.00	pc	$1.00	1.00	$1.00	pc	$1.00
labels	3.00	$0.05	pc	$0.15	3.00	$0.05	pc	$0.15	3.00	$0.05	pc	$0.15
hang tag	1.00	$0.05	pc	$0.05	1.00	$0.05	pc	$0.05	1.00	$0.05	pc	$0.05
packaging	1.00	$0.05	pcs	$0.05	1.00	$0.05	pcs	$0.05	1.00	$0.05	pcs	$0.05
labor	29.50	$0.05	SAM	$1.48	29.50	$0.08	SAM	$2.36	29.50	$0.05	SAM	$1.48
total				$10.39				$11.57				$10.39
commission %		0.07		$0.73		0.05		$0.58		0.07		$0.73
duty %		0.16		$1.78		0.00		$0.00		0.16		$1.78
shipping	1.00	$0.50	pc	$0.50	1.00	$0.50	pc	$0.40	1.00	$0.50	pc	$0.50
total CoG				$13.39				$12.55				$13.39
wholesale mark up		0.50		$13.39		0.50		$12.55		0.50		$13.39
wholesale price				$26.78				$25.10				$26.78
trade discount %				48.50%				49.81%				48.50%
list price				$52.00				$50.00				$52.00

This Production cost sheet has been updated with information used in the final production of the dress from Figure 9.2. In the simulation, the product development team evaluated the risks of starting production in a country where they had no agent, experience, or knowledge. They agreed to do research, contact agents and other resources, and proceed with a small pilot in the next season.

Figure 13.3
This production cost sheet has been updated with information used in the final production of the dress from Figure 9.3. The postproduction costing information from this dress will be used to help costing similar styles in the future.

BEYOND DESIGN

Delivery: 10/31/2024 | Capsule Name: Modern Mosaic | Size Scale: Missy

style# desc	sizes/ scale	colors	materials (M)	labor (L)	commission	duty/duty% of M&L	shipping	CoG/ % of WH	OE&P/ % of WH	wholesale price (WH)	TD/ % of LP	list price (LP)
 BD2338 Dress print	6-12	tile	$8.91	$1.48	$0.73	$1.78	$0.50	$13.40	$13.40	$26.79	$25.21	$52.00
	missy	mosaic			7.00%	16.00%		50.00%	50.00%	51.52%	48.48%	
 BD2339 Jacket eyelet	6-12	indigo/white	$8.75	$3.50	$0.86	$0.92	$0.50	$14.53	$14.53	$29.05	$28.95	$58.00
	missy				7.00%	16.00%		50.00%	50.00%	50.09%	49.91%	
 BD2340 Slim pant print	6-12	tile	$5.44	$1.50	$0.49	$1.19	$0.50	$9.11	$9.11	$18.23	$17.77	$36.00
	missy	mosaic			7.00%	16.00%		50.00%	50.00%	50.63%	49.37%	
 BD2341 Top mesh	one size	lapis	$4.75	$1.00	$0.40	$0.98	$0.50	$7.64	$7.64	$15.27	$14.73	$30.00
	missy				7.00%	16.00%		50.00%	50.00%	50.91%		
 BD2342 Slim pant eyelet	6-12	indigo/white	$5.44	$1.75	$0.50	$1.21	$0.50	$9.41	$9.41	$18.82	$17.18	$36.00
	missy				7.00%	16.00%		50.00%	50.00%	52.27%	47.73%	
 BD2343 Wrap Dress burnout	6-12	clay	$8.38	$1.50	$0.69	$1.69	$0.50	$12.76	$12.76	$25.53	$24.47	$50.00
	missy	terra			7.00%	16.00%		50.00%	50.00%	51.05%	48.95%	
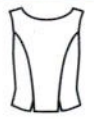 BD2344 Fitted top eyelet	6-12	white/lapis	$3.00	$1.50	$0.32	$0.77	$0.50	$6.09	$6.09	$12.17	$11.83	$24.00
	missy	white/terra			7.00%	16.00%		50.00%	50.00%	50.71%	49.29%	
 BD2345 Skirt mesh	6-12	lapis/indigo	$3.75	$1.75	$0.39	$0.89	$0.50	$7.28	$7.28	$14.55	$13.45	$28.00
	missy				7.00%	16.00%		50.00%	50.00%	51.97%	48.03%	
 BD2346 Cowl top burnout	S-M-L	clay	$2.81	$1.00	$0.27	$0.65	$0.50	$5.23	$5.23	$10.46	$9.54	$20.00
	missy	terra			7.00%	16.00%		50.00%	50.00%	52.29%	47.71%	
 BD2347 Slim skirt eyelet	6-12	white/lapis	$3.56	$1.50	$0.35	$0.87	$0.50	$6.78	$6.78	$13.56	$12.44	$26.00
	missy	white/terra			7.00%	16.00%		50.00%	50.00%	52.16%	47.84%	

Figure 13.4

Line List with estimated costs based on products developed for the Line and Assortment Plans in Chapter 7, including the dress from Figure 9.3 and all of the pages of the tech pack in Chapters 10 and 11.

| DESCRIPTION: dress, fit & flare, short sleeve, ribbon belt, metal clasp
TEXTILE:
jersey print polyester | Style# 233876
Delivery 10-31-2024 |
| | B D Productions Inc.
Los Angeles CA USA |

OPERATIONS BREAKDOWN (LABOR WORKSHEET)

section	operation	SAM
cutting	cut shell	1.50
	fuse facing block	0.50
	re-cut facings	0.50
bodice prep	join side front bodice panels to front bodice	1.00
	join side back bodice panels to center back bodice panels	1.00
skirt prep	join side front skirt panels to front skirt panel	1.10
	join side back skirt panels to center back skirt panels	1.10
join bodice to skirt	join bodice sections to skirt sections @ front and back	1.06
prep backs	serge center back seam for zipper opening	0.80
	stay stitch thread loops to side back panel	0.64
	stay stitch center back seam below zipper	0.32
	join center back seam below zipper	0.50
	set concealed zipper	1.44
shoulder	join shoulder seams (shell)	0.75
	join shoulder seams (neck facing)	0.72
facing	set labels to back facing	0.54
	set neck facing and understitch	2.15
	tack facing to shoulder seam	0.64
side seams	join side seams from underarm to bottom hem	1.40
sleeve	join inseam on sleeve	0.70
	serge sleeve hem edge	0.70
	topstitch sleeve hem	1.20
	set sleeves	1.32
hem	serge bottom edge	0.95
	topstich bottom edge	1.26
belt	close belt ends	0.32
	tack clasp to belt ends	0.96
trim/inspect		1.50
press		2.00
pack		1.00
	total	**29.57**

Figure 13.5

This is the operations breakdown for the dress described in Figure 9.3. An operations breakdown is not the same as the sewing instructions in a tech pack. Sewing instructions are descriptive and related to the design of the garment. Breakdowns are lists of all the movements needed to complete a product with exact times attached in fractions of a minute. The sum total of each individual time is the engineered time. That is multiplied by the wage per hour of the sewers making the product to determine the direct labor cost. Most apparel wholesalers do not have factories in which to conduct time studies, so they use lists generated by consultants or factory simulators.

"lower needle," "walk two steps." The **direct labor** of the garment is calculated by adding up all the times needed to construct the garment (in fractions of a minute) into **Standard Allowed Minutes (SAMs)**. With so few factories remaining in the US in which to observe productive sewing methods, some brands use software that simulates a factory environment to visualize the assembly process. As precise as this process may sound, it can only measure one possible scenario. The actual factory bidding for the contract may use different assembly procedures or may lack comparable skill levels or automation. In addition, the factory's costing system may not be comparable to the brand's, and that may obscure an estimate of the value of the sewing labor.

Regardless of how carefully a garment is engineered and how efficiently it is assembled, the fact remains that apparel production is labor intensive. In order to compete, brands perceive that they must seek sources of production from facilities in those parts of the world where wages are the lowest (Figure 13.6).

Indirect Production Costs

Sourcing specialists are aware that good management and efficient practices have an impact on the hidden labor costs in a vendor's factories. They look for ISO certification or, when they inspect factories personally, they look for up-to-date equipment and communication technology, current engineering, and quality assurance methodology, as well as worker skill development and fair labor practices.

Sourcing specialists may discover opportunities to keep costs down by working with factories that manage their operating expenses to maximum efficiency for the product. Production facilities use a variety of methods for calculating operating expenses. Their challenge is to earn enough money to cover their costs and earn a profit, while not making their prices so high that they are no longer competitive. Some operating costs such as rent are fixed; they stay the same regardless of the quantity or complexity of the units produced. **Fixed costs** increase in inverse proportion to the number of units produced—the greater the number of units made, the smaller the unit cost for fixed expenses because the fixed amount is spread over more units. Some operating expenses are **variable costs** because they may increase for products that require additional labor, water, energy, machinery, or specialized skills such as mixing dyes to match color standards.

Factories that make commodity products, such as tee shirts or jeans, have mostly fixed costs with few variables. They might use **direct costing**, a method in which all operating expenses for a period are summed then divided by the number of units produced to calculate an average fee which is added as a fixed amount to every product. The only variable costs are the materials and labor.

Some production facilities produce a wide variety of continually changing products that demand variable amounts of set-up costs such as planning, machinery downtime, multiple samples, and frequent communication with the client. These facilities may use **absorption costing**, a method that assesses operating expenses as a percentage relative to the value of the labor. This method assumes that the percentage is high enough to cover setup costs without the necessity of recording the cost of each activity individually.

Ethiopia: Lowest Pay in the Global Garment Supply Chain

Rising wages in Asia have contributed to Western brands' interest in manufacturing in Africa

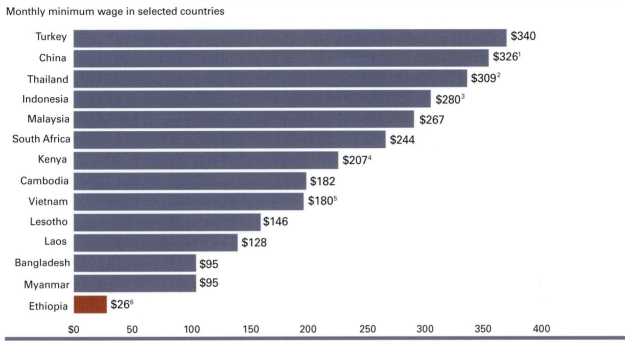

Monthly minimum wage in selected countries

Country	Wage
Turkey	$340
China	$326[1]
Thailand	$309[2]
Indonesia	$280[3]
Malaysia	$267
South Africa	$244
Kenya	$207[4]
Cambodia	$182
Vietnam	$180[5]
Lesotho	$146
Laos	$128
Bangladesh	$95
Myanmar	$95
Ethiopia	$26[6]

[1] In Shenzhen [2] In Chonburi and Rayong [3] In Jakarta [4] In Nairobi and Mombasa [5] Hanoi and Ho Chi Min City [6] Ethiopia has no legal minimum; $26 is the customary base wage, which is sometimes supplemented by incentive payments. Sources: Just-Style and NYU Center research

Figure 13.6
Monthly wages for selected apparel-producing countries. (Adapted from Barrett & Baumann-Pauley, 2019).

Some companies find that **activity-based costing** is a more accurate reflection of the variable operating expenses for each type of product. It measures each indirect cost (such as administration, marketing, and engineering) and charges that cost to individual products. For example, a tee shirt would not be charged as much for marker making as a plaid jacket. This method is complicated and time-consuming to apply and is more apt to be employed by larger businesses with multiple factories (Figure 13.7).

Materials Costs

During the sampling process, computerized patternmaking, grading, and marker-making activities reveal the actual materials consumption and clarify options for improvement, allowing merchandisers, technical designers, and designers to consider their options. For example, if the same textile is available in a wider width, will the savings in utilization outweigh the higher price? If the shape of odd or oversized pieces is changed so that they lock together better in the marker, will the perceived quality or design intent of the product be lost? (see Figure 11.4).

In the process of selecting materials, it is sometimes possible to substitute a fabric or trim that costs less without sacrificing the aesthetic vision of the designer, the brand image, or the functionality of the garment. However, decisions to use less costly

Figure 13.7

Factory costing methods. In this simulation, the labor and materials for three shirts are the same. Three factories have calculated their price for the client, each using a different method of assigning markup (operating expenses + profit). They must price low enough to compete with other vendors and yet not underprice so far that they go out of business.

	A	B	C
	• classic tailored shirt • cotton/poly broadcloth	• classic tailored shirt • cotton/rayon dobby poplin	• Tuxedo shirt • poly/spandex satin

Factory 1: DIRECT COSTING

materials	$5.00	$5.00	$8.00
direct labor	$5.00	$6.50	$7.00
expenses = flat amount charged per garment	$6.50	$6.50	$6.50
total = price to client	**$16.50**	**$18.00**	**$21.50**

Factory 1 charges an across-the-board flat fee for expenses. Direct costing is common in factories where the same basic product is made continuously. The only variation in the cost is the labor and materials. Even though the novelty poplin will demand some what more handling, the rate is the same as the broadcloth shirt. The satin shirt will need planning, training of operators, machine set up and special handling, yet there is no increase in expenses. Although the price Factory 1 offers to the client for shirt C is much lower than Factories 2 and 3, Factory 1 will probably lose money if they take the work.

Factory 2: ABSORPTION COSTING

materials	$5.00	$5.00	$8.00
direct labor	$5.00	$6.50	$7.00
total labor and materials	$10.00	$11.50	$15.00
expenses = 40% of price to client	$6.67	$7.67	$10.00
total = price to client	**$16.67**	**$19.17**	**$25.00**

Factory 2 uses absorption costing. They charge an across-the-board percentage of the price to the client as overhead. The percentage is an estimate. The percentage may be adequate when competing with Factory 1 in the basic tailored shirt category, but it may be too low to capture all of the indirect costs of Shirt C.

Factory 3: ACTIVITY BASED COSTING

materials		$5.00		$5.00		$8.00
direct labor		$5.00		$6.50		$7.70
total materials and labor		$10.00		$11.50		$15.70
indirect labor = 25% of labor	$1.25		$1.63		$1.93	
rent/utilities = 65% of labor	$3.25		$4.23		$5.01	
taxes and fees = 10% of materials	$1.00		$1.15		$1.57	
professional services = 15% of labor	$0.75		$0.98		$1.16	
shipping = rate based on packing requirements of client	$0.50		$0.50		$1.00	
total expenses		$6.75		$8.48		$10.66
total = price to client		**$16.75**		**$19.98**		**$26.36**

Factory 3 calculates expenses by breaking them down into categories.

• Indirect labor is charged in relation to the direct labor cost: if the product takes more labor, it will need more planning, training, machine set up, inspection and other support.

• Rent and utilities are charged in relation to direct labor : if the product is in the factory longer, it w ill use more space and power.

• Shipping costs are higher for Shirt C because the client wants it shipped on a hanger.

• Taxes and fees wil l be related to the value of materials.

Activity based costing is more accurate than direct or absorption costing, but it is more time consuming to record the detail   s.

materials are not without risks. For example, applied textile finishes that can imitate structural design, such as embossing or flocking, are not permanent. Textiles made of inexpensive fibers such as acetate will shrink, fade, and deteriorate quickly with cleaning and wear. Knit textiles fabricated with extra tension to save yarn can shrink several inches in length after washing. The risks of returns and damaged brand image from poor-quality material substitutions may not be calculable in advance, so the product development team may choose to make other changes to design or merchandising parameters instead.

An allowance for waste is customarily added to the utilization reported after marker making. Sourcing specialists may suspect that a production facility needs to improve materials management when they consistently report high yardage consumption or repeatedly ship fewer pieces than ordered. It may be necessary to request that the facility conduct an internal audit of cutting room practices such as splicing, spreading, and fabric inspection to reduce waste. In CMT factories where common trims such as thread or elastic and packaging materials are ordered in bulk quantities, mismanagement can occur between production runs. Requesting reports of inventory management practices can stop damage, loss, and theft.

Bulk Discounts

When labor or materials estimates from suppliers are too high, sourcing professionals can review the line as a whole. They can work with merchandisers and ask them to eliminate some styles from the line or consolidate expected orders into fewer styles to increase quantity per style. In this way they can negotiate bulk discounts for labor or materials. They may also suggest reducing the number of color offerings in order to meet minimums and avoid extra charges. The merchandisers will weigh these ideas up against the loss of novelty and variety in the line.

Another way to keep production costs down is to follow the traditional production method, cut-to-stock or **make-to-stock (MTS)**. In the MTS system, brands negotiate lower labor and materials costs by investing in materials and booking factory capacity in advance of receiving orders. They look at past sales and current trend reports to guide their decisions. They hope that the risk of not finding buyers for their product will be mitigated by having the product in hand when the buying season starts and being able to capture sales. The trend over the last few decades has been for brands to wait to ask vendors to order materials and cut fabric only after they receive distributors' orders. This lean manufacturing method, called cut-to-order or **make-to-order (MTO)**, has been supported by advances in communication and manufacturing technology. MTO has the advantage of lower risk, but prices are higher, lead times are longer, and materials may be harder to get in smaller quantities.

Transportation Costs

Transportation, fees, and tariffs for materials can be reduced by sourcing materials as close to the production factory as possible. Besides the shipping costs of fuel and labor, every time a product crosses a border or checkpoint it is subject to taxation. The efficiency and quality of the supply chain in a country or region can impact costs. The size and timing of a shipment also have an effect.

The duty that the US government assigns to imported apparel varies for each garment based on criteria such as type of fabric, fiber content, garment category (sleepwear, swimwear, etc), and demographic characteristics such as age and gender, as well as on the prevailing trade agreement governing trade relations with the exporting nation. Product development teams use the internet-based Harmonized Tariff Schedule to search for the duty that applies to each style in their line or collection. Small details can change the category, so when the assigned duty of a garment is high, small changes in the design, fiber content, or textile construction may change the duty considerably (Figure 13.8).

When a preliminary cost sheet is developed, the product development team is likely to use a set cost that reflects the country of origin and the customary charges from freight forwarders or brokers. If the vendor is paying for all charges, then these costs will be included in the vendor's price. The brand and vendor should ascertain who is paying for which services while negotiating the vendor's price. Transportation to the

Figure 13.8
Explanation of the Harmonized Tariff Schedule for a dress made from synthetic fibers like the one described in Figure 9.3.

Explanation of the Harmonized Tariff Schedule (HTS) for a dress made of synthetic fibers						
section		paper products	textiles and apparel	footwear		The Harmonized Tariff Schedule covers many kinds of products from agricultural and mineral raw materials to airplanes. Textiles and apparel products are in Section XI.
		X	XI	XII		
chapter		knits	wovens			Section XI covers mainly fibers and fabrics. Chapter 61 deals with knitted and crocheted apparel. Chapter 62 covers woven apparel.
		61	62			
heading		outerwear	daywear	shirts blouses	underwear pajamas	Chapter 62 is divided into headings defined by end-use (outerwear, daywear, athletic wear, underwear, etc.) and by gender. 6204 is "Women's or girls' suits, ensembles, suit-type jackets, blazers, dresses, skirts, divided skirts, trousers, bib and brace overalls, breeches and shorts (other than swimwear)"
	Male	6201	6203	6205	6207	
	Female	6202	6204	6206	6208	
sub-heading	suits	ensembles	dresses	skirts	pants	Heading 6204 is divided by types of garments, suits, ensembles, dresses, skirts and pants. This category is used for most women's everyday and formal clothing. The dresses are designated by a .4.
	6204.1	6204.2 & 3	6204.4	6204.5	6204.6	
fiber content	wool	silk	synthetic	artificial	cotton	The 6204.4 subheading is divided by fiber content. Animal fibers are .41. Cotton fibers are .42, etc. Additional designations referring to a variety of other categories such as textile construction or age range of consumer and are added with more digits.
	6202.41.20	6204.41.10	6204.43.40	6204.44.40	6204.42.30	
general rate of duty	13.60%	0.00%	16.00%	16.00%	8.40%	
special rate of duty	free	free	free	free	free	The HTS lists special duty rates for countries that hold unilateral or multilateral trade relations with the U.S.A. In this case, Australia, Bahrain, Canada, Chile, Colombia, Israel, Jordan, South Korea, Morocco, Mexico, Oman, Panama, Peru, Singapore can export synthetic dresses to the U.S.A without paying duty.
synthetic fiber blend general rate of duty		36% wool 6204.43.30	36% silk 6204.43.20			Within the 6204.43 designation, there are two fiber blends with lower duty rates, silk being the lowest.
		14.90%	7.10%			

The HTS for a dress like the one in Figure 9.2 made of synthetic fibers shows a general duty rate of 16%. The cost sheet in Figure 13.3 lists a total for labor, material and commission of $11.12. 16% duty would equal $1.78. When the product development team does the preliminary costing, they look for alternatives. In this case, they may consider making the product in one of the countries with a trade agreement that allows them to export this product without duty. The sourcing team would look at the pros and cons of importing from these countries. The team may also consider sourcing a textile made with 30% silk. The duty is 7.1% which would lower the duty to $.78. Looking for lower duty is only one strategy for arriving at a competitive price. Note: This table is a simulation of a possible scenario for importing apparel into the USA. Duty percentages change when trade agreements change and should be verified and updated each time a cost sheet is written.

vendor's port, exit fees, and taxes are probably best paid for by the vendor who can negotiate more easily in their own country. Once the product is on the ship, the charges can be paid by either party. Brands may want to pay charges in their own country after the product lands. As brands take on more charges, they have more control over shipping activities; if vendors handle all charges, they take on more risk. There are many acronyms for the various arrangements for payment of shipping charges. Smaller companies without resources to hire logistics professionals may choose Delivered Duty Paid (DDP), where all services are handled by the vendor. Larger companies that import large quantities may chose Free on Board (FOB) so that they can negotiate shipping costs for all their shipments with one shipping company (Figure 13.9).

Shipping charges vary according to the size of the shipment. All international ports use standardized containers to make shipping efficient. Shipping is less expensive if the brand uses a Full Container Load (FCL). The shipping cost from Shenzhen, China, to Los Angeles might be as low as $0.13–$0.18 for a tee shirt. Less than Container Load (LCL) might be as high as $0.40–$0.50 per tee shirt. Clearly, bigger brands (or distributors acting as brands) have an advantage over smaller companies. Insurance also adds to shipping fees, around 2 percent of an FOB price, and is of such importance that it should not be neglected.

Distance is a major factor in shipping costs. The farther a garment must travel, the more it costs in fuel and time onboard ship and at moorage in ports during fueling. Chapter 12 discusses the hidden costs of long shipping times from distant ports. Longer shipping times mean the brand may not be able to respond to market changes and will have to finance products longer while they are in transit. However, transportation costs are still less than 10 percent of the cost of goods and even lower for larger brands who can take advantage of bulk pricing, so moving a product closer to home to save shipping costs may not outweigh other costs such as labor.

Cost of Discounts to Distributors

When a sales rep from a brand approaches a buyer, they will provide a line list with the **suggested retail price (list price)** for each product offered. The list price is calculated to cover the brand's costs, operating expenses, and profit, but it is also based on an estimate of a reasonable at-market price. The list price is just a starting point. The buyer and brand's sales rep will negotiate discounts that benefit both parties. They will start with the **trade discount**, the amount that the distributor needs to run the warehouse and store, pay for marketing, and make a profit—in other words, an amount roughly equivalent to the distributor's gross margin. Gross margins vary widely depending on the type of product, distribution, and channel or business and are usually in the range of 30 to 60 percent.

The brand's sales rep may offer a **seasonal discount** to encourage the distributor to place orders to be manufactured at times when the factory is slow. This kind of discount may coincide with times when the distributor needs to attract customers with a special sale or compete with others with similar deals. Seasonal discounts may also be

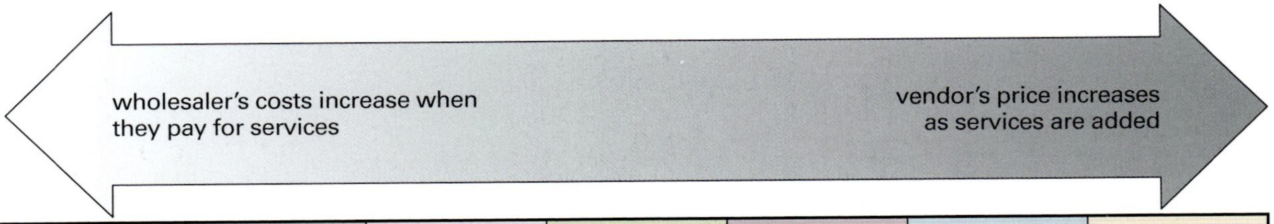

services necessary for shipping goods from foreign port to USA	Ex Point of Origin	Free Along Side (FAS)	Free on Board (FOB)	Cost and Freight (CNF/C&F)	Cost, Insurance, Freight (CIF)	Landed Duty Paid (LDP)	Delivered Duty Paid (DDP)
cost of production	Vendor pays	Vendor pays	Vendor pays	Vendor pays	Vendor pays	Vendor pays	Vendor pays
transport to port	Wholesaler pays	Vendor pays	Vendor pays	Vendor pays	Vendor pays	Vendor pays	Vendor pays
exit fees and taxes	Wholesaler pays	Wholesaler pays	Vendor pays	Vendor pays	Vendor pays	Vendor pays	Vendor pays
loading on ship	Wholesaler pays	Wholesaler pays	Vendor pays	Vendor pays	Vendor pays	Vendor pays	Vendor pays
ocean freight	Wholesaler pays	Wholesaler pays	Wholesaler pays	Vendor pays	Vendor pays	Vendor pays	Vendor pays
marine insurance	Wholesaler pays	Wholesaler pays	Wholesaler pays	Wholesaler pays	Vendor pays	Vendor pays	Vendor pays
duty on arrival at destination port	Wholesaler pays	Wholesaler pays	Wholesaler pays	Wholesaler pays	Wholesaler pays	Vendor pays	Vendor pays
transport to destination beyond port	Wholesaler pays	Wholesaler pays	Wholesaler pays	Wholesaler pays	Wholesaler pays	Wholesaler pays	Vendor pays

vendor's price increases as services are added

wholesaler's costs increase when they pay for services

vendor's risk increases as services are added

wholesaler's control over handling of merchandise increases when they pay for services

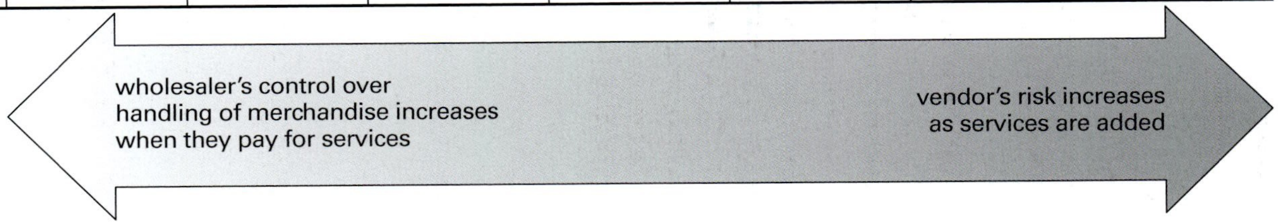

Figure 13.9
Explanation of who pays for various services in common categories of shipping arrangements.

offered by a brand in order to compete with others during a holiday season or during calendar sales events such as back-to-school.

A **quantity discount** benefits both the distributor, who gets to keep unit costs down, and the brand, who gets to sell more product while engaging production facilities on terms that benefit from the economies of scale and efficiency that large orders afford. **Promotional discounts** are offered to distributors in exchange for the cost of promoting the brand. Brands may offer **introductory allowances** to distributors to entice them to try a new product. Brands sometimes negotiate **invoice payment terms**, granting additional discounts to distributors when they agree to pay their bills early so that brands can save finance charges. As the selling season closes and the distributor must reduce the ticket price of the product to clear out inventory, they may ask the brand to accept reductions in the invoice price. The distributor justifies this **markdown money** with proof that goods are not selling due to poor quality, late deliveries, or styling that does not excite the customer.

Distributors will deduct **chargebacks** from a brand's invoice, usually for mislabeled products or late delivery. This practice started in the 1970s but increased as larger distributors demanded more detailed and precise packaging and labeling of shipments for automated warehouses. Friction increased as brands accused distributors of applying arbitrary chargebacks and putting the onus on the brand to disprove the charge. In the early 2000s, after lawsuits were filed against distributors, groups such as the Fashion Association in New York and the Vendor Compliance Federation were founded to look for mutually beneficial standards and practices. Nevertheless, chargebacks have become increasingly common and smaller businesses continue to struggle to meet such demands.

DISTRIBUTION COSTS

Massive store closures in the early 2020s and the expansion of e-commerce forced brands to rethink their distribution strategies, seeking the right mix of brick-and-mortar stores and e-commerce solutions for selling their products. When developing a distribution strategy, a brand will consider many factors such as their relationship with the customer, availability of goods, access to quality data. Cost is an aspect of them all.

Retail Brick and Mortar Costs

Of the many variables in calculating the expense of selling products on-ground, the costs of renting space and hiring people are unavoidable.

Payroll Costs

Payroll is one of the highest expenses in the on-ground P&L. Typically, around 18 percent of the retail price of a garment compensates people who unpack deliveries, prepare products for presentation, listen to the needs of the customer, make suggestions, search the store for possible choices, service the sale and returns, and clean up the fitting rooms (Rodrigue, 2021). Even a small retail store needs at least one person present during usual retail hours (anywhere from 48–72 hours a week). Higher-priced merchandise will require people to sell who have higher sales skills and experience and who will be paid more. Regardless of the direct hourly wage, payroll also includes indirect costs of benefits, commission, payroll taxes, training, etc. For brands that are willing to invest in face-to-face interaction with customers, the rewards are high and on-ground stores will probably continue to be a part of the distribution network.

Store Costs

Paying rent and related expenses is unavoidable for on-ground stores. Rent will include the storefront, storage space for inventory, toilets, and parking. The price per square foot is related to

- the amount of "foot-traffic" expected (will enough potential customers pass your door?)
- the mix of businesses (are there theaters and restaurants nearby?)
- the caliber and size of the neighboring stores (are the passers-by already shopping in this location going to have the taste and resources to buy your product?)
- ease and security of parking
- services provided by the landlord such as security, valet, seasonal decorations, promotions, events

Rent, liability, and insurance are fixed costs and usually absorb about 15 percent of the retail price of a garment. Variable costs related to the space such as utilities and services such as window cleaning and consumable store supplies such as hand sanitizer account for about 8 percent (Rodrigue, 2021).

Some independent stores rent space to outsiders to offset the cost of high rents. Some stores strike deals with brands who want to have their own store-within-a-store staffed by their own trained sales associates. This arrangement can be beneficial for the brand and the store. The brand maintains control over its image and collects its own sales data. The store recoups some of its rent and attracts customers who may buy its own products. Some stores make consignment deals with small and upcoming brands to showcase their products in a dedicated space. The store provides the sales staff and co-markets the products. The brand pays a percentage of the retail price, usually between 50–60 percent to the store. The store benefits by testing a new brand with low risk. Should the products not sell, the brand owns the merchandise and will seek other venues for their sale. Should the products be successful, the brand may become a regular supplier to the store. Whether the products sell or not, the brand benefits by testing the market and gathering data.

Warehousing Costs

Most bulk production is shipped to a warehouse, stored until needed, and then shipped in bulk to individual stores. Handling in and out of the warehouse is charged per pallet and includes the labor and equipment. Shipping is charged per box or pallet through the shipping company. Storage is charged like rent, by the square foot per increment of time. This cost, roughly 3percent of the retail price of a product, was at one time easy to calculate. It became an unexpectedly devastating expense during the pandemic of 2020 as stores cancelled orders or did not have the funds to pay for them. Investment in the production and storage of cancelled orders resulted in the bankruptcy of many brands, forcing liquidation of stock to recover costs and make room for new shipments. Because of this brands and stores have been developing new sales strategies that are based on smaller order quantities. For example, stores that want to ship directly to consumers may create that capability within the store, using the storeroom as a small warehouse and shipping station. Small brands are experimenting with striking deals with such stores, paying them a fee for holding a small quantity of product that can be packed and shipped on demand (Chen, 2020).

Cost of Goods

Brands do not expect to make a profit on the sale of goods to their own stores. This allows the store to have a higher profit margin. Independent retailers have been experimenting with brands that can offer smaller orders with short lead times to avoid the cost of markdowns and unsold store inventory. Consignment is another way for independent retailers to have product in their store with no risk of owning the product if it does not sell.

Marketing Costs

The cost of marketing for a branded store will be less than an independent retailer. The brands' marketing department will have already developed plans and fixtures for the decoration of the store, how to merchandise the product, and how to conduct outreach. Brands may consider selling a portion of their product on-ground in their own stores as a marketing tool to drive sales to online or vice versa. Selling in independent stores is also a way for a brand to test a market, however, lack of consistency for gathering sell-through data makes an on-ground channel a poorer partner than an online one when it comes to quick response in managing risks associated with too much or too little inventory.

Brands may contribute to co-marketing with a store, especially if the brand has a store-within-a store arrangement, but apart from this, independent stores do not have the marketing scope or reach of big brands or national retailers. Independents must generate interest and loyalty with print and media advertising, social media, co-marketing with neighbors, participation in local events and causes. These local connections have become increasingly important for attracting customers who support small and local businesses as a part of their commitment to sustainable practices (Nishimura, 2020).

Cost of Returns

Returns have always been a large cost in on-ground stores; however, there is always the possibility of reselling the return. A person who walks into a store to return an item is a potential customer for a new item. On-ground stores can also help avoid returns in the first place by training sales associates to be sure that the customer is satisfied with their purchase before buying it. Customers who buy multiple sizes online to find the one that fits can try on several sizes in the store, thereby eliminating the return of the sizes that do not fit.

E-commerce Costs

In e-commerce sales, the cost of goods will be roughly the same as that for brick-and-mortar. Selling products online eliminates the next largest expenses borne by on-ground stores—rent and payroll. Yet, e-commerce has many expenses that when added up make it a competitor to on-ground sales but not the clear winner. For that reason, brands sell their products in multiple channels to maximize their sales in a variety of markets.

Web Platform Costs

In e-commerce, the brick-and-mortar store is replaced by a digital store. Large brands have in-house IT departments who build and maintain their sales platforms. Smaller brands are not technology experts, so they subscribe to services such as Shopify, Wix, and Alibaba that provide them with the tools they need to reach their customers to sell and deliver their products. These companies offer menus of service that range from very basic packages for startups to complex, customized offerings for more mature businesses. There is usually an initial subscription and then monthly maintenance fees. Some fees vary depending on traffic. Such services may include

- website hosting
- templates for website design
- search engine optimization to keep the brand in front of the customer
- transaction security
- integration of orders from multiple sources such as social media, phone, and email and directing them to single drop-ship sites
- the ability to add services as the business grows
- the ability to conduct business in multiple currencies.

Selling on marketplace sites such as ASOS, Flubit, Alibaba, and Amazon provide small and startup brands with exposure without having to invest in their own web platform. These sites may sell their product with others or on dedicated brand sites. Even large brands sell on marketplace sites as a form of marketing and gathering data. Some specialty brands sell on curated sites such as Beklina, Inkloo, or Flora & Fauna where customers with specific tastes, interests, needs, or points of view want to view products that have been preselected by experts or afficionados. Big name luxury brands might be featured next to startup brands with the same cache. The percentage of sales taken by these sites varies.

Customer Acquisition and Retention Costs

A brand cannot rely on generating sales only from having products represented in online stores. It must generate interest and loyalty on social media, sales events in on-ground stores, involvement in events that support charities or causes, and garner support from celebrities. Retention will rely on multiple strategies such as the use of data collection and analysis and their application to product suggestions. Liberal return policies are crippling some online businesses, prompting them to allow returns only within a window. Shipping costs have prompted some brands to decentralize warehouse locations to reduce shipping time and fees. All of these costs are indirect. They cannot be measured against the sale of a product that is offered on multiple platforms. For this reason, calculating marketing cost has become a complex science.

Warehousing Costs

The boxes in a warehouse that handles bulk product are huge and remain closed. A fulfillment warehouse that services e-commerce and other DTC orders has open bins and boxes where a product is picked based on a single order and send on to be packed for shipping. Warehouses try to keep costs down by using robotic pickers, eliminating paper pick orders with Electronic Data Interchange (EDI), and employing 3D visualization software to select boxes. Some warehouses have been experimenting with pop-up fulfillment centers to deal with fluctuating demand. These centers provide an opportunity for startups to try DTC without having to have huge minimums.

SUSTAINABILITY

It is predicted that by 2024, 14 percent of the apparel market will be handled through recommerce (Murphy, 2021). Some recommerce supply chains have been around for a long time such as thrift stores and alteration and repair shops. New business models, emerging rapidly to respond to the demand for circularity, rely on technology and partnerships. Some of the expenses for selling goods by recommerce are similar to those found on the P&Ls of businesses that sell new products. The greatest difference is in costs associated with acquiring goods.

Cost of Reselling New Products

One source of procuring products for recommerce distribution is brands and retailers who have warehouses full of bulk products that never made it to a sales site or sales floor due to overstock or cancellations. These products are undamaged and often available in complete size runs and color choices. They are still in their original packaging with original labels and swing tags. Companies such as B-Stock contract with brands to manage the auction of these large lots to resellers. Resellers pay a fraction of the original bulk price for the goods and usually arrange to pay for the freight to their own warehouse. Once the reseller owns the product and has paid the fee for a resale certificate in their state, they can distribute it in any channel. Companies that do this can be small and local, others are large, international companies such as T.J. Maxx (USA), Marshalls (USA and Canada), T.K. Maxx (Europe and Australia), or e-commerce sites such as Overstock.com. They may choose to pay a licensing fee to the original brand so that they can legally use its logos and name for advertising (O'Brien, 2018).

Some brands and retailers have leftover new stock that is no longer in complete size runs or color assortments and may include damaged, returned, or out-of-style items. It is not easy to sell these items through their own linear distribution systems as new product. Patagonia, Levi's, REI, North Face, Carhartt, and Prana work with Trove (USA) and Renewal Workshops (USA and Netherlands), leaders in the recommerce supply chain. In addition to processing garments for resale they specialize in protecting brand value in the secondary market through authentication. This process can be time consuming and costly because it calls for expertise in the identification of fakes and may require testing. Brands such as Ralph Lauren, Yoox and Puma are already investing in the infrastructure to support the secondary market by adding QR codes or RFID chips when they produce garments so that authentication can eventually be automated (Murphy, 2021).

Whether the product is destined to be sold with brand pedigree or relabeled, the processing costs include

- removal of packaging
- inspection and sorting
- sewing labor which may include repair, preparing for label changes, or sewing in new labels
- repackaging
- remarketing which may include photos, descriptions, and pricing
- customer service
- picking, packing, and shipping

The costs accrued by preparing goods for the secondary market may be more than the customer wants to pay. Some brands such as Burberry and H&M chose to destroy products rather than invest in reprocessing. Their customers and the press let these brands know that such practices are unacceptable (Khomami, 2018). Brands are increasingly seeking options other than destruction to signal their commitment to circularity.

Rental models such as Rent the Runway (RTR) avoid costs for brand authentication because the product never leaves their ownership. They do incur costs for their robust e-commerce platforms that use recommendation software to reduce customer dissatisfaction (and therefore lost business and returns). When they started in business, RTR offered one-on-one shopping and styling advice both online and in brick-and-mortar stores. However, due to high cost, and losses related to the pandemic, they had to close all of their stores in 2020, using the locations for drop-off only. Costs such as inspection, stain removal, steam cleaning, and mending are high due to the skill level and time needed to keep the products looking as good as new. Acquisition cost of new products can be mitigated by negotiating deals with brands. RTR now buys its products from vendors on a consignment basis to reduce investment in styles that are not popular (Hollis, 2021).

Cost of Reselling Used Products

Brands struggle to maintain the integrity of their identity in the secondary market when the source of the product is a single person. Vestiaire Collective, a recommerce marketplace that connects private sellers of luxury items with private buyers, pays the seller to ship the product to their facility where it is subjected to a rigorous authentication process by experts. The company pays for shipping to the buyer and shares up to 80 percent of the selling price with the seller.

Sites such as The RealReal, ThreadUP, and Poshmark also provide a marketplace that connects private buyers and sellers. They do not authenticate, so the seller takes legal responsibility for the legitimacy of what they are selling. These recommerce marketplaces have features that offer buyers and sellers a tradeoff between convenience or cash. Services might include pick up from seller, shipping to buyer, paying sales tax, handling returns, sorting and donating products that will not be sold, writing product descriptions, bidding, or building sales within the site's community. As the secondary online market continues to evolve, the number of recommerce marketplaces is increasing. They are differentiating themselves with the types of services they provide and types of products they handle as well as the method and amount of payout.

Some businesses such as Plato's Closet, Crossroads Trading, or Buffalo Exchange use the "pawn shop" model where the seller gets instant cash for their used item. This system allows the store a steady flow of fresh merchandise from which they can select or reject. This type of on-ground store must budget for marketing costs to continually reach out to their individual suppliers. They generally pay more to rent stores with high foot traffic of both buyers and sellers. They may purchase some new bulk product to maintain consistency of inventory on the sales floor (Murphy, 2021).

Donors of used products to nonprofit organizations such as Goodwill Industries or Oxfam may benefit from earning a tax write-off or coupon for shopping. In addition, they may be happy in the knowledge that they are keeping textile waste out of landfills. For a nonprofit organization to continue to do its good work, it must cover its costs, which may include training and employing people from marginalized communities. Apart from the expense of running retail stores, costs might include

- awareness: campaigns to encourage people to donate their clothing rather than throw it in the garbage
- collection: bins in public places and trucks to pick up donations from bins and homes
- space: once goods are collected, they have to be processed and staged for sale
- sorting: a very labor intensive and skilled process
- washing, restoring, and repairing
- preparing in bales for bulk sales at auction
- preparing for store sale by gender, age, etc. and adding a price tag

Nonprofit organizations are not the only resellers who repair used clothing. Some brands, such as Levi's SecondHand, Patagonia's Worn Wear, and Eileen Fisher's Renew, have developed recommerce platforms for their own products where they collect and sell previously owned clothing. Their expenses include the usual costs of e-commerce as well as authentication, cleaning, repair, remarketing, and shipping. They offer gift cards, credit, or coupons, which reduces income earned from new products. These resale channels bring in enough revenue to be self-supporting. Patagonia reports that Worn Wear was profitable within two years of its inception. By offering their own refurbished products with all their brand attributes at an affordable price, brands can attract new customers and track their buying habits (Murphy, 2021).

Take-back programs that offer to recycle used clothing in exchange for new products also benefit from building relationships with new customers. Knickey, who sells organic cotton underwear, reports having recruited about one quarter of their customers from those who send in old undies (any brand) in exchange for a new pair (Wicker, 2019).

Figure 13.10
Canadian recommerce company, Pre-loved, has been crafting unique fashion for more than twenty years, blending reclaimed vintage clothing with deadstock and overrun fabric waste from the apparel industry.

Cost of Transforming Used Products and Textile Waste

About half of donated clothing is in good enough condition to be resold. When apparel products make their way back into the supply chain and cannot be resold, they might be candidates for upcycling into other items. Eileen Fisher's Resewn collection deconstructs take-back garments into one-of-a-kind designs and North Face's Remade program sells "creatively repaired" items. Patagonia makes new products from various forms of textile waste in its ReCrafted program and in partnership with independent companies such as Frankie Collective, a Canadian team of apparel designers and technicians (Chua, 2021). Because of the high labor costs and rental fees for storage space, upcycling by larger brands is financially feasible if the original product is high value and already in demand (Wicker, 2019). Smaller brands such as Fanfare, Antiform, Don Kaka, and Pre-loved have built viable businesses on the ethos of the circular economy, the spirit of creating community, and the desire for clothing with a story (Figure 13.10). Although they are creating wearable art which demands a high level of expensive skilled labor, they can balance these costs with the low cost of acquiring discarded materials and the marketing power of social media which leverages word-of-mouth and drives customers to pop-up trunk shows and events (Radin, 2019).

Cost of Recycling

Clothing that cannot be resold or upcycled is sorted again by color and fiber, stripped of trims, and sent to be sold as rags. Products that are not even useful as rags may be shredded and reformed into padding for furniture, mattresses, carpet pads, or appliances or used for insulation in homes and cars. Some fibers can be shredded or broken down and respun into new yarn. Sorting and stripping apparel for use as rags or shredding demands a high amount of skilled labor. New technologies are emerging that can sort textile waste by fiber but they are not in widespread use. Products that do not have a positive economic return or cannot be recycled are sent to landfills or incinerated (Leblanc, 2019).

SUMMARY

Today brands generate expenses and income from activities in multiple distribution channels and supply chain partners including planning, production, distribution, and recommerce. A standard financial tool, the Profit and Loss Statement, is useful in managing this complex environment. Product developers are instrumental in developing cost sheets in stages as products are planned, designed, sampled, and produced. In each of the elements of a cost sheet, decisions can be made to uphold brand standards or contain costs. Some of those costs relate directly to the production to the product; some relate to activities that indirectly impact the cost. As new distribution channels emerge, brands may decide to lose income from some channel to build brand identity and attract customers. Some aspects of building a profitable recommerce business may resemble older business models but others, such acquiring goods, are new.

KEY TERMS

absorption costing

activity-based costing

chargebacks

cost of goods sold

costs and expenses

direct costing

direct costs

direct labor

fixed costs

gross margin

gross sales

income or revenue

introductory allowances

invoice payment terms

Life Cycle Assessment (LCA)

make-to-order (MTO)

make-to-stock (MTS)

markdown money

net sales

operating expenses

operating profit

other expenses or income

post-production costing

production cost

Profit and Loss Statement (P&L)

profit before taxes

promotional discount

quantity discount

recommerce

returns and allowances

seasonal discount

Standard Allowed Minutes (SAMs)

suggested retail price (list price)

trade discount

Triple Bottom Line (TBL)

variable costs

Case Study 13.1
The Environmental Profit and Loss Statement

The last line on a Profit and Loss Statement, the profit, is sometimes called the "bottom line". Environmentalist John Elkington suggested substituting the traditional "bottom line" with the **Triple Bottom Line**, to take into account the full measure of the resources being consumed or damaged by a company, as well as the contribution it is making to the world:

- Planet: environmental stewardship
- People: social responsibility
- Profit and loss: traditional accounting bottom line (Elkington, 1997)

Luxury apparel giant, Kering, launched its Environmental Profit & Loss Account (EP&L) in 2013, a working model for calculating the Triple Bottom Line which they use to guide business strategy and progress toward neutral environmental impact.

Environmental Profit & Loss Account (EP&L)

Kering's EP&L Account is a tool used for measuring the environmental impact of activities for all of their brands, from the beginning to end of their supply chain. Subsidiaries Gucci and Stella McCartney publish their own separate EP&Ls using the same methodology, which highlights six aspects of environmental damage: carbon emissions, water use, water pollution, land use, air pollution, and waste. These are examined each year in relation to each stage of production and distribution: raw materials, processing, manufacturing, assembly, operations, and retail. The data is gathered and analyzed to quantify the impact on people and planet. These measurements are translated into a monetary equivalent so that they can be reported in a language that shareholders, executives, and customers can relate to. When the amounts are formatted in graphs and tables, they can illustrate progress of each brand over time and in comparison with each other (Kering, 2021a).

Kering uses its EP&L to drive sustainability strategy, allowing the company to prioritize its efforts on areas that are causing the most damage and to form to a coherent plan. Early EP&Ls showed that over 90 percent of negative environmental impact was the result of unsustainable production and processing of raw materials in agriculture, mining, and forestry. Although they do have initiatives for sustainable practices in retail and warehousing their focus is on supporting regenerative systems that not only mitigate climate change but also promote biodiversity and support all people to thrive (Donaldson, 2018).

For Gucci, some of their top measurable goals include increased use of organic and recycled fibers and extending circularity programs such as Scrap-Less. In 2015, Gucci set a goal of reducing its total greenhouse gas emissions by 50 percent by 2025. As of 2019, Gucci has reduced its emissions "all the way to the end of the supply chain" by 39 percent relative to growth (Equilibrium, 2021).

Collaboration

Creating and using an EP&L for any company is an exercise in collaboration. From reporting to analyzing to sharing information, the project of cleaning up the planet is too big for any brand to manage alone.

EP&L reports are based on indicators that are developed by scientists and academics. The knowledge base is highly complex, continually expanding and being refined. Building the metrics for an EP&L calls for collaboration with environmental nonprofit organizations and research groups who compile and analyze data in reports such as **Life Cycle Assessments (LCAs)**, which catalog and evaluate the environmental impact of each stage of producing, distributing, and disposing of a specific product.

It is well known that the production of cellulosic fibers made from pulp has a devastating effect on water and land use. In 2017, Stella McCartney commissioned a Life Cycle Assessment from SGS Global Services to obtain a detailed understanding of the environmental impact of cellulosic fibers made from pulp from ten different sources including managed forests, rainforest, and bamboo and recycled fiber from several regions. This report helps Stella McCartney refine sustainability goals regarding water and land use and make informed decisions to reach its targets. The company makes its findings available open source to provide

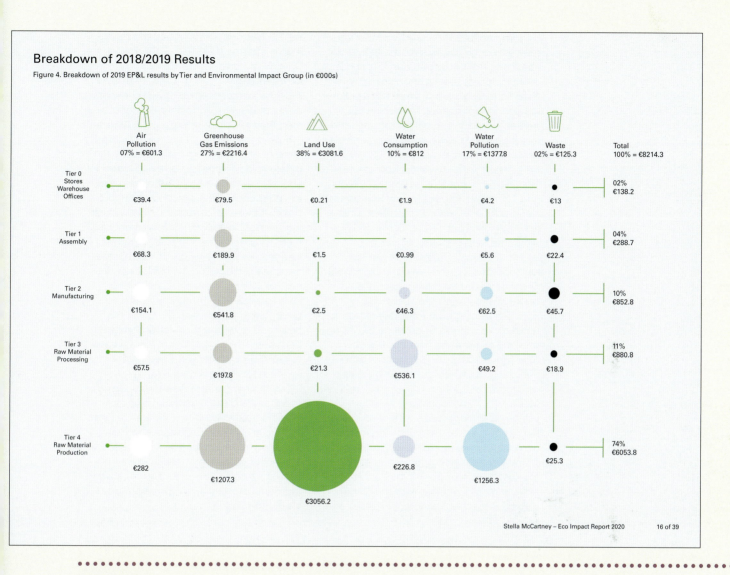

Breakdown of 2018/2019 Results

Figure 4. Breakdown of 2019 EP&L results by Tier and Environmental Impact Group (in €000s)

	Air Pollution 07% = €601.3	Greenhouse Gas Emissions 27% = €2216.4	Land Use 38% = €3081.6	Water Consumption 10% = €812	Water Pollution 17% = €1377.8	Waste 02% = €125.3	Total 100% = €8214.3
Tier 0 Stores Warehouse Offices	€39.4	€79.5	€0.21	€1.9	€4.2	€13	02% €138.2
Tier 1 Assembly	€68.3	€189.9	€1.5	€0.99	€5.6	€22.4	04% €288.7
Tier 2 Manufacturing	€154.1	€541.8	€2.5	€46.3	€62.5	€45.7	10% €852.8
Tier 3 Raw Material Processing	€57.5	€197.8	€21.3	€536.1	€49.2	€18.9	11% €880.8
Tier 4 Raw Material Production	€282	€1207.3	€3056.2	€226.8	€1256.3	€25.3	74% €6053.8

Stella McCartney – Eco Impact Report 2020   16 of 39

Figure CS13.1

Eco Impact Report 2020 from Stella McCartney, "Breakdown of 2019EP&L results by Tier and Environmental impact Group." The large green dot in Tier 4 under Land Use shows an environmental hotspot: water pollution caused by copper mining (used for hardware). Note that Raw Material Production accounts for 74 percent of the brand's environmental impact.

transparency for anyone wishing to examine the firm's process and to support other companies to make their own decisions (Schultz & Surech, 2017).

In 2017, apparel industry giants such as The Gap, PVH, and Target put competition aside and joined together to create the Apparel Impact Institute (AII). Its purpose is to unify and increase industry efforts focused on narrowly defined issues concerning water, energy, and pollution. In 2020, AII launched a platform for Italian luxury apparel and footwear brands to work together, funding and expanding their environmental initiatives through Clean by Design (Warren, 2021).

Some goals can be reached most efficiently through collaboration with international nonprofit organizations. Gucci has come to realize that its efforts to achieve its EP&L goal of carbon neutrality are not enough. Although they have done considerable work in avoiding, reducing, and restoring the damage done by greenhouse gasses, they have been faced, at least for the present, with unavoidable emissions. They have chosen to offset to reach their goals. They work together with the United Nations REDD+ project to protect forests from being logged in Cambodia, Indonesia, Kenya, and Peru (Chua, 2020).

In their early EP&Ls, Stella McCartney found that cashmere had the most negative environmental impact of any of the raw materials they used. Compared to wool, cashmere requires twenty times more animals to produce the same quantity of sweaters. The popularity of cashmere has pushed producers in Mongolia to expand pasture for goats, destroying natural grassland. In 2016 Stella McCartney replaced all virgin cashmere used in their collections with regenerated Re.Verso™, a cashmere yarn regenerated from factory waste. (Stella McCartney, 2016). Kering is going further by supporting sustainable pastoral practices in Mongolia in a collaboration with the Natural Capital Project at Stanford University and the US National Aeronautics and Space Administration (NASA).

Leadership

Big luxury brands did not invent the sustainability movement and they have contributed their fair share to waste, pollution, and misuse of resources. Critics have accused them of greenwashing and exploiting the passions of eco-consciousness of Generation Z for their own profit. Managing their activities using EP&L accounting can put some of these accusations to rest because the science behind the measurements and the data collected are available on their websites and those who wish to can study the methodology and conclusions of the reports. Kering, Stella McCartney, and Gucci are leading the way by taking risks by exposing and owning their past mistakes and revealing their current financial behaviors. They are also forming alliances to remedy past errors and sharing their research for all brands to use.

Kering encourages new businesses to use the EP& L to guide their business practices by partnering with accelerators such as Plug and Play in California and Fashion for Good in Amsterdam (Gunther, 2020). They offer guidance on their website on setting up an EP&L and an app for costing individual products with sustainable materials (Kering 2021b).

References

Elkington, J. (1997), Cannibals with forks: The triple bottom line of 21st century business. Oxford: Capstone.

Kering. (2021a), What is an EP&L? https://www.kering.com/en/sustainability/environmental-profit-loss/what-is-an-ep-l/ (accessed February 21, 2021).

Kering. (2021b), My EP&L https://www.kering.com/en/sustainability/environmental-profit-loss/app-my-ep-l/ (accessed February 23, 2021).

Donaldson, T. (2018), "Sourcing Scoop: Kering Sustainability Leader on Really Navigating Sustainable Sourcing," *Sourcing Journal*, December 7. https://sourcingjournal.com/topics/sourcing/kering-helen-crowley-sustainable-sourcing-129665/ (accessed February 20, 2021).

Equilibrium. (2021), Environmental Profit and Loss accounting. Gucci. https://equilibrium.gucci.com/environmental-profit-and-loss-accounting/ (accessed February 23, 2021).

Gunther, C. (2020), "Kering shines light on sustainability efforts," *Vogue Business*. January 30. https://www.voguebusiness.com/sustainability/kering-shines-light-on-sustainability-efforts-luxury (accessed February 23, 2021).

Schultz, T. & Surech, A. (2017), Life Cycle Assessment Comparing Ten Sources of Manmade Cellulose Fiber. https://cdn.scsglobalservices.com/files/resources/SCS-Stella-LCA-MainReport-101017.pdf (accessed February 22, 2021).

Stella McCartney. (2016), Stella McCartney Environmental Profit and Loss. December 5. https://www.stellamccartney.com/cloud/smcwp/uploads/2017/09/Stella-McCartney-EPL-Report-2016-FINAL.pdf (accessed February 23, 2021).

Stella McCartney. (2020), Eco Impact Report. https://www.stellamccartney.com/cloud/smcwp/uploads/2020/09/EcoImpact_2020.pdf (accessed February 22, 2021).

Warren, L. (2021), "Apparel Impact Institute Taps Luxury Giants to Make Italian Fashion More Sustainable," *Sourcing Journal*. February 3. https://sourcingjournal.com/denim/denim-business/apparel-impact-institute-italian-sustainable-fashion-program-stella-mccartney-kering-259616/ (accessed February 20, 2021).

DISCUSSION QUESTIONS

1. Review the discussion of balancing the cost of goods and gross margin in a retail Profit and Loss Statement. Look at Figure 13.1. The simulation reflects a drop in gross margin in May. Look at the figures highlighted in orange. What caused that? What did the buyer do in June to bring the gross margin closer to the retailer's expected 52 percent?

2. Imagine that you are the production manager of a CMT facility that produces athleisure clothing for women. Generally, the textiles used are consistent, changing only in color from style to style. Even the general silhouette of the tops, bottoms, and jackets is similar. The detailing, however, such as the seaming, embroidery, pocket shape and location, ribbing cuffs, and Velcro and zipper closures, change often. Review the three methods of production costing. Choose the one you think will capture the real operating expenses and allow your operation to make a profit.

3. Choose a major brand with whose products you are familiar. Search online for a product that you might buy. Choose a product that will be easy to find, for example Levi's 501 jeans. Find every site that you can where the product is sold. Go to the brand's own site and find the stores that sell the brand and find a store near you. Call them to see if they have the product in the store. For every location and e-commerce site where you find the product, write down the price and the shipping cost. Is the price (including shipping) the same in all distribution channels? What do you think accounts for variance in the price? Where would you choose to buy this product? Why?

ACTIVITIES

1. Review the section of this chapter on phases of wholesale costing. Think of the key players on the product development team and choose one. Imagine that you are that person. Imagine that you are working with an OEM vendor. List your interactions with team members and the vendor in each of the three costing phases. For example, suppose you are a technical designer. Where will costing information come from? What information will you be looking for? What blanks will you fill in on the preliminary cost sheet? What will you do if the labor cost is too high? With whom will you consult? Who will make the final decision about the production cost?

2. Study the line list in Figure 13.4. This simulation suggests balancing the cost of goods and gross margin by seeking lower-duty categories through changes in materials or country of origin. Study the line sheet, review the text, and find another strategy.

3. Ask each student in the class to identify an issue that they feel passionate about (environmental, social, political) or an affinity group with whom they identify. Ask each student to look for curated marketplace e-commerce sites that serve the group that shares their interests. Ask them to present three sites to the group, comparing the sites as to whether they would buy products from them and why.

STUDiO RESOURCES

- Take the chapter quiz with scored results and personalized study tips.
- Review glossary flashcards to build your vocabulary.

REFERENCES

Barrett, P.M., and Baumann-Pauley, D. (2019), Made in Ethiopia: Challenges in the Garment Industry's New Frontier. https://issuu.com/nyusterncenterforbusinessandhumanri/docs/nyu_ethiopia_final _online?e=31640827/69644612 (accessed March 24, 2021).

Chen, C. (2020), "7 Ways to Make E-Commerce More Profitable," *Business of Fashion*, November 12. https://www.businessoffashion.com/articles/retail/e-commerce-margins-profitable-pandemic (accessed February 10, 2021).

Chua, J.M. (2021), "Frankie Collective Converts Castoff Patagonia Garments into Sexy Streetwear," *Sourcing Journal*, January 22. https://sourcingjournal.com/topics/sustainability/frankie-collective -patagonia-upcycling-repurposed-streetwear-textile-waste-256755/ (accessed February 11, 2021).

Hollis, S. (2021), "How Rent The Runway Built an $800 Million Business in a Mom-and-Pop Industry," *Jilt.com*, January 14. yhttps://jilt.com/blog/rent-the-runway-logistics/ (accessed March 12, 2021).

Khomami, N. (2018), "Burberry destroys £28m of stock to guard against counterfeits," *The Guardian*, July 19. https://www.theguardian.com/fashion/2018/jul/19/burberry-destroys-28m-stock-guard-against -counterfeits (accessed February 15, 2021).

Leblanc, R. (2019), "How Clothing Recycling Works," *The Balance*, February 27. https://www .thebalancesmb.com/how-garment-recycling-works-2877992 (accessed February 12, 2021).

Murphy. N. (2021), "There's A Quiet Revolution Underway with Recommerce," *Forbes*. https://www .forbes.com/sites/niallmurphy/2021/02/17/theres-a-quiet-revolution-underway-with-recommerce/ (accessed February 28, 2021).

Nishimura, K. (2020), "In Banner Year for DTC, Are Brands Really Fleeing Wholesale?" *Sourcing Journal*, December 2. https://sourcingjournal.com/topics/retail/nuorder-wholesale-fashion-brands -ecommerce-coronavirus-dtc-247973/ (accessed February 1, 2021).

O'Brien, M. 2018. Is it legal to buy products from stores and resell them online as new? June 29. https:// www.obrienpatents.com/legal-buy-products-stores-resell-online-new/ accessed February 28, 2021).

Pre-loved. (2021), About us. https://getpreloved.com/blogs/news/how-we-do-it (accessed February 15, 2021).

Radin, S. (2019), "What's behind the rise of upcycled garments?" *Fashionista*, January 16. https:// fashionista.com/2019/01/upcycled-clothing-sustainable-fashion-trend (accessed March 15, 2021).

Rodrigue, J-P. (2021). "Comparison Between Retail and E-commerce Cost Structures for a $150 Apparel Piece," *The Geography of Transport Systems*. https://transportgeography.org/contents/chapter7/ logistics-freight-distribution/ecommerce_cost_structure-2/ (accessed February 10, 2021).

Wicker, A. (2019), "Fashion's growing interest in recycling clothing," *Vogue Business*, August 21. https://www.voguebusiness.com/companies/fashion-brands-recycling-upcycling-resale-takeback -sustainability (accessed February 12, 2021).

GLOSSARY

3D matching technology. Used to create a 3D shape by comparing the two photos taken at different angles.

absorption costing. A method of costing that assesses operating expenses as a percentage relative to the direct labor value. This method assumes that the percentage is high enough to cover set-up costs without the necessity of recording the cost of each activity individually.

achromatic. Neutrals without color; black, white, and gray are considered achromatic.

activity-based costing. A method of costing which measures each indirect cost (such as administration, marketing, and engineering) and charges that cost to individual products.

additive color-mixing system. A structure that explains how colored light is mixed. It is used in theater lighting, on television screens, and on computer monitors. When using the additive mixing system to mix colored light, red, green, and blue or blue-violet are the primaries; yellow, magenta, and cyan are the secondaries. When all three of the additive primaries are mixed, the human eye sees white. The greatest range of color can be produced using the additive mixing system.

aesthetic properties. Characteristics of textiles that convey meaning to the consumer through their expression in apparel products by means of drape and hand, luster, surface interest, and other properties.

African Growth and Opportunity Act (AGOA). A non-reciprocal trade agreement between the US and sub-Sahara Africa nations, permitting them to export goods (many of which are apparel) to the USA duty-free.

analogous. A color harmony that consists of colors positioned next to each other on the color wheel.

apparel supply chain. The flow of all information, products, materials, and funds between different stages of creating and selling a product to the end-user.

applied design. Textile surface design that is added to the surface of finished goods.

Association of Southeast Asian Nations (ASEAN). A trade bloc including Indonesia, Malaysia, the Philippines, Singapore, Thailand, Brunei, Vietnam, Laos, Myanmar, and Cambodia.

assortment plan (range plan). A document that further defines the line plan using the line concept as a unifying theme. An assortment plan is a detailed chart that shows the number of styles, fabrics, colors, and sizes that will be included in the line. Each style is illustrated and paired with fabric swatches. If the style is to be made in more than one size run (e.g., misses and petites or tall), that is also indicated since every combination will be a separate SKU.

asymmetric balance. Describes a garment that is different on each side. Asymmetry may be achieved by an off-center closing or a pocket detail on only one side of the garment. Coordinating garments should be similarly balanced or neutral with no visible center point.

athleisure. Athletic-inspired apparel worn for leisure wear.

authenticity. A term used to describe a business that is true to its values in relation to its products and services, its supply chain partners, and its final customers.

auxiliary businesses. Specialty businesses that support the apparel product development process by filling in process voids that a brand does not have the capacity to perform in-house. Auxiliary businesses include, but are not limited to, design bureaus, software providers, sourcing agents, factors (credit agents), patternmaking services, testing labs, consultants, and advertising agencies. Auxiliary businesses are also a good resource when demand for a task is greater than the in-house team can handle and still meet deadlines.

avant-garde design. Describes the work of designers who break the rules, innovate with new technology, and are masters of fabric manipulation. They value an interdisciplinary approach to design and are more concerned with creativity than commercial viability.

B Corporation™. A business, certified by B Lab, to have standards of verified, overall social and environmental performance, public transparency, and legal accountability.

balance. Refers to the distribution of the visual weight of objects, color, texture, and bulk in a garment, giving it a sense of stability or equilibrium. It is determined by dividing a silhouette vertically down the middle.

balance (pattern). A characteristic expressed when gravity can act upon all parts of a garment equally so that they are able to hang without pitching or twisting to the front, back or side.

basic goods. Textiles used by a brand for the core products of a line that do not change radically from year to year in quality or appearance.

basic product (commodity). Product that is produced in high volume, with predictable demand, and is very price sensitive; the consumer can purchase it from a variety of competitors. Since these products change minimally from season to season, design decisions can be made early, providing a longer production lead time. This longer lead time in combination with high volume means product can be produced at relatively low unit cost offshore.

bilateral trade agreements. Pacts struck between two nations or between a nation and a trade block for mutual benefit in trade.

bill of materials (BOM). A section of a tech pack in which textiles, trims, labels and packing materials are listed with description, sizes, quantities, and other information needed to ensure that the product is made according to the design.

block patterns (slopers). The simplest pattern pieces needed to make a garment. In a dress, the pieces would include a front, back, and sleeve with no style lines, design detail, or finishing pieces such as facings. Blocks include ease for comfort and movement, but no extra fabric for silhouettes that extend beyond the body shape.

bobbin. A small spool in the bottom of a single needle lockstitch machine that carries one of the threads that make up the stitch.

body form (mannequin, dress form). Full or scaled representations of the whole body or partial sections (such as torso or legs) which are placed on a stand to facilitate patternmaking, draping, and fitting activities.

body model (avatar). A digital representation of a three-dimensional body.

booked seam. The most common configuration of fabric in industrial sewing in which two layers of fabric are lined up along their cut edges and inserted into the machine.

BOPIS or BOPUS. Two acronyms for buy online, pick up instore.

bottom weight. Textiles weighing more than 6.0 ounces per square yard; they are used in products such as pants, skirts, jackets, etc.

bound seams. Fabric edges on garment parts that are cleaned by the application of a separate piece of fabric.

braid. Textile trims made of heavy cord wrapped by filament or metal yarns; often used for military or formal looks.

brand. The name, logo, tagline, and/or other unique feature that identifies a businesses' goods or services with a promise to its customers that is distinct from its competitors.

brand equity. Refers to the value that accrues to a brand for customers, who may be willing to spend more for the promise of a brand-name product, and as a corporate asset that can be leveraged in launching new product categories, influencing mergers and acquisitions, maximizing revenue streams, and justifying capital investment.

brand extension. The practice of using an existing brand's reputation to promote a new service or product. This can be achieved by expanding a brand's assortment or launching a new product category or service under an existing brand label.

brand image. The consumer's set of assumptions and feelings about products and/or services provided under the brand name.

brand portfolio. The management of multiple brands by a single company. Each brand is managed as a separate entity so that the average consumer is generally unaware of the business relationship.

brand/product positioning. A marketing strategy that crafts a brand image to highlight the brand's products and services in a way that customers perceive it to be more desirable than the competition. Brand positioning matches product characteristics (size range, fit, colors, logos, fabrication, styling) to decisions regarding channels of distribution, distribution partners, location, presentation (website design, social media, and/or store design), and pricing.

brand umbrella. A group of brands that are owned by the same company and that ownership is transparent or obvious to the final consumer.

branding. A competitive strategy used to create, communicate, and strengthen a brand's promise to its target market. Branding integrates a brand's visual identity, product differentiation, level of service, marketing, and market positioning in the minds of the consumer.

break point. The point along the front edge of the garment at which the lapel begins to roll back.

breakline. The line on which the lapels turn back.

buck (utility press). Press with two parts that open and close like an oyster. They press tailored products with pressure and steam.

business functions/operations. High- level groupings of processes that describe the workings of a business.

business plan. A document that makes a case for the market and operational feasibility of a new company or division in order to attract investors or secure loans.

busted seam (butterflied). A seam whose edges are prefinished before it is stitched and pressed with the seam allowances open.

callouts (blowups). Separate drawings in a larger scale that magnify an area so that a patternmaker or sample maker can understand exactly what is expected.

computer vision technology. Used to process and analyze digital information from photos to create fitting avatars of retail customers.

capsule collection. Smaller collections of ten to thirty pieces, delivered every two to six weeks—rather than seasonal collections that are released all at one time.

cardigan. Sweaters that have a front opening.

chain stitch machine. Forms a stitch where one thread is forced by a needle through layers of fabric and then interlooped with a thread from a looper underneath.

channel. A chain of businesses or intermediaries through which a product or service is distributed.

channel strategy. A brand's plan for moving a product or service through one or more chains of commerce to the final customer.

chargebacks. Distributors will deduct chargebacks from a brand's invoice, usually for mislabeled products or late delivery.

chatbots. Computer programs that simulate human conversation through voice commands or text chats, which assist with shopping or customer service.

chroma. A color's saturation, or degree of departure from the neutral of the same value. It is determined by the amount of pigment in a color. Hues at 100 percent intensity are fully saturated with pigment; when there is no pigment present, a gray of equal value to the color is left.

chromatic. Describes something that has even the slightest amount of a hue.

circular supply chain (closed loop). A zero-waste supply chain that reuses, recycles, or composts all materials. It requires product developers to design out waste and pollution, keeping products and materials in use and regenerating natural systems.

clienteling. A technique whereby sales associates use devices to establish long-term relationships with customers based on data about their preferences, behaviors, and purchases.

cluster models. A type of predictive analytics that uses algorithms to segment audiences based on past brand engagement, past purchases, and demographics.

CMT (cut-make-trim). A vendor who cuts fabric provided by the client, assembles and finishes the product and ships it.

co-branding. A term that refers to the practice of marketing a product or service under two brand names linking the competitive advantage of both brands. The terms of the agreement may be for a single collection or for a term of three to five years, renewable at the discretion of both parties.

collaborative supply chain. An interactive network of manufacturing specialists who join forces operationally to integrate complementary resources in response to a market opportunity. The goal is to strike strong and mutually beneficial long-term relationships with suppliers while retaining the ability to pivot to meet market needs.

collar. Component part that surrounds the neck and is attached permanently or temporarily to the neckline of the garment.

color. The visual perception of an object as a result of the way in which it reflects certain wavelengths of light seen by the retina of the eye. Visible light consists of a narrow band of wavelengths within the electromagnetic spectrum, which also includes television and radio waves, X-rays, ultraviolet light, and infrared light.

colorants. Pigments and dyes that work by reflecting, absorbing, or transmitting light energy that our eye recognizes as color.

color blocked garment. A garment whose pieces are cut from contrasting color fabric.

color constancy. A feature of the human color perception system that refers to the perceived color of something appearing relatively constant regardless of the light source.

color harmonies. A term that refers to how colors are used in combination with one another in patterns and prints.

color inconstancy. The phenomenon of a single-color sample reading as a slightly different color under different light sources. Color inconstancy is related to the color hue rather than the color recipe.

color management. The process of controlling the outcome of a color, from the initial concept (a chip, swatch, yarn, or sample) to the final production output, in a way that is acceptable to the consumer.

color solids. A visual representation of color that shows how colors relate to one another in respect to their attributes of hue, value, and chroma. Each color in a color solid can be identified using the color system's numerical notation system, which identifies the specific color in color space. The resulting notation system facilitates the visual identification, matching, and reproduction of colors.

color standard. A visual fabric reference with color code data to which dyed samples can be measured and compared for accurate color reproduction.

color temperature. A term used to describe a color's apparent warmth or coolness in relation to another color. Yellow, orange, and red are traditionally known as warm colors, whereas green, blue, and violet are considered cool colors. Intermediate colors such as red-violet and yellow-green are considered temperate colors, but they can migrate toward the warm or cool temperatures depending on the proportion of colors mixed.

color-matching system. A method for identifying the range of color that can be produced on a given material such as paper, cotton, wool, polyester, or silk and, in some cases, the dye formula to obtain that color.

colorways. The range of colors or color combinations in which a style or design is available.

competitive advantage. Refers to attributes that allow an organization to outperform its competitors.

complementary. A color harmony that consists of colors opposite one another on the color wheel.

complex subtractive color-mixing system. A structure that explains how thick films of color are mixed.

component parts. Elements of a garment that are not part of its basic structure but add aesthetic interest or provide functionality. Examples include collars, cuffs, pockets, and belts.

Computer Aided Design (CAD). Software for creating original design sketches, layout of merchandising boards, color management and illustrations for the tech pack.

computer vision technology. The science behind some of applications that extract information about customers' measurements from scans or photos to make sales recommendations.

concept board. A collection of images, sketches, color references, and swatches that express the design direction a brand is exploring for a particular delivery. Concept boards may be physical or digital depending on how they will be shared.

concept review. A checkpoint for the design team to present their ideas to the merchandising, sales, and marketing teams to ensure that design assortments are in sync with line plan expectations.

concept store. A specialty retailer, generally located in a fashion capital, that curates its selection to define the newest brands, designers, and trends influencing fashion.

concession strategy. A leasing agreement between a retailer and a brand whereby the retailer leases out designated space to the brand which can then operate somewhat autonomously, curating its product and services and staffing with its own personnel.

contemporary designer. Designers/brands that offer clothes with a younger vibe and somewhat lower price point than found at designer RTW. They distinguish themselves with a less traditional color palette, more streetwear influence, and a more relaxed fit.

content curation. The ways in which information is presented to an audience and the interaction that follows.

continuous improvement. A concept originally formulated by W. Edward Demming, one of the founders of modern quality assurance, involves defining opportunities for improvement, testing solutions, measuring the impact, and sharing the learning. Continuous improvement is a core idea of production methods such as Six Sigma, Kanban, Kaizen, Toyota Production System (TPS), and Lean Manufacturing.

contour. The form of a fiber down its length.

conversational commerce. Represents the intersection of messaging and shopping. It uses text messaging and chat apps like Facebook messenger, WhatsApp, and WeChat with the goal of turning the purchase journey into a two-way conversation rather than a one-way deluge of repetitive promotional messaging.

coordinated group lines. A mix of items organized around fabric groups and intended to be purchased and worn together.

coordinates. A term that refers to groups of items that are designed to stimulate the purchase of multiple pieces, e.g., a skirt or pant that pairs with a shirt or sweater and a jacket.

copyright law. In the US, this body of law provides legal protection for authors of non-useful, original compositions, including literary, dramatic, artistic, and musical works. Copyright protection is generally denied to clothing on the grounds that garment designs are intrinsically useful articles. Copyrights can be obtained for two-dimensional fabric designs, unique combinations of knit stitches, patterns on lace, original graphics on a tee shirt, and on occasion, the unique design of ornamental trims such as buttons and buckles. When a work qualifies for copyright protection, protection extends only to the particular manner of expression of the work; it does not extend to the underlying themes or concepts.

core values. The ideals that guide a business. Authentic values help to make an emotional connection with stakeholders.

cost of goods sold. The dollar value of unsold inventory from a previous accounting period plus the amount paid to obtain new merchandise.

Cost of Poor Quality (COPQ). The money spent in fixing problems that could have been avoided in the first place.

cost per wear. A metric that divides the price of a garment by the number of times the garment was worn.

cost sheet. A document created during the early stages of the product development process and used throughout as a dynamic record of decisions made about costs that make up the wholesale price.

costs and expenses. One of the ways that businesses keep track of the cost of their business activities is by recording the money that they spend.

country report. A research document that provides information upon which a company can base its decisions about which countries to work in.

courses. Rows of loops formed by hooked needles in a knitting machine that run perpendicular to the selvedge of the textile.

coverstitch machine. Forms a stitch where two or three threads are forced by needles through layers of fabric and then interlooped with a thread from a looper underneath. An additional looper thread may be added on the top.

croquis sketch. Croquis is the French word for sketch. A quick sketch of the figure with a loose drawing of the clothes being designed. Croquis figures are generally elongated, drawn anywhere from nine to twelve heads high as opposed to a more realistic figure, which is traditionally eight heads high.

cross-sectional shape. The silhouette of a fiber viewed at 90 degrees to its length.

crowdsourcing. The process of obtaining input into a decision, usually on a digital platform, from a community of platform users.

cultural appropriation. Refers to the use of the customs, practices, or ideas of a nondominant culture in a way that neither respects their original meaning nor gives credit to their source, or reinforces stereotypes or contributes to oppression.

customer data analytics. The science of analyzing data points from multiple sources regarding customer behavior; these data points help brands to understand each customer's needs and preferences in order to make strategic marketing decisions. Data analytics uses predictive modeling, data visualization, artificial intelligence, and machine learning to segment buyers based on actual behavior which informs marketing in the development of targeted messaging and promotions delivered at the right time, on the right platform, and on the right device.

customer engagement. The ongoing, value-driven relationship between the customer and the brand achieved through providing positive, memorable experiences at every consumer intersection.

customer journey. A roadmap that tracks every interaction with the brand. The stages of that journey are generally identified as pre-purchase awareness and consideration; purchase/acquisition; post-purchase service and customer retention; and evolution into loyalty and advocacy.

customer lifetime value (CLV). A measure of the total revenue a customer can bring to the brand over the course of their lifetime. One-time customers offer little CLV; repeat customers generate increasing value and offer more return on marketing investment.

customer relationship management (CRM). Refers to all strategies, techniques, tools, and technologies used by a business to develop, retain, and acquire customers. CRM manages interactions with existing as well as past and potential customers and consolidates customer data across channels.

customs union. A trade agreement in which members trade without restrictions, and members are required to negotiate trade with outside countries with uniform policies.

cut order plan (cutting ticket). A document generated by the production department of a firm confirming the exact style, sizes, and precise quantities that are to be cut to complete a contract order.

cut-and-sew construction. Describes the construction of knit garments where the pieces are cut from yardage rather than knit to shape. Ribbings, when used, are sewn on with a seam rather than linked. The fit varies from tight-fitting tube tops to oversized tee shirts, sweatshirts, and hoodies.

cutting instructions. A section of the tech pack that lists all of the pattern pieces needed to make one garment, provides clarity regarding unusual cutting layouts, and alerts the marker maker, spreader, and cutter about fabric that has special requirements.

deadstock fabric. Fabrics that remain from previous collections.

decorative embellishments. A means of manipulating the fabric of the garment, such as smocking, quilting, tucking, appliqué, and embroidery. These embellishments may be added at the fabric yardage stage or strategically applied to a cut piece.

demand forecast. The projection of achievable sales revenues based on historical sales data, strategic growth goals, quality and capacity of supply chain, and market analysis. Also known as a sales forecast.

demographics. Statistics about a given population with respect to age, gender, marital status, family size, income, spending habits, occupation, education, religion, ethnicity, and region.

derivative design. A design process where designers adapt the ideas of runway designers or other brands functioning more as a stylist than a designer. Derivative designs provide the consumer with looks that are similar to what is available at more expensive price points.

design. The organization of design elements, using design principles, to create products that are aesthetically pleasing to the observer.

design ease. The number of inches added or removed from a garment measurement (over and above the corresponding body measurement and functional ease) to create the silhouette and design concept.

design elements. The building blocks of design, intrinsic to every product, including apparel. The design elements are line, color, texture, pattern, silhouette, and shape.

design piracy. The practice of taking an idea designed by others and reinterpreting the look for their own brand.

design principles. Guidelines that help designers work with the design elements to compose a composition that is pleasing to the eye. Design principles include proportion, balance, emphasis or focal point, rhythm, and harmony or unity.

design specifications (design specs). A set of visual and written directions from which to create a first prototype of a new style.

designer ready-to-wear (RTW). The most expensive garments that can be bought off the rack. These brands are more profit oriented than haute couture and may be produced in quantities that vary from one hundred garments to several thousand; they are beautifully designed, impeccably made, and use high-quality fabrics.

detail. Component parts, decorative embellishments, and trims that add interest to garments.

diamond plan. A merchandising strategy in which basics represent only a small portion of a brand's product mix, key items make up the bulk of their offerings, and cutting-edge items are again represented at the top. Increasingly, this structure is expected of brands that compete in the fashion arena.

diffusion line. A luxury brand strategy utilized to reach a broader market by launching a secondary line at a more affordable price point.

digital marketplace. A website or app that facilitates shopping from many different sources. The marketplace does not take ownership of inventory. They are experts at presenting a brand's inventory and facilitating transactions, which are fulfilled by the brand.

digital printing. A method of creating a surface design directly onto a textile in which micro-sized droplets of dye are applied to the fabric through inkjet print heads.

digital twin. Technology that is used to create virtual replicas of processes, tasks, products, or services to run simulations that inform decisions, facilitate remote implementations, and prepare multiple scenarios for an uncertain future. It bridges the physical and virtual world.

digital wallets. Mobile apps that allow payment using a mobile phone, which stores credit or debit card information rather than using cash or the actual credit card. Also known as E-wallets.

direct costing. A method of costing in which all operating expenses for a period are summed, then divided by the number of units produced to calculate an average fee, which is added as a fixed amount to every product.

direct costs. Costs related to the expenses producing individual products. They include only the materials and labor needed to assemble a specific garment.

direct labor. An element of costing a garment which is calculated by adding up all the times needed to construct the garment (in fractions of a minute) into Standard Allowed Minutes (SAMs).

direct sourcing. The process of engaging the services of apparel vendors from cut, make, and trim factories to full package vendors without using an intermediary or agent.

direct-to-consumer channels (DTC). A brand that sells product to final consumers through signature stores, outlet stores, or digital channels that they operate.

disruptive technology. When innovation and new technology significantly alter the way consumers, industries, and businesses operate.

diversification. A strategy in which a firm expands its product mix to capitalize on brand recognition or experience in a particular segment of the business.

diversity imperative. A call for inclusivity and equity at all levels of fashion, up and down the supply chain, in corporate culture, on the runway, and from the consuming public.

double-welt pocket (bound pocket or besom pocket). Slash pockets with two welts, one sewn to the top edge of the slash and the other sewn to the bottom edge of the slash. Welts are typically $3/16$ to $1/4$ inch wide. Bound pockets are accessed in an opening between the two welts.

downstream. Points in the supply chain that manage distribution to the final consumer.

drag lines. Unintended folds that form horizontally across the bust, hip, or shoulder, often due to a lack of functional ease.

drape. The tendency of a textile to cling to or stand away from a body when acted upon by gravity.

draping. A method of patternmaking in which fabric is shaped around a body form to create a garment prototype.

dress. One- or two-piece garments that fall from the shoulder or high bust and continue to surround the torso of the body, ending anywhere from the mid-thigh to the floor.

dumping. A practice of selling off goods that have lost value in the open market to a country that has no import restrictions, thereby threatening the value of the same product in the local economy.

durability. The strength of a textile exhibited through time and use. A durable textile lasts because it resists the mechanical stress of abrasion, cutting, ripping, and tearing.

dye. A colorant that chemically bonds with the substrate.

ease. The amount of difference between body measurements of the intended wearer and the corresponding measurements of the finished garment.

economic integration. A process that starts when trade partners lower tariffs or quotas for some products and may expand to unrestricted movement of goods, the creation of shared financial institutions, or even a common currency.

edge finish. Configuration of fabric that hides the raw edge of a panel of fabric using the fabric itself, not a separate piece.

Enterprise Resource Planning systems (ERP). Software programs that include all the applications needed to run a business such as accounting, human resources, corporate governance, customer services, sales, distribution, procurement, and design. ERPs store, share and analyze information using a single data base that updates all linked applications simultaneously.

e-government. The use of web-based communication that governments use to provide or support the delivery of services and information.

elastic. A narrow textile that is braided, woven, or knit with insertions of elastomeric filament such as rubber or spandex.

emboss. A type of textile design in which hot rollers with engraved surfaces impress dimples, ridges, pleats, and other shapes into the surface of a finished textile.

enclosed seam. A configuration of edges of fabric that are sewn together and then turned back on themselves, concealing the raw edges. This seam is common on the edge of collars and cuffs.

engraved roller printing. A method of creating a surface design on a textile that utilizes steel cylinders coated with an outer layer of copper, into which a design is etched. Each color in the print requires a separate roller.

exclusive brands. Private brands or brands with which a retailer has a licensing agreement that gives the retailer all rights to distribute product under that brand name in a particular product category or categories.

experience management software. Computer applications that allow businesses to measure customer impressions through feedback and then use that feedback to improve the customer journey.

exports. Goods or services that are produced or performed in one country and sold outside of its borders.

fabric costs. Fabric costs generally make up 35 to 50 percent of a domestically produced gar-ment and 50 to 70 percent of a garment sourced offshore.

fabric story. The textiles chosen for the entire apparel line or a group within it reflecting a season, theme or mood or end-use.

fabrication. The process of selecting textiles and trims for each style and group in a line.

fall. The part of the collar that turns over the stand or garment.

fallout. Scraps of fabric that are left after the patterns are all cut out of the fabric. They are generally thrown out.

fashion. A culturally endorsed form of aesthetic expression and communication that changes within the context of time and place and reflects the prevailing ideas within a society or group.

fashion calendar. A seasonal schedule that is created to manage the timing of fashion presentations, buying markets, and product deliveries.

fashion forward product. Product geared to a store's leading-edge customers; this product may have limited distribution online and in prime store locations. Fashion forward product helps a brand test product trends for upcoming seasons. It is generally made in relatively small quantities and may be more complex in design, making these items the most expensive to produce and therefore carrying the highest risk.

fashion system. The structures, organization, and activities employed to promote change and novelty in apparel, generally for economic gain. The fashion system encourages the ongoing identification of new trends; promotes seasonal runway shows and fashion presentations; and drives new product development and distribution that propels customers to continually want new product whether or not what's in their closets is still functional.

fast fashion. The design, creation, and marketing of trend-driven apparel quickly and inexpensively.

feedstock. Raw material from virgin or recycled sources used to make new fiber.

fiber. The raw material that makes up textiles. Fibers are tiny and hair-like. They must be small and flexible enough to be spun into yarns and stable enough to be woven into fabric.

field-size metamerism. Describes a pair that is a good color match when viewed from a distance or in a sample that is very small but does not match when viewed up close or in a larger size.

filament. Very, very long fibers.

first pattern. A pattern used for the first sample whose dimensions are based on the target measurements based on the sample size.

first sample. A sample cut with the first patterns and cut from sample fabric.

fit. A customer's perception about whether a garment fulfills their expectations for consistency, proportion, ease of movement, comfort, balance, smoothness, and availability.

fit model. An individual who is chosen to test prototypes for a product development company by trying them on and commenting. Ideally they will have the target girth and height measurements of the sample size and no exaggerated features.

fit session. A meeting at which a sewn garment is put onto a form or a real body and observed by one or more of the product development team to assess conformity with specifications and standards.

fixed costs. Business costs that increase in inverse proportion to the number of units produced—the greater the number of units made, the smaller the unit cost for fixed expenses.

flap pocket. A slash pocket that includes a flap that is sewn to the top edge of the slash and that falls over the pocket opening. The pocket flap must be lifted to provide access to the pocket. Flap pockets may be combined with upper or lower pocket welts. Sometimes flaps are attached to a garment to give the look of an inside pocket even though there is no inside pouch. This technique saves costs by making the garment simpler to produce. It may also be desirable when the garment fabric cannot support a functional pocket.

flat pattern method. A method of developing a style or silhouette by manipulating block patterns.

flat seam. A specialized type of seam for athletic wear made on machinery that butts raw edges of fabric together and creates a web of stiches to hold the pieces together.

float. A sketch drawn over an underdrawing for proportions but without adding the body itself.

floats. Warp or weft yarns in twills and satin can be designed to skip over each other, creating long sections of yarn so that the surface can be smoother or more broken and the textile is more flexible.

floor-ready. A trend in retailing that demands that vendors perform all preparation of the product for sale to facilitate distribution.

focal point (emphasis). Describes the first place on the garment to which the eye is drawn. It may be created through a convergence of lines, a combination of colors, or a detail.

folder (assist). A device made of sheet metal that guides strips of fabric or fabric edges, folding them into shapes such as plackets, bindings, and hems immediately before stitching on a machine.

free trade. An international business environment in which importers and exporters can buy and sell products and services without restrictions of duty or quota.

Free Trade Agreements (FTAs). Multinational pacts whose goals include the reduction or elimination of tariffs and other barriers to trade among countries within a free trade area.

free trade zones. Property owned by a host government set aside for foreigners to conduct business with freedom from import duties, relaxation of some local regulations and taxes, relaxed export procedures, and added security.

front-hip pocket. A pocket typically found on jeans and pants that features a style line that is cut into the garment front at the hip and faced to form the opening. Many variations can be achieved with this pocket style. The style-line of the pocket is generally topstitched.

full package vendors. Manufacturers or contractors who provide pattern and sample making services based on client requirements and source all the materials, factory labor, and services needed to produce garment contracts.

full-fashion construction. Refers to knit garments in which some part of the garment has been knit to shape. At a minimum, sweater lengths are linked together so that the ribbing can be attached through linking as opposed to serging. In other sweaters, shaping for the armscye and neckline are also knit to shape.

functional ease. The number of inches added to a garment over and above the corresponding body measurement when drafting a pattern to allow for movement and comfort.

fusible interlining. Support fabric that has heat sensitive dots of resin on one side that melt when heat is applied, allowing it to be uniformly bonded to the shell.

gamut. The entire range of colors that can be achieved within a medium or on a substrate.

General Agreement on Trades and Tariffs (GATT). A multilateral trade agreement set up in 1948 by twenty-three nations to eliminate tariffs and quotas.

generational cohort. A group whose members share significant historical and social experiences at a similar stage in life that shape their values and behavior. The study of generational cohorts combines understanding gleaned from both demographic and psychographic data.

generational marketing. The study of how the values, motivations, and life experiences of a generational cohort shape its purchasing behavior, reach, and market influence.

geometric metamerism. A phenomenon that occurs when identical colors appear different when viewed at different angles.

geometry (mesh) processing. Algorithms that reconstruct a 3D shape, using computer vision technology and photos. They can be used to create a fitting avatar from photos taken on the customer's cell phone.

gorge line. The seam where the collar and the lapel are joined.

grade rules. A list of incremental changes to pattern measurements from one size to the next that are applied to a base pattern within a sizing system to achieve a graded set of production patterns. The increase or decrease between one size and the next on a specific measurement is called "the grade."

grading. The process of creating a complete set of production patterns for each size in a range using grade rules to expand the distance proportionally between landmark points on the coordinate grid.

gross margin. Net sales – cost of goods sold = gross margin.

gross sales. All of the money earned from sales in a period of time (month, quarter, year).

hand (handle). The aesthetic property that is experienced when a textile is crushed in the hand and then released.

hardware. Trims such as buttons, buckles, rings, chains, and grommets can be made of any rigid material that can be carved, molded, punched, etched, engraved, covered, laminated, painted, or dyed.

harmony (unity). The sum of all of the design elements working together in a garment to produce a pleasing aesthetic appearance and to give a feeling of unity to the design.

haute couture. A legally protected designation in Paris that can only be used by houses registered with the French Ministry of Industry. Haute couture designers must adhere to a strict set of standards administered by the Chambre Syndicale de la Haute Couture that require each house to employ at least fifteen people in a Paris atelier and present a minimum of thirty-five new designs twice a year. Haute couture garments are made of the highest quality fabrics, often require handwork, and are custom made, requiring one or more fittings.

head ends. Sample of a woven textile sent by a vendor for approval before continuing to the next step of production.

hero products. A small number of well-designed products that represent a brand's DNA and solve a design problem; hero products can serve as a gateway to the marketplace.

high street. A UK term used to describe mass market chain stores that offer trend-right and affordable fashion that can be readily found on any main street. High street brands are the equivalent to chain stores typically found in US malls.

horizontal integration. A growth strategy that prioritizes the acquisition or licensing of companies or brands that make or sell similar products to expand market penetration, reduce competition, access technology, and take advantage of business synergies. It may be used to acquire brands at the same price level, which reduces competition, or to penetrate multiple price points in the same product category, which expands reach.

hue. The property of light by which the color of an object is classified as one of the hue families of the light spectrum. There is a natural order of hues that follows the sequence of hues seen in a rainbow. That order goes from red to orange to yellow, then green, blue, and purple. Purple does not appear in the rainbow, but it completes the human perception of the hue families. Hue families can be arranged in this order to form a color circle.

hyperspectral imaging. The use of sensors to collect color information as a set of images, rather than a single image. It breaks a print down into many different images across the electromagnetic spectrum. The result is an accurate analysis of each color in the pattern.

illuminant metamerism. The perceived change in color between a pair of samples that match under one light source but do not a match under another.

illuminant. Refers to the light source used when measuring color.

implied warranty. An unwritten expectation that a garment will do what it is designed to do, e.g., a coat will provide warmth.

imports. Goods or services that are produced or performed in one country and brought in by businesses or residents of another.

income or revenue. Money that a business receives over a period of time as recorded in a Profit and Loss Statement (P&L).

indirect channels. Brick and mortar stores or digital channels that buy product wholesale and then assign a retail price before selling it to the final consumer.

influencer marketing. The use of endorsements and product mentions from individuals who have a dedicated social following and are viewed as experts within their niche.

in-house. A method of obtaining first patterns and samples within the same location and same business unit as the marketing and design functions.

in-seam pocket. Pockets in which the opening is designed into an existing seam of the garment. They are most frequently found in vertical garment side seams or princess seams, but they may also be found in horizontal yoke or waist seams. These pockets provide function without disrupting the lines of the garment.

inside pocket. Pockets in which the pouch falls inside the garment with only an opening visible from the outside.

intellectual property. A branch of law that protects "creations of the mind" such as novel inventions, ornamental aspects of useful products, literary and artistic works, photographs, and brand names, trademarks, and logos. It is an extremely nuanced aspect of the law. The US law is distinct in the protections it offers from the UK, the EU, and other countries.

interlining. A general industry term that includes knit, woven, and nonwoven products that are held behind the shell fabric by fusing or sewing in. The term "interfacing" is more commonly used for home sewing products.

intermediate colors. The colors created when a primary color is mixed with a secondary color that is next to it on the color wheel. Also called tertiary colors.

interpretive design. Describes the work of skilled designers who are inspired by the zeitgeist, translating macro and micro trends into wearable, functional designs.

introductory allowances. Brands may offer introductory allowances to distributors to entice them to try a new product.

invoice payment terms. Discounts granted by brands to distributors when they agree to pay their bills early.

item lines. Product assortments created to be sold one piece at a time rather than as a coordinated outfit.

item driven. Describes an environment in which customers tend to buy more single garments than coordinated ensembles.

jacket. A short coat worn for indoor or outdoor use.

jacquards. Complex woven textiles made on looms that allow many possible arrangements of warp and weft yarns to create intricate designs.

jobbers. Middlemen who buy textiles and other materials in bulk and sell in smaller quantities at higher prices.

joint venture. An offshore facility owned by a US company in partnership with a business based in another country.

knit-down. Sample of a knitted textile sent by a vendor for approval before continuing to the next step of production.

knitted textiles (knits). Made on knitting machines by interlooping one or more continuous yarns. Knits vary by the direction in which the loops are formed.

knock off design. The lowest level of creativity, characterized by copying the ideas of others, generally in less expensive fabric and poor-quality construction.

lab dip. A sample of the fabric or trim specified for a design, dyed to match the color standard. Lab dips must be approved before production yardage is dyed.

label. A piece of material that is attached to garments or an area of screen printing that provides written information or a visual message for the consumer.

lapel. A part of the garment front that is designed to attach to the collar and turn back over the garment.

lapped seams. A classification of configurations of fabric in which two or more pieces are folded and stitched together.

lay. A stack of plies of fabric ready to be cut into parts that will be sewn into garments.

lead time. The length of time spent from the date that an order is placed for a product until it is the hands of the customer. Lead time includes turnaround time for production as well as logistics such as order processing and shipping.

Least Developed Countries (LDCs). Countries that are deemed by the United Nations to have the lowest indicators of socioeconomic development.

licencee. A vendor who provides all services to create and distribute a product, including design, development, manufacturing, marketing, and sales.

licensing agreements. Legal agreements that grant a business partner exclusive rights to produce or sell products under a proprietary brand name.

Life Cycle Assessment (LSA). Reports that catalog and evaluate the environmental impact of each stage of producing, distributing, and disposing of a specific product.

lifestyle brands. Brands that go beyond their origins in a single product category to include additional apparel and accessory categories, perfumes, cosmetics, travel packages or experiences, or home goods, all related to a particular lifestyle.

line. A design element that determines the silhouette of the garment and the shapes formed within the garment. Internal garment lines may be created through the use of garment seams and edges; fabric patterns and textures; and details such as tucks, pleats, darts, gathers, and linear trims. Lines have several aspects that determine their character. These include length, boldness, thickness, and direction. The impact of line is further defined by how frequently it is repeated, its placement, and whether it is used symmetrically or asymmetrically.

line review. A meeting where merchants or buyers quantify their orders, taking into consideration product needed for marketing campaigns, visual merchandising displays, and the assortments required for their distribution plan.

lining. A lightweight fabric with a smooth surface can be added to the inside of the garment to cover the raw edges of seams and help the shell fabric slide easily and yet maintain its drape.

livestream shopping. Reminiscent of television shopping networks, streamed events are used to create a sense of community, promote new merchandise, and create a sense of exclusivity and scarcity. They take advantage of consumers' increasing fascination with video and social media. Participants are offered the first opportunity to buy limited edition merchandise.

lockstitch machine. Forms a stitch where one thread is forced by a needle through layers of fabric and then interlaced with a thread from a bobbin underneath.

loyalty program. A marketing strategy designed to retain customers and motivate them to buy.

luster. An aesthetic property that is perceived as the amount of light reflected from the textile surface.

luxury market. A category of goods and services that are highly desirable, due to their cost. These products are perceived to have superior value, quality, and craftsmanship that project status and taste.

macro trends. Long-term paradigm shifts that affect a major segment of the population through the evaluation of current events in order to identify and anticipate directional shifts in business strategies, lifestyles, consumer behavior, and global dynamics. Macro trends evolve over a longer period of time and tend not to be discipline specific. They tend to reveal the root cause of lifestyle and behavioral change.

make. The perceived quality of the combined effect of textile, components, seaming, fit, and finish in a garment.

make-to-order (MTO). A supply chain strategy in which brands wait to ask vendors to order materials and cut fabric only after the brand receives distributors' orders.

make-to-stock (MTS). A suppy chain strategy in which brands invest in materials and book factory capacity in advance of orders.

manual method. A traditional method for making final or graded patterns by hand using tag board and making markers by drawing around each piece of pattern on marker paper.

manufactured fibers. Spun by forcing liquid forms of dissolved or melted compounds through tiny holes in a spinneret.

markdown money. Reductions on suppliers' invoices demanded by distributors when goods are not selling due to poor quality, late deliveries, or styling that does not excite the customer.

marker. A large piece of paper onto which graded patterns are traced by hand from tagboard patterns or printed by computer-driven plotter. The outlines guide the cutter to accurately cut the stack of fabric underneath. The image of such an arrangement of patterns is called a "nest" in a digital marker-making program.

market segmentation. The ability to break down markets into increasingly smaller, well-defined groups based on data collected regarding customer behavior and preferences.

market trends analysis. A study that helps to anticipate any demographic shifts or market conditions that might impact customer traffic and engagement. These market trends can be triggered by new technology, economic factors, political changes, and social developments.

markets of one. A strategy that targets each customer as a single market, making them feel special by delivering personalized customer service.

mass customization. The application of mass-production techniques to the production of a single customer-configured garment in order to maximize choice and minimize cost.

mass market. A mass market strategy attempts to cater to the highest number of customers, making up for lower margins with high volume. It may be used to describe a brand, a price point, or a retailer/distribution channel.

measurement chart. A list found in a specification package with target finished garment measurements that guide the patternmaker to create a first pattern. After the sample is approved for production, the measurement chart is graded for each size.

merchandise budget. A budget that identifies how much inventory needs to be in stock and ready for distribution week by week in order to meet sales goals. It factors in an estimated cost of goods, anticipated initial margins, and seasonal reductions. This early planning must be synchronized with marketing efforts and helps sourcing to reserve sufficient manufacturing capacity.

merchandise plan (line plan). A document that anticipates the merchandise inventory levels required to maximize sales potential and return on investment. It serves as a guide for the design team setting parameters that help it to create the right product with the right balance and that it can be delivered to the right channels at the right price.

micro trends. Directional tendencies that are fairly pervasive within a specific sphere of influence and/or for a particular audience. These shifts tend to be more discipline specific and the changes may be observed for a season or several years, depending on the audience.

Minimum Order Quantity (MOQ). The smallest order a supplier can make and still make a profit.

minimums. The smallest order a supplier can make and still make a profit.

mission statement. A concise declaration that reflects a company's heritage by articulating why it's in business, the customer it serves, and what makes it special.

modular manufacturing system. A method of garment factory organization in which small teams of operators work together on small quantities of product conducting multiple tasks at one machine.

monochromatic. Color harmonies that utilize a single hue in a variety of tints and shades.

multi-brand retailers. Retailers that carry a variety of wholesale brands. They may also carry private brands alongside their wholesale brands.

multichannel. Refers to product that is distributed through a combination of stores and digital channels.

nanometer. A measurement equal to one millionth of a millimeter; it is the unit of measurement used to measure light waves. The human eye perceives colors at wavelengths in a range from 400 nanometers (which we see as deep blue) to about 700 nanometers (which we see as deep red).

nanoparticles. Fibers, tubes, whiskers, or other forms that are less than 100 nanometers in any direction.

narrow textiles. Fabrics with all of the characteristics of wide textiles but made on looms no wider than 12 inches.

natural fibers. Fibers cultivated and harvested from animal and plant sources.

near-shoring (proximity manufacturing). A strategy focused on producing product closer to the market where it will be sold.

neoprene. A laminate of foam rubber and synthetic jersey.

net sales. Gross sales – returns/allowances = net sales

nonwoven textiles. Created by entangling fibers and then pressing them into a smooth fabric.

notch. The triangular shape between the lapel and the collar formed where the gorge line connects the collar and the lapel.

novelty goods. Textiles that feature fresh print designs, new knit stiches and yarns, or new weaving patterns used to bring interest to a fashion line.

observer metamerism. A phenomenon that occurs when two observers perceive a color match differently—to one's eye the pair matches and to the other's eye the pair does not match. This difference in perception could be due to color blindness in one of the observers, differing sensitivity to light in the medium- and long-wavelength-sensitive cones in the retina, yellowing of the lens, or macular degeneration.

OEM (original equipment manufacturer). A vendor who sources and finances materials from specified sources and, in addition, provides cutting, sewing, finishing, and packing.

off-the-card. An order placed with a supplier that is chosen from products that are offered for sale with no changes or customization.

omnichannel merchandising. A strategy focused on creating a unified customer experience across all possible points of customer engagement for a seamless experience.

open-source design. The development of ideas, technology, and systems without the retention of intellectual property rights.

operating expenses. All the costs that a company must pay to run its business.

operating profit. Gross margin – operating expenses = operating profit.

order orchestration. The ability to fulfil a purchase from either an e-commerce distribution center or a store. Being able to track inventory across all channels helps to avoid overstocks instore that require significant end-of-season markdowns while incurring stockouts for the same merchandise online.

organic cotton. Cotton fiber cultivated with natural methods that reduce water consumption by 91%, uses no synthetic pesticides, herbicides, or fertilizers.

ornamental stitching. A classification of stitches that are decorative and do not necessarily function to hold fabric together into a garment.

other expenses or income. Money spent or earned for activities not related to its core business.

outlet stores. Brand-owned stores that provide a means of controlling the distribution of excess goods.

outside pocket. Pockets in which the pouch or bag of the pocket is visible from the outside of the garment.

pants. Bifurcated garments worn by men, women, and children. Pant legs vary from skintight leggings to wide, elephant leg pants or palazzo pants. The pants category also includes active sportswear such as biker shorts, yoga pants, and ski pants, to name just a few.

patch pocket. A piece of fabric that is topstitched to the outside of a garment to form a pouch.

pattern (for cutting). A set of paper or electronic shapes that are used as templates to guide the cutting of fabric panels that will be sewn into a product.

pattern (textile). A repeated decorative design that can be constructed into the fabric—through weaving, knitting, or felting—or applied to the fabric surface through printing, embossing, and other specialty techniques such as devoré or laser cutting.

pattern and sample making services. Contract firms who develop patterns and samples for companies who choose not to have their own in-house sample studios.

pattern design software (PDS). Digital tools for creating patterns, size and grading charts, grading patterns, and making markers.

pattern drafting. A process for making patterns for clothing that starts by taking measurements from a body and transferring them to a coordinate grid. Landmark points are connected in a closed figure to form patterns.

payment gateways. Digital services that offer a simple and secure way for businesses to collect digital payments.

pigments. A colorant that lays on the surface of the substrate.

plain weaves. Woven textiles with warp and weft yarns arranged in the simplest patterns.

ply. In cutting: A single layer of fabric laid on top of others to make create a stack (lay) for cutting.

ply. Thin uniform yarns that can be spun together to make stronger yarns. Plies of very different textures can be spun together to make novelty yarns.

pocket. Extra fabric attached to the inside or outside of a garment to form a pouch with a top or side opening. Pockets play both decorative and functional roles in garment design.

polymer. Long chain of molecules.

post-production costing. Historical information from profit and loss statements of previous seasons and detailed cost information about specific products guide product development for future seasons.

predictive analytics. A subset of data analytics that leverages artificial intelligence (AI), machine learning, data models, and algorithms on data assets to predict future behaviors. It assists marketers in understanding consumer behaviors and trends, predicting future shifts, and planning marketing campaigns.

Preferential Trade Arrangements (PTAs). Non-reciprocal pacts made for the benefit of developing nations.

preliminary cost estimate (precost). A cost developed before a sample has been made using historical cost information, materials vendor information and current labor, shipping, and overhead costs.

price point (price zone). Refers to an understanding of the price range that the intended target customer is willing to pay for the value offered.

primary colors. The minimum number of hues that can be mixed to make the greatest number of other colors.

printing. The application of a design or pattern to a fabric using dyes or pigments applied in limited areas.

private brands (exclusive brands, own brands). Product brands developed for exclusive distribution by a particular retailer. Chain stores such as Zara and Lululemon sell only private brands. Private brands sold by mass merchants and department stores typically compete with wholesale brand products also carried by the retailer.

private label brands. Private brands developed to compete with wholesale brands also sold by the same retailer.

product development. An end-to-end process that includes marketing, merchandising, creative and technical design, sourcing, production, and distribution planning of goods that have a perceived value for a well-defined consumer group. These goods should be made to reach the marketplace, in the right quantity, when consumers are ready to buy.

product differentiation. To distinguish a product or service from others in order to make it more desirable in the marketplace.

product drops. A strategy that was introduced by savvy streetwear brands. Brands specify a day each week or month when limited edition stock will be released at flagship stores and/or online. In-the-know customers wait in line to snag pieces that will be in limited supply.

product experience management. A strategy used to deliver the right content, when and where it is needed, to drive sales, build loyalty and grow market share.

product lifecycle management (PLM). Applications that integrate the product development process with supply chain management, enabling internal and external teams to communicate and collaborate on product-related information in order to define roles, streamline processes, meet deadlines, ensure quality, and authenticate product integrity from initial concept to a product's retirement.

product placement. A strategy that positions brand products in print images, movies, videos, or tv shows in order to get noticed.

product search filters. These systems help customers to refine their search by gender, category, brand, price, size, color, and reviews.

production cost. The information on a cost sheet that has been updated with the production cost at the same time that the final tech pack is created.

production patterns. A set of graded patterns ready for marker making. Manual patterns are cut in tag. Electronic patterns are images on a screen.

production yardage. The bulk quantity of textiles needed to produce an order for apparel products, made to the brand's technical specifications.

Profit and Loss Statement (P&L). A business document for recording the money that it spends (costs and expenses) and receives (income or revenue) over a period of time.

profit before taxes. Operating profit + / – other expenses or income = profit before taxes.

progressive bundle system. A method of garment factory organization in which small parts are completed first, then attached to larger sections and finally assembled into a whole garment.

promotional discount. Promotional discounts are offered to distributors in exchange for the cost of promoting brand.

propensity models. A type of predictive analytics that evaluates a consumer's likelihood to engage with a website, act on an offer, or make a purchase.

proportion. The relationship or scale of all of a garment or ensemble's parts to each other and to the body as a whole. Horizontal lines, such as yoke and waistline seams or jacket and top edges, divide a garment or ensemble into sections. The ancient Greeks judged proportions by the rule of the golden mean. They believed that ratios of 2:3, 3:5, and 5:8 were the most pleasing to the eye.

psychographics. The study of the social and psychological factors that influence consumer lifestyles; this information reveals more behavioral motivations and buying practices. The social aspects of lifestyle include reference groups, life stage, hobbies, interests, and activities. Psychological aspects include personality, attitudes, and level of class consciousness.

pullover. Sweaters that are pulled on over the head.

pyramid plan. A merchandising strategy in which basic styles and core items that carry little risk and can be ordered in large quantities and assortments make up the biggest part of a brand's seasonal line. In the middle level of the pyramid is where product developers interpret current fashion trends for their core customer; these key items are critical to maintaining brand loyalty. The top of the pyramid consists of cutting-edge items that help to create an image and expose the customer to new trends in fashion and technology. These items are not produced in great quantities.

QR code. An arrangement of black and white squares printed on a surface that can be read by a camera or smartphone which directs the user to a URL.

qualitative research. Subjective research that relies on methodologies such as observation, self-reporting, and case studies in which experiences are recorded as a narrative to describe observed behaviors within the context of environmental factors.

quality assurance. Defect prevention rather than defect detection.

quantitative research. An objective methodology in which data are collected about a sample population and analyzed to generalize behavioral patterns statistically.

quantity discount. A negotiated price paid by a distributor who pays less per unit costs for a bulk order. The brand can make up the loss at facilities that benefit from the economies of scale and efficiency from bulk orders.

quota. A system in which a nation limits the quantity of goods that can be imported by defined categories in a specific period.

recommendations filtering. A type of predictive analytics that evaluates past browsing sessions and purchases to understand where there may be additional sales opportunities.

recommerce. The process of selling previously owned, new, or used products to private or business customers for the purpose of reusing, repairing, or recycling.

regenerated fibers. Fibers that start as agricultural products that are chemically transformed into liquid and then spun into fiber.

returns and allowances. Money lost when a distributor has to mark down a product after a return or to resolve a customer complaint.

RFID tags. Radio frequency identification tags.

rhythm. The natural movement of the eye through the related elements of a garment. Rhythm can be achieved by strong silhouette lines; through the use of color, line, or shape; or through the use of repetition, radiation, or gradation.

roll line. The line where the collar fall turns over the stand.

rotary screen printing. Most common and least costly method of industrial printing in which ink (paste) is pumped into the hollow space inside of a cylinder that is made of a fine metal screen whose surface is blocked in some areas to prevent the paste from printing. The paste is pressed out onto the fabric through the holes of the screen. Each color is printed with a separate roller.

Rules of Origin Certificate. A document that proves the country of origin of fibers used in a product so it can be eligible for reduced or removed tariffs under yarn forward rules.

sample yardage. Small quantity of fabric to make one or more garments to test design ideas and patterning. Because it comes from textile shows or sales reps, it may not conform to the brand's quality standards.

seam. Configuration of parts and/or edges of fabric that when stitched, transform raw fabric into a garment or product and add to its visual design.

seam allowance. The distance between the needle and the raw edges of fabric panels.

seam classification. A system of naming seams in relation to the way fabric is configured.

seasonal discount. A seasonal discount offered by a brand to encourage a distributor to place orders at times when factories are slow.

seasonal product. Product that differentiates a brand and establishes its fashion aesthetic. Seasonal product is generally produced in moderate quantities. Product developers prefer to put off decision making until the last minute to better predict demand. Prices must be competitive, but consumers may pay more for this product's on-trend aesthetic or brand image.

seasonless fashion model. A new approach to fashion that slows down the product development and consumption cycle and does not conform to seasonal trends or schedules. Seasonless fashion focuses on core pieces that are developed to have a longer shelf life, delivered in smaller quantities at intervals throughout the year, without the expense and pageantry of an expensive fashion presentation.

secondary colors. The colors created when two primary colors are mixed together.

separates. A term that refers to items that are designed to be purchased as individual pieces rather than a coordinated outfit.

serging machines (overlock). A classification of machines that cut a clean edge and then form a web of stitches over the edge to keep it from raveling. Some sergers also stitch a row of reinforcement or an extra row of chain stitching.

sewing instructions. A section of a tech pack in which standards are listed for stitch types and seam types. Measurements are given for seam and hem depths, topstitch gauges and stitches per inch.

shade. A darker color achieved by mixing a color with black to decrease the value and darken the color. Navy blue and forest green are examples of shades.

shade sorting. The process of grouping shade variations together for distribution to specific customers or regions for more satisfactory color matching.

shape. Smaller sections within a silhouette defined by seam lines, details, and garment edges. Shapes add design interest, help to achieve fit, allow for the combination of fabrics and textures, and add functionality.

shaping device. Darts, seams, pleats, and gathers that help to mold a garment to the contours of the body.

short supply. A term used in trade agreements to allow relaxation of rules regarding eligibility of products for tariffs if the material in question is not commercially available.

signature stores. Brand-owned stores that provide a direct line to the brand's ultimate consumer and the data points that accompany those interactions.

silhouette. The outer shape of a garment. Silhouettes are sometimes described by letters such as A, H, T, V, or Y, in which the silhouette follows the shape of the letter. Silhouettes may also be described as specific shapes (trapezoid, tent, hourglass, pear, or bell) or identified from periods in history (empire or flapper).

silhouette. The term used to describe the outline or outer shape of a garment.

simple subtractive color-mixing system. A structure that explains how thin films of color are mixed.

size recommendation software. Digital applications (apps) that match customers to products that are more likely to meet their expectations for size and fit.

size system. A list of body measurements that correspond to letters or numbers.

skirt. A garment that hangs from the body at or near the waist and covers the hips and upper legs but is not bifurcated to go around each leg separately as do pants.

slash pocket. Pockets where the opening is slashed into the garment body and finished with a flap or welt, with the pocket pouch hidden inside the garment.

slow fashion. More of a concept than a market, slow fashion prioritizes the sustainable use of resources, ethical treatment of supply chain partners, quality that encourages long-term wear, recycling, and reuse, involving the consumer in design.

slow steam policy. A general agreement struck in 2007 among shipping companies to reduce fuel costs and greenhouse gas emissions by restricting ocean speed.

sneakerization. Describes the process of transforming or redefining a product line that is losing its relevance into a cutting-edge specialty product.

social enterprise. A business that has specific social objectives that serve its primary purpose. Social enterprises seek to maximize profits while maximizing benefits to society and the environment. Their profits are principally used to fund social programs.

sourcing. The continuous review of the need for goods and services against the purchasing opportunities that meet quantity, quality, price, sustainability, and delivery parameters, in order to leverage purchasing power for the best value. Any goods that a brand can't produce or functions that a brand can't perform cost effectively are outsourced to other vendors.

sourcing agent. A vendor who provide all the services necessary for production, including sourcing of fabrics and trims, product testing, color matching, sample making, grading, marker making, cutting, garment assembly, finishing, shipping, and export.

sourcing mix. The combination of resources and vendors a company utilizes for production of their product line.

special instructions. A section of a design spec or tech pack which specify the standards for non-sewing processes that are not done on the sewing floor such as pleating, embroidery, garment wash or dyeing.

specification library. A database in an electronic Product Lifecycle Management system that stores information about materials and drawings of past styles that can be drawn on when developing a new design spec.

spectrophotometers. An instrument that compares the amount of light used to illuminate an object with the amount of light that is reflected back from that object. A ratio is calculated at each wavelength in the visible spectrum in order to measure color accurately. Spectrophotometers are the preferred instrument for color identification, detection of metamerism, and color formulation. Handheld versions can help a designer document and read color inspiration without having to buy or collect physical samples.

spinneret. A device with tiny holes through which liquefied compounds are forced to create fibers.

stakeholder. Every individual, group, or organization that affects or is affected by the fashion system and product development process. Stakeholders include raw materials providers, manufacturers, service providers, brands, retailers, governments, industry associations, nonprofits, and academia as well as consumers, employees, and investors.

stand. The part of the collar that fits close to the neck.

standard (core) body size. A set of body measurement for the size that most closely represents the ideal shape of the target customer or the median size of a range.

Standard Allowed Minutes (SAMs). The direct labor of the garment is calculated by adding up all the times needed to construct the garment (in fractions of a minute) into Standard Allowed Minutes (SAMs).

Standard Inspection Procedure (SIP). A method of inspection that prescribes a specific order in which to look at the garment and the criteria to use at each point.

standards. Characteristics of products and processes that are used as the basis for making decisions. Standards define expectations for quality of materials and performance.

staple. Short fibers.

stitch. Row of continuous strands of thread that interlace or interloop in order to hold fabric together or create a pattern that shows on the surface of the garment.

stitch classification. A system of naming stitches formed by machines in relation to the way the machine interlaces or interloops the thread.

store brands. Private brands developed for retailers that only sell their own private brands.

strategic planning. A top-level management activity that is used to set priorities, focus energy and resources, strengthen operations and ensure that stakeholders are working toward common goals.

stretch. The ability of a yarn, fiber, or textile to elongate with stress and to recover its original shape and size when the stress is removed.

strike-off. A sample of a yarn-dyed fabric or a full repeat of a print that is submitted to a product developer to approve registration (the actual color placement on the fabric); a computer-aided design (CAD) file with a color key of all colors that appear within the print.

structural design. Textile design that is visible on the surface and is woven or knitted into the textile in the fiber, yarn, or construction stages of production.

style line. The shape of the outer edge of the collar.

stylist. Refers to designers who adapt the work of others.

sublimation printing (heat transfer printing). A textile printing technique in which dispersed dyes are first digitally printed on special transfer paper, which is then placed on the fabric and passed through a machine at about 400 degrees Fahrenheit. The temperature and pressure cause the dye to vaporize and transfer onto the fabric.

substrate. In color terminology, refers to the material on which one is attempting to apply color. Different materials require different colorants.

subtractive color-mixing system. A structure that describes how pigments are mixed. Paints, inks, dyes, and other color media all absorb certain wavelengths of light, which enable an object to absorb some light waves and reflect back others. The more pigments that are blended, the more light is absorbed and the less light is reflected.

suggested retail price (list price). A price is calculated to cover the brand's costs, operating expenses, and profit, but it is also based on an estimate of a reasonable at-market price.

superimposed seams. A classification of configurations of seams in which two or more pieces of fabric are laid together and stitched.

support materials. Generate contrast by restricting the drape of some parts of the garment while leaving the original drape for other parts.

surface interest. An aesthetic property created by breaking up a surface into contrasting units of light reflection.

sustainability movement. Promotes change in the fashion system that support environmental integrity, social justice, and economic fairness. These changes would impact planning, design, production, distribution, and consumption of fashion products and services.

sustainability properties. Characteristics of the material itself or its production that ensure that it does not cause harm to the environment or people throughout its life cycle.

sweater set (twin set). Coordinated sweaters sold as two pieces, typically a sleeveless knit shell that can be worn with or without the cardigan sweater with which it is paired.

SWOT analysis. A strategic planning technique for assessing the internal strengths and weaknesses as well as external opportunities and threats for a business going forward.

symmetric balance. Describes a garment that appears to be the same on both sides. A symmetrically balanced garment can be easily changed with accessories and can be readily mixed and matched with other symmetrical garments in the wardrobe.

synthetic fibers. Spun from melted thermoplastic compounds distilled from petrochemicals.

tag board (oak tag, tag). Heavy manila cardboard used for making manual patterns.

tariffs. Import and export taxes or duties.

target market. A well-defined customer group to which a business wants to sell.

technical flat (flat). An accurate drawing of the front and back of a proposed garment as it appears in two dimensions spread out on a flat surface, used in tech packs. They visually define the proportions, details, and construction techniques required for production purposes.

technical specification (tech pack). A set of visual and written instructions that evolves throughout the development process and is finalized before a product goes into mass production. They clearly define expectations for the final product and the methods used to achieve it.

Tex. A direct numbering system for classifying thread by its diameter. Tex 24 and 27 are used for sportswear and Tex 80 is used for jean topstitch.

texture. The term used to describe the surface or hand of a fabric and can be attributed to a combination of the fabric's characteristics—fiber, yarn, construction, weight, and finish.

thermal management. A group of textile properties that give apparel products the ability to keep the body at its ideal temperature regardless of exterior conditions, activity level, or health.

thread. A strong, slender form of yarn used for stitching garments.

thread count. A system for reporting the number of yarns within a square inch or centimeter of a textile: warp x weft. Sometimes the counts of warp and weft are added and reported as single number.

three-dimensional patternmaking software. Digital applications for displaying virtual images of garments based on existing patterns on avatars to test design concept and fit.

thumbnail sketch. Small, quick sketch of a design or design detail.

time and action calendar. A schedule that begins with market dates that are set by the industry or, in the case of retail product developers, the delivery dates when new merchandise must hit the stores and works backwards to set deadlines for each stage of the product development process.

tint. A pale color achieved by mixing a color with white paint, water, or white light; a commercial printer achieves a tint by leaving more space between dots. Tints are sometimes called pastels; examples include pink and peach.

tolerance. The allowable amount of variance from the stated measurement.

tops. 1. In the broader meaning, tops must have a front and back bodice; some also have sleeves. Tops include tee shirts, sweaters, shirts and blouses, vests, indoor and outdoor jackets, and coats. Jackets, coats, and dresses are considered tops because they must fit the body torso; they are tops rather than bottoms because they are developed from torso pattern blocks. 2. In the narrower sense, for import and export classification purposes, the tops category generally includes tee shirts, sweatshirts, hoodies, tank tops, crop tops and the like as opposed to sweaters which are knit to shape.

top-weight. Textiles typically weighing less than 6.0 ounces per square yard, chosen for blouses, soft dresses, knit tops, etc.

touchpoint. Any interaction with a brand that might alter the way that the customer feels about the product, brand, business, or service positively or negatively.

traceability. The ability to track each component of an item throughout the supply chain from the raw material, to the thread, to the final garment.

trace-off (rub-off, reverse engineering). A method of developing a pattern for one garment that involves copying its dimensions and details exactly and making a new pattern.

trade agreements. Agreements made between countries to lower or remove barriers to each other's markets.

trade bloc. An intergovernmental trade organization.

trade discount. An amount added to a distributor's suggested retail price that is roughly equivalent to the distributor's gross margin.

trade dress. A broader term than trademark that covers the totality of elements in which a product or service is packaged and presented. Trade dress can include the shape and appearance of a product or its packaging, the cover of a book or magazine, or the unique layout and appearance of a business establishment.

trademark. Any word, name, symbol, device, color, or combination thereof that is adopted and used by a manufacturer or merchant to identify goods and distinguish them from those manufactured and sold by others.

transparency. A strategy that holds brands accountable to know what is happening up and down the supply chain and to communicate this knowledge both internally and externally. Transparency helps to end the use of hidden supply chains that abuse workers, hire underage children, and pay sub-standard wages in order to meet a brand's price and deadline requirements.

transshipment. An illegal practice of shipping goods made in one country with the label of a country with more favorable export agreements.

trend. The observable change of direction in ideas, values, purchasing behavior or style.

trend analysis. A means of anticipating consumer demand; it identifies paradigm shifts that cause us to look at things differently. Not only does it promote newness but in a business sense, it helps to mitigate risk.

trickle-across theory. Describes a process where there is little lag time between fashion adoption from one group to another—from one price point to another.

trickle-down theory. An observation that many new fashion ideas start on designer runways appealing to fashion leaders who have the money and taste level to wear new looks. As new ideas gain visibility, they are reinterpreted at lower and lower price points.

trickle-up theory. Explains the phenomenon of street fashions that originate with avant-garde consumer groups rather than a designer or product developer.

Triple Bottom Line (TBL). Environmentalist John Elkington suggested substituting the traditional "bottom line" (profit) with the Triple Bottom Line (including people and planet) to take into account the full measure of the resources being consumed or damaged by producing products.

turnaround time. The time required for making, dyeing, and finishing the fabric and trims, in order to meet the delivery date determined by the production schedule. Compare to lead time that includes logistics.

underdrawing (lay figure). A well-proportioned pose that can be slid under a page and used as a template to help control proportions and the location of garment details. When using an underdrawing, the design idea is drawn first and then the visible head, arms, and legs are added. There is no need to draw in facial features or hair.

under-pressing. A method of pressing seams and darts on the inside of the garment shortly after they are sewn and before the garment is pressed during finishing.

unilateral trade agreements or actions. Trade policies adopted by one country toward another without reciprocity.

Unit Production System (UPS). A method of garment factory organization in which an overhead transporter carries a part or section of a garment to each operator's station in sequence.

United States-Mexico-Canada Agreement 2018 (USMCA). A Free Trade Agreement which features the duty-free exchange of goods and a unified, simplified import and export system among its partners Mexico, Canada, and the United States.

upstream. The supply side of the supply chain that provides raw materials.

utilitarian properties. Characteristics that make the product useful to the consumer, including safety properties such as resistance to flame or chemicals; value properties such as low cost, easy care, and durability; and comfort properties such as stretch, flexibility, softness, weight, and thermal management.

value. The quality by which we distinguish light colors from dark colors.

value chain. A supply chain in which managers look for opportunities to add significant benefit to the product rather than negotiating solely on price.

variable costs. Costs that increase for products that require additional water, energy, machinery, or specialized skills such as mixing dyes to match color standards.

vendor compliance. The evaluation of vendor performance in delivering products that meet clients' standards and specifications.

vertical integration. A strategy whereby a company seeks to own its suppliers, distributors, or retail locations in order to control the supply chain's value and efficiency. Companies may follow a vertical integration strategy if they feel it will enhance their access to production capacity, improve quality, or offer economies of scale.

vest. A sleeveless version of a jacket.

virtual sampling technology. Computer software that allows designers to approve the color, fit, styling, and proportions of a design that only exists digitally—not as a physical sample.

vision statement. A declaration of the organization's goals for the future; it is aspirational. A vision statement is critical to planning because in outlining goals, it guides decision making and resource allocation in the planning that follows.

visual search tools. Enable users to take a screenshot of a look they've seen on the web, on influencers, or social media and find the actual item or similar items, with relevant shopping links.

voice commerce. The use of voice commands as a digital assistant to search for and purchase products digitally.

wales. Vertical chains of loops formed in a knitted textile as the loop from one course is interlooped with the loop from a previous course.

warp. Yarns that are used in a textile loom to create the base structure of the textile. They are arranged down the length of the loom, parallel to the selvedge. Garments cut with the warp running vertical to the ground are on the warp or length grain.

warp knits. Textiles knitted from multiple yarns arranged in the warp direction which are pulled in many directions to interconnect with other loops, forming stable, strong fabrics.

weft. Yarns are carried across a woven textile loom in a shuttle and interlaced at right angles to the warp. Garments cut with the weft running vertical to the ground are on the weft or cross grain.

weft knits. Textiles formed when a yarn passes over a series of hooked needles that pull the yarn into a row of loops called courses.

weight. Measured by cutting a swatch of a specific size and putting it on a scale and then calculating the number of ounces per yard or grams per meter. Also a subjective response to what the user senses is appropriate for a product.

welt pocket. A slash pocket finished with a single welt, typically $\frac{1}{4}$ inch to $1\frac{1}{2}$ inches wide, that is attached to the bottom edge of the slash and flips up over the pocket to cover the opening. This pocket is accessed from the top of the welt. Narrow welt pockets are sometimes used on the back of men's or women's pants. Wider welts are frequently found on tailored jackets, coat dresses, and coats.

white label. A product or service designed and produced by one company that other companies rebrand to make it appear as if they produced it.

wholesale (bulk) price. The amount charged by a wholesale (bulk) product development company or manufacturer when the garment is sold to a retailer or distributor.

wholesale brand. Brands that design, produce, and market products under a proprietary label and distribute those products to retailers or third parties, who sell them to the final consumer. Mass merchants, department stores, specialty stores, chain stores, and boutiques frequently carry wholesale brands.

World Trade Organizaton (WTO). A voluntary international organization formed in 1995 that helps importers and exporters conduct business through negotiated agreements and rules.

woven textiles (wovens). Constructed on looms with two or more sets of yarns, the warp and the weft, interlaced at right angles to each other.

written warranty. A legally binding written claim by the brand that a product will perform in a particular way.

WTO Appellate Body. A court that will hear arguments and make a ruling. It can authorize remedies for the injured member such as allowing them to raise tariffs.

WTO Rules of Global Trade. The largest multilateral trade agreements in the world.

yarn forward rule. A rule in a trade agreement that requires that all the steps of production (excluding fiber) must be conducted within partner countries unless a component product is in short supply.

yarns. Long, thin arrangements of fibers, suitable for being fabricated into textiles, held together by twisting.

zero waste. An approach to design in which an attempt is made to eliminate all fallout from cutting as a part of a commitment to sustainability.

zippers. Continuous closure with interlocking teeth mounted in twill tape or other textile and made of various materials that are opened and closed with a slider connected to a pull.

CREDITS

CHAPTER 5

5.0 SSPL/Getty Images
5.1a YOSHIKAZU TSUNO/AFP/ Getty Images
5.1b YOSHIKAZU TSUNO/AFP/ Getty Images
5.2a–e Iannaccone / WWD / © Conde Nast
5.3a & b Fairchild Books
5.4 Courtesy of Pantone LLC
5.5–5.11 Fairchild Books
5.12 Anna Blazhuk/Moment/Getty Images
5.13 Courtesy of Color Solutions Internations (www.csicolors.com)
5.14–5.16 Fairchild Books
5.17 & 5.18 Courtesy of X-rite
5.19 Sultan Mahmud Mukut/SOPA Images/LightRocket via Getty Images

CHAPTER 6

6.0 15Jtextile2 Maestri / WWD / © Conde Nast
6.1 4e 6.1 Courtesy of Deborah Vandermar
6.1a.1 shutterstock_343609208 Slay / Shutterstock.com
6.1a.2 shutterstock_172887056 Zuraimy / Shutterstock.com
6.1a.3 iStock_98801209_LARGE Paffy69 / iStock.com
6.1a.4 shutterstock_91515653 Suphatthra China / Shutterstock.com
6.1a.5 shutterstock_267178250 Mr Doomits / Shutterstock
6.1a.6 dreamstime_m_14622618 © Muharrem Zengin / Dreamstime.com
6.2 zoranm / iStock.com
6.3 Catherine Yeulet / iStock.com
6.4 dreamstime_m_61337388 Gasparij / Dreamstime.com
6.5 shutterstock_287057366 ProStockStudio / Shutterstock.com
6.6-6.11 Courtesy of Deborah Vandermar
6.12 ivkatefoto / Shutterstock.com
6.13 Courtesy of Akris
6.14–6.18 Courtesy of Deborah Vandermar
6.18a Shamleen / Shutterstock.com
6.18b-k Courtesy of Deborah Vandermar

6.19 Courtesy of Deborah Vandermar
6.19c gerenme / iStock.com
6.20a Courtesy of Patricia Nugent
6.20b SuperStock
6.20c Inmagine Asia
6.20d SuperStock
6.21a Amnarj Tanongrattana / Shutterstock.com
6.21b Amnarj Tanongrattana/ Shutterstock.com
6.21c S3studio/Getty Images
6.22-6.24 Courtesy of Deborah Vandermar
6.25a Claudio Lavenia/Getty Images
6.25b Victor VIRGILE/Gamma-Rapho via Getty Images
6.25c THONGCHAI PITTAYANON / Shutterstock.com
6.25d MagMos / iStock.com
6.25e OmiStudio / Shutterstock.com
6.26 Courtesy of NASA
6.27a Will & Deni McIntyre / Corbis Collection / Getty Images
6.27b WWD / © Conde Nast
6.28 KM6064 / iStock.com
6.29 & 6.30 Courtesy of Deborah Vandermar
6.31 Photo courtesy of Cocon / 37.5
6.32 Courtesy of Deborah Vandermar
6.33 Lars Niki/Corbis via Getty Images
6.34 United Nations Department of Global Communications
6.35 Universal History Archive/ Universal Images Group via Getty Images
6.36 United Nations Department of Global Communications
6.37 Charley Gallay/Getty Images for Outerknown
6.38 United Nations Department of Global Communications
6.39 United Nations Department of Global Communications
6.40 www.fibersort.eu
6.41 Nataliya Petrova/NurPhoto via Getty Images
6.42 Courtesy of Deborah Vandermar
6.43 United Nations Department of Global Communications
6Box6.1 Men's Tailoring FPO Courtesy of Deborah Vandermar
6CS6.1 Design for Good

CHAPTER 7

7.0 Yagi-Studio/E+/Getty Images
7.1 & 7.2 Fairchild Books
7.3 Chris Rose / Alamy Stock Photo
7.4 & 7.5 Fairchild Books
7.6 Courtesy of Deborah Vandermar
7.7 Courtesy of Donna Ricco
7.8a & b Fairchild Books
7.9a Mitra / WWD / © Conde Nast
7.9b JP Yim/Getty Images
7.10 Vittorio Zunino Celotto/Getty Images
7.11 US Government
7.12 Kevork Djansezian / Getty Images
7.13 Courtesy of Statista
7.14 Wally Skalij / Los Angeles Times via Getty Images

CHAPTER 8

8.0 Lane Oatey/Blue Jean Images/ Getty Images
8.1a Thomas Monaster/NY Daily News via Getty Images
8.1b Estrop/Getty Images
8.1c Victor VIRGILE/Gamma-Rapho via Getty Image
8.2 Daniel C Sims/Getty Images
8.3 Art-Y/DigitalVisionVectors/ Getty Images
8.4 lechatnoir/E+/Getty Images
8.5 Fairchild Books
8.6 FilmStudio/E+/Getty Images
8.7 Per-Anders Pettersson/Getty Images
8.8 & 8.9 Fairchild Books
8.10a Victor Boyko/Getty Images
8.10b Maestri / WWD / © Conde Nast
8.11a–d Courtesy of Steven Stipelman
8.12 Courtesy of Sandra Keiser
8.13 & 8.14 Courtesy of Deborah Vandermar
8.15 Courtesy of Somarta
8.16 Dave Hogan/Hulton Archives/ Getty Images
8.17–8.26 Courtesy of Deborah Vandermar
8T8.1 Fairchild Books

CHAPTER 8 APPENDIX

All illustrations rendered by Graphic World, Inc., based on drawing provided by Deborah Vandermar/ Fairchild Books

Part 3 Xurxo Lobato/Cover/Getty
Images

CHAPTER 9

9.0 GOODLUZ / Alamy Stock
Photo
9.1 Courtesy of Deborah Vandermar
9.2 Courtesy of Gerber Technology
9.3–9.5 Courtesy of Deborah
Vandermar
9.6 MARTIN BUREAU/AFP via
Getty Images
9.7 Courtesy of Deborah Vandermar
9.8 Fancy Photography / Veer
9.9a Courtesy of Deborah Vandermar
9.9b WWD / © Conde Nast
9.9c & d Courtesy of Deborah
Vandermar
9.10a Courtesy of Lectra
9.10b Courtesy Gerber Technology
9.11a Courtesy of Optitex
9.11b Courtesy of Gerber
Technologies
9.11c Courtesy of Optitex
9.11d Courtesy Gerber Technology
9.12 Courtesy of Optitex
9CS Courtesy of beproduct.com

CHAPTER 10

10.0 Wavebreakmedia/Alamy Stock
Photo
10.1 Via Trading Corporation
10.2a Courtesy of FitAnalytics
10.2b Courtesy of ShotFitMatch
10.2c yuoak/DigitalVision Vectors/
Getty images"
10.2d a-r-t-i-s-t/DigitalVision
Vectors/Getty Images"
10.2e Courtesy of3DLook
10.3 Julia Xanthos/NY Daily News
via Getty Images
10.4a Jameswimsel/Dreamstime.com
10.4b Courtesy Alvanon
10.5 Marcus Kuhn
10.6 © WWD / Condé Nast
10.7 Courtesy of Deboah Vandermar
10.8 Courtesy of Optitex
10.9a & b Optitext 2D/3D Integrated
Platform
10.10 Courtesy of Myrna Garner
10.11 & 10.12 Courtesy of Deboah

Vandermar
10.13a–g Courtesy of Browzwear
10.14a & b Courtesy of Nervous
System, Inc.
CS 10.1 & CS10.2Courtesy of
Alvanon
Chapter 10 Appendix Courtesy of
Alvanon

CHAPTER 11

11.0 Ann Johansson/Corbis via Getty
Images
11.1 Courtesy of Deborah Vandermar
11.2 Courtesy of Gerber Technologies
11.3 Courtesy of Deborah Vandermar
11.4a–c Courtesy of Colleen Moretz
11.5a Edward Wong/South China
Morning Post via Getty Images
11.5b WWD / © Conde Nast
11.6–11.9 Courtesy of Deborah
Vandermar
11.10 Tonello Photography/
Shutterstock.com
11.11a–c Courtesy of VEIT
11.12a David Walter Banks/For The
Washington Post via Getty Images
11.12b ANNE-CHRISTINE
POUJOULAT/AFP via Getty
Images
11.13–11.16 Courtesy of Deborah
Vandermar
11.17 Scott Olson/Getty Images
11.18 Courtesy of Deborah
Vandermar
11.19a © Colin Young-Wolff /
PhotoEdit
11.19b Courtesy of Myrna Garner
11.19c Courtesy of ASTM
11.20 Mark Dadswell/Getty Images
11.21 WWD / © Conde Nast
11.22 minemero / iStock.com
11.23 Fairchild Books
11.24 WWD / © Conde Nast
11CS 11.1 & 2 Courtesy of ISAIC,
Industriatl Sewing and Innovation
Center
Chapter 11 Appendix American &
Efird, Inc.

Part 4 MR.Cole_Photographer/
Moment/Getty Images

CHAPTER 12

12.0 Olivier Asselin / Alamy Stock
12.1 Shamleen/Shutterstock.com
12.2 Open Apparel Registry
12.3 Maitre / WWD / © Conde Nast
12.4a Berton Chang/South China
Morning Post via Getty Images
12.4b Courtesy of Sandra Keiser
12.5 Courtesy of Deborah Vandermar
12.6a alvarez/E+/Getty Images
12.6b © Gerber Technology
12.6c ClarkandCompany/iStock.com
12.7a SlobodanMiljevic/iStock Photo
12.7b kzenon/iStock.com
12.7c idealistock/iStock.com
12.8 © Joerg Boethling / Alamy
12.9 Courtesy of Deborah Vandermar
12.10 ABDULLAH APU/AFP via
Getty Images
12.11 Ashley Cooper/The Image
Bank Unrelased/Getty Image
12.12 K M Asad/LightRocket via
Getty Images
12.13 Hoxuanhuong/Dreamstime.
com
12.14a Rijans007
12.14b Bayazid Akter / Dreamstime.
com
12.15 Hk Rajashekar/The India
Today Group/Getty Images
12.16 Courtesy of Deborah
Vandermar
Chapter 13

CHAPTER 13

13.0 GettyImages-1030324482.jpg
NICOLAS ASFOURI/AFP via
Getty Images
13.1–13.5 4e 13.3.pdf Courtesy of
Deborah Vandermar
13.6 New York University Stern
Center for Human Rights
13.7–13.9 Courtesy of Deborah
Vandermar
13.10 Edward James/FilmMagic/
Getty Images
13CS Stella McCartney. 2020. Eco
Impact Report

INDEX